# Strategic Physical Distribution Management

The Irwin Series in Marketing
*Consulting Editor*  Gilbert A. Churchill  *University of Wisconsin, Madison*

# Strategic Physical Distribution Management

**Douglas M. Lambert**
*Department of Marketing and Transportation Administration*
*The Graduate School of Business Administration*
*Michigan State University*

**James R. Stock**
*Division of Marketing*
*College of Business Administration*
*University of Oklahoma*

1982

**RICHARD D. IRWIN, INC.**  Homewood, Illinois  60430

© RICHARD D. IRWIN, INC., 1982

*All rights reserved.* No part of this publication may be reproduced, stored in a retrieval system, or transmitted, in any form or by any means, electronic, mechanical, photocopying, recording, or otherwise, without the prior written permission of the publisher.

ISBN 0-256-02549-5
Library of Congress Catalog Card No. 81—82878
*Printed in the United States of America*

1 2 3 4 5 6 7 8 9 0 MP 9 8 7 6 5 4 3 2

*To Bernard J. LaLonde*
*Teacher, Mentor, Colleague, and Friend*

# Preface

The events of the past few years have led to the realization that physical distribution has a significant impact on our standard of living. Approximately 20 percent of the GNP of the United States can be directly attributed to distribution and distribution related activities—this equates to over $420 billion! Distribution activities provided more than 14 million jobs in the United States in 1980. Excluding public sources, investment in transportation and distribution facilities has been estimated to approximate $300 billion. Certainly, distribution is big business in terms of its consumption of land, labor, and capital, and its impact on the standard of living.

Curiously, it has been only recently (since 1960) that interest in physical distribution has arisen in the business community. At its present stage of development physical distribution can be likened to marketing during the late 1950s and early 1960s. At that point in the development of marketing thought the marketing concept was beginning to take shape in the minds and actions of management. It was recognized that customer satisfaction and profitability were mutually inclusive rather than mutually exclusive terms. Firms began to reorganize and to place responsibility for all the marketing activities at the senior executive level. At the same time, academicians and their students embraced the marketing concept and provided the business community with a continuing flow of highly trained marketing professionals. These enterprising men and women have combined their talents to produce an industrialized society which is felt by many observers to be the world leader in marketing theory and practice.

What does all this have to do with physical distribution? Simply, marketing has performed magnificently to generate customer demand for a plethora of products, services, and ideas, but it has failed to focus adequately on the supply side of the marketing equation. Traditionally, we have been more successful at generating demand in the marketplace than we have been in satisfying that demand once it was created. Recently, business firms have come to recognize that successful implementation of the marketing concept requires that the physical distribution activity be managed well. The new management focus on profitability rather than sales volume will increase the importance of physical distribution in the future.

*Strategic Physical Distribution Management* approaches the topic from a managerial perspective. In each chapter basic physical distribution concepts are operationalized in a format that is useful for management decision making. Of course, the basics—terms, concepts, principles—are covered, but they are examined in light of how they interrelate and interface with other functions of the firm. Examples of corporate application of concepts are included in each chapter in order to provide you, the practitioner and the student, with a text which will enable you to develop a knowledge of how the physical distribution activity can be managed to properly implement the marketing concept.

Within this book you will find a good balance of theory and practical application. All the traditional physical distribution functions have been included. However, there are several important topics that are unique to this text or are approached in a different way. For example, the financial control of physical distribution is discussed in a separate chapter as well as interwoven throughout all chapters. We have purposely taken this direction because of the impact of physical distribution on the firm's profitability. Because physical distribution ultimately affects marketing's ability to generate and satisfy demand and thus create customer satisfaction, the customer service activity is emphasized early in the book. Also, customer service can be considered the output of the physical distribution function. For this reason it provides a focal point for the entire book and is included in each of the 14 chapters.

A number of important topics not covered in other texts are covered in this book, including: order processing and management information systems; materials management; financial control of distribution performance; physical distribution organizations; international physical distribution; and the strategic physical distribution plan. Our goal in providing coverage of these topics in addition to the traditional activities is to provide you with a grasp of the totality of the physical distribution process.

The book is divided into three major sections. Part One provides an introduction to the physical distribution process by examining distribution's role in the economy and the firm and introducing the concept of integrated physical distribution management. In Part Two, the functional areas of distribution are presented from a customer service perspective with the financial implications emphasized throughout. The topics of transportation, warehousing, inventory management, order processing and information systems, materials management, and customer service are discussed in detail, always with a view toward how they can be effectively managed. Part Three emphasizes the strategic aspects of physical distribution management from both domestic and international perspectives. Chapter topics include Financial Control of Distribution Performance, Physical Distribution Organizations, International Physical Distribution, and The Strategic Physical Distribution Plan.

The pragmatic applied nature of the book, its managerial orientation and its how-to-do-it appendixes should make it a must-have reference book for present and future distribution professionals. The end-of-chapter questions and the case material require you to apply the material presented in each chapter. The questions, problems, and cases are structured to challenge your managerial skills. They are integrative in nature and examine issues that are important to today's physical distribution executive.

*Douglas M. Lambert*
*James R. Stock*

# Acknowledgments

Any work of this magnitude is seldom the exclusive work of one or two individuals. A number of persons from the practitioner and academic communities have provided invaluable input into the writing of this text. Several individuals from the business sector made a number of helpful comments on the manuscript which enabled the authors to properly blend theory into practice. These persons included: Donald J. Allison, division manager, physical distribution, Johns-Manville Canada, Inc.; Bruce D. Becker, director corporate distribution, The Stanley Works; George A. Gecowets, vice president/executive director, National Council of Physical Distribution Management; Bernard J. Hale, vice president, distribution planning, Bergen Brunswig Corporation; M. Chris Lewis, industry analyst, American Telephone and Telegraph Company, Business Marketing, Market Management Division; Eugene L. Sailer, director of manufacturing, General Mills, Inc.; and Douglas E. Zemke, division marketing manager, AT&T Long Lines. Many of our academic colleagues were extremely helpful in suggesting changes and providing input into the text, including: Professors James A. Constantin of the University of Oklahoma; Gilbert A. Churchill, Jr., of the University of Wisconsin, Madison; Saeed Samiee of Kent State University; and Paul H. Zinszer of the University of Oklahoma.

Special thanks must go to the many people at Michigan State University and the University of Oklahoma who provided editorial, graphical, and clerical support. At Michigan State University we especially appreciate the support of Dean Richard J. Lewis of the Graduate School of Business Administration, Professor Donald A. Taylor, chairman, Department of Marketing and Transportation Administration, for providing an atmosphere which allows faculty members to be productive, and Gary Farha, an M.B.A. student, who read page proofs. At the University of Oklahoma recognition is given to the support of Dean Lawrence McKibbin, College of Business Administration; Professor Malcolm Morris, director, Division of Marketing; and Cindy Gray, Peggy Haynes, Paul Lewis, Julie Rojas, Margaret Smith, Alice Watkins, Caroline Wells, and Patricia Wickham, all staff personnel.

We are grateful to a number of persons and companies who were most gracious in providing us with exhibits, case materials, and other assistance:

American Telephone and Telegraph Company; USCO Services, Inc.; Professor Donald J. Bowersox, Michigan State University; Larry Hile, vice president—material, Nalley's Fine Foods; Herbert Hodus, vice president physical distribution, Child World; J. T. Kelly, director of distribution, Maryland Cup Corporation; Wynn Robin, corporate distribution manager, Miles Laboratories, Inc.; Professor Stuart U. Rich, University of Oregon; Professor Karl M. Ruppenthal, University of British Columbia; Jay U. Sterling, doctoral candidate, Michigan State University; and, Professor Martin R. Warshaw, University of Michigan. Our students at Michigan State University and the University of Oklahoma as well as the hundreds of business executives who have attended our seminars have had a strong influence on the content of this book.

Without the support of our families, the task of writing a text would be impossible. The first author wishes to thank his parents, John D. and Mary Lambert, who over the years represented a continuing source of love and encouragement. They provided motivation to a teenager who lacked it and still provide gentle reminders "not to work too hard" to one whose enthusiasm often leads to over-commitments. His wife, Lynne, was a constant source of love and moral support. As his sole source of manuscript assistance she deserves most of the credit for his ability to meet the always optimistic deadlines.

The second author wishes to thank his parents, William and Frances Stock, who were instrumental in instilling the work ethic necessary to complete this text. His wife, Katheryn, was a constant source of encouragement, providing both moral support and manuscript assistance. Special thanks goes to his daughter, Elizabeth, for giving up so many hours of time with her daddy so that he could write.

Finally, we wish to express our warmest appreciation to Bernard J. LaLonde, Riley Professor of Marketing and Logistics and Associate Dean, College of Administrative Science, The Ohio State University. It was his love for the discipline of physical distribution and his leadership during and since our doctoral programs at The Ohio State University that have made this text a reality. For those who know "Bud," no explanation is necessary. For those who have missed the experience, no words can explain it. We are most fortunate to be able to call him our teacher, mentor, colleague, and friend.

To all of those persons who provided assistance and to the publishers and authors who graciously granted permission to use their material, we are indeed grateful. Of course, responsibility for any errors or omissions rests with the authors.

*D. M. Lambert*
*J. R. Stock*

# Contents

**PART ONE** .......................... 1

1. **Distribution's Role in the Economy and the Firm** ............. 2

   Channels of Distribution: *A Typical Channel of Distribution. Physical Distribution and Channel Management.* Physical Distribution's Role in the Economy. Physical Distribution's Role in the Firm: *Definition of Physical Distribution Management.* Development of Physical Distribution Management: *Historical Development. Factors Underlying the Development of Interest in Physical Distribution Management. Operationalizing a Physical Distribution Management System.*

2. **The Integrated Physical Distribution Management Concept** .. 30

   Reasons for Growth of the Physical Distribution Function. Physical Distribution and the Marketing Function: *Price. Product. Promotion. Place.* The Total Cost Concept: *Customer Service Levels. Transportation Costs. Warehousing Costs. Order Processing and Information Costs. Production Lot Quantity Costs. Inventory Carrying Costs.* Physical Distribution and Corporate Profit Performance: *The Strategic Profit Model.* An Example of Integrated Physical Distribution Management. Conducting a Marketing and Physical Distribution Audit. Developing a Physical Distribution Strategy. Areas Where Physical Distribution Performance Can Be Improved: *Forecasting. Order Processing and Communications Systems. Customer Service. Inventory Management. Transportation. Warehousing.*

**PART TWO** .......................... 53

3. **Customer Service** ................... 54

   What is Customer Service?: *Customer Service Definitions. Elements of Customer Service. Some Key Industry Demographics.* Relationship of Customer Service to Successful Marketing. Customer Service and the Integrated Physical Distribution Management Concept: *Cost of Lost Sales. Implementing Cost/Service Trade-offs.* Conducting a Customer Service Audit: *An ABC Analysis of Customer Service.* Developing and Reporting Customer Service Standards. Impediments to an Effective Customer Service Strategy. Improving Customer Service Performance.

   **Appendix A:** Customer Service Audit, 81

   **Appendix B:** Customer Service/Physical Distribution Audit, 84

   **Appendix C:** Customer Service Questionnaire, 95

4. **The Transportation System** ........ 100

   *Time and Place Utility. Transportation/Physical Distribution/Marketing Interface.* The U.S. Transportation System: *Alternative Transport Modes. Intermodal Combinations. Legal Forms of Transportation Carriers. Transportation Regulation. Traffic and Transportation Management.*

   **Appendix A:** Section-by-Section Summary of the Motor Carrier Act of 1980, 131

   **Appendix B:** Standing Congressional Committees Having Jurisdiction over Transportation, 135

**Appendix C:** Transportation Responsibilities in the Executive Branch, 137

**Appendix D:** Department of Transportation—Organization and Responsibilities, 139

**Appendix E:** Federal Transportation Regulatory Agencies, 141

5. **Decision Strategies in Transportation** .................... 144

Developing Cost-Effective Transportation. The Transportation-Mode Selection Decision: *Problem Recognition. Search Process. Choice Process. Postchoice Evaluation.* Shipper Response to Transportation Regulatory Reform: *Response to Motor Carrier Reforms. Response to Rail Carrier Reforms. Response to Air Carrier Reforms.* The Private versus For-Hire Decision: *Define the Problem. Develop Transport Objectives. Collect Pertinent Information. Determine Present Cost. Analyze Present Operations. Develop Alternatives. Determine Private Fleet Costs. Consider Indirect Factors. Summarize Alternatives. Make the Decision.* Leasing. Evaluation of Mode/Carrier Performance. Designing an Optimal Transportation System.

**Appendix:** Key Issues Affecting Future Transportation Decision Making, 176

6. **Warehousing** ..................... 180

*Nature and Importance of Warehousing. Types of Warehousing.* Warehousing Operations: *The Functions of Warehousing. Warehouse Layout and Design. Warehouse Handling Systems. Packaging.* Decision-Making Strategies in Warehousing: *Public versus Private Warehousing. Measurement and Improvement of Warehouse Performance. Warehouse Site Selection.*

**Appendix A:** Problem 1—Where Should In-Process Parts Be Stored for Minimum Travel Costs? 227

**Appendix B:** Problem 2—How Do You Assign Storage Locations to Minimize Travel? 230

7. **Financial Impact of Inventory** ...... 232

Financial Aspects of Inventory Strategy: *Inventory and Corporate Profitability. Inventory and Least Total Cost Physical Distribution.* Inventory Carrying Costs: *Calculating Inventory Carrying Costs.* The Impact of Inventory Turnover on Inventory Carrying Costs.

**Appendix A:** Inventory Carrying Costs—Six Case Studies, 261

**Appendix B:** Inventory Carrying Costs—Forms for Data Collection, 265

8. **Inventory Management** ............ 274

Basic Inventory Concepts: *Why Hold Inventory? Inventory as a Buffer. Types of Inventory.* Basic Inventory Management: *Inventory Management under Conditions of Certainty. Inventory Management under Uncertainty. Calculating Safety Stock Requirements. Inventories and Customer Service. Production Scheduling. Symptoms of Poor Inventory Management.* Improving Inventory Management: *ABC Analysis. Forecasting. Inventory Models. Order Processing Systems.* Impact of an Inventory Reduction on Corporate Profit Performance.

9. **Order Processing and Information Systems** .......................... 306

Customer Order Cycle: *How Do Customer Orders Enter the Firm's Order Processing Function? The Path of a Customer's Order.* The Communications Function: *Advanced Order Processing Systems.* Integrating Order Processing and the Company's Physical Distribution Management Information System. Basic Need for Information. Designing the Information System. A Distribution Data Base for Decision Making. Financial Considerations.

10. **Materials Management** ............ 338

Scope of Materials Management Activities: *Purchasing and Procurement. Production Control. Inbound Traffic and Transportation. Warehousing and Storage. MIS Control. Inventory Planning and Control. Salvage and Scrap Disposal.* Administration and Control of Materials Management: *Materials Requirements Planning (MRP).*

**Appendix:** Evaluating Suppliers in a Typical Manufacturing Firm, 365

**PART THREE** ......................... 367

11. **Financial Control of Distribution Performance** ..................... 368

The Importance of Accurate Cost Data: *Total-Cost Analysis. Controlling Physical Distribution Activities. Case Studies.* Solving the Problem of Insufficient Cost Data: *Standard Costs and Flexible Budgets. Budgetary Practices. Productivity Standards. Physical Distribution Costs and the Corporate Management Information System. The Role of the Order Processing System.* Cost Justification of Physical Distribution System Changes.

**Appendix A:** An Application of Standard Costs in Physical Distribution, 392

**Appendix B:** Developing Standard Costs and Flexible Budgets for Warehousing, 397

12. **Physical Distribution Organizations** .................... 402

    Importance of an Effective Physical Distribution Organization. Types of Physical Distribution Organizational Structures. Decision-Making Strategies in Organizing for PDM: *Components of an Optimal Physical Distribution Organization. An Approach to Developing an Optimal Physical Distribution Organization. Measuring the Effectiveness of the Physical Distribution Organization.*

13. **International Physical Distribution** ...................... 430

    International Distribution Channel Strategies: *Exporting. Licensing. Joint Ventures. Ownership.* Management of the Export Shipment: *Export Facilitators. Documentation. Terms of Trade. Free-Trade Zones.* The International Marketplace: *Uncontrollable Elements. Controllable Elements—Strategic. Controllable Elements—Managerial.* Financial Aspects of International Physical Distribution. Managing International Physical Distribution Activities.

14. **The Strategic Physical Distribution Plan** .................. 466

    Developing a Strategic Physical Distribution Plan: *Formulating the Channel Strategy. Formulating the Physical Distribution Plan. Evaluation and Selection of Individual Physical Distribution Channel Members. Performance Evaluation and Channel Modification.* Future Challenges: *Distribution Accounting. A Need for Broader-Based Management Skills. Energy/Ecological Issues. Regulatory Trends. International Physical Distribution. Consumerism.*

    **Appendix:** Transportation Planning—An Overview, 492

**CASES** ................................. 497

1. The Dow Chemical Company, 498
2. Smith Chemical Company, 501
3. Acme Office Products, Inc., 507
4. Favored Blend Coffee Company, 517
5. McGraw-Hill Book Company (A): Location of Western Region Warehouse, 524
6. Giles Laboratories, 536
7. Western Plywood Corporation: Logistics Problems of a Softwood Plywood Producer, 543
8. Riverview Distributing Company, Incorporated (B), 553
9. Ferle Foods, Inc., 559

**Author Index** .......................... 577

**Subject Index** .......................... 579

# Part One

# 1 Distribution's Role in the Economy and the Firm

Introduction

Channels of Distribution
   A Typical Channel of Distribution
   Physical Distribution and Channel Management

Physical Distribution's Role in the Economy

Physical Distribution's Role in the Firm
   Definition of Physical Distribution Management
      Time and place utility
      Efficient movement to customer
      Marketing oriented
      Proprietary asset
      Activities included in physical distribution management

Development of Physical Distribution Management
   Historical Development
   Factors Underlying the Development of Interest in Physical Distribution Management
   Operationalizing a Physical Distribution Management System

Summary

**Objectives of this chapter:**

To show how physical distribution activities interface with the economic system at the macro (societal) and micro (firm) level

To identify the relationship between physical distribution and marketing

To explore the historical development of the physical distribution function

To examine the strategic function of physical distribution management in the modern corporation

## INTRODUCTION

There are perhaps few areas of study which have as significant an impact on a society's standard of living as does physical distribution. Almost every sphere of human activity is affected, directly or indirectly, by the physical distribution process.

> How often have you gone to the supermarket for milk, eggs, or bread, and not found what you wanted on the shelf?
>
> Have you ever placed an order through the mail, over the telephone, or in person, and received the wrong merchandise?
>
> Have you ever shipped a package to someone in the same city or across the country and had the item arrive damaged, or perhaps not arrive at all?
>
> When was the last time you were promised delivery of an item within a few days and it took a few weeks?

Often we do not think of the role that physical distribution plays in our lives until a problem occurs. How fortunate it is that we usually find the items we want in the supermarket, receive the correct order, undamaged, and at the time it was promised.

As consumers, business persons, educators, government workers, or whatever the vocation, it is important that we understand the physical distribution process. In this chapter you will be shown how physical distribution activities interface with the economic system at the macro (societal) and micro (firm) levels. You will be shown how to identify the relationship between physical distribution and marketing. The historical development of the physical distribution function will be presented, which will aid you in your examination of the strategic function that physical distribution management has in the modern corporation.

## CHANNELS OF DISTRIBUTION

*The Exchange Process*

In any society—industrialized or nonindustrialized—goods must be physically moved or transported between where they are produced and where they are consumed. Except in very primitive cultures, where household needs were met by producing the products necessary to carry out the family's daily activities, the *exchange process* has become the cornerstone of economic activity. Exchange takes place when there is a discrepancy be-

**Why Channels Develop**

tween the amount of goods available and the amount of goods needed. If a number of individuals or organizations within the society have a surplus of goods which someone else needs, then a basis for exchange is developed.

As an outcome of many exchanges taking place between the producers and consumers of goods, the marketing channel develops. The development of channels can be explained in terms of four related steps in an economic process:

1. Intermediaries arise in the process of exchange because they can increase the efficiency of the process.
2. Channel intermediaries arise to adjust the discrepancy of assortments through the performance of the sorting process.
3. Marketing agencies hang together in channel arrangements to provide for the routinization of transactions.
4. Also, channels exist to facilitate the searching process as well as the sorting process.[1]

Figure 1-1 shows how the presence of a channel intermediary can reduce the number of transactions or exchanges. Since some cost can be assigned to each exchange, the channel with 14 market contacts is significantly more cost efficient than the channel with 40 market contacts.

**FIGURE 1-1** How Intermediaries Reduce the Cost of Market Contact between Supplier and Customer

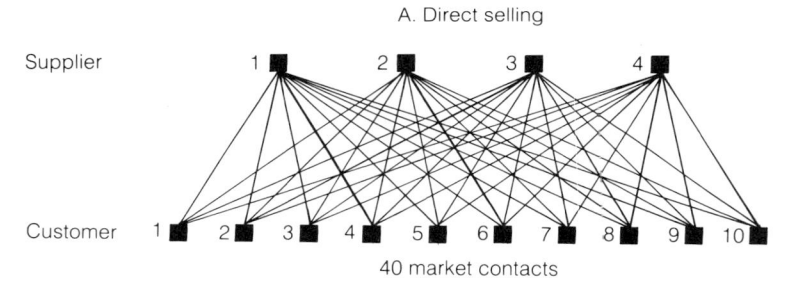

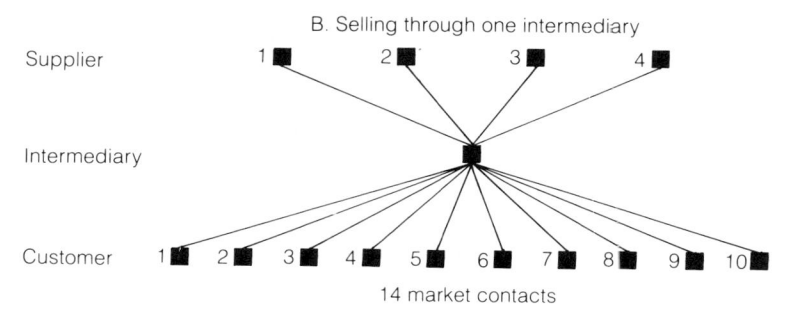

A. Direct selling

40 market contacts

B. Selling through one intermediary

14 market contacts

Source: Douglas M. Lambert, *The Distribution Channels Decision* (New York: National Association of Accountants, 1978), pp. 15–16. Copyright © 1978 by National Association of Accountants. All rights reserved.

---

[1] Philip Kotler, *Principles of Marketing* (Englewood Cliffs, N.J.: Prentice-Hall, 1980), p. 219.

In addition to increasing the efficiency of the exchange process, intermediaries bridge the gap between the producer and consumer by taking the goods produced by the producer and making them available to the consumer in the correct size, quantity, style, and variety. Generally, producers have available a large quantity of a limited variety of goods, while the consumer desires a limited quantity of a large variety of goods.

Channel intermediaries enable many exchange processes to become routinized. Because they are performing the same or similar functions for the producers of like goods and their consumers, standardized procedures can be developed which facilitate the exchange process and make the channel more efficient. Typical examples of routinization include communications, procedures, delivery schedules, billing, credit, and many others.

Finally, channels facilitate the search process because the number of contacts within the channel is reduced. For example, the customers in Figure 1–1 must only search out a single intermediary instead of trying to locate each of four suppliers. By reducing the amount of search a larger number of exchanges can occur more frequently.

### A Typical Channel of Distribution

*A Channel of Distribution Defined*

A *channel of distribution* or *marketing channel* can be defined as "the set of all firms and individuals that cooperate to produce, distribute, and consume the particular good or service of a particular producer."[2] It is important to recognize that the channel of distribution and the process of physical distribution be understood as interdependent marketing activities which, when combined into one system, culminate in a satisfied customer.

A channel of distribution can be structured in a multitude of ways. Figure 1–2 illustrates the major types of firms that would be included in a marketing channel. All of the marketing channel members combine to provide the customer (industrial or consumer) with the right product at the right place at the right time in the right condition for the right cost.

### Physical Distribution and Channel Management

*The PD/Marketing Interface*

A number of relationships exist between physical distribution and the marketing channel. Bert Rosenbloom has identified four areas of interface as follows:

> Defining what kinds of physical distribution service standards the channel members want.
> 
> Making sure that the proposed physical distribution program designed by the firm meets the channel members' service standards.
> 
> Selling the channel members on the physical distribution program.
> 
> Monitoring the results of the physical distribution program once it has been instituted.[3]

Schematically, these interfaces are represented in Figure 1–3.

---

[2] Ibid., pp. 47–48.

[3] Bert Rosenbloom, *Marketing Channels: A Management View* (Hinsdale, Ill.: Dryden Press, 1978), p. 241.

**FIGURE 1-2** Typical Channels of Distribution

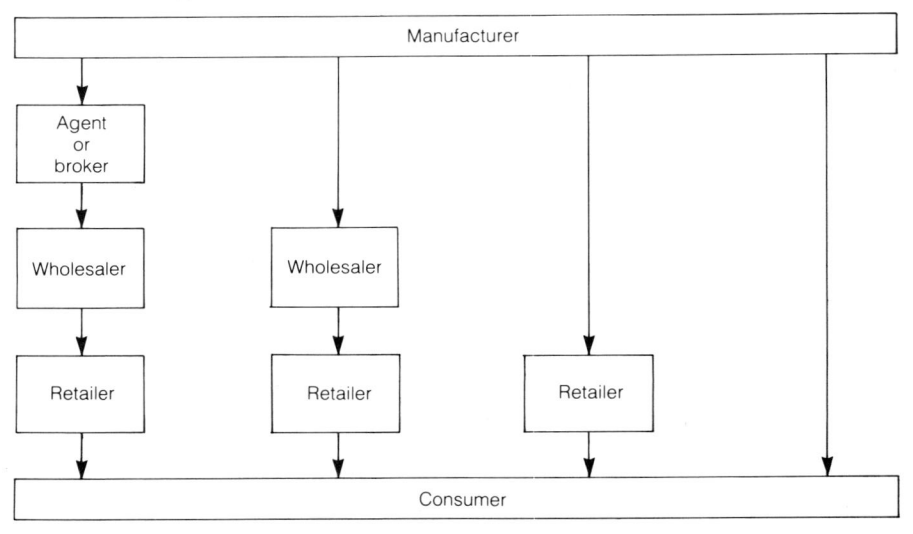

```
                    Manufacturer
         │             │             │              │
         ▼             │             │              │
      Agent            │             │              │
        or             │             │              │
      broker           │             │              │
         │             ▼             │              │
         ▼          Wholesaler       │              │
     Wholesaler       │              │              │
         │            │              │              │
         ▼            ▼              ▼              │
      Retailer     Retailer       Retailer          │
         │            │              │              │
         ▼            ▼              ▼              ▼
                    Consumer
```

**FIGURE 1-3** Interfaces between Physical Distribution and Channel Management Viewed Sequentially

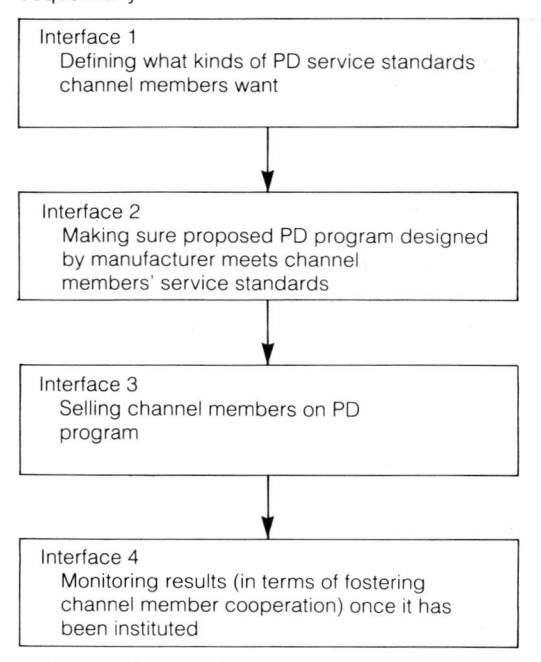

Interface 1
  Defining what kinds of PD service standards channel members want

↓

Interface 2
  Making sure proposed PD program designed by manufacturer meets channel members' service standards

↓

Interface 3
  Selling channel members on PD program

↓

Interface 4
  Monitoring results (in terms of fostering channel member cooperation) once it has been instituted

Source: *Marketing Channels: A Management View* by Bert Rosenbloom. Copyright © 1978 by Bert Rosenbloom. Reprinted with permission of Holt, Rinehart & Winston.

It is beyond the scope of this book to examine marketing channels in depth. At this point, let us suffice to say that the distribution process takes place within the marketing channel and that physical distribution management and channel management are closely related.

## PHYSICAL DISTRIBUTION'S ROLE IN THE ECONOMY

The rising affluence of consumers has given rise to national and international markets for goods and services. Literally thousands of new products have been introduced during this century which are sold and distributed to customers in every corner of the world. Business firms have greatly increased in size and complexity to meet the challenges of expanded markets and the proliferation of new products. Multiplant operations have replaced single-plant production. The distribution of products from point of origin to point of consumption has become an enormously important component of the GNP of industrialized nations.

*The Growing Cost of Distribution*

Using the United States as an example, in recent years, the contribution of manufacturing to GNP has declined to a point where it accounts for about half the total. Conversely, distribution has grown to where it contributes more than 20 percent of GNP. During 1978, U.S. industry spent more than $200 billion on the transportation of goods, more than $125 billion on warehousing, more than $75 billion on inventory carrying charges, and nearly $20 billion to administer, communicate, and manage the distribution process—a total of over $420 billion.[4] Distribution and related activities provided more than 14 million jobs in the United States in 1980, about 14 percent of the total labor force.[5] Excluding public sources, investment in transportation and distribution facilities has been estimated to approximate $300 billion.[6] Certainly, distribution is big business in terms of its consumption of land, labor, and capital and its impact on the standard of living.

*PD and the Nation's Productivity*

As a significant component of GNP, distribution has impact on the rate of inflation, interest rates, productivity, energy cost and availability, and consumerism. In a study commissioned by the National Council of Physical Distribution Management (NCPDM) in 1978 and completed by an international management consulting firm specializing in physical distribution management (A. T. Kearney, Inc.), it was reported that an average company in the U.S. could improve its productivity by 20 percent and some firms identified opportunities for 35 percent improvement—or more. A. T. Kearney, Inc., conservatively estimated that if the distribution process could be improved by as little as 10 percent, a $40 billion savings could be realized.[7]

---

[4] Wendell M. Stewart and James E. Morehouse, "Improving Productivity in Physical Distribution—A $40 Billion Goldmine," in *Proceedings of the Sixteenth Annual Conference of The National Council of Physical Distribution Management*, October 16–18, 1978, pp. 4–5.

[5] John J. Coyle and Edward J. Bardi, *The Management of Business Logistics*, 2d ed. (St. Paul, Minn.: West Publishing, 1980), p. 39.

[6] D. Philip Locklin, *Economics of Transportation*, 7th ed. (Homewood, Ill.: Richard D. Irwin, 1972), p. 12.

[7] Stewart and Morehouse, "Improving Productivity," pp. 2 and 5.

The amount is staggering. Improvements in our nation's productivity have positive effects on the prices we pay for goods and services, the balance of national payments, the value of the dollar, industry profits (higher productivity implies lower costs of operation to produce and distribute an equivalent amount of product), the availability of investment capital, and economic growth that leads to a higher level of employment.

> There has been an increase in productivity over the past two decades for the United States and many of her major trading partners. It is based on data supplied by the *Bureau of Labor Statistics*. Productivity has been improving at the rate of 9 percent per year in Japan and more than 5 percent per year in West Germany and in France. Even in the United Kingdom, it has been improving at a rate of more than 3 percent per year. But in the United States, productivity improvement has averaged only about 2 percent per year. Continuation of these differences in productivity growth rates spell disaster for the American way of life. To survive and prosper, U.S. industry must move aggressively to improve productivity in all sectors of the economy and in all functions of business, particularly distribution.[8]

With respect to energy cost and availability, the distribution sector consumes an enormous quantity of energy resources. As a result, given the natural laws of supply and demand, distribution has an upward influence on energy prices due to its large usage of those resources. The federal Council for Science and Technology has stated that transportation (including distribution) currently consumes 25 percent of all the energy and 50 percent of all the petroleum production in the United States.[9] It is expected that the distribution sector will continue to utilize increasing quantities of energy resources in the foreseeable future which will add additional upward pressure on energy prices and further complicate the existing procedures for allocating energy resources among various user groups.

## PHYSICAL DISTRIBUTION'S ROLE IN THE FIRM

In recognition of the fact that distribution is a significant component of a country's economy, it would be beneficial at this point to define, in specific terms, what is meant by the term *distribution*.

### Definition of Physical Distribution Management

A review of the trade and academic press over the past decade reveals that the process we have referred to thus far as "distribution" has been given a variety of names:

| | |
|---|---|
| Physical distribution | Materials management |
| Physical distribution systems | Marketing logistics |
| Physical distribution management | Rhochrematics |
| Distribution engineering | Distribution |

---

[8] Ibid., p. 4.

[9] James R. Stock, "The Energy/Ecology Impacts on Distribution," *International Journal of Physical Distribution and Materials Management* 8, no. 5 (1978), 250.

| | |
|---|---|
| Business logistics | Logistics |
| Business logistics management | Logistical management |
| Distribution logistics | Industrial logistics |

The authors have no preference for any of the above terms inasmuch as they all have, at one time or another, referred to essentially the same thing; that is, "the management of the flow of goods from point-of-origin to point-of-consumption." However, the most widely referenced term has been *physical distribution management*. One of the largest and most prestigious groups of distribution professionals, the National Council of Physical Distribution Management, with a membership in excess of 3,000, has used *physical distribution management* to describe the function. As expressed by George Gecowets, vice president/executive director of NCPDM:

> Today . . . physical distribution has emerged as the term most generally used by top management—and those of us who work in the profession—to describe the total cost concept of material flow (logistics, materials management, whatever). More people use this term—more than any other—to describe the total movement and storage function. . . . Most people who use the term *physical distribution* intend for it to mean "inbound" as well as "outbound" movements in the context in which they use it.[10]

In light of the fact that the term *physical distribution management* is the most widely accepted term used by distribution professionals, the authors have used it as the title of this book and accept the NCPDM's definition:

**Physical Distribution Management Defined**

> Physical distribution management is the term describing the integration of two or more activities for the purpose of planning, implementing and controlling the efficient flow of raw materials, in-process inventory and finished goods from point-of-origin to point-of-consumption. These activities may include, but are not limited to, customer service, demand forecasting, distribution communications, inventory control, material handling, order processing, parts and service support, plant and warehouse site selection, procurement, packaging, return goods handling, salvage and scrap disposal, traffic and transportation, and warehousing and storage.[11]

Figure 1—4 illustrates the components of physical distribution management.

Efficient management of the flow of goods from point-of-origin to point-of-consumption at the macro (society) or micro (firm) levels involves successfully planning, implementing, and controlling a multitude of distribution activities. The activities shown in Figure 1—4 may involve raw materials (subassemblies, manufactured parts, packing materials, basic commodities), in-process inventory (product partially completed and not yet ready for resale), and finished goods (completed products ready for sale to intermediate or final customers). Effective physical distribution management results

---

[10] George A. Gecowets, "Physical Distribution Management," *Defense Transportation Journal* 35, no. 4 (August 1979): 11.

[11] National Council of Physical Distribution Management, *NCPDM Comment* 9, no. 6 (November—December 1976): 4—5.

**FIGURE 1–4** Components of Physical Distribution Management

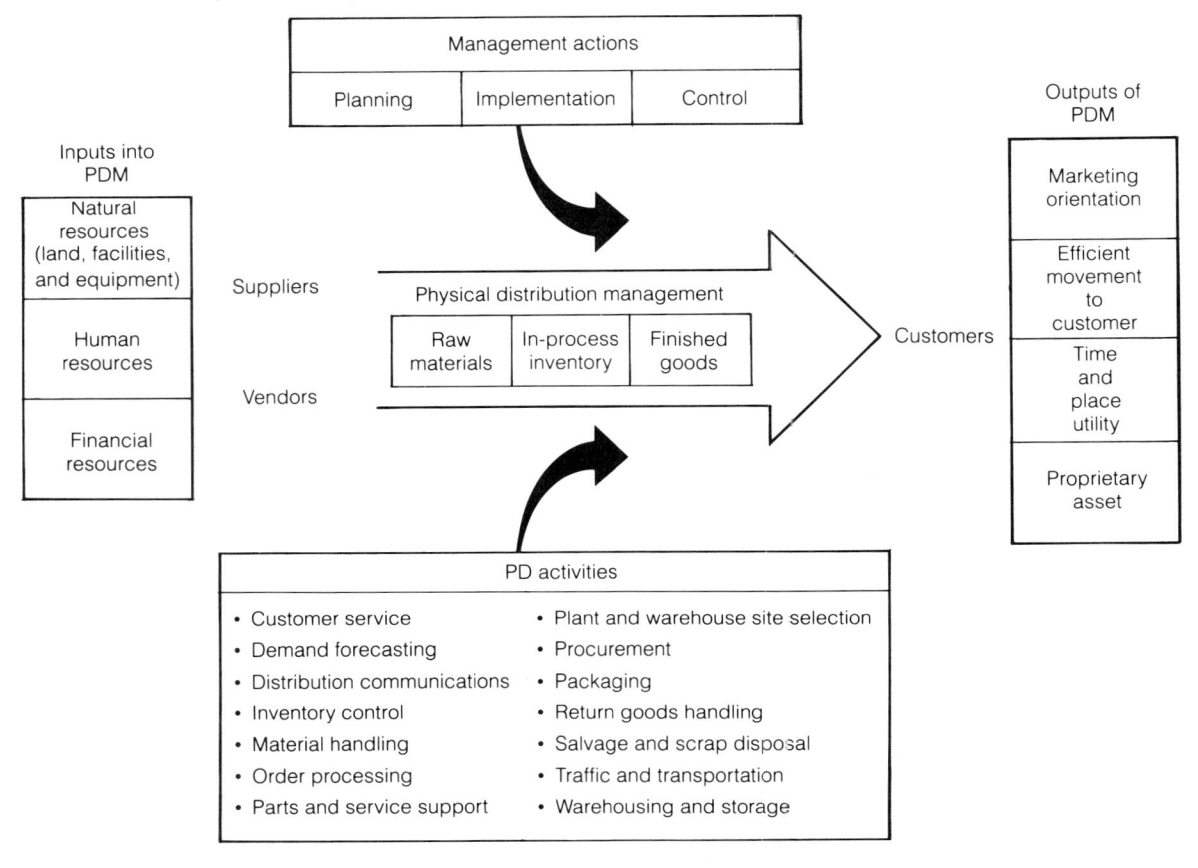

```
                    ┌─────────────────────────────────────┐
                    │        Management actions            │
                    ├──────────┬──────────────┬───────────┤
                    │ Planning │Implementation│  Control  │
                    └──────────┴──────────────┴───────────┘
Inputs into                                                              Outputs of
  PDM                                                                      PDM
┌──────────────┐                                                       ┌──────────────┐
│  Natural     │                                                       │  Marketing   │
│  resources   │                                                       │  orientation │
│(land,facilities,│                                                    ├──────────────┤
│and equipment)│                                                       │  Efficient   │
├──────────────┤  Suppliers  ┌─────────────────────────┐               │  movement    │
│   Human      │             │Physical distribution mgt │               │     to       │
│  resources   │             ├──────┬─────────┬────────┤  Customers    │  customer    │
│              │             │ Raw  │In-process│Finished│               ├──────────────┤
├──────────────┤             │materials│inventory│goods │               │    Time      │
│  Financial   │  Vendors    └──────┴─────────┴────────┘               │    and       │
│  resources   │                                                       │   place      │
│              │                                                       │   utility    │
└──────────────┘                                                       ├──────────────┤
                                                                       │ Proprietary  │
                                                                       │    asset     │
                                                                       └──────────────┘
                    ┌─────────────────────────────────────┐
                    │            PD activities             │
                    ├──────────────────────────────────────┤
                    │ • Customer service                   │
                    │ • Demand forecasting                 │
                    │ • Distribution communications        │
                    │ • Inventory control                  │
                    │ • Material handling                  │
                    │ • Order processing                   │
                    │ • Parts and service support          │
                    │ • Plant and warehouse site selection │
                    │ • Procurement                        │
                    │ • Packaging                          │
                    │ • Return goods handling              │
                    │ • Salvage and scrap disposal         │
                    │ • Traffic and transportation         │
                    │ • Warehousing and storage            │
                    └──────────────────────────────────────┘
```

**Physical Distribution Adds Value to Products**

in the addition of time and place utility to products, an efficient movement of products to customers, enhancement of the marketing efforts of the firm, and can be treated, in accounting terms, as a proprietary asset of the company.

*Time and place utility.* When products are produced by manufacturing they possess some value or utility because an assembled item is worth more than the unassembled components or raw materials that comprise the item. As an illustration, a completed automobile is much more valuable to a consumer than the unassembled component parts. The value, or utility, of making materials available in a completed state is termed *form utility.* However, to a customer interested in purchasing an automobile, the product must have not only form utility, it must be available in the right place, at the right time, and be available for purchase. The value added to products, over and above that added by manufacturing (form utility), has been referred to as the addition of "place, time, and possession utility." Place and time utility are generally thought to be provided by the distribution activity, while marketing provides possession utility.[12]

Place utility is defined as the value created or added to a product by making something available for purchase or consumption in the right place. Certainly, physical distribution is directly responsible for adding place utility to products as it efficiently moves raw materials, in-process inventory, and finished goods from point-of-origin to point-of-consumption. Time utility is thought of as the value created by making something available at the right time. Products are not as valuable to customers if they are not available at the precise time when they are needed. For example, a food processing company must have raw materials (food items), packaging materials, and other items available before the production process begins, or if already begun, before existing supplies of these component parts run out. Failure to receive these items at the proper time can cause costly production shutdowns and place the firm in a disadvantageous competitive position. As will be seen in the remaining chapters of this book, distribution activities combine to add place and time utility to products.

Possession utility, while not a result of the physical distribution process, is nonetheless important because it is the value added to a product by allowing the customer to take ownership of the item. The offering of credit, quantity discounts, and delayed payments enable the customer to assume possession of the product and provide a culmination to the distribution process.

*Efficient movement to customer.* Grosvenor Plowman, retired vice president of traffic for the U.S. Steel Corporation and now a distribution consultant, has referred to the "five rights" of a physical distribution system. The five rights include the supply of the right product at the right place at the right time in the right condition for the right cost to those customers consuming the product.[13] The use of the statement *right cost* deserves consideration. While Plowman's first four rights are analogous to the form, time, place, and possession utilities mentioned, the addition of the cost component is immensely important to the physical distribution process. The significance of the cost aspect was voiced by Peter Drucker two decades ago when he stated:

> Almost 50 cents of each dollar the American spends for goods goes for activities that occur after the goods are made, that is, after they have come in finished form.... Economically ... distribution is the process in which physical properties of matter are converted into economic value; it brings the customer to the product.[14]

The Five Rights of PD

---

[12] The official definition of *marketing* by the American Marketing Association is "the performance of business activities that direct the flow of goods and services from producer to consumer or user." See Committee on Definitions, *Marketing Definitions: A Glossary of Marketing Terms* (Chicago: American Marketing Association, 1960).

[13] Gecowets, "Physical Distribution Management," p. 5.

[14] Peter F. Drucker, "The Economy's Dark Continent," *Fortune* 65, no. 4 (April 1962): 103.

While some individuals might disagree with the 50-cent cost estimated by Drucker, the cost involved in adding time and place utility is substantial. Figure 1–5 provides another estimate of the distribution cost component. The figure implies that physical distribution is the third-largest cost of doing business for a typical firm.

**FIGURE 1–5** Average Cost and Utility Created by Major Corporate Functions—One Way of Viewing the Major Costs of Doing Business

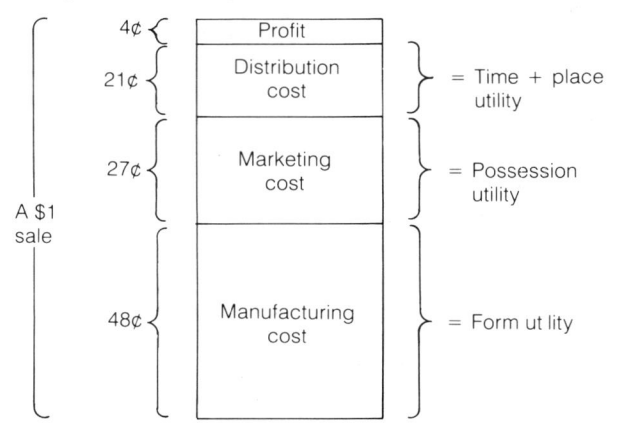

A $1 sale:
- 4¢ Profit
- 21¢ Distribution cost } = Time + place utility
- 27¢ Marketing cost } = Possession utility
- 48¢ Manufacturing cost } = Form utility

Source: Bernard J. LaLonde, John R. Grabner, and James F. Robeson, "Integrated Distribution Systems: A Management Perspective," in *International Journal of Physical Distribution*, October 1970, p. 46.

**A Shoe Company Improves Distribution Efficiency**

The cost of performing the physical distribution function has led companies such as the Thom McAn Division of the Melville Shoe Corporation to examine their distribution activities with the intent of reducing costs, improving profitability, and increasing the efficient movement of product to their customers. With a large distribution network that included over 1,000 retail stores throughout the United States, Thom McAn was able to achieve the following efficiencies which had substantial impact on the profitability of the company:

An increase in productivity of 35.3 percent over the past four years.

A vast improvement in service at a lower cost: The cost of an outbound delivery as a percent of sales dropped from 2.23 percent in 1971 to 1.46 percent in 1974.

The total distribution facility cost, including labor, dropped from 2.26 percent of sales in 1971 to 1.68 percent of sales in 1974.

The total distribution cost; including total delivery and facility costs, went down from 4.89 percent of sales in 1971 to 3.06 percent in 1974.

Despite economic conditions and a slight reduction in sales over the previous year, total physical distribution costs in 1974 were under 1973.[15]

[15] Dennis J. Hennessey, "What Faith Hath Wrought,' *Handling and Shipping*, 17, no. 5 (May 1976): 56.

*Home Furnishings Manufacturer Lowers Distribution Costs*

A major manufacturer of home furnishings in the hard-goods area examined its distribution activity for the purpose of efficiently serving its customers and in the process, contributed to the profitability of the company. During the period 1971–76, the company was able to make its distribution system more efficient in the following areas:

1. Distribution department personnel declined by 35 percent in the face of a substantial increase in volume and an assumption of several new responsibilities.
2. The internal operating budget, which is closely tied to manpower declined by almost $1 million in real terms.
3. Transportation costs, which had increased over 50 percent since 1971, had actually declined 20 percent.

These and other distribution system changes resulted in a cumulative savings of over $50 million for the five-year period, 1971–76.

*Marketing Concept*

**Marketing oriented.** During the 1950s, a philosophy referred to as the "marketing concept" was formulated and adopted by a number of successful companies such as General Electric, Procter & Gamble, IBM, McDonalds, United Airlines, and Whirlpool Corporation. The concept simply stated that the "customer is the boss!" In essence, the marketing concept "is a customer needs-and-wants orientation backed by an integrated marketing effort aimed at generating customer satisfaction as the key to satisfying organizational goals."[16]

*PD, a Key to Successful Marketing*

As part of the marketing effort of the company, distribution plays a key role in satisfying the firm's customers and achieving a profit for the company as a whole. Figure 1–6 represents the marketing concept from a physical distribution management perspective. Customer satisfaction involves maximizing time and place utility to the firm's suppliers, intermediate customers, and final customers. Integrated effort requires that the company coordinate its marketing activities (product, price, promotion, and distribution) to achieve synergistic results, that is, a total which is greater than the sum of its parts. The essence of achieving true integration is the "total cost concept" which examines the cost trade-offs that can occur between and within the marketing and distribution activities. A comprehensive treatment of this important issue will be presented in Chapter 2. The final component of the marketing/physical distribution management concept—company profit—recognizes the need of the firm to achieve an acceptable level of long-term profits. From a financial perspective, the optimal means of achieving this profitability is to reduce total distribution costs as much as possible while still maintaining an adequate level of customer service or satisfaction.

*PD Creates Customer Goodwill*

**Proprietary asset.** An efficient and economical physical distribution (PD) system is similar to a tangible asset on a corporation's books. Additionally, it cannot be readily duplicated by the firm's competitors. The ability of a company to provide its customers with products quickly and at low cost

---

[16] Kotler, *Principles of Marketing*, p. 23.

**FIGURE 1-6** Marketing/Physical Distribution Management Concept

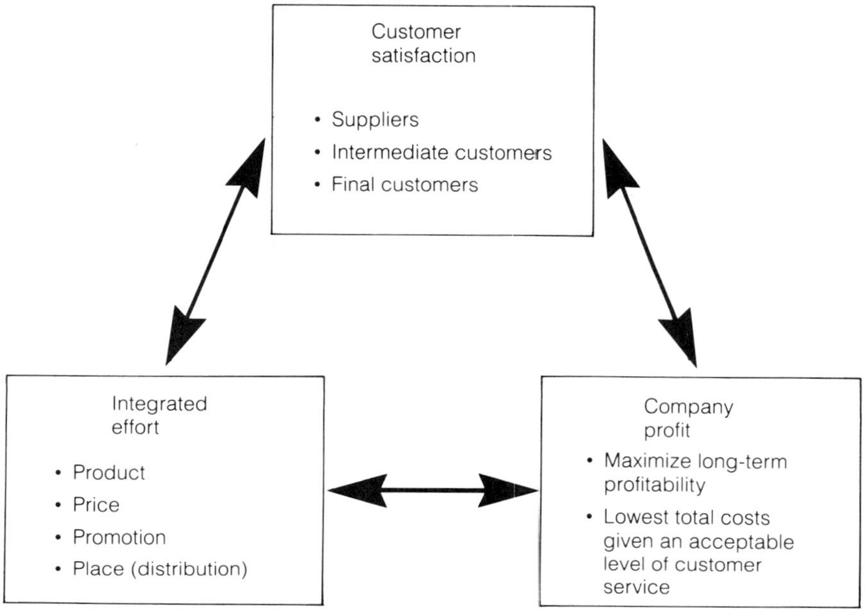

```
                    Customer
                   satisfaction

                  • Suppliers
                  • Intermediate customers
                  • Final customers


    Integrated                         Company
      effort                            profit

  • Product                        • Maximize long-term
  • Price                            profitability
  • Promotion                      • Lowest total costs
  • Place (distribution)             given an acceptable
                                     level of customer
                                     service
```

can enable the firm to achieve market share advantages over its competitors. This can be achieved by selling the product at a lower cost as a result of distribution efficiencies or by providing a higher level of service to customers, thereby creating customer goodwill. If this were to be shown on a firm's balance sheet it would be found under *intangible assets* which includes items such as patents, copyrights, trademarks, and investment in research and development.

*Activities included in physical distribution management.* A variety of activities are involved in the flow of product from point-of-origin to point-of-consumption. While these specific activities will be discussed at length in subsequent chapters, a brief description of each is in order at this point.

*1. Customer service.* In the pioneering study by Bernard LaLonde and Paul Zinszer (1976) which examined the state-of-the-art of customer service in major U.S. corporations, the authors defined customer service as "a customer-oriented philosophy which integrates and manages all of the elements of the customer interface within a predetermined optimum cost-service mix."[17] Customer service acts as the binding and unifying force for all of the activities of physical distribution management. It is such an integral part of the entire distribution process that Chapter 3 of this book has been devoted to it. Under the broad umbrella of customer service come any

<small>Customer Satisfaction Is Important to the Firm</small>

---

[17] Bernard J. LaLonde and Paul H. Zinszer, *Customer Service: Meaning and Measurement* (Chicago: National Council of Physical Distribution Management, 1976), p. iv (hereafter cited as NCPDM).

activities which impact on the level of satisfaction obtained by the firm's customers or suppliers. Since each element of a firm's physical distribution system can affect a customer's receipt of the right product at the right place in the right condition for the right cost at the right time, the service activity involves the integrated management of the distribution activities in such a manner so as to provide the necessary level of customer satisfaction at the lowest possible total cost.

*The Importance of Demand Forecasting*

2. *Demand forecasting.* Demand forecasting involves a determination of the amount of product, and accompanying service, which customers will require at some point in the future. The need to know precisely how much product will be demanded is important to all facets of the firm's operations—marketing, manufacturing, and physical distribution. Within marketing, forecasts of future demand are integrally related with determining promotional strategies, allocation of sales force effort, pricing strategies, and market research activities. Manufacturing requires forecasts to determine production schedules, purchasing and acquisition strategies, and in-plant inventory decisions.

Physical distribution management is concerned with the flow of product from point-of-origin to point-of-consumption, and forecasts of demand are necessary to determine how much of each item the company produces must be moved or transported to the various markets served by the firm. Also, physical distribution must know where the demand will originate so that the proper amount of product can be placed or stored in each market area. Knowledge of future demand levels will enable physical distribution managers to allocate their resources (budgets) to those distribution activities which will service that demand. Decision making under uncertainty is suboptimal in most cases because it is extremely difficult to allocate resources among distribution activities without knowing what products and services will be needed. Therefore, it is imperative that some type of demand forecasting be undertaken by the firm and the results communicated to the firm's marketing, manufacturing, and physical distribution departments. Such forecasts may be developed using a variety of techniques including sophisticated computer models, trend analysis, projects based upon sales force estimates, or other methods.

*Effective Communication Is Vital*

3. *Distribution communications.* Today's company manages a complex communications system. Effective communication must take place between (a) the firm and its customers, suppliers, and vendors; (b) the major functional components of the company—marketing, manufacturing, physical distribution, and finance/accounting; (c) the various distribution-related activities such as customer service, traffic and transportation, warehousing and storage, order processing, and inventory control; and (d) the various subcomponents of each distribution activity (e.g., within inventory control would be in-plant inventory, inventory in transit, and inventory in field warehouses). Communication is the vital link which coordinates and integrates the entire physical distribution process with the firm's customers. Accurate and timely communication is the cornerstone of successful physical distribution management.

A firm's communication system may be extremely sophisticated because it utilizes a computerized management information system (MIS), either online or offline, or it may be as simple as word-of-mouth communication between individuals. Whatever the system used, it is vital that information be available and communicated to those individuals who have a "need to know."

4. *Inventory control.* The inventory-control decision is critical because of the financial aspects of maintaining a sufficient supply of product to meet the needs of customers as well as manufacturing requirements. Maintaining raw materials, parts, and finished goods in inventory not only consumes space but also capital resources. Money tied up in inventory is not available for use elsewhere. In a subsequent chapter on inventory, the financial aspects of inventory control will be examined in detail, but at this point it is sufficient to point out that most authors estimate that inventory carrying costs average approximately 25 percent of inventory value; however, depending on the type of product, the amount can range from 14 percent to over 50 percent of the inventory value.[18] Successful inventory control involves determining the level of inventory necessary to achieve the desired level of customer service while giving full consideration to the cost of performing the other physical distribution activities.

5. *Material handling.* Material handling is concerned with every aspect of the movement or flow of raw materials, in-process inventory and finished goods within a plant or warehouse. The objectives of material handling are typically recognized as:

**Objectives of Material Handling**

To eliminate handling wherever possible;

To reduce travel distance to an absolute minimum;

To increase speed of processing by providing uniform flow free of bottlenecks;

To reduce goods in process in order to provide a faster turnover of working capital; and

To minimize losses from waste, breakage, spoilage, and theft.[19]

Costs are incurred by a firm every time an item is handled. Generally, handling adds no value to a product. Consequently, these operations should be kept to a minimum. For items with low unit value, the proportion of material handling costs to total product cost can be significant. "Poor material handling can lead directly to product damage, customer dissatisfaction, production delays, and idle employees."[20]

**The Firm's Central Nervous System**

6. *Order processing.* "Order processing may be compared to the human body's central nervous system, triggering the distribution process and directing the actions to be taken in satisfying order demand."[21] The

---

[18] For a comprehensive review of the inventory carrying cost literature see Douglas M. Lambert, *The Development of an Inventory Costing Methodology: A Study of the Costs Associated with Holding Inventory* (Chicago: NCPDM, 1975).

[19] Richard J. Tersine and John H. Campbell, *Modern Materials Management* (New York: Elsevier North-Holland, 1977), p. 194.

[20] Ibid.

[21] A. T. Kearney, Inc., *Measuring Productivity in Physical Distribution* (Chicago: NCPDM, 1978), p. 186.

components of the order processing activity may be broken down into three groups: (a) operational elements such as order entry/editing, scheduling, order-shipping set preparation, and invoicing; (b) communication elements such as order modification, order status inquiries, tracing and expediting, error correction, and product information requests; and (c) credit and collection elements including credit checking and accounts receivable processing/collecting.[22] The speed and accuracy of a firm's order processing activity has a great deal to do with the level of customer service provided by the company. Advanced order-processing systems are able to reduce the time between placement of a customer's order and the shipment of that order from a warehouse or storage facility. In many firms this process is performed by computer with direct transmission of orders to the company via WATS telephone lines, teletype, or video, cathode-ray tube terminals. Advanced systems, although initially expensive to the company, can substantially increase order-processing accuracy and reduce order-response time. Often, the system can be cost justified by savings in other physical distribution expenses such as inventory, transportation, and/or warehousing, or by improvements in customer service which increase sales.

7. *Parts and service support.* In addition to the movement of raw materials, in-process inventory, and finished goods, physical distribution must be concerned with the many activities associated with the repair and servicing of products. The responsibility of physical distribution does not end once the product is delivered to the customer. As part of the marketing activity of the firm, the customer must be provided with servicing after the sale has been made. This involves providing replacement parts when product breakdowns or malfunctions occur. For example, in the automobile market, the dealerships must have efficient service departments which offer complete servicing and repair of most domestic and foreign automobiles. Adequate supplies of spare and replacement parts are vital to the service and repair activity. Physical distribution is responsible for making sure those parts are available when and where the customer needs them. In the industrial marketplace where the product may be a piece of manufacturing equipment, down time can be extremely costly to the customer if the product failure results in a production-line slowdown or shutdown. In that instance, the firm supplying the space or replacement part must be able to respond to the problems quickly and decisively. Adequate parts and service support is extremely important whenever after-the-sale support is part of the marketing effort of the firm.

8. *Plant and warehouse site selection.* Whether facilities are owned, leased, or rented, the location decision for plants and/or warehouses (storage facilities) is extremely important.

> Site selection affects total corporate costs to an even greater degree in the decade of the 1970s [and 1980s] with its fuel crises, foreign competition, inflation, etc. Increasing transportation costs have developed into a continual headache—especially for companies that cannot raise consumer prices.[23]

---

[22] Ibid., p. 191.
[23] "Site Selection Checklist," *Distribution Worldwide* 73, no. 2 (February 1974): 28.

The strategic placement of plants and warehouses can improve the firm's customer service levels by locating facilities near the company's markets. Also, proper facility location can reduce transportation costs by moving product from plant to warehouse, plant to plant, or warehouse to customer in a manner that will take advantage of volume-related transportation rates.

The first consideration in site selection is determining the location of the firm's various markets. The needs of the customers and the location of raw materials, component parts and subassemblies, should be major considerations when locating plant and warehouse facilities. This is because the company must be concerned with inbound movement and storage of materials in addition to outbound flows. A multiplicity of other important factors include: labor rates; transportation services; city, county, and state taxes; security; legal aspects; local factors such as the attitude of the local community toward new industry; land cost; and availability of utilities.

9. *Procurement.* Every company relies to some extent on materials and services supplied by other firms.

*Procurement—a $350-Billion Business*

The great majority of U.S. industries spend from 40 to 60 percent of their revenues for materials and services from outside sources. It has been estimated that U.S. industries purchased materials totaling over $350 billion per year in the early 1970s. For the same period, capital expenditures amounted to another $20 billion and year-end inventory exceeded $100 billion. The magnitude of these figures emphasizes the importance of purchasing and procurement on the U.S. economy as well as to individual organizations.[24]

Procurement can be defined as the acquisition of materials and services to insure the operating effectiveness of the firm's manufacturing and distribution processes. The procurement function includes the selection of supply source locations, determination of the form in which the material is to be acquired, timing of purchases, price determination, quality control, and many other activities. In recent years, a changing economic environment marked by wide variations in the availability and cost of materials has made procurement an even more important activity of the physical distribution process.

10. *Packaging.* Packaging performs two basic functions—a marketing function and a physical distribution function. In a marketing sense the package acts as a form of promotion or advertising. The size, weight, color, and information on the package serve to attract customers and convey meaningful knowledge about the product being offered for sale. From a physical distribution perspective, packaging serves a dual role. First, the package protects the product from damage while it is being stored or transported. Second, the package can aid in the efficient storage and handling of the product. Packaging can make it easier to store and move products by reducing handling, and thereby reducing materials-handling costs. When firms are involved in international distribution the packaging activity becomes even more important. Products marketed in foreign countries

*Packaging Serves a Dual Role*

---

[24] Tersine and Campbell, *Modern Materials Management*, p. 82.

travel greater distances and undergo more handling operations. Also, the handlings may occur under conditions much less favorable than in the United States. In many countries management must deal with a lack of adequate material-handling equipment and must rely on poorly trained personnel. In general, domestic packaging is not strong enough to withstand the rigors of export shipment.[25]

*Reverse Distribution*

11. *Return goods handling.* The handling of return goods, which is often referred to as *reverse distribution,* is an important part of the physical distribution process. Items may be returned to the seller due to product defects, overages, incorrect items received by the buyer, and other reasons. Reverse distribution has been likened to going the wrong way on a one way street because the great majority of product shipments flow in one direction. Most distribution systems are ill-equipped to handle product movement in a reverse channel. Some distribution professionals have speculated that the cost to move a product back through the system from consumer to producer may cost as much as nine times the cost to move the same product from producer to consumer. In many industries where products are returned for warranty repair, replacement, or recycling, reverse distribution costs may be high. Often, the returned goods cannot be transported, stored, and/or handled as easily, resulting in higher physical-distribution costs. Reverse distribution promises to become even more important as customers demand more flexible and lenient return-of-goods policies from companies.

12. *Salvage and scrap disposal.* As a by-product of the manufacturing and distribution processes, waste materials are produced. If this material cannot be used to produce other products, it must be disposed of in some manner. Whatever the by-product—scrap materials, residues, or radioactive wastes—it is part of the physical distribution processes to effectively and efficiently handle, transport, and store the material. In those instances where the by-products are reusable and have value as recyclable materials, physical distribution administers the flow of that material to those locations where they can be remanufactured or reprocessed.

*Transportation Is an Important Component of Distribution*

13. *Traffic and transportation.* One of the major components of the physical-distribution process is the movement or flow of goods from point-of-origin to point-of-consumption, and perhaps their return as well. The traffic and transportation activity refers to the management of the movement of products and includes components such as selecting the method of shipment—air, rail, water, pipeline, truck; choosing the specific path (routing) to be taken by the product; complying with various local, state, and federal transportation regulations; and being aware of both domestic and international shipping requirements.

Transportation is an important responsibility in physical distribution management, both from the cost standpoint and from the service standpoint.

Ford Motor Company is an example of the broad utilization made of transpor-

---

[25] Charles A. Taff, *Management of Physical Distribution and Transportation,* 5th ed. (Homewood, Ill.: Richard D. Irwin, 1972), p. 267.

tation. On any given day, Ford has in transit up to 50,000 finished vehicles and almost 1 billion finished parts bound for assembly plants and parts depots. In addition, over 14 million tons of raw materials and semifinished parts are transported each year.

All shipments, both inbound raw materials and fabricated parts and outbound finished products on which the company pays transportation costs, are handled by the physical distribution department. The physical distribution manager should have a knowledge of the various modes of transport and services and routing offered by each mode and by carriers within the modes. Special services, such as diversion and reconsignment of shipments while in transit and transit privileges granted by some carriers on certain kinds of shipments which may be stopped in transit for storing, processing, fabricating, or other activities and reforwarded at the lower through rate, should be developed and used by the physical distribution manager where they will be advantageous to his company. He should be familiar with the rates charged by various carriers and the procedures to be followed in rate negotiations. His general knowledge of transportation will be of valuable aid in determining if he should institute company transportation as a means of paring transportation costs, as a trade-off in the physical distribution system, or in improving transportation service. It will also be to his advantage to have familiarity with the special facets of international distribution.[26]

In many companies, transportation may be the single, largest cost of the physical distribution process.

*14. Warehousing and storage.* Unless products are needed by customers at precisely the instant that they are produced, they must be stored at the plant or in the field. Generally, the greater the time lag between when the product is produced and when it is consumed, the larger the level or amount of inventory required. Warehousing and storage encompass those activities necessary to manage the space needed to hold or maintain inventories. Specific components of the storage activity include own-lease-rent decisions, warehouse layout and design, product mix considerations, safety and maintenance, security systems, personnel training, productivity measurement, and others.

## DEVELOPMENT OF PHYSICAL DISTRIBUTION MANAGEMENT

### Historical Development

Evidence suggests that physical distribution was first written about in the early 1900s. John Crowell (1901) discussed the costs and factors affecting the distribution of farm products in a government report entitled *Report of the Industrial Commission on the Distribution of Farm Products*.[27] Later, in a text entitled *An Approach to Business Problems* by Arch Shaw (1916), the

---

[26] Ibid., p. 15.

[27] John F. Crowell, *Report of the Industrial Commission on the Distribution of Farm Products*, vol. 6 (Washington, D.C.: Government Printing Office, 1901).

strategic aspects of physical distribution were discussed.[28] In 1922, the role of distribution in marketing was identified by Fred Clark in *Principles of Marketing*,[29] and in 1927 the term *physical distribution* was first used in a text by Ralph Borsodi entitled *The Distribution Age*.[30] The book defined physical distribution in a way similar to its use today.

> There are two uses of the word distribution which must be clearly differentiated . . . first, the use of the word to describe physical distribution such as transportation and storage; second, the use of the word distribution to describe what is better termed marketing.[31]

With the onset of World War II, physical distribution, or logistics, as it was called in the military, was further developed and refined. Used in conjunction with a new corporate philosophy that originated in the 1950s—"the marketing concept"—physical distribution came to be associated, to an even greater degree, with the customer service and cost components of a firm's marketing efforts.

In 1956, a study of the economics of air freight added an additional dimension to the field of physical distribution.[32] The study introduced the concept of total cost analysis. Air freight is a high-cost form of transportation. However, use of air freight in lieu of other transport modes could result in lower inventory and warehousing costs as a firm distributed directly to its customers.

The decade of the 1960s brought with it a number of developments in physical distribution. In 1961 the first text on physical distribution management was written by Edward Smykay, Donald Bowersox, and Frank Mossman.[33] The book examined physical distribution from a systems perspective and discussed the total cost concept. The National Council of Physical Distribution Management (NCPDM) was formed in 1963 "to develop the theory and understanding of the physical distribution process, promote the art and science of managing physical distribution systems and to foster professional dialogue and development in the field operating exclusively without profit and in cooperation with other organizations and institutions."[34]

During the remainder of the 1960s and continuing into the 1980s, a multitude of texts, articles, monographs, journals, and conferences, were devoted to the subject of physical distribution management. One of the

---

[28] Arch W. Shaw, *An Approach to Business Problems* (Cambridge, Mass.: Harvard University Press, 1916).

[29] Fred E. Clark, *Principles of Marketing* (New York: Macmillan, 1922).

[30] Ralph Borsodi, *The Distribution Age* (New York: D. Appleton, 1927).

[31] Ibid., p. 19.

[32] Howard T. Lewis, James W. Culliton, and Jack D. Steele, *The Role of Air Freight in Physical Distribution* (Boston: Harvard Business School, 1956).

[33] Edward W. Smykay, Donald J. Bowersox, and Frank H. Mossman, *Physical Distribution Management* (New York: Macmillan, 1961).

[34] Information supplied by the National Council of Physical Distribution Management indicates a 1981 membership of over 3,200 distribution practitioners and academicians.

earliest writings to examine the accounting/physical distribution interface was Michael Schiff's *Accounting and Control in Physical Distribution Management*, published in 1972.[35] The study was instrumental in creating an awareness that accounting and financial information is vital to the distribution activity. In 1976 the landmark study by LaLonde and Zinszer entitled *Customer Service: Meaning and Measurement* was published.[36] For the first time, the topic of customer service was explored in detail. As part of the marketing concept, customer satisfaction requires a complete understanding of what customer service is all about. Two years later, in 1978, the issue of distribution productivity was examined by A. T. Kearney, Inc., under sponsorship of NCPDM. The state-of-the-art appraisal of this important aspect of physical distribution was entitled *Measuring Productivity in Physical Distribution*.[37] These NCPDM sponsored studies are continuing to influence the physical distribution profession and it will be many years before their significance can be fully appraised.

For the readers interest, Table 1–1 identifies some of the more important events in the development of physical distribution management.

### Factors Underlying the Development of Interest in Physical Distribution Management

A number of factors have been identified as reasons underlying the recognition of the subject of physical distribution management as being important to society and the firm. Among the most important factors were: advances in computer technology and quantitative techniques; development of the systems approach and total cost analysis concept; recognition of physical distribution's role in the firm's customer service program; erosion of many firms' profits resulting in their examining functional areas where cost savings might be realized; the profit leverage resulting from increased distribution efficiency; and general economic conditions since the 1950s.

Undoubtedly, a multiplicity of factors operating independently, yet having joint and synergistic effects, were instrumental in bringing about interest in physical distribution management. Certainly, a recognition of the cost and service impacts of the distribution process were important. For example, distribution costs can be a significant portion of a typical firm's sales dollar as was shown in Figure 1–5. However, for firms in specific industries, the impact can be even more pronounced. Distribution costs for an industrial nondurable goods producer can be much higher than for a pharmaceutical company. If we examined the various components of the physical distribution process we would probably find that it was the transportation component that consumed a significantly smaller percentage of the pharmaceutical company's distribution costs. Generally, the

Distribution — a Significant Cost to the Firm

---

[35] Michael Schiff, *Accounting and Control in Physical Distribution Management* (Chicago: NCPDM, 1972).

[36] LaLonde and Zinszer, *Customer Service*.

[37] A. T. Kearney, Inc., *Measuring Productivity*.

**TABLE 1–1** Historical Development of Physical Distribution Management

| Date(s) | Event | Significance |
|---|---|---|
| 1901 | John F. Crowell, *Report of the Industrial Commission on the Distribution of Farm Products,* vol. 6 (Washington, D.C.: Government Printing Office) | The first text to deal with the costs and factors affecting the distribution of farm products |
| 1916 | Arch W. Shaw, *An Approach to Business Problems* (Cambridge, Mass.: Harvard University Press) | The text discussed the strategic aspects of physical distribution |
| 1922 | Fred E. Clark, *Principles of Marketing* (New York: Macmillan) | The text defined marketing as those efforts which affect transfers in the ownership of goods and care of their physical distributions |
| 1927 | Ralph Borsodi, *The Distribution Age* (New York: D. Appleton) | One of the first texts to use the term *physical distribution* and to describe it as presently utilized |
| 1941–45 | World War II | Military logistics operations demonstrated how distribution activities could be integrated into a single system |
| 1945 | Delta Nu Alpha Transportation Fraternity founded | The first national fraternity organized to encourage and promote education in transportation |
| 1946 | American Society of Traffic and Transportation (AST&T) founded | The first professional transportation testing and certification society |
| 1950s | Initial development of the marketing concept | Corporations began to emphasize customer satisfaction at a profit. Customer-service element later became the cornerstone of physical distribution management |
| 1954 | Paul D. Converse, "The Other Half of Marketing, "*Twenty-sixth Boston Conference on Distribution* (Boston: Boston Trade Board) | A leading business and educational authority pointed out the need for academicians and practitioners to examine the physical distribution side of marketing |
| 1956 | Howard T. Lewis, James W. Culliton, and Jack D. Steele, *The Role of Air Freight in Physical Distribution* (Boston: Harvard Business School) | Introduced the concept of total cost analysis to the area of physical distribution |
| Early 1960s | Introduction of Sylvania Company's "unimarket" concept | Earliest reported company effort to adopt and implement physical distribution management concept. Sylvania utilized one distribution center for U.S. market in combination with an air freight transportation system |
|  | Michigan State University and Ohio State University institute undergraduate and graduate programs in physical distribution | The first formal educational programs developed to train physical distribution practitioners and educators |

**TABLE 1–1** (continued)

| Date(s) | Event | Significance |
|---|---|---|
| 1961 | Edward W. Smykay, Donald J. Bowersox, and Frank H. Mossman, *Physical Distribution Management* (New York: Macmillan) | One of the first texts on physical distribution. The systems approach to physical distribution management and the total cost concept were discussed in detail |
| 1962 | Peter Drucker, "The Economy's Dark Continent," *Fortune* 65, no. 4 (April 1962): 103, 265, 266, 268, 270 | A leading business and educational authority recognized the importance of distribution in the United States. Many scholars believe this article had significant impact on the practitioner community |
| 1963 | The National Council of Physical Distribution Management (NCPDM) founded | Largest and most prestigious national organization devoted to physical distribution management |
| 1969 | Donald J. Bowersox, "Physical Distribution Development, Current Status, and Potential," *Journal of Marketing* 33, no. 1 (January 1969): 63–70 | Integrated physical distribution management concept examined for the first time from a historical (past, present, and future) perspective |
| 1972 | Michael Schiff, *Accounting and Control in Physical Distribution Management* (Chicago: NCPDM) | Created an awareness of the importance of accounting and financial information to successful physical distribution management |
| 1976 | Douglas M. Lambert, *The Development of an Inventory Costing Methodology: A Study of the Costs Associated with Holding Inventory* (Chicago: NCPDM) | Identified the cost components of one of the largest physical distribution expense items and developed a methodology whereby firms could calculate their inventory carrying costs |
| 1976 | Bernard J. LaLonde and Paul H. Zinszer, *Customer Service: Meaning and Measurement* (Chicago: NCPDM) | The first comprehensive state-of-the-art appraisal of the customer service activity in major U.S. corporations |
| 1978 | A. T. Kearney, Inc., *Measuring Productivity in Physical Distribution* (Chicago: NCPDM) | The first comprehensive state-of-the-art appraisal of productivity measurement in physical distribution |

product value (dollars per pound) is much higher for pharmaceuticals than it is for industrial nondurables (raw materials and industrial products used in the manufacture of end products). As a result, distribution costs will be a smaller percentage of a firm's sales dollar for the pharmaceutical company. To illustrate, suppose a product shipment is valued at $10,000 for the pharmaceutical company and $2,000 for the industrial nondurables company. Because of factors such as market conditions, level of competition, transportation modes utilized, product perishability such as damageability and shelf life, inventory carrying costs, and handling characteristics, the pharmaceutical company may pay only $500 to distribute their product while the industrial nondurable-goods firm pays $250. In absolute terms the pharmaceutical company has paid more, but as a percentage of product value or sales, they have paid only 5 percent as opposed to 12.5 percent paid by the industrial nondurable-goods firm.

In addition to the distribution expense of the firm, the profit squeeze and potential profit leverage that can result from increased efficiency in distribution, have contributed significantly to the development of interest in physical distribution management.

As markets constantly expanded during the 1950s and 1960s, emphasis was upon increased sales. As the tempo of domestic and international competition increased, a "profit squeeze" was reflected in many American firms' balance sheets. This prompted many firms to look for cost reduction opportunities along with market expansion opportunity. For example, if the firm makes 2 percent net from $1 sales, then a saving of 2 cents in logistics is equivalent to $1 expansion in sales (Table 1–2). This is assuming that all fixed costs remain constant. A $2

**TABLE 1–2** Profit Leverage Provided by Physical Distribution Cost Reduction

*If Net Profit on the Sales Dollar is 2.0 Percent Then . . .*

| A Saving of | Is Equivalent to a Sales Increase of |
|---|---|
| $      0.02 | $          1.00 |
|          2.00 |           100.00 |
|      200.00 |       10,000.00 |
|   2,000.00 |     100,000.00 |
| 20,000.00 |  1,000,000.00 |

Source: Bernard J. LaLonde, John R. Grabner, and James F. Robeson, "Integrated Distribution Systems: A Management Perspective," *International Journal of Physical Distribution*, October 1970, p. 46.

distribution cost saving is equivalent to $100 in sales expansion and likewise a $2,000 saving in distribution cost is equivalent to $100,000 in additional sales. The profit leverage argument makes a persuasive argument to management for reviewing cost reduction opportunities available from integrated distribution management.[38]

### Operationalizing a Physical Distribution Management System

Within any individual company, physical distribution management approaches will vary depending upon the specific characteristics of the company and its products. In Chapter 12 we will explore the question of how a

---

[38] Bernard J. LaLonde, John R. Grabner, and James F. Robeson, "Integrated Distribution Systems: A Management Perspective," *International Journal of Physical Distribution*, October 1970, p. 46.

firm can organize its physical distribution system, but in general, Figure 1–7 shows a typical approach that a manufacturing firm might take. The diagram illustrates the organizational aspects (planning, control, and execution) of a physical distribution management system and the interrelationships and interdependencies of the functional systems that sustain and support its activities.[39] While the exact organizational structure will vary by

**FIGURE 1-7** Operational Elements of a Physical Distribution System

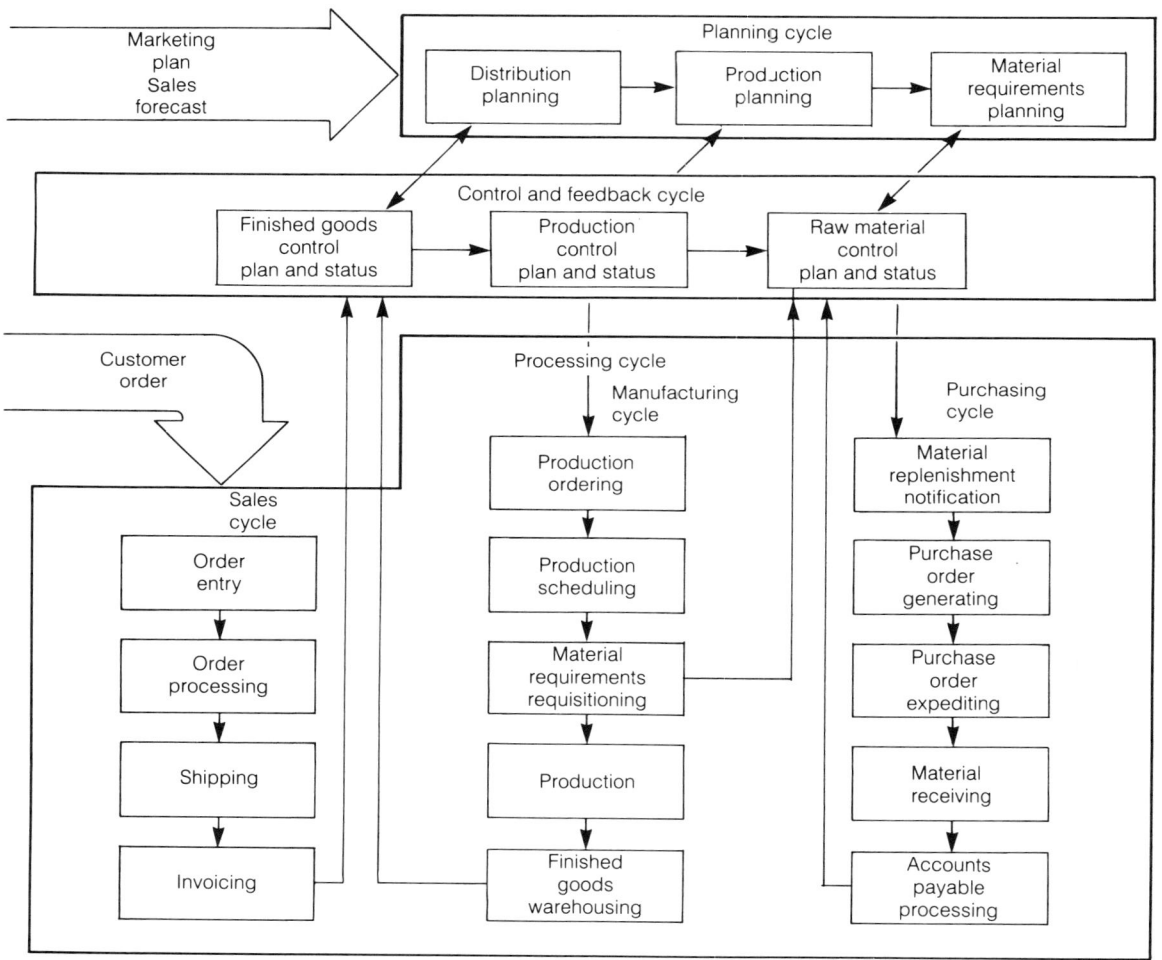

```
Marketing plan / Sales forecast →  Planning cycle:
    Distribution planning → Production planning → Material requirements planning

Control and feedback cycle:
    Finished goods control plan and status → Production control plan and status → Raw material control plan and status

Customer order → Processing cycle

Sales cycle:
    Order entry → Order processing → Shipping → Invoicing

Manufacturing cycle:
    Production ordering → Production scheduling → Material requirements requisitioning → Production → Finished goods warehousing

Purchasing cycle:
    Material replenishment notification → Purchase order generating → Purchase order expediting → Material receiving → Accounts payable processing
```

Source: Harrison H. Appleby, "Organizing the Logistics Function to Optimize Benefits," in *Proceedings of the Sixteenth Annual Conference of the National Council of Physical Distribution Management*, October 16–18, 1978, p. 184.

---

[39] Harrison H. Appleby, "Organizing the Logistics Function to Optimize Benefits," in *Proceedings of the Sixteenth Annual Conference of the National Council of Physical Distribution Management*, October 16–18, 1978, p. 183.

organization it is important that whatever the system, it be as efficient as possible from a cost and service perspective.

In the face of higher costs of operation and increasing pressures from customers for better levels of service, the physical distribution organization must evolve and change to meet the challenge. An understanding of the factors which make organizations effective and a knowledge of how those factors interrelate are the first steps toward developing an optimal distribution system in a company.

## SUMMARY

In this chapter you were shown how physical distribution activities interface with the economic system at the macro (societal) and micro (firm) levels. The relationship between physical distribution management and a firm's channel of distribution was discussed.

Physical distribution management was defined as the integration of two or more activities for the purpose of planning, implementing, and controlling the efficient flow of raw materials, in-process inventory, and finished goods from point-of-origin to point-of-consumption. The relationship between physical distribution and marketing was examined with special emphasis given to the creation of time and place utility. The importance of physical distribution to the firm from a cost standpoint was also examined.

Examples of physical distribution activities included customer service, demand forecasting, distribution communications, inventory control, material handling, order processing, parts and service support, plant and warehouse site selection, procurement, packaging, return goods handling, salvage and scrap disposal, traffic and transportation, and warehousing and storage.

The historical development of physical distribution management was examined in light of the strategic function of PM in the modern corporation. With this as background you are prepared to examine the integrated PDM concept, the total cost concept, and the marketing and physical distribution audit which are the subjects of Chapter 2.

## QUESTIONS AND PROBLEMS

1. A number of relationships exist between physical distribution and the marketing channel. Identify the relationships that exist.

2. Identify how improvements in physical distribution productivity can influence the economic position of individual consumers and the population as a whole.

3. Physical distribution has been described as an activity which adds time and place utility to products. Indicate how physical distribution affects time and place utility.

4. The definition of physical distribution management used in this book includes a variety of activities involved in the flow of product from point-of-origin to point-of-consumption. Briefly describe each of the following activities included in physical distribution management:

a. Customer service.
   b. Demand forecasting.
   c. Distribution communications.
   d. Inventory control.
   e. Material handling.
   f. Order processing.
   g. Parts and service support.
   h. Plant and warehouse site selection.
   i. Procurement.
   j. Packaging.
   k. Return goods handling.
   l. Salvage and scrap disposal.
   m. Traffic and transportation.
   n. Warehousing and storage.

5. What factors have influenced business to recognize that physical distribution management is important to society and the firm?

6. Physical distribution cost reductions can provide significant profit leverage. If a firm has a net profit on its sales of 5 percent, what sales increase would be required to match a physical distribution cost reduction of $1,000? In what areas of physical distribution would the cost reduction be most likely to occur?

# 2 The Integrated Physical Distribution Management Concept

Introduction

Reasons for Growth of the Physical Distribution Function

Physical Distribution and the Marketing Function
    Price
    Product
    Promotion
    Place

The Total Cost Concept
    Customer Service Levels
    Transportation Costs
    Warehousing Costs
    Order Processing and Information Costs
    Production Lot Quantity Costs
    Inventory Carrying Costs

Physical Distribution and Corporate Profit Performance
    The Strategic Profit Model
        Net Profit
        Asset Turnover
        Return on Assets
        Financial Leverage
        An Application

An Example of Integrated Physical Distribution Management

Conducting a Marketing and Physical Distribution Audit

Developing a Physical Distribution Strategy

Areas Where Physical Distribution Performance Can Be Improved
    Forecasting
    Order Processing and Communications Systems
    Customer Service
    Inventory Management
    Transportation
    Warehousing

Summary

**Objectives of this chapter:**

To show how physical distribution influences economic and corporate performance

To show how to implement the integrated physical distribution management concept using total cost analysis

To show how to conduct a marketing and physical distribution audit

To show how to recognize areas where physical distribution performance can be improved

## INTRODUCTION

In an inflationary economy marked by rising energy costs, potential energy and material shortages, high interest rates and capital rationing, and a declining growth rate in productivity, the maintenance of corporate profit growth and return on investment is becoming increasingly difficult. Consequently, it has become necessary for management to investigate alternative methods of revenue generation and cost reduction. Many firms have discovered that few areas offer the potential for profit improvement that can be found in the physical distribution function. This is because physical distribution costs can exceed 25 percent of each sales dollar at the manufacturing level.[1] In many companies physical distribution has not been managed as an integrated system, and successful implementation of the integrated physical distribution management concept can lead to significant improvements in profitability.[2] The foundation of the integrated physical distribution management concept is *total cost analysis* which has been defined as "the minimization of the sum of the costs of transportation, warehousing, inventory, order processing and communications, and production lot quantity cost while achieving a desired customer service level."

The purpose of this chapter is to show you: how physical distribution influences economic growth and corporate performance; how the integrated physical distribution management concept can be implemented using total cost analysis; how to conduct a marketing and physical distribution audit; and how to recognize areas where physical distribution performance can be improved.

During the past two decades physical distribution has emerged as a separate and dynamic discipline. Many major corporations have acknowledged the importance of physical distribution by placing responsibility for integrating distribution activities at the vice president level.[3] Basically, the

---

[1] Bernard J. LaLonde, John R. Grabner, and James F. Robeson, "Integrated Distribution Systems: A Management Perspective," *International Journal of Physical Distribution*, October 1970, p. 134.

[2] Alan H. Gepfert, "Business Logistics for Better Profit Performance," *Harvard Business Review* (November–December 1968), pp. 75–84, and Jack Farrell, *Physical Distribution Case Studies* (Boston: Cahners Books International, 1973).

[3] A quick scan of the membership roster of the National Council of Physical Distribution Management confirms this, also see Bernard J. LaLonde and Martha Cooper, "Career Patterns in Distribution: Profile 1979," *Proceedings of the Seventeenth Annual Conference of the National Council of Physical Distribution Management*, October 1979, pp. 15–42.

**Integration of PD Activities Smoothes Corporate Interfaces**

integrated physical distribution management concept refers to the administration of the various distribution activities as an integrated system. In firms that have not adopted a systems integrative approach, physical distribution is a fragmented and often uncoordinated set of activities spread throughout various organizational functions with each individual function having its own set of priorities and measurements.[4] A number of firms including Johns-Manville, Quaker Oats, and Whirlpool Corporation have found that total distribution costs can be reduced, customer service improved, and interdepartmental conflicts substantially reduced by the integration of such distribution-related activities as: customer service, transportation, warehousing, inventory management, order processing, and production planning. Without this integrated approach inventory tends to build up at the following critical business interfaces:

Supplier—purchasing.
Purchasing—production.
Production—marketing.
Marketing—distribution.
Distribution—intermediary.
Intermediary—consumer/user.

In a manufacturing environment inventory commonly builds up at these interfaces for the following reasons:

1. Purchasing management is often rewarded for achieving low per unit costs for raw materials and supplies.
2. Production management is usually compensated based on achieving the lowest possible per-unit production costs.
3. Salespeople like to have large inventories of product in the field and as close to the customer as possible in order to offer the fastest possible order-cycle time and minimize the difficulties associated with working closely with customers to forecast their needs.
4. In many companies the only physical distribution cost which has been closely monitored is transportation cost. With upward pressure on transportation rates caused by higher energy and labor costs, there is even more incentive for transportation managers to ship products by truckload or even better by the railcar in order to obtain lower rates. Generally, these large shipments of products require increased inventories at both the origin and destination (for example at the manufacturer and retailer).
5. Both consumers/users and intermediaries may attempt to reduce their own inventories by purchasing more frequently, thereby forcing inventories and the associated carrying costs back in the channel of

---

[4] Alan H. Gepfert, "Business Logistics for Better Profit Performance," *Harvard Business Review* (November—December, 1968), pp. 75—84 and Jack Farrell, *Physical Distribution Case Studies* (Boston: Cahners Books International, 1973).

distribution toward the manufacturer. This is particularly true in times when cash-flow management is a major concern of intermediaries.

The central coordination of the various components of physical distribution management forces cost trade-offs to be made between and among customer service levels, transportation, warehousing, inventory management, order processing, and production planning.

## REASONS FOR GROWTH OF THE PHYSICAL DISTRIBUTION FUNCTION

Although physical distribution is a function that has always been performed by manufacturers and marketing intermediaries, it was not until the late 1950s that management began to direct a considerable amount of attention to physical distribution. The increase in interest in distribution was the result of: (1) the proliferation of products that came about as a result of acceptance of the marketing concept and the desire to segment markets; (2) the profit squeeze experienced in the late 1950s; (3) the existence of the computer technology required to handle large volumes of data; (4) the growing acceptance of the systems approach as a method of management; (5) the application of mathematical techniques for solving business problems; and (6) the success achieved in military logistics managing transportation inventory and warehousing systems.[5]

The economy of the 1970s resulted in even greater pressure on profitability. Inflation rates hit record highs for the United States with annualized rates approaching 20 percent in 1980 and 1981. This record inflation was fueled by energy dependency on OPEC oil and declining growth rates in national productivity.[6] Usually improvements in productivity can be achieved through technological change. Recession and a prime interest rate that reached 20 percent, however, placed severe constraints on corporate investment.

In this type of economic climate, management must look for ways to improve the profitability of existing business. This is because in most companies it is not possible to achieve corporate profit and return on investment objectives by increasing sales. Consequently top management focuses its attention on cash-flow management and asset management. The implications for physical distribution, which is relatively more labor intensive

---

[5] See Lewis M. Schneider, "Milestones on the Road of Physical Distribution," in *Readings in Business Logistics*, ed. David M. McConaughy (Homewood, Ill.: Richard D. Irwin, 1969), pp. 51–63, and Bernard J. LaLonde, John R. Grabner, and James F. Robeson, "Integrated Distribution Systems: A Management Perspective," *International Journal of Physical Distribution*, October 1970, pp. 133–39.

[6] "A Sudden Break in the Spiral," *Newsweek*, May 19, 1980, pp. 54, 59; and Wendell M. Stewart and James E. Morehouse, "Improving Productivity in Physical Distribution—A $40 Billion Goldmine," from *Proceedings of the Sixteenth Annual Conference of the National Council of Physical Distribution Management*, October 16–18, 1978, p. 5.

and energy intensive than the other areas of most firms, are obvious.[7] Physical distribution costs can exceed 25 percent of a manufacturer's sales revenue and account for over 30 percent of a manufacturer's investment in assets. Because physical distribution has not received the same attention as other areas of the firm, profits can be increased and return on investment improved by integrating physical distribution activities using total cost analysis.

## PHYSICAL DISTRIBUTION AND THE MARKETING FUNCTION

Profitable business development requires that management allocate scarce resources to physical distribution and the other elements of the marketing mix.[8] This is because the total dollars spent on the various components of the marketing mix influence the company's market share and profitability. The more dollars that a company invests in the marketing mix relative to its competitors the larger the market share achieved, assuming that all competitors spend their dollars equally effectively. However, this is rarely the case. Significant advantage can be achieved by allocating dollars to the marketing mix more efficiently and effectively than competitors. The cost trade-offs that management must make are summarized in Figure 2−1. The objective is to allocate resources to the price, product, promotion, and place components of the marketing mix in a manner that will lead to the greatest long-run profits.

*Physical Distribution and the Marketing Mix*

### Price

The price component refers to the price that the manufacturer receives for its product. It is important for management to determine how the purchase behavior of intermediaries and ultimate consumers will be affected by changes in price. When a manufacturer demands faster payment of accounts receivable or otherwise changes the financial terms of sale, management is in effect changing the price of its products, which may impact demand. The price that the manufacturer receives for its products will differ depending on the channel of distribution used.

### Product

Product refers to the package of benefits that the consumer receives from the purchase. The manufacturer may allocate dollars to research and development in order to be able to continually bring new products to the market. The quality of the product will influence its demand in the market place as

---

[7] David Ray, "Distribution Costing—The Current State of the Art," *International Journal of Physical Distribution* 6 no. 2 (1975): 88; and James R. Stock, "The Energy Ecology Impacts on Distribution," *International Journal of Physical Distribution and Materials Management* 8, no. 5 (1978): 249−83.

[8] This material is taken from Douglas M. Lambert, "Improving Profitability by Managing Marketing Costs," a paper presented at the American Marketing Association Accounting/Marketing Conference, 1981.

**FIGURE 2-1** Cost Trade-offs Required in a Physical Distribution System

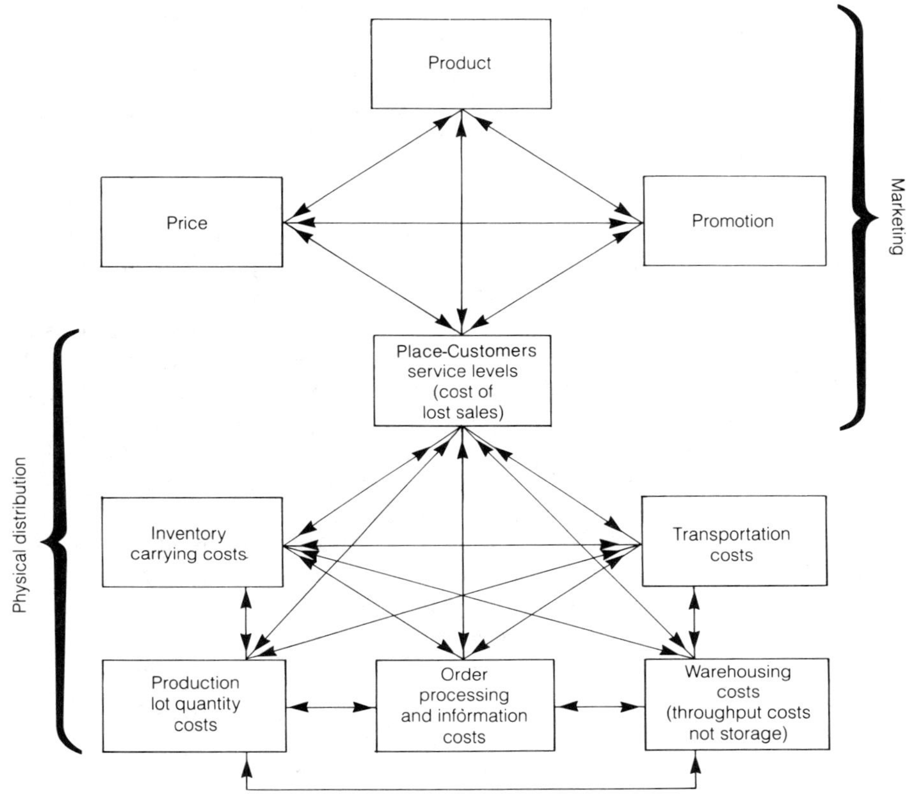

Objective: Minimize total costs

Total costs = Transportation costs + Warehousing costs
+ Order processing and information costs + Production lot quantity costs
+ Inventory carrying costs + Cost of lost sales

Source: Adapted from Douglas M. Lambert, *The Development of an Inventory Costing Methodology: A Study of the Costs Associated with Holding Inventory* (Chicago: National Council of Physical Distribution Management, 1976), p. 7.

well as the price that can be charged for it. Reducing quality will lower manufacturing costs and increase short-run profits but may erode long-run profitability. Marketers must consider the impact of product attributes on demand.

**Promotion**

Promotion refers to both advertising and sales promotion. Increasing expenditures for advertising will increase sales but at some point additional advertising expenditures will not increase sales enough to justify the expenditure. The amount of sales support required will depend upon the channel of distribution used. For example, direct sales require that the manufacturer spend more dollars on sales people than if an indirect channel is used. The size of the salesforce will influence the size of the potential market and the manufacturer's market share. However, increased expenditures for promotion must lead to increased contribution as a result of increased sales if the additional expense is to be justified.

### Place

The place component represents the manufacturer's expenditure for customer service which is the output of the physical distribution system. The area of customer service represents physical distribution's interface with the demand creation portion of marketing. Physical distribution represents the demand-supply part of marketing. Customer service not only impacts the place component of the marketing mix, but also influences the price of the product. Product availability and order-cycle time can be used to differentiate the product and may influence the market price if customers are willing to pay more for better service. In addition, physical distribution costs are added to product costs and as such may affect the market price set by the company.

*Customer Service is Critical for Successful Marketing*

Figure 2—1 illustrates the cost trade-offs that are required to successfully implement the integrated physical distribution management concept. It will be used throughout this text as the financial model for making physical distribution decisions.

## THE TOTAL COST CONCEPT

Total cost analysis is the key to managing the physical distribution function.[9] Management should strive to minimize the total costs of physical distribution rather than attempt to minimize the cost of each component. Attempts to reduce the cost of individual physical distribution activities may be suboptimal and lead to increased total costs.[10] For example, consolidating finished goods inventory in a small number of distribution centers will reduce inventory carrying costs and warehousing costs but may lead to a substantial increase in freight expense or lower sales volume as a result of reduced levels of customer service. Similarly, the savings associated with large volume purchases may be less than the increased inventory carrying costs.

It is important that management consider the total of all of the costs of physical distribution described in Figure 2—1. Figure 2—2 illustrates how different field-warehouse systems, as measured by the number of field locations, can affect various other physical distribution costs as well as total

---

[9] This section draws heavily from Douglas M. Lambert, *The Development of an Inventory Costing Methodology: A Study of the Costs Associated with Holding Inventory* (Chicago: National Council of Physical Distribution Management, 1976), pp. 5–15 and 59–67.

[10] See Marvin Flaks, "Total Cost Approach to Physical Distribution," *Business Management* 24 (August 1963): 55–61, and Raymond LeKashman and John F. Stolle, "The Total Cost Approach to Distribution," *Business Horizons* 8 (Winter 1965): 33–46.

**FIGURE 2-2** The Total Cost Approach

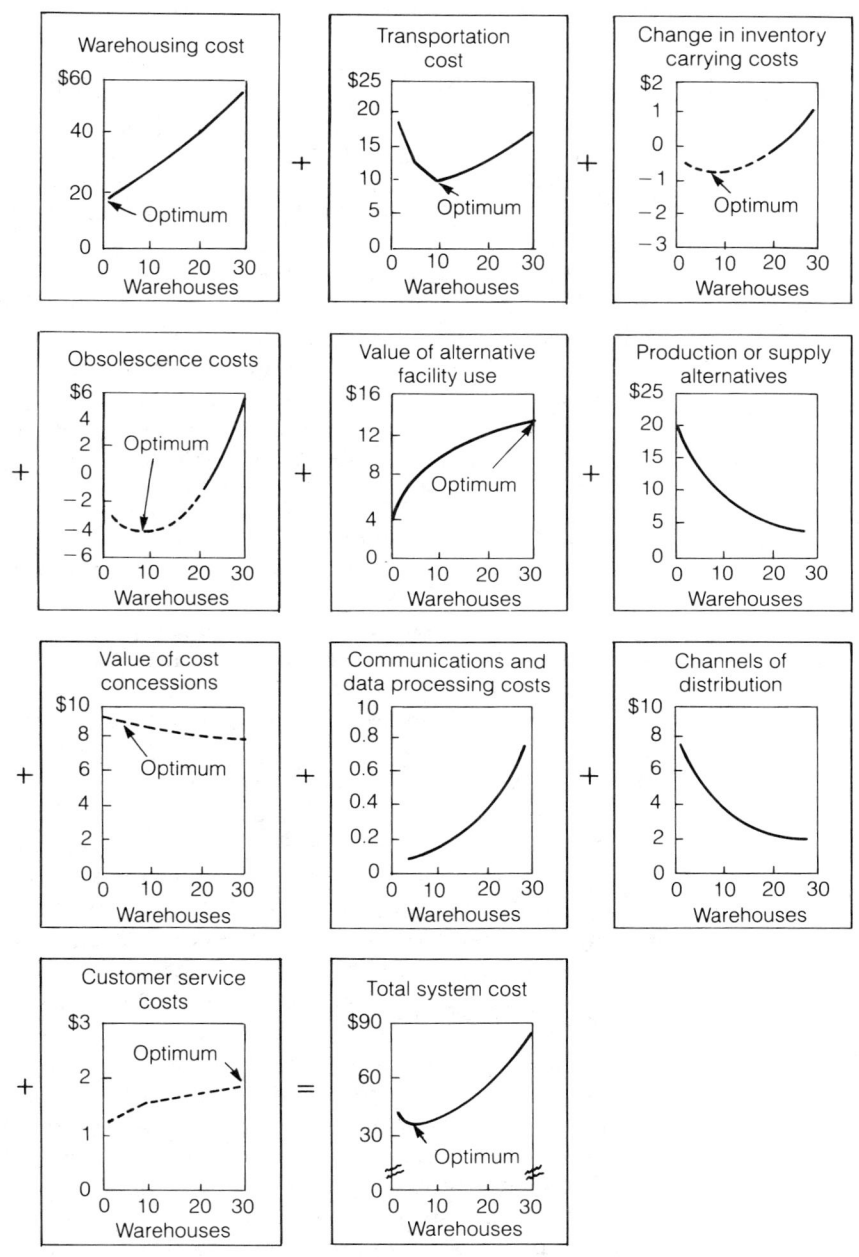

Source: Raymond LeKashman and John F. Stolle, "The Total Cost Approach to Distribution," *Business Horizons* 8 (Winter 1965): 33–46.

costs. Depending upon which individual cost is traded off with warehousing costs a certain number of warehouses would be optimum.

> The sum of all of these curves—each with its own optimum—is one final curve that defines the total cost. That in turn defines the optimum number of warehouses for this operation, when all considerations are taken into account. Except by chance coincidence, this point will differ from the optimum of each of the component curves. Obviously, a piecemeal approach to cost reduction will not yield the maximum profit impact achieved by this total cost approach.[11]

*Total Cost Analysis is the Key to Integrated Physical Distribution Management*

Reductions in the cost of physical distribution activity invariably lead to increased costs of other cost components. Effective management and real cost savings can be accomplished only by viewing physical distribution as an integrated system and minimizing its total cost. The cost categories introduced in Figure 2 − 1 are: customer service levels (the cost of lost sales); transportation costs; warehousing costs; order processing and information costs; production lot quantity costs; and inventory carrying costs.

**Customer Service Levels**

The cost associated with customer service levels is the cost of lost sales (not only the margin lost by not meeting the current sales demand, but the present value of all future contributions to profit forfeited when a customer is lost due to poor availability) which is indeed difficult, if not impossible, for most business people to measure. For this reason, it is recommended that only the measurable costs associated with back-ordering or expediting be included in this category. The objective then becomes one of minimizing the total costs, given a level of customer service. With this type of information, it is possible for management to make a knowledgeable judgment concerning the likelihood of recovering, through increased sales, the increase in total system costs brought about by an increase in customer service levels. Another possibility, of course, would be to reduce spending in some other component of the marketing mix, promotion for example, in order to maintain profits with a similar sales volume. Likewise, with decreases in customer service levels, profitability can be improved or other components of the marketing mix may enjoy increased levels of expenditure in an effort to maintain or improve market position.

It becomes apparent that even though the cost of lost sales associated with customer service are elusive, if management determines customer service levels based on customer needs and on understanding of the interaction between customer service and the other marketing-mix elements, that better decisions are possible. The goal is to determine the least-total-cost method of physical distribution given the customer service objectives, which requires that good cost data are available for the other five cost categories shown in Figure 2 − 1.

---

[11] Ibid.

### Transportation Costs

The next category of costs are those associated with the transportation function. These costs can be dealt with in total or on an incremental basis. Transportation costs, if not currently available in any other form, can be determined by a statistical audit of freight bills for common carriers or from corporate accounting records for private fleets. Transportation costs and how to collect them will be dealt with in depth in Chapter 5.

### Warehousing Costs

Warehousing costs are comprised of all of the expenses that can be eliminated or must be increased as the result of a change in the number of warehousing facilities. There has been a great deal of confusion in the literature about these costs. Many authors have included warehousing costs in inventory carrying costs.[12] However, this is a misconception since most of these costs will not change with the level of inventory stocked, but rather with the number of stocking locations. Nevertheless, the converse is true. The number of warehouses employed with the distribution system will have an impact on the levels of inventory held. In addition, these costs, in the case of leased or owned facilities, take the form of step-functions. Consequently, their inclusion in inventory carrying costs requires a recalculation of the carrying cost percentage each time a decision involves the possibility of opening or closing a warehouse. The most straightforward method is to separate the warehousing costs into two distinct categories: those related to throughput and those related to storage. Throughput costs are the costs associated with selling product in a given market by moving it into and out of a warehouse in that market. Examples of throughput costs are the charges that public warehousers assess for product handlings into and out of their facilities. These charges are related to how much product is sold in that market and are distinct from storage space costs which public warehousers assign to their customers based on the amount of inventory stored in the facility. The former group of costs should be included in warehousing costs so that the increments can be easily added or subtracted with changes in distribution system configuration.

### Order Processing and Information Costs

Order processing and information costs include the cost of issuing and closing orders, the related handling costs, and associated communication costs. The important thing to remember when establishing these costs is to include in the analysis only those costs that will change with the decision that is being made.

### Production Lot Quantity Costs

Production lot quantity costs are those costs that will change as a result of a change in the distribution system and usually will include some or all of

---

[12] This will be documented in Chapter 7, Financial Impact of Inventory.

the following:

1. Production preparation costs.
   a. Set-up time.
   b. Inspection.
   c. Set-up scrap.
   d. Inefficiency of beginning operation.
2. Lost capacity due to changeover.
3. Materials handling, scheduling, and expediting.

The production-preparation costs and lost-capacity costs are usually available since they are used as inputs to production planning. The other costs can be approximated by taking the incremental total costs incurred for two different levels of activity and dividing by the increment in volume. Regression analysis is another technique that can be used to isolate fixed and variable costs components. The number obtained can be used as an input to the design of a physical distribution system.

**Inventory Carrying Costs**

Conceptually, inventory carrying costs have been one of the most difficult costs to determine, and next to the cost of lost sales probably the most difficult. Inventory carrying costs should include only those costs that vary with the level of inventory stored and can be categorized into the following groups: (1) capital costs which is the company's opportunity cost of capital multiplied by the variable out-of-pocket investment in inventory; (2) inventory service costs such as insurance and taxes on the inventory; (3) storage space costs; and (4) inventory risk costs including obsolescence, damage, pilferage, and relocation costs. These costs are discussed in great detail in Chapter 7.

## PHYSICAL DISTRIBUTION AND CORPORATE PROFIT PERFORMANCE

We can expect that the economic climate of the 1980s will result in a continued interest on the part of top management in asset management and cash flow management. Table 2−1, which contains selected financial data for 10 manufacturers of consumer packaged goods, shows that accounts receivable average 20 percent of total assets for these firms and that inventory investment represents 27 percent of their assets on average. Combined they comprise from 36 percent to 56 percent of the assets of the 10 firms. The two most common strategies that result from the desire to improve cash flow and return on assets are: (1) to reduce accounts receivable; and (2) to reduce the investment in inventory. These two actions improve cash flow and reduce the company's investment in assets. However, the reduction of the terms of sale, or simply enforcing the stated terms of sale, in effect changes the price component of the firm's marketing mix. Also, simply reducing the level of inventory can significantly increase the cost of physical distribution if current inventories have been set at a level that

**TABLE 2-1** Selected Financial Data for 10 Manufacturers of Consumer Packaged Goods ($ millions)

| Company | Fortune 500 Ranking | Sales | Net Profits | Total Assets | Accounts Receivable | Inventory Investment | Accounts Receivable as a Percent of Assets | Inventories as a Percent of Assets |
|---|---|---|---|---|---|---|---|---|
| Borden | 82 | $ 4,595.8 | $ 147.8 | $2,643.3 | $ 49.95 | $ 506.0 | 19% | 19% |
| Bristol-Myers | 117 | 3,158.3 | 270.6 | 2,209.4 | 517.4 | 545.2 | 23 | 25 |
| Colgate-Palmolive | 64 | 5,130.4 | 173.2 | 2,578.1 | 566.8 | 769.7 | 22 | 30 |
| Consolidated Foods | 62 | 5,342.9 | 127.7 | 2,263.4 | 495.3 | 730.5 | 22 | 32 |
| General Foods | 55 | 6,012.0 | 255.8 | 2,978.5 | 669.5 | 1,003.0 | 22 | 34 |
| Johnson & Johnson | 74 | 4,837.4 | 400.7 | 3,342.5 | 643.8 | 848.8 | 19 | 25 |
| Procter & Gamble | 24 | 10,772.0 | 1,083.0 | 6,553.4 | 879.3 | 1,488.1 | 13 | 23 |
| Quaker Oats | 160 | 2,405.2 | 96.4 | 1,334.2 | 315.8 | 342.5 | 24 | 26 |
| Ralston Purina | 72 | 4,886.0 | 163.0 | 2,246.5 | 296.7 | 566.4 | 13 | 25 |
| Standard Brands | 128 | 3,018.5 | 104.4 | 1,608.4 | 319.9 | 555.9 | 20 | 35 |

Note: All figures are for 1980.

allows the firm to achieve least-total-cost physical distribution for a desired level of customer service.

The arbitrary reduction of accounts receivable and/or inventories in the absence of technological change or changes in the physical distribution system can have a devastating impact on corporate profit performance. For example, changing the terms of sale can affect the company's customers in two ways. First, it changes the manufacturer's price and therefore the competitive position of its products, which may lead to decreased sales. Second, it further complicates the cash flow problems of the wholesalers and/or retailers the manufacturer sells its products to. Forcing faster payment of invoices causes the other channel members to improve their cash flow by reducing their inventory investment. This leads to increased physical distribution costs for the manufacturer and the wholesalers/retailers as a result of the more frequent smaller orders being placed by intermediaries.

Similarly, a manufacturer's policy of arbitrarily reducing inventory levels, increasing inventory turns, in the absence of a system change may escalate transportation costs as the physical distribution system scrambles to achieve the specified customer service levels. This is assuming, of course, that the company was efficiently and effectively distributing its products prior to the policy change on inventory investment. Alternatively, the pressure to reduce expenses may preclude the use of premium transportation as a means of achieving the desired customer service levels with less inventory. In this case, customer service levels would be eroded with the possible outcome being a decrease in market share. In either set of circumstances, the increased costs of transportation or lost sales contribution could far exceed the savings in inventory carrying costs.

However, if management concentrates on systems changes that improve physical distribution efficiency or effectiveness it may be possible to satisfy all of the firm's objectives. For example, many companies have not kept pace with technology in the area of order processing. By replacing an outdated, mail-based, order processing and communication system with advanced technology a firm may be able to achieve some or all of the following: (1) increased customer service levels; (2) lower inventories; (3) improved speed of collections; (4) decreased transportation costs; (5) lower warehousing costs; and (6) improvements in cash flow and return on assets.

One very useful way of determining how a proposed systems change will influence profit performance and return on assets is by using the strategic profit model (see Figure 2–3).

### The Strategic Profit Model

The strategic profit model demonstrates that return on net worth, that is, the return on shareholders' investment plus retained earnings, is a function of three factors which are controllable by management: (1) net profit, (2) asset turnover, and (3) financial leverage.

*Net profit.* Net profit as a percent of sales is a measure of how efficiently and effectively products are manufactured and sold. However net profit alone is not a satisfactory measure of performance. For example, would you

---

Return on Net Worth = Net Profit Percentage × Asset Turnover × Financial Leverage

**FIGURE 2-3** The Strategic Profit Model

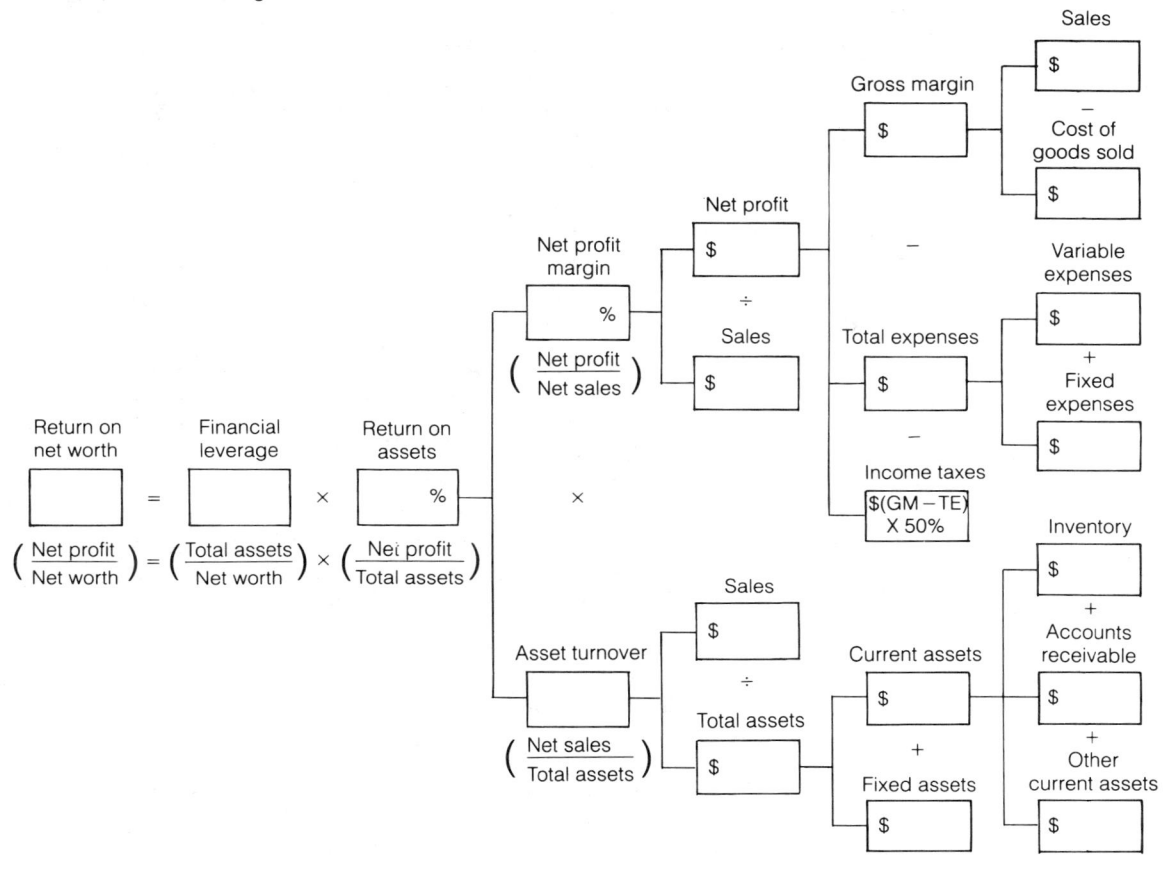

want to purchase stock in a company with a 2 percent net profit or one with a 10 percent net profit? In order to answer this question, it would be necessary to know the sales volume of the firm in question as well as the investment required to achieve that level of sales. The assets employed by a firm can be controlled by management and efficient utilization of such assets also should be measured.

*Asset turnover.* Asset turnover, sales divided by total assets, shows how efficiently assets are employed in order to generate a level of sales.

*Return on assets,* which is determined by multiplying the net profit margin by asset turnover, relates profitability to the value of the assets employed.

*Financial leverage.* Financial leverage is calculated by dividing total assets by the net worth of the firm. It is a measure of how management uses financing which is obtained from sources outside the firm to increase the return on net worth, shareholders equity plus retained earnings.

Simply stated, if money can be borrowed at a cost of 10 percent before taxes, 5 percent after taxes, and can be invested in assets that provide a return of 15 percent after taxes, earnings per share will be larger if expansion is financed by borrowed money and cash from operations rather than by selling shares. The important measure for shareholders is return on net worth, which is equal to the return on assets multiplied by the financial leverage ratio. The strategic profit model can be used to illustrate how a physical distribution system change will impact upon the firm's profit performance.

*An application.* Refer to Table 2−1 and the financial data presented for Consolidated Foods. In 1980 the company had a net profit of $127.7 million on sales of $5,342.9 million for a net profit on sales of about 2.39 percent. Total assets were $2,263.4 million and return on assets was 5.64 percent. If an advanced order transmittal, order entry, and processing system would allow the company to reduce out-of-pocket costs associated with transportation, warehousing, and inventory by about $10 million before income taxes, the costs of such a system, assume $1 million before taxes, would be more than recovered. If the company's effective tax rate was 50 percent, the aftertax saving would be $4.5 million [($10 million − $1 million) × 50 percent]. In addition, if such a system would make it possible to reduce accounts receivable by as much as $25 million and inventories by $75 million, improvements in both cash management and return on assets would result.

If the $100 million could be invested at a rate of return of 20 percent after taxes the following benefits would be realized:

1. Net profit would increase by $24.5 million ($100 million at 20 percent plus $4.5 million) to 2.85 percent of sales.
2. Return on assets would increase from 5.64 percent to 6.72 percent.

In order to have had a similar impact on return on assets, a sales increase of approximately $1,025 million or 19.2 percent would be required.

Improvements in return on assets and cash flow achieved by increasing productivity have the additional benefit of not forcing other channel members to react in a fashion that will impact negatively on channel efficiency. Of course, the primary benefit to the manufacturer's own operation is that the cost savings associated with a reduction in accounts receivable or inventory are not offset by the costs of reduced service levels or increased transportation costs.

## AN EXAMPLE OF INTEGRATED PHYSICAL DISTRIBUTION MANAGEMENT

In the late 1960s a major manufacturer of consumer durable goods established a physical distribution function in order to "merge areas formerly independent of each other into a unified system which controlled the destiny of all finished product from its production scheduling through shipment to its distributors."[13] The objectives of the new PD function were to:

---
[13] This material was provided by Jay Sterling, doctoral candidate, Department of Marketing and Transportation, Michigan State University.

1. Design an overall distribution system concept to effectively and economically distribute the corporation's merchandise now and in the future.
2. Consider all elements of distribution to achieve these objectives.

The distribution task was defined as embracing or closely related to:

Physical distribution including transportation, order processing, inventory control, and warehousing.

Data processing and data communications.

Sales forecasting and retail feedback.

Production planning and scheduling.

Accounting.

One of the first things that the company did upon formation of the physical distribution function was to completely restructure the system of accounting for distribution costs. The payment of freight bills on finished product, which was formerly paid by individual manufacturing divisions, was transferred to corporate headquarters and a series of prepaid expense accounts was established. Also, payment of warehouse bills on finished product stored at field warehouses was transferred from the control of manufacturing divisions to corporate headquarters and a series of prepaid accounts similar to prepaid freight was created.

Since one of the major benefits of integrating the physical distribution function is the cost savings that are possible, management reports were developed to document the costs of each physical distribution activity and for the total system. The primary concern of management was to use this information to stimulate cost savings to improve the company's procedures and operations.

*A Major Firm Saves $15 Million with Integrated Physical Distribution*

By 1970, the new physical distribution function was the largest cost-savings area within the firm, with annual savings approaching $15 million. This was comprised of $9 million in operating expenses and a $6 million improvement in working capital as a result of lower inventories. A member of the firm's management made the following statement in a presentation at a national NCPDM meeting:

> In conclusion, I would like to leave you with this thought:
> For a physical distribution function to truly succeed we *must* discard the idea that former tools of measuring costs and performance levels can be transferred to a PD concept. No longer can we talk of:
>
> 1. Freight costs for the traffic department.
> 2. Warehousing costs for the warehouse function.
> 3. Operating costs for each individual department, such as order processing or EDP.
>
> The least expensive way to distribute a product does *not* necessarily result in the lowest possible cost in freight, warehousing, administration, or data processing areas as individual functions. Therefore, financial control in respect to physi-

cal distribution equals the effective management of the total system of distributing a company's product to the retailer or ultimate consumer.

We refer to this objective as *Maximum product availability at minimum overall cost*.[14]

## CONDUCTING A MARKETING AND PHYSICAL DISTRIBUTION AUDIT

An important prerequisite to successful implementation of integrated physical distribution management is a marketing and physical distribution audit. An audit program should be conducted on a routine basis although the length of time between audits may vary among firms. In many cases, firms will become involved in special studies which include an audit, but these should not be considered substitutes for the regularly scheduled audits.

Audits are required if the firm is to successfully adapt to the changing business environment. Knowledge of past behavior and current policies and practices as well as competitive and environmental behavior are important for future planning. This is accomplished by evaluating corporate objectives and plans given the audit results. A good audit should include evaluation of the external market as well as internal operations.

*External Market Audit*

The items that should be included in the external market audit are: customer service levels demanded in the market place; market requirements; product mix; and competition. In the category of *customer service* it is important to determine: response time requirements, that is, the time that the customer expects to wait after placing an order before receiving the products as well as the accepted ranges of variability in this time; information requirements which may include the ability to determine product availability at the time of order placement, order status, advance information on price changes, and shipping data; distribution system flexibility including the ability to expedite an order, the ability to backorder and/or the ability to substitute in the event of a stockout; and, various other customer service requirements.

In the *market requirements* category it is important to determine: if there are new potential markets for the products, and their location; if there are identifiable market segments for the company's products; how market needs differ by such business segments as geographic area, customer, and product; and demand elasticity with regard to various marketing mix strategies.

The *product mix* category considers the impact on the firm of such factors as product safety requirements; new products; new lines of business; and product balance.

Finally, it is necessary to obtain information about the *competition* including company-specific data such as customer service levels offered: distribution policies; distribution patterns; and location and strengths. The elements of the external market audit are summarized in Figure 2—4.

---

[14] Ibid.

**FIGURE 2-4** Elements of the External Market Audit

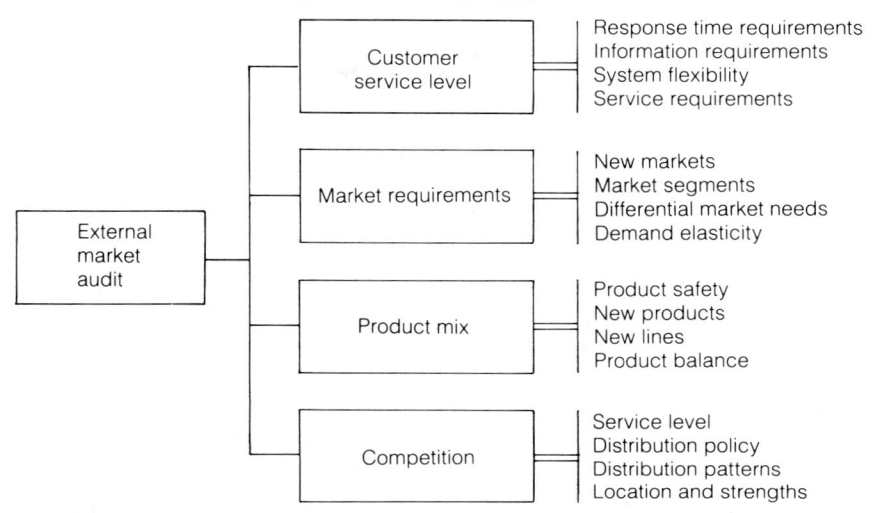

External market audit
- Customer service level
  - Response time requirements
  - Information requirements
  - System flexibility
  - Service requirements
- Market requirements
  - New markets
  - Market segments
  - Differential market needs
  - Demand elasticity
- Product mix
  - Product safety
  - New products
  - New lines
  - Product balance
- Competition
  - Service level
  - Distribution policy
  - Distribution patterns
  - Location and strengths

Source: Bernard J. LaLonde, Riley Professor of Marketing and Logistics, The Ohio State University, 1973.

**FIGURE 2-5** Elements of the Internal Operations Audit

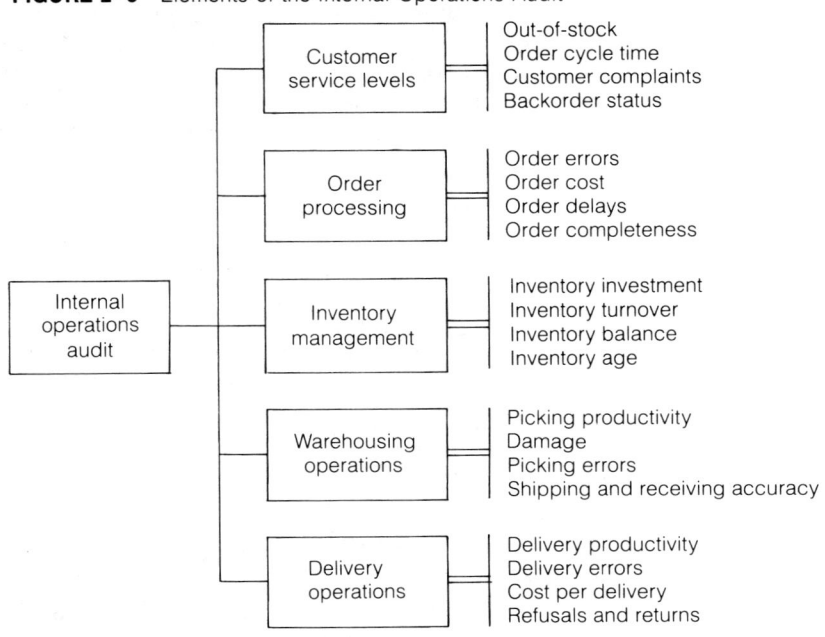

Internal operations audit
- Customer service levels
  - Out-of-stock
  - Order cycle time
  - Customer complaints
  - Backorder status
- Order processing
  - Order errors
  - Order cost
  - Order delays
  - Order completeness
- Inventory management
  - Inventory investment
  - Inventory turnover
  - Inventory balance
  - Inventory age
- Warehousing operations
  - Picking productivity
  - Damage
  - Picking errors
  - Shipping and receiving accuracy
- Delivery operations
  - Delivery productivity
  - Delivery errors
  - Cost per delivery
  - Refusals and returns

Source: Bernard J. LaLonde, Riley Professor of Marketing and Logistics, The Ohio State University, 1973.

**Internal Operations Audit**

Once the external market audit has been completed, the next step is to perform an internal operations audit. The internal audit should include investigation of existing customer service levels; the order processing system, inventory management practices, warehouse operations, and delivery operations (see Figure 2 — 5). A detailed internal operation audit is included in Chapter 3 as Appendix B.

When the two audits have been completed, internal procedures should be modified to take advantage of market opportunities and to remove existing system inadequacies.

## DEVELOPING A PHYSICAL DISTRIBUTION STRATEGY

Once the marketing and physical distribution audit have been completed, the strengths and weaknesses of the current operations identified, and market opportunities recognized, objectives must be formulated for the physical distribution function. The next step is to develop a physical distribution strategy in order that the objectives be achieved. At this point, various alternatives must be considered. For example, it may be possible to achieve the desired objectives, perhaps a 95 percent in-stock product availability and 72-hour delivery,[15] with a motor-carrier based system with few field warehouses or with a rail and motor carrier combination which requires more field warehouses and inventory. When the costs associated with various structural alternatives have been established, management must select the physical distribution structure that is the most likely to accomplish the specified objectives at least total cost.

With the physical distribution structure determined, management must establish criteria for the evaluation and selection of individual channel members and methods of evaluating their performance. Then, individual channel members should be selected and performance measured. In instances where performance is not adequate the following questions should be asked:

1. Can performance be improved?
2. Would a change of intermediaries solve the problem?
3. Is a change of channel structure required?

If the answer to the first question is yes, corrective action should be taken. Otherwise, the second question must be asked. If changing a particular intermediary such as a warehouse or carrier will not suffice, a system design change may be necessary.

The entire process should be repeated as a routine part of the planning process beginning with the marketing and physical distribution audit.

## AREAS WHERE PHYSICAL DISTRIBUTION PERFORMANCE CAN BE IMPROVED

**Opportunities for Improving Productivity**

There are a number of areas that offer particularly good opportunities to improve physical distribution productivity including: (1) forecasting, (2)

---

[15] That is, on the average 95 percent of the items ordered by a customer will be delivered within three days after the manufacturer has received the order.

order processing and communications systems, (3) customer service, (4) inventory management, (5) transportation, and (6) warehousing.

**Forecasting**

Forecasting demand for products is necessary if production is to be scheduled and the required inventories made available at a reasonable cost where customers expect to make the purchase. If physical distribution is to successfully provide time and place utilities, management must be able to forecast by individual item by market area for a specific period. In recent years, the area of forecasting has been studied extensively and methods of making predictions more objective and reliable have been developed.[16] However, many companies are still relatively unsophisticated in their approach to this very important physical distribution activity and consequently it offers significant potential for improving their operations.

**Order Processing and Communications Systems**

The order is the device that sets the physical distribution system in motion. Order processing is the nerve center that guides the flow of products to customers and cash to the firm. Many firms have not capitalized on the latest technology in order-processing and communications systems. The implementation of an advanced order-processing system by such a firm could lead to significant productivity gains by: improving customer service; reducing costs by eliminating errors and redundancy; and, improving cash flow by making the order flow more efficient. Order processing and information systems will be the topic of Chapter 9.

**Customer Service**

In the highly competitive business environment of the 1980s customer service is a critical component of the marketing mix. An important component of customer service is the communication that takes place between the vendor and customer. Also, customer service levels can be improved by inventory management techniques that improve product availability as well as order communications and transportation systems that shorten the order cycle time. Chapter 3 will be devoted to a thorough presentation of the customer service activity and how it should be managed.

**Inventory Management**

Inventory can account for more than 35 percent of a firm's assets. Improved inventory management can free capital for use in other investments and the rate of return that could be obtained on such investments is the opportunity cost associated with the inventory. In addition, out-of-pocket carrying costs such as insurance, taxes, storage costs, and inventory risk costs can raise the total to more than 40 percent of the inventory value. Advanced order-processing systems and computerized inventory-management packages are just two ways inventory levels can be reduced.

---

[16] Those interested in an in-depth review of forecasting techniques should refer to Steven C. Wheelwright and Spyros Makridakas, *Forecasting Methods for Management* (New York: John Wiley & Sons, 1973).

Also, savings can be obtained by decreasing the labor costs associated with inventory management and reducing the number of backorders and the related costs. Backorders result when orders cannot be completely filled within the specified order cycle time. Inventory management will be given detailed treatment in Chapters 7 and 8.

### Transportation

Transportation usually represents the largest single expense of physical distribution. Substantial savings can be realized by the company that embarks on a program of transportation consolidation. Also by implementing an advanced order-processing system as much as three or four days may be made available for planning more efficient and less costly movement of products. Chapter 5 will explore methods of improving management of the transportation activity.

### Warehousing

Many of the accounting techniques developed in management accounting for manufacturing operations, for example standard costs and flexible budgets, have direct applicability in warehousing. The productivity improvements that are possible in warehousing will be discussed in Chapter 6.

## SUMMARY

In this chapter you were shown the importance of the integrated physical distribution management concept and the reasons for its growth. Also, you were shown how integrated physical distribution management can be implemented in a firm using total-cost analysis and how to measure the impact of physical distribution decisions on corporate profit performance. Examples were used to show how firms have implemented physical distribution management. The marketing and physical distribution audit were presented as the basis for developing a strategic physical distribution plan. Finally, the chapter closed with a description of areas that offer significant potential for improving physical distribution performance. With this as background you are now ready for in-depth treatment of the major physical distribution activities beginning with customer service, the subject of Chapter 3.

## QUESTIONS AND PROBLEMS

1. What factors in the business environment make physical distribution so important for companies in the 1980s.

2. What are the cost categories that must be considered if integrated physical distribution management is to be implemented using total cost analysis?

3. The two most common management strategies that result from the desire to improve cash flow and return on assets are: (1) to reduce accounts receivable, and (2) to reduce the investment in inventory. What are the shortcomings associated

with arbitrarily reducing accounts receivable and/or inventories in the absence of a change in the firm's physical distribution system?

4. How can the strategic profit model be used to show the financial impact of a change in the structure of the physical distribution system?

5. What area(s) of physical distribution do you believe offer(s) the most potential for improving performance? Explain why.

6. Using the 1980 financial data for Bristol-Myers (Table 2−1) show how return on assets would be affected if the company was to implement an advanced order processing system capable of reducing accounts receivable by $30 million and inventories by $50 million. For your analysis, assume that the money could be invested in other assets that would generate a return of 20 percent after taxes and that the increased communications cost of $200,000 per year would be offset by similar savings in transportation and warehousing costs.

7. Based upon your calculations in question 6, what percentage increase in annual sales would be necessary in order to obtain the same return on net worth?

# Part Two

# 3 Customer Service

Introduction

What Is Customer Service?
  Customer Service Definitions
  Elements of Customer Service
    Pretransaction elements
    Transaction elements
    Posttransaction elements
  Some Key Industry Demographics

Relationship of Customer Service to Successful Marketing

Customer Service and the Integrated Physical Distribution Management Concept
  Cost of Lost Sales
  Implementing Cost/Service Trade-offs

Conducting a Customer Service Audit
  An ABC Analysis of Customer Service
  Developing and Reporting Customer Service Standards

Impediments to an Effective Customer Service Strategy

Improving Customer Service Performance

Summary

Appendixes
A. Customer Service Audit
B. Customer Service/Physical Distribution Audit
C. Customer Service Questionnaire

**Objectives of this chapter:**

To show how to define customer service

To show the importance of the customer service function to the marketing and physical distribution effort of the firm

To show how to calculate cost/service trade-offs

To show how to conduct a customer service audit

To identify opportunities for improving customer service performance

## INTRODUCTION

Customer service represents physical distribution's interface with the demand creation portion of marketing and the place component of the firm's marketing mix. Consequently, the customer service level provided by a firm will have a direct impact on that firm's market share, its total physical distribution costs, and hence, its ultimate profitability. For this reason, it is imperative that customer service be an integral part of the design and operation of any physical distribution system.

In this chapter, you will be shown: how to define customer service; the importance of the customer service function to the marketing and physical distribution effort of the firm; how to calculate cost/service trade-offs; how to conduct a customer service audit; and how customer service performance can be improved.

## WHAT IS CUSTOMER SERVICE?

A Definition of Customer Service

The meaning of *customer service* varies from one company to another and often is viewed quite differently by vendors and their customers. Customer service may be defined in terms of a number of variables but in many firms it is assumed to mean one of the following:

1. The elapsed time between the receipt of an order at the supplier's warehouse and the shipment of the order from the warehouse.
2. The minimum size of order, or limits on the assortment of items in an order which a supplier will accept from its customers.
3. The percentage of items in a supplier's warehouse which might be found to be out-of-stock at any given point.
4. The proportion of customer orders filled accurately.
5. The percentage of customers, or volume of customer orders, which describes those who are served (whose orders are delivered) within a certain time period from the receipt of the order at the supplier's warehouse.
6. The percentage of customer orders which can be filled completely upon receipt at a supplier's warehouse.
7. The proportion of goods which arrive at a customer's place of business in saleable condition.

8. The elapsed time between the placement of an order by a customer and the delivery of goods ordered to the customer's place of business.
9. The ease and flexibility with which a customer can place an order.[1]

Customer service involves both tangible, measurable elements and intangible, difficult to measure elements such as the attitude of a business toward the customer in the service it provides. John Gustafson and Raymond Richard note four main categories of customer service performance:

1. Time—order-cycle time.
2. Dependability—consistency and reliability, accuracy, and quality of goods on arrival.
3. Communications—feedback on expectations and deviations from the norm, on information flow from order through invoice, and on order reminders.
4. Convenience—in ordering, in information flow, in materials handling, shipments, schedules, carriers, and in being able to cancel or complain.[2]

In broad terms customer service can be considered the measure of how well the physical distribution system is performing in creating time and place utilities for a product including post sale support of the product. Customer service can be defined as:

1. An activity that has to be managed such as order processing, invoicing, or handling customer complaints.
2. Performance measures such as the ability to ship complete within 48 hours 95 percent of the orders received.
3. A corporate philosophy whereby customer service is treated as an element of the total corporate philosophy rather than as an activity or a set of performance measures.[3]

**Customer Service Definitions**

In a landmark study of customer service funded by the National Council of Physical Distribution Management, cooperating corporate executives were asked to "define customer service as it applies to physical distribution in your company." The following were typical responses:

> Activity related: Order entry, tracing, proof of delivery, invoicing, order processing, broker contact.—Food manufacturer.
>
> All of the activities required to accept, process, deliver and bill customer orders and to follow up on any activity that erred.—Chemicals and plastics manufacturer.

---

[1] James L. Heskett, "Controlling Customer Logistics Service," *International Journal of Physical Distribution* 1, no. 3 (June 1971): 140–45.

[2] John F. Gustafson and Raymond Richard, "Customer Service in Physical Distribution," *Transportation and Distribution Management*, June 1964 pp. 34–37.

[3] Bernard J. LaLonde and Paul H. Zinszer, *Customer Service: Meaning And Measurement* (Chicago: National Council of Physical Distribution Management, 1976), pp. 156–59.

*Performance related:* Make shipments to customers of product ordered within 10 days of receipt of order.—Food manufacturer.

Percent of orders received and processed in 48 hours with no backorders.—Pharmaceuticals manufacturer.

*Corporate-philosophy related:* A complex of activities involving all areas of the business which combine to deliver and invoice the company's products in a fashion that is perceived as satisfactory by the customer and which advance our company's objectives.—Food manufacturer.

"Customer Service" Means Different Things to Different People

Customer service cannot be defined in precise terms that tell us exactly what customer service is and what it isn't. It can mean different things to different types of operations. . . . Customer service is each and all of the following:

1. An organizational unit—a department that receives and disseminates complaints for proper handling.
2. After the sales function brings new customers, customer service is what we do to hold on to them, to keep them satisfied and coming back again to buy more of our products and services.
3. Customer service, the quality of the service, and the kind of service we offer, attracts new customers.
4. Customer service is not just a function or an activity—it is a *philosophy* and *attitude*. It is something we must believe in, in order to have a beneficial influence in every policy and decision we make.
5. Customer service is a potential, an opportunity. It is the basis on which we must build our business. We can make money on customer service by:
    a. Giving the quality or level of service that will attract new customers and hold them—the quality they want and will pay for but haven't been getting.
    b. Offering new services to attract and hold customers, services they want and will pay for but haven't been getting.
6. Finally, customer service must be a plan of action, not a means of pacification. Those responsible for customer service must have the ability to effect its performance.—Chemicals and plastics manufacturer.[4]

It must be remembered that "successful implementation of the marketing concept requires both obtaining customers and keeping them" while satisfying the long-range profit and return-on-investment objectives of the firm. Although the creation of demand, obtaining customers, is often thought of solely in terms of sales and advertising, the product, and price, customer service can have a significant impact on demand. In addition, it is customer service that determines whether or not the customers will remain customers. Both order getting and order filling (physical distribution) are required for the long-range financial success of the firm.

### Elements of Customer Service

There are a number of elements that are commonly associated with customer service, although the degree of importance attached to each of them will vary from company to company depending upon customer

---

[4] LaLonde and Zinszer, *Customer Service*, pp. 203–17.

needs. For example, Peter Gilmour developed the following list of customer service elements:

1. *Availability of item* represents the ability of the supplier to satisfy customer orders within a time limit generally accepted by the industry for the particular item (for example, a chemical from stock; an expensive piece of equipment in six weeks).
2. *After sales service and back-up* includes speedy and ready replacement of defective or damaged items; commissioning of equipment if the customer experiences difficulties; subsequent follow-up to ascertain if user is happy with the purchase.
3. *Efficient telephone handling of orders and queries* includes the availability of personnel within the organization who can be quickly accessed for intelligent handling of customer queries, whether of a technical nature or about availability, price, or status of an earlier order. Also includes the training of operator/receptionist to immediately recognise the right contact to best handle the customer's call.
4. *Order convenience* represents the efficiency, accuracy, and simplicity of paperwork necessary to conform to legal requirements and interface with the firm's and the customer's business systems.
5. *Competent technical representatives* involves training, background knowledge, and presentation of representatives calling on customers.
6. *Delivery time* is the elapsed time for the normal ordering procedure between receipt by the supplier of a firm commitment for an order and receipt of the goods by the customer. Naturally only ex-stock items are included here.
7. *Reliability* means the supplier's commitment to maintain a promised delivery schedule and to advise customers if such deliveries subsequently cannot be made on time.
8. *Demonstrations of equipment* represents willingness of the supplier to allow a prospective customer to examine a particular piece of equipment on his own premises prior to signing a purchase contract. Also includes the willingness and competence of the supplier's staff to demonstrate equipment without any purchase commitment.
9. *Availability of published material.*[5]

Bernard LaLonde and Paul Zinszer categorized the elements of customer service into three groups:

1. Pretransaction elements.
2. Transaction elements.
3. Posttransaction elements.[6]

The customer service elements identified by LaLonde and Zinszer are summarized in Figure 3−1 and are explained individually on the following pages.

---

[5] Peter Gilmour, "Customer Service: Differentiating By Market Segment," *International Journal of Physical Distribution* no. 3 (1977):145.

[6] LaLonde and Zinszer, *Customer Service*, pp. 272−82.

**FIGURE 3-1** Elements of Customer Service

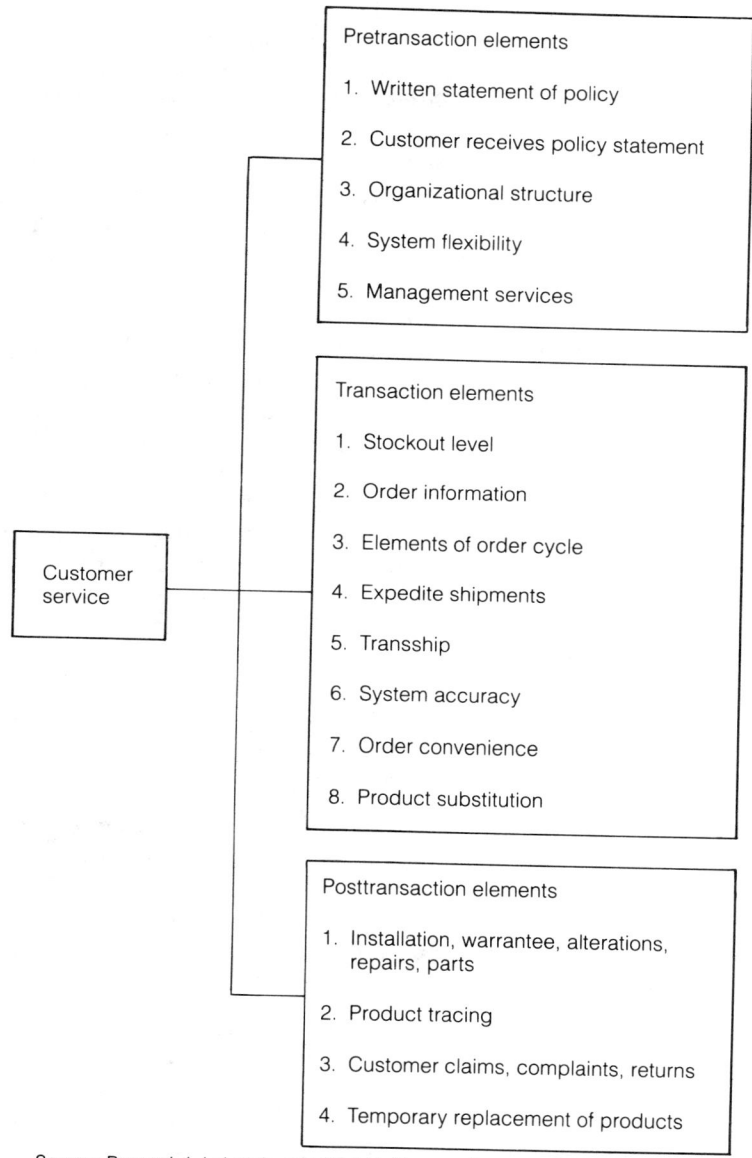

Customer service

**Pretransaction elements**
1. Written statement of policy
2. Customer receives policy statement
3. Organizational structure
4. System flexibility
5. Management services

**Transaction elements**
1. Stockout level
2. Order information
3. Elements of order cycle
4. Expedite shipments
5. Transship
6. System accuracy
7. Order convenience
8. Product substitution

**Posttransaction elements**
1. Installation, warrantee, alterations, repairs, parts
2. Product tracing
3. Customer claims, complaints, returns
4. Temporary replacement of products

Source: Bernard J. LaLonde and Paul H. Zinszer, *Customer Service: Meaning and Measurement* (Chicago: The National Council of Physical Distribution Management, 1976), p. 281.

Customer Service Before the Sale

***Pretransaction elements.*** The pretransaction elements of customer service tend to be nonroutine, policy related, and require management input. These activities, although not specifically involved with physical distribution, have a significant impact on product sales. The specific elements of pretransaction customer service include:

1. *A written statement of customer service policy.* The customer service policy statement should be based on customer needs, define service standards, determine who reports the performance measurements to whom and with what frequency, and be operational.
2. *Provide customers with a written statement of service policy.* It makes little sense to provide customers with a level of service designed to improve market penetration and then fail to inform the customer of what is being provided. A written statement reduces the likelihood that the customer will have unrealistic expectations of distribution system performance. It also provides the customer with information on how to communicate with the manufacturer if specified performance levels are not attained.
3. *Organization structure.* Although there is no organization structure best suited to successful implementation of a customer service policy, the organization should facilitate communication and cooperation between and among those functions involved in implementing the customer service policy. In addition, customers should be provided with the name and phone number of a specific individual who can satisfy their need for information. The individuals who manage the customer service components must have the appropriate responsibility and authority and must be rewarded in such a manner as to encourage corporate interfaces.
4. *System flexibility.* Flexibility is required in order for the system to effectively respond to unplanned events such as snow storms, shortages of raw materials and/or energy, and strikes.
5. *Management services.* Training manuals and seminars designed to help the customer improve inventory management, ordering, or merchandising are elements of customer service.

All of the above pretransaction elements of customer service are essential components of a successful marketing strategy.

*Customer Service at the Time of Sale*

***Transaction elements.*** The transaction elements are comprised of those activities which are normally associated with the customer service function including:

1. *Stock-out level.* The stock-out level is a measure of product sales lost due to a low level of product availability. Stock-outs should be recorded by product and by customers in order to determine where problems exist. When stock-outs occur customer goodwill can be maintained by arranging for suitable product substitution and/or expediting the shipment when the product is received in stock.
2. *Order information.* Order information is the ability to provide the customer with fast and accurate information about such considerations as inventory status, order status, expected shipping and delivery dates and back-order status. A back-order capability allows the identification and expedition of orders which require immediate attention. The number of back orders and their associated order cycle times can be used as a measure of system performance. The ability to back order is

important because the alternative may be to force a stock-out. The number of back orders should be recorded by customer and by product categories in order to identify and correct poor system performance.

3. *Elements of the order cycle.* The order cycle is the total elapsed time from initiation of the order by the customer until delivery to the customer has been accomplished. Individual components of the order cycle include order communication, order entry, order processing, order picking and packing, and delivery. Because it is the total order cycle time that is of concern to the customer, it is important to monitor and manage each of the components of the order cycle in order to determine the cause of variations in total order cycle time.

4. *Expedite shipments.* Expedited shipments are those that receive special handling in order to reduce the normal order cycle time. Although expedited shipments cost considerably more than those handled in the standard manner, the cost may be significantly less than that incurred when a customer is lost due to poor product availability. It is important for management to determine which customers qualify for expedited shipments and which ones do not. Presumably, such a policy would be based on how much individual customers contribute to the manufacturer's profitability.

5. *Transhipments.* Transhipments are the transporting of product between field locations to avoid stock-outs. They are often made in anticipation of customer demand.

6. *System accuracy.* System accuracy refers to the accuracy of quantities and products ordered as well as billing. Mistakes are costly to both manufacturer and the customer and errors should be recorded and reported as a percentage of the number of orders handled by the system.

7. *Order convenience.* Order convenience refers to the degree of difficulty that a customer experiences when placing an order. Problems may result from confusing order forms or nonstandard terminology and both can lead to errors and poor customer relations. An appropriate performance measurement is the number of errors as a percentage of the number of orders. These problems can be reduced or eliminated by conducting field interviews with customers.

8. *Product substitution.* Substitution occurs when the product ordered is replaced by the same item in a different size or with another product that will perform as well or better. For example, a customer may order a case of Clairol Herbal Essence shampoo for normal hair in 12-ounce bottles. If the customer is willing to accept 8-ounce bottles or 16-ounce bottles when a stock-out is experienced, the manufacturer is able to increase the customer service level as measured by product availability within some specified time period. Two product substitutions allow the manufacturer to increase the customer service level from 70 percent to 97 percent with no change in inventory (see Figure 3−2). However, if the customer service level attained by the firm was 97

**FIGURE 3-2** Impact of Substitution on Service Level

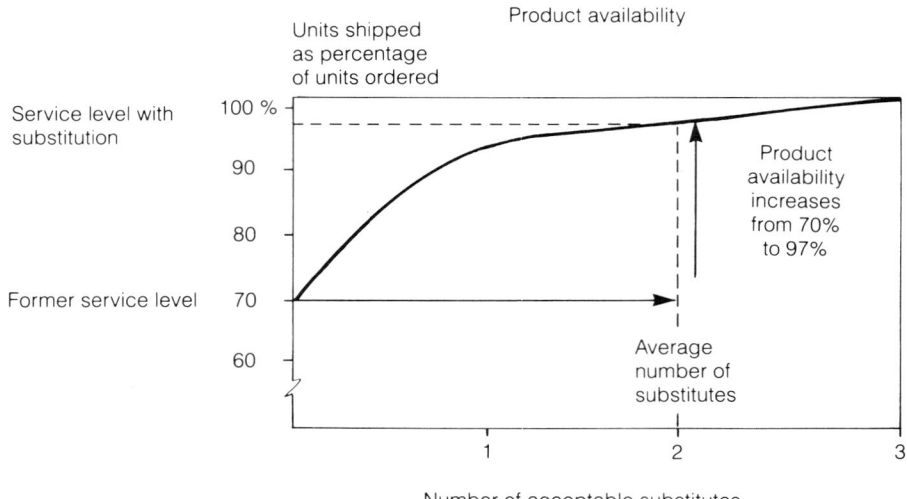

*[Graph: Units shipped as percentage of units ordered (Product availability) vs. Number of acceptable substitutes. Curve rises from 70% at 0 substitutes (Former service level) through approximately 97% at 2 substitutes (Average number of substitutes, Service level with substitution). Product availability increases from 70% to 97%.]*

percent without product substitution, two product substitutions would enable the manufacturer to maintain the 97 percent service level with a 28 percent reduction in inventory.

In order to develop an appropriate product-substitution policy, the manufacturer should work closely with customers to inform them and/or gain concurrence. Product substitution records should be kept so that performance can be monitored. A successful product substitution program requires good communication between the manufacturer and customers.

The transaction elements of customer service are the most visible because of the direct impact they have on sales.

**Customer Service after the Sale**

*Posttransaction elements.* The posttransaction elements of customer service support the product after it has been sold. The specific posttransaction elements include:

1. *Installation, warranty, alterations, repairs, parts.* These elements of customer service can be a significant factor in the decision to purchase and they should be evaluated in a manner similar to the transaction elements. To perform these functions, the following are necessary:
    a. Assistance in seeing that the product is functioning as expected upon initiation of use by the consumer.
    b. Availability of parts and/or repairmen.
    c. The field force is supported by documentation to assist in performing their jobs as well as accessibility to a supply of parts.
    d. There is an administrative job validating warranties.[7]

---

[7] LaLonde and Zinszer, *Customer Service*, p. 278.

2. *Product tracing.* Product tracing is a necessary component of customer service. In order to protect themselves from possible litigation, manufacturers must be able to recall potentially dangerous products from the market place. For example, in 1978, Carnation Company found it necessary to recall 14.1 million breakfast bars, Avon Products recalled 104,000 units of skin cream, Kraftco recalled 48,000 units of mayonnaise, and Revlon recalled 11,000 hair relaxers. Product tracing is required in order to identify the users of defective products.
3. *Customer claims, complaints, returns.* Usually, physical distribution systems are designed to move product in one direction, toward the customer. Nevertheless, almost every manufacturer experiences some returned goods and the nonroutine handling of these items is expensive. A corporate policy should exist which specifies how claims, complaints, and returns should be handled. Also, data on claims, complaints, and returns should be maintained in such a way as to provide product development, marketing, physical distribution and other corporate functions with valuable consumer information.
4. *Product replacement.* Temporary placement of product with customers waiting for receipt of a purchased item or waiting for a previously purchased product to be repaired is an element of customer service.

The posttransaction elements of customer service also can play a significant role in the purchase decision.

### Some Key Industry Demographics

*Manufacturers and Merchandisers Evaluate Customer Service Elements*

The importance of major customer service elements in manufacturing industries is summarized in Table 3−1. Senior physical distribution executives were asked to distribute 100 points among the elements of customer service which are important in generating sales for their business. In total, 105 manufacturing firms and 30 merchandising firms responded. The element of customer service perceived to be the most important was product availability which received approximately 43 percent of the total points from both groups. The element that received the second-highest ranking was order cycle time. The average importance of order cycle time, based on the 105 manufacturers was 19.4 percent. The corresponding percentage for merchandisers was 25.5 percent. The other elements of customer service in order of the importance given to them by manufacturers and merchandisers were: distribution system information, distribution system flexibility, distribution system malfunctions, and post sale product support. Table 3−1 also contains examples of common measurements that are used to monitor the level of performance achieved for the various elements of customer service.

## RELATIONSHIP OF CUSTOMER SERVICE TO SUCCESSFUL MARKETING

*Customer Service and the Marketing Mix*

The elements of the marketing mix that management can adjust to improve a firm's marketing effort and profit performance are: the product

**TABLE 3-1** Relative Importance of Elements of Customer Service as Perceived by Senior Physical Distribution Executives in Manufacturing and Merchandising

| Element | Importance Manufacturing | Importance Merchandising | Measurement Units |
|---|---|---|---|
| 1. Product availability | 42.7 | 43.1 | Units, Cases, Lines, Orders, Sales ($), or Profit ($) Stocked Out by Time Period |
| 2. Order cycle time | 19.4 | 25.5 | Time — Variance — Consolidation Saved ($) |
| a. Entry | 4.2 | 6.1 | |
| b. Processing | 5.1 | 4.7 | |
| c. Pick and ship | 4.9 | 7.9 | |
| d. Transit time | 5.2 | 6.8 | |
| | | | Report frequency — Response time — Number of inquiries — Action taken |
| 3. Distribution system information | 12.4 | 11.8 | |
| a. Inventory status | 4.5 | 4.5 | |
| b. Order status | 3.6 | 3.2 | |
| c. Data base | 3.8 | 3.9 | |
| d. Other | 0.5 | 0.2 | |
| | | | Number — Percent of orders — $ cost — Additional cost — Contribution margin versus cost |
| 4. Distribution system flexibility | 11.6 | 10.1 | |
| a. Expedite order | 4.1 | 3.5 | |
| b. Back order | 2.6 | 2.0 | |
| c. Substitute | 1.6 | 2.2 | |
| d. Faster transportation | 2.7 | 2.4 | |
| e. Other | 0.6 | 0.0 | |
| 5. Distribution system malfunctions | 8.0 | 7.2 | Number — Percent of orders — Action taken — Cost |
| a. Administration errors (credit) | 2.1 | 1.1 | |
| b. Picking errors | 1.5 | 1.5 | |
| c. Shipping errors | 1.2 | 2.3 | |
| d. Warehouse damage | 1.2 | 0.8 | |
| e. Company shipping damage | 0.8 | 0.7 | |
| f. Carrier-ship damage | 0.9 | 0.8 | |
| g. Other | 0.3 | 0.0 | |
| 6. Post sale product support | 5.1 | 2.3 | Percent in stock, number back ordered, days down, response time, average number of trips, number of times contacted per year, response time |
| a. Repair parts | 1.1 | 0.4 | |
| b. Repair service | 1.1 | 0.2 | |
| c. Technical advice | 2.0 | 1.5 | |
| d. Other | 0.9 | 0.2 | |
| 7. Other | 0.8 | 0.0 | |
| Points | 100 | 100 | |

Source: Adapted from: Bernard J. LaLonde and Paul H. Zinszer, *Customer Service: Meaning and Measurement* (Chicago: National Council of Physical Distribution Management, 1976) p. 118.

(including research and development); the price; the promotional effort (sales promotion and advertising); and the place (channels of distribution). The channel of distribution cannot be determined without careful consideration of physical distribution since the ultimate profitability of a particular channel strategy will be influenced by the cost of physical distribution.[8] For example, a manufacturer's decision to sell through wholesalers rather than directly to retail accounts can lead to: (1) lower transportation costs because larger volumes will be shipped; (2) lower inventory carrying costs by shifting a portion of the inventory investment to the wholesaler; (3) lower order-processing and handling costs as a result of receiving fewer orders for larger quantities; (4) reduced field warehousing costs; and (5) lower bad debts. These savings must be compared to the difference in revenue associated with selling to wholesalers rather than directly to retailers.

Customer service can be thought of as the output of the physical distribution function. It is a measure of the effectiveness of the physical distribution system in creating time and place utilities for a product. The level of customer service offered by a firm will not only determine whether existing customers will remain customers but how many potential customers will become customers. Nevertheless, the level of customer service chosen by a firm is often the result of industry norms, management judgment, or past practices, and is often not what the customer wants nor what would maximize corporate profitability.[9]

A survey conducted by *Progressive Grocer* magazine showed considerable variability with respect to consumers' willingness to switch brands of grocery products when faced with a stock-out. For many products, however, over 50 percent of the respondents would switch brands or buy elsewhere.[10] Other research has shown that retail and wholesale buyers are sensitive to small variations in product availability and order cycle time provided by manufacturers.[11]

The entire marketing effort of the firm can be rendered ineffective by poorly conceived customer service policies and yet this seems to be a forgotten component of the marketing mix. What is the advantage of having a well-researched and needed product, priced to sell and promoted well, if customers cannot find it on the shelf at the retail level? It is essential that a firm adopt a customer service policy that is based on customer needs, is consistent with overall marketing strategy, and advances the long-range profit objectives of the corporation.

---

[8] For a detailed treatment of the impact of physical distribution costs on channel design, operations, and performance measurement, refer to chapters 7, 8, 9, and 10 of Donald J. Bowersox, M. Bixby Cooper, Douglas M. Lambert, and Donald A. Taylor, *Management in Marketing Channels* (New York: McGraw-Hill, 1980).

[9] Harvey M. Shycon and Christopher R. Sprague, "Put a Price Tag on Your Customer Service Levels," *Harvard Business Review* (July–August 1975): 71–78.

[10] "The Out-of-Stock Study," *Progressive Grocer: The Magazine of Super Marketing* 47 (October 1968).

[11] Ronald P. Willett and Ronald Stephenson, "Determinants of Buyer Response to Physical Distribution Service," *Journal of Marketing Research* 6 (August 1969): 283.

## CUSTOMER SERVICE AND THE INTEGRATED PHYSICAL DISTRIBUTION MANAGEMENT CONCEPT

The sum of the expenditures for physical distribution activities such as transportation, warehousing, order processing, and inventory management can be viewed as the company's expenditure for customer service. To successfully implement cost trade-off analysis, it is necessary to compare the total cost of performing physical distribution activities with the cost of lost sales experienced at different customer service levels.[12]

### Cost of Lost Sales

In consumer goods companies, it is difficult to determine the cost of lost sales associated with different levels of customer service. Usually customer service levels are measured between the manufacturer and intermediaries excluding the consumer, the person who purchases the product at the retail level. For example, a stock-out at the manufacturer-wholesaler interface may not result in the wholesaler stocking out the retail accounts that it services. This will depend on the safety stock carried by the wholesaler. The retailer's inventories also may prevent the consumer from facing a stock-out at the retail level.

*Stock-outs Can Mean Lost Revenues to the Firm*

*Determining the Cost of Lost Sales*

In order to determine the cost of lost sales at the retail level, it is necessary to know what the consumer is likely to do when faced with a stock-out. Figure 3–3 is a model that illustrates possible consumer reactions when faced with a stock-out at the retail level. For example, if a consumer enters a retail store wanting to purchase Clairol Herbal Essence shampoo for normal hair in a 12-ounce bottle and faces a stock-out, a number of reactions are possible. First, the customer could switch stores and purchase the product. While the probability of this happening for shampoo may seem to be low, there are a number of products for which the consumer may be willing to switch stores.[13] The manufacturers of infant formula do not advertise their products using national media. Rather, they advertise by giving the product to hospitals and doctors who give it to new mothers. Because of the high perceived risk associated with the purchase of a nutritional product for a baby, the mother will specify the brand given to her by the doctor or used while she and the baby were at the hospital.[14] Although the two leading brands of products may have the identical ingredients the consumer would rather switch stores than switch brands. This information is critical when formulating a customer service strategy. While the penalty to the manufacturer for stocking out the retailer may be very low, there is a high cost to stocking out a doctor or a hospital. For example, if a doctor switches from Ross Laboratories' product, Similac, to Mead-Johnson's product, Enfamil, Ross Laboratories has lost all of the future new mothers with which that doctor might come into contact. Similarly, if a hospital is lost as a result of

---

[12] The total cost concept was explained in Chapter 2.

[13] Consumers may be quite willing to switch stores for a shampoo that exhibits special properties. For example, if it is the only shampoo that will solve a person's dandruff problem.

[14] In fact many doctors further reduce the likelihood of brand switching by telling the mother *not* to switch the brand of formula.

**FIGURE 3-3** Model of Consumer Reaction to a Repeated Stock-out

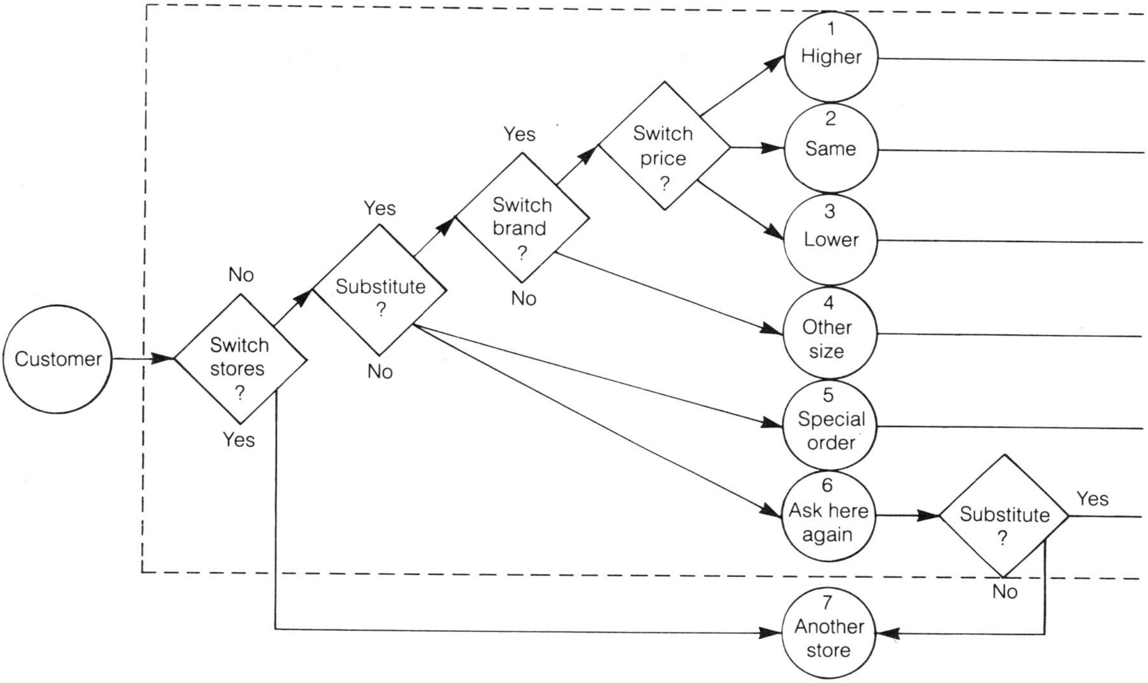

Source: Clyde K. Walter, "An Empirical Analysis of Two Stockout Models," Ph.D. dissertation, The Ohio State University, 1971.

poor product availability or any other aspect of customer service, the supplying company will have lost all future contribution to profit that would have been made by mothers who gave birth at that hospital and decided to use an infant formula. The customer service implications are clear. Hospitals and doctors require a high level of customer service because the associated costs for a stock-out are very high. Retailers, on the other hand, will most likely lose the sale if they experience a stock-out on Similac.

Since retail management must be conscious of how their institutions are positioned against competitors, they must be concerned about how often a stock-out occurs on items for which consumers are willing to switch stores. Frequent stock-outs on such items could cause consumers to permanently switch their shopping loyalties to another retail establishment.[15] With this information, the manufacturer could offer lower customer service levels, as measured by the length of the order cycle, to retail accounts and the retailers would be required to carry higher inventory levels in order to satisfy their customers.

---

[15] A recent study of 7,189 shoppers found that those experiencing stock-outs left the store with lower store image and satisfaction beliefs and purchase intentions decreased. See Paul H. Zinszer and Jack A. Lesser, "An Empirical Evaluation of the Role of Stock-Out on Shopper Patronage Processes," *1980 Educators Conference Proceedings*, (Chicago: American Marketing Association, 1980), 221–24.

In most cases the consumer will not be willing to accept the inconvenience of switching retail outlets which brings us to the second decision point, substitution. Consumers must decide if they are willing to substitute for the item. Returning to the example of the consumer who wanted to purchase Clairol Herbal Essence shampoo, the consumer's willingness to postpone the purchase until the next shopping trip will depend upon the inventory position at home. If there is still a full bottle or a portion of a bottle at home, the purchase decision may be postponed; otherwise, substitution will take place. Placing a special order for a product such as shampoo would be unlikely.

However, for some items the majority of consumers are willing and may even expect to place a special order. For example, Whirlpool and Sears, in a special study, found that consumers did not expect to take delivery of major appliances the same day. In fact, most consumers were willing to wait from 7 to 10 days for delivery. The implications of this finding are significant in terms of the logistical system required to satisfy the demand. First, only floor models of appliances need to be carried at the retail level. Second, it is only necessary to carry inventory of fast-moving standard items at retail distribution centers. All other products are manufactured only when orders have been communicated to the manufacturer after having been initiated at the retail level by customers. Once manufactured, the product is shipped to the manufacturer's mixing warehouse, from there to a Sears distribution center, and from the distribution center to the consumer. All of this takes place within the required 7 to 10 days.

Implementation of this system brought about substantial reduction in system-wide inventories without sacrificing the necessary customer service. It was no longer necessary to predict the color, size, and features desired by the consumer at each location because the system responded to orders and not to the anticipation of orders. While this type of system may not be possible for all consumer products, it is illustrative of how consumer research can be used to establish a customer service policy.

Although switching stores occurs when consumers experience a stockout on an item which commands a high level of brand preference, for other products consumers will substitute size or brand when faced with a stockout at the retail level. In Figure 3−2 you were shown how customer service levels could be increased from 70 percent to 97 percent with no corresponding increase in inventories, if customers were willing to accept two product substitutions. When this is the case, customer service levels should not be measured on each stock-keeping unit, such as the 12-ounce bottle of Clairol Herbal Essence shampoo for normal hair, but on all sizes of Clairol Herbal Essence shampoo for normal hair.[16]

The final option available to consumers who face a retail stockout is to switch brands. When they do, they may choose another one that sells for about the same price, substitute a higher-price item, or substitute a lower-

---

[16] Stock-keeping units are individual units of product and are considered as such because they differ from others in shape, size, color, or some other characteristic.

price item. In some cases, one national brand is substituted for another. When substitution takes place the retailer does not lose a sale and depending on the substitution strategy employed by the consumer may not experience any negative impact on either sales or profits. If the manufacturer knows that consumers are willing to substitute size, it should be possible to use this information to convince retailers and wholesalers that they also should be willing to accept these substitutes.[17]

However, if brand switching takes place, the manufacturer will definitely lose at least the contribution that would have been realized if the customer had not experienced the stock-out. By stocking out and putting the consumer in the position of switching brands, the manufacturer is, in effect, allowing the competitor to conduct product sampling and at the same time receive direct compensation for it. In addition, the possibility exists that once the consumer tries the substituted brand it will become first choice in the future. If this is the case, the manufacturer has lost the present value of all future contributions to profit that would have been realized had the consumer not experienced the stock-out and changed purchase behavior. Determining this exact figure may be very difficult if not impossible for most manufacturers. How then can distribution cost trade-off analysis be implemented?

### Implementing Cost/Service Trade-offs

The cost trade-offs required for implementation of the integrated physical distribution management concept are illustrated in Figure 3 — 4. In order to achieve least-cost physical distribution, it is necessary to minimize the total of the following costs: transportation costs, warehousing costs (these costs are variable with sales or are fixed, they do not include variable storage costs), production lot quantity costs (for example, reductions in field inventory levels may result in increased production set-ups at plant locations), inventory carrying costs (which include storage costs that vary with inventory levels), order processing and information costs, and the cost of lost sales.

*Higher Customer Service Levels Must be Offset by the Contribution Margin on Increased Sales*

Although it may not be possible to determine the cost of lost sales with any degree of certainty, it still is possible to implement least-cost physical distribution management. Provided that management knows the costs associated with the remaining costs categories, it is possible to minimize the total of these costs given a specified level of customer service. Consequently, the costs associated with improving the level of service can be compared to the increase in sales required to recover the additional costs. For example, consider a company that is currently offering a 95 percent customer service level (however the company measures service performance) and is accomplishing it at least total physical distribution cost. If sales management insisted that service levels must be increased to 97 percent in order for the

---

[17] For a review of the literature on consumer response to stock-outs as well as a proposed research methodology see W. E. Miklas, "Measuring Customer Response to Stock-Outs," *International Journal of Physical Distribution and Materials Management* 9, No. 5 (1979): 213 — 42.

**FIGURE 3-4** Cost Trade-offs Required in a Physical Distribution System

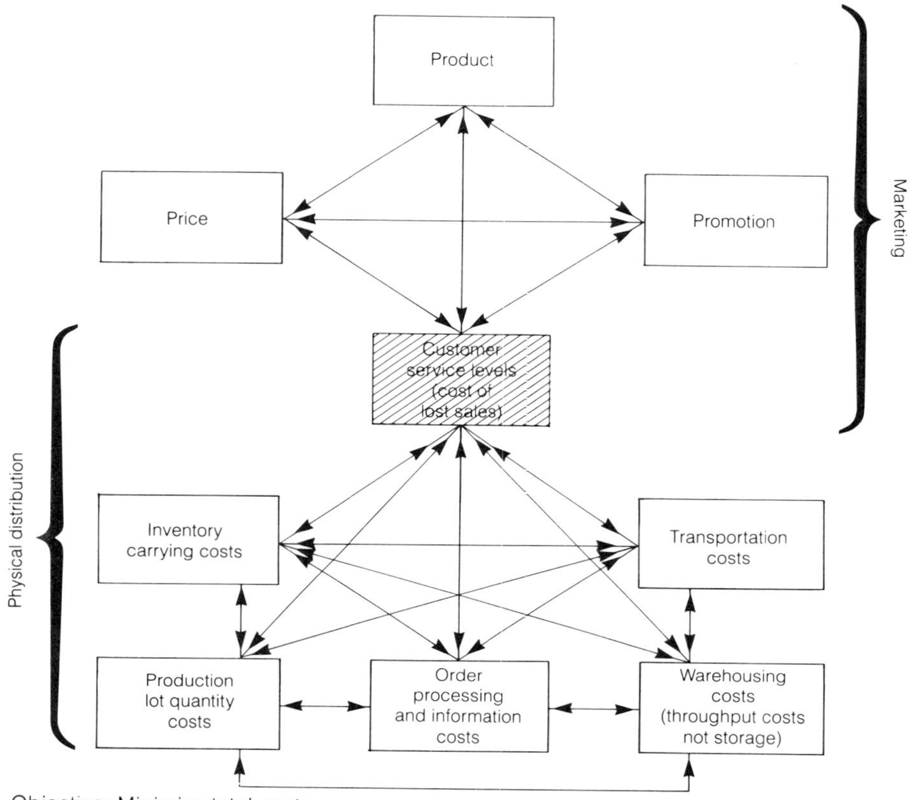

Objective: Minimize total costs

Total costs = Transportation costs + Warehousing costs
+ Order processing and information costs + Production lot quantity costs
+ Inventory carrying costs + Cost of lost sales

Source: Adapted from: Douglas M. Lambert, *The Development of an Inventory Costing Methodology: A Study of the Costs Associated with Holding Inventory* (Chicago: National Council of Physical Distribution Management, 1976), p. 7.

company to achieve its market-penetration objectives, the cost of the most efficient method of physical distribution could be calculated for the new service objective and compared to the current cost. Assume that the cost associated with the most efficient distribution system which could be used to achieve the 97 percent service goal was $2 million higher than the existing system cost. If the sale of additional product would yield a 25 percent contribution to fixed costs and profit, that is, for each $1 in revenue the company experienced 75 cents in out-of-pocket manufacturing, marketing, and physical distribution costs, what additional sales volume would be required in order to recover the additional physical distribution costs? The point at which the company would break even on the service improvement can be calculated by dividing the additional cost incurred by the contribution margin ($2 million divided by 25 percent). Therefore the company would require a sales increase of $8 million per year just to recover the additional costs incurred. The likelihood of this occurring could be estimated by determining what an $8 million sales increase would represent as a percentage increase in sales. That is, a 2 percent increase in sales volume might be viewed as a very likely occurrence whereas a 20 percent sales increase might be considered very unlikely given the competitive situation.

Another approach would be to take advantage of occasions such as product not passing quality inspection, strikes, snowstorms, shortages, or other events to determine the impact on retail sales of decreases in service levels throughout the channel of distribution. Before, during, and after measures will provide the manufacturer with valuable insights into the impact of various customer service levels on retail sales.

*Wholesalers and Retailers Influence Marketing Success*

In addition, it should be remembered that although the manufacturer's ultimate goal should be to provide needed products to the ultimate consumer, the manufacturer rarely engages in direct transactions with the consumer. However, the manufacturer reaches the consumer through wholesalers and retailers. Consequently, it is important to determine how retailers or wholesalers will react to service failures. Marcus Bennion in case studies of six wholesaling institutions, all with annual sales in excess of $500 million, found that a number of short-run and long-run reactions were possible when buyers experienced a stock-out (see Figure 3 − 5).[18] It is necessary for the manufacturer to determine what reactions its customers might take when faced with a stock-out in order to evaluate the costs and benefits associated with various service policies. An excellent starting point is to conduct a customer service audit.

## CONDUCTING A CUSTOMER SERVICE AUDIT

The customer service audit is a means of evaluating the level of service being provided. The audit not only allows the evaluation of existing service but provides a benchmark for appraising the impact of changes in customer service policy. The audit is designed to identify the important elements of customer service, the manner in which performance is controlled, and the internal communication system.

An example of a customer service audit is included in Appendix A. The goal of the customer service audit is to discover the following:

*The Goals of a Customer Service Audit*

1. The corporate statement of customer service objectives.
2. The information that the firm provides to its customers with regard to customer service standards.
3. The elements of customer service.
4. The internal customer service reporting system.
5. The customer service performance measurements used.

---

[18] Marcus Lyndsay Bennion, "An Investigation of Wholesale Buyer Reaction to Manufacturer Customer Service Failures in the Grocery Channel," Ph.D. dissertation, Michigan State University, 1980.

**FIGURE 3-5** Generalized Model of Reactions to Customer Service Failures

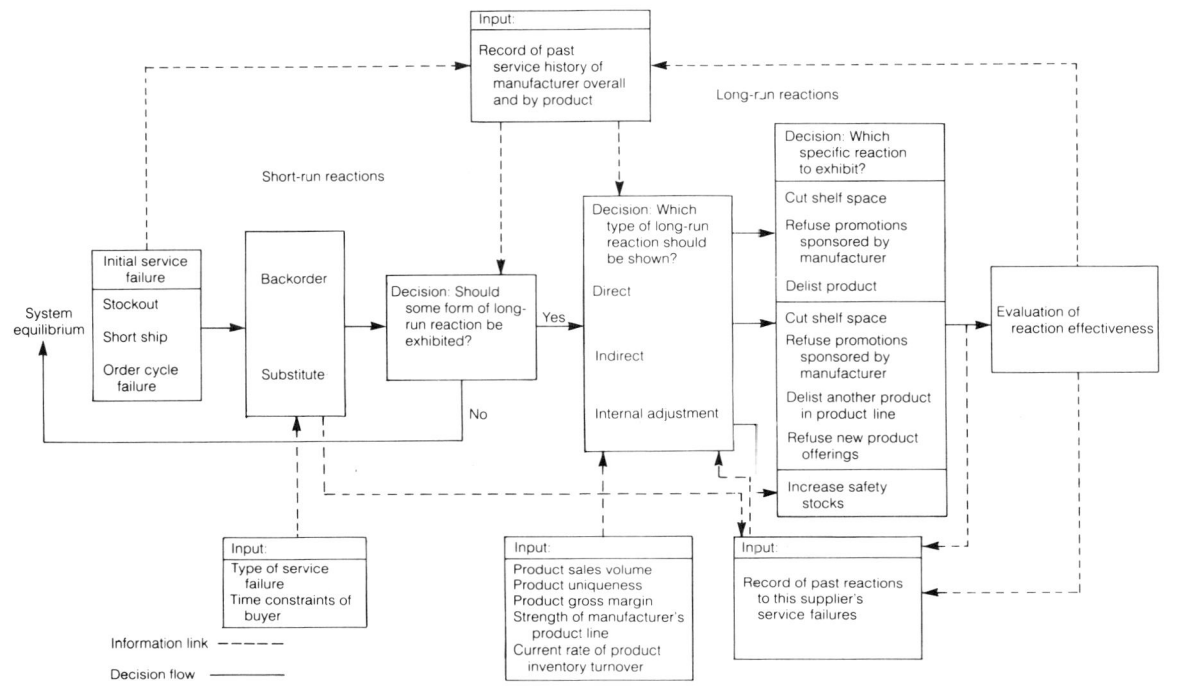

Source: Marcus Lyndsay Bennion, "An Investigation of Wholesale Buyer Reaction to Manufacturer Customer Service Failures in the Grocery Channel," Ph.D. dissertation, Michigan State University, 1980, p. 163.

A more comprehensive customer service audit which incorporates an overall physical distribution audit is presented in Appendix B:

Customer service questionnaires such as the one contained in Appendix C also provide useful information for establishing policy and developing reports. The questionnaire in Appendix C can be used to determine what the manufacturer's management views as important aspects of customer service and how manufacturer XYZ compares with its competitors on the various aspects of customer service. These results can be compared to the results obtained by surveying the manufacturer's customers. Usually there will be significant discrepancies between what management believes to be important and what is important to the customers. With this knowledge, emphasis can be redirected toward those aspects of customer service deemed to be important by the customer. If the manufacturer lags behind its competitors on elements that are important to its customers, corrective action can be taken.

With the knowledge provided by the questionnaires, customer service levels can be adjusted to meet the specific needs of customers. Peter Gilmour has reported the successful segmentation of markets by the supplier providing differential service levels.[19] One method of analyzing markets to determine the profit impact of differential customer service levels is ABC analysis.

### An ABC Analysis of Customer Service

**Prioritizing Customer Service Levels by Account/Product Profitability**

The ABC analysis used to improve customer service efficiency is similar to the ABC analysis used for inventory planning.[20] The logic behind this approach is that some customers and products are more profitable to the manufacturer than others. Consequently, higher levels of customer service should be maintained for the most profitable customer-product combinations.[21]

Table 3–2 illustrates a customer-product contribution matrix which is used to classify customers and products according to their impact on the manufacturer's profit performance. It is interpreted as follows:

1. Product line A is the firm's most profitable, followed by B, C, and D.
2. Customers in category I are the most profitable for the manufacturer and may number no more than 5 or 10 customers.
3. Customers in category V are the least profitable customers because of the small quantities purchased each time or small annual sales volume and they could number in the hundreds or thousands.
4. The most profitable customer-product combination is product line A being sold to customers in category I, the next most profitable is product line B sold to customers in category I, the next is A sold to customers in category II and so on until the least profitable product-customer relationship, product line D sold to customers in category V.

**TABLE 3-2** A Customer-Product Contribution Matrix

| Customer Classification | Product A | B | C | D |
|---|---|---|---|---|
| I | 1 | 2 | 6 | 10 |
| II | 3 | 4 | 7 | 12 |
| III | 5 | 8 | 13 | 16 |
| IV | 9 | 14 | 15 | 19 |
| V | 11 | 17 | 18 | 20 |

Source: Bernard J. LaLonde and Paul H. Zinszer, *Customer Service Meaning and Measurement* (Chicago: National Council of Physical Distribution Management, 1976), p. 181.

---

[19] Gilmour, "Customer Service," pp. 141–48.

[20] ABC analysis for inventory planning is discussed in Chapter 8.

[21] A method for obtaining profitability on a segmental basis is discussed in Chapter 9.

The customer-product contribution matrix is operationalized in a manner similar to that shown in Table 3−3. Priority range 1 to 5 is assigned an in-stock standard of 100 percent, a delivery standard of 48 hours, and orders are shipped complete 99 percent of the time. The reason that the

**TABLE 3-3 Operationalizing a Customer-Product Contribution Matrix**

| Priority Range | In-stock Standard | Delivery Standard (hours) | Order Completeness Standard |
|---|---|---|---|
| 1-5 | 100% | 48 | 99% |
| 6-10 | 97.5 | 72 | 97 |
| 11-15 | 95.0 | 96 | 95 |
| 16-20 | 90 | 120 | 93 |

Source: Bernard J. LaLonde and Paul H. Zinszer, *Customer Service: Meaning and Measurement* (Chicago: National Council of Physical Distribution Management, 1976), p. 182.

order completeness standard is not 100 percent, when the in-stock standard is 100 percent, is that customers in category I also order products in priority range 6 to 10.

The lowest priority range, 16 to 20, has an in-stock standard of 90 percent, a delivery standard of 120 hours, and an order completeness standard of 93 percent. This method recognizes the need to provide the most profitable customers with service levels that will encourage continuation of their business. For example, you do not want to stock-out your most profitable customers on your most profitable product line. Less profitable accounts can be made more valuable by reducing the associated costs of servicing them relative to the top-priority business.

### Developing and Reporting Customer Service Standards

Once the important elements of customer service have been determined, it is necessary to develop standards of performance and regularly report results to the appropriate levels of management. William Hutchinson and John Stolle offered the following four steps as requirements for the measurement and control of customer service performance:

*Measuring and Reporting Customer Service Performance Are Important*

1. Establish quantitative standards of performance for each service element.
2. Measure actual performance for each service element.
3. Analyze variance between actual services provided and the standard.
4. Take corrective action as needed to bring actual performance into line.[22]

Cooperation of customers is essential if information about the speed, dependability, and condition of the delivered product is to be obtained. To

---
[22] William H. Hutchinson, Jr., and John F. Stolle, "How to Manage Customer Service," *Harvard Business Review*, November−December 1968, pp. 85−96.

be effective, the customer must be convinced that service measurement/monitoring is valuable as a means of improving future service.

Figure 3−6 contains a number of possible measures of service performance. The emphasis placed on individual elements by any manufacturer

**FIGURE 3-6**   Possible Measures of Customer Service Performance

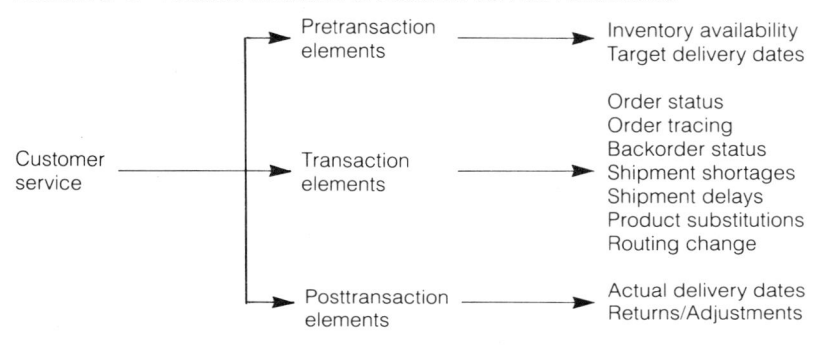

Customer service →
- Pretransaction elements → Inventory availability / Target delivery dates
- Transaction elements → Order status / Order tracing / Backorder status / Shipment shortages / Shipment delays / Product substitutions / Routing change
- Posttransaction elements → Actual delivery dates / Returns/Adjustments

must be based on what that manufacturer's customers believe to be important. Such service elements as inventory availability, delivery dates, order status, order tracing, and back-order status require good communications between the manufacturer and its customers. Because many companies have not kept pace with technology in order processing, this area offers significant potential for improving customer service. Consider how much communications can be improved by a system where customers telephone their orders to customer service representatives who are equipped with CRTs. Immediate information can be provided on inventory availability and product substitution can be arranged if a stock-out exists. Also, target delivery dates can be communicated to the customers.

*Automated Order Processing Improves Customer Service*

Examples of customer service standards are reported in Figure 3−7. The particular standards chosen should best reflect what the customer needs rather than what management may think customers need. Performance should be measured and compared to the standard and this information should be reported to the appropriate levels of management on a regular and timely basis. Table 3−4 provides a format that can be used when trying to evaluate and/or understand an existing customer service reporting system or for the design of a new system of customer service management reports.

A manufacturer's order-processing system and accounting-information system can provide much of the information necessary for developing a customer-product contribution matrix and for the implementation of the customer service management reports. These important interfaces will be discussed in detail in Chapter 9, Order Processing and Information Systems, and Chapter 11, Financial Control of Distribution Performance.

**TABLE 3-4** A Framework for Outlining the Customer Service Management Reporting System

| Customer Service Element(s) | Used As a Performance Measurement | Appears on a Formal Report | Data Sources | Who Gets Report – For Information | Who Gets Report – For Action | Exception or Detailed Report | Frequency Created |
|---|---|---|---|---|---|---|---|
| 1. Product availability | | | | | | | |
| 2. Order cycle time | | | | | | | |
|    Customer to company | | | | | | | |
|    Order entry to shipping | | | | | | | |
|    Customer order to delivery | | | | | | | |
| 3. Distribution system information | | | | | | | |
|    Status | | | | | | | |
|    Order status | | | | | | | |
|    Data base for forecasting | | | | | | | |
| 4. Distribution system flexibility | | | | | | | |
|    Expedite | | | | | | | |
|    Back order | | | | | | | |
|    Substitute | | | | | | | |
|    Transportation | | | | | | | |

|   |   |   |   |   |   |
|---|---|---|---|---|---|
| 5. Malfunction |   |   |   |   |   |
| Administrative errors (i.e., pricing, promotion, transcription) |   |   |   |   |   |
| Picking errors |   |   |   |   |   |
| Shipping errors |   |   |   |   |   |
| Warehouse damage |   |   |   |   |   |
| Company shipping damage |   |   |   |   |   |
| Carrier shipping damage |   |   |   |   |   |
| 6. Post-sale support invoice errors (adjustments) |   |   |   |   |   |
| Returns |   |   |   |   |   |
| Allowances |   |   |   |   |   |
| Technical advice |   |   |   |   |   |
| 7. Other |   |   |   |   |   |

Note: When used in combination with appendixes B and C this provides a framework for determining where in the communications-information system changes are needed.

Source: American Telephone and Telegraph Company, Business Marketing, Market Management Division, 1980.

**FIGURE 3-7** Examples of Customer Service Standards

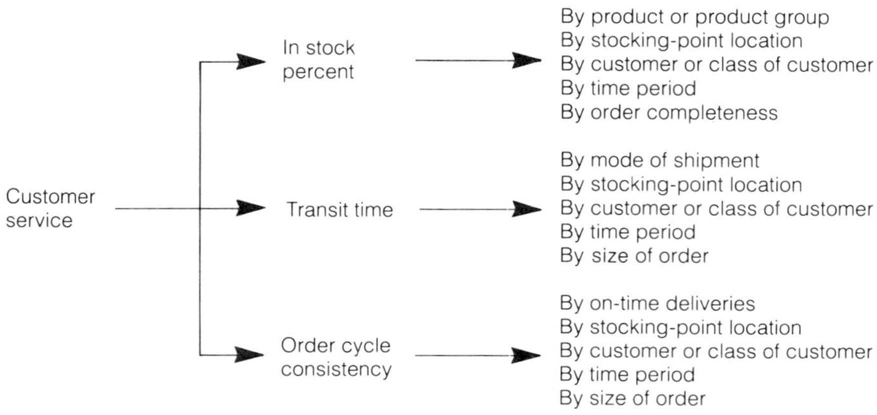

```
Customer service
├── In stock percent
│     ├── By product or product group
│     ├── By stocking-point location
│     ├── By customer or class of customer
│     ├── By time period
│     └── By order completeness
├── Transit time
│     ├── By mode of shipment
│     ├── By stocking-point location
│     ├── By customer or class of customer
│     ├── By time period
│     └── By size of order
└── Order cycle consistency
      ├── By on-time deliveries
      ├── By stocking-point location
      ├── By customer or class of customer
      ├── By time period
      └── By size of order
```

## IMPEDIMENTS TO AN EFFECTIVE CUSTOMER SERVICE STRATEGY

In many companies an effective customer service strategy has not been attained. Even the best-managed firms may be guilty of one of the following:

*Eleven Hidden Costs of Customer Service*

1. Misdefining customer service.
2. Overlooking customer profitability.
3. Unrealistic customer service policies.
4. Failing to research.
5. Burying customer service costs.
6. Misusing customer service as a sales incentive.
7. Blurred lines of authority.
8. Equating warehouses with customer service.
9. Adding bodies rather than systems.
10. Undertrained, undercompensated personnel.
11. Misreading the seller's market.[23]

Failure to segment markets in terms of the service offered may be a costly practice. Often firms are hesitant to offer different levels of service for fear of violating the Robinson-Patman Act. This is because it is necessary to cost-justify such policies and most firms do not have the necessary cost information.[24]

Customer service can be misused by sales people who promise faster delivery as a further incentive to place an order. However, most customers

---

[23] Warren Blanding, "The Hidden Eleven Costs of Customer Service," *Transportation and Distribution Management* 14, no. 4 (July–August 1974): 6–10.

[24] See Douglas M. Lambert, *The Distribution Channels Decision* (New York: The National Association of Accountants and Hamilton, Ontario: The Society of Management Accountants of Canada, 1978); Douglas M. Lambert and John T. Mentzer, "Is Integrated Physical Distribution Management a Reality?" *Journal of Business Logistics* 2, no. 1 (1980): 18–27; and, Douglas M. Lambert and Howard M. Armitage, "Distribution Costs: The Challenge," *Management Accounting* (May 1979), pp. 33–37 and 45.

value reliability and consistency in filling orders more than the actual speed of delivery. Consequently, attempting to decrease the order cycle on an ad hoc basis increases transportation costs for the expedited shipments as well as order assembly costs by disrupting normal work flow. In addition, very little benefit is realized by the customer or the company. When salesmen override customer service policies on shipping dates, lead times, shipping points, transportation modes, and units of sale, orders for other customers are disrupted and distribution costs increase. In other situations, salespeople have been known not to "sell" the services being provided by the company.

Another impediment to an effective customer service strategy is a lack of customer orientation. Robert Sabath has argued that:

> . . . . many "service levels" are usually set arbitrarily, and often much too high—generally, far higher than any customer would set them. So the first step is to banish the costly misconception that all customers seek or need improved service. It is far more likely that current service levels are more than adequate but are poorly defined; it may be that only a very few products in a large line need, say a 95 percent service level, and that 75 percent is highly satisfactory for all other products.[25]

When one considers the vast sums of money that are spent researching products and advertising appeals, it makes little sense for a firm not to adequately research the levels of customer service that are necessary for profitable long-range business development.

Finally, the economic environment of the late 1970s and the 1980s has caused top management to push for more inventory turns and lower accounts receivable. As was pointed out in the last chapter both of these reactions can lead to decreased levels of customer service and eventually lower corporate profitability.

## IMPROVING CUSTOMER SERVICE PERFORMANCE

The levels of customer service offered by a firm can be improved by the following actions: (1) thoroughly researching the customers needs; (2) setting service levels that realistically trade-off revenues and expenses; (3) making use of the latest technology in order-processing systems; and, (4) measuring and evaluating the performance of individual distribution activities.

An Effective Customer Service Strategy Requires a Thorough Understanding of Customers

It is imperative that an effective customer service strategy be based on an understanding of what the customer considers service to be. The customer service audit and surveys of customers are a must.

> Many customer service surveys show that customers define service differently than suppliers and prefer a lower but more reliable service level than that currently offered. Under these circumstances, there is no reason why a firm can't

---

[25] Robert E. Sabath, "How Much Service Do Customers Really Want?" *Business Horizons*, April 1978, p. 26.

improve service as the customers perceive it and at the same time cut costs. To improve service as measured by this objective standard is often less costly than to improve service as measured by arbitrary in-house standards.[26]

Once the customers' views of service have been determined, it is necessary to select a customer service strategy that advances the long-range profit and return on investment objectives of the firm.

> It should be clear that the optimum service level is not always the lowest cost level. The optimum level is one that retains customers at the lowest possible costs—and meets the company's growth needs. Defined this way, an optimum service level may be achieved by trading off some PD cost savings for more valuable marketing advantages or manufacturing efficiencies. The point is that with objective, customer-defined service levels and a good handle on costs, everyone knows exactly what is being traded and what is received in return.[27]

Many firms have antiquated order-processing systems and automating order processing represents a significant opportunity for improving customer service. The primary advantage of automating the order processing system is to reduce the order cycle time. Given that most customers prefer a consistent delivery cycle to a shorter one, it usually will not be necessary or wise to reduce the order cycle time. By using the additional time internally, for planning, this will not only lead to potential savings in transportation, warehousing, and inventory costs, but automation will improve customer service by providing the following benefits to the customer:

1. Better product availability.
2. More accurate invoices.
3. The ability to lower safety-stock levels and the associated carrying costs.
4. Improved access to information on order status.

In short, automated order processing systems enhance the ability to perform all of the transaction and posttransaction elements of customer service.

Finally, the development of an effective customer service program requires the establishment of customer service standards that

1. Reflect the customer's point of view.
2. Provide an operational and objective measure of service performance.
3. Provide management cues for corrective action.[28]

The impact of individual distribution activities such as transportation, warehousing, inventory management, and order processing on the level of customer service also should be measured and evaluated. Regular reports should be sent to the appropriate levels of management showing achievement. Actual performance must be compared to standards and corrective action taken when performance is inadequate. To be successful, efficient, and timely information flow is necessary. It is also critical to have well-

---

[26] Ibid., p. 32.
[27] Ibid., p. 32.
[28] LaLonde and Zinszer, *Customer Service*, p. 180.

defined accountability within the organization since the information alone will not guarantee improved decision making.

## SUMMARY

In this chapter you were shown how to define customer service. Although the importance of the individual elements of customer service will vary from company to company, the common elements that are of concern to most companies were explained. Industry data showed how physical distribution executives rated the importance of each element. Also stressed was the need for a customer service policy that is consistent with marketing and physical distribution strategies. The successful implementation of the integrated physical management concept is dependent upon knowledge of the costs associated with different distribution system designs and the relationship between system design and customer service levels. You were shown how management can obtain better knowledge of the costs and revenues associated with different levels of customer service and how to implement cost/service tradeoffs.

The customer service audit was introduced as a method of:

1. Determining the existing service levels.
2. Determining how performance is measured and reported.
3. Appraising the impact of changes in customer service policy.

Questionnaires were suggested as a means of finding out what management and customers view as important aspects of customer service. The chapter closed with a discussion of common roadblocks to an effective customer service strategy and some ways for improving performance. In the next chapter you will be shown how transportation influences the efficiency and effectiveness of the physical distribution function.

## Appendix A: Customer Service Audit

### Part I—General Information

1. Do you have a specific statement of customer service policy?
   _____ Yes  _____ No  _____ Other (specify) _____

   If yes:
   a. Do you provide your customers and potential customers with a copy of your customer service policy?
      _____ Yes  _____ No  _____ Other (specify) _____

2. Can you provide us with a definition of customer service as viewed by your company?
   _____
   _____
   _____

Source: Paul H. Zinszer, University of Oklahoma, 1978.

3. Do you use a standard cost for a customer order? _____Yes _____No
   a. If yes: What cost do you use? $_____
   What cost categories are included in customer order costs? _____
   _____

4. Do you use a standard cost for a stock-out order? _____Yes _____No
   a. If yes: What cost do you use? $_____
   What cost categories are included in the stock-out order costs? _____
   _____

5. Do you use a standard cost for a back-ordered order? _____Yes _____No
   a. If yes: What cost do you use? $_____
   What cost categories are included in the back-order costs? _____
   _____

## Part II—Customer and Internal Reporting System

| Presale Elements | Customer | | Management | | | Channel of Communications | Source of Communications | Comments |
|---|---|---|---|---|---|---|---|---|
| | I | TR | I | P | TP | | | |
| Inventory availability | | | | | | | | |
| Target delivery date | | | | | | | | |

| Sale Elements | Customer | | | | Management | | | | Channel of Communications | Source of Communications | |
|---|---|---|---|---|---|---|---|---|---|---|---|
| | I | E | P | TR | I | E | P | TP | | | |
| Order status | | | | | | | | | | | |
| Order tracing | | | | | | | | | | | |
| Back-order status | | | | | | | | | | | |
| Shipment shortages | | | | | | | | | | | |
| Product substitutions | | | | | | | | | | | |
| Routing changes | | | | | | | | | | | |

| Postsale Elements | Customer | | Management | | | | Channel of Communications | Source of Communications | |
|---|---|---|---|---|---|---|---|---|---|
| | I | TR | I | E | P | TP | | | |
| Actual delivery date | | | | | | | | | |
| Returns/adjustments | | | | | | | | | |

**Definitions:**
    I—Inquiry.
  TR—Time of response (e.g., immediate, 24 hours, one week).
    E—Exception—report provided indicating less than expected performance.
    P—Periodic—routine report.
  TP—Time period associated with periodic report.
      Channel of communications—telephone, interoffice memo, mail, telex, etc.
      Source of communications—shipping location, stocking location, sales, etc.

**Example of answers**
Yes.
12 hrs.
Yes.
Yes.
1 week.

## Part III—Customer Service Performance Measurement

| Element | (1) Activity Considered Part of Customer Service Functions - Yes | (1) No | (2) Is Activity Measured - Yes | (2) No | (3) Describe Unit of Measurement | (4) Performance Standard to Be Achieved | (5) Are Reports Generated on This Activity - Yes | (5) No | (6) Frequency of Reports | (7) Distribution of Report | (8) Corporate Function Controlling Activity | (9) Reporting Element |
|---|---|---|---|---|---|---|---|---|---|---|---|---|
| Inventory availability | | | | | | | | | | | | |
| Stock-out rate | | | | | | | | | | | | |
| Order completeness rate | | | | | | | | | | | | |
| Emergency orders | | | | | | | | | | | | |
| Back orders | | | | | | | | | | | | |
| Trans shipments | | | | | | | | | | | | |
| Product substitutions | | | | | | | | | | | | |
| Total transit time | | | | | | | | | | | | |
| Total order cycle time | | | | | | | | | | | | |
| Complaints | | | | | | | | | | | | |
| Credits/returns | | | | | | | | | | | | |
| Errors experienced in Ordering | | | | | | | | | | | | |
| Billing | | | | | | | | | | | | |
| Shipping | | | | | | | | | | | | |
| Order picking | | | | | | | | | | | | |
| Customer misunderstanding | | | | | | | | | | | | |
| Other | | | | | | | | | | | | |
| Claims | | | | | | | | | | | | |
| Damage in transit | | | | | | | | | | | | |
| Product warranty | | | | | | | | | | | | |
| Product shortages | | | | | | | | | | | | |
| Other | | | | | | | | | | | | |
| Shipments refused | | | | | | | | | | | | |

### Explanation of Terms Used in Customer Service Audit

**Part I 3,4,5:** The costs referred to in questions 3, 4, and 5 include not only the processing of the order, but the movement of the goods.

**Part II Customer:** Refers to the ability of the customer to either initiate or receive response from the distribution system.

**Management:** Refers to the ability of appropriate management functions (sales, marketing, physical distribution) queuing the system.

**Channel of Communications:** This may differ by customer versus sales and management, e.g., telephone, telex, mail, interoffice memo.

**Source of Communications:** Where in the system the particular activity occurs, e.g., shipping location, management information system, sales, etc.

**Part III Col. (3)** Describe Unit of Measurement: What units are used to measure the activity, e.g., percent of sales, dollar, percent of total freight, etc.

**Col. (4)** Performance Standard to Be Achieved: This is the measurements associated with the units described in (3).

**Col. (7)** Distribution of Report: What departments in the organization receive the report. Suggested definitions of departments are:

    IPD—Internal physical distribution only.
    PD—Physical distribution.
    M—Marketing.
    S—Sales.
    P—Planning.
    PM—Production.
      Additional departments may be used.

**Col. (9)** Reporting Element: What department initiates the report—refer to (7) for definitions of departments.

# Appendix B: Customer Service/Physical Distribution Audit

1. How many product/package combinations do you ship? _____
2. What is your geographical market? _____
   _____
3. Do you have a written customer service policy?
   Yes _____
   No _____
   Other (specify) _____
4. Do customers receive a copy of this policy?
   Yes _____
   No _____
   Other (specify) _____
5. May we have a copy of this policy?
   Yes _____
   No _____
   Other (specify) _____

Source: M. Chris Lewis, Industry Analyst, American Telephone and Telegraph, Business Marketing, Market Management Division, 1981.

3 / *Customer Service* **85**

6. Indicate how inventory moves through your distribution system for the products which you are describing. Use approximate figures if necessary.

| Location | Number of Facilities | Average Annual Inventory at Location | Percent of Annual Volume Shipped Directly to Customer |
|---|---|---|---|
| Plant | | | |
| Company operated warehouse | | | |
| Public warehouse | | | |

7. What are your total annual warehousing costs? _____

   a. What percentage of total warehousing costs can be attributed to:

   | | |
   |---|---|
   | In plant warehouses | _____ |
   | Field private | _____ |
   | Field public | _____ |
   | Total warehousing costs | 100% |

   b. What cost categories are included in total warehousing costs associated with company-operated facilities? Do you use standard costs for labor? Other? Please be specific. _____

   c. If they use standard costs, ask:
   How do your current results compare to your standard costs?

   d. If there is a variance, ask:
   What corrective action plans are underway? _____

   e. What type of payment arrangement do you have with the public warehouse(s) for handling charges? For storage charges? _____

   f. What are the per-unit handling charges at the public warehouse(s)? Per-unit storage costs? _____

8. What is your total annual freight bill? _____
    a. Percent of freight bill attributed to company-operated transportation? _____
    b. What cost categories are included in transportation costs associated with company-operated vehicles? _____
    _____

    c. For what do you use company-operated vehicles? Intracompany hauling? Company to customers? Please explain. _____
    _____
    _____

    d. Do you pay freight charges on incoming raw materials?
       Yes _____ If yes: _____ percent of freight bill?
       No _____
       Other (explain) _____

    e. Provide the following information concerning product movement in your distribution system. Use approximate figures if necessary.

| Freight Movement | Percent of Freight Bill | Percent of Number of Shipments | \multicolumn{5}{c}{Percent of Weight Shipped by Mode} | |
|---|---|---|---|---|---|---|---|---|
| | | | CL | Piggy-back | TL | LTL | Other (describe) _____ | |
| Plant to customer | | | | | | | | = 100% |
| Plant to warehouse | | | | | | | | = 100 |
| Warehouse to customer | | | | | | | | = 100 |
| | 100% | 100% | | | | | | |

9. Can you provide us with a definition of customer service as viewed by your company? _____
    _____

    a. Do you provide different levels of customer service by product or customer?
       _____ Yes _____ No  If yes, please explain specifically.
       _____
       _____
       _____

10. Is there enough seasonal variation in demand for this product that the shipping characteristics would change throughout the year? _____ Yes _____ No

11. Do your customer service standards change? _____ Yes _____ No  If yes, please explain why—seasonal demand for your products, etc. _____
    _____
    _____
    _____

12. What cost categories do you include in inventory carrying costs?

| Cost Categories | Check if Included in Carrying Costs | Cost as a Percent of Inventory Value |
|---|---|---|
| Cost of money | | |
| Average monthly inventory* | | |
| Taxes | | |
| Insurance | | |
| Variable storage | | |
| Obsolescence | | |
| Shrinkage | | |
| Damage | | |
| Relocation costs | | |
| Total carrying Costs percentage | | |

* Valued at variable costs delivered to the distribution center.

13. Do you have a precalculated cost for cutting a customer order?
    _____ Yes _____ No
    If yes, what cost do you use? _____
    What cost categories are included in customer order costs? _____
    _____
    _____
    _____

14. Do you use a standard cost for a stock-out order (cost of lost sale?)
    _____ Yes _____ No
    If yes, what cost do you use? $ _____
    What cost categories are included in stock-out order costs? _____
    _____

15. Do you use a standard cost for a back-ordered order? _____ Yes _____ No
    If yes, what cost do you use? $ _____
    What cost categories are included in backorder costs? _____
    _____

16. Do you use a standard cost for an expedited order? _____ Yes _____ No
    If yes, what cost do you use? $ _____
    What cost categories are included in expedited order cost? _____
    _____

If they have one or more standard costs, ask:

17. How do your current results compare to your standard costs?
    Ask this in regard to *each* standard cost.

    _____
    _____
    _____
    _____
    _____
    _____
    _____

18. If there is a variance what corrective action plans are underway?
    Ask this in regard to each variance.

    _____
    _____
    _____
    _____

19. We realize that all elements of the marketing mix are important but we would like you to distribute 100 points among the following marketing variables. (The greater number of points indicating greater importance in achieving sales for your firm.)

    | | |
    |---|---|
    | Product | _____ |
    | Price | _____ |
    | Customer service | _____ |
    | Advertising, sales effort | _____ |
    | | 100 points |

20. Diagram your company's organizational chart (or provide a photocopy). Show the functions of physical distribution, marketing, production, purchasing, top management, or their equivalents. Include any function which your company presently defines as customer service (or customer relations, distribution services, etc.). If your company subdivides the physical distribution activities show where they report. Show staff responsibility with a dashed line and line responsibility with a solid line. If appropriate, you may describe only a division or subsidiary of your company if most of the corporate functional areas described above are included within it.

    a. *Who Has Responsibility For:*   *Who Do They Report To?*
       Warehouse? _____   _____
       Finished goods inventory? _____   _____
       Transportation? _____   _____
       Order processing? _____   _____
       Customer service? _____   _____

    b. If your company designates a particular area as customer service (or customer relations, distribution services, etc):
       (1) How many people are assigned to the area? _____
       (2) Describe the major responsibilities of these individuals:
           _____
           _____
       (3) To what department does this area report? _____
       (4) If possible, please provide us with all job descriptions which include customer service/customer relations in the title.
           _____
           _____
           _____

21. Relative to your company's order cycle time:
    a. How frequently do you monitor the order cycle (check one)
       _____ Every order  _____ Routinely sample  _____ Never  _____ Other (specify)
       _____

    b. Indicate (using letters from the diagram below, e.g., B to C) which components are part of your measurement.
       _____ to _____ .

| Customer Places Order | Order Receipt | Order Processed | Order Shipped | Order Received by Customer |
|---|---|---|---|---|
| A | B | C | D | E |

22. If measured indicate the average time and variance in days or hours (specify which) taken by your system between:

    *Average*                         *Variance (fastest to slowest time frames)*

    A and B = _____ hrs/days           _____ hrs/days
    B and C = _____ hrs/days           _____ hrs/days
    C and D = _____ hrs/days           _____ hrs/days
    D and E = _____ hrs/days           _____ hrs/days

    a. Your estimate of the average total order cycle A to E is _____ hrs/days.
    b. Your estimate of the total variability (range) for the total order cycle A to E is _____ hrs/days (e.g., 6–23 days or 1–5 days).

23. Is order processing centralized in one location or decentralized. Explain.
    Centralized _____   Where? _____
    Decentralized _____   Number and types of locations _____
    _____
    _____

24. How many orders do you process each month? _____
    What is the range from month to month?

    *Total Company (number of orders)*              *This location (number of orders)*

    Low month _____     _____
    High month _____     _____
    Average month _____     _____

    a. What is the dollar value of a typical order? Number of line items? _____
       _____

25. What percentage of customer orders are placed by outside salespeople? (percent of total received)
    _____ (percent orders placed by outside salespeople)
    Total company _____
    This location  _____
    a. What percentage of total customer orders are placed by inside salespeople/order clerks *who call the customer* to get the order?
       _____ (percent orders company initiated via tel-sell method)
       Total company _____
       This location  _____
    b. What percentage of total customer orders are placed by customers?
       _____ (percent orders placed by customers)
       Total company _____
       This location  _____

26. In terms of methods of order entry:
    *How* do each of these groups above enter orders? If they use multiple methods, please indicate the percentage of *their* total entered via each method.

| Order Entry Methods | Outside Salespeople | | Customers | | Inside Sales/Order Clerks | |
|---|---|---|---|---|---|---|
| | Total Company | This Location | Total Company | This Location | Total Company | This Location |
| Mail (0/0) | | | | | | |
| Telephone (0/0) | | | | | | |
| Other (specify) | | | | | | |
| Total | 100% | 100% | 100% | 100% | 100% | 100% |

Please explain "other" order entry methods or any of respondent's comments about order entry below.
_____
_____
_____
_____
_____

a. How many departments enter customer orders? Please specify which departments as well.
_____

b. How many order-entry locations exist in the company? Specify. Plants, DCs, Sales offices.
   Total number of order entry locations_____
_____
_____
_____

   Number of this type location _____
_____
_____
_____

27. Once received by the firm does the order taker:
    _____ Fill out a preprinted order form? If yes, ask for a copy.
    _____ Enter the order into the computer via a data terminal offline?
    _____ Enter the order into the computer via a data terminal online?
    _____ Other (specify):
    _____

   a. Does the order taker:
      _____ Verify credit?
      _____ Verify inventory availability?
      _____ Assign inventory to the order?
      _____ Make product substitutions?
      _____ Price the order?
      _____ Confirm delivery date?

_____ Attempt to increase order size to achieve an efficient shipping quantity?
_____
_____

_____ Other (specify) _____
_____

b. Are the following reference files manual or computerized?

| File | Manual | Computerized |
|---|---|---|
| Customer | | |
| Product | | |
| Prices | | |
| Promotions | | |
| Inventory | | |
| Ship schedules | | |
| Credit | | |
| Other | | |

How are these files updated? Frequency of updates?

| File | Frequency | Manual | Computerized |
|---|---|---|---|
| Customer | | | |
| Product | | | |
| Prices | | | |
| Promotions | | | |
| Inventory | | | |
| Ship schedules | | | |
| Credit | | | |
| Other | | | |

c. How does the order taker access these files? When—while on the telephone or after hanging up?
_____ Manual look up.
_____ Via data terminal.
_____ Other (specify) _____
_____
_____

28. Are orders processed:
    _____ Batch processed?
    _____ Individually processed?
    If batch processed, explain in detail. Number of orders per batch? Cut-off times? Batches per day, per week? etc.
    _____
    _____
    _____
    _____
    _____

29. How does the order taker transmit order information to:
    *Transportation,* so that they can determine route, loading sequence, and ship date? _____
    _____

    *Warehouse* for picking and packing? _____
    _____

    a. Who else does the order taker send order information to? How is it transmitted? What does this department do with this information. Probe.
    _____
    _____

30. Are orders batch picked?
    _____ Yes
    _____ No
    _____ Other (specify) _____

    *If yes,* How are picking lists developed and by whom are they developed? Probe.
    _____
    _____
    _____
    _____

31. How are transportation routes/trucks scheduled and by whom? Probe.
    _____
    _____
    _____
    _____

32. After picking, is a copy of the packing list transmitted to:
    _____ Invoicing          How transmitted? _____
    _____ Transportation     How transmitted? _____
    _____ Sales              How transmitted? _____
    _____ Other (specify) _____
    _____
    _____

33. How are inventory levels at the DCs set? Average inventory in units? Variable delivered cost of one unit of product? Probe.
    _____
    _____
    _____
    _____

34. Are DC inventory records:
    _____ Manual?
    _____ Computerized, offline?
    _____ Computerized, online?

35. How is the inventory file updated to reflect new product received and product shipped? Probe.
    _____
    _____
    _____
    _____

36. In reference to the replenishment of inventory at the DCs:
    a. How do you know when it is time to order product for the DC? How do you know how much to order? How do you communicate your replenishment need to the plant? Explain.
    _____
    _____
    _____

    b. What is your average replenishment cycle in hrs/days? Variability (range) in hrs/days?

    |  | Average Cycle | Variability (range) |
    |---|---|---|
    | This location | _____ hrs/days | _____ hrs/days |
    | Total company | _____ hrs/days | _____ hrs/days |

37. What formal reports are generated regarding inventory? _____
    _____

    a. Data source? How is this file updated? Frequency? _____

    b. Compiled manually or computer generated? _____

    c. Exception or detailed report? _____

    d. Frequency created? _____

    e. Who gets these reports and for what, information or action? _____
    _____

38. Do salespeople or customers receive an order acknowledgement?

    _____ Sales       When? _____   How transmitted? _____
    _____ Customers   When? _____   How transmitted? _____
    _____ Both        When? _____   How transmitted? _____
    _____ Neither

39. Do you have an established method of communications for your customers to contact you about some aspect of their order after the order has been entered?
    Yes _____
    No _____
    Other (specify) _____

40. Do you have a *single* point of contact for customers or do certain departments handle different types of inquiries/complaints?
    _____
    _____
    _____

41. Please explain the communications methods customers use. Do they call you, send a letter, or do something else?
    Communications channel _____
    (mail, telephone, other)
    If multiple methods are used estimate the percentage of the total each method accounts for.
    Mail _____
    Telephone _____
    Other (specify) _____
    a. If telephone, is it a long distance call?
        No _____
        Yes _____
        Sometimes _____   Estimate long distance calls as a percentage
                                        of total calls _____
    b. If long distance, who pays for the call?
        Customer _____
        Company _____          Toll-free? _____
                                               Collect? _____
                                               Other? (Specify) _____
                                               _____
                                               _____
    c. Do you provide customers with a telephone number? If so, how do you make them aware of it?
        Yes _____
        No _____

42. Do your competitors have an established method of communication for their customers who want to contact them about some aspect of their order after the order has been entered?
    Yes _____
    No _____
    Other (specify) _____
    _____

43. Of the total number of customer orders you process each month, what percentage are:
    _____ Shipped complete?
    _____ Contain product substitutions?
    _____ Back orders?
    _____ Expedited orders (rush orders)?
    _____ Cancelled?
    _____ Delivered on date promised?

44. Indicate the relative degree of competition which your products experience in the marketplace. (1 = little competition; 7 = intensive competition).
    Degree of competition = _____

45. Who are your major competitors? What products do they sell? To whom? _____
    _____
    _____
    _____
    _____

46. How do they distribute their products? What types of services do they offer customers? Why would someone purchase your competitors products over yours? _____
    _____
    _____
    _____

47. What is your total annual sales volume?  $ _____

# Appendix C: Customer Service Questionnaire

Listed below are a number of factors which manufacturers may provide to their customers. Please evaluate each of the factors on a scale of 1–5 on the importance of the individual factor to you as a retailer/wholesaler. If there are other important factors under the general heading (example: Product availability), please write in the factor and evaluate its importance. Also evaluate the XYZ Company, as compared to other manufacturers of similar products who supply your firm, on each of the elements of customer service by checking (✔) the appropriate response.

| Item | Importance (please circle one) Not Important — Very Important | Rating of XYZ Company (please check one) Much Better than / Better than / About the Same as / Worse than / Much Worse than |
|---|---|---|
| **A. Product availability** | | |
| 1. Completeness of order (percent of order shipped) | 1 2 3 4 5 | ___ ___ ___ ___ ___ |
| 2. Fill rate (percent of orders shipped complete) | 1 2 3 4 5 | ___ ___ ___ ___ ___ |
| 3. Other _____ | 1 2 3 4 5 | ___ ___ ___ ___ ___ |
| **B. Order cycle time** | | |
| 1. Short order cycle time | 1 2 3 4 5 | ___ ___ ___ ___ ___ |
| 2. Minimum variation between expected arrival date and actual arrival date | 1 2 3 4 5 | ___ ___ ___ ___ ___ |
| 3. Other _____ | 1 2 3 4 5 | ___ ___ ___ ___ ___ |
| **C. Assistance in ordering** | | |
| 1. Sales person's help in order preparation | 1 2 3 4 5 | ___ ___ ___ ___ ___ |
| 2. Assistance with inventory management | 1 2 3 4 5 | ___ ___ ___ ___ ___ |
| 3. Adherence to special shipping instructions | 1 2 3 4 5 | ___ ___ ___ ___ ___ |
| 4. Adherence to special packaging instructions | 1 2 3 4 5 | ___ ___ ___ ___ ___ |
| 5. Ability to expedite orders | 1 2 3 4 5 | ___ ___ ___ ___ ___ |
| 6. Use of a substitution policy for out-of-stock merchandise | 1 2 3 4 5 | ___ ___ ___ ___ ___ |
| 7. Efficient order entry procedures | 1 2 3 4 5 | ___ ___ ___ ___ ___ |
| 8. Order entry personnel | 1 2 3 4 5 | ___ ___ ___ ___ ___ |
| 9. Other _____ | 1 2 3 4 5 | ___ ___ ___ ___ ___ |
| **D. Financial terms** | | |
| 1. Adequate cash discount | 1 2 3 4 5 | ___ ___ ___ ___ ___ |
| 2. Adequate payment period | 1 2 3 4 5 | ___ ___ ___ ___ ___ |
| 3. Reasonable minimum order quantities | 1 2 3 4 5 | ___ ___ ___ ___ ___ |
| 4. Prepaid shipments | 1 2 3 4 5 | ___ ___ ___ ___ ___ |
| 5. Seasonal dating programs | 1 2 3 4 5 | ___ ___ ___ ___ ___ |
| 6. Speed and accuracy in billing | 1 2 3 4 5 | ___ ___ ___ ___ ___ |

Source: Adapted from Bernard J. LaLonde and Paul H. Zinszer, *Customer Service: Meaning and Measurement* (Chicago: The National Council of Physical Distribution Management, 1976) pp. 254–56.

|  | | Importance<br>(*please circle one*) | | | | | Rating of XYZ Company<br>(*please check one*) | | | | |
|---|---|---|---|---|---|---|---|---|---|---|---|
| Item | | Not<br>Important | | | | Very<br>Important | Much<br>Better<br>than | Better<br>than | About<br>the<br>Same<br>as | Worse<br>than | Much<br>Worse<br>than |
| | 7. Expedient recognition of debits and credits | 1 | 2 | 3 | 4 | 5 | ___ | ___ | ___ | ___ | ___ |
| | 8. Handling of claims | 1 | 2 | 3 | 4 | 5 | ___ | ___ | ___ | ___ | ___ |
| | 9. Other _____ | 1 | 2 | 3 | 4 | 5 | ___ | ___ | ___ | ___ | ___ |
| E. | General marketing support | | | | | | | | | | |
| | 1. Knowledgable sales representatives | 1 | 2 | 3 | 4 | 5 | ___ | ___ | ___ | ___ | ___ |
| | 2. Adequate pretesting of new products before introduction | 1 | 2 | 3 | 4 | 5 | ___ | ___ | ___ | ___ | ___ |
| | 3. Results of market research available as a marketing tool | 1 | 2 | 3 | 4 | 5 | ___ | ___ | ___ | ___ | ___ |
| | 4. Marketing assistance | 1 | 2 | 3 | 4 | 5 | ___ | ___ | ___ | ___ | ___ |
| | 5. Availability of promotion and pricing materials | 1 | 2 | 3 | 4 | 5 | ___ | ___ | ___ | ___ | ___ |
| | 6. Other _____ | 1 | 2 | 3 | 4 | 5 | ___ | ___ | ___ | ___ | ___ |
| F. | Information availability | | | | | | | | | | |
| | 1. Order status | 1 | 2 | 3 | 4 | 5 | ___ | ___ | ___ | ___ | ___ |
| | 2. Advance information on price changes | 1 | 2 | 3 | 4 | 5 | ___ | ___ | ___ | ___ | ___ |
| | 3. Advance information on new product introduction | 1 | 2 | 3 | 4 | 5 | ___ | ___ | ___ | ___ | ___ |
| | 4. Availability of inventory status | 1 | 2 | 3 | 4 | 5 | ___ | ___ | ___ | ___ | ___ |
| | 5. Availability of cost, weight, cube, etc. information | 1 | 2 | 3 | 4 | 5 | ___ | ___ | ___ | ___ | ___ |
| | 6. Advance information on shipping delays | 1 | 2 | 3 | 4 | 5 | ___ | ___ | ___ | ___ | ___ |
| | 7. Advance information on order deletions and substitutions | 1 | 2 | 3 | 4 | 5 | ___ | ___ | ___ | ___ | ___ |
| | 8. Other _____ | 1 | 2 | 3 | 4 | 5 | ___ | ___ | ___ | ___ | ___ |
| G. | Physical distribution | | | | | | | | | | |
| | 1. Adequate carton identification | 1 | 2 | 3 | 4 | 5 | ___ | ___ | ___ | ___ | ___ |
| | 2. Order filling accuracy | 1 | 2 | 3 | 4 | 5 | ___ | ___ | ___ | ___ | ___ |
| | 3. Advance notice of change in packaging quantities | 1 | 2 | 3 | 4 | 5 | ___ | ___ | ___ | ___ | ___ |
| | 4. Reasonably small shelf package quantities | 1 | 2 | 3 | 4 | 5 | ___ | ___ | ___ | ___ | ___ |
| | 5. Unitized or palletized shipments where possible | 1 | 2 | 3 | 4 | 5 | ___ | ___ | ___ | ___ | ___ |
| | 6. Procedures for damaged merchandise | 1 | 2 | 3 | 4 | 5 | ___ | ___ | ___ | ___ | ___ |
| | 7. Other _____ | | | | | | | | | | |

3 / Customer Service    97

| Item | Importance (please circle one) Not Important / Very Important | Rating of XYZ Company (please check one) Much Better than / Better than / About the Same as / Worse than / Much Worse than |
|---|---|---|
| H. Other | | |
| 1. _____ _____ _____ | ..... 1  2  3  4  5 | ___  ___  ___  ___  ___ |
| 2. _____ _____ _____ | ..... 1  2  3  4  5 | ___  ___  ___  ___  ___ |
| 3. _____ _____ _____ | ..... 1  2  3  4  5 | ___  ___  ___  ___  ___ |
| I. Other | | |
| 1. _____ _____ _____ | ..... 1  2  3  4  5 | ___  ___  ___  ___  ___ |
| 2. _____ _____ _____ | ..... 1  2  3  4  5 | ___  ___  ___  ___  ___ |
| 3. _____ _____ _____ | ..... 1  2  3  4  5 | ___  ___  ___  ___  ___ |

Please allocate 100 points among the following major elements of customer service. Make your allocation on the basis of the relative importance of the elements to our program of service to you.

*Element*  *Point Allocation*

1. Product availability ................................................. _____
2. Order cycle time .................................................... _____
3. Assistance in ordering .............................................. _____
4. Financial terms ..................................................... _____
5. General marketing support ........................................... _____
6. Information availability ............................................ _____
7. Physical distribution ............................................... _____
8. Other _____
   ................................................................... _____
   TOTAL ............................................................. 100

Annual purchases from all suppliers of items supplied by the XYZ Company?
$ _____

## QUESTIONS AND PROBLEMS

1. What is customer service?

2. Customer service can be defined as: an activity, a performance measure, or a corporate philosophy. What do you believe would be the advantages and disadvantages of each of these types of definitions?

3. Explain the importance of the pretransaction, transaction, and posttransaction elements of customer service.

4. Explain the relationship of customer service to successful marketing.

5. How can management implement the cost/service trade-offs required to successfully achieve integrated physical distribution management?

6. Why is the customer service audit important when evaluating a corporation's customer service strategy?

7. Explain how ABC analysis can be used to improve efficiency of the customer service activity.

8. Why does automating the order processing system represent such an attractive opportunity for improving customer service? How will this service improvement be accomplished?

9. How might a firm go about improving customer service performance?

10. Given the following information, what percentage increase in sales would be necessary in order to break even, if customer service levels are increased from 90 percent to 95 percent in-stock availability?

    a. Transportation costs increase by $200,000.
    b. Inventory levels increase by $2 million.
    c. Warehousing costs increase by $50,000.
    d. The inventory carrying-cost percentage is 45 percent of the inventory value.
    e. Annual sales are currently $50 million.
    f. The contribution margin on the company's products average 30 percent of the selling price.

# 4 The Transportation System

Introduction
  Time and Place Utility
  Transportation/Physical Distribution/Marketing Interface

The U.S. Transportation System
  Alternative Transport Modes
    Air
    Motor
    Pipeline
    Rail
    Water
    Freight Forwarders
  Intermodal Combinations
    TOFC/COFC
    Fishyback
  Legal Forms of Transportation Carriers
    Common Carriers
    Contract Carriers
    Exempt Carriers
    Private Carriers
  Transportation Regulation
    Regulatory Reforms and Their Impact on Shippers
    Transportation Rate Structures
    Accessorial Service Charges
  Traffic and Transportation Management

Summary

Appendixes
A. Section-by-Section Summary of the Motor Carrier Act of 1980
B. Standing Congressional Committees Having Jurisdiction over Transportation
C. Transport Responsibilities in the Executive Branch
D. Department of Transportation-Organization and Responsibilities
E. Federal Transportation Regulatory Agencies

**Objectives of this chapter:**

To provide a thorough understanding of the transportation function and its importance to physical distribution

To identify the alternative transport modes and intermodal combinations available for product movement

To develop an understanding and awareness of how the transportation sector is influenced by regulation

To understand the functions and importance of traffic management in the physical distribution process

## INTRODUCTION

It is difficult to imagine an industrialized society without an efficient transportation system. As consumers we often take for granted that products will move from where they are produced to where they are consumed with a minimum of difficulty in terms of time and cost. The transportation segment of most industrialized economies is so pervasive that we often fail to comprehend the magnitude of its impact on our way of life. Approximately 20 percent of U.S. expenditures for goods and services (GNP) are made for transportation.[1] In 1978 this amounted to $455.6 billion. Transportation also accounts for a large share of the total federal taxes collected by the government. An estimated 13.5 percent, or $48.3 billion, of federal taxes were derived from transportation sources in 1977. During 1978, total business expenditures for new transportation-related plant and equipment were $23.8 billion or 15.5 percent of total business outlays. In 1978, about 11 percent of the civilian work force, 10.6 million persons, were employed in transportation or transportation-related industries.

Also, transportation is a major consumer of the nation's industrial production. It consumes 75 percent of all rubber produced, 67 percent of all lead, 53 percent of all petroleum, 36 percent of all zinc, 28 percent of all steel, 22 percent of all aluminum, 17 percent of all cement, and 15 percent of all copper. During the present period of energy shortages and escalating prices, the role of transportation in the movement and consumption of petroleum is of considerable significance.

The role of transportation in our society was perhaps expressed best by D. F. Pegrum:

> The unique position which transportation occupies in economic activity arises from the reduction by it of the resistances of time and space to the production of economic goods and services. The significance of this in terms of the allocation of economic resources is indicated by the fact that probably at least one third of our national wealth is directly devoted to transportation. So important is it that without it organized human activity would be impossible; complete stoppage of a

---

[1] The statistics cited in this section were developed by the Transportation Association of America. See Transportation Association of America, *Transportation Facts and Trends,* 15th ed. (Washington, D.C., July 1979), p. 1.

community's transport services is the quicket way to assure complete paralysis of cooperative effort; economic, political, and social.[2]

Since 1947 the transportation sector has grown by 130 percent to over 2.5 trillion ton-miles in 1979 (see Table 4-1).[3] Figure 4—1 shows how transportation—represented as intercity ton-miles—has grown over the years relative to population, GNP, industrial production, and passenger traffic.

In this chapter you will be provided with an overview of the transportation function and its importance to physical distribution. Alternative transport modes and intermodal combinations available for product movement

**TABLE 4-1.** Estimated Distribution of Intercity Ton-Miles

| Mode | 1979 (billions of ton-miles) | Percent of Total 1979 | 1960 | 1940 |
|---|---|---|---|---|
| Rail | 918 | 36 | 44 | 61 |
| Motor carrier | 614 | 25 | 22 | 10 |
| Air | 6 | — | — | — |
| Water | 410 | 16 | 17 | 19 |
| Pipeline | 588 | 23 | 17 | 10 |
| Total | 2,536 | 100 | 100 | 100 |

Source: Transportation Association of America, *Transportation Facts and Trends*, 15th ed. (Washington, D.C., July, 1979), p. 8, and Transportation Association of America, *What's Happening in Transportation*, Supplement, "Transport Review for 1979," (Washington, D.C., January 22, 1980).

**FIGURE 4-1** Economic and Transportation Trends since 1947

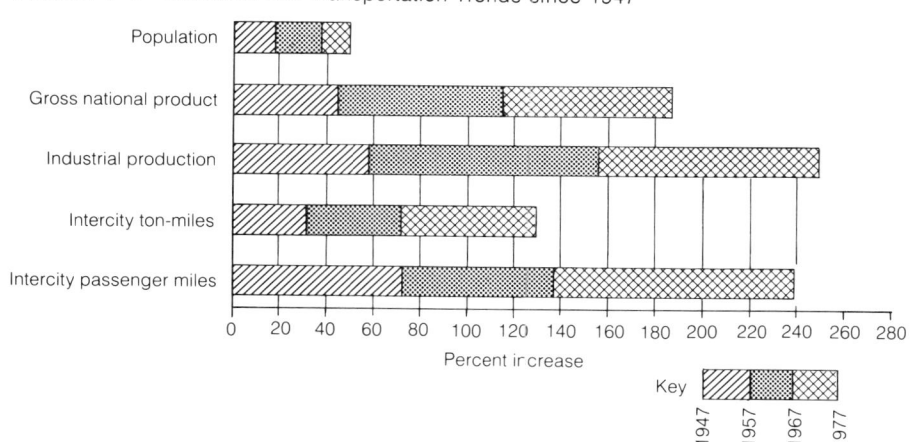

Source: Transportation Association of America, *Transportation Facts and Trends*, 15th. ed. (Washington, D.C., July 1979), p. 2.

[2] Dudley F. Pegrum, *Transportation Economics and Public Policy*, 3d ed. (Homewood, Ill.: Richard D. Irwin, 1973), p. 19.

[3] Ton-miles are the statistical units used to measure the volume of freight traffic moved between points. One ton transported one mile would be equivalent to 1 ton-mile.

will be identified. You will see how transportation is affected by regulation. Additionally, the functions and importance of traffic management in the physical distribution process will be discussed.

### Time and Place Utility

*Transportation Adds Value*

Physical distribution involves the movement of product from point-of-origin to point-of-use or consumption. A product produced at one point has very little value to the prospective customer unless it is moved to the point where it is consumed. Movement is accomplished by the transportation activity. Movement across space or distance creates value or place utility. Time utility is mostly created or added by the warehousing and storage of product until it is needed. However, transportation also creates time utility by how fast a product moves from one point to another. This is known as *time-in-transit*. If a product is not available at the precise time it is needed, difficulties may arise. Most distribution managers are familiar with the problems associated with the late arrival of needed items. UPS, Federal Express, and Flying Tiger Line are examples of successful companies which were able to increase the time and place utility of their customers' products.

### Transportation/Physical Distribution/Marketing Interface

It has been stated that transportation broadens the market(s) of a firm. Expressed another way, transportation serves to move a firm's products to markets that often are geographically separated by great distances. By doing so it adds to the customer's general level of satisfaction which is an important component of the marketing concept. Because transportation creates place utility and contributes to time utility, both of which are necessary for successful marketing, its availability, adequacy, and cost have an effect on several business decisions unrelated to managing the transportation function itself.[4] As expressed by a noted transportation scholar, the decisions affected by transportation include:

*Decisions Affected by Transportation*

*Product decisions.* For those firms that deal in tangible products, one such decision is the product decision or the decision as to what product or products to produce or to distribute. The transportability of a product in terms of its physical attributes and the cost, availability, and adequacy of transportation should enter into any product decision.

*Market area decisions.* Closely related to the product decision for firms dealing in tangible products is the decision relative to where the product(s) should be sold. This can be affected by transportation availability, adequacy, and cost plus the physical characteristics of the product(s) itself.

*Purchasing decisions.* What to purchase and where to purchase can be affected greatly by transportation considerations, regardless of the nature of the firm, whether it be a manufacturer, wholesaler, retailer, service organization, mining company, or whatever. The goods involved may be parts, raw materials, supplies, or finished goods for resale. The availability, adequacy, and cost of transportation plus the transportation characteristics of the goods involved have a bearing on the "what and where" decision.

---

[4] Donald V. Harper, *Transportation in America: Users, Carriers, Government,* © 1978, pp. 13–14. Reprinted by permission of Prentice-Hall, Inc., Englewood Cliffs, New Jersey.

*Location decisions.* Although decisions relative to where plants, warehouses, offices, stores, and other business units should be located are influenced by many factors, transportation availability, adequacy, and cost can be extremely important in such decision making. The significance of the transportation factor varies widely from industry to industry and from firm to firm, but transportation usually is worthy of some consideration in making location decisions.

*Pricing decisions.* Since transportation is a cost factor in business operations, it can have a bearing on the pricing decisions made by business firms, especially those firms that have a cost-oriented pricing policy. In fact, because transportation is one of the nation's "basic" economic activities, price changes in transportation can have a serious effect on the prices of industry in general. This does not mean that in any individual firm there is an automatic cause-and-effect relationship between transportation cost changes and the firm's prices, but transportation cost is one of the factors that usually should be considered in pricing decisions.[5]

For products such as sand, coal, and other basic raw materials, transportation can account for 50 percent or more of the cost of the item. For items such as computers, business machines, and electronic components, the cost may be less than 1 percent. Generally, as transportation's share of product cost increases, it becomes more important to effectively and efficiently manage the firm's transportation activity.

## THE U.S. TRANSPORTATION SYSTEM

*There Are Five Basic Modes of Transportation*

A variety of options exist for the individual, firm or country that must move its product from one point to another. Any one or more of five transportation modes—air, motor, pipeline, rail, water—may be selected. In addition, there are certain modal combinations that are available including rail-motor (piggyback), motor-water (fishyback), motor-air, and rail-water. Such intermodal combinations offer services not generally available when using a single transport mode. Finally, there are other transporters, sometimes called indirect, special, or auxiliary carriers, which offer a variety of services to shippers. These transporters include freight forwarders, shipper cooperatives, parcel post, United Parcel Service (UPS), and other parcel services. Usually special carriers act as transportation middlemen and use one or more of the basic modes for moving their customer's products.

### Alternative Transport Modes

*Air.* Domestically, air transporters move less than 1 percent of the ton-mile traffic. Revenues to the air carriers resulting from the movement of freight approximate 2.4 percent of the total freight bill.[6] Although air freight is being used by increasing numbers of shippers for regular service, most view air transport as a premium, emergency service. Air-freight rates have been escalating in recent years due to higher aviation fuel prices to a point

---

[5] Ibid., pp. 13–14.

[6] Transportation Association of America, *Transportation Facts and Trends*, p. 4.

where rates exceed those of motor carriers by more than 10 times and those of rail by more than 25 times. However, in those instances where an item must be delivered to a distant location quickly, air freight offers the shortest time-in-transit of any mode. For most shippers, however, shipments which are so time sensitive are relatively few in number or frequency.

Modern aircraft have cruising speeds between 500 and 600 miles per hour and have international capabilities. The average length of haul domestically is 1,115 miles, although international movements may be many thousands of miles. Domestic air freight competes directly with motor carriers to a great extent, and rail carriers to a much lesser degree. Internationally, where countries are separated by large expanses of water, the major competitor of air freight is water carriage.

*Air Freight Is Growing*

Although many airlines have freighter aircraft, for most, freight is incidental to passenger traffic. For these airlines, freight travels on a space-available basis on aircraft which also carry passengers. Exceptions are air freight companies such as Flying Tiger Line, Seaboard World, and Airlift International which are classified as all-cargo carriers. Approximately 25 percent of all domestic and international air freight was transported by all-cargo carriers in 1978.[7] This percentage represented a sizable increase over 1968 when only 10 percent of all air freight was handled by the all-cargo carriers.

Generally, air carriers transport products which are of high value and low density or weight. Air freight could not be cost justified for low-value items because the high price of air freight would represent too much of the product cost. As an example, an electronic component and a textbook may weigh the same although their cost may differ significantly. If it costs the same to air freight them from point A to point B, then the transportation charges will consume a greater portion of the textbook's total cost and a smaller portion of the electronic component's cost. Usually, as mentioned, products shipped via air freight are not of high density or weight. Unlike rail cars or truck trailers which have capacities that may exceed 100–125 tons, the lift capacity of aircraft—how much weight the aircraft may carry given its design capability—is much less. This is because most air freight is shipped in the holds or bellies of passenger aircraft. At the present time, the only aircraft which can compete domestically on a lift basis with the other modes is the all-cargo 747 which can carry over 100 tons. The limited capability of most aircraft means that air freight shipments usually cube-out before they weigh-out. That is, the volume capacity is reached before the lift capacity.

Although air transport provides rapid time-in-transit, terminal and delivery delays and congestion may appreciably reduce this advantage. On a point-to-point basis, motor transport often may equal or better the total transit time of air freight. It is the total transit time which is important to the shipper rather than the transit time from terminal-to-terminal. Generally, the frequency and reliability of air service is very good since the majority of freight is moved on passenger flights. Usually, coverage of service is limited

[7] Compiled using statistics cited in Air Transport Association of America, *Air Transport 1979* (Washington, D.C., June 1979), pp. 6–8.

**Motor Carriage Is the Most Widely Used Mode**

to movements between major points although limited service is available to smaller cities.

The volume of air freight has grown rapidly over the years and shows continuing growth even in the face of higher rates. Undoubtedly, as customers demand higher levels of service in the future, and as international shipments increase, air freight will continue to have a strategic role in the distribution plans of many firms.

*Motor.* During the late 1960s, motor carriage replaced rail carriage as the dominant form of freight transport in the United States. Almost half of all freight is transported by motor carriers. Motor carriers transport over three quarters of the tonnage of agricultural products, such as fresh and frozen meats (80.7 percent), dairy products (80.5 percent), bakery products (84.3 percent), confectionary and related items (86.4 percent), beverages and flavoring extracts (84.3 percent), and cigars (84.2 percent). Many manufactured products are also transported by motor carriers, including toys, amusement, sporting, and athletic goods (72.5 percent); watches, clocks, and parts (79.1 percent); farm machinery and equipment (73.3 percent); radios, TVs, phonographs, and records (73.2 percent); carpets and rugs (80.9 percent); clothing (82.3 percent); drugs (71.5 percent); and office and accounting machines (84.0 percent).[8] Most consumer goods are transported by motor carrier.

Usually, motor carriers compete with air for small shipments, and rail for large shipments. An efficient motor carrier can compete with an air carrier on point-to-point service when shipment size is less than 10,000 pounds and the distance involved in the movement is 1,000 miles or less.[9] The ability of motor carriers to compete with air carriers on these shipments is due to greater efficiency in terminal and pickup/delivery operations.

In a study released by the American Trucking Associations in 1977, the percent of total manufactured tonnage transported by motor carriage was 44.6 percent. Rail-dominated tonnage was 28.8 percent. The remainder, or 26.6 percent, was competitive between rail and truck.[10] Based on a study of 89 commodity groupings from the *1972 Census of Transportation, Commodity Transportation Survey*, Ronald Roth identified, by distance and shipment size, products modally dominated and intermodally competitive. Table 4–2 shows the degree of competition between rail and motor carriage. Table 4–3 shows the areas of competition between all modes except water and pipeline.

The average length of haul for motor carriers in 1978 was 301 miles.[11] Some national carriers have average hauls several times as long while some intracity carriers may average 11 miles or less."[12]

---

[8] American Trucking Associations, *American Trucking Trends, 1979–1980* (Washington, D.C., 1981), p. 20.

[9] The generally accepted term applied to shipments weighing less than 10,000 pounds is *LTL* or *less-than-truckload*. *TL* or *truckload* is the designation for larger shipments.

[10] Ronald D. Roth, "An Approach to Measurement of Modal Advantage," a presentation to the Transportation Research Board Annual Meeting, January 1977.

[11] Transportation Association of America, *Transportation Facts and Trends*, p. 14.

[12] Roy J. Sampson and Martin T. Farris, *Domestic Transportation: Practice, Theory and Policy*, 4th ed. (Boston: Houghton Mifflin, 1979), p. 64.

**TABLE 4-2** Distribution of Shipment Size and Distance Modally Dominated and Intermodally Competitive for All Products, 1972

|  | Under 1000 pounds | 1,000-9,999 Pounds | 10,000-29,999 Pounds | 30,000-59,999 Pounds | 60,000-89,999 Pounds | 90,000 pounds or more |
|---|---|---|---|---|---|---|
| Less than 100 miles | Truck | Truck | Truck | Truck | Competitive | Competitive |
| 100-199 miles | Truck | Truck | Truck | Truck | Competitive | Rail |
| 200-299 miles | Truck | Truck | Truck | Truck | Competitive | Rail |
| 300-499 miles | Truck | Truck | Truck | Truck | Competitive | Rail |
| 500-999 miles | Truck | Truck | Competitive | Competitive | Rail | Rail |
| 1,000-1,499 miles | Truck | Truck | Competitive | Competitive | Rail | Rail |
| 1,500 miles or more | Truck | Truck | Competitive | Competitive | Rail | Rail |

Legend: Truck dominant / Competitive / Rail dominant

Source: "An Approach To Measurement of Modal Advantage," by Ronald D. Roth, director of the department of research, ATA, 1977. Based on data from U.S. Department of Commerce, Bureau of the Census, *1972 Census of Transportation, Commodity Transportation Survey*. Used with permission of the Research and Economics Division of the American Trucking Associations, Inc., Washington, D.C.

**TABLE 4-3** Competition for Intercity For-Hire Truck Service

| Category | Under 100 Pounds | 100 to 500 Pounds | LTL over 500 Pounds | "Standby" Truckload* | Truckload | Truckload Special Equipment |
|---|---|---|---|---|---|---|
| General commodity carriers | X | X | X | X | X | X |
| Specialized commodity carriers and SCDs |  |  |  |  |  | X |
| Private fleets | X | X | X | X | X | X |
| Contract carriers | X | X | X | X | X | X |
| Rail |  |  |  |  | X | X |
| Piggyback (TOFC) |  |  |  |  | X | X |
| Freight forwarders and shipper associations | X | X | X | X |  |  |
| Specialized small shipment carriers | X | X |  |  |  |  |
| Air cargo and passenger airlines | X | X | X | X |  |  |
| UPS, Parcel Post, Bus | X |  |  |  |  |  |

*"Standby" Truckload refers to truckload service provided by general commodity carriers who offer truckload service at class or column commodity rates. Typically, they carry truckloads which cannot be handled by the shipper's private fleet or specialized carrier because of balance or capacity problems, e.g., at peak periods.

Source: John F. Throckmorton and Paul M. Mueller, *Motor Carrier Marketing Management*, Part I (Washington, D.C.: Sales and Marketing Council of American Trucking Associations, 1980), p. 27.

---

**Motor Carriers Offer Flexibility and Versatility**

Motor carriers are more flexible and versatile than other modes. The flexibility of motor carriers is made possible by a network of over 3.5 million miles of roads, thus enabling them to offer point-to-point service from almost any origin-destination combination. Motor carriers are very versatile in that virtually any product that will fit on a truck, including some for which equipment modifications are necessary, can be transported. The flexibility and versatility of motor carriers has enabled them to become the dominant form of transport in the United States.

In general, motor carriage offers the customer fast, reliable service with little damage or loss in transit. Motor carriers give much faster service than railroads and compare favorably with air carriers on short hauls. Loss and/or damage ratios for motor carriers are substantially lower than for rail and are slightly higher than for air freight. There is no other mode which can provide the market coverage offered by motor carriers.

The industry can be classified into two major types: general freight carriers and specialized motor carriers. General freight carriers generated 59.6 percent of all truck traffic revenues in 1979 and included intercity common carriers and other general freight carriers.[13] Specialized motor carriers generated 40.5 percent of revenues and included several types of carriers: heavy machinery, liquid petroleum, refrigerated products, agricultural commodities, motor vehicles, building materials, household goods, and other specialized carriers.[14] Figure 4−2 shows the distribution of revenue by type of carrier for 1979.

The amount of freight being transported by motor carriers has been steadily increasing over the years. That trend is likely to continue in the years ahead. Motor carriage is a vital part of most firms' distribution network. The characteristics of the motor carrier industry are compatible with the service requirements of the firms' customers. As long as the industry is able to provide fast and efficient service at rates between rail and air, motor carriage will continue to prosper.

*Pipeline.* Pipelines account for over 23 percent of all domestic U.S. intercity freight traffic measured in ton-miles.[15] Pipelines are able to transport only a limited number of products including natural gas, crude oil, petroleum products, chemicals, and slurry products.[16] Natural gas and crude oil account for the majority of pipeline traffic. Slurry products, usually coal slurry, accounts for only a small percentage of pipeline shipments. The coal is ground into a powder, suspended in water, transported through a pipeline, and at destination is removed from the water and readied for use. In light of the world's dependence on energy products, it is likely that pipelines will become even more important in the future. This will be particularly true for coal slurry as some countries attempt to shift away from natural gas- or petroleum-based energy systems towards a coal-based system.

There are over 440,000 miles of intercity pipeline in the United States.[17]

> Pipelines Will Become More Important in the Future

---

[13] Carriers may be classified into several categories based upon whether or not they are regulated by the government. Four categories exist—common, contract, exempt, private—which will be discussed later in this chapter.

[14] James F. Notman, Jr., *1980 Financial Analysis of the Motor Carrier Industry* (Washington, D.C.: American Trucking Associations, 1980), p. 6.

[15] Transportation Association of America, *Transportation Facts and Trends*, p. 8.

[16] *Slurry* is usually thought of as a solid product which is suspended in a liquid, often water, which can then be transported more easily.

[17] Donald F. Wood and James C. Johnson, *Contemporary Transportation* (Tulsa, Okla.: Petroleum Publishing, 1980), p. 213.

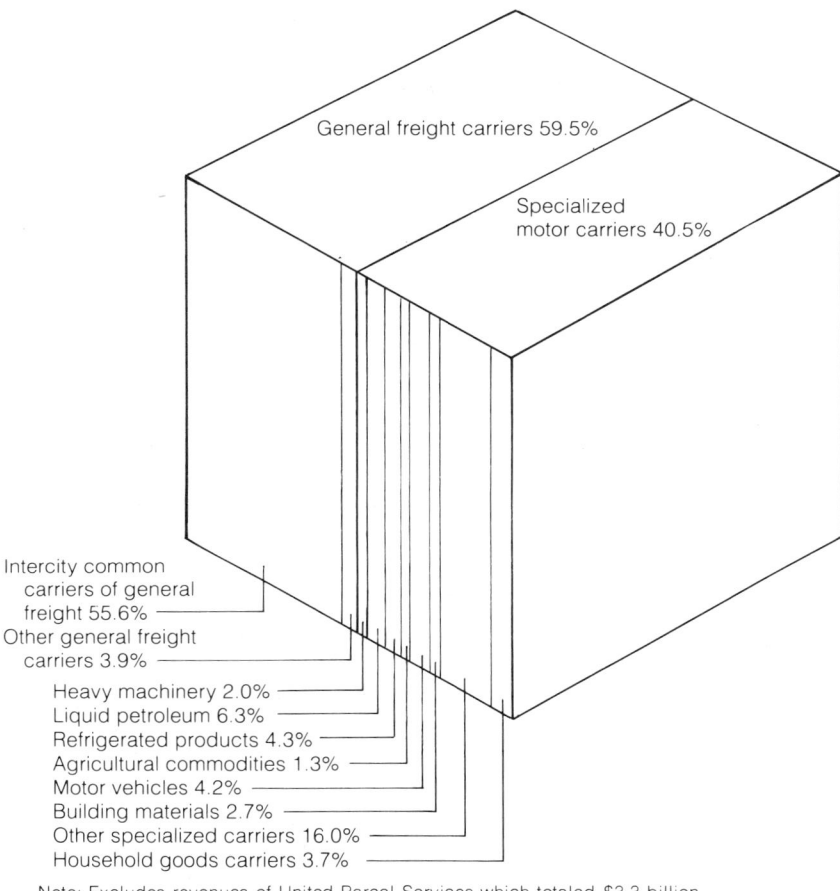

**FIGURE 4-2**  Distribution of Revenues by Type of Carrier, 1979

General freight carriers 59.5%
Specialized motor carriers 40.5%

Intercity common carriers of general freight 55.6%
Other general freight carriers 3.9%
Heavy machinery 2.0%
Liquid petroleum 6.3%
Refrigerated products 4.3%
Agricultural commodities 1.3%
Motor vehicles 4.2%
Building materials 2.7%
Other specialized carriers 16.0%
Household goods carriers 3.7%

Note: Excludes revenues of United Parcel Services which totaled $3.3 billion.
Source: James F. Notman, Jr., *1980 Financial Analysis of the Motor Carrier Industry* (Washington, D.C.: American Trucking Associations, Inc., 1980), p. 6. Used with permission of the Research and Economics Division of the American Trucking Associations, Inc., Washington, D.C.

The average length of haul is 276 miles for crude pipelines and 343 miles for product pipelines.[18] Pipelines offer the shipper an extremely high level of service dependability at relatively low cost. The ability of pipelines to deliver their product on time is due primarily to the following factors:

- The flows of products within the pipeline are monitored and controlled by computer.
- The loss and/or damage ratio due to pipeline leaks or breaks is extremely low.
- Climatic conditions have minimal effect on products moving in pipelines.
- Pipelines are not labor intensive; therefore, strikes or employee absences have little effect on their operation.

---

[18] Transportation Association of America, *Transportation Facts and Trends*, p. 14.

The cost and dependability of pipelines compared with other transport modes has stimulated shipper interest in moving other products via pipeline. Certainly, if a product is, or can be, in liquid, gas, or slurry form, it is capable of being transported by pipeline. As the costs for other modes increase, additional consideration by shippers will be given to pipelines as a mode of transport for nontraditional products.

*Rail.* In 1978 railroads carried over 1.4 billion tons of freight over a network of track totalling approximately 200,000 miles. Railroads accounted for 35.8 percent—873 billion ton-miles—of the intercity freight traffic.[19] Since World War II when rail transported about 70 percent of the ton-mile traffic, its share of the market has continually declined. Most of the freight which was once shipped via rail has shifted over to motor carriers. Some traffic has been lost to water and pipeline carriers which generally compete with railroads for bulk commodities.

The bulk of rail traffic comes from low-value, high-density products such as paper and allied products, chemicals and plastics, lumber, iron and steel, metal cans, canned foods, and nonferrous metals. In addition, the railroads carry over three quarters of all motor vehicles as a percent of intercity ton-miles.

Railroads have an average length of haul of 587 miles.[20] Rail service is available in almost every major metropolitan center throughout the world and in many smaller communities as well. However, the rail network is not nearly as extensive as the highway network in most countries. Therefore, rail transport lacks the versatility and flexibility of motor carriers since it is limited to fixed track facilities. As a result, railroads provide terminal-to-terminal service, like air transport, in lieu of point-to-point service.

<u>Rail Is Low in Cost</u>

Rail transport is generally low-cost relative to air and motor carriers. For most shipments, rail compares favorably with other modes on loss and/or damage ratios, but is at a significant disadvantage relative to motor carriers in transit time and frequency of service. In the United States, railroads travel at an average speed of 20 miles per hour. This is primarily due to delays on sidings or in terminals and the generally poor condition of rail roadbeds. Trains travel on time-table schedules which means that departures are less frequent than those of a motor carrier. In situations where the shipper has strict arrival and departure requirements, railroads are at a competitive disadvantage relative to motor carriers. Some of this disadvantage may be overcome through the use of piggyback or trailer-on-flatcar (TOFC) service which offers the economies of rail movement coupled with the flexibility of trucks. Truck trailers are delivered to the rail terminals where they are loaded on rail cars. At the destination terminal they are off-loaded and delivered to the consignee, the customer who receives the shipment. TOFC service will be examined in further detail later in this chapter.

An additional deficiency that railroads have relative to motor carriers is

---

[19] Ibid., pp. 8, 10.
[20] Ibid., p. 14.

equipment availability. Railroads use each others' cars and at times, this equipment may not be located where it is most needed. Rail cars may be unavailable because of loading or unloading, moving within railroad sorting yards, repairs, standing idle, or lost within the vast rail network. "In 1978, the average daily utilization was three hours and five minutes. An average rail car in 1978 traveled only 59.5 miles, moving at an average speed—including stops—of under 20 miles per hour. This means a car is in use only about 13 percent of the time."[21] Some of these problems have been overcome through the use of computer routing and scheduling, upgrading of equipment, roadbeds, and terminals, improvements on rail car identification systems, use of unit trains, and shipper-owned or leased cars.[22] Railroads own approximately 80 percent of their car fleet. The remaining 20 percent are either leased or owned by shippers. Shippers which own or lease cars are typically heavy users of rail and are especially sensitive to rail car shortages because of unique market and/or competitive conditions.

It is uncertain whether the railroads can recapture the traffic lost to trucks, pipelines, and water carriers. Certainly, improvements in equipment and facilities, upgrading of roadbeds, and better monitoring and control of rail fleets are necessary. The inherent relative energy efficiency of railroads over motor carriers coupled with the fact that the majority of coal is transported by rail offers a promise of better things to come and perhaps a rebirth of the rail industry.

*Water.* Water transportation can be broken down into several distinct categories: (1) inland waterway such as rivers and canals; (2) Great Lakes; (3) coastwise and intercoastal ocean; and (4) international deep sea. Water carriage competes primarily with rail since the majority of commodities carried by water are semiprocessed or raw materials. "Water carriage by nature is particularly suited for movements of heavy, bulky, low-value-per-unit commodities which can be loaded and unloaded efficiently by mechanical means in situations where speed is not of primary importance, where the commodities shipped are not particularly susceptible to shipping damage or theft, and where accompanying land movements are unnecessary."[23]

Water movement is primarily engaged in inbound transportation. Bulk materials such as iron ore, grains, pulpwood products, coal, limestone, and petroleum, are transported internationally or domestically to points where they can be used as inputs into the manufacturing process.

Other than in international deep-sea transport, water carriers are limited in their movement by the availability of lakes, rivers, canals, or intercoastal waterways. Depending upon the locale, water carriage may account for a large share of freight movement or only an insignificant amount. For example, in the United States, 591 billion ton-miles, or 24 percent of the total

---

[21] Wood and Johnson, *Contemporary Transportation*, p. 187.

[22] Unit trains are trains of great length carrying a single product in one direction. Examples of commodities transported by unit trains include coal, grains, U.S. mail, automobiles, fruits, and vegetables.

[23] Sampson and Farris, *Domestic Transportation*, p. 79.

intercity freight, is moved by water.[24] In Europe water carriage is much more important because of the vast system of navigable waterways and the accessibility of major population centers by water routes. In West Germany, waterways account for more than 30 percent of all traffic transported and in Belgium and Holland the percentage is substantially higher.[25] The average length of haul varies tremendously depending upon the type of water transport. For inland waterways, it is 376 miles; for Great Lakes shipping, 535 miles; and for coastwise and intercoastal shipping, 1,367 miles.[26] When international deep sea movements occur, the length of haul can be many thousands of miles.

*Water Carriage Is Best Suited for High-Bulk, Low-Value Commodities*

Water carriage is perhaps the most inexpensive method of shipping high-bulk, low-value commodities. As stated by Roy Sampson and Martin Farris:

> From the individual shipper's viewpoint, the principal advantage of using water transportation for domestic shipments in preference to land transport is low freight rates. Sometimes, in addition, water carrier facilities are more suitable for handling (loading and unloading) certain kinds of bulk commodities. A principal disadvantage, even for bulk shipments, is the generally slower and less frequently scheduled service available from water carriers. Goods in transit represent funds tied up in inventories—speed is money to the shipper. Also, slowness and less frequent departures and arrivals on the part of water carriers virtually preclude the filling of rush orders and sometimes require that shippers carefully plan their production and shipping schedules in advance. Then too, water carriage typically gives pinpoint area coverage.
>
> Where it is available, water carriage generally serves only major points and bypasses many smaller intermediate communities. Also, delays due to adverse weather conditions frequently must be anticipated . . . unless the shipper and the consignee are located directly adjacent to water facilities, goods must be transported to and from water by land carriers. This may involve extra handling expenses. That is, goods must be loaded onto a land carrier, hauled to the water carrier's dock, and reloaded onto the river carrier's vessel. At destination, the goods must be unloaded from the water carrier, hauled to the consignee's place of business, and again unloaded from the land vehicle. In addition to the extra handling charges, terminal fees of various kinds may also be incurred.[27]

Due to the inherent limitations of water carriers it is unlikely that the role of water transport in domestic and international commerce will change appreciably in the future. However, international developments have made marine shipping increasingly important. The development of the very large crude carriers (VLCCs), or supertankers, has enabled marine shipping to assume a vital role in the transport of petroleum between the oil-producing and oil-consuming countries. Because of the importance of energy re-

---

[24] Transportation Association of America, *Transportation Facts and Trends*, p. 8.

[25] James R. Stock, "The Energy/Ecology Impacts on Distribution," *International Journal of Physical Distribution and Materials Management* 8, no. 5 (1978): 259.

[26] Transportation Association of America, *Transportation Facts and Trends*, p. 14.

[27] Roy J. Sampson and Martin F. Farris, *Domestic Transportation: Practice, Theory, and Policy*, 4th edition, pp. 78–79. Reprinted by permission of Houghton Mifflin Company.

sources to industrialized nations, water carriage will continue to play a significant role in the transportation of energy resources in the future.[28]

*Freight forwarders.* Although freight forwarders are not one of the five basic modes of transport, they are a viable shipping alternative for most companies. Freight forwarders are divided into three types: (1) surface-freight forwarders which use rail, motor, and domestic water carriers; (2) air-freight forwarders which use domestic and/or foreign air carriers; and (3) foreign freight forwarders which primarily use international water carriers.

Freight Forwarders Act as Transportation Wholesalers

Forwarders act much in the same capacity as wholesalers in the marketing channel. They purchase transport services from any one or more of the five modes and consolidate small shipments from a number of shippers into large shipments that move at lower rates. These companies offer shippers lower rates than could be obtained directly from the carrier because small shipments generally cost more per pound to transport than do large shipments. In some instances, the freight forwarder is able to provide faster and more complete service than a carrier. In any given year, over 20 million shipments are handled by freight forwarders.

### Intermodal Combinations

In addition to the five basic modes of transport and freight forwarders, there are a number of modal combinations available to the shipper. The more popular combinations are: (1) trailer-on-flat-car (TOFC) and container-on-flat-car (COFC), or piggyback; and (2) fishyback which is a water/truck combination. Theoretically, intermodal movements combine the cost and/or service advantages of two or more modes in a single product movement.

*TOFC/COFC.* Although technically there are some differences, TOFC, COFC, and intermodal are generally referred to as piggyback service by most distribution executives. In piggyback service, a motor-carrier trailer or a container, under which an axle can be placed for movement by a truck tractor, is placed on a rail flatcar and transported from terminal-to-terminal. At the terminal facilities, the pickup and delivery functions are performed by a motor carrier. Thus, piggyback service combines the low cost of long haul rail movement with the flexibility and convenience of truck movement.

A variety of piggyback services are available to shippers and can be summarized as follows:

> Plan I: This plan is available to for-hire motor carriers (common and contract). The railroad provides the motive power, flatcar, and right of way. The railroad does not participate in the origination of the commodity inside the trailer; the for-hire motor carrier originates the shipment and has all shipper responsibility.
>
> Plan II: This is an all rail plan in which the railroad offers piggyback service to the shipping public. The railroad provides the trailer and pickup and delivery service—door-to-door service. The railroad originates the shipment and has all shipper responsibility.

---

[28] Stock, "Energy/Ecology Impacts," p. 259.

Piggyback

Plan II¼: Plan II¼ is a modification of Plan II in which the railroad continues to provide the trailer but offers either pickup or delivery, but not both. This is useful when the shipper or consignee owns or leases a truck. A lower rate is charged for Plan II¼ than for Plan II.

Plan II½: This is another hybrid of Plan II. The trailer is still provided by the railroad but neither pickup nor delivery is provided. This is a ramp-to-ramp service and a lower charge is assessed than that for either Plan II or II¼.

Plan III: The railroad furnishes the flatcar, motive power, and right of way, but the shipper provides the trailer. Under this plan the shipper is incurring the cost of the trailer ownership and the rates for Plan III are lower than Plan II rates.

Plan IV: Under this plan the railroad provides ramp-to-ramp service of the shipper's trailer and flatcar. The shipper makes a greater investment (trailer and flatcar) in the transportation equipment and a rate lower than both Plans II and III is charged.

Plan V: This is a truly coordinated plan offered by cooperating railroads and for-hire motor carriers. The two modes publish joint rates (one rate) for an origin-destination link and each participates in the movement and revenue.[29]

The greatest majority of piggyback traffic moves under Plans II¼ and II½. Fewer, but substantial, amounts move under Plan IV. Figure 4–3 shows the percentage of total piggyback movements under each plan over a 10-year period, 1967–77.

As evidenced by the variety of piggyback plans available, there are many participant groups which, in combination, provide service to the shipper. The participants include the motor carrier, freight forwarder, consolidators, shipper association, cartage company, rail carrier, car lessor, trailer lessor, and the primary shipper.[30] An overview of the participating groups involved in piggyback service is shown in Table 4–4.

In recent years shippers have increased their usage of piggyback service. Piggyback carloadings were over 1.7 million in 1978, 3.3 million in 1979, and a projected market of 10 to 12 million carloadings by 1990.[31] (See Figure 4–4.) The future holds enormous potential for piggyback. In analyzing the prospects for piggyback service in the next decade, Booz, Allen and Hamilton, Inc. undertook a study of the TOFC/COFC industry and concluded that:

> The TOFC market could realistically grow at an annual rate of 11 to 12 percent until 1990, becoming as large as 10 to 12 million trailer-loads, or nearly quadruple the current market.

---

[29] Reproduced by permission from *The Management of Business Logistics*, 2d ed., by John J. Coyle and Edward J. Bardi, copyright © 1976, 1980, West Publishing Company, pp. 223–24. All rights reserved.

[30] Shippers' associations are nonprofit organizations which perform services similar to freight forwarders and serve only their members.

[31] Booz, Allen & Hamilton, *Piggyback: The Efficient Alternative for the 80's* (New York: Transamerica Interway, 1980), pp. xv–xvi.

**FIGURE 4–3** Shift in Importance of TOFC Service Plans

| Plan | Description | 1967 | 1977 |
|---|---|---|---|
| Plan I | Railroad carries trailers owned by motor common carriers, ramp to ramp. | 8% | 10% |
| Plan II | Railroad carries its own trailers under its own truck competitive tariffs and furnishes pickup and delivery | 43% | 9% |
| Plan II¼ | Railroad provides either pickup or delivery, but not both. | | |
| Plan II½ | Railroad performs ramp-to-ramp service only. Railroad does not furnish pickup and delivery. | 10% | 43% |
| Plan III | Railroad carries trailers owned by shipper ramp to ramp at published rates. | 18% | 9% |
| Plan IV | Railroads carry trailers owned or leased by shippers on flatcars also owned or leased by shippers at flat charge per car, whether trailers are loaded or empty. | 12% | 19% |
| Plan V | Railroad carries its own or motor comon carrier trailers under through billing at joint rail-truck rates. | 3% | 2% |
| Other | Variations of other plans. | 6% | 9% |

Source: Booz, Allen & Hamilton Inc., *Piggyback: The Efficient Alternative for the 80's* (New York: Transamerica Interway Inc., 1980), p. 9–10.

**TABLE 4-4** Participants and Roles in the Piggyback System

| | Supplies car | Supplies trailer | Performs pickup | Performs delivery | Performs line-haul | Designs service | Sells service | Operates terminal | Provides full service |
|---|---|---|---|---|---|---|---|---|---|
| Primary shipper | ● | ● | ● | ● | | | | | |
| Motor carrier | | ● | ● | ● | | | | ● | |
| Freight forwarder | | ● | ● | ● | | | ● | | |
| Consolidators other | | | | | | | ● | | |
| Shipper association | | ● | ● | ● | | | ● | | |
| Cartage company | | | ● | ● | | | | | |
| Rail carrier | ● | ● | ● | ● | ● | ● | ● | ● | ● |
| Car lessor | ● | | | | | | | | |
| Trailer lessor | | ● | | | | | | | |

Source: Booz, Allen & Hamilton, *Piggyback: The Efficient Alternative for the 80's* (New York: Transamerica Interway, 1980), p. 22.

**FIGURE 4-4** Piggyback Carloading, 1955–1978

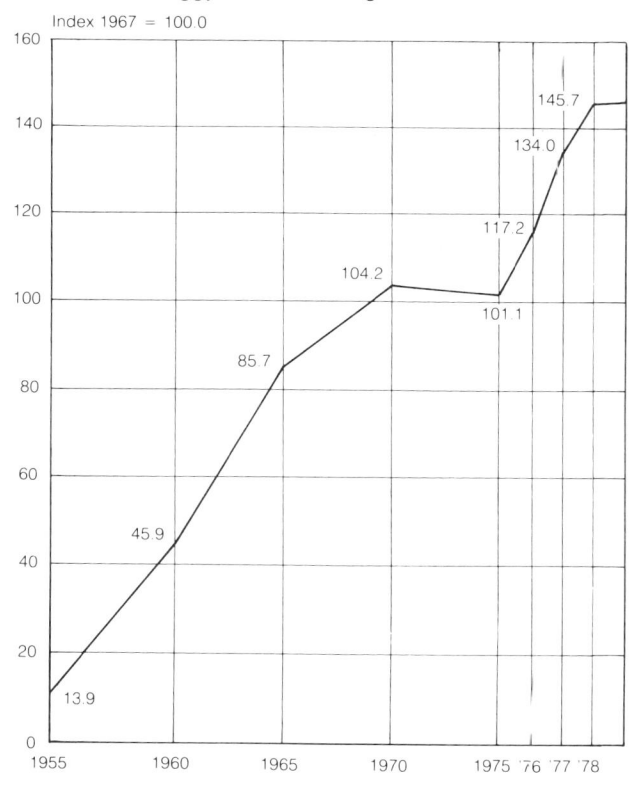

Index 1967 = 100.0

| | Cars loaded | Index |
|---|---|---|
| 1955 | 168,150 | 13.9 |
| 1960 | 554,115 | 45.9 |
| 1965 | 1,034,377 | 85.7 |
| 1967 | 1,207,242 | 100.0 |
| 1968 | 1,337,149 | 110.8 |
| 1969 | 1,344,123 | 111.3 |
| 1970 | 1,257,993 | 104.2 |
| 1971 | 1,199,137 | 99.3 |
| 1972 | 1,330,932 | 110.2 |
| 1973 | 1,535,374 | 127.2 |
| 1974 | 1,511,717 | 125.2 |
| 1975 | 1,220,637 | 101.1 |
| 1976 | 1,415,132 | 117.2 |
| 1977 | 1,617,315 | 134.0 |
| 1978 | 1,758,358 | 145.7 |

Note: Cars loaded with trailers and containers, excluding mail and express.

Source: *Weekly Carloading Report*, Car Services Division, Association of American Railroads; Research Review, no. 222, ATA. The figure was published in American Trucking Associations, Inc., *American Trucking Trends*, 1979–1980 (Washington, D.C.: ATA, 1981), p. 41.

Shippers will support increased TOFC use if reasonable service improvements are made.

Operating improvements currently being carried out in some railroads will make TOFC more cost competitive; some companies already have found ways of streamlining operations and realizing major savings.

*The Outlook for TOFC Is Bright*

Regulatory changes that will promote a modern integrated intermodal system are increasingly likely; such change is vital to stimulating growth of TOFC.[32]

An additional facet of piggyback service which will effect its growth will be the continuing worldwide energy crisis. Fuel shortages and higher energy prices substantially increased the demand for piggyback after 1973. Piggyback, in addition to its other services, is more energy efficient than strictly motor carriage because it involves the line-haul energy savings of rail. As energy shortages occur more frequently and as prices continue their dramatic rise, piggyback will become an even more viable alternative for the movement of products.

*Fishyback*

*Fishyback.* Fishyback refers to the movement of truck trailers, rail cars, or containers by water carriers. Intermodal movements involving water carriers generally occur with international shipment although some domestic moves take place. For example, Canadian National provides service between the Canadian Maritime provinces utilizing vessels which carry truck trailers or containers.[33]

The bulk of fishyback movements internationally involve containers. The shipper in one country places his cargo into an owned or leased container at his own facility or point-of-origin.[34] Then, the container is transported via rail or motor carrier to a water port for loading onto a containership. After arrival at the destination port it is unloaded and tendered to a rail or motor carrier in that country and subsequently delivered to the customer or consignee. The shipment leaves the shipper and arrives to the customer with minimal container handlings and absolutely no handling of the items within the container. With the use of containers in intermodal distribution, the need for manpower is reduced, in-transit damage and pilferage is minimized, time-in-transit is shortened because of reduced port turnaround time, and the shipper is able to take advantage of volume shipping rates.

Other forms of intermodalism exist although they have not developed as extensively as piggyback and fishyback. Reflective of the importance of intermodal transportation is Table 4–5 which identified the types of companies which participate in these movements as well as the enormous capital tied up in intermodal equipment such as trailers, containers, and container chassis.

[32] Ibid., p. xiv.

[33] "Canadian Coastal Containers," *Distribution Worldwide* 76, no. 3 (March 1977): 65–66.

[34] Containers typically are 8 × 8 × 20 feet or 8 × 8 × 40 feet in size and compatible with conventional motor or rail equipment.

**TABLE 4-5** Intermodal Equipment in the United States—Early 1981

| Participating Firms | Number of Firms | Trailers | Containers | Chassis |
|---|---|---|---|---|
| Motor carriers | 45 | 74,015 | 6,634 | 141 |
| Ship lines | 40 | 11,536 | 839,786 | 116,310 |
| Leasing firms | 32 | 93,028 | 925,477 | 47,560 |
| Railroads | 47 | 94,687 | 2,916 | 2,906 |
| Other (air and private carriers) | 6 | 0 | 1,793 | 420 |
| Total | 170 | 273,257 | 1,776,606 | 167,337 |

Source: American Trucking Associations, Inc., "Intermodal Equipment Update," *Research Review*, no. 233 (April 15, 1981), p. 3. Tabulations of intermodal equipment made from the ATA's Equipment Interchange Association *International Registry of Trailer, Container and Chassis Equipment;* from the rail-sponsored *Intermodal Equipment Registry;* and from the Maritime Administration of the U.S. Department of Commerce, *Inventory of American Intermodal Equipment, 1981.* Used with permission of the Research and Economics Division of the American Trucking Associations, Inc., Washington, D.C.

### Legal Forms of Transportation Carriers

In addition to classifying alternative forms of transportation on the basis of mode, carriers can be classified on the basis of the four legal forms of transportation: (1) common carriers, (2) contract carriers, (3) exempt carriers, and (4) private carriers. The first three forms are for-hire carriers and the last is owned by the shipper. For-hire carriers transport freight which belongs to others and are subject to various federal, state, and local statutes and regulations. Private carriers transport their own goods and supplies in their own equipment and are exempted from most regulations with the exception of those dealing with safety and taxation. Figure 4−5 identifies the various legal forms of carriers within each of the five basic modes.

*Common, Contract, Exempt, and Private Carriers*

*Common carriers.* Common carriers offer their services to any shipper(s) to transport products between designated points using published rates. In order to legally operate, they must be granted authority from the appropriate federal regulatory agency. This authority would specify the type of commodities which could be carried and the service routes the carrier could traverse.[35] With the deregulation of the major transportation modes in the United States during the late 1970s and early 1980s, carriers have been provided with much more flexibility with respect to market entry, routing, and rate making.

Common carriers must offer their services to the general public on a nondiscriminatory basis, that is, to serve all shippers of the commodities they carry under their authority. Common carriers are required to publish rates, supply adequate facilities, provide service to all points prescribed in its certificate of authority unless withdrawal is authorized by the appropriate regulatory agency, deliver the goods entrusted to their care within a reasonable time, charge reasonable rates, and refrain from discrimination.

*Contract carriers.* A contract carrier is a for-hire carrier that does not hold itself out to serve the general public; rather, it serves one or a limited

---

[35] Carriers may be irregular-route common carriers or regular-route common carriers. An irregular-route carrier may use any route to service the origin/destination points within his or her authorized territory. A regular-route carrier must travel prescribed routes between his or her origin and destination points. The routes are spelled out in detail in the carrier's certificate.

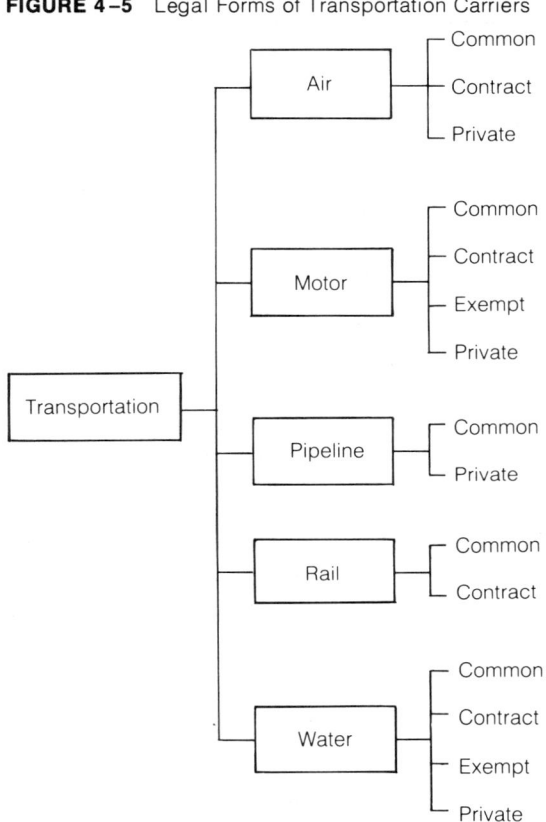

**FIGURE 4-5** Legal Forms of Transportation Carriers

```
Transportation ─┬─ Air ──────┬─ Common
                │            ├─ Contract
                │            └─ Private
                │
                ├─ Motor ────┬─ Common
                │            ├─ Contract
                │            ├─ Exempt
                │            └─ Private
                │
                ├─ Pipeline ─┬─ Common
                │            └─ Private
                │
                ├─ Rail ─────┬─ Common
                │            └─ Contract
                │
                └─ Water ────┬─ Common
                             ├─ Contract
                             ├─ Exempt
                             └─ Private
```

number of shippers under specific contractual arrangements. Operating authorities which contract carriers obtain from the federal government authorize the carriers to serve particular areas and transport certain types of commodities. The contract between the shipper and the carrier requires that the carrier provide a specified transportation service at a specified cost. In most instances, contract-carrier rates are lower than common-carrier rates because the carrier is transporting commodities which it prefers to carry and is provided with a known, predetermined amount of traffic from its clients. In the case of a common carrier future demand is always uncertain inasmuch as the firm's clients cannot be completely predicted in advance.

*Exempt carriers.* An exempt carrier is a for-hire carrier that is not regulated with respect to routes, areas served, and rates. The exempt status is determined by the type of commodity hauled and the nature of the operation. Examples of exempt carriers include companies transporting unprocessed agricultural and related products such as farm supplies, livestock, fish, poultry, and agricultural seeds. Also, carriers of newspapers are given exempt status. The exempt status was originally established to allow farmers to transport their products using public roads; however it has since been extended to a wider range of products. Exemptions are also provided to water carriers if their cargoes are liquids being transported in tank vessels or if in a single ship or barge not more than three bulk commodities such as coal, ore, and grains, are being moved. In addition, local cartage firms operating locally, that is, in a municipality or "commercial zone" surrounding a municipality are exempt.

Generally, exempt carriers offer lower rates than common or contract carriers. However, because very few commodities relative to the multitude of products available to consumer and industrial markets are given exempt status, the exempt carrier is not a viable form of transport for most companies.

*Private carriers.* A private carrier is not for-hire and is not subject to federal economic regulation. With private carriage, the firm is providing its own transportation. As a result, the company must own or lease the transport equipment, operate its own facilities, and in most cases, must be the owner of the products being transported. From a legal standpoint, the most important factor which distinguishes private carriage from the for-hire carriers is the restriction that the transportation activity must be incidental to the primary business of the firm. Prior to 1980, intercorporate hauling for compensation was not permitted. After passage of the Motor Carrier Act of 1980 this restriction was eliminated for companies with private fleets hauling goods for wholly owned subsidiaries. Today, the majority of private carrier operations utilize motor carriage, including Sears, Bendix Corporation, Levi Strauss & Co., and Pizza Hut.

Private carriage has increased significantly in recent years because the flexibility and economy offered are difficult for common carriers to match. The major advantages of private carriage are cost and service related. Robert V. Delaney, manager distribution planning and analysis for International Paper Company (formerly manager—business development at Pet, Inc.), has stated that private carriage offers five advantages over other alternatives: (1) reliable service, (2) transaction control or management of working capital, (3) operating flexibility, (4) market penetration, and (5) cost control.[36] Later in this chapter the private versus for-hire transportation decision will be examined and the pros and cons of private carriage will be presented fully.

## Transportation Regulation

*Regulation Affects Transportation Costs, Service, and Safety*

In many countries, including the United States, the transportation sector is regulated with respect to economics, service, and safety.[37] Because transportation is such an essential part of a country's economic system, many governments have determined that it is their responsibility to insure that the transportation sector operate fairly and efficiently, and without unfair discrimination against its users. As a result many laws and regulations have

---

[36] H. G. Becker, Jr., "Private Carriage: Facts and Trends, Some Reasons Why," *Handling & Shipping* 17, no. 7 (July 1976): 25–26.

[37] Portions of this section were taken from James R. Stock, "Regulations, Regulators, and Regulatory Issues: A Motor Carrier Perspective," *Transportation Journal* 18, no. 3 (Spring 1979): 65–73.

been enacted to promote the economic well-being of the industry. Additional regulations have been enacted which insure that the transport modes provide reasonable levels of service to their users. Safety regulations provide for the safe operation of transportation equipment, protection for employees of carriers, and protection for the general public.

Transportation regulation is truly an issue which generates a polarity of opinion, with almost no one indifferent. This reaction can be expected given the impact transportation regulation has on both carriers and shippers. Robert Lieb summed it up by saying:

> The impact of regulatory controls on the structure, conduct, and performance of the domestic transportation system is pervasive. Although regulatory guidelines vary somewhat across the modes, they typically influence such factors as market entry, abandonment of service, pricing, security issuance, carrier consolidation, and introduction of new services.[38]

Over the years, the degree to which the transportation sector has been regulated has varied. In the United States since 1977 the trend has been towards less regulation of transportation. The Airline Deregulation Acts of 1977 and 1978 effectively removed most airline controls, exclusive of those pertaining to safety. Nearly all of the statutes controlling airline fares, routes, and competitive practices were eliminated. Motor carriers were deregulated by the Motor Carrier Act of 1980 which eliminated many economic and service restrictions previously placed on motor carriers. A summary of the Motor Carrier Act is provided in Appendix A. Also in 1980, the railroads were partially deregulated as a result of passage of the Railroad Transportation Policy Act (Staggers Rail Act) of 1980. A summary of the various motor, rail, and air cargo regulatory reforms and their impact on the shipping community is presented in the next section.

*Regulatory reforms and their impact on shippers.* The impact of regulatory reform on shippers and their response to those impacts are of immense importance to companies. "These are the issues that will assist shippers in formulating concrete plans and programs for dealing with regulatory reform and for improving their distribution operations."[39] As a basis for discussing the various regulatory reforms and their impact on shippers, the following order of presentation will be used: (1) motor carrier reform; (2) rail carrier reform; and (3) air carrier reform.

*Motor Carrier Act of 1980 Deregulated the Trucking Industry*

1. *Motor carrier reform.* As summarized in Appendix A, the basic areas of motor carrier reform are: (a) zone of rate freedom, (b) easing of market entry restrictions, (c) intercorporate hauling, (d) contract carriage, and (e) rate bureaus. The modifications in each of those areas as outlined by the Motor Carrier Act of 1980 had their greatest impact on carrier rates, service levels, and the use of private trucking. Table 4-6 identifies the major

---

[38] Robert C. Lieb, "Promoting Change in Transportation Regulation," *Business Horizons* 18, no. 3 (June 1975): 91.

[39] Paul E. Fulchino and George T. Mauro, "Reform Impacts and Strategic Shipper Responses," in *Proceedings of the Eighteenth Annual Conference of the National Council of Physical Distribution Management*, October 13-15, 1980, p. 368.

**TABLE 4-6** Motor Carrier Reform—Price Impacts

| Type Carrier/Freight | Initial Impact | Cause |
|---|---|---|
| Truckload | | |
|   General freight | Reduced rates | Increased competition<br>PTOs |
|   Special commodities | Reduced rates | Contract<br>Owner-operators<br>Special commodities<br>Increased number of contract rate actions |
| Dense-corridor LTL | Reduced rates | Major carrier/intermodal competition for market share |
| Low-density and rural LTL | | |
|   Over 500 pounds | Rates increase with inflation | Major carrier departure, less efficient "entering" carriers |
|   Under 500 pounds | Rates increase above inflation | |
| Low-density, long-haul LTL | Rates increase above inflation | Carrier departures |
| Local LTL cartage | Rates increase above inflation | Less efficient entering competitors, higher operating costs |
| Long-haul small package | Rates increase with or below inflation | Stable competition, favorable operating costs |
| Short-haul small package | Rates increase above inflation | Higher operating costs |

Source: Paul E. Fulchino and George T. Mauro, "Reform Impacts and Strategic Shipper Responses," in *Proceedings of the Eighteenth Annual Conference of the National Council of Physical Distribution Management*, October 13-15, 1980, p. 370.

impacts that regulatory reform will have on carrier rates. Generally, rates will be reduced in highly competitive areas—densely populated regions, large volumes, regular movements—and increased in less competitive areas—LTL shipments, short hauls, irregular movements.

Specific forecasts of motor carrier rates during the 1980s are not widely available although one forecast by Drake Sheahan/Stewart Dougall, Inc. published in *Handling & Shipping Magazine* (see Table 4-7) suggests that TL and LTL rates will amost double by 1985. The implication for shippers is clear—the prices paid for major freight categories will be substantially higher in the years ahead and will require even more stringent financial control and evaluation of the firm's transportation budget.

"Motor carrier service impacts will be felt by shippers in all segments of for-hire motor carriage—a result, primarily, of changes in competitive forces. In addition, entirely new types of services (service options) are likely to appear."[40] Table 4-8 identifies some of the expected service impacts

---
[40] Ibid., p. 371.

**TABLE 4-7**  Trucking Cost and Rate Forecast

A. Base forecast cost factors (percentage increase)

|  | 1980 | 1981 | 1982 | 1983 | 1984 | 1985 |
|---|---|---|---|---|---|---|
| Labor cost | 11 | 13 | 12 | 13 | 13 | 8 |
| Fuel cost | 35 | 13 | 10 | 10 | 12 | 12 |
| Materials and supplies | 11 | 11 | 10 | 10 | 12 | 12 |
| Depreciation | 8 | 5 | 5 | 5 | 5 | 5 |
| Miscellaneous cost | 9 | 10 | 8 | 9 | 9 | 9 |

B. Percentage of trucking costs by functional cost area

|  | TL 1978 | TL 1985 | LTL 1978 | LTL 1985 |
|---|---|---|---|---|
| Labor | 44.9 | 44.7 | 76.3 | 77.7 |
| Fuel | 11.8 | 18.0 | 2.9 | 4.5 |
| Materials and supplies | 16.7 | 16.9 | 5.0 | 5.3 |
| Depreciation | 11.2 | 7.3 | 5.7 | 3.7 |
| Miscellaneous | 15.4 | 13.1 | 10.1 | 8.8 |
| Total | 100.0 | 100.0 | 100.0 | 100.0 |

C. Base trucking rate increase forecast (percentage)

|  | TL | LTL |
|---|---|---|
| 1980 | 14 | 12 |
| Annual average through 1985 | 11 | 11 |
| Cumulative increase through 1985 | 92 | 89 |

Source: Data from Drake Sheahan/Stewart Dougall, Inc., Chicago, as reported in Robert C. Heiden, "Trucking: A New Equation," *Handling & Shipping Management* 22, no. 1 (January 1981): 52.

resulting from regulatory reform. Again, much like the impact in the rate area, service levels will generally improve where competition is keenest and decline where competition is absent or minimal.

Motor carrier reform will produce some of its most substantial direct effects in the area of private trucking, because of intercorporate hauling reform provisions. . . . Four important private trucking operation (PTO) impacts appear likely:

Significant PTO activity in intercorporate hauling

Moderate interest in for-hire . . . activity by large, sophisticated, private fleets organized as transportation subsidiaries

Increasing competition between PTOs and contract carriers

Growing need for accurate, timely, and flexible PTO cost/performance monitoring systems

Shippers who operate private fleets and who desire to capitalize on regulatory reform opportunities are going to be forced to operate these fleets more and more as sophisticated, competitive transportation businesses. Similarly, when selecting

**TABLE 4-8**  Motor Carrier Reform—Service Impacts

| Type Carrier/Freight | Initial Impact | Cause |
|---|---|---|
| Truckload | | |
|    General freight | Improved service | More TL carriers |
|    Special commodities | Improved service | More TL carriers |
| Dense-corridor LTL | | |
|    Over 500 pounds | Service maintained with more options, fast LTL | Major carrier competition |
|    Under 500 pounds | Service maintained | |
| Low-density and rural LTL | | |
|    Over 500 pounds | Service deterioration | Exit of major efficient carriers |
|    Under 500 pounds | Service deterioration | |
| Low-density, long-haul LTL | Service deterioration | Exit of major carriers |
| Local LTL cartage | No change | Not applicable |
| Long- and short-haul small package | Improved service | Increased competition, increased air-cargo pickup distance, UPS weight limit raised |

Source: Paul E. Fulchino and George T. Mauro, "Reform Impacts and Strategic Shipper Responses," in *Proceedings of the Eighteenth Annual Conference of the National Council of Physical Distribution Management*, October 13–15, 1980, p. 371.

transportation services, shippers without fleets will be forced to give greater attention to the possibility of using other firms' private fleets.[41]

2. *Rail carrier reform.*   The Staggers Rail Act of 1980 was primarily concerned with improving the financial condition of the railroads. As a result, the most significant impact of rail reform on the shipper is in the area of pricing.

*Staggers Act of 1980 Allowed Rate Freedom to the Railroads*

The governing principle for setting rates is to be that rates will be set in a free market environment governed by intermodal and intramodal competition. ICC jurisdiction over maximum rates will be limited to situations where "market dominance" is exercised by railroads. Market dominance is defined solely in terms of the ratio of revenue to variable cost. Challenges to rates on the basis of reasonableness can only be made if the rate exceeds a specified revenue-to-variable cost ratio. That ratio will ultimately be determined on an annual basis by the ICC, but it must fall into the range of 170 to 180 percent.[42]

As a result of rail carrier rate reform, rates are expected to almost double by 1985. Table 4–9 shows rail costs and rate forecasts for the period 1980–85.

In the area of service impacts, two notable items are important. First, the legal forms of rail carriage have been expanded. Contracts for rail service are

[41] Ibid., pp. 371–72.
[42] Ibid., p. 376.

**TABLE 4-9** Rail Cost and Rate Forecast
A. Base forecast cost factors (percentage increase)

|  | 1980 | 1981 | 1982 | 1983 | 1984 | 1985 |
|---|---|---|---|---|---|---|
| Labor cost | 10 | 8 | 7 | 7 | 9 | 8 |
| Fuel cost | 53 | 24 | 19 | 20 | 22 | 22 |
| Materials and supplies | 17 | 13 | 12 | 12 | 13 | 6 |
| Depreciation | 2 | 2 | 2 | 2 | 2 | 2 |
| Miscellaneous cost | 9 | 10 | 7 | 7 | 9 | 9 |
| Return on investment | 4 | 4 | 4 | 4 | 4 | 4 |

B. Percentage of rail costs by functional cost area

|  | 1978 | 1985 |
|---|---|---|
| Labor | 52.8 | 44.4 |
| Fuel | 6.9 | 19.3 |
| Materials and supplies | 21.8 | 23.4 |
| Depreciation | 4.4 | 2.1 |
| Miscellaneous | 14.1 | 10.8 |
| Total | 100.0 | 100.0 |

C. Base rail rate increase forecast (percentage)

| | |
|---|---|
| 1980 | 15 |
| Annual average thru 1985 | 10.5 |
| Cumulative thru 1985 | 90 |

Source: Data from Drake Sheahan/Stewart Dougall, Inc., Chicago, as reported in Patrick Gallagher, "Railroads: Rough Track Ahead," *Handling & Shipping Management* 22, no. 1 (January 1981): p. 38.

---

now legalized resulting in contract rail carriage as well as common carrier rail service. Second, shippers and rail carriers are now allowed to jointly determine limits of carrier liability for loss and damage claims and establish deductible clauses in such liability agreements.

*Airlines Deregulated in 1977 and 1978*

3. *Air carrier reform.* The Airline Deregulation Acts of 1977 and 1978 basically involved three areas of reform: (a) rate freedom, (b) industry and market entry/exit freedom, and (c) elimination of minimum liability for damage. These particular reform components are expected to cause three primary impacts on shippers of air cargo:

1. Higher rates except at major hubs.
2. Greater service availability except in small communities.
3. Reduced carrier liability.[43]

With respect to all of the deregulated transport modes, the regulatory bodies and agencies that were in existence before the various reforms were still in place after the reforms, although some of their functions were transferred to other agencies. A summary of the agencies, bureaus, commissions, and committees, and their responsibilities as of mid-1981 is shown in Appendixes B through E. The groups with the most interface, or direct control over transportation, include the Department of Transportation (DOT), Interstate Commerce Commission (ICC), Civil Aeronautics Board (CAB), Federal Maritime Commission (FMC), and Federal Energy Regulatory Commission

---

[43] Ibid., p. 379.

(FERC). Among them, all of the five basic modes of transportation, plus freight forwarders, are regulated in some fashion—economic and/or safety.

*Transportation rate structures.* Common carriers of freight are subject to some form of rate regulation unless they are among the deregulated modes of the transportation sector. Generally, regulated common carriers publish their rates through a rate bureau which is a committee established by the carriers of a mode serving a specific region of the country. Rate bureaus establish and publish rates for their members although each carrier may establish their own rates if they so desire. This collective rate making allows for more uniform prices or rates to shippers.[44] At the present time, most major transportation modes (air, rail, and motor) are able to adjust their rates freely, within prescribed limits, without regulatory agency involvement.

*Three Basic Rate Structures—Distance, Volume, and Value-of-Service*

There are three basic rate structures in operation in the United States. The first rate structure is related to *distance.* That is, rates increase with distance but do not increase as fast as distance increases. In its simplest form, distance rates are the same for all origin-destination pairs. An example of such a uniform rate is the postal rate charged for a one ounce first-class letter. Another distance measure is built on the tapering principle. Rates increase with distance, but not proportionally, because terminal costs and other carrier fixed costs remain the same regardless of distance. Because of the high fixed costs associated with rail, railroad rates experience a greater tapering with distance than do motor carrier rates.

Other distance rates are established for *key points* whereby several points may be grouped together for rate purposes even though the distances to these points may be different. When key-point rates are established for rail they are the maximum rates to be charged for intermediate points. These rates have resulted in part as an effort to meet rates of competitors and in an effort to simplify rate publications and administration.

The second type of rate structure is related to *volume.* This is in recognition of the fact that economies of scale are present with large-volume shipments. Volume can be reflected in the rate structure in a number of ways. Rates may be quoted on the quantity of product shipped. Shipments below a prescribed minimum volume are charged the same *any-quantity* flat rate. Shipment above a specified volume receive truckload (TL) or carload (CL) rates and those between these extremes receive less than vehicle-load (LTL and LCL) rates. Also high volume can be used as justification for quoting a shipper special rates on particular commodities.

The third type of rate structure is related to the *value-of-service* provided. This process amounts to charging what the traffic will bear and it establishes the upper limit of the rate. For example, say two manufacturers compete for business in a market area. Manufacturer A is located in the market area and sells its product for $2.50 a unit and earns a contribution of

---

[44] Rate bureaus have been exempted from the antitrust laws by the Reed-Bulwinkle Act of 1948.

50 cents per unit. If manufacturer B incurs the same costs exclusive of transportation costs but is located 400 miles from the market, 50 cents per unit represents the maximum that manufacturer B can afford to pay for transportation to the market. Also if two forms of transportation available to manufacturer B were equal in terms of performance characteristics, the higher-priced service would have to meet the lower rate to be competitive.

The charges assessed by carriers can be divided into two classes: line-haul rates which are charged for the movement of goods between two points that are not in the same local pickup and delivery area; and, accessorial charges which cover all other payments made to carriers for transporting, handling, or servicing a shipment. Line-haul rates can be grouped into three types: (1) class rates, (2) exception rates, and (3) commodity rates.

**Class Rates**

*Class rates* simplify the number of transportation rates required by grouping products into classes for the purposes of pricing. A specific product classification is referred to as its *rating*. The charge to move a specific product classification between two locations is referred to as the *rate*. By identifying the class rating for a product, the rate per hundredweight between any two points can be determined.

**Exception Rates**

*Exception rates*, or exceptions to the classification, are special rates that provide the shipper with lower rates than the published class rates. Exception rates were introduced in order to provide a special rate for a specific area, origin-destination, or commodity when competition or volume justified the lower rate. When an exception rate is published, the classification that normally applies is changed. Usually all services associated with the shipment are the same as the class rate when an exception rate is used.

**Commodity Rates**

*Commodity rates* apply when a large quantity of a product is shipped between two locations on a regular basis. These rates are published on a point-to-point basis without regard to product classification. Most rail freight in the United States moves via commodity rates. However, the commodity rate is not used frequently by motor carriers.

*Accessorial service charges.* In addition to line-haul rates, carriers assess charges for a number of special services including (1) demurrage and detentions, (2) split delivery, (3) transit privileges, (4) diversion and reconsignment, and (5) protective service. *Demurrage and detention* refer to charges against the shipper or consignee for delay of a rail car or vehicle beyond the specified time for loading or unloading. *Split delivery* service is provided by motor carriers. It allows the shipper to pool a number of orders to make a large shipment for individual delivery within the limits of a specific split-delivery area. Special split-delivery charges are made for each delivery made within the area. *Transit privileges* apply to goods that require some handling or processing at an intermediate point between origin and destination. When transit privileges exist, the shipment is charged a through rate from origin to destination plus a transit privilege charge. Another type of transit privilege permits the shipper to stop a shipment at an intermediate point to unload a portion of the shipment. A business that purchases from two suppliers can, where the tariff provisions permit, have a truck or rail car partially loaded at one source of supply and then moved to the other supplier to complete the load. The rate from the original point to the destination usually applies to the entire shipment. An exception occurs if the rate from the second supplier to the destination is the higher of the two. In such a case the highest rate applies to the entire shipment. *Diversion and reconsignment* refer to a change in the routing of a shipment and a change of the consignee, respectively. The purpose of diversion is to permit shipments to be delivered to any one of a number of destinations sometime after the shipment originates but before it reaches the originally designated destination. It is a method of allowing the shipper to use the carrier as a warehouse. Both diversion and reconsignment are services provided by railroads and motor carriers for a specified charge. *Protective service* may include refrigeration, heater service, ventilation, or any other service to protect the product being shipped from changes in temperature.

In general, transportation rates are determined by examining a variety of factors which might affect the carrier's cost to move the products. Table 4-10 identifies some of the factors considered when determining rates.

**TABLE 4-10** Factors Affecting Transportation Rate Levels

Liability to loss, damage, waste, or theft in transit
Risks due to hazards of carriage
Expense of, and care in, handling
Density and distribution of population
Geographical characteristics of territories
Types of industrial development (type of products)
Concentration of industrial development
Concentration of sources of raw materials
Balance or imbalance of freight traffic in territory
Predominant type of traffic (type, volume, weight, value)
Seasonal movement of traffic
Distances goods must be transported
Nature of intermode and intramode competition
Costs of performing transportation services (labor, fuel, equipment)
Likelihood of injury to other freight with which it may come in contact
Kind of container or package used to protect the product

**Traffic and Transportation Management**

The physical distribution manager must be familiar with the characteristics of the types of service provided by commercial carriers in order to determine the best mix of modes for the company. This requires that the company's transportation needs be analyzed giving full consideration to the impact that transportation has on other physical distribution components such as inventory, warehousing, production-lot-quantity costs, and customer service.

**TABLE 4-11** Typical Activities Assigned to a Traffic Department

| Almost Always | Frequently | Sometimes |
|---|---|---|
| Negotiate freight rates and transportation contracts | Appear before the commission or bureaus | Supervise packaging operations |
| Determine and monitor freight classifications | Conduct transportation surveys | Control company automobiles and aircraft |
| Develop and implement innovative shipping or transportation methods or techniques | Supervise warehouse operations | Supervise import-export transportation activities |
| Control freight loss and damage | Supervise shipping and receiving operations | Supervise intra-plant transportation |
| Control demurrage | Run private trucking operations | Assist in marketing product to carriers |
| Determine transportation mode and route | Prepare shipping documents | |
| Develop and administer order or shipment consolidation programs | Arrange for passenger reservations and household moves | |
| Provide weight or rate quotations | Assist purchasing in supplier chargeback programs | |
| Trace or expedite shipments | Participate in import-export transportation activities | |
| Audit freight bills | Secure and, where applicable, control transportation fleet equipment | |
| Make minor transportation studies | | |
| Advise on warehouse type or location | | |
| Advise on shipping operations | | |
| Advise on transportation-packaging relationship | | |
| Advise on shipping document preparation | | |

Source: Donald W. Weitz, "Organizing the Traffic Function," Technical Paper no. 55 (New York: Drake Sheahan/Stewart Dougall, June 1972), p. 12.

Five Functions of Traffic and Transportation Management

The specific functions of traffic and transportation management include:

1. Knowledge of rates and rate negotiation.
2. Routing and carrier selection. When selecting carriers, the management must consider the volume of products being shipped, the services that are provided by each mode, and the reliability and consistency of pick-up and delivery associated with each mode.

3. Knowledge of regulatory agencies and how various regulations governing modes will affect company operations.
4. The operation of a private fleet when it can be cost-justified in terms of cost or service improvement.
5. Cooperation with carriers to improve transportation productivity. This type of institutional cooperation can be illustrated by explaining a system that Spector Motor Freight has developed in cooperation with its customers. The system makes it possible for a customer of Spector Motor Freight to access Spector's computer for the purposes of tracing a shipment. For example, if a manufacturer receives an inquiry from one of its customers with regard to the expected delivery date of a shipment, the company's traffic department can access Spector's computer and obtain shipment location and estimated arrival time.

The typical activities assigned to the traffic department are numerous and varied. Table 4–11 shows some of the activities in which the traffic department is involved based upon their frequency of occurrence.

In order to be effective, the traffic function must interface with other departments within, and outside of, the physical distribution area. Examples of areas of interface include accounting (freight bills), engineering (packaging, transportation equipment), legal (warehouse and carrier contracts), manufacturing (interplant transport), purchasing (expediting, supplier negotiation), sales (service standards), shipping (carrier performance), receiving (claims and documentation), and warehousing (equipment supply and scheduling).[45]

## SUMMARY

In this chapter you were provided with an understanding of the transportation function and its importance to physical distribution. Transportation, in conjunction with warehousing, adds time and place utility to products. The five basic modes of transportation—air, motor, pipeline, rail, and water—provide movement of products between where they are produced and where they are consumed.

The physical distribution manager must be aware of the characteristics of each basic mode as well as all modal combinations. The regulatory network was shown to be an important aspect of the transportation system and one which impacts on the selection of a particular mode and/or carrier.

An important part of this chapter was designed to provide you with an overview of the traffic management function. The traffic management function involves administration of all aspects of the firm's transportation system. In Chapter 5, the information contained in this chapter will form the basis for making a variety of cost and service decisions within the firm.

---

[45] Donald W. Weitz, "Organizing the Traffic Function," Technical Paper no. 55 (New York: Drake Sheahan/Stewart Dougall, June 1972), p. 12.

# APPENDIX A: Section-by-Section Summary of the Motor Carrier Act of 1980

*Congressional finding.* States that a safe, sound, competitive, and fuel-efficient motor carrier system is vital to the economy and national defense, that current transportation law is in need of revision, that in some cases existing regulation has been counterproductive, that the ICC should be given explicit direction and well-defined parameters for regulation of the motor carrier industry, and that the ICC should not attempt to go beyond the powers vested in it by the Interstate Commerce Act.

This section also requires the appropriate committees of Congress to hold annual oversight hearings on the effect of this legislation during the next five years after enactment.

*National transportation policy.* Adds to the National Transportation Policy the goal of promoting competitive and efficient transportation service in order to achieve the following objectives: meet needs of shippers, receivers, and consumers; allow a variety of price and service options; allow the most productive use of equipment and energy resources; enable adequate profits and fair wages; provide and maintain service to small communities and small shippers; maintain a privately-owned motor carrier system; promote minority participation; and promote intermodal transportation.

*Entry.* Authorizes issuance of certificates if the commission finds the applicant fit, willing, and able, if the applicant shows additionally that the service proposed will serve a useful public purpose, responsive to public demand or need—unless the protestants show the service to be inconsistent with the public convenience and necessity.

*Restrictions on operating authority.* Within 180 days after enactment, the commission must eliminate gateway and circuitous route limitations and implement procedures to process individual motor carrier applications to remove certificate operating restrictions. The latter procedure would be designed: to allow the broadening of the categories of property authorized; to authorize service to intermediate points; to provide round-trip authority in lieu of one-way authority; to eliminate narrow territorial limitations; and to eliminate other unreasonable restrictions wasteful of fuel, inefficient, or contrary to the public interest. Fuel efficiency and small-community service would be major factors in restriction removal cases.

*Exemptions.* Adds to the exempt agricultural commodities list: fish or shellfish by-products not intended for human consumption; and livestock and poultry feed, agricultural seeds, and plants if transported to a site of agricultural production or to a business selling agricultural goods.

All incidental-to-air motor freight operations are exempted and new exemptions are added for used pallets, shipping containers, and devices; natural crushed vesicular rock to be used for decorative purposes; and wood chips.

*Food transportation.* Permits sellers of food and grocery products using a uniform zone-delivered pricing system to compensate customers who pick up purchased products, if such compensation is available to all customers on a nondiscriminatory basis, and if the compensation does not exceed the actual delivery cost to the seller. The ICC is directed to mon-

Source: American Trucking Associations, "Section-by-Section Summary of New Motor Carrier Act," *Transport Topics*, no. 2343 (July 7, 1980), pp. 20–21.

itor the extent to which any savings realized are passed on to the ultimate consumer, and may require reports and other information for that purpose.

*Private carriage.* Intercorporate hauling for compensation is permitted for wholly owned subsidiaries if notice is given to the commission containing a list of participating subsidiaries and an affidavit of 100 percent ownership; the notice is published in the *Federal Register*, and a copy of the notice is carried in the cabs of vehicles providing the transportation.

*Contract carriers.* Entry rules are modified by deleting the number of shippers as a consideration in granting a permit for property carriers. Protests are limited and master permit proceedings are prohibited. A provision enabling the master permitting of one-truck processed food haulers is included, and is subject to the same requirements as included for master certification.

Permit restrictions are eased regarding particular industry or geographic area limitations, and regarding existing limitations on holding both a permit and certificate to transport property over the same route or in the same area.

*Zone of rate freedom.* Creates a 10 percent up-or-down zone of rate flexibility within which the commission may not investigate, suspend, revise, or revoke any rate on the basis of reasonableness. This zone can be increased by 5 percent if the commission finds sufficient competition and additional benefits from more flexibility. After two years, the zone would be adjusted to account for changes in the Producer Price Index.

*Released rate.* Enables common carriers individually to offer released-rate alternatives without ICC approval. The commission may require carriers to keep in effect regular rates as an option.

*Rule of ratemaking.* Directs the commission to adopt revenue standards which allow carriers to "achieve revenue levels that will provide a flow of net income, plus depreciation, adequate to support prudent capital outlays, assure the repayment of a reasonable level of debt, permit the raising of needed equity capital, attract and retain capital in amounts adequate to provide a sound motor carrier transportation system in the United States, and take into account reasonable estimated or foreseeable future costs."

*Rate bureaus.* Defines "single-line rate" as a rate, charge, or allowance proposed by a single motor common carrier of property that is applicable only over its line and for which the transportation can be provided by that carrier. After January 1, 1981, only those carriers with authority to participate in the rate proposal may vote. After January 1, 1984, discussion of and voting upon single-line rates would be prohibited, except that if the Motor Carrier Ratemaking Study Commission (see below) does not submit a final report before January 1, 1983, the date would be postponed until July 1, 1984. The single-line rate prohibition does not apply to general rate adjustments, changes in commodity classifications, changes in tariff structures, and tariff publishing services.

A "Motor Carrier Ratemaking Study Commission" would be established to make a full and complete study of collective ratemaking and of the need or lack of need for continued antitrust immunity. The 10-member commission would be comprised of six congressional members and four members appointed by the President. Of the latter, two must be motor carriers.

*Lumping.* Prohibits coercion to load or unload vehicles and includes strong civil and criminal penalties for violations. Language is also included requiring the parties to agree as to who is responsible for loading and unloading. A joint study on lumping practices is authorized.

*Written contracts (exempt for-hire carriage).* Authorizes the ICC, in cooperation with the Secretary of Agriculture, to require the use of written contracts for exempt agricultural transportation and for brokerage services.

*Motor carrier brokers.* Adopts a general fit, willing, and able test for licensing of brokers—other than household goods brokers.

*Finance exemptions.* Increases the thresholds for ICC jurisdiction over the carrier issuance of securities and assumptions of indebtedness. The present $1 million threshold is raised to $5 million for securities; the present $200,000 threshold is raised $1 million for notes. The threshold is also raised for ICC jurisdiction over consolidations and mergers from the present $300,000 to $2 million (aggregate cross revenue).

*Uniform state regulation.* Directs the Department of Transportation and the ICC, in consultation with the states, to develop recommendations to provide a more efficient and equitable state regulatory system regarding licensing, registration, and filings. These recommendations are to be made within 18 months after enactment.

*Pooling.* Adds a new provision to existing law providing for expedited consideration of pooling arrangements by the commission. Carriers would file the agreement not less than 50 days before its effective date. Prior to its effective date, the commission would be required to determine whether the agreement is of major transportation importance, or will unduly restrain competition. If neither factor is found to exist, the agreement shall be approved. If either factor exists, more formal consideration would be given.

*Mixed loads.* Allows carriers to transport in the same vehicle mixed loads of regulated and exempt commodities. The provision also makes clear that such mixing does not affect the unregulated status of the exempt property nor the regulated status of the property being transported pursuant to a commission-issued certificate or permit.

*Joint rates and through routes.* Authorizes the commission to require the establishment of through routes and joint rates between motor carriers of property, and between those carriers and water carriers. The commission cannot require carriers to include in a through route substantially less than the entire length of its route unless unreasonable circuity is involved. The new provision also ensures that the carriers will not be subjected to unfair or unreasonable demands to provide such service. Further, it requires all carriers participating in coordinated service to promptly pay divisions or make interline settlements with other carriers that are party to the service arrangement. Finally, if participating carriers become unduly delinquent in the settlement of such divisions or interline settlements, the coordinated service may be suspended or cancelled under rules prescribed by the commission.

This provision also authorizes freight forwarders to enter into contracts with rail carriers or water common carriers for certain transportation. Currently, freight forwarders may contract only with motor common carriers.

*Temporary authority and emergency temporary authority.* Authorizes the commission to grant temporary authority for up to 270 days and emergency temporary authority for up to 30 days. The commission may extend the emergency temporary authority for an additional 90 days.

*Cooperative associations.* Allows agricultural cooperative associations to haul up to 25 percent of their total interstate tonnage in nonfarm, nonmember goods, in movements incidental and necessary to their primary business as cooperative associations. The current percentage is fifteen.

*Procedural reform.* Establishes expedited commission hearing and appellate procedures to govern motor carrier cases.

For cases involving applications for operating authority, the new provision imposes deadlines at each stage of the decision-making process.

In order to further expedite commission cases, the new provision eliminates the multileveled appeals of commission decisions required by the current statute.

*Enforcement.* Extends the current three-year deadline for formal investigations for rail carriers to all carriers. If the investigation is not concluded in three years, it is automatically dismissed.

This section also clarifies when a freight loss or damage claim is disallowed for purposes of filing court action. The new provision states that an offer of compromise will not constitute such a disallowance unless the carrier specifically informs the claimant, in writing, that its claim is disallowed and gives reasons for the disallowance. Further, any communications received from a carrier's insurer will not constitute a disallowance, unless the insurer, in writing, informs the claimant that the claim is being disallowed, gives reasons, and informs the claimant that the insurer is acting on behalf of the carrier.

*Merger procedures.* Establishes deadlines for each step involved in the commission merger proceedings. For example, evidentiary proceedings must be completed within 240 days and a final decision reached by 180 days thereafter.

*Small-community service study.* Requires the commission to conduct a study of service to small communities with emphasis on communities having a population of 5,000 or less. The study is to include an analysis of the common carrier obligation to provide service to small communities, an assessment of whether the commission is enforcing the obligation, and an evaluation of the effect of this legislation on service to small communities. Further, the commission shall make specific recommendations regarding ways to ensure motor carrier service to small communities. The commission's report is due September 1, 1982. The section authorizes the appropriation of such sums as are necessary to conduct the study and make the report.

*Minimum financial responsibility for motor carriers.* Transfers from the ICC to DOT the authority to establish financial responsibility for bodily injury and property damage by motor carriers.

*Imposition of state tax on motor carrier transportation property.* Prohibits as a burden on interstate commerce the assessment, levying, or collecting of taxes on motor carrier property in a manner different than that of other commercial and industrial property. It applies to motor carrier property owned or used by a motor carrier of freight providing transportation in interstate commerce.

*Business entertainment expense.* Allows carriers to incur business entertainment expenses without being held in violation of the statute's prohibition against unreasonable rate discrimination. The allowed expenses are the same as those which could be lawfully incurred by a person or corporation not subject to the commission's jurisdiction. However, such entertainment expenses shall not be taken into account in determining the cost of service or the carrier's rate base.

***Coordinated transportation services.*** Permits motor carriers to deliver to or receive from a rail carrier a trailer moving in trailer-on-flat-car service at any point on the route of the rail carrier, if the motor carrier is authorized to serve the origin and destination points of traffic.

***Job referral.*** Directs the Secretary of Labor to maintain a list of jobs available with regulated motor carriers, and to assist persons previously employed by such carriers in finding other employment. The secretary may require motor carriers to file reports, data, and other information, but may not prohibit motor carriers from filling any openings before they are published on the list. Nor can motor carriers be required to hire employees from such list.

## APPENDIX B: Standing Congressional Committees Having Jurisdiction over Transportation

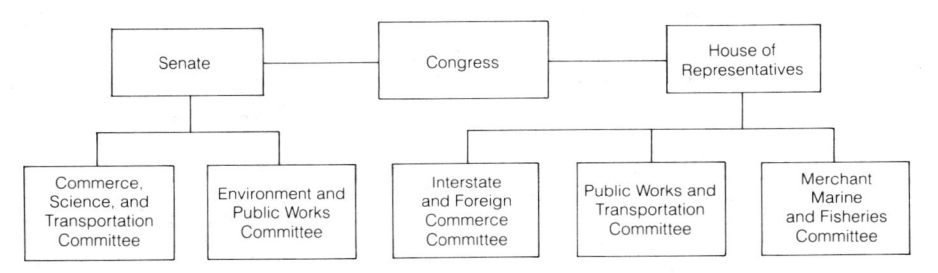

```
                            Congress
            ┌──────────────────┼──────────────────┐
         Senate                                House of
                                            Representatives
   ┌────────────┬────────────┐      ┌────────────┬────────────┬────────────┐
 Commerce,    Environment          Interstate   Public Works   Merchant
 Science, and  and Public           and Foreign  and           Marine
 Transportation Works               Commerce     Transportation and Fisheries
 Committee    Committee             Committee    Committee     Committee
```

The present standing committee structure of Congress includes several committees which have both direct and indirect jurisdiction over policies affecting the transportation industry. The organizational chart above indicates the positions of these committees within the structure of the Congress. The table of functions points up the major areas of the transportation industry covered by the various committees, as well as the similarity of their respective jurisdiction.

---

*Senate Committee*

Commerce, Science, and Transportation
  Regulation of interstate railroads, buses, trucks, oil pipelines, freight forwarders, domestic water carriers, and domestic and international air carriers. Inland waterways. Promotion of civil aviation, including subsidies and airport construction.

*House Committee*

Interstate and Foreign Commerce
  Jurisdiction over railroads and the Railway Labor Act (which also covers airline labor). Air pollution.

*Merchant Marine and Fisheries*
  Same basic jurisdiction over international water transport as Senate Commerce Committee, plus unregulated domestic oceangoing water transportation and water pollution. Approve Maritime Administration programs.

---

Source: Transportation Association of America, *Transportation Facts and Trends*, 15th ed. (Washington, D.C., July 1979), p. 33.

## APPENDIX B  (*continued*)

International water carriers generally, including registering and licensing of vessels and small boats; navigation and the laws relating thereto; measures relating to subsidies; and the inspection and safety of vessels. Approve Maritime Administration programs.

Environment and Public Works
Projects for the benefit of water navigation and rivers and harbors. Measures relating to the construction or maintenance of highways. Air and water pollution.

Public Works and Transportation
Same basic jurisdiction as the Senate Environment and Public Works Committee, plus jurisdiction over interstate buses, trucks, oil pipelines, freight forwarders, water carriers, as well as urban mass transport and domestic and international air carriers.

Legislation affecting transportation also comes within the jurisdiction of several other congressional committees, such as:

| | |
|---|---|
| Appropriations | Actual appropriation of funds |
| House Government Operations / Senate Governmental Affairs | Transportation operations of Federal agencies |
| Judiciary | Rules and procedures for regulatory agencies |
| House Post Office and Civil Service / Senate Governmental Affairs | U.S. Postal Service, including parcel post |
| House Ways and Means / Senate Finance | Financial matters, with House committee originating all tax bills |
| House Education and Labor / Senate Human Resources | Transport labor generally, including mediation or arbitration of disputes. (Note House Interstate and Foreign Commerce Committee's jurisdiction over rail labor) |
| Senate Banking, Housing, and Urban Affairs | Urban mass transport (note similar jurisdiction of House Public Works and Transportation) |

# APPENDIX C: Transportation Responsibilities in the Executive Branch

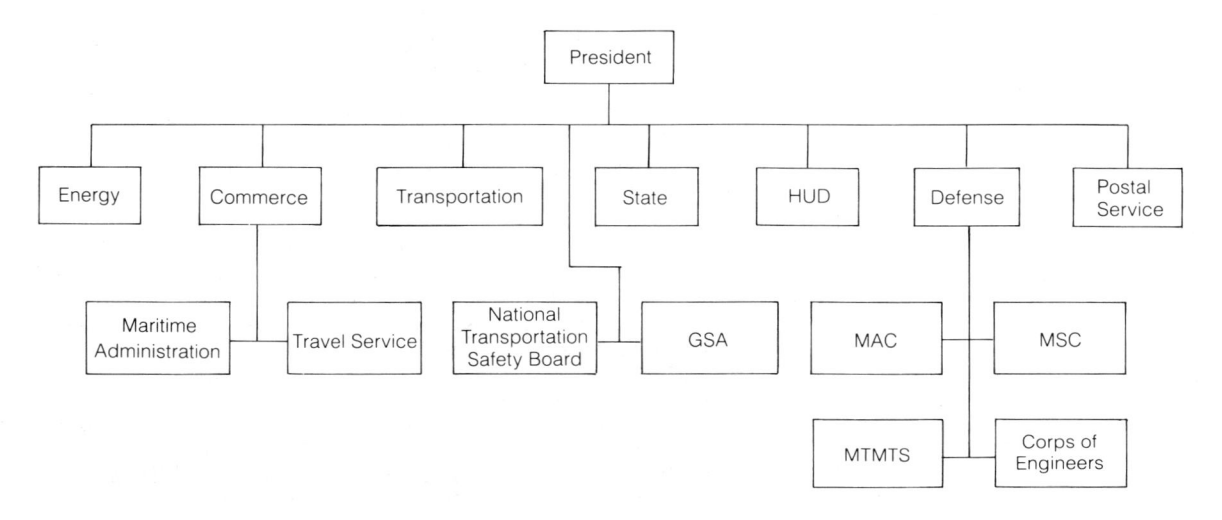

```
                                    President
        ┌───────┬───────┬───────────┬────┴────┬────────┬────────┬────────┐
      Energy  Commerce  Transportation  State   HUD    Defense   Postal
                │            │                           │       Service
         ┌──────┴──────┐     │                    ┌──────┴──────┐
      Maritime      Travel   │                   MAC           MSC
    Administration  Service  │                    │             │
                      National                    │             │
                      Transportation──GSA        MTMTS      Corps of
                      Safety Board                           Engineers
```

| Office or Agency | Responsibility |
| --- | --- |
| President | Rules on matters relating to international air transport by U.S. air carriers and foreign air carrier operations to the United States. Appoints members of federal agencies and appoints chairmen of the CAB, ICC, and FMC. |
| Department of State | Develops policy recommendations and approves policy programs concerning international aviation and maritime transportation. |
| National Transportation Safety Board | Promotes transportation safety by conducting independent accident investigations involving all modes of transport; by regulating accident reporting procedures; and by recommending changes for improvement. Reviews on appeal suspensions/denials of licenses issued by DOT agencies. |
| Department of Housing and Urban Development | Administers variety of federally aided housing and community development programs, consulting with and advising Department of Transportation in order that DOT urban transport programs are compatible with HUD programs. |
| Department of Energy | Develops and implements national energy policies. Administers, through Economic Regulatory Administration, petroleum and natural gas pricing, allocation, and import/export controls. Assures availability of energy supplies, and performs regulatory functions not assigned to Federal Energy Regulatory Commission. |
| U.S. Travel Service | Develops, plans, and carries out a comprehensive program designed to stimulate and encourage travel to the United States by residents of foreign countries. |

Source: Transportation Association of America, *Transportation Facts and Trends,* 15th ed. (Washington, D.C., July, 1979), p. 34.

| | |
|---|---|
| Maritime Administration | Promotes merchant marine; grants ship mortgage insurance; determines ship requirements, ocean services, routes, and lines essential for development and maintenance of the foreign commerce of the United States; maintains the National Defense Reserve Fleet; develops ship designs, marine transportation systems, advanced propulsion concepts, and ship mechanization and management techniques. Its Maritime Subsidy Board awards subsidies, determines the degree of services and specific routes of subsidized operators. |
| U.S. Postal Service | Provides postal services throughout the United States, contracts for mail transport services, and takes final action, subject to judicial review, on recommendations of independent Postal Rate Commission on rates and mail classifications. Made independent agency of Executive Branch in 1970, with 11-member Board—9 appointed by President and confirmed by Senate. |
| General Services Administration | Develops and operates transportation programs within the federal government; provides and procures transportation services; develops and implements procedures for improving motor-equipment management, operation, and rehabilitation programs of the federal government including assigning, regulating or performing the operation of interagency motor pools and motor transport systems. |
| Military Sealift Command | Provides ocean transportation for personnel and cargo of the Department of Defense and, as directed, for other agencies and departments of the United States. Also operates ships in support of scientific projects and other programs of the federal government. |
| Military Airlift Command | Provides air transportation for personnel and cargo for all the military services on a worldwide basis; in addition furnishes weather, rescue, and photographic and charting services for the Air Force. |
| Military Traffic Management and Terminal Service | Directs military traffic management, land transportation, and common-user ocean terminal service within the United States, and for worldwide traffic management of the DOD household goods moving and storage program. Provides for the procurement and use of freight and passenger transportation service from commercial for-hire transportation companies operating between points in the continental United States, except for long-term contract air-lift service. |
| Corps of Engineers | Constructs and maintains river and harbor improvements. Administers laws for protecting navigable waterways. |

# APPENDIX D: Department of Transportation— Organization and Responsibilities

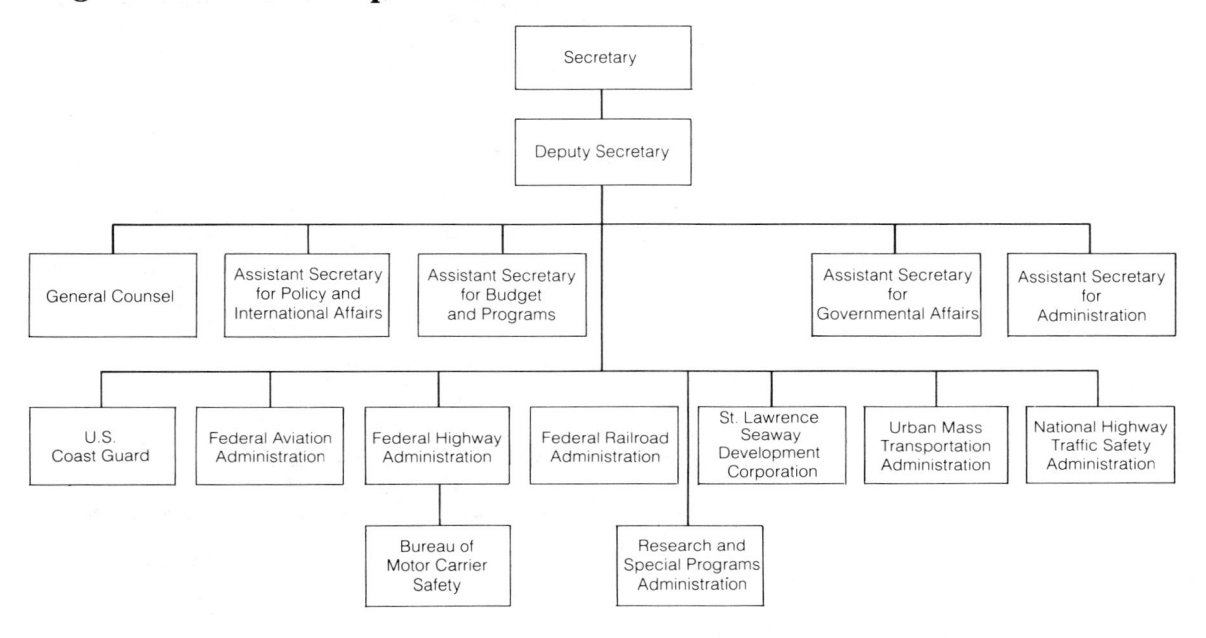

```
                              Secretary
                                 |
                           Deputy Secretary
```

Organization chart branches from Deputy Secretary to:
- General Counsel
- Assistant Secretary for Policy and International Affairs
- Assistant Secretary for Budget and Programs
- Assistant Secretary for Governmental Affairs
- Assistant Secretary for Administration

Operating administrations:
- U.S. Coast Guard
- Federal Aviation Administration
- Federal Highway Administration (→ Bureau of Motor Carrier Safety)
- Federal Railroad Administration
- St. Lawrence Seaway Development Corporation (→ Research and Special Programs Administration)
- Urban Mass Transportation Administration
- National Highway Traffic Safety Administration

| Office or Agency | Responsibility |
| --- | --- |
| Secretary of Transportation | Principal assistant to president in all matters relating to federal transportation programs. His office directly handles public and consumer affairs, deepwater ports, civil rights, contract appeals. |
| Deputy Under Secretary | Acts for and exercises the power of the secretary and is responsible for the supervision and coordination of the activities of the department as directed by the secretary. |
| General Counsel | Chief legal officer of DOT and final authority on questions at law. Represents DOT before regulatory agencies, supervises legal aspects of DOT legislative programs, coordinates legal resources. |
| Assistant Secretary for Policy and International Affairs | Formulates transport policy and implementing plans; coordinates U.S. interests in international transportation affairs; analyzes social, economic, and energy aspects of transport; assesses performance of transport system; coordinates environment and safety programs; handles DOT's interest in domestic and foreign marine transport. |
| Assistant Secretary for Budget and Programs | Supervises DOT's transition to zero-based budgeting, to hold down costs through annual budget reviews. |
| Assistant Secretary for Governmental Affairs | Maintains liaison with the Congress, coordinates DOT's legislative activities, and assures effective communication and coordination with other federal agencies, as well as state and local governments. |

Source: Transportation Association of America, *Transportation Facts and Trends,* 15th ed. (Washington, D.C., July, 1979), p. 35.

| | |
|---|---|
| Assistant Secretary for Administration | Supervises and implements DOT policies relating to personnel and training, management systems, procurement, and contracting, installations and logistics, and investigations and security. |
| U.S. Coast Guard | Maintains network of rescue vessels, aircraft, and communications facilities to protect lives and property on high seas and navigable waters of the United States. Enforces federal laws governing navigation, vessel inspection, port safety and security, marine environmental protection, and resource conservation. Enforces ship construction and safety standards, and regulates Great Lakes' pilotage. |
| Federal Aviation Administration | Promotes civil aviation generally, including R&D, and promulgates and enforces safety regulations. Develops and operates the airways, including facilities. Administers federal airport program. |
| Federal Highway Administration | Administers federal-aid highway program of financial assistance to states for highway construction. Develops and administers program to promote highway safety, including financial aid to states. Administers highway beautification program and highway programs on federal territorial lands. Coordinates and helps fund research and development programs on wide variety of highway problems. |
| Federal Railroad Administration | Consolidates U.S. support of rail transport, administers and enforces rail safety regulations, administers rail financial-aid programs, conducts research and development to improve rail service. Responsible for DOT R&D Test Center at Pueblo, Colorado, and operations of U.S.-owned Alaska Railroad. |
| St. Lawrence Seaway Development Corporation | Administers operation and maintenance of the U.S. portion of St. Lawrence Seaway, including toll rates. |
| Urban Mass Transportation Administration | Responsible for developing comprehensive coordinated mass transport systems for metropolitan and urban areas, including R&D and demonstration projects; aid for technical studies, planning, engineering, and designing; and financial aid to local transit for operations. |
| National Highway Traffic Safety Administration | Implements motor vehicle safety programs and issues standards prescribing levels of safety for motor vehicles and their equipment. Conducts test programs to assure compliance with standards and need for them. Helps fund state/local motor vehicle safety programs, maintains national poor-drivers' register, sets fuel economy standards for autos, in cooperation with EPA/DOE, and assesses penalties. |
| Research and Special Programs Administration | Directs DOT's programs relating to technology R&D, data collection, transport security, university research, transport facilitation (including international), hazardous materials, and pipeline safety. |
| Bureau of Motor Carrier Safety | Regulates safety performance of interstate commercial motor carriers, including movement of hazardous materials, and cargo security/noise abatement programs. Makes road checks and prosecutes violators. |

# APPENDIX E: Federal Transportation Regulatory Agencies

The federal transportation regulatory agencies are arms of the legislative branch of the government. They are *not* courts. They do have recourse to the courts in order to enforce their orders, although they exercise quasi-judicial powers as well as quasi-legislative powers. Their members are appointed by the president with Senate approval at salaries of $50,000 with chairmen receiving $2,500 more. Not more than a majority of one can be from any political party.

### Interstate Commerce Commission

The ICC was created in 1887 by the Act to Regulate Commerce. Its official complement of 11 members is being reduced unofficially to 9 by allowing two vacancies to remain unfilled. Commissioners serve for seven years. The chairman is appointed by the president, and the vice chairman is elected by the members.

| Regulates | Major Functions |
|---|---|
| Railroads (1887), express companies, sleeping car companies (1906). Motor carriers (1935). (Private carriers and carriers of agricultural commodities exclusively are exempt, as are motor vehicles used by farm co-ops.) Water carriers (1940) operating coastwise, intercoastal, and on inland waters of the United States. (Carriers of liquid and/or dry bulk commodities are exempt.) Coal slurry pipelines (1906, in conjunction with oil pipelines, which have been transferred to Federal Energy Regulatory Commission)—common carrier only. Freight forwarders (1942). (Nonprofit shippers' associations are exempt.) | Regulates, in varying degrees by mode, surface carrier operations, including rates, routes, operating rights, abandonments, and mergers. Conducts investigations and awards damages where applicable and administers railroad bankruptcy. Prescribes uniform system of accounts and records and evaluates property owned or used by carriers subject to the act. Authorizes issuance of securities or assumption of obligations by carriers by rail and certain common and contract carriers by motor vehicle. Develops preparedness programs covering rail, motor, and inland waterways utilization. |

### Civil Aeronautics Board

The CAB, as it exists today, is an outgrowth of the Civil Aeronautics Act of 1938, presidential reorganization plans of 1940 and the Federal Aviation Act of 1958. There are five board members, each serving a term of six years. The chairman and vice chairman are appointed by the president.

| Regulates | Major Functions |
|---|---|
| U.S. domestic and international air carriers. (In 1977, domestic air cargo operations were removed from regulation; and, starting in 1978, domestic air passenger regulation is to be phased out: fares in 1981, routes in 1983, and CAB itself in 1985.) Foreign air carrier operations, to, from, and within the United States. | Regulates carrier operations, including rates, routes, operating rights and mergers. Determines and grants subsidies. Assists in the development of international air transport and grants, subject to Presidential approval foreign operating certificates to U.S. carriers and U.S. operating permits to foreign carriers. |

Source: Transportation Association of America, *Transportation Facts and Trends*, 15th ed. (Washington, D.C., July, 1979), p. 36.

### Federal Maritime Commission

The present FMC was established by Presidential Reorganization Plan 7 of 1961, but most of its regulatory powers are similar to those granted predecessor agencies by the Shipping Act of 1916 and subsequent statutes. It consists of five members serving four-year terms. The president names the chairman. The vice chairman is elected annually by members.

| Regulates | Major Functions |
| --- | --- |
| All U.S.-flag and foreign-flag vessels operating in the foreign commerce of the U.S. and common carriers by water operating in domestic trade to points beyond the continental United States. | Regulates services, practices and agreements of water common carriers in international trade and rates and practices of water common carriers operating in domestic trade to points beyond the continental United States. (Note entry and route-designation functions of Maritime Subsidy Board.) |

### Federal Energy Regulatory Commission

The FERC was created by the Department of Energy Organization Act of 1977 as a component of the Department of Energy but with independent regulatory powers. Its five members serve four-year terms. The chairman is appointed by the president, and the vice chairman is elected annually by the members.

| Regulates | Major Functions |
| --- | --- |
| Oil pipelines—common carrier only (transferred from ICC). Natural gas pipelines—(transferred from Federal Power Commission). | Regulates rights, rates, abandonments, and mergers of oil and natural gas pipelines and the charges for sale of natural gas. Establishes valuations for oil pipelines. |

## QUESTIONS AND PROBLEMS

1. Physical distribution management is concerned with the addition of time and place utility to products. More specifically, each of the physical distribution functions contributes to the creation of time and place utility. Define what is meant by time and place utility and identify how the transportation function adds utility to products.

2. Basic transportation modes can be defined and compared based upon their characteristics including (1) service(s) provided, (2) cost, (3) availability, and (4) products transported. Briefly discuss the five modes on each characteristic.
    a. Air.
    b. Motor.
    c. Pipeline.
    d. Rail.
    e. Water.

3. Although freight forwarders are not one of the five basic modes of transport, they are a viable shipping alternative for most companies. Discuss the role and functions of freight forwarders in the transportation system.

4. In addition to the five basic modes of transport and freight forwarders, there are a number of modal combinations available to the shipper. Among the most widely used are trailer-on-flat-car (TOFC) and container-on-flat-car (COFC). These combinations are referred to as piggyback movement. Describe piggyback movement from a cost, service, and availability perspective, and identify its major strengths and weaknesses.

5. Three types of for-hire transportation carriers exist: common, contract, and exempt. Briefly define and describe the characteristics of each carrier type.

6. An issue of extreme importance to the distribution sector in recent years has been the question of regulation versus deregulation of the transportation industry. Briefly identify the viewpoints of shippers and carriers on the regulation of major transportation activities.

7. Identify the major activities undertaken by the traffic department in a typical firm and briefly discuss how the traffic function interfaces or relates with other physical distribution activities.

# 5 Decision Strategies in Transportation

Introduction

Developing Cost-Effective Transportation

The Transportation-Mode Selection Decision
   Problem Recognition
   Search Process
   Choice Process
   Postchoice Evaluation

Shipper Response to Transportation Regulatory Reform
   Response to Motor Carrier Reforms
   Response to Rail Carrier Reforms
   Response to Air Carrier Reforms

The Private versus For-Hire Decision
   Define the Problem
   Develop Transport Objectives
   Collect Pertinent Information
   Determine Present Cost
   Analyze Present Operations
   Develop Alternatives
   Determine Private Fleet Costs
   Consider Indirect Factors
   Summarize Alternatives
   Make the Decision

Leasing

Evaluation of Mode/Carrier Performance

Designing an Optimal Transportation System

Summary

   Appendix: Key Issues Affecting Future Transportation Decision Making

**Objectives of this chapter:**

To show how to measure transportation costs and performance

To show how to recognize opportunities for reducing transportation costs in the firm

To show how to improve the performance of the firm's transportation system

## INTRODUCTION

A thorough understanding of the transportation system is a prerequisite to successful physical distribution decisionmaking. Transportation is an essential part of any distribution system and must be effectively managed if the firm is to satisfy its customers and achieve an acceptable rate of return on its investment. It is integrally related to the other components of physical distribution as shown in Figure 5 — 1. In this chapter you will be shown how to measure transportation costs and performance. Also, opportunities for reducing transportation costs in the firm will be identified. Finally, you will be shown how to improve the performance of the firm's transportation system.

The physical distribution executive is faced with a multitude of transportation-related decisions. For example, how should the cost and service aspects of the transportation activity be measured? Which modes/carriers should the company select? How will transportation regulatory reform impact the firm? Should the company use for-hire or private transportation? Is leasing a feasible alternative for the firm? What is the best way to evaluate mode/carrier performance? These are some of the more important questions which must be answered if the company's transportation activities are to be most productive.

## DEVELOPING COST-EFFECTIVE TRANSPORTATION

*Transportation Costs Must Be Identified*

Ideally, transportation costs should be fully identified, reported quickly and accurately, and readily accessible for routine operation and long-range planning. Effective cost measurement is vital to the success of a firm's transportation system.

The machinery group of FMC Corporation is an example of a company that has examined the cost aspects of their transportation system. FMC management posed a series of questions which required specific cost information.

Where are most products being shipped?

What areas supply what operations' materials needs?

Are products being shipped at minimal cost?

Do service levels meet customer requirements?

Have proper rate codes been assigned and negotiated?

Have freight consolidation programs been developed?

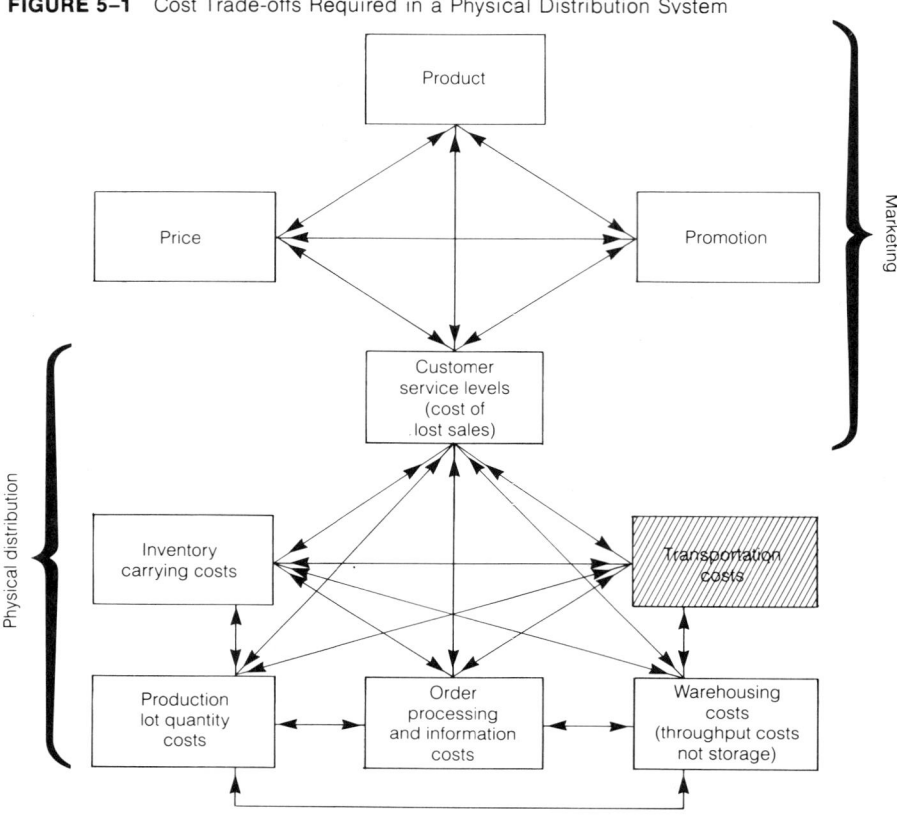

**FIGURE 5-1** Cost Trade-offs Required in a Physical Distribution System

Objective: Minimize total costs.

Total costs = Transportation costs + Warehousing costs
+ Order processing and information costs + Production lot quantity costs
+ Inventory carrying costs + Cost of lost sales

Source: Adapted from Douglas M. Lambert, *The Development of an Inventory Costing Methodology: A Study of the Costs Associated with Holding Inventory* (Chicago: National Council of Physical Distribution Management, 1976), p. 7.

What are FMC's private fleet requirements as compared to the current fleet?

Can an overall cost—effective customer-oriented transportation system and its organization be defined for FMC machinery group?[1]

The approach taken by FMC in answering their questions is shown in Figure 5–2 and is in a form which can be applied to almost any multi-product firm with plants located in various geographical areas. For FMC, and

---
[1] Michael Heschel, "Developing Cost-Effective Transportation," *Transportation and Distribution Management* 15, no. 6 (November/December 1975): 31.

**FIGURE 5-2** An Approach to Solving Transportation-Related Problems

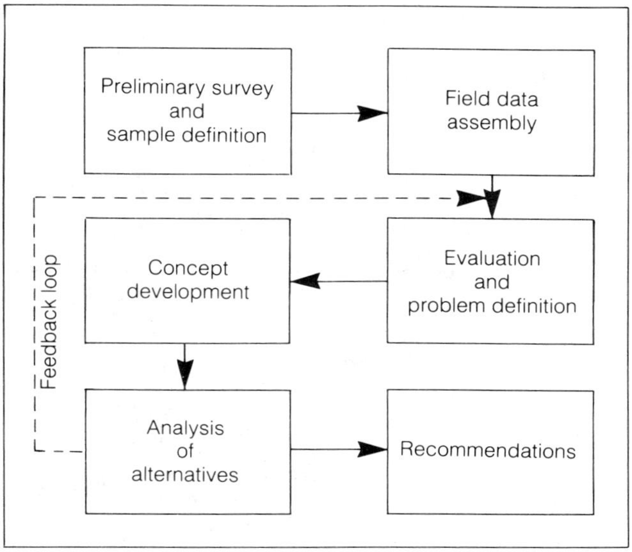

```
Preliminary survey         Field data
and                  →     assembly
sample definition                
        ┌ - - - - - - - - - - - ↑
        │                       │
Feedback│  Concept        Evaluation
loop    │  development ←  and
        │                 problem definition
        │       │
        │       ↓
        │  Analysis
        └→ of          →  Recommendations
           alternatives
```

Source: Michael Heschel, "Developing Cost-Effective Transportation," *Transportation and Distribution Management* 15, no. 6 (November/December, 1975): 31.

for any firm that has adopted the integrated physical distribution management concept, the overall objective of the approach presented in Figure 5-2 was to obtain the optimal cost-service mix for the company. As a result of their analyses, FMC was able to identify:

Important operations.

Areas with high freight patterns.

Freight quantities and patterns by plant.

Common freight areas for plants.

Modes of transportation and tonnage by plant and location.

Inbound and outbound area, locations for potential backhaul.

Tonnage by type of product.[2]

The knowledge gained by FMC allowed the company to reduce overall transportation costs through the use of increased consolidations, piggyback routings, common pickup and delivery, traffic department reorganizations, changes in the operations of the firm's private fleet, and more effective packaging.

*The Bill of Lading Is the Basic Shipping Document*

Figure 5-3 illustrates the source and type of data which a firm can accumulate to examine the cost-effectiveness of their transportation system. As shown in the figure, the bill of lading provides much of the needed

[2] Ibid., p. 33.

**FIGURE 5-3** Elements of a Shipment File

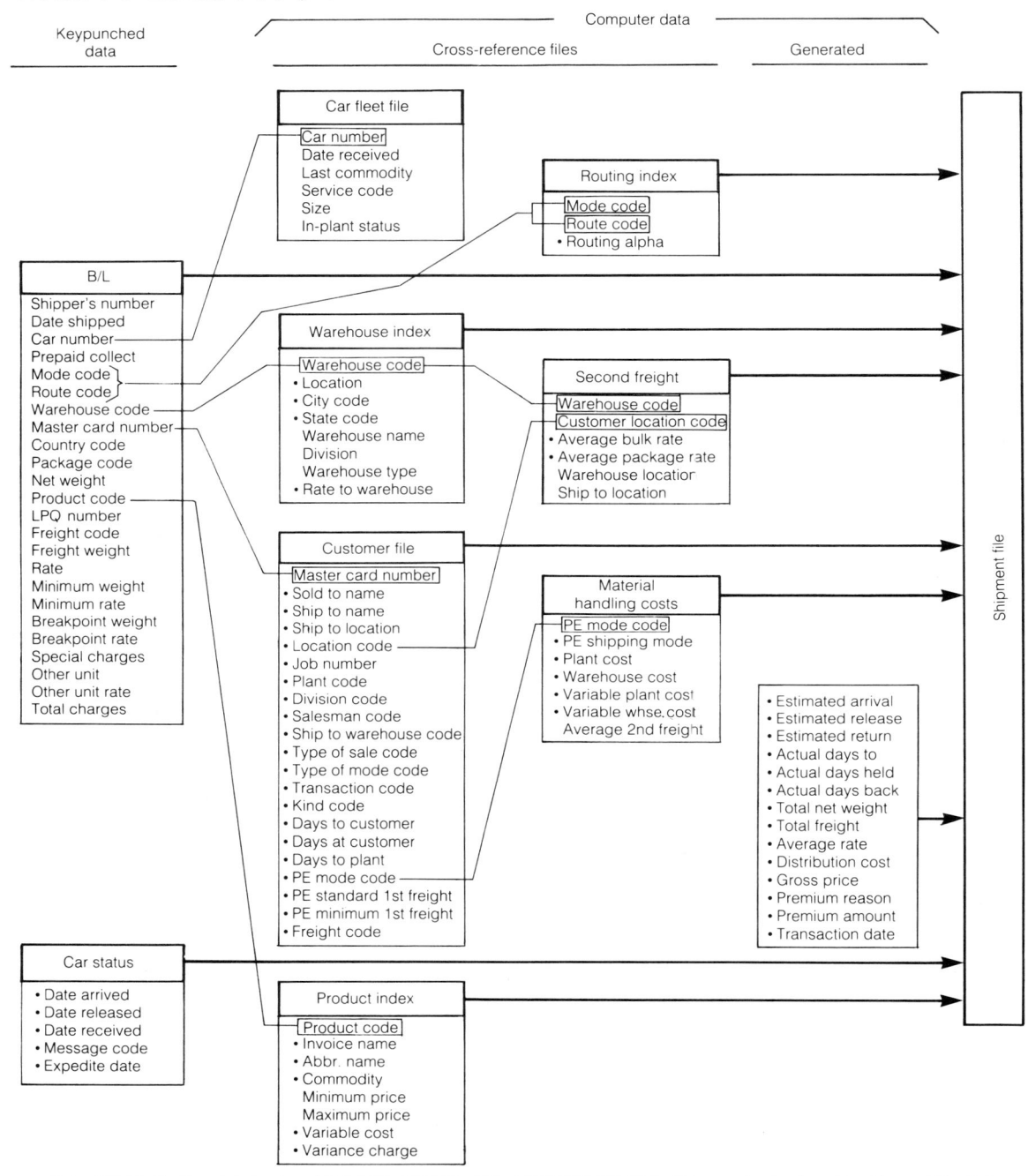

| Keypunched data | Cross-reference files | Generated |
|---|---|---|

**Car fleet file**
- Car number
- Date received
- Last commodity
- Service code
- Size
- In-plant status

**Routing index**
- Mode code
- Route code
- Routing alpha

**B/L**
- Shipper's number
- Date shipped
- Car number
- Prepaid collect
- Mode code
- Route code
- Warehouse code
- Master card number
- Country code
- Package code
- Net weight
- Product code
- LPQ number
- Freight code
- Freight weight
- Rate
- Minimum weight
- Minimum rate
- Breakpoint weight
- Breakpoint rate
- Special charges
- Other unit
- Other unit rate
- Total charges

**Warehouse index**
- Warehouse code
- Location
- City code
- State code
- Warehouse name
- Division
- Warehouse type
- Rate to warehouse

**Second freight**
- Warehouse code
- Customer location code
- Average bulk rate
- Average package rate
- Warehouse location
- Ship to location

**Customer file**
- Master card number
- Sold to name
- Ship to name
- Ship to location
- Location code
- Job number
- Plant code
- Division code
- Salesman code
- Ship to warehouse code
- Type of sale code
- Type of mode code
- Transaction code
- Kind code
- Days to customer
- Days at customer
- Days to plant
- PE mode code
- PE standard 1st freight
- PE minimum 1st freight
- Freight code

**Material handling costs**
- PE mode code
- PE shipping mode
- Plant cost
- Warehouse cost
- Variable plant cost
- Variable whse. cost
- Average 2nd freight

- Estimated arrival
- Estimated release
- Estimated return
- Actual days to
- Actual days held
- Actual days back
- Total net weight
- Total freight
- Average rate
- Distribution cost
- Gross price
- Premium reason
- Premium amount
- Transaction date

**Car status**
- Date arrived
- Date released
- Date received
- Message code
- Expedite date

**Product index**
- Product code
- Invoice name
- Abbr. name
- Commodity
  Minimum price
  Maximum price
- Variable cost
- Variance charge

→ Shipment file

Note: All bill of lading data is placed in the shipment file. Only asterisked data from other sources is placed in shipment file. Balance of data is for manual reference or report purposes.

Source: Michael Schiff, *Accounting and Control in Physical Distribution* (Chicago: National Council of Physical Distribution Management, 1972), p. 4-66.

information.[3] The system was designed for a company engaged in manufacturing industrial consumables but it could be used by almost any manufacturing operation. As evidenced by Figure 5–3, a large amount of specific cost data is needed. The system is based on standards or norms for each of the company's product moves. The standards were defined as the "least cost, most practical movement, of a product to a customer destination."[4]

On a regular basis, the company examined computer-generated reports on shipment performance relative to standard. As a result they were able to pinpoint those shipments which were moving at less-than-optimal levels. A summary of the benefits directly attributable to the system developed by the company can be summarized as follows:

> Customer service has benefitted from the distribution cost reporting system. By having distribution cost figures readily available, alternate distribution patterns have been developed to improve service, at no additional cost.
>
> Close inspection and audit of exception and standard reports since the system became operational have effected substantial savings in fringe areas. These have been in (1) identifying excessive charges by carriers, (2) identifying charges incorrectly paid by the company, rather than the recipient, and (3) identifying and taking corrective action on extra freight charges such as weekend charges, charges for auxiliary equipment, and demurrage.
>
> In order to gain Marketing's cooperation in an effort to reduce distribution costs, the information contained in the freight standard and exception reporting system was displayed in a different format that was of value to Marketing, to help achieve the foregoing beneficial results.
>
> The sequence of the Freight Standards Report was changed to show, for each product, the customers in ascending order of freight costs. In the case of products sold on a delivered basis, it made relative return of the same product to various customers apparent to Marketing product groups. With this information, the cooperation of Marketing was gained in the areas of customer selection and service levels. With the interest developed in Marketing in the area of distribution costs, further gains were made by supplying more freight information. Freight rates were furnished to Marketing product groups for those customers that were not ordering in the most economical size or mode of shipment. Progress has been made, and continues to be made, by Marketing to change customer order patterns to the most economical distribution means.[5]

All firms must have an understanding of the cost elements of their transportation system. That understanding allows the company to identify opportunities for improvements in distribution costs and/or customer service. It also allows a firm to establish distribution cost performance measures which are needed to evaluate the transportation system. The specific costs, or the forms in which they are collected, may vary by firm depending upon

---

[3] The bill of lading is the basic document used when shipping by common carrier. The bill of lading (B/L) performs three functions: It (1) is a receipt for the shipment; (2) contains the contract specifying the obligations of the carrier and the shipper; and (3) serves as evidence of title for the goods being shipped.

[4] Michael Schiff, *Accounting and Control in Physical Distribution* (Chicago: National Council of Physical Distribution Management, 1972), p. 4–65 (hereafter cited as NCPDM).

[5] Ibid., p. 4–69.

the markets served, the product line, and the level of customer service provided; however, they are absolutely vital to the physical distribution executive administering the transportation function.

## THE TRANSPORTATION MODE SELECTION DECISION

During the past several years the traffic manager has been faced with an economic situation characterized by uncertainty, inflation, energy shortages, materials shortages, and the profit squeeze.[6] The role of the traffic manager has expanded considerably during this period as the importance of the logistics function has been recognized by a larger number of companies. Commensurate with this expanded role and in conjunction with the era of uncertainty which has existed, the importance of making the right traffic decisions has increased considerably.

From a corporate standpoint the era of uncertainty has made wrong traffic decisions much more costly in terms of lost sales, profits, and customer goodwill. From a societal standpoint these decisions have sometimes had adverse impacts on energy, pollution, and other such global problems. As an example of a traffic decision which has had significant impact on the firm and society, especially when the wrong decision has been made, is the mode-choice selection decision.

Existing economic and resource constraints necessitate that the most efficient and productive mode-choice decisions be made by every firm. Because of the impact of transportation mode choice on customer service, time-in-transit, consistency, inventories, packaging, warehousing, energy consumption, pollution caused by transportation, and other factors, transportation decision makers must develop the best possible mode strategies. Because managers have not been faced with the decisions of selecting between modes, except infrequently, a knowledge of the process underlying such a decision becomes extremely important.

*A Model of Transportation Mode Selection*

In a study of 357 shippers, James Stock and Bernard LaLonde were able to model the mode-selection decision process and to identify the factors which influenced the selection of a particular mode or modes. The model developed is shown in Figure 5–4. It was discovered that four separate and distinct decision stages occurred in the mode-selection decision: (1) problem recognition, (2) search process, (3) choice process, and (4) postchoice evaluation.

### Problem Recognition

As shown in Figure 5–4, the problem-recognition stage of the mode-choice process was triggered by a variety of factors such as customer orders, dissatisfaction with an existing mode, changes in the distribution patterns of the firm, and many others. Examples of factors which could stimulate the problem-recognition stage were presented to respondents. Traffic managers

---

[6] This discussion draws upon James R. Stock and Bernard J. LaLonde, "The Transportation Mode Decision Revisited," *Transportation Journal* 17, no. 2 (Winter 1977): 51–59.

**FIGURE 5-4** Mode Selection Decision Model

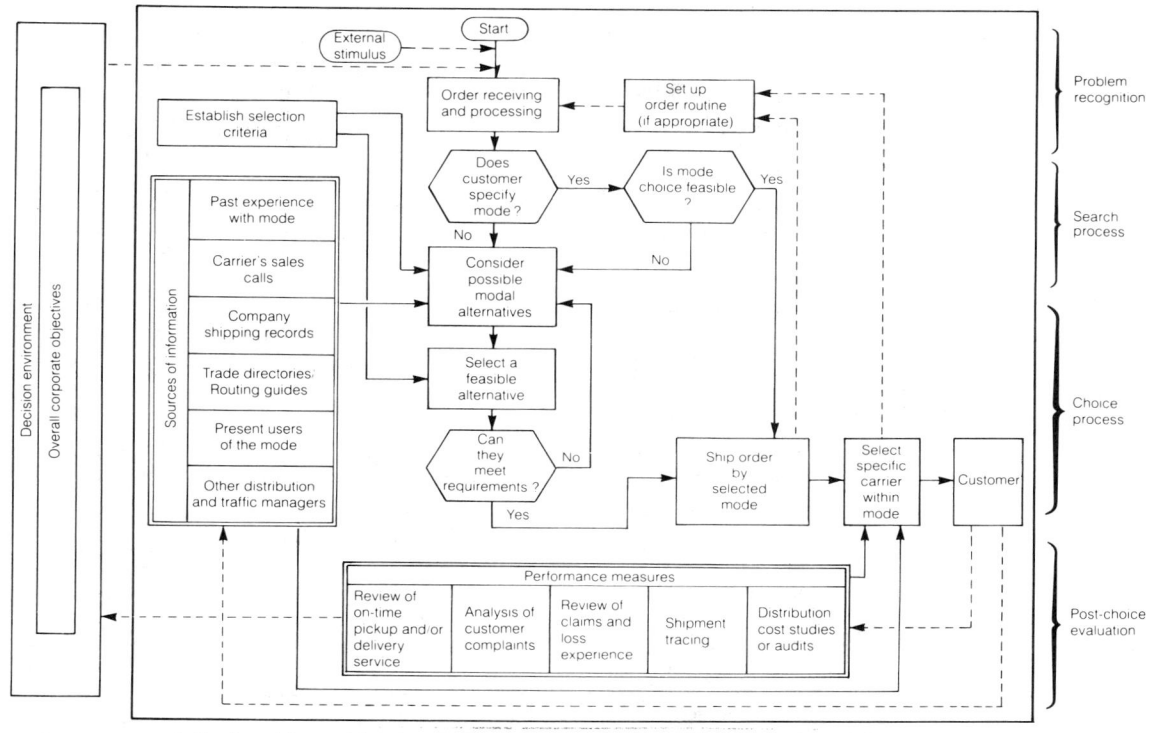

Source: James R. Stock and Bernard J. LaLonde, "The Transportation Mode Decision Revisited," *Transportation Journal* 17, no. 2 (Winter 1977):53. Material from the *Transportation Journal* is used with the express permission of the American Society of Traffic and Transportation, Inc.

were asked to rate the items from zero (0) to 100 with the most important and least important factors given the highest and lowest scores respectively. All other factors were assigned scores between the extreme points. Table 5−1 shows the mean importance scores for various situations or factors which could cause firms to alter modal patterns, such as change modes, select new modes, or shift traffic between modes. As evidenced by Table 5−2, customer service factors rated highest. Once the problem-recognition stage has been entered into by the traffic and/or distribution manager, an order routine is followed, if appropriate, for the decision process continues to a search stage. For those cases where the customer does not specify the mode, a search is undertaken for a feasible transportation alternative.

### Search Process

A variety of information sources are scanned by the traffic manager to be used as inputs into the mode-choice process. A number of possible sources are presented in Figure 5−4 and Table 5−2.

The extent of the search process may be minimal if the decision maker uses only past experience as an information source. As more sources of

**TABLE 5-1** Factors Causing Firms to Switch to Another Transportation Mode

| Situation | Mean Importance Score |
|---|---|
| Desire to improve customer service | 84.4 |
| Deterioration of service provided by mode | 79.8 |
| Desire to reduce overall distribution costs | 77.2 |
| Poor pickup and delivery by an existing mode | 76.3 |
| Customer complaints | 76.1 |
| Desire to reduce transit time | 72.2 |
| Changing needs of customers | 64.7 |
| Unsatisfactory claims and/or loss experience | 63.5 |
| Expansion to new market territories or elimination of old markets | 53.5 |
| Solve emergency conditions | 48.6 |
| Existing modes unable to provide additional services | 48.4 |
| Irritation caused by a change in the operational procedures of a mode | 47.9 |
| Development of new product requiring different modes | 42.6 |
| Change in company's geographical distribution plans | 42.2 |
| Changes in corporate transportation policy | 37.6 |
| Increases in traffic volume exceeded present modal capacity or flexibility | 36.1 |
| Packaging cost reduction | 35.7 |
| Desire to distribute existing traffic volume among a larger/smaller number of modes | 30.5 |
| Contact with carrier salesmen | 28.7 |

Source: James R. Stock and Bernard J. LaLonde, "The Transportation Mode Decision Revisited," *Transportation Journal* 17, no. 2 (Winter 1977):54. Material from the *Transportation Journal* is used with the express permission of the American Society of Traffic and Transportation, Inc.

**TABLE 5-2** Value Scores for Sources of Information about Modes

| Information Source | Mean Importance Score |
|---|---|
| Past experience with mode | 83.4 |
| Carrier's sales calls | 61.7 |
| Company shipping records | 61.1 |
| Trade directories/routing guides | 49.8 |
| Present users of the mode | 47.2 |
| Other distribution and traffic managers | 46.9 |
| Present or potential customers of the firm | 44.1 |
| Marketing/sales department | 39.4 |
| Trade magazines and journals | 32.1 |
| Local traffic clubs | 26.0 |
| Tariff bureaus | 24.4 |
| Direct mail advertising | 23.0 |
| Local or national newspapers and magazines | 19.6 |
| Accounting and finance department | 16.5 |
| Outside consultants | 13.5 |
| Yellow pages | 8.8 |

Source: James R. Stock and Bernard J. LaLonde, "The Transportation Mode Decision Revisited," *Transportation Journal* 17, no. 2 (Winter 1977): 55. Material from the *Transportation Journal* is used with the express permission of the American Society of Traffic and Transportation, Inc.

information are cited, however, the time expended in the search process may be considerable. At the point where a sufficient number of sources have been examined to satisfy the traffic manager's requirements for information, the decision becomes one of using the information obtained to select a particular modal alternative.

**Choice Process**

The task facing the traffic manager at this stage is to decide upon a feasible alternative among the several modes available. Using those information sources considered relevant and which are available, the manager determines which of the available modes can meet the requirements of shipment. Generally, service related factors are the major determinants of mode choice. Table 5–3 identifies a number of selection criteria used in the

**TABLE 5–3** Selection Criteria Used to Evaluate Mode Choices

| Selection Criteria | Mean Importance Score |
|---|---|
| Consistent, on-time pickup and delivery | 92.4 |
| Freight charges | 79.8 |
| Time-in-transit | 79.1 |
| Points served by mode, including routing authority | 73.9 |
| Frequency of service | 72.1 |
| Loss and/or damage history | 69.2 |
| Timely acceptance of shipments of all sizes | 65.6 |
| Door-to-door delivery | 61.9 |
| Shipment tracing capability | 61.8 |
| Prompt claim service | 60.8 |
| Adaptability to specific company needs | 53.5 |
| Availability of standard equipment | 50.6 |
| Serviceability at off-line points | 50.2 |
| Local reputation of carrier firm(s) | 47.1 |
| Availability of special equipment and services | 41.0 |
| Possible future rate increases by mode due to higher fuel costs | 36.2 |
| Information services offered | 35.0 |
| Consolidation and/or breakbulk services | 33.9 |
| Vulnerability of mode to current or future energy/ecology problems | 25.1 |
| Competence of solicitors | 24.5 |
| Acceptability by other organization members | 22.6 |
| Energy efficiency (e.g., fuel economy) of mode | 21.1 |
| Environmental impact(s) of mode | 11.7 |

Source: James R. Stock and Bernard J. LaLonde, "The Transportation Mode Decision Revisited," *Transportation Journal* 17, no. 2 (Winter 1977):56. Material from the *Transportation Journal* is used with the express permission of the American Society of Traffic and Transportation, Inc.

evaluation of a mode. As the recent transportation literature has suggested, and evidenced by Table 5–3, consistency of service has become the most important single criterion for evaluating modal alternatives. The mode which best satisfies the traffic manager's decision criteria is then selected and the shipment is routed via that mode. In those cases where a similar decision may occur in the future, such as with a repeat order from a customer, an order routine may be established so that the same mode-choice decision will not have to be repeated. Order routines eliminate the inefficiencies associated with making the same decision repeatedly.

**Postchoice Evaluation**

Once the mode and carrier choice has been completed, some procedure of evaluation is employed to determine the performance level of the mode/carrier. Depending upon the individual firm, the postchoice evaluation process may be nonexistent or extremely detailed. For the majority of firms, the degree of postchoice evaluation lies somewhere between the two extremes. It is the rate company that does not at least respond to customer complaints about modes/carriers and this is one form of postchoice evaluation. Many firms use more sophisticated techniques such as cost studies and audits. Respondent firms are asked to identify and indicate the importance of procedures used by them in evaluating mode performance. Table 5−4

**TABLE 5-4** Procedures Used by Firms in Evaluating Mode Performance

| Procedures Used to Evaluate Modal Performance | Mean Importance Score |
|---|---|
| Review of on-time performance of delivery service | 82.1 |
| Review of on-time performance of pickup service | 80.8 |
| Analysis of customer complaints | 72.9 |
| Review of claims and loss experience (including claims handling) | 56.8 |
| Shipment tracing | 49.6 |
| Distribution cost studies or audits | 41.7 |

Source: James R. Stock and Bernard J. LaLonde, "The Transportation Mode Decision Revisited," *Transportation Journal* 17, no. 2 (Winter 1977):57. Material from the *Transportation Journal* is used with the express permission of the American Society of Traffic and Transportation, Inc.

reveals the importance of several procedures. In some cases, these evaluative procedures may lead to the problem-recognition stage if the mode and/or carrier is performing unsatisfactorily. Firms which primarily used private carriage also employed many of these evaluative procedures as part of their self-evaluation.

As shown in Figure 5−4 an integral part of the mode-choice model is the feedback mechanism. In addition to performance measures providing one method of information feedback, feedback can occur from other sources. The decision environment which lies external to the modal-selection decision also provides inputs into the process such as sales personnel feedback, interdepartmental communications, etc. The feedback can be used as input an any point in the model as evidenced in Figure 5−4. The importance of the feedback mechanism is that it occurs concurrently and independently of performance measures. The mode-choice decision is a universal process in that while the factors entering into the process may vary across national boundaries, the basic structure remains consistent irrespective of these differences. Therefore, the model of mode choice illustrated in Figure 5−4 can be applied in any situation, domestic or international, which requires that a transportation mode choice be made.

## SHIPPER RESPONSE TO TRANSPORTATION REGULATORY REFORM

The specific transportation regulatory reforms affecting the motor, rail, and air cargo sectors were discussed in Chapter 4. In this section the response—current and forecasted—of the shipper community is presented. Some of the responses have had, or will have, substantial impact on the mode-selection decision.

### Response to Motor Carrier Reforms

Three major areas of shipper response include: (1) organization and systems realignments; (2) freight volume opportunity development programs (distribution, marketing, production/purchasing/packaging); and (3) private trucking operations.[7] An outline of shipper response in each area is provided below:

I. Organization and systems realignments.
   A. Assignment of key executive responsibility for development of regulatory reform strategies.
   B. Problems identifying distribution requirements in terms of total landed costs and service levels:
      1. Develop product-distribution profiles by product and market.
      2. Compare requirements with regulatory reforms to identify impacts on your distribution operations.
      3. Develop distribution monitoring system:
         a. To provide repetitive cost/service profiles.
         b. To test system alternatives.
      4. Provide top management with an initial estimate of the potential costs of regulatory reform.
      5. Measure actual service received from major carriers; identify all the freight your firm is moving by each carrier—to provide negotiating leverage.
      6. Appoint a carrier negotiator.
II. Freight volume opportunity development programs.
   A. Distribution:
      1. Evaluate shipper associations.
      2. Pursue innovative consolidation programs.
      3. Devise warehouse options to shorten LTL final shipping distances.

---

[7] Paul E. Fulchino and George T. Mauro, "Reform Impacts and Strategic Shipper Responses," in *Proceedings of the Eighteenth Annual Conference of the National Council of Physical Distribution Management, October 13–15, 1980*, p. 372.

B. Marketing:
   1. Evaluate dropping of small-volume products or markets.
   2. Focus management attention on volume products and markets.
   3. Establish volume-order discounts.
   4. Relax service standards.
   5. Revise terms of freight.
   6. Consult with customers to smooth their order patterns.
C. Production/purchasing/packaging:
   1. Make sure site-selection programs consider new transportation environment's cost and service realities.
   2. Include raw materials in regulatory response programs.
   3. Consider receiver associations for consolidating inbound freight.
   4. Evaluate packaging concepts and loading facilities to increase shipment sizes and reduce carrier waiting times.

III. Private trucking operations (PTO).
   A. Reevaluate benefits available from establishing a PTO.
   B. Establish accurate PTO cost and operations monitoring system.
   C. Evaluate PTO opportunities to service rural markets on backhauls.
   D. Contact contract carriers to solicit price/service opportunities that may affect your actual or proposed PTO.
   E. Contact other PTOs that might be interested in your freight as a backhaul.[8]

## Response to Rail Carrier Reforms

As a result of rail carrier regulatory reforms a number of shipper responses are possible. These responses can be grouped into five major categories: (1) ascertaining the cost structure of servicing railroads; (2) individual rate making; (3) service contracts (to guarantee service reliability and to increase control); (4) insurance coverage for cargo; and (5) shipper/carrier negotiations. An outline of shipper response in each area is provided below:

I. Ascertaining the cost structure of servicing railroads.
   A. Secondary source information:
      1. ICC published cost data.
      2. Association of American Railroads (AAR) indexes of railroad material prices and wage rates.
      3. ICC Rail Cost Inflation Index (required under the Staggers Act).
      4. Individual railroad data.
   B. Primary source information:
      1. Data gathered from customers of your firm.
      2. Data gathered from other firms within your industry.
      3. Market research studies.
II. Individual rate making.
   A. Consider splitting shipments among railroads.
   B. Use waybills to specify routings favorable to the shipper's position.

---
[8] Ibid., pp. 372–74.

C. Consider the transportation implications of corporate decisions relating to:
    1. Plant locations.
    2. Warehousing strategies.
    3. Marketing policies.
    4. Customer relations practices.
III. Service contracts.
    A. Build individual shipment or aggregate volume.
    B. Seek service "quid pro quos."
    C. Monitor ICC filings for innovative provisions of existing contracts that might be adopted.
    D. Incorporate incentives/penalties for nonperformance.
IV. Insurance coverage for cargo.
    A. Commercial insurance.
    B. Self-insurance.
    C. Shipper insurance cooperatives.
V. Shipper/carrier negotiations.
    A. Be prepared to negotiate.
        1. Know your carriers.
        2. Know your available options.
        3. Define your acceptable "price-service envelope."
        4. Give the negotiator the authority to make deals.
    B. Build your volume.
        1. Concentrate shipments by:
            a. Locating plants with shipment volume in mind.
            b. Developing appropriate warehousing and distribution schemes.
            c. Increasing order quantities.
        2. Consolidate shipments, perhaps using:
            a. Freight forwarders.
            b. Consolidators.
            c. Shipper associations.[9]

## Response to Air Carrier Reforms

Shipper Response to Air Carrier Reforms

Table 5–5 identifies shipper responses to three areas—rates, service, and damage liability—affected by air-cargo regulatory reform. Generally, the responses tend to reduce the negative effects of each area and involve some of the same strategies employed in response to motor and rail carrier reforms.

Undoubtedly, the preceding discussion can not include every possible strategy for responding to transportation carrier reform. There are many factors or issues which can affect future transportation decision making. The major factors are national transportation policy, economic trends, regulatory trends, and technology trends.[10] Each factor is composed of many

---
[9] Ibid., pp. 376–78.

[10] Ronald S. Potter, "Transportation Planning: An Overview," in *Proceedings of the Eighteenth Annual Conference of the National Council of Physical Distribution Management, October 13–15, 1980*, pp. 228–33.

**TABLE 5-5** Shipper Responses to Three Areas Affected by Air-Cargo Reform

| Rates | Service | Damage Liability |
|---|---|---|
| Use freight forwarders | Ship through major hubs | Self-insure |
| Truck to major hubs | Negotiate with carriers for requirements | Form insurance cooperatives with other shippers |
| Plan shipments for nonprime time | | |
| Consolidate shipments for volume discounts | | |

Source: Paul E. Fulchino and George T. Mauro, "Reform Impacts and Strategic Shipper Responses," in *Proceedings of the Eighteenth Annual Conference of the National Council of Physical Distribution Management*, October 13–15, 1980, p. 379.

subelements which must be considered by shipper firms as they make the myriad of transportation decisions that comprise their strategic physical distribution plan. A summary of each factor and subelements is provided in Appendix A.

## THE PRIVATE VERSUS FOR-HIRE DECISION

*The Make-or-Buy Decision in Transportation*

A furniture manufacturer ships 85–90 percent of its finished goods by private trucks even though it can only generate backhauls on 10 percent of its runs. The company could utilize specialized furniture carriers or general commodity common carriers. The common carriers discourage the business through lack of equipment and extensive transit times because rates are too low to make furniture transport profitable. Specialized carriers provide lower rates, but service is much worse. The specialized carriers charge lower rates by consolidating small shipments to a single city area. As a result, transportation times increase drastically. Since the furniture company wants more timely service, even at higher cost, it opts to enter private carriage.

An Oregon manufacturer of kraft paper bags sells the products in the San Francisco area. Competitors offer fast deliveries of small orders. To meet the competition, the company ships by private carriage at the expense of 35 percent higher costs and empty backhauls. The company claims that inconsistent common carrier service is not capable of meeting competition. The common carrier cannot supply the service profitably under the present regulatory structure. Thus the company is forced to use private carriage.

An industrial-machinery manufacturer lowers transport costs by utilizing private carriers. Most of its shipments are LTL (less-than-carload lots) and would be subject to high common carrier rates. In shipping via private carrier, the company relaxes transport times to gain high equipment use and consolidate shipments.[11]

[11] Case examples adapted from Robert M. Sutton, Donald W. Weitz, and Ronald S. Potter, *Case Studies of Private Motor Carriage*, Report No. DOT-OS-30017 (Washington, D.C.: U.S. Government Printing Office, November 1973).

There can be a variety of reasons underlying a firm's decision to utilize private carriage in lieu of for-hire carriage. George Agamemnon, a retired distribution executive from Burlington Industries, was quoted in *Handling & Shipping* as follows:

> . . . if you are at that point of considering private trucking[12] as your next move, your prime motivation will be to seek a better transit service for distribution of your customer shipments than you now experience. if financial gain is your motivation, be very careful, it isn't always available. Many shippers have engaged in private trucking to their benefit; others, unfortunately, to their dismay . . . the move to private carriage is fraught with decision making. There are many pros and cons.[13]

Some of the more frequently mentioned pros and cons of private carriage are shown in Table 5–6.

Private carriage should not be viewed strictly as a transportation decision; rather, it is also a financial decision. There are two stages in evaluating the financial considerations of private carriage. The first involves an evaluation or comparison of current cost and service data of the firm's for-hire carriers with that of a private carrier operation.

The feasibility study should begin with the evaluation of the current transportation situation along with corporate objectives toward potential future market expansion. Objectives should include a statement outlining historical, current, and desired service levels as well as environment issues such as legal restrictions and the general trend of the economy.

A suggested outline which organizes the 10 steps that one must take to fully evaluate problems in distribution and develop alternatives to solve those problems follows:

*Ten Steps in the Evaluation of Private Carriage*

1. Define the problem.
2. Develop transport objectives.
3. Collect pertinent information.
4. Determine present cost.
5. Analyze present operations.
6. Develop alternatives.
7. Determine private fleet cost.
8. Consider indirect factors.
9. Summarize alternatives.
10. Make the decision.[14]

### Define the Problem

Difficulties can originate from any one or more members of the transportation system—customer, carrier, and/or shipper. Does the customer re-

---

[12] Many authors use the terms *private carriage* and *private trucking* interchangeably because the overwhelming majority of shipments made by private carriers involve the use of owned or leased trucks.

[13] H. G. Becker, Jr., "Private Carriage: Facts and Trends, Some Reasons Why," *Handling & Shipping* 17, no. 7 (July 1976): 24.

[14] See Barrie Vreeland, *Private Trucking From A to Z* (New York: Commerce and Industry Association Institute, 1968), p. 6.

**TABLE 5-6** Advantages and Disadvantages Associated with Private Trucking

Advantages
    New market availability
    Reduced inventory levels
    Quality service
    Immediate help in emergencies
    Less or no packing requirements
    Ability to meet customer demands
    Control of freight enroute
    More security
    Advertising on equipment
    Private trailers serve as warehouses
    Ease of tracing
    Reduced loss and damage claims
    Overall cost should be lower
    Hedge against truck strikes
    Sales advantages
    Return on investment
    Control of routing
    Flexibility
    Control and supervision of labor
    Consolidations from many plants to same customer
    Seven-day operations
    Cost controls
    Train own personnel to meet needs

Disadvantages
    Cost of administrative overhead
    Substantial capital investment
    Costly equipment maintenance if not on full-maintenance lease
    DOT safety requirements
    Seasonal fluctuations in traffic
    Labor problems, if unionized
    Full cost responsibility on loss and damage to product
    Private carriage schedules are rather difficult to plan
    Taxes, fuel, and other such
    Cash-flow problems
    Purchasing problems
    Lease versus ownership
    Hazardous-materials regulations
    Injury to relations with motor common carrier
    Licensing problems
    Reciprocity problems
    Use of and contracting for cartage agents
    Need for specialized equipment
    Changes in sales terms
    Insurance coverage, cargo and equipment
    Accident reporting and handling

Source: H. G. Becker, Jr., "Private Carriage: Facts and Trends, Some Reasons Why," *Handling & Shipping*, 17, no. 7 (July 1976): 24–25.

ceive adequate service, undamaged goods, on time, and at a reasonable cost? Does the carrier have the required route flexibility and operational capability to deliver the product economically? Do volumes prevent delivery of the desired service level at a competitive price? Does the carrier's equipment and facilities meet the requirements of the channel members? The problem may also arise from the seller's operation—facility and dock equipment may be overburdened or underutilized, the company may be responsible for management and scheduling problems, or simply have a poor logistics system.

### Develop Transport Objectives

These objectives should center around two measures. The first, customer-service level—delivery consistent and fast as well as additional services which may be required. The second should focus upon the firm's cost objectives for the total distribution process—order processing, communications, warehousing, inventory, transportation, and the return of damaged goods. Goals should be established for each of these functions in both effectiveness and efficiency.

### Collect Pertinent Information

This requires the gathering of data which is relevant to the three parties involved. Inventory data and shipping procedures, product characteristics, origin and destination, volumes and weight, and cost associated with the shipment of the products. From the customer's viewpoint, one should look at complaints received, quantifiable service-level data, and competitive actions.

### Determine Present Cost

It is necessary to use a total cost approach which not only determines the cost of transportation but encompasses the total distribution network. The determination of operating cost should include the cost of order processing, packaging, shipping, transportation, and the expense attributed to damaged goods and returns. In addition, the current cost of inventory-investment, insurance, taxes, inventory risk, and building cost directly associated with the inventory function should be included.

The determination of these current costs will serve as the point of comparison against the private trucking option or other possible alternatives.

### Analyze Present Operations

This includes the review of both the qualitative and quantitative data which has been gathered in the attempt to uncover poor cost/service relationships. This step includes the analysis of customer order patterns, transportation patterns, cyclical or seasonal variations, and potential for backhauls. Also included is the evaluation of ton-mile cost and review of specific transportation costs which exceed standard.

### Develop Alternatives

Step six begins with a review of cost and service levels of functions where a problem has been identified and suggestions of alternative courses of action to solve those problems. Three basic alternatives are almost always available in this process. They are: (1) do nothing; (2) invest the available capital in other areas of the firm which may yield an even higher return; and (3) the use of funds to improve the current system.

The improvement of distribution operations need not necessarily include the implementation of a private fleet operation but rather adjustments such as improving order processing, negotiating new carrier rates, or improving packaging—all of which may yield the same benefits of private trucking at a much lower cost.

### Determine Private Fleet Costs

All costs associated with private trucking should be accounted for as well as their effects upon the cost of the total firm. Any added savings or cost generated in inventory, personnel, or production because of the use of private trucking should be added to or deducted from the cost of this alternative. Costs for the private trucking function include equipment cost, labor cost, and other expenses such as maintenance, insurance, and vehicle taxes.

### Consider Indirect Factors

There are many nonmonetary factors that may influence the decision to go to a private trucking operation. They include company image, advantages over competition, advertising value of the trucks, the effects upon the employees and unions, the management skills required to develop and control the system, carriers' willingness to accept remaining freight, potential for rate renegotiation, and corporate policy toward equipment selection, maintenance, and replacement. Also to be included are a wide range of environmental factors not under the control of the firm such as legal (ICC), economic, and technical change.

### Summarize Alternatives

"The summary should outline the cost, capital requirements and indirect factors (advantages and disadvantages) for the present method, for an alternative improved method that would *not* be a major change to your existing operation, and finally for a private fleet operation."[15]

### Make the Decision

The final step is to make a decision based on the summary as well as from other available inputs such as internal management, outside experts, and the experience of other firms who have had private fleets.

Despite the quantitative information available, no decision can be cut and dried. There are a large number of factors to be considered which are

---
[15] Ibid., p. 7.

left to judgment and the willingness of the decision maker to assume some level of risk.

In the discussion of the transportation-selection decision it was pointed out that a cost/benefit analysis must be performed to determine whether private trucking was to be used. Any financial analysis should consider the time value of money. The analysis of cash flows that must be performed is illustrated in Table 5 — 7. The favorable net cash inflows (cash inflows minus

**TABLE 5-7** Financial Consideration of the Decision to Switch to Private Trucking

|  | Amount |
|---|---|
| Capital requirements | |
|   Cost of buying or leasing fleet | _____ |
|   Cost of maintenance facilities | _____ |
|   Cost of terminal facilities | _____ |
| Annual cash inflows | |
|   Savings over using public carriers | _____ |
|   Reduction in lost sales | _____ |
|   Reduction in inventory carrying costs due to more efficient routing | _____ |
|     Total | _____ |
| Annual cash outflows | |
|   Fuel | _____ |
|   Labor—drivers | _____ |
|   Labor—maintenance and terminal | _____ |
|   Insurance—trucks | _____ |
|       —drivers | _____ |
|       —maintenance and terminal facilities | _____ |
|   License fees | _____ |
|   Parts supply | _____ |
|   Utilities | _____ |
|   Supervision | _____ |
|   Administrative—billing, telephone, accounting | _____ |
|     Total | _____ |
| Annual cash inflows − Annual cash outflows | _____ |

cash outflows) must be calculated for the life of the investment decision and discounted using the company's minimum acceptable rate of return on new investment. The sum of these discounted cash flows must be compared to the initial capital requirement to determine if the investment is financially sound.

Once the company has made the decision to engage in private carriage, the next step would be to devise a plan of implementation and a procedure for system control. Implementation would begin with a review of the structure of the organization or group responsible for operation of the private fleet. The activities to be performed would be assigned to groups or individuals along with a timetable for the phasing in of the project. Because of the risk involved, most firms begin with a low level of activity followed by intermediate reviews of results and subsequent modification of the plan. The process is repeated until full implementation is achieved.

In the study conducted by Robert Sutton, Donald Weitz, and Ronald Potter, companies which had recently entered into private carriage had all developed a plan which included but was not limited to the following elements:

**Implementing the Private Carriage Decision**

1. An outline and structure of the organization responsible for the overall project implementation.
2. A list of activities to be performed and the assignment of responsibilities for such performance.
3. A schedule that provides a sequence of specific events as well as the overall phasing of the program.
4. Details of the control system designed to record, report, and evaluate implementation activities.
5. A budget to include all administrative and operational costs associated with starting the operation and bringing it on stream.[16]

Control of private motor transportation should center around the measure of performance against standards with the ability to identify specific problem areas. Vreeland identified two areas of cost to be considered. Direct cost of the operation are those associated with the amount of distance traveled or ton-miles. Indirect costs are charged against the department whether the trucks run or not. To the truck manager the direct costs of operation are the only relevant ones. The transportation indirect costs are the responsibility of the distribution manager.

If one desires to use a total-cost concept in order to charge cost against the product and customer, a cost per mile may be calculated spreading fixed cost associated with distribution of the product and adding the variable cost per mile. This information may also be useful to compare budgeted against actual or the comparison of your operation to common carrier statistics and industry averages. One should recognize the limitations in the value of the information generated, however, due to the wide variations of cost and service requirements across industries and divisions within an industry.

Companies involved in private trucking must be aware of the potential problems which a private fleet can cause, especially those which impact on the firm's profitability. In a series of articles published in *Handling & Shipping*, an industrial research team from the GMC Truck and Coach Division of General Motors Corporation presented findings from a number of studies of actual truck operating and maintenance figures from fleet operations of a variety of companies.[17] The research team developed a list of eight potential problems which might cause problems for any firm engaged in private trucking:

---

[16] Sutton et al., *Case Studies*, p. 15.

[17] See "Profit Leaks in Truck Transportation," *Handling & Shipping* 18, nos. 10 and 11 (October and November 1977), and 19, nos. 3, 4, 5, and 6 (March, April, May, and June 1978).

Eight Profit Leaks in Truck Transportation

1. Lack of exacting vehicle selection.
2. Lack of attention by top management.
3. Lack of planned vehicle replacement.
4. Lack of analysis of useful records.
5. Lack of strong maintenance policies.
6. Lack of clear performance standards.
7. Lack of skillful dispatching.
8. The human factor (hiring, firing, leasing, and training).

Problems in one or more of the eight areas might result in lower corporate profitability for the firm.

## LEASING

In a study conducted by Sutton, Weitz, and Potter of 10 manufacturers in selected industries, 9 of the 10 leased all or part of their fleets. The study also found that tractor leasing was more common than trailer leasing. Several factors were mentioned for this practice:

Evaluating the Leasing Decision

1. Investment in a trailer is significantly less than the investment in a tractor.
2. The trailer life is typically several years longer than the tractor life.
3. Trailers require a minimal amount of maintenance.
4. Much of the maintenance associated with trailer ownership is not covered under full-service lease agreements, since it results from damage associated with loading and unloading.[18]

Leasing also seems particularly attractive to a new fleet operation as it provides ease of entry and predictable-cost and service levels. In contracting for the use of a full-service fleet, inexperienced management can know exactly the cost for transportation services and budget accordingly. Sutton, Weitz, and Potter revealed evidence which supported the idea that as the firm's truck operation matures and management skills improve, there is a trend away from leasing toward the total ownership of fleet equipment. Table 5–8 contains terms commonly used in leasing.

Other advantages of leasing include the possibility of the adjustment of vehicle resources for business cycles and seasonality through special lease agreements. Also, if the fleet is to be small, the avoidance of investing in maintenance equipment and facilities for so small a number of vehicles should be a consideration. A final consideration is that of transportation obsolesence either by the fact that new technology has improved the vehicles or because the firm has outgrown its distribution and transportation system.

Private truck ownership may be preferred if capital is available and it can be shown that vehicle investment will yield a favorable return. Included in this analysis would be the tax advantages of depreciation, interest, and

---

[18] Sutton et al., *Case Studies*, p. 20.

**TABLE 5-8** The Language of Leasing

The DM or TM who finds himself hurled into the center of the lease versus buy question can quickly sink beneath the waves of terminology involved with leasing.

Here, in brief, are some of the words he'll have to command, along with their definitions.

*Lease*—A term financing arrangement in which a company (the lessee) has unrestricted use of specified equipment owned by a financing organization (the lessor). The lessee makes scheduled payments to the lessor, usually for terms of three to eight years. At the end of the lease term, the equipment can either be purchased, returned to the lessor, or leased again, depending on contract specifications.

*Capital lease*—According to standards set by the Financial Accounting Standards Board, a capital lease is one that transfers ownership benefits and risks from the lessor to the lessee, either through the value of lease payments or the length of the lease term. For accounting purposes, a capital lease must be capitalized on the equipment user's balance sheet as an asset offset with a liability and amortized.

*Operating lease*—For accounting purposes, any lease that does not qualify as a capital lease.

*Chattel mortgage*—An instrument by which the borrower (mortgagor) legally owns the equipment but gives the lender (mortgagee) a lien on this property as security for the financing. The borrower's use of the property is unimpaired, and once the obligation is repaid, the lien is removed.

*Leveraged lease*—This method normally is used for acquiring equipment costing $1 million or more. The owner/lessor forms a syndicate of outside investors that provides the major portion of the equipment cost (usually 70 to 80 percent); the lessor provides the remainder. Outside investors receive a return on their investment and the lessor receives the full value of tax and depreciation on the equipment. The lessee enjoys lower-cost financing because only the outside investor portion has to be repaid. Leveraged leases generally have initial terms of seven years or longer.

*Master lease*—A blanket agreement that offers predetermined terms and conditions for multiple-equipment deliveries over a given period of time. Each new equipment acquisition does not require a new contract.

*Sale and leaseback*—A company sells its equipment to a financing organization, then leases it back and uses it while repaying the debt.

*Asset-based finance*—A secured lending arrangement such as equipment finance wherein funding is secured by an underlying asset.

*Bargain purchase option*—A clause in some contracts that gives the lessee the opportunity to buy the equipment at a specific time, so inexpensively that it is likely to be exercised.

*Bargain renewal option*—A clause in a contract that allows the lessee to extend the lease term at a significant reduction in payments. Again, this option is likely to be exercised by the lessee.

*Depreciation*—The amount of equipment cost allowed by the Internal Revenue Service as a deductible expense.

*Dry lease*—This term originated in aircraft leasing where a dry lease provided only financing while a wet lease provided fuel and maintenance services as well.

**TABLE 5–8** *(continued)*

*Equipment finance*—An umbrella term that encompasses leasing and related financing methods such as chattel mortgages, sale and lease-backs, and security agreements, equipment finance vehicles provide fixed-rate financing over medium or extended terms.

*Estimated economic life*—Also called *useful life.* An objective evaluation of how long a piece of equipment will be functional, based on stated expected use and care by the lessee.

*Estimated residual value*—What is believed at the leases' inception will be the fair value of the property at the lease's end.

*Fair value*—The price for which leased equipment could be sold in a transaction between unrelated parties. This can be determined by independent appraisal or "arm's length" negotiation between buyer and seller.

*Full payout lease*—A lease in which the cash flow returns to the lessor: (1) the asset's acquisition cost; (2) the cost of financing; (3) overhead, and (4) an acceptable return on investment.

*Nonpayout lease*—A lease in which the lessor depends upon an unguaranteed future value of the equipment to earn an acceptable return on its investment.

*Lessee's incremental borrowing rate*—The interest rate the lessee would have paid on similar term-debt financing for the leased equipment.

Source: Tom Dulaney, "The Lease Vs. Buy Question," *Distribution* 79, no. 2 (February 1980):34.

investment tax credit. Other advantages might include the ability to buy needed equipment at a discounted cost through reprocity, the utilization of currently owned maintenance equipment and facilities, increased flexibility and freedom of utilization, and potential to provide special customer services that the lessor would not allow.

### EVALUATION OF MODE/CARRIER PERFORMANCE

Successful administration of the traffic function requires that day-to-day performance of for-hire carriers and private carriage be measured and controlled. Operating standards in terms of speed of service, size of order shipped, on-time delivery, transit time variability, and damage must be established and individual carrier performance must be measured. In cases where performance standards are not being met, corrective action must be taken.

In a survey of members of the National Council of Physical Distribution Management, Douglas Lambert and James Stock asked senior physical distribution executives to report on mode usage by their firms and how carrier performance was measured. The largest single group of firms were in the packaged goods industry. Of the firms surveyed, 93 percent used common or contract motor carriage. The next most commonly used modes were UPS/Parcel Post (69 percent), common carrier rail (67 percent) and private carrier (63 percent).

**Carrier Performance Measurement Is Vital**

The data that were used to measure transportation performance are summarized in Table 5−9. Those data that appear on a formal report are shown in Table 5−10. By comparing the responses in Tables 5−9 and 5−10, it becomes apparent that most carrier performance measurement is

**TABLE 5−9** Data Used to Evaluate Transportation Performance (percent response, N = 363)

| Data | Do Not Use | Presently Using | Currently Developing | Planning to Develop within Next 18 Months |
|---|---|---|---|---|
| Common/contract Carriers | | | | |
| Damage claims | 28.6 | 65.0 | 4.7 | 1.7 |
| Transit time | 31.9 | 59.8 | 5.2 | 3.0 |
| Customer complaints | 34.9 | 59.5 | 2.8 | 2.8 |
| Shipment tracing | 37.2 | 60.1 | 1.4 | 1.4 |
| On-time delivery performance | 38.3 | 55.6 | 3.6 | 2.5 |
| Shipment expediting | 46.5 | 50.7 | 1.7 | 1.1 |
| Billing accuracy | 47.7 | 48.8 | 2.8 | 0.8 |
| Equipment availability | 51.7 | 46.0 | 1.7 | 0.6 |
| On-time pickup performance | 50.4 | 44.6 | 3.0 | 1.9 |
| Data from freight payment system | 43.3 | 47.4 | 6.9 | 2.5 |
| Equipment condition | 60.9 | 37.5 | 1.1 | 0.6 |
| Assigned rail cars | 73.0 | 26.2 | 0.6 | 0.3 |
| Sanitation | 73.8 | 23.7 | 1.9 | 0.6 |
| Postcard survey of customers | 70.8 | 22.6 | 3.0 | 3.6 |
| Cost per ton mile | 72.2 | 19.8 | 3.6 | 4.4 |
| Form letter to customer regarding performance | 83.5 | 11.3 | 1.9 | 3.3 |
| Utilization | 57.0 | 38.6 | 3.6 | 0.8 |
| On-time delivery performance | 63.6 | 33.6 | 1.7 | 1.1 |
| Transit time | 63.4 | 34.7 | 1.7 | 0.3 |
| Damage | 65.2 | 33.6 | 0.8 | 0.3 |
| Customer complaints | 67.8 | 30.6 | 0.8 | 0.8 |
| Cost per ton mile | 65.1 | 30.9 | 3.3 | 0.8 |
| On-time pickup performance | 72.7 | 25.1 | 1.1 | 1.1 |

accomplished on an informal basis and not by using data that appear on formal reports.

The exact format for data collection is not as important as the need to have the information available in some form.

Over the past several years, transportation measurement has evolved almost on a company by company basis. As specific problem areas were encountered and needs were perceived, measures were developed to address those problems and needs. It is extremely difficult to apply the term *better* to a set of measurements since this highly subjective term must be defined in terms of the importance of measurement (or the importance of the activity being measured) versus the cost of obtaining that measurement. For example, a project expenditure of several thousand dollars to develop industrial-engineered labor standards for a small (2−3 truck) private fleet might be of questionable justification.

It is possible, however, to discuss the evolution of productivity measurement

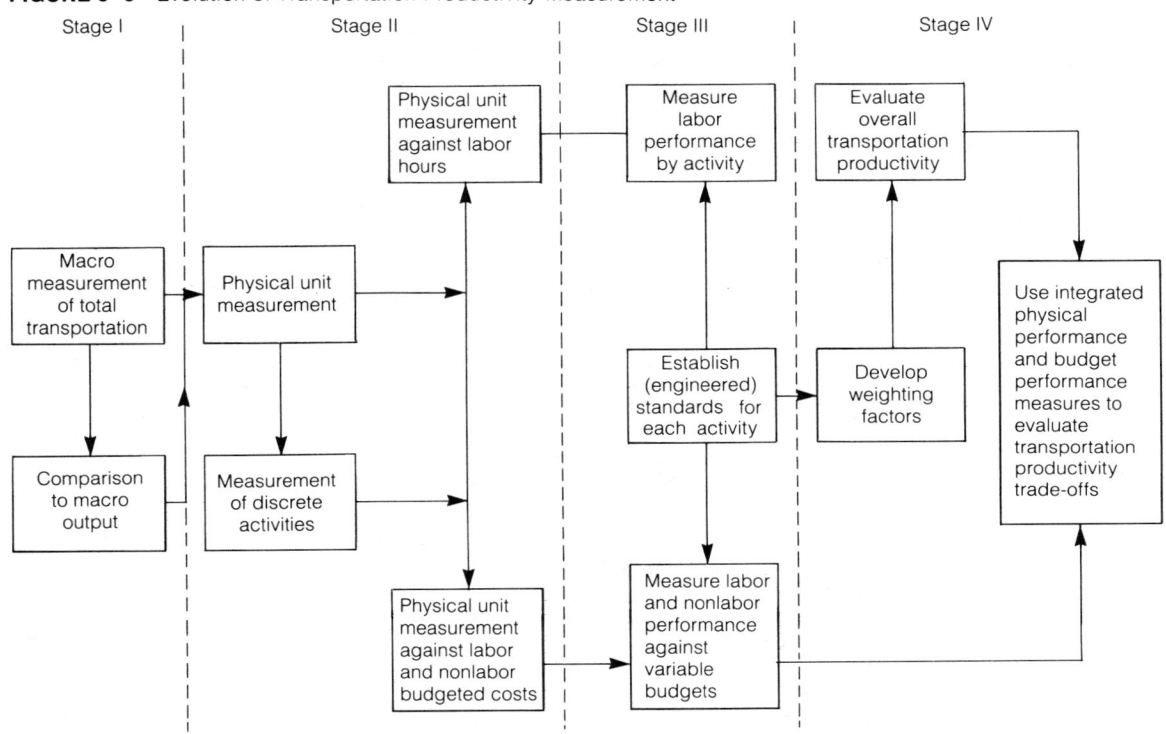

**FIGURE 5-5** Evolution of Transportation Productivity Measurement

Source: A. T. Kearney, Inc., *Measuring Productivity in Physical Distribution* (Chicago: National Council of Physical Distribution Management, 1978), p. 80.

in terms of "sophistication." Figure 5–5 displays a schematic representation of the evolution of effectiveness measurement. This evolutionary process may be viewed as occurring in four separate stages.

Stage I is the development and use of raw data in terms of dollars. Characteristic of this data is that it is usually provided by some other functional area, e.g., sales or finance, it is usually nonphysical in nature, and the time increment measured is relatively long, e.g., monthly or quarterly. At this stage, this cost data is often compared to some type of macro output such as dollar sales. Thus, a common Stage I measure might be total transportation costs as a percent of sales.

In Stage II physical measures and activity budgets are introduced for transportation activities. Units such as weight, stops, orders, miles, etc., are tracked within the transportation activities over shorter time intervals, such as days, or weeks. At this point, these physical units can be measured against transportation labor and nonlabor costs to track cost per pound, per mile, per stop, or per ton-mile. The introduction of time-phased activity budgets is now possible with this information.

Stage III begins with the establishment of empirical or historical "goals" for the overall transportation operation. These goals could be in the form of physical units or period operational costs, but in either case can now lead to the first measurement of performance (actual versus standard).

**TABLE 5–10** Transportation Performance Data that Appear on a Formal Report

| Response | Percent Response (N = 363) |
|---|---|
| Common/contract carriers | |
|     Damage/claims | 43.0 |
|     Data from freight payment system | 33.6 |
|     Transit time | 30.9 |
|     On-time delivery performance | 29.5 |
|     Shipment tracing | 28.1 |
|     Customer complaints | 27.8 |
|     Billing accuracy | 25.1 |
|     Equipment availability | 19.6 |
|     On-time pickup performance | 19.3 |
|     Shipment expediting | 19.0 |
|     Assigned rail cars | 17.1 |
|     Post card survey of customers | 14.6 |
|     Equipment condition | 13.5 |
|     Cost per ton mile | 11.8 |
|     Sanitation | 8.8 |
|     Form letter to customers regarding performance | 7.2 |
| Private carriers | |
|     Utilization | 25.1 |
|     Cost per ton mile | 21.2 |
|     Damage | 19.6 |
|     Transit time | 19.3 |
|     On-time delivery performance | 18.2 |
|     Customer complaints | 15.4 |
|     On-time pickup performance | 13.5 |

The development of industrial-engineered standards for labor and nonlabor inputs by activity is usually the next step in further sophistication. Transportation requirements can then be converted to standard hours of work, vehicle loads, or dollars of cost, for instance. This development leads to performance measurement of labor, and nonlabor inputs by activity. It should be noted that productivity trade-offs between activities can be analyzed quantitatively using this data. Less transportation labor in the loading activity (in exchange for increased nontransportation labor) can result in greater capacity for purely transportation activities (e.g., driving).

Stage IV is the last step in the development of a productivity measurement system. In Stage IV, physical performance data is merged with financial data to provide management with an overall view of the transportation operation. Information provided by a Stage IV system would include actual versus budgeted cost analyses as well as variance analyses highlighting the reasons for budgetary variance (e.g., standard versus actual unit cost, standard versus actual output).

Armed with this type of measurement system, management is in a position to control ongoing operations as well as to test alternatives and seek trade-offs to present operations.[19]

---

[19] A. T. Kearney, Inc., *Measuring Productivity in Physical Distribution* (Chicago: NCPDM, 1978), pp. 79, 81.

Illustrations of how a firm might collect and array data on transportation performance are presented in Tables 5—11 through 5—13 and Figures 5—6 through 5—9. Most firms will probably utilize a variety of methods, procedures, and reporting forms to evaluate mode/carrier performance. The tables presented would be representative of reporting forms used by companies which evaluate and monitor transportation performance variables such as transit time variability, on-time delivery, and loss and/or damage. Each table could be easily modified (where applicable) to show trends by adding a dimension, or axis, representing the time parameter.

## DESIGNING AN OPTIMAL TRANSPORTATION SYSTEM

*Transportation Audit Pinpoints Important Areas of Decision Making*

No single transportation system is "best" for every company because each firm has its own unique set of products, markets, customers, and facilities. The individual company must develop a system which is both "cost and service optimal" for itself. As an approach which a typical firm

**TABLE 5-11** An Approach to Analyzing On-Time Delivery (number of shipments)

| Promised Transit Time (days) | On Time | Days Late |||||
|---|---|---|---|---|---|---|
| | | 1 | 2 | 3 | 4 | 5 or More |
| 1 | | | | | | |
| 2 | | | | | | |
| 3 | | | | | | |
| 4 | | (The number of shipments* in each group would be entered in this table. Any time period (daily, weekly, monthly) that would be appropriate to the company could be used.) |||||
| 5 | | |||||
| . | | |||||
| . | | |||||
| . | | |||||
| N | | |||||
| Total | | | | | | |

\* Can be based upon all modes combined, a single mode, a single carrier, or by origin-destination.

**TABLE 5-12** Loss and/or Damage Rates for Various Modes/Carriers

| Mode/Carrier | Number of Shipments | Shipments Lost or Damaged ||  Loss and/or Damage Value | Freight Charges | Loss/Damage as Percent of Total |
|---|---|---|---|---|---|---|
| | | Number | Percent | | | |
| Rail CL | | | | | | |
| Rail LCL | | | | | | |
| Motor TL | | | | | | |
| Motor LTL | | | | | | |
| TOFC | | | | | | |
| Air | | | | | | |
| Freight forwarder | | | | | | |

**TABLE 5-13** Loss and/or Damage Rates for Various Product Groups and Modes/Carriers

| Product | Mode/Carrier | | | | | | Freight Forwarder | Total ($) | Percent of Total |
| --- | --- | --- | --- | --- | --- | --- | --- | --- | --- |
| | CL | LCL | TL | LTL | TOFC | Air | | | |
| Product A | | | | | | | | | |
| Product B | | | | | | | | | |
| Product C | | | | | | | | | |
| Product D | | | | | | | | | |
| · | | | | | | | | | |
| · | | | | | | | | | |
| · | | | | | | | | | |
| · | | | | | | | | | |
| · | | | | | | | | | |
| Product N | | | | | | | | | |

**FIGURE 5-6** Average Transit Time Performance for Various Transportation Carrier Options

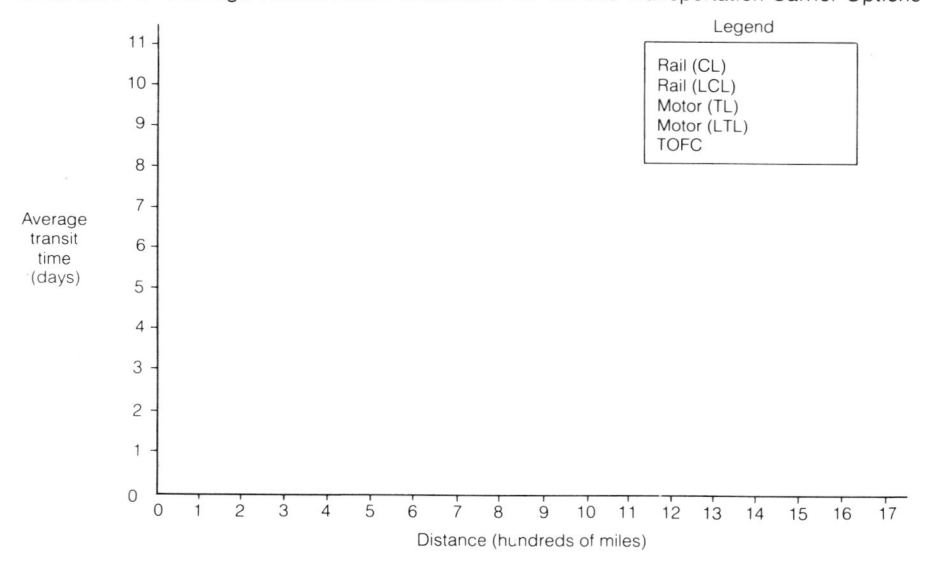

Legend:
Rail (CL)
Rail (LCL)
Motor (TL)
Motor (LTL)
TOFC

Average transit time (days) vs. Distance (hundreds of miles)

might take, a transportation system audit is presented in Table 5–14. Each component of the physical distribution system is capable of being audited. Such an audit should be performed periodically.

A transportation system audit provides the firm with an overview of the various transportation components of their physical distribution network. The audit serves to identify and pinpoint the important areas of transportation decision making.

In conducting an audit, the firm needs to examine the cost and service aspects of the transportation system. Theoretically, the transportation decision is fairly simple, that is, how to move products to the customer from the firm. Unfortunately, the theory is complicated by the reality, in that, cus-

**FIGURE 5-7** Comparison of Transit Time Variability across a Variety of Modes

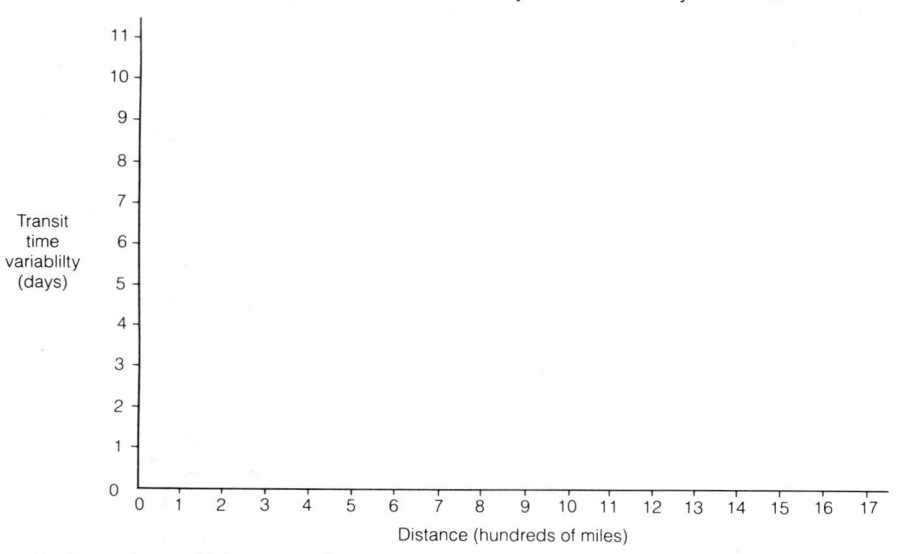

Each mode would be arrayed on a separate chart or the same chart. The mode which exhibited a tighter or narrower range of variability would be the most desirable option.

**FIGURE 5-8** Comparison of Transit Time Variability Utilizing a Stated Standard of Performance

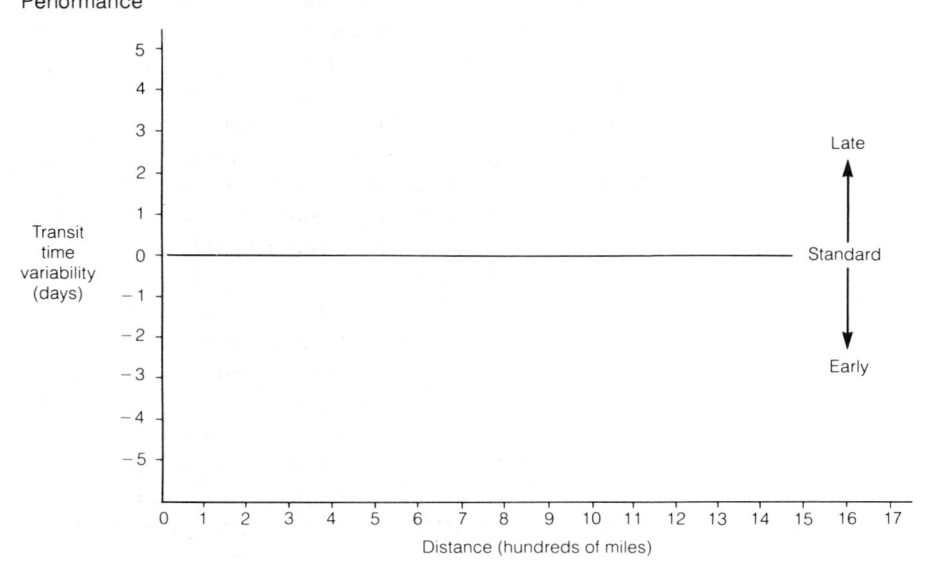

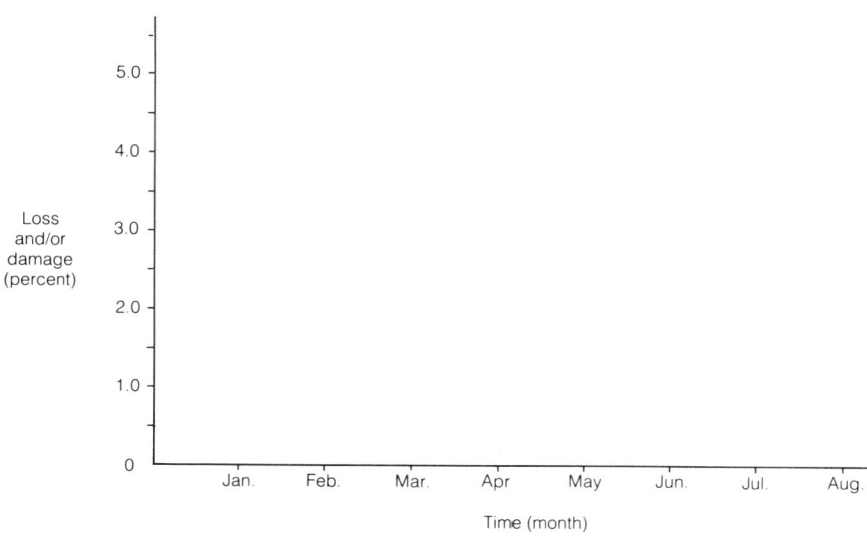

**FIGURE 5-9** Loss and/or Damage Rates for Various Modes/Carriers over Time

tomers order in different quantities, they order different products, and they can be located in multiple locations. Other factors which complicate the process include multiple stocking points, inventory levels, mode/carrier characteristics, and irregular ordering patterns by customers.

The items included in Table 5-14 illustrate the myriad of factors which must be considered as a firm plans, implements and controls a transportation system. Product considerations will impact on the selection of a particular mode and carrier. Some products, because of size, weight, durability, value, etc., are not compatable with certain transportation modes or carriers. It is vital that the company identify the product/mode interfaces that exist in order to select the mode or carrier offering the best cost and service package.

Similarly, it is important for the firm to identify the characteristics of all potential modes and carriers. Usually there are a number of transportation options available to the company and it is essential that each option be explored sufficiently so as to make the optimal mode/carrier choice. When sufficient for-hire carriers are not available, the audit must include examination of the private carrier option. Even when for-hire carriage is present the firm should consider the private carrier option in case the cost/service equation is unfavorable to the company.

Even after a specific transportation network is established, the system must be constantly monitored and evaluated. A thorough transportation system audit includes identification of performance standards, the measurement of cost and service components, and the procedures for planning, implementation, and control of the entire transportation network. Of necessity, such an evaluation must take place within the context of the overall physical distribution system of the firm. A discussion of how the transporta-

**TABLE 5-14** The Transportation System Audit

1. Product considerations
   a. Size
   b. Weight
   c. Durable
   d. Value
   e. Freight classification
2. Customer service considerations
   a. The company's existing service levels
   b. Service levels provided by the firm's major competitors
   c. Probable reactions of customers and competitors to the proposed system
3. Distance of the firm from its markets
4. Modal considerations
   a. Time in transit
   b. Frequency of service
   c. Dependability of service
   d. Capability of mode
   e. Availability of service
   f. Special services offered
   g. Past experience with the mode
   h. Freight charges
   i. Cost of loading and unloading
   j. Packaging costs
   k. In-transit losses
   l. Damage levels
5. The impact of the mode selected on
   a. The cost of carrying inventory
   b. Warehousing costs
   c. Order-processing costs
   d. Production lot quantity costs
6. The cost of private carriage versus the cost of common carriage
7. Once the mode is selected which specific carriers should be used?
   a. Volume of traffic
   b. Market's serviced by each carrier
   c. Routing alternatives
   d. Special services provided
   e. Number of product handlings before shipment reaches its final destination
   f. Current freight rates
   g. Projected freight rates
8. How often should the transportation system be reexamined? What procedure(s) should be used?
9. What performance standards exist and can the transportation system components be measured?

tion component fits into the total physical distribution strategic plan is discussed further in Chapter 14.

## SUMMARY

In this chapter, various transportation decision strategies were discussed which influenced the firm's cost/service offering. Vital transportation decision strategies included the mode/carrier selection process, use of private versus for-hire carriage, leasing versus owning, and evaluating mode/carrier performance.

You were shown how to measure transportation costs and performance, and how to recognize opportunities for reducing transportation costs and/or improving performance of the transportation function. An example of a transportation audit was provided. With this background you are prepared to examine the warehousing activity, which is closely related to the transportation function.

## Appendix: Key Issues Affecting Future Transportation Decision Making

A. National transportation policies
  1. Railroads will be aided:
    a. Loan guarantees.
    b. Subsidies.
    c. Research and planning.
    d. User charges on inland waterways.
    e. Trucks viewed as less energy efficient.
    f. Rail network rationalization.
  2. Regulation.
    a. More even-handed toward the modes.
    b. Pricing more flexible.
    c. Burden of proof shifting to shippers in many instances.
    d. Administrative procedures will be streamlined.
    e. Single regulatory agency doubtful.
B. Economic trends
  1. Mergers:
    a. Some will occur in rail industry.
    b. Limited motor carrier activity.
  2. Railroads will continue to lose market share to motor carriers.
  3. Capital investment:
    a. Shortage of capital will be critical, particularly for railroads.
    b. The stronger railroads will be able to attract capital funds for equipment, will be easier to find them for roadbed and fixed plant.
    c. Motor carriers in better position as equipment financing (which constitutes 25 percent of investment) becomes easier.
    d. Higher ROI needed by railroads to attract equity financing.
  4. Deferred maintenance:
    a. Will continue to inhibit competitiveness of railroads.
    b. Government assistance will be needed, particularly for less affluent carriers.
  5. Operating expenses:
    a. Labor and fuel will continue to be largest and most critical.
    b. Cost saving measures will be more effective in fuel area than in labor.

Source: Ronald S. Potter, "Transportation Planning: An Overview," in *Proceedings of the Eighteenth Annual Conference of the National Council of Physical Distribution Management, October 13–15, 1980*, pp. 228–33.

6. Operating subsidies will temporarily defer abandonment of some light-density rail trackage.
7. Elimination of discriminatory taxation of railroad property will provide limited relief.

C. Regulatory trends
   1. Rail
      a. Rates:
         (1) ICC willing to rethink its prior position on contract rates and in a proper case find them lawful (ExParte 358F, Change of Policy, Railroad Contract Rates).
         (2) ICC deregulated movement of fresh fruits and vegetables (ExParte 346, Sub. 1, March 1979).
         (3) Greater tendency by railroads toward selective rate increases by commodity in lieu of general across the board increases.
         (4) Recent legislation (4-R Act, February 1976) encouraged more innovative ratemaking, granted ICC authority to eliminate regulation which is not needed. Little impact due to market dominance issues.
         (5) Currently proposed administration legislation (s.796) would give broad freedom to railroads to set rates:
            (a) Rely on market forces for ICC policy.
            (b) Set rates at market-determined levels.
            (c) Sanction shipper-carrier contracts.
            (d) Eliminate ICC suspension power.
            (e) Eliminate port equalization.
            (f) Repeal long- and short-haul clause.
      b. Abandonment
         (1) Increased ability to abandon marginal lines granted by 4-R Act. Federal subsidies to continue operations authorized for five years.
         (2) Proposed legislation provides three years retention of present system. Thereafter, railroads can abandon lines by notifying public. However, they must continue service if subsidy offered.
      c. TOFC
         (1) Railroads encouraging this service, but much emphasis being placed on utilizing shipper trailers.
         (2) Round-trip pricing appearing particularly on transcontinental traffic.
   2. Motor Carrier
      a. Rates
         (1) Restrictions placed on role and power of rate bureaus (ExParte 297).
         (2) ICC changing formula for determining reasonableness of rates from operating ratio to return on investment. (I&S M-29772, Southern Motor Carriers Rate Conference, November 1978.)
         (3) More cost-oriented rate making occurring, particularly by irregular route carriers publishing their own tariffs.
      b. Entry
         (1) ICC eliminated maximum limitation of eight shippers for contract carriers. New rule has no fixed ceiling; each case to be decided on own merits. Set standards for determination:
            (a) Performs exclusively one type of service usable only by a particular shipper or industry.
            (b) Serves exclusively firms affiliated with one another.
            (c) Assigns equipment to exclusive use of each person served for at

least 30 days. (ExParte MC-119, Policy Statement Regarding the "Rule of Eight" in Contract Carrier Applications, January 1979).
- (2) Rate competition allowed as justification for new operating authorities (ExParte MC-116, Change of Policy Consideration of Rates in Operating Rights Application Proceedings, November 1978).
- (3) Dual authority—common and contract—by a carrier now authorized.
- (4) ICC has enlarged the size of commercial zones.
- (5) ICC has changed protest standards to shift the burden of proof to existing carriers and restricted protests to carriers actively participating in movements involved in an application.
- (6) ICC Task Force report has proposed deregulating entry for 12 specialized industry segments (December 1978).
- (7) Proposed legislation will remove all restrictions on ICC certificates:
  - (a) Backhaul restrictions.
  - (b) Prohibitions on intermediate stops.
  - (c) Gateway restrictions.
  - (d) Commodity restrictions.
- (8) Proposed legislation will shift "burden of proof" to protestants in entry cases.

c. Private carriage
- (1) ICC has allowed private carriers to become for-hire carriers on their backhaul routes (Toto case—March 1978).
- (2) ICC is becoming more amenable to allowing private carriers to convert to contract carrier status.
- (3) ICC has proposed to allow intercorporate hauling when subsidiaries are at least 80 percent owned (ExParte MC-122, July 1979).
- (4) Restriction on backhaul allowance by shippers of food or grocery products have been eased.

d. Exemptions from regulations
- (1) Increased agricultural commodities exemptions.
- (2) Increased maximum nonmember interstate hauling of agricultural commodities from 15 to 25 percent.
- (3) Exempts traffic incidentals to rail and air travel.

e. Administration
- (1) Places additional restriction on ICC.
- (2) Requires minimum liability insurance for carriers.
- (3) Establishes monitoring procedures to guide future legislations.

3. Safety regulations:
  a. Increased weight limits for motor carriers must be broadly adopted by the states for major savings to be achieved.
  b. No additional federal increases in size and weight seen in near future.
  c. Some additional states will allow double and triple bottoms.
  d. Possible reduction in maximum hours of service for truck drivers.

4. Energy and Environmental Regulations:
  a. 55 m.p.h. speed limit will continue and enforcement may be more strict.
  b. Increased noise and emission standards are likely.
  c. Gasoline tax uncertain, but prospects are diminishing.
  d. Voluntary energy conservation measures will prevail.
  e. Railroads less adversely impacted than motor carriers.

D. Technology trends
  1. No revolutionary development:
    a. Few dramatic changes in size, speed, or capacity over next several years.

b. Advances will be concentrated in communication, management information systems, and automated terminal functions.
2. Intermodal developments will make minor progress:
   a. Rail TOFC
   b. International
3. Incremental improvements are possible in both rail and motor carrier modes:
   a. Greater productivity major goal.
   b. Increases in fuel efficiency will be sought.
   c. Meeting environmental constraints will receive increased attention.
4. Barriers to technological development are more institutional than technical:
   a. Greater deterrent will be lack of capital as large-scale investments will be needed to meet new social requirements without increasing productivity.
   b. Regulatory provisions inhibit innovation.
   c. Conflicting and impractical environmental and energy standards consume time and resources.
   d. Labor restrictions and fragmentation in industry will slow pace of technological change.

## QUESTIONS AND PROBLEMS

1. In the problem recognition stage of the transportation-mode selection decision, it was the opinion of most traffic executives that service factors were generally more important than cost factors in causing firms to switch to another transportation mode. What reasons can you suggest for the fact that service factors are more important than cost factors?

2. In the evaluation of transportation modes, *consistency of service* is significantly more important to shippers than *time-in-transit*. Differentiate between the two terms and identify some possible reasons why consistency of service would be considered to be more important than time-in-transit.

3. It was stated in the chapter that private carriage should not be viewed strictly as a transportation decision. Rather, it is also a financial decision. Briefly explain the factors which underlie such a statement.

4. When a firm decides to engage in private transportation, the company can either purchase or lease their equipment. Briefly identify the advantages/disadvantages of leasing transportation equipment versus owning the equipment outright.

5. It is vitally important that a firm be able to evaluate the efficiency and/or productivity of its transportation network. Figure 5–5 shows the evolution of transportation-productivity measurement. At the present time, most firms are in Stage I or II. Briefly explain what Stages III and IV represent and identify some reasons why only a few companies have evolved to the final two stages.

6. An Oregon manufacturer of kraft paper bags sells its products in the San Francisco area. The degree of competition is intense and competitors are able to offer fast deliveries of small orders. In the past, common carrier service has been inconsistent, although with deregulation of the motor carrier industry by The Motor Carrier Act of 1980, service is expected to improve. Identify the motor transport options available to this company and indicate the advantages/disadvantages associated with each option.

# 6 Warehousing

Introduction
  Nature and Importance of Warehousing
  Types of Warehousing

Warehousing Operations
  The Functions of Warehousing
  Warehouse Layout and Design
  Warehouse Handling Systems
    Standard Systems
    Automated Systems
  Packaging

Decision-Making Strategies in Warehousing
  Public versus Private Warehousing
    Advantages of Public Warehousing
    Disadvantages of Public Warehousing
    Public Warehousing Services
    Advantages of Private Warehousing
    Disadvantages of Private Warehousing
    A Financial Comparison of Public versus Private Warehousing
  Measurement and Improvement of Warehouse Performance
  Warehouse Site Selection

**Summary**

**Appendixes**
A. Problem 1—Where Should In-Process Parts Be Stored for Minimum Travel Costs?
B. Problem 2—How Do You Assign Storage Locations to Minimize Travel?

**Objectives of this chapter:**

To show how warehousing can be used to improve physical distribution efficiency

To show how to make efficient and effective warehousing decisions

To show how warehousing policies affect a firm's performance

To show how to improve warehousing performance

## INTRODUCTION

Warehousing is an integral part of every physical distribution system and plays a vital role in providing a desired level of customer service at the lowest possible total cost (see Figure 6–1). The warehousing or storage

**FIGURE 6–1** Cost Trade-offs Required in a Physical Distribution System

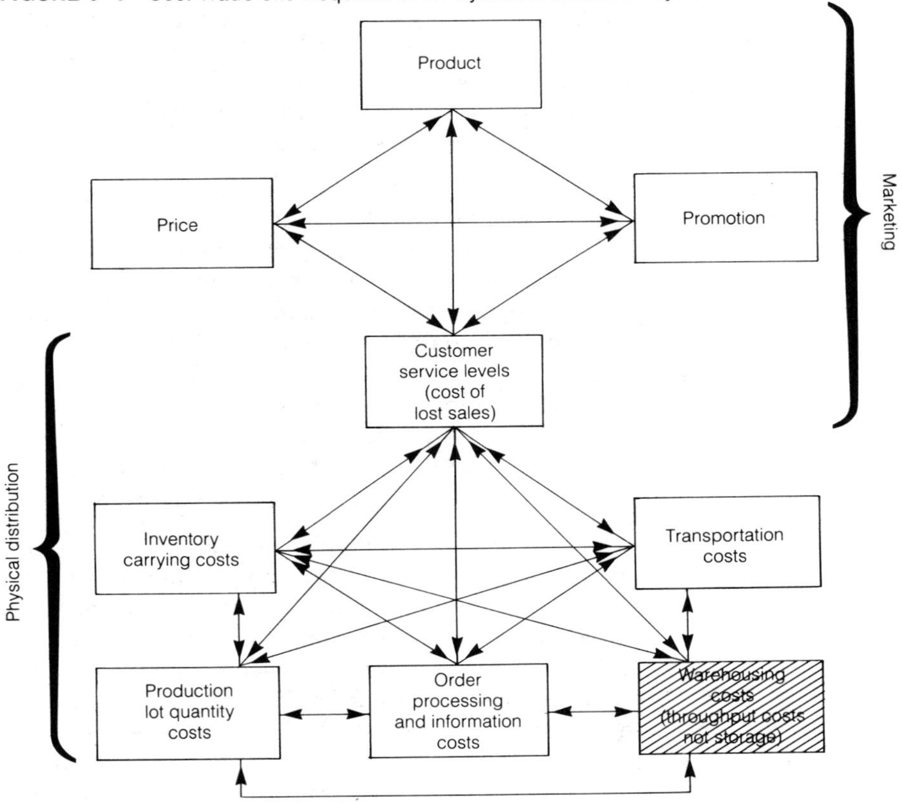

Objective: Minimize total costs.

Total costs = Transportation costs + Warehousing costs
+ Order processing and information costs + Production lot quantity costs
+ Inventory carrying costs + Cost of lost sales

Source: Adapted from Douglas M. Lambert, *The Development of Inventory Costing Methodology: A Study of the Costs Associated with Holding Inventory* (Chicago: National Council of Physical Distribution Management, 1976), p. 7.

activity is the link between the producer and the customer. Over the years, warehousing has evolved from a relatively minor facet of a firm's distribution system to one of the most important functions. Expressed simply, "warehousing is the function of storing goods between the time they are produced and the time they are needed."[1]

In this chapter you will be shown how warehousing can be used to improve a firm's physical distribution efficiency and how a PD manager can make the most efficient and effective warehousing decisions. In addition, you will be shown how various warehousing policies affect financial performance and how to improve that performance.

### Nature and Importance of Warehousing

Warehousing is used for the storage of inventories during all phases of the distributive process. Basically, there are two types of inventories that can be placed into storage: raw materials (physical supply) and finished goods (physical distribution). Also, there may be inventories of goods-in-process although in most firms they would constitute only a small portion of a company's total inventories.

*Why Use Warehousing?* Why is it necessary to hold inventories in storage? In general, the warehousing of inventories is necessary for the following reasons:

1. To achieve transportation economies.
2. To achieve production economies.
3. To take advantage of quantity purchase discounts.
4. To maintain a source of supply.
5. To support the firm's customer service policies.
6. To meet changing market conditions (e.g., seasonality, demand fluctuations, competition).
7. To overcome the time and space differentials that exist between producers and consumers.
8. To accomplish least-total cost physical distribution commensurate with a desired level of customer service.

Transportation economies are possible for both the physical supply system and the physical distribution system. In the case of physical supply, small orders from a number of suppliers may be shipped to a consolidation warehouse near the source of supply in order to achieve a truckload or carload shipment to the plant (see Figure 6–2) which is normally a considerably greater distance from the warehouse. The warehouse is located near the sources of supply so that the LTL rates apply only to a short haul and the volume rate is used for the long haul from the warehouse to the plant.

Warehouses are used to realize similar transportation savings in the physical distribution system. In the packaged goods industry manufacturers often have multiple plant locations with each plant manufacturing only a portion of the company's product line. Usually, these companies also maintain a number of field-warehouse locations from which mixed ship-

---

[1] Creed H. Jenkins, *Modern Warehouse Management* (New York: McGraw-Hill, 1968), p. 1.

**FIGURE 6-2** Transportation Consolidations Made Possible by Warehousing

A. Physical supply system

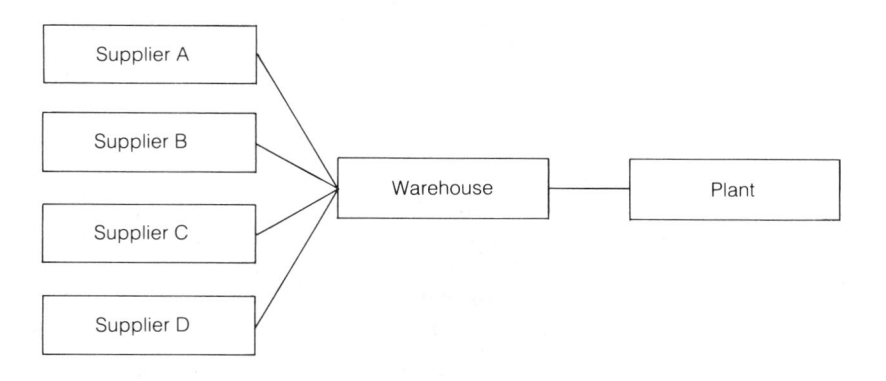

B. Physical distribution system

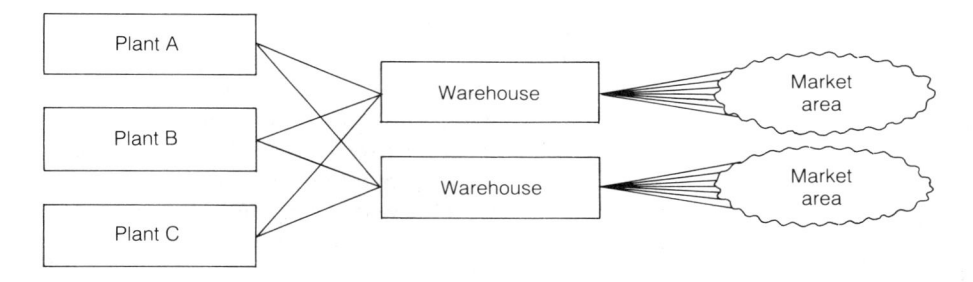

ments of the entire product line can be made to customers. Shipments from plants to field warehouses are normally by rail in full carload quantities of the products manufactured at each plant. Orders from customers, comprised of various items in the product line are shipped by truck at truckload or LTL rates. The use of field warehouses results in lower transportation costs than direct shipments to customers and the savings are often significantly larger than the increased cost of warehousing and the associated increase in inventory carrying costs.

Production economies are realized when long production runs are made. Short production runs minimize the amount of inventory that is held throughout the physical distribution system by producing to meet current demand. However, there are increased costs of set-ups and line changes associated with short production runs. Also, if a plant is operating near or at capacity, frequent line changes may mean that the manufacturer cannot produce enough product to meet demand. If so, the associated cost of lost sales (the lost contribution to profit on sales that cannot be made) would be the result of short production runs.

The production of large quantities of product for each line change results in a lower per-unit cost on a full-cost basis as well as more units for a given plant capacity. However, long production runs lead to larger inventories and increased warehouse requirements. Consequently, the production-cost savings must be balanced with the increased physical distribution costs in order to achieve least total cost.

Warehousing also is necessary if a manufacturer is to take advantage of quantity purchase discounts on raw materials. Not only is the per-unit price lower as a result of the discount but if the manufacturer pays the freight, transportation costs will be less on a volume purchase because of transportation economies. Likewise, similar discounts and savings would accrue to retailers or wholesalers purchasing from manufacturers.

Holding inventories in warehouses may be necessary in order to maintain a source of supply. For example, the timing and quantity of purchases is important in keeping suppliers especially in times of shortages. Also, it may be necessary to hold an inventory of items that may be in short supply as the result of a strike against one of the company's suppliers, damage in transit, or vendor stock-outs.

Customer service policies such as a 48-hour delivery standard may require a number of field warehouses in order to minimize total costs while achieving the standard.

Changing market conditions also may make it necessary to warehouse product in the field. This is due primarily to the inability to accurately predict consumer demand and the timing of retailer and wholesaler orders. By keeping some excess inventory in field-warehouse locations the company can respond quickly to meet demand that exceeds forecast. In addition, the excess inventory allows the manufacturer to fill customer orders when shipments to restock the field warehouses arrive late.

The majority of firms utilize warehousing in order to accomplish least total cost physical distribution. The use of warehousing enables management to select the transportation modes and inventory levels that, when combined with communication and order processing systems and production alternatives, result in minimizing total costs while providing a desired level of customer service.

The factors that influence a firm's warehousing policies include: the industry; the firm's philosophy; capital availability; product characteristics such as size, perishability, product lines, substitutability, and the obsolescence rate; economic conditions; seasonality of demand; and the production process being used.

**Types of Warehousing**

In general, firms have a variety of warehousing alternatives available. Some companies may market products directly to customers and thereby eliminate warehousing in the field. Mail-order catalogue companies would be one example of an industry that utilizes warehousing only at a point-of-origin such as sales headquarters or plant. However, most firms warehouse

**Two Types of Warehousing—Private and Public**

products at some intermediate point between plant location(s) and customers. When product storage occurs in the field, a firm is faced with two warehousing options: "owned" or "leased" facilities called *private warehousing*, or rented facilities called *public warehousing*.

There are important customer-service and financial considerations which must be examined by firms as they choose between the private versus public warehousing alternatives. For example, operating costs for a public warehouse tend to be higher because of the inclusion of a profit factor, selling, and advertising costs. However, there is no initial investment in facilities required when public warehousing is used. From a customer-service perspective, private warehousing can generally provide higher service levels because of more specialized facilities and equipment, and better familiarity with the firm's products, customers, and markets.

In general, there are six types of public warehouses: (1) general merchandise warehouses for manufactured goods; (2) refrigerated or cold-storage warehouses; (3) bonded warehouses; (4) household-goods and furniture warehouses; (5) special-commodity warehouses; and (6) bulk-storage warehouses. Each type provides users with a broad range of specialized services.

The general merchandise warehouse is probably the most common form. It is designed to be used by manufacturers, distributors, and customers for storing practically any kind of product.

Refrigerated or cold-storage warehouses are those providing a temperature-controlled storage environment. Usually, they are used for preserving perishable items such as fruits and vegetables, however a number of other items such as frozen-food products, some pharmaceuticals, and furs require this type of facility.

Some general-merchandise warehouses or special-commodity warehouses are known as bonded warehouses. These warehouses undertake surety bonds from the U.S. Treasury and place their premises under the custody of an agent of the Treasury. In short, goods such as imported tobacco and alcoholic beverages are stored in a public warehouse, although the government retains control of the goods until they are distributed to the marketplace. At that time, the importer must pay customs duties to the federal Internal Revenue Service. The advantage of the bonded warehouse is that import duties and excise taxes need not be paid until the merchandise is sold.

Household-goods warehouses are used for storage of personal property rather than merchandise. The property is typically stored for an extended period, although an exception to this is when moving and storage companies employ these services as a temporary layover option. Within this category of warehouse, there are several types of storage alternatives. First, is the open storage concept. The goods are stored on a cubic-foot basis per month out on the open floor of the warehouse. Typically, household goods are confined to this type of storage. A second kind of storage is private-room or vault storage where users are provided with a private room or vault to lock in and secure goods. A third kind, container storage, provides the user with a container into which goods are packed. This affords better protection of the product than does open storage.[2]

Special-commodity warehouses are used for particular agricultural products, such as grains, wool, and cotton. Ordinarily each of these warehouses handles one kind of product and offers special services particular to that product. Commodity warehouses are characterized by:

1. They are warehouses used for products that originate from a number of scattered points and are gathered for sale in a particular market area.
2. The items themselves are stored in the terminal points for a considerable length of time.
3. The commodities are stored in bulk on an interchangeable basis, that is, commodities of the same quality and grade are considered the equal of any other units.
4. Frequently the commodity warehouse provides services such as cleaning grain, compressing cotton, etc.[3]

Bulk storage warehouses provide tank storage of liquids and open or sheltered storage of dry products such as coal, sand, and chemicals. The services provided by such warehouses may include filling drums from bulk, or mixing types of chemicals with others to produce new compounds or mixtures.[4]

Private warehouses may be owned or leased. Financial considerations usually will determine which option is the best for any particular firm. Whether leased or owned, a number of advantages may be realized by a firm when private warehousing is used:

*Advantages of Private Warehousing*

1. Greater flexibility in design to meet the specific needs of the owner.
2. Greater control of the operation to insure that warehousing is conducted efficiently. The company has direct control of personnel and operating responsibility is within the company. Warehouse policies and objectives can be coordinated with sales and production.
3. Lower cost per unit provided that the volume of throughput is consistent and large. This is possible because the public warehouse must recover advertising and selling costs while many of the other operating expenses would be the same.
4. Using the field warehouse to house a local sales office or field purchasing organization resulting in lower total costs for the combined facility. This occurs because the combined operation can more fully utilize basic services such as offices, switchboards, duplicating equipment, data processing and clerical staffs, and administrative functions.
5. Provides the manufacturer with in-the-field contact with customers, a visible presence in the marketplace.

---

[2] William J. Schultz, *American Marketing* (Belmont, Calif.: Wadsworth Publishing, 1962), p. 367.

[3] John H. Frederick, *Using Public Warehouses* (Philadelphia, Pa.: Chilton, 1957), pp. 15–17.

[4] Ibid., p. 17.

Many companies find it advantageous to use a combination of public and private warehouses. The private warehouses are used to handle the basic inventory levels required for least-cost distribution in markets where the volume justifies ownership. Public warehouses are used in those areas where volume is not sufficient to justify ownership and/or to store peak requirements. Public warehouses typically charge on the basis of cases or hundredweight stored or handled. Consequently, when the volume of activity is sufficiently large, public warehousing charges will exceed the cost of a private facility, making ownership more attractive.

## WAREHOUSING OPERATIONS

Warehousing serves an important role in the physical distribution system of a firm. In combination with other distribution activities, it serves to provide the firm's customers with an adequate level of service. Obviously, the primary role of warehousing is to store products. However, warehousing provides break-bulk and consolidation services as well. These activities emphasize product flow rather than storage. Fast and efficient movement of large quantities of raw materials, component parts, and finished goods through the warehouse are the goals of every distribution system.

### The Functions of Warehousing

*Warehousing Has Two Basic Functions— Movement and Storage*

Warehousing has two basic functions: movement and storage. The movement function can be further divided into four handling activities: (1) receiving, (2) transfer, (3) order selection, and (4) shipping.[5] The *receiving* activity includes the physical unloading of products from the transportation carrier. It includes the updating of warehouse inventory records, inspection for damage, and verification of the count against orders and shipping records. *Transfer* involves the physical movement of the product into the warehouse for storage, movement to areas for specialized services such as consolidation, and movement to the loading dock for outbound shipment. Customer *order selection* is the major movement activity and involves the regrouping of products into the assortments desired by the customers. Packing slips also are detailed at this point. The last movement activity, *shipping*, consists of physically moving the assembled orders into carrier equipment, adjusting inventory records, and checking on orders to be shipped.

The second function of warehousing—storage—can be performed on a temporary or a nontransaction basis. *Temporary* storage emphasizes the movement function of the warehouse and includes only the storage of product which is necessary for basic inventory replenishment. Temporary storage is required regardless of the actual inventory turnover. The extent of temporary inventory storage will depend upon the design of the physical distribution system and the variability experienced in lead-time and demand. *Permanent* storage is the storage of inventory in excess of that re-

---

[5] Donald J. Bowersox, *Logistical Management* (New York: Macmillan, 1974), p. 212.

quired for normal replenishment. The most common conditions which lead to permanent storage are (1) seasonal demand, (2) erratic demand, (3) conditioning of products such as fruits and meats, (4) speculation, and (5) special deals such as quantity discounts.

In summary, the major functions of warehousing—movement and storage—include all of the following activities:

1. Inventory control.
2. Purchasing.
3. Order entry.
4. Receiving.
5. Inspection.
6. Redistribution.
7. Put-away.
8. Storage.
9. Replenishment.
10. Order selection.
11. Checking.
12. Packing and marking.
13. Staging and consolidation.
14. Shipping.
15. Clerical/administration.[6]

*Inventory control* is concerned with how much inventory is on hand and available for shipment to customers, plants, or other warehouses. *Purchasing*, which is typically performed by the manufacturing group, affects warehouse operations through the types and volumes of items acquired, and through the processing and record-keeping functions that accompany purchasing transactions. *Order entry* is the process of entering orders into the firm's order-processing system for the purpose of initiating the order cycle. Mistakes or errors in order entry generally grow in magnitude as they progress through the distribution system. Incorrect entry of orders often results in duplication in the other warehousing and distribution activities. *Receiving* is where it all begins. "The warehouse that can't receive inventory efficiently and correctly identify the material will pay for this later on when they attempt to find out what really happened. This is also the ideal place to get control of inventory allocated to back orders. If back orders are filled as goods are received, the inventory will be used as intended."[7]

Making sure that the items received at the warehouse are undamaged, of the proper size or type, and that the order is complete, are the objectives of the *inspection* activity. *Redistribution* refers to the transshipment of items to other company warehouses or plants. The firm is able to take advantages of transportation economies by receiving large shipments at the warehouse and then reshipping smaller quantities to those points where they are needed. *Put-away* is the physical process of taking goods received and placing them within the warehouse in the locations where they are to be stored.

*Storage* is what warehousing is all about. It is the most basic warehousing activity and is defined as the depositing of goods in a facility for safekeeping. *Replenishment* is the process of relocating goods from a bulk storage area to an order-pick storage area. An important warehousing task is to keep track of inventory levels efficiently so that replacements may be obtained. *Order selection* can be referred to as order picking. It involves the

---

[6] "More Effective Warehouse Inventory Management with Front-End Control," *The Howard Way Letter* 1, no. 1 (October 1979), p. 1.

[7] Ibid., p. 2.

accurate and timely selection of product for shipment from the warehouse. Successful completion of all of the warehousing activities already mentioned would eliminate the need for *checking*. However, errors and mistakes do occur within any warehouse operation and it is usually necessary to conduct a check of previous activities. This function is analogous to the quality-control function in manufacturing.

*Packing and marking* involves the preparation of the goods for shipment. Products are placed in boxes, cartons, or containers; palletized and/or stretch-wrapped (the process of wrapping products in a plastic film); and are marked with information needed for shipment such as origin, destination, shipper, consignee, and package contents. *Staging and consolidation* is concerned with preparing the goods for shipment and usually takes place on the loading dock or staging area of the warehouse. The actual loading and movement of the product occurs in the *shipping* activity.

The final activity, *clerical and administrative,* occurs in conjunction with all of the warehousing activities. Each activity must be administered effectively and efficiently. In addition, there is an enormous amount of clerical duties which must be performed in conjunction with each warehouse activity. In spite of numerous attempts by business firms to reduce the paperwork flow in the distribution process, the amount of paperwork that needs to be completed is enormous. It is for this reason, and many others, that firms have attempted to automate the clerical function whenever possible.

Figure 6–3 displays the relationship of each of the 15 warehousing

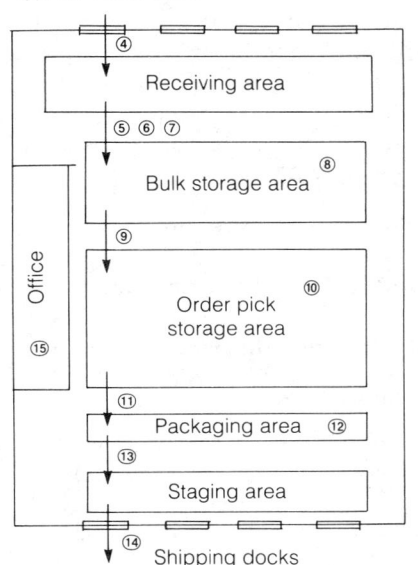

**FIGURE 6–3** Activities Performed in a Typical Warehouse

Source: A. T. Kearney, Inc., *Measuring Productivity in Physical Distribution* (Chicago: National Council of Physical Distribution Management, 1978), p. 96.

activities. For the most part, inventory control, purchasing, and order entry are decisions made prior to the goods being received at the warehouse.

**Warehouse Layout and Design**

Where things are located in the distribution system, and more particularly in the warehouse(s), has a critical effect on system efficiency and productivity. A good warehouse layout can (1) increase output, (2) improve product flow, (3) reduce costs, (4) improve service to customers, and (5) provide better employee working conditions.[8] Illustrative of some of the issues involved in effective warehouse layout include the following.

*Benefits Resulting from Good Warehouse Layout*

- A liquid and powdered bleach manufacturer is expanding a regional plant and warehouse by 50,000 square feet. *The problem:* What's the best location for the palletizers for each of the three primary products; and what is the best layout for the warehouse?
- A multiproduct warehouse is served by numerous truck and rail docks. *The problem:* How to revise the layout to minimize the handling needed for storage and retrieval?
- A paint manufacturer is planning a new warehouse for over 600 stockkeeping units (SKUs) of finished goods, with block storage for fast-movers plus racks and shelves for the rest. *The problem:* How to create a layout and handling system for two-year demand projections, and do it quickly while also considering requirements for five years out?[9]

The optimal warehouse layout and design for a firm will vary by the type of products being stored, the financial resources of the company, the competitive environment, and customer needs. However, irrespective of the preceding factors, it is imperative that the firm develop an optimal warehousing system for itself utilizing a logical and consistent decision strategy.

Bergen Brunswig Corporation, a large nationwide firm distributing pharmaceuticals and hospital supplies, has developed a seven-step approach to organized warehouse layout planning.

*A Seven-Step Approach to Warehouse Layout Planning*

1. Obtain at least a five-year projection of product-line growth, or longer if available.
2. Analyze the product line, quantities moved, flow of material, and space required.
3. Analyze material-handling equipment requirements.
4. Establish space requirements, including five-year projections when possible.
5. Establish relationships and closeness of all functions—shipping, receiving, order picking, packing, inventory storage, returned goods, etc.

---

[8] Mike Shumey, "Ways to Improve Productivity in a Physical Distribution Warehouse," in *Proceedings of the Sixteenth Annual Conference of the National Council of Physical Distribution Management, October 16–18, 1978,* p. 138.

[9] James A. Tompkins and John A. White, "Location Analysis—More than Just Plant Layout!" *Modern Materials Handling* 32, no. 9 (September 1977): 64. Copyright 1977 by Cahners Publishing Company, Division of Reed Holdings, Inc.

6. Draw several overall alternative layouts.
7. Select the best layout and provide detailed layout.[10]

It is important that a firm establish some procedure, manual or computerized, to develop effective and efficient warehouse layout.

Illustrative of some of the most popular computerized programs are CRAFT, COFAD, COSFAD, PLANET, CORELAP, and ALDEP. Table 6–1 iden-

**TABLE 6-1**  Most Popular Computerized Layout Programs and What They Do

| Type | Title | Acronym | What It Does |
| --- | --- | --- | --- |
| 1. Improvement, quantitative | Computerized relative allocation of facilities technique | CRAFT | Minimizes the volume-distance product |
|  | Computerized facilities design | COFAD | Minimizes the materials handling system cost |
|  | Computerized Safety and Facilities Design | COSFAD | Minimizes risk |
| 2. Construction, qualitative | Plant layout analysis and evaluation technique | PLANET | Maximizes closeness of related departments |
|  | Computerized relationship layout planning | CORELAP | Maximizes closeness relationships |
|  | Automated layout design program | ALDEP | Maximizes closeness relationships |

Two basic groups are available to help you improve existing layouts or create new ones from scratch. CRAFT, COFAD, and COSFAD are improvement routines which locate departments in an existing layout following quantitative criteria: volume-distance, cost, and risk. They minimize these factors. PLANET, CORELAP, and ALDEP are construction routines which help you develop layouts from scratch, based on maximizing qualitative activity relationships.

Source: James A. Tompkins and John A. White, "Location Analysis—More than Just Plant Layout," *Modern Materials Handling* 32, no. 9 (September 1977):69. Copyright 1977 by Cahners Publishing Company, Division of Reed Holdings, Inc.

tifies each computer routine and briefly explains its use. The computer programs are classified into two major categories: (1) *improvement*—a layout is initially input into the computer and improved upon in successive iterations; and (2) *constructive*—a layout is built up from scratch given certain conditions specified by the decision-maker.[11] Examples of two layout problems and their solutions are presented in Appendixes A and B. Both examples attempt to minimize travel distance within the storage facility. The examples can be worked through manually although more complex situations readily lend themselves to computer analysis.

---
[10] Shumey, "Ways to Improve Productivity," pp. 138–39.
[11] Tompkins and White, "Location Analysis," pp. 68–69.

Whatever layout is finally selected by the company for its warehouse, it is vital that all available space be utilized as fully and efficiently as possible. "Good space utilization practices begin with a layout designed to provide the optimum balance between space utilization and handling efficiency."[12] Some useful guidelines have been established by Bergen Brunswig Corporation which are appropriate for firms of all types. They include:

1. Space requirements for all products should be carefully calculated.
2. Make use of high-level storage, where practical.
3. Aisle dimensions are important. Aisles too narrow restrict flow of material and effective use of equipment. Aisles too wide simply waste space.
4. Make use of vertical overhead space for conveying material from one area to another.
5. Use mezzanines for order picking, or other warehousing functions.
6. Use space utilization standards to evaluate amount of space actually needed, amount of space used, and as a guide in evaluating expansion requirements.
7. Standards may be expressed as the ratio of cubic feet occupied to net usable storage space, or as percent usable square feet of total space.[13]

**Warehouse Handling Systems**

Closely related to warehouse layout and design is the storage and retrieval (S/R) system utilized by the firm. Efficient movement and storage within a warehouse requires the correct layout as well as the right S/R equipment. The following examples illustrate the relationship.

A high-rise automatic storage and retrieval system is being designed for an automotive parts supplier. *The problem:* How to locate items in the racks to minimize the average storage and retrieval time?

A pharmaceutical manufacturer plans to link production and finished-goods warehousing with a driverless tractor system. *The problem:* How many unloading stations are needed, and where should they be?[14]

"Every storage system must accommodate unit loads (mostly on pallets), individual cases (also called secondary packages), and individual shelf units (or primary packages). The complications begin because there are so many different items... The challenge is to come up with a rational system that can accommodate all the differences in the storage mix while minimizing costs."[15] Basically, warehouse storage systems can be classified into two categories: (1) standard or nonautomated; and (2) automated. The specific

---
[12] Shumey, "Ways to Improve Productivity," p. 143.
[13] Ibid., p. 143.
[14] Tompkins and White, "Location Analysis," p. 64.
[15] Walter F. Friedman, "Efficient Storage Systems," *Distribution Worldwide* 77, no. 12 (December 1978), p. 31.

type of equipment selected by a firm is dependent on many factors. Some of the more pertinent questions a firm should ask itself are the following:

**Before Selecting Warehouse Storage Systems Several Questions Need to Be Answered**

1. Is there excessive manual handling by employees?
2. Is high storage space being wasted?
3. Is present equipment antiquated and in need of repair?
4. Do forklifts require excessively wide aisles to swing palletized loads?[16]
5. Is there congestion in material-staging areas?
6. Are labor costs higher than other warehouses in the same line of business?
7. Is equipment flexible enough to handle changes in operating procedures?
8. What are the maintenance requirements and cost of the various handling systems?
9. Can acquisition of the handling system be economically justified?
10. Are spare parts and service available?[17]

*Standard systems.* The forklift truck is a vital part of almost every warehouse operation. It is the basic piece of equipment in all but the fully automated warehouse. Forklift trucks can be of various types as shown in Figure 6–4. The four examples presented in Figure 6–4 illustrate the fact that warehouse layout and warehouse handling systems are integrally intertwined. The simplest type of forklift truck, the counterbalanced truck, requires 10,000 square feet of space to handle 1,000 pallets of material. It is the least expensive forklift; under $5,000. The swing-reach truck requires only 4,600 square feet to handle 1,000 pallets but costs about $60,000. The warehouse decision maker must examine the cost trade-offs involved between the variety of available systems and determine which alternative is most advantageous from a cost/service perspective.

Other examples of standard systems include hand trucks, electric tractors, carts, cranes, platform trucks, etc. In each example there is direct human involvement (operation) with the piece of equipment.

*Automated systems.* "True automation in every sense of the word in a distribution center would involve automatic control of warehousing functions, from automated unloading of goods at the receiving dock, to identification and sortation, storing, picking, packing, and finally loading completed orders into the delivery trucks. In actual practice . . . most "automated" distribution warehouses have integrated some computer controlled equipment with the manually controlled functions."[18]

Many firms including United Parcel Service, Sears, John Deere, Ralston Purina, and others, have employed automated S/R systems (AS/R) in their warehouse operations. Examples of S/R systems used by firms include conveyors, case-picking equipment, driverless trucks, sorting equipment, and packaging equipment.

---

[16] Forklift trucks are the most common type of material handling equipment used in warehousing. Examples of several forklifts are shown in Figure 6–4.

[17] Shumey, "Ways to Improve Productivity," pp. 140–41.

[18] Ibid., p. 141.

**FIGURE 6–4** Space Required to Store 1,000 Pallets with Four Types of Lifts

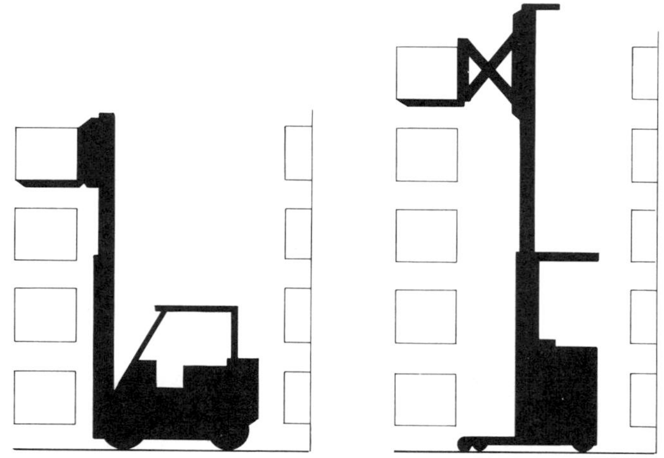

Counterbalanced truck
10,000 square feet
... Needs wider aisles to maneuver and has shorter reach than other models

Reach-fork truck
6,660 square feet
... Operates in aisles 4 feet to 6 feet narrower than a counterbalanced truck

In a survey by *Handling & Shipping* magazine of possible owners of S/R systems, it was found that approximately 15 percent of all firms have S/R systems.[19] Generally, the food, paper, primary metals, and machinery industries were more likely to have S/R systems. Almost one quarter of the companies without S/R systems anticipated the acquisition of such equipment within the foreseeable future.

The most important advantages which users mentioned about their S/R systems were savings in space, lower operating costs, better control of inventory, and reduction in manpower (see Table 6–2). Serious disadvantages which were mentioned included equipment failures or down time, loads lost in system, delays in debugging or adjustments, and training of employees (see Table 6–3). It was interesting that over one third of S/R system users reported no disadvantages whatsoever.

A case illustration of a company which has utilized an automatic S/R system is Farmers Union Central Exchange Inc. (Cenex). Cenex is a farmers cooperative, located in Minnesota and serving almost 1,000 customers located in the western United States. The company stocks over 27,000 items, ranging from wrenches to refrigerators. In a 183,000-square-foot addition to an existing warehouse, Cenex installed automatic S/R equipment. Figure 6–5 shows the warehouse configuration used by Cenex. As a result of the

---

[19] John Spencer, "You'd Better Believe . . . Some Facts about Storage/Retrieval Systems," *Handling & Shipping* 18, no. 6 (June 1977), pp. 65–71.

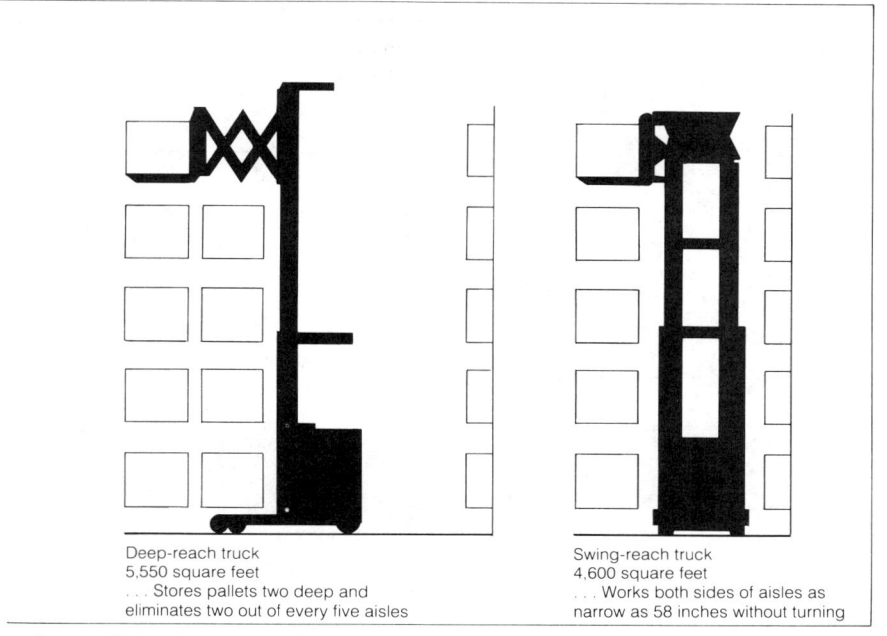

Deep-reach truck
5,550 square feet
... Stores pallets two deep and eliminates two out of every five aisles

Swing-reach truck
4,600 square feet
... Works both sides of aisles as narrow as 58 inches without turning

Source: Walter F. Friedman, "Efficient Storage Systems," *Distribution Magazine* 77, no. 12 (December 1978), pp. 32–33.

**TABLE 6-2** Experience with the System—Three Most Important Advantages Users Say They Enjoy from Their S/R Systems

| Advantage | \multicolumn{3}{c}{Percent of Users Rated Advantage Named at Left as} |
|---|---|---|---|
| | First | Second | Third |
| Saving in space required | 36.2 | 15.0 | 10.9 |
| Lower operating cost | 17.0 | 10.6 | 15.2 |
| Better control of inventory | 15.0 | 17.0 | 8.7 |
| Reduction of manpower required | 10.6 | 19.1 | 13.1 |
| More capacity without adding floor space | 8.5 | 15.0 | 8.7 |
| Faster operation | 6.4 | 10.6 | 17.4 |
| Fewer items lost | 2.1 | 6.4 | 0.0 |
| Less damage in handling | 2.1 | 2.1 | 4.4 |
| Better security for product stored | 2.1 | 0.0 | 6.5 |
| Reduced cost of storage building | 0.0 | 2.1 | 13.1 |
| Elimination of paperwork | 0.0 | 2.1 | 0.0 |
| Bases | (47) | (47) | (47) |

Source: John Spencer, "You'd Better Believe . . . Facts about Storage/Retrieval Systems," *Handling & Shipping* 18, no. 6 (June 1977), p. 68.

**TABLE 6-3** Experience with the System—Serious Disadvantages Which Users Say They Have Experienced with Their S/R Systems

|  | This Percent of Users Name and Rank Disadvantages Listed at Left Thus:* | | |
|---|---|---|---|
| Disadvantages | First | Second | Third |
| None (so answered—not a blank reply) | 34.6 | 0.0 | 0.0 |
| Equipment failures, down time | 20.4 | 14.2 | 0.0 |
| Loads lost in system | 10.2 | 0.0 | 0.0 |
| Delays in debugging, adjustment | 8.1 | 14.2 | 25.0 |
| Training of employees | 6.1 | 23.8 | 12.5 |
| Delays in installation | 4.0 | 4.8 | 0.0 |
| Poor service from major contractor | 4.0 | 0.0 | 12.5 |
| Higher installed cost than expected | 2.1 | 4.8 | 12.5 |
| Higher operating cost than expected | 2.1 | 0.0 | 25.0 |
| Problems with OSHA | 2.1 | 0.0 | 0.0 |
| Problems with insurer | 2.1 | 4.8 | 0.0 |
| Loads damaged by equipment | 0.0 | 4.8 | 12.5 |
| Employee sabotage | 2.1 | 0.0 | 0.0 |
| Equipment maintenance more costly than expected | 0.0 | 23.8 | 12.5 |
| Can't use whole system because inventory isn't cyclical | 2.1 | 0.0 | 0.0 |
| Problem to maintain diverse products | 0.0 | 4.9 | 0.0 |
| Bases | (49) | (21) | (8) |

* Note base of percent.
Source: John Spencer, "You'd Better Believe . . . Facts about Storage/Retrieval Systems," *Handling & Shipping* 18, no. 6 (June 1977), p. 68.

new system, orderpicking productivity increased by more than 20 percent, customer order "fill time" was reduced to one day, and "fill rate" increased to 92 percent.[20]

Warehouse handling systems, whether automated or manual, are an important part of the firm's total distribution system. A company can realize a number of benefits by utilizing good material-handling equipment including:

Benefits Can Result from Good Material Handling Equipment

1. Increased productivity per employee through increased output.
2. Reduced operating expenses.
3. Optimized machine utilization.
4. Increased space utilization.
5. Reduced damage to inventory.
6. Increased customer service levels.
7. Reduced employee fatigue.
8. Reduced accidents.
9. Improved flow of material.[21]

[20] "A High-Variety Warehouse with High Productivity and Low Cost!" *Modern Materials Handling* 43, no. 11 (November 1977), p. 76.
[21] Shumey, "Ways to Improve Productivity," p. 140.

**FIGURE 6-5** A High-Variety Warehouse

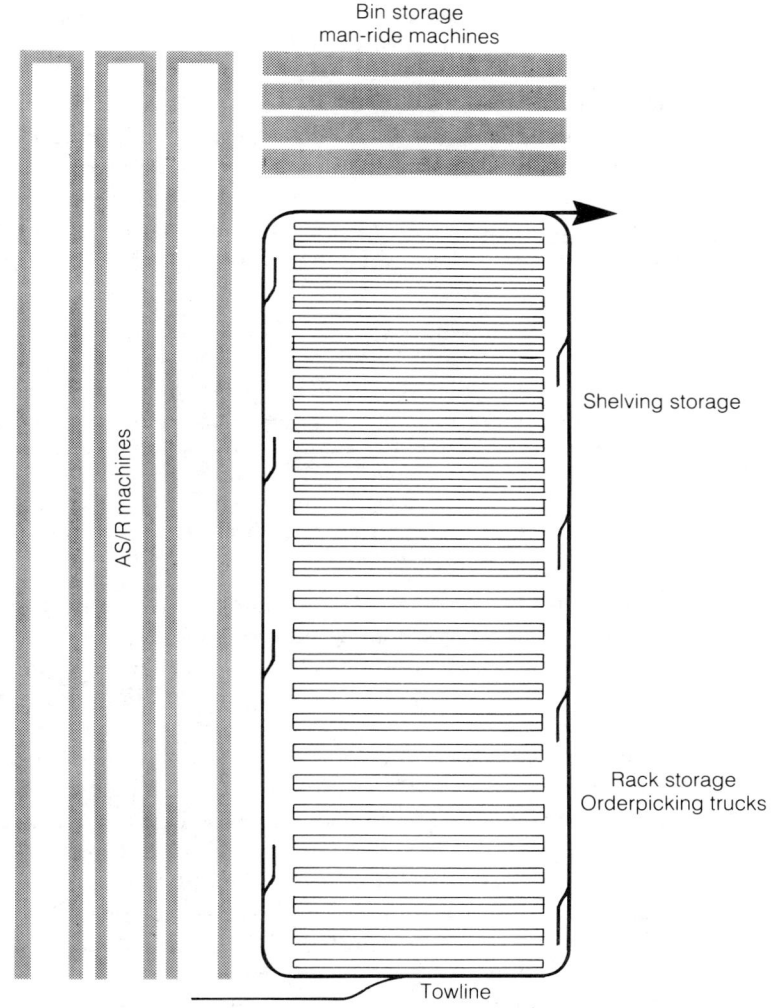

The idea was to store active stock for picking in minimum space without sacrificing access. Picking areas are also segregated by item size. Research stock, in pallet loads, is in the AS/R system at left. From the AS/RS, loads go by lift truck to the towline to picking areas. Slow movers go by truck directly to picking areas, bypassing the AS/RS. Picking areas include bin storage for small parts, served by man-ride machines with special towcarts; shelving for case-lot picking, served by orderpicking trucks and towcarts; and pallet racks for pallet loads and fast-moving case-lots, served by orderpicking trucks and pallets.

Source: "A High-Variety Warehouse with High Productivity and Low Cost!" *Modern Materials Handling* 32, no. 11 (November 1977), p. 78. Copyright 1977 by Cahners Publishing Company, Division of Reed Holdings, Inc.

### Packaging

**Packaging Performs Marketing and Distribution Functions**

Packaging serves two basic functions, marketing and distribution. Its marketing function is one in which the package provides information to the customer about the product and promotes the product through the use of color, sizing, etc. Its distribution function is simply to keep the product free from damage as it is transported and stored within the firm's distribution system.

> It may be that the packaging trade-offs are the least used trade-offs in physical distribution. Package an item one way and you can safely expose it to shock, vibration, weather, soiling, and no harm will be done to it—that kind of packaging can save in transportation costs and storage costs. Package another way, and you save on packaging, but you must spend more for better storage conditions, vehicles that cause less shock and vibration, more careful handling; the extra costs may be offset a little by lighter weight and smaller space requirements. Does industry look at these opportunities? Or does it pass them by, satisfied with conventional acceptance of packaging as it is?[22]

The optimal package should be one which optimizes service, cost, and convenience. The package should be designed to provide the most efficient storage of product. Good packaging ". . . affects materials handling in terms of load stability and compatibility with the different forms of mechanization and automation . . . it satisfies warehousing requirements through dimension and stackability for good pallet patterns and efficient storage."[23]

In a study of a variety of industries, *Handling & Shipping* magazine asked companies to identify the factors which governed good package design. Table 6—4 identifies those factors mentioned most frequently by business firms. The factors can be conveniently categorized into the following characteristics: (1) standard quantities, (2) pricing (cost), (3) product or package adaptability, (4) protective level, and (5) handling ability. The importance placed on each of the factors shown in Table 6—4 by a firm, as well as the cost/service trade-offs made, will vary by industry. For example, a food processor will be more concerned with having a package that minimizes shipping and storage costs than will a computer manufacturer because of the differences in products (cost, physical characteristics, etc.). The computer manufacturer on the other hand will place more emphasis on the protective aspects of packaging because of the fragile, and expensive, nature of computer systems.

The distribution package results from many components of the firm's operations and is represented pictorially in Figure 6—6.

---

[22] John F. Spencer, "A Picture of Packaging in the Context of Physical Distribution," *Handling & Shipping* 18, no. 10 (October 1977), p. 43.

[23] Walter F. Friedman, "The Total Package," *Distribution Worldwide* 74, no. 2 (February 1975), p. 53.

**TABLE 6-4** Factors Which Influence Package Design Decisions

| Factor | Percent of Firms Mentioning the Factor |
|---|---|
| Minimize damage to package contents | 77% |
| Minimize shipping/packaging cost | 73 |
| Design package for handling with lift trucks | 63 |
| Protect contents of package from shock, impact | 63 |
| Minimize shipping cost | 55 |
| Meet carriers' requirements | 47 |
| Identification of contents | 43 |
| Weights and shapes appropriate for manual handling | 41 |
| Column strength of package, for stacking | 41 |
| Meet needs for export | 40 |
| Meet customers' specifications | 39 |
| Compatibility with existing handling and warehousing systems | 37 |
| Protection from external moisture | 36 |
| Conform to regulations on hazardous materials | 36 |
| Dimensions for good pallet patterns | 35 |
| Protection of contents from vibration | 33 |
| Dimensions for best use of space in trucks, railcars, etc. | 33 |

Source: John F. Spencer, "A Picture of Packaging in the Context of Physical Distribution," *Handling & Shipping* 18, no. 10 (October 1977), p. 47.

Developing the Distribution Package

What is involved in designing the distribution package?

The ultimate goal is to develop a package that optimizes service, cost and convenience factors for all elements of the marketing and physical distribution system. In the broadest approach, distribution packaging begins with the design of the product, and it ends with the re-use or disposal of the package.

More narrowly, it concentrates on the shipping container—which might be a corrugated box, cargo cage, van container, truck, covered hopper, or tank car. It also covers any inner containers or protectors as well as the individual consumer package.

Design of the distribution package involves proper product identification with the size, type and location of the item code or Universal Product Code and with other package information to assure correct selection, sorting and shipping. It relates to transportation through package density and efficient cube use; it satisfies warehousing requirements through dimension and stackability for good pallet patterns and efficient storage; it affects materials handling in terms of load stability and compatibility with the different forms of mechanization and automation; it has impact on the customer's distribution system in terms of the ability to receive and integrate merchandise with his warehouse operating system, particularly with less than full case order picking.

The interactions of distribution packaging become complex with product protection, which applies not only in the manufacturer warehouse but also in rail or truck or other forms of transport, in the customer warehouse with many different forms of mechanized or automated materials handling, and in the consumer outlet or other end-use environment.

Distribution packaging must also consider total distribution costs, including freight rates, handling and storage efficiency, and end-use costs of opening and disposal of the package and assembly or other preparation of the product.

**FIGURE 6-6** The Distribution Package is the End Result of Many Interactions and Must Be Looked at in Terms of the Total Picture for Full Efficiency

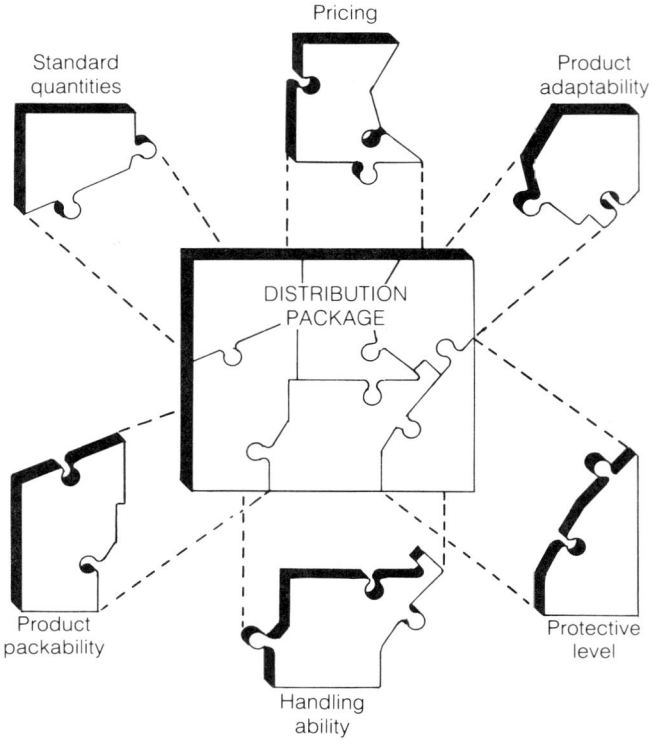

[Puzzle-piece diagram with central piece labeled "DISTRIBUTION PACKAGE" connected to surrounding pieces labeled: Pricing, Standard quantities, Product adaptability, Product packability, Protective level, Handling ability]

Source: Walter F. Friedman, "The Total Package," *Distribution Worldwide* 74, no. 2 (February 1975), p. 55.

The intangibles of the distribution package are important in terms of customer convenience—those hard-to-measure end-use benefits that allow smooth interface with merchandising, production, or other aspects of the customer's distribution system.

The cost of materials and producing a package, of course, is also a prime factor in any packaging system, but the optimum system is one that considers all the requirements we have outlined at the lowest total cost. Obviously, this involves a good deal more than simple design.

It means that you have to mediate conflicts, evaluate trade-offs, and reach a fair balance. It means that you have to question basic manufacturing, marketing, and distribution assumptions so that invalid claims can be eliminated in favor of meaningful requirements.

It means that you have to measure warehousing and transportation and handling costs against packaging costs and all of them against product protection. And it means that you have to weigh manufacturing efficiencies and marketing decisions against distributor and retailer needs. It means that you have to be willing to pay a premium in one area in order to introduce badly needed benefits in another area—and thereby gain a very real marketing edge.[24]

---
[24] Ibid., p. 54.

## DECISION-MAKING STRATEGIES IN WAREHOUSING

*Should Warehousing Be Owned, Rented, or Leased?*

Effective warehouse management involves a thorough understanding of the functions of warehousing, the merits of public versus private warehousing alternatives, the financial and service aspects of warehousing decisions, a knowledge of methods which can improve warehousing performance, and a strategy for locating warehousing facilities at the most-optimal locations.

Warehousing decisions may be strategic or operational. Strategic decisions are those that deal with the allocation of distribution resources over an extended time period in a manner that is consistent and supportive of overall enterprise policy and objectives. They can take two forms, either long range or project type. An example of a long-range strategic decision is physical distribution system design. A project type decision might deal with consolidation of branch warehouses into a regional distribution center. Other examples of typical strategic decisions include: (1) should warehousing be owned, leased, rented, or some combination; (2) should the warehousing function be "spun off"; and (3) should the company install new materials handling equipment or continue to utilize more labor.

Operational decisions are those decisions that are used to manage or control physical distribution performance. Typically, these decisions are routine in nature and involve time horizons of one year or less. Due to the short time horizon involved these decisions have less uncertainty than strategic decisions. Also, they relate to the coordination and performance of the physical distribution system. Given a system design, operational decisions are related to efficient and effective performance of the system. For example, a warehouse manager would be concerned with increasing costs and/or declining productivity in the shipping department.

### Public versus Private Warehousing

One of the most important warehousing decisions is whether public or private facilities should be utilized. In order that the proper decision be made from a cost and service standpoint it is necessary that the warehousing manager understand the advantages and disadvantages of each alternative.

*Advantages of public warehousing.*

*Eight Advantages of Public Warehousing*

The benefits that may be realized if a firm uses public warehouses rather than privately owned or operated warehouses include: (1) conservation of capital; (2) the ability to increase warehouse space to cover peak requirements; (3) reduced risk; (4) economies of scale; (5) flexibility; (6) tax advantages; (7) knowledge of costs for storage and handling; and (8) to minimize labor disputes.

*Conservation of capital.* One of the major advantages of public warehouses is that they require no capital investment on the part of the user. The user avoids the investment in buildings, land, and material handling equipment as well as the costs associated with starting up the operation and hiring and training personnel.

*Meeting peak distribution requirements.* If a firm has any seasonality in its operations, the public warehouse option allows the user to contract for as much storage space as needed to meet peak requirements. A private warehouse, on the other hand, has a constraint on the maximum amount of product that can be stored and is likely to be underutilized during a portion of each year.

Since most firms experience substantial variations in inventory level due to seasonality in demand or production, sales promotions, or other factors, public warehousing offers the distinct advantage of allowing storage costs to vary directly with volume.

*Reduced risk.* Usually companies plan for a distribution facility to have a life of from 20 to 40 years. Consequently, by investing in a private warehouse, management assumes the risk that the facility will become obsolete due to changes in technology or changes in the volume of business.

*Economies of scale.* Public warehouses are able to achieve economies of scale that would not be possible for a small firm to attain. This is because public warehouses handle the warehousing requirements of a number of firms and their volume allows the employment of a full-time basic warehousing staff. Also, building costs are nonlinear and a firm pays a premium to build a small facility. Additional economies of scale can be provided by using more expensive but more efficient material handling equipment and by providing administrative and other expertise.

Public warehouses are able to offer a number of specialized services more economically than a private warehouse. These specialized services include:

- Broken-case handling which is breaking down manufacturers' case quantities to enable orders for less-than-full case quantities to be filled.
- Packaging of manufacturers' products for shipping. A variation of this is performed by Distribution Centers Inc., a public warehousing firm, for the California Growers Association. Product is shipped to the Atlanta distribution center in the "brights," cans without labels, and the labels are put on the product at the public warehouse as orders are received from customers.
- Damaged product and product being recalled by the manufacturer are consolidated at the warehouse for shipment to the manufacturer in carload or truckload quantities. In addition to the documentation and prepacking that may be necessary, the public warehouse frequently performs the rework of damaged product.
- Equipment maintenance and service.
- Stock spotting of product for manufacturers with limited or highly seasonal product lines. Stock spotting involves shipping a consolidated carload of inventory to a public warehouse just prior to a period of maximum seasonal sales.
- A break-bulk service whereby the manufacturer combines the orders of different customers located in a market and ships them at the carload

or truckload rate to the public warehouse where the individual orders are separated and local delivery is provided.

Finally, economies of scale are made possible by the consolidation of small shipments with other noncompetitors using the same public warehouse. The public warehouse consolidates orders from a specific customer for the products of a number of different manufacturers on a single shipment. This results in lower shipping costs as well as reduced congestion at the customer's receiving dock. Also, customers who pick up their orders at the public warehouse are able to obtain the products of several manufacturers with one stop, if the manufacturers use the same facility.

*Flexibility.* Another major advantage offered by public warehouses is flexibility. Owning or holding a long-term lease on a warehouse can become a burden if business conditions necessitate changes in locations. Public warehouses require only a short-term contract and thus long-term commitments are avoided. The short-term contracts available from public warehouses make it easy to change field-warehouse locations if there is a change in the marketplace such as a shift in the population, a change in the relative cost of various modes of transportation, a change in the volume of a product sold, or a change in the company's financial position.

In addition, a firm that uses public warehouses does not have to hire or lay-off warehouse employees as the volume of business changes. A public warehouse also provides the personnel required for extra services when they are necessary without having to hire them on a full-time basis.

Finally, public warehousing makes it possible for the manufacturer to experiment with a warehouse location to determine its contribution to the firm's distribution system and to discontinue the operation with relative ease if cost savings or performance objectives are not realized.

*Tax advantages.* In most states there is a definite advantage to not owning property in the state because such ownership means that the firm is doing business in the state and is subject to various state taxes. These taxes can be substantial. Consequently, if the firm does not currently own property in a state it may be advantageous to use a public warehouse. Also, certain states do not charge property tax on inventories in public warehouses and this tax shelter applies to both regular warehouse inventory and storage-in-transit inventories. A *free-port* provision enacted in some states allows inventory to be held for up to one year, tax free. Finally, there is no real estate tax payable by the manufacturer. Of course the public warehouse pays real estate tax and this must be included in the warehouse rates but, it is smaller on a per-unit throughput basis because of the significantly larger volume of business possible.

*Knowledge of storage and handling costs.* When a manufacturer uses a public warehouse, storage and handling costs are known because a bill is received each month. Also, it is possible to forecast costs for different levels of activity because the costs are known in advance. Firms that operate their own facilities often find it very difficult to determine the fixed and variable costs and the basis for variability.

*To minimize labor disputes.* The courts have ruled that a labor union does not have the right to picket a public warehouse when the union is involved in a labor dispute with one of the customers of that public warehouse. Thus using a public warehouse has the advantage of insulating the manufacturer's distribution system from a labor dispute.

**Public Warehousing Has Its Disadvantages**

***Disadvantages of public warehousing.*** A number of disadvantages may be associated with the use of public warehousing. First, using public warehouses may require a more complex administration. Another frequently mentioned disadvantage is lack of control. However, this disadvantage may be overstated for the following reasons: (1) in many markets competition may be so intensive that a public warehouse operator, with a large account on a relatively short-term contract, has a definite incentive to perform well; and (2) the public warehouse operation may be held responsible, under the terms of the contract, for pilferage and damage, which brings these costs to zero for the user.

Effective communications may be a problem with public warehouses because computer terminals manufactured by various competitors are not compatible with all computer systems. A warehouse operator may be hesitant to add another terminal for just one customer. Additionally, lack of standardization in contractual agreements makes communication regarding contractual obligations difficult.

Finally, the space or specialized services desired may not always be available in a specific location. Most public warehouse facilities only provide local service and are of limited use to a firm that distributes regionally or nationally. Consequently, a manufacturer that wants to use public warehouses for national distribution may find it necessary to deal with several different operators and monitor several contractual agreements.

***Public warehousing services.*** A number of services are offered by a public warehouse. In a study of public warehouse users and nonusers, James Stock and Earl Carrara identified five categories of service being offered: (1) facility characteristics, (2) warehouse services, (3) transportation services, (4) clerical services, and (5) miscellaneous factors.[25]

Many studies of public warehousing have asked companies to rate the importance of various services and products. Unfortunately, such information is not always useful because it is difficult to determine with a level-of-importance measure whether or not a potential customer will or will not use a public warehouse if the service or characteristic they require is lacking. Stock and Carrara attempted to overcome the problem by determining if a company would utilize a general-merchandise public warehouse if a particular factor was absent.

**User Perceptions of Public Warehousing Services**

Table 6–5 shows management perceptions of the importance of nine *facility characteristics.* Potential public-warehousing customers considered the protection of their product extremely important as evidenced by the large number of companies that considered sprinkler systems and security

---

[25] James R. Stock and Earl A. Carrara, "How To Choose a Public Warehouse," *Distribution* 79, no. 4 (April 1980), pp. 42–46.

**TABLE 6-5** Importance of Facility Characteristics in Selecting a Public Warehouse

| | Necessity of Item | | |
|---|---|---|---|
| Characteristics | Absolutely Necessary | Important but Not Absolutely Necessary | Not Important and Not Necessary |
| Availability of sprinkler system ($N = 358$) | 60.9% | 29.6% | 9.5% |
| Sophisticated security systems ($N = 361$) | 32.7 | 51.2 | 16.1 |
| Special handling equipment ($N = 359$) | 34.5 | 36.5 | 29.0 |
| Availability of pallet racks ($N = 360$) | 31.7 | 33.9 | 34.4 |
| Downtown location ($N = 357$) | 1.1 | 10.4 | 88.5 |
| Availability of refrigerated space ($N = 354$) | 5.6 | 5.1 | 89.3 |
| Availability of freezer space ($N = 353$) | 3.1 | 2.8 | 94.1 |
| Suburban location ($N = 357$) | 7.3 | 29.7 | 63.0 |
| Availability of office space on premises ($N = 354$) | 11.0 | 16.1 | 72.9 |

systems as being absolutely necessary or very important. A significant number of firms considered the availability of pallet racks and special handling equipment as important and/or absolutely necessary. With respect to location, a significant number of companies felt that a suburban location was superior to a downtown location. Many public warehouses do not offer office space on premises although 11.0 percent of public warehousing customers felt that the availability of office space was absolutely necessary.

Over the years, the public-warehousing industry has added many distribution services. Table 6-6 identifies some of the more important *warehouse services* which customers are demanding and which the modern public warehouse is offering more frequently.

Lease of specific blocks of space, pool distribution, shipment consolidation, and preventive sanitation programs are considered important by public warehouse users and nonusers. Temperature and humidity control systems are also considered very necessary. An ability to handle hazardous materials and store bulk commodities is thought necessary by a significant number of firms; however, for most public warehouses additional facility expense would be required to store/handle such materials. Also, the impact that storage of those types of products would have on products already stored would be unknown.

Packaging and labeling capability is considered to be absolutely necessary by almost 20 percent of the firms. There is a concept in marketing called *functional shiftability* which states that marketing/distribution functions can be shifted within the channel of distribution but cannot be elimi-

**TABLE 6-6** Importance of Warehouse Services in Selecting a Public Warehouse

| | Necessity of Item | | |
|---|---|---|---|
| Service | Absolutely Necessary | Important but Not Absolutely Necessary | Not Important and Not Necessary |
| Lease of specific blocks of space ($N = 353$) | 33.7% | 35.1% | 31.2% |
| Bulk material handling and storage ($N = 355$) | 25.1 | 21.4 | 53.5 |
| Packaging and labeling capability ($N = 352$) | 19.6 | 23.6 | 56.8 |
| Pool distribution ($N = 352$) | 10.8 | 23.9 | 65.3 |
| Temperature control ($N = 358$) | 24.3 | 28.2 | 47.5 |
| Humidity control ($N = 356$) | 18.5 | 32.1 | 49.4 |
| Shipment consolidation ($N = 355$) | 17.5 | 36.9 | 45.6 |
| Recooperage ($N = 346$) | 9.5 | 31.0 | 59.5 |
| Ability to handle hazardous materials ($N = 358$) | 15.4 | 12.8 | 71.8 |
| Prevention sanitation programs ($N = 350$) | 20.6 | 23.7 | 55.7 |

* Recooperage is the recovery of damaged merchandise and is essentially a repackaging/labeling operation performed by the public warehouse.

nated. Traditionally manufacturers have packaged and labeled their products in-plant. However, with the proliferation of products (sizes, styles, assortments, branded, and unbranded) in recent years, manufacturers have been forced to carry larger amounts of inventory in order to effectively service their customers. Because the public warehouse is generally a "step closer" to the final customer in the channel of distribution, it is possible to assume the packaging/labeling function and thereby reduce the total amount of manufacturers' inventory while at the same time improving order-cycle time through quicker response time. At the present time very few public or private warehousing operations have packaging/labeling capability.

Five aspects of *transportation service* are identified in Table 6-7. Although many firms felt that it was a definite advantage for a public warehouse to own or manage local cartage service, the presence of good working relationships with the various transport modes was considered sufficient. Generally, good rail service was perceived to be less essential than good motor-carrier service. In fact, a majority of firms believed that access to good rail connectors and direct service by a specific rail line were not important and not necessary in their decision to select a public warehouse. The availability of warehouse-owned or -managed local cartage was important or absolutely necessary to many companies. Some public warehouses have responded by entering into contractual arrangements with local/regional transporters, and/or acquiring local carriers in areas where pick-up/delivery service was marginal or poor. Control over local cartage can be a significant marketing advantage in a highly competitive market.

**TABLE 6-7**  Importance of Transportation Services in Selecting a Public Warehouse

|  | Necessity of Item |  |  |
|---|---|---|---|
| Service | Absolutely Necessary | Important but Not Absolutely Necessary | Not Important and Not Necessary |
| Access to good rail connectors ($N = 355$) | 15.8% | 29.3% | 54.9% |
| Good location with respect to motor-carrier terminals ($N = 362$) | 57.2 | 33.7 | 9.1 |
| Availability of warehouse-owned or -managed local cartage ($N = 358$) | 17.3 | 48.6 | 34.1 |
| Direct service by specific rail line ($N = 355$) | 6.5 | 19.1 | 74.4 |
| Good relationship with local carriers or cartage companies ($N = 364$) | 51.4 | 36.5 | 12.1 |

**TABLE 6-8**  Importance of Clerical Services in Selecting a Public Warehouse

|  | Necessity of Item |  |  |
|---|---|---|---|
| Service | Absolutely Necessary | Important but Not Absolutely Necessary | Not Important and Not Necessary |
| Availability of computer facilities ($N = 351$) | 11.7% | 34.5% | 53.8% |
| Freight-bill payment ($N = 350$) | 12.3 | 32.0 | 55.7 |
| Inventory reports at specified intervals ($N = 356$) | 58.1 | 21.7 | 20.2 |
| Notification of low stock levels ($N = 351$) | 31.9 | 29.1 | 39.0 |
| Shipment routing ($N = 351$) | 27.4 | 34.7 | 37.9 |
| Customer billing ($N = 348$) | 11.2 | 16.1 | 72.7 |

Table 6–8 shows that *clerical services* were extremely important to firms considering the use of public warehousing. The modern public warehouse provides much more than storage space. Increasingly the users of public warehousing are demanding a variety of clerical services that traditionally were performed elsewhere in the channel of distribution (the concept of functional shiftability).

Firms require a lot more information today than in past years—and a lot more-sophisticated information too! The availability of computer equipment on-site is a definite plus factor. A computer software system, supported by the appropriate hardware, will become even more important in the future as the public warehouse assumes more clerical functions. The optimal system should have the capacity to perform traffic-management functions (rating, routing, mode/carrier selection), inventory control (report inventory levels, prepare out-of-stock reports), and accounting functions (billing, payments).

Most companies do not consider public warehousing cost as the sole criterion for selecting a particular warehouse. Service factors are vitally important to the public warehouse user. Of course, costs are still very important and will continue to be, given the need for firms to be cost efficient in order to remain competitive. As shown in Table 6–9, there are advan-

**TABLE 6-9** Importance of Miscellaneous Factors in Selecting a Public Warehouse

|  | Necessity of Item ||| 
| --- | --- | --- | --- |
| Factor | Absolutely Necessary | Important but Not Absolutely Necessary | Not Important and Not Necessary |
| Ability to provide rate quotations on any basis ($N = 349$) | 25.8% | 40.1% | 34.1% |
| Resident management ($N = 348$) | 33.9 | 41.4 | 24.7 |
| Lowest rates in the area ($N = 345$) | 20.0 | 60.9 | 19.1 |
| Import/export capability ($N = 345$) | 17.4 | 32.5 | 50.1 |
| Consultation services ($N = 343$) | 6.4 | 30.0 | 63.6 |
| Bonded space ($N = 345$) | 26.4 | 28.1 | 45.5 |

tages in being the public warehouse with the lowest rates in town, but not all firms select the cheapest warehouse in which to place their products. What is important is that a public warehouse be competitive with its rates and if they're higher, be able to cost justify them to prospective clients.

Related to this item is an ability to provide rate quotations on any basis. At a minimum, a public warehouse should be able to quote rates on a square-foot, pallet, or cubic-foot basis. However, few warehouses quote rates for basic storage, storage plus all the extra services, *or* the services alone. Today an automobile purchaser can buy the car of his/her choice with few options, with every option, or anywhere in-between. The buyer can also know exactly how much each option will cost and can then make an intelligent, rational decision on which option(s) to purchase.

In most public warehouses, the buyer (user firm) generally has only two options—basic storage only or basic storage plus all the options. There usually is no in-between. Many users of public warehousing pay for services they do not need. This leads some companies to place their products in public warehouses that offer fewer services than they really require, but at a lower price. The philosophy of one price fits all, is fast becoming obsolete. The public warehouse of the future will have a price list which specifically identifies the various rates being charged for each of the services being offered.

**Six Advantages of Private Warehousing**

***Advantages of private warehousing.*** Private warehouses have many advantages over public warehouses although the major advantage is the greater degree of *control* exercised by the company owning the goods. The firm has direct control, and responsibility, of the product until the customer takes possession or delivery.[26] This greater degree of control allows the firm to more easily integrate the warehousing function into the total distribution system of the company.

With this warehouse control comes a greater degree of *flexibility*. This is not flexibility from the perspective of being able to reduce or increase storage space quickly; rather, it is flexibility in being able to design and operate the warehouse to exactly fit the needs of customers and characteristics of the product. Companies with highly specialized products requiring special handling and/or storage may not find public warehousing feasible. In those instances the firm must utilize private warehousing or ship direct to customers. Also, the warehouse can be modified through expansion or renovation to facilitate product changes, or it can be converted to a manufacturing plant or branch office location.

Another prominent advantage of private warehousing is that it can be *less costly* over the long term than public warehousing. Operating costs can be 15 – 25 percent lower if sufficient throughput or utilization is achieved. The generally accepted industry norm for the utilization rate of a private warehouse is 75 – 80 percent. If a firm could not achieve at least a 75 percent utilization rate, it would generally be more appropriate to use public warehousing. Of course, it should be apparent that good management control is a prerequisite to keeping private-warehousing costs at a minimum.

By employing private warehousing a firm can make greater use of its present *manpower resources*. It is possible to utilize the expertise of the technical specialists within the firm. Also, the company's employees will be the individuals working in the warehouse. Generally, greater care in handling and storage occurs when the firm's own work force operates the warehouse. It should be noted however, that some public warehouses will allow a firm to utilize its own employees in the handling and storage of products within the confines of the public warehouse.

*Tax benefits* can also be realized when a company owns its warehouses. Depreciation allowances on building and equipment can substantially reduce the cost of a structure or apparatus over its life.

Finally, there may be certain *intangible benefits* associated with warehouse ownership. When a firm distributes its products through a private warehouse, it can give the customer a sense of permanence and continuity of business operations. The customer sees the company as a stable, dependable, and lasting supplier of products. This can mean marketing advantages for the firm.

**Private Warehousing Is Not for Everyone**

***Disadvantages of private warehousing.*** Many experts feel that the major drawback to private warehousing is the same as one of its main

---

[26] Charles A. Taff, *Management of Physical Distribution and Transportation,* 5th ed. (Homewood, Ill.: Richard D. Irwin, 1972), p. 173.

advantages—*flexibility*. A private warehouse may be too costly because of its fixed size and costs. Irrespective of the level of demand experienced by the firm, the size of the private warehouse is restricted in the short term. A private facility can not expand and contract to meet increases or decreases in demand. When demand is low the firm must still assume the fixed-cost expense as well as lower productivity associated with unused warehouse space.

If a firm uses only private warehouses, it also loses flexibility in its strategic location options. Changes in market size, location, and preferences are often swift and unpredictable. If a company cannot adapt to these changes in its warehouse structure it may lose a valuable business opportunity. Customer service and sales could also fall if a private warehouse was not able to adapt to changes in the firm's product mix.

Because of the prohibitive costs involved, many firms are simply unable to generate enough *capital* to build or buy a warehouse. A warehouse is a long-term, often risky investment and may be difficult to sell because of its customized design. Also, depending on the nature of the firm, return on investment may be greater if funds are channeled into other profit-generating opportunities.

Many *costs* are incurred in building a warehouse. An extensive and costly site analysis must precede any building. The warehouse must be designed around the products to be contained, and their handling. Expensive research and analysis are necessary to complete this step. Start up costs will be high because of the need to hire and train employees. Also material-handling equipment must be selected, purchased, maintained, and repaired—all time and cost consuming activities.

*A financial comparison of public versus private warehousing.* The primary advantages of public and private warehouses are summarized in Table 6—10. These factors must be considered in light of the characteristics of each individual firm. A further consideration in the decision is the rate of return that will be provided by the private warehouse alternative. The investment in a corporate-owned warehouse should generate the same rate of return as other investments made by the firm. Table 6—11 illustrates the type of financial analysis that must be performed. To simplify the analysis for this example, it was assumed that annual operating costs would not change over the life of the investment and that straight line depreciation would be taken for tax purposes. However, in reality, warehousing costs would be expected to change from year to year and accelerated depreciation would be used for tax purposes in order to maximize cash inflow in the early years. An investment tax credit also would apply. To simplify the need for making assumptions about cost behavior too far into the future, a five- to seven-year time horizon normally would be used.

### Measurement and Improvement of Warehouse Performance

In order to achieve maximum efficiency from the warehousing function, performance of both public and private facilities must be measured and controlled. One method involves the development of standard costs and flexible budgets for private facilities. This is accomplished by isolating the

**TABLE 6–10** Summary of Factors Influencing the Public/Private Warehousing Decision

|  | Public Warehouses | Private Warehouses |
|---|---|---|
| Operating costs | Higher due to inclusion of profit factor, selling, and advertising costs | 10% to 25% lower if sufficient volume |
| Initial investment | None | Large facility, startup, equipment, train personnel |
| Control | Good due to incentive to perform on short-term contract | Direct responsibility over personnel and procedures |
| Risk | Minimal | Risk of obsolescence due to change in technology or demand |
| Tax advantages | Free-port states real estate taxless, no property advantage | Depreciation allowance |
| Economies of scale | Possible due to serving many customers | Dependent on company's volume |
| Consolidation of shipments | Can consolidate to warehouse and from warehouse to customer | None |
| Storage and handling costs | Know exact charges for decision making | Generally only estimated |

behavior of costs on a fixed and variable basis. Another possibility is the development of warehousing ratios such as productivity ratios, efficiency ratios, and effectiveness ratios. These methods are summarized in Figure 6–7 and they will be discussed further in Chapter 11, Financial Control of Distribution Performance.

In the NCPDM-sponsored study on productivity measurement in physical distribution, three types of warehousing measures were developed.

> Productivity is the ratio of real output to real input. Examples are cases handled per labor-hour and lines selected per equipment-hour.
>
> Utilization is the ratio of capacity used to available capacity. Examples are percent of pallet spaces filled in a warehouse and employee hours worked versus employee hours available.
>
> Performance is the ratio of actual output to standard output (or standard hours earned to actual hours). Examples are cases picked per hour versus standard rate planned per hour and actual return on assets employed versus budgeted return on assets employed.[27]

---

[27] A. T. Kearney, Inc., *Measuring Productivity in Physical Distribution* (Chicago: National Council of Physical Distribution Management, 1978), p. 95.

**TABLE 6-11** Comparative Analysis of the Financial Impact of the Public versus Private Decision

Consider only the costs that differ between the alternatives

For example

| Cost Category | Options | |
|---|---|---|
| | Public | Private |
| Investment in warehouse and equipment | — | X |
| Annual operating costs excluding depreciation | M | N |
| Tax implications of depreciation | — | K |

Where

$X = \$3,000,000$
$M = \$2,700,000$
$N = \$2,300,000$

Fixed = $\$950,000$
Variable = $\$1,350,000$

Depreciation = $150,000 (assuming straight-line depreciation and a useful life of 20 years)

Income taxes = 40% of net income
$K = 60,000 \, (150,000 \times 40\%)$

Also assume:
1. The required rate of return is 16% after taxes.
2. The land cost for the warehouse is $1,000,000 but the estimated value in 20 years is $10,000,000 after taxes.
3. The building will have a estimated salvage value of $2,000,000 at the end of 20 years. Since the building will have been fully depreciated, this amount is taxable at 40%.

After-Tax Analysis of Public versus Private Decision

| | | Present-Value Discount Factors, 16% | Total Present Value | Sketch of Cash Flows (end of year, 000,000s) |
|---|---|---|---|---|

Sketch of Cash Flows time points: 0  1  2  3  4 ......20

**A. Public**

| | | | | |
|---|---|---|---|---|
| Recurring cash operations costs | $ 2,700,000 | | | |
| Income tax savings, 40% | 1,080,000 | | | |
| After-tax operating costs | $ 1,620,000 | 5.929 | $ (9,604,980) | ($1.62) ($1.62) ($1.62) ($1.62) ......($1.62) |
| Total present value of all cash flows | | | $ (9,604,980) | |

**B. Private**

| | | | | |
|---|---|---|---|---|
| Recurring cash operating costs | $ 2,300,000 | | | |
| Income tax savings, 40% | 920,000 | | | |
| After-tax operating costs | $ 1,380,000 | 5.929 | $ (8,182,020) | ($1.38) ($1.38) ($1.38) ($1.38) ......($1.38) |

Assume straight-line depreciation of $150,000 per year:

| Deduction | Income tax savings |
|---|---|
| $150,000 | $60,000 |

| | | | | |
|---|---|---|---|---|
| | $60,000 | 5.929 | 355,740 | $0.06 $0.06 $0.06 $0.06 $0.06 |

Initial investment:

| | | | | |
|---|---|---|---|---|
| building and equipment | 3,000,000 | 1.000 | (3,000,000) | ($3.0) |
| Residual value, all subject to tax because book value will be zero | 2,000,000 | | | |
| Less: 40% income tax | 800,000 | | | |
| Net cash inflow | $ 1,200,000 | 0.051 | 61,200 | |

Land:

| | | | | |
|---|---|---|---|---|
| Initial investment | 1,000,000 | 1.000 | (1,000,000) | ($1.0) |
| Net disposal value after taxes | 10,000,000 | 0.051 | 510,000 | $1.20    $10.00 |
| Total present value of all cash flows | | | $(11,252,080) | |

Difference in favor of public warehouse ... $ 1,657,100

**FIGURE 6-7** Operating Ratios for Warehousing

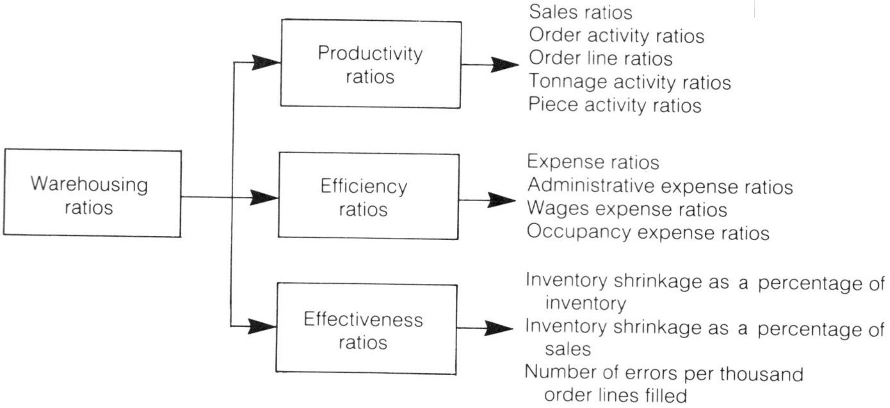

Warehousing ratios
- Productivity ratios
  - Sales ratios
  - Order activity ratios
  - Order line ratios
  - Tonnage activity ratios
  - Piece activity ratios
- Efficiency ratios
  - Expense ratios
  - Administrative expense ratios
  - Wages expense ratios
  - Occupancy expense ratios
- Effectiveness ratios
  - Inventory shrinkage as a percentage of inventory
  - Inventory shrinkage as a percentage of sales
  - Number of errors per thousand order lines filled

Source: Bernard J. LaLonde, Riley Professor of Marketing and Logistics, The Ohio State University, 1975.

**Perhaps the most important, and difficult, measure is *productivity*.**

Over the past several years, productivity measurement has evolved almost on a company by company basis. As specific problem areas were encountered and needs were perceived, measures were developed to address these problems and needs. It is extremely difficult to apply the term *better* to a set of measurements since this highly subjective term must be defined in terms of the importance of measurement (or the importance of the activity being measured) versus the cost of obtaining that measurement. For example, a project expenditure of several thousand dollars to develop industrial engineered labor standards for a two- or three-man warehouse might be of questionable justification. However, it is possible to discuss, in terms of "sophistication," the evolution of productivity measurement.

Figure 6-8 displays a schematic representation of the evolution of warehouse productivity measurement. This evolutionary process may be viewed as occurring in four separate stages.

*Four Stages in Productivity Measurement*

Stage I pertains to the development and use of raw data in terms of dollars. Characteristic of this data is that it is usually provided by some other functional area, e.g., sales or finance, it is usually nonphysical in nature, and the time increment is relatively long, e.g., monthly or quarterly. At this stage, this cost data is often compared to some type of macro output, such as dollar sales. Thus, a common stage I measure might be, total warehousing costs as a percent of sales.

In stage II physical measures and activity budgets are introduced for warehouse activities. Units such as weight, lines, orders, etc., are tracked within the warehousing activities over shorter time intervals, such as days or weeks. At this point, these physical units can be measured against warehouse labor hours, and warehouse labor and nonlabor costs. The introduction of time-phased activity budgets is now possible with this data base.

Stage III initially sees the establishment of empirical or historical "goals" for the overall warehouse and warehouse activities. These goals could be in the form of physical units or period operating costs, but in either case can now lead to the first measurement of performance.

**FIGURE 6-8** Evolution of Warehouse Productivity Measurement

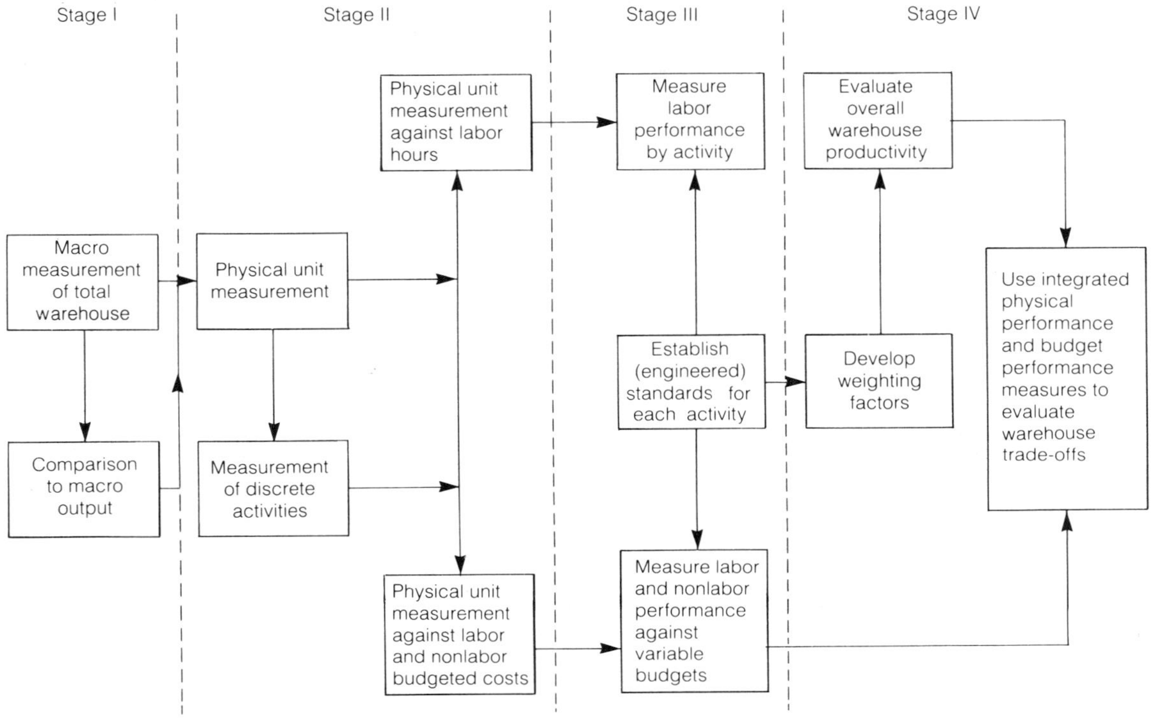

Source: A. T. Kearney, Inc., *Measuring Productivity in Physical Distribution* (Chicago: National Council of Physical Distribution Management, 1978), p. 135.

The development of industrial engineered standards for labor and nonlabor inputs by activity is usually the second step in stage III sophistication. This development leads to performance measurement not only of labor, but also nonlabor input, by activity. It should be noted that productivity trade-offs between warehousing activities can be quantitatively gauged at this level. Increased labor performance in the checking activity, for example, can cause decreased facility productivity in the packing and marking activity. Thus, improvement in methods analysis can lead to improved measurement in an attempt to "optimize" net warehousing productivity.

Stage IV of sophistication may best be defined as the establishment of "weighting factors" for each warehouse activity input. These factors are then used to develop a "total factor" productivity equation. This equation takes into consideration the relative importance of each input to the total warehouse activity as well as the relationship with other activity inputs. Cost relationships are also included in this equation. As a result of these interrelationships and weighting factors, this approach is generally considered to be the most sophisticated in gauging warehouse productivity.[28]

---

[28] Ibid., pp. 133–34

A number of techniques or systems have been developed by firms to measure warehouse productivity, utilization, and performance. *Warehousing Review* magazine has suggested a fairly simplistic approach to productivity measurement. Table 6–12 shows how to identify areas which need

**TABLE 6–12**

| Work measurement report | | | | | | | Performance goal | |
|---|---|---|---|---|---|---|---|---|
| Operation | Measurement unit | Standard units/ man-hour | Actual units | Actual man-hours | Actual units/ man-hour | Percent of standard | Comments | Column A units per man-hour | Column B units per man-hour |
| 1. Receive and store | Cartons | 50 | 7,280 | 182.0 | 40 | 80 | Inbound Trailer Delayed | 36 39 42 35 45 | 41 41 42 41 45 |
| 2. Replenish | Cartons | 25 | 3,328 | 128.0 | 26 | 104 | | 46 47 (40) 37 36 | 47 46 41 41 41 |
| 3. Pick | Dozens | 42 | 7,600 | 190.0 | (40) | 95 | | | |
| 4. Ship | Dozens | 80 | 7,650 | 102.0 | 75 | 94 | | 39 40 42 48 48 | 41 41 42 48 48 |
| 5. Miscellaneous | — | — | — | 5.5 | — | — | | | |
| 6. Labor pool | — | — | — | 9.5 | — | — | Fork Truck Down | 45 38 38 39 40 | 45 41 41 41 41 |
| 7. Total hours | — | — | — | 614.0 | — | — | | 820/20 = 41 (Actual average) | 855/20 = 43 (Potential average) |
| 8. Productivity | Dozens | 17.8 | — | — | 12.4 | 70 | | | |

Source: "A Quick Way To Boost Warehouse Productivity," *Warehousing Review* 3, no. 4 (April/May 1972):5–6. Reprinted by permission of the American Warehousemen's Association from *Warehousing Review* I, no. 4, p. 3.

productivity improvement and establish realistic performance goals. The report can be used as follows:

> *To measure performance,* have warehouse supervisors record labor assigned to each major function. This is often done hourly, but pick whatever time interval is most appropriate. At the end of the day or shift, a clerk relates the manpower data to records of the units handled during the same period. In the report—from a small garment maker—units are cartons and dozens. Elsewhere, they might be bags or cases. Key figure is "actual units per man-hour."
>
> *To improve performance,* give warehouse supervisors a goal they know they can achieve. One way: Substitute average performance over a 20-day period (41) for each day the actual results fell below this. "Target" average is 43.[29]

In addition to a variety of other measures, the consumer-products division of a large, multinational firm examines warehouse performance from a customer-service perspective. Table 6–13 identifies some of the warehousing components of customer service used by the company. For each month

---
[29] "A Quick Way To Boost Warehouse Productivity," *Warehousing Review* 1, no. 2 (April/May 1972), pp. 5–6.

**TABLE 6–13** Customer Service Level Reviews—Metropolitan Warehouse, Los Angeles

|  | 1981 Jun. | 1981 Jul. | 1981 Aug. | 1981 Sept. | 1981 Oct. | 1981 Nov. | 1981 Dec. | 1982 Jan. | 1982 Feb. | 1982 Mar. | 1982 Apr. | Total | Average | Standard |
|---|---|---|---|---|---|---|---|---|---|---|---|---|---|---|
| Order picking error |  |  |  |  |  |  |  |  |  |  |  |  |  |  |
| Wrong product substituted |  |  |  |  |  |  |  |  |  |  |  |  |  |  |
| Mark-out |  |  |  |  |  |  |  |  |  |  |  |  |  |  |
| Duplicated shipment |  |  |  |  |  |  |  |  |  |  |  |  |  |  |
| No record of shipment |  |  |  |  |  |  |  |  |  |  |  |  |  |  |
| Miscellaneous |  |  |  |  |  |  |  |  |  |  |  |  |  |  |
| Subtotal |  |  |  |  |  |  |  |  |  |  |  | — | — |  |
| Over, short, and damaged |  |  |  |  |  |  |  |  |  |  |  |  |  |  |
| Trace shipments |  |  |  |  |  |  |  |  |  |  |  |  |  |  |
| Total |  |  |  |  |  |  |  |  |  |  |  | — | — |  |

of the review period the total number of customer service errors is tabulated. This enables the warehouse manager or other distribution executive to spot any trends which have occurred or may now be occurring. An average for the review period is determined and compared to established standards. Significant deviations from standard are analyzed in depth by management and corrective action taken if necessary. Additionally, the firm is able to examine the effects that changes in warehousing policies or procedures have on customer-service levels.

It is important, irrespective of the method used, that some measure of warehousing performance be determined by a firm. In a survey of 363 members of the National Council of Physical Distribution Management, Lambert and Stock asked senior physical distribution executives to report the data that were used by their firms to evaluate warehousing performance, the performance data that appeared on a formal report, and the usefulness of the various data used to evaluate warehousing performance. The results of the survey are summarized in Tables 6–14, 6–15, and 6–16. Although total costs were the most often mentioned method of evaluating both public and private warehousing and were considered to be the most useful per-

**TABLE 6-14** Data Used to Evaluate Warehousing Performance

|  | Percent Response (N = 363) ||||
| --- | --- | --- | --- | --- |
| Data | Do Not Use | Presently Using | Currently Developing | Planning to Develop within Next 18 Months |
| Public warehouses: | | | | |
| Total cost | 49.6 | 48.5 | 1.7 | 0.3 |
| Handling costs per unit | 52.3 | 44.6 | 1.9 | 1.1 |
| Storage costs per unit | 53.1 | 43.5 | 2.8 | 0.6 |
| Accuracy and promptness of inventory reports | 58.7 | 39.9 | 1.4 | — |
| Annual warehouse inspection | 57.0 | 40.2 | 2.5 | 0.3 |
| Damage/claims | 59.5 | 38.0 | 1.1 | 1.4 |
| On-site audits | 60.6 | 36.9 | 1.9 | 0.6 |
| Sanitation/housekeeping | 60.1 | 36.6 | 2.2 | 1.1 |
| Warehouse operations performance | 60.0 | 36.4 | 2.5 | 1.1 |
| Customer complaints | 65.0 | 33.3 | 1.4 | 0.3 |
| Billing accuracy | 66.9 | 31.1 | 1.7 | 0.3 |
| Consolidation of outbound freight | 65.9 | 30.9 | 2.5 | 0.8 |
| Salesman's comments | 70.8 | 27.5 | 1.1 | 0.6 |
| Safety and environmental factors | 73.3 | 24.5 | 1.9 | 0.3 |
| Cost measured against standard | 71.1 | 22.3 | 4.7 | 1.9 |
| Company used (Leased) distribution centers: | | | | |
| Total cost | 38.8 | 60.1 | 0.8 | 0.3 |
| In-stock availability | 45.2 | 52.3 | 1.7 | 0.8 |
| Inventory turns | 47.4 | 50.1 | 2.5 | — |
| Damage/claims | 57.8 | 39.7 | 1.7 | 0.8 |
| Order cycle availability | 56.5 | 38.6 | 3.0 | 1.9 |
| Cost by product | 66.9 | 28.4 | 3.6 | 1.1 |

**TABLE 6-15**  Warehouse Performance Data that Appear on a Formal Report

| Response | Percent Response (N = 363) |
|---|---|
| Public warehouses: | |
| Total cost | 33.1 |
| Handling costs per unit | 30.6 |
| Storage costs per unit | 28.9 |
| Accuracy and promptness of inventory reports | 23.7 |
| Annual warehouse inspection | 23.4 |
| Warehouse operations performance | 20.9 |
| Damage/claims | 20.4 |
| On-site audits | 18.7 |
| Sanitation/housekeeping | 17.6 |
| Cost measured against standard | 16.5 |
| Consolidation of outbound freight | 15.2 |
| Billing accuracy | 14.6 |
| Customer complaints | 14.6 |
| Safety and environmental factors | 13.2 |
| Salesman's comments | 8.9 |
| Company owned (leased) distribution centers: | |
| Total cost | 44.7 |
| In-stock availability | 36.9 |
| Inventory turns | 35.8 |
| Order cycle availability | 27.3 |
| Damage/claims | 24.2 |
| Cost by product | 21.5 |

formance measure, only 33 percent of the firms reported having such data on a formal report for judging public warehouses. The corresponding figure for private warehouses was 45 percent. Similar descrepancies between data used and the data appearing on a formal report were found to varying degrees for all of the measures of performance used. This would support the conclusion that performance evaluation of warehousing takes place primarily on an informal basis.

As suggested by the multitude of warehouse performance measures being used by firms, it is necessary that performance data are available and used as the basis for corrective action. It is not sufficient to merely identify problem areas, rather it is vital that appropriate actions be taken by the firm to improve poor performance whenever possible. Therefore, a company should have decision strategies developed to handle most problem areas before the problems develop. This is the essence of contingency planning.

There is no single approach that a firm can pursue. Management action is determined by a variety of factors such as customer-service levels, competition, product mix, and many others. There is however, universal acceptance of the principle that problems should be pinpointed based upon cause and effect. Once pinpointed, various controls and/or corrective actions can be taken to improve warehouse performance.

**TABLE 6–16** Degree of Usefulness of Data Used to Measure Warehousing Performance

| | | Percent Response | | | | | |
|---|---|---|---|---|---|---|---|
| Data | Number of Respondents | Very High 5 | 4 | 3 | 2 | Very Low 1 | Mean Response |
| Public warehouses: | | | | | | | |
| Total cost | 205 | 63.4 | 22.9 | 8.8 | 1.5 | 3.4 | 4.4 |
| Storage costs per unit | 194 | 51.5 | 29.9 | 11.3 | 3.1 | 4.1 | 4.2 |
| Handling costs per unit | 192 | 52.1 | 28.6 | 12.5 | 2.6 | 4.2 | 4.2 |
| Accuracy and promptness of inventory reports | 172 | 48.8 | 27.9 | 14.5 | 5.2 | 3.5 | 4.1 |
| Warehouse operations performance | 166 | 42.8 | 33.1 | 18.7 | 1.2 | 4.2 | 4.1 |
| Annual warehouse inspection | 176 | 39.2 | 29.5 | 19.9 | 5.7 | 5.7 | 3.9 |
| Sanitation/housekeeping | 160 | 39.4 | 29.4 | 18.1 | 4.4 | 8.7 | 3.9 |
| On-site audits | 165 | 30.3 | 33.9 | 22.4 | 7.9 | 5.5 | 3.8 |
| Billing accuracy | 149 | 32.9 | 33.6 | 18.1 | 9.4 | 6.0 | 3.8 |
| Customer complaints | 146 | 33.3 | 28.6 | 24.5 | 8.2 | 5.4 | 3.8 |
| Damage/claims | 168 | 25.6 | 38.1 | 23.8 | 5.4 | 7.1 | 3.7 |
| Consolidation of outbound freight | 147 | 34.0 | 29.9 | 20.4 | 4.1 | 11.6 | 3.7 |
| Cost measured against standard | 127 | 31.5 | 33.9 | 20.5 | 4.7 | 9.4 | 3.7 |
| Safety and environmental factors | 132 | 22.7 | 25.0 | 30.3 | 9.8 | 12.1 | 3.4 |
| Salesman's comments | 127 | 13.4 | 24.4 | 32.3 | 15.0 | 15.0 | 3.1 |
| Other | 17 | 52.3 | 41.2 | 0.0 | 0.0 | 5.9 | 4.4 |
| Company owned (leased) distribution centers: | | | | | | | |
| Total cost | 244 | 68.0 | 21.3 | 10.2 | .4 | 0.0 | 4.6 |
| In-stock availability | 217 | 63.1 | 24.4 | 8.3 | 3.2 | .9 | 4.5 |
| Inventory turns | 213 | 49.8 | 26.8 | 16.0 | 6.1 | 1.4 | 4.2 |
| Order cycle availability | 186 | 48.9 | 28.5 | 14.0 | 5.4 | 3.2 | 4.2 |
| Cost by product | 144 | 50.7 | 28.5 | 11.1 | 3.5 | 6.3 | 4.1 |
| Damage claims | 174 | 28.2 | 30.5 | 29.9 | 8.6 | 2.9 | 3.7 |

### Warehouse Site Selection

One of the most significant questions that distribution managers must answer is: "How many warehouses should the company have and where should they be located?" If public warehouses are to be used, the startup costs for a new warehouse often can be ignored when making location decisions. Warehouses must be positioned in such a way as to provide the desired level of service at the least distribution cost. If it can be shown that physical distribution costs are linear with respect to volume, then linear programming can be used to determine the number of warehouse sites from among a large group of demand points. Simulation is another technique that can be used to determine the number and location of field warehouses and a number of computer packages are available to do this.

The site selection decision can be approached from a macro and a micro perspective. The macro perspective examines the issue of where to locate warehouses geographically (in a general sense) so as to improve the firm's

**Site Selection from A Macro Perspective**

market offering (improve service or reduce cost). The micro perspective examines factors which pinpoint specific locations within the larger geographical areas identified from the macro view.

In a macro approach developed by Edgar Hoover (1938), three types of location strategies were identified: (1) market positioned; (2) production positioned; and (3) intermediately positioned.[30] The *market-positioned* strategy locates warehouses nearest to the final customer. This maximizes customer service levels and enables the firm to utilize transportation economies (TL and CL shipments) from plants or sources of supply to each warehouse location. The factors which influence the placement of warehouses near the market areas served include transportation costs, order-cycle time, time sensitivity of the product, order size and local transportation availability, and service levels.

*Production-positioned* warehouses are those which are located in close proximity to sources of supply or production facilities. Although these warehouses generally cannot provide the same level of customer service offered by market-positioned warehouses, they serve as collection points or mixing facilities for products manufactured at a number of different plants. For multiproduct companies transportation economies result from consolidation of shipments into TL or CL quantities. The factors which influence the placement of warehouses close to the point of production include perishability of raw materials, number of products in the firm's product mix, assortment of products ordered by customers, and transportation consolidation rates.

The final location strategy places warehouses at a midpoint between the final customer and the producer. Customer service levels for *intermediately-positioned* warehouses are typically higher than the production-positioned facilities and lower than market-oriented facilities. This strategy is often followed when a firm must offer high customer service levels and has a varied product offering being produced at several plant locations.

**Site Selection from A Micro Perspective**

From a micro perspective, more specific factors must be examined. If private warehousing is to be used, it will be necessary to consider:

1. The quality and variety of transportation carriers serving the site.
2. The quality and quantity of available labor.
3. Labor rates.
4. The cost and quality of industrial land.
5. The potential for expansion.
6. The tax structure.
7. Building codes.
8. The nature of the community environment.
9. The costs of construction.
10. The cost and availability of utilities.

---

[30] Edgar M. Hoover, *The Location of Economic Activity* (New York: McGraw-Hill, 1948), p. 11.

If the firm wants to use public warehousing, it will be necessary to consider:

1. The facility characteristics.
2. The warehouse services provided.
3. The availability or proximity to motor carrier terminals.
4. The availability of local cartage.
5. Other companies using the facility.
6. The availability of computer services and communications.
7. The type and frequency of inventory reports.

**Benchmarks for Site Selection**

One of the most comprehensive overviews of the warehouse-site selection decision was published by *Distribution Worldwide* magazine. The publication identified three primary considerations that needed to be examined when determining warehouse sites: (1) marketing aspects; (2) traffic (transportation economics); and (3) location or consolidation objectives.[31] Table 6–17 shows the types of questions a firm must ask, and answer, when it proposes to open a warehousing facility in a new location. The numerous items included in Table 6–17 indicate the complexity of the warehouse

**TABLE 6–17**  Benchmarks for Site Selection

I. Preliminary study
　A. Marketing aspects
　　General service areas
　　Volume forecast
　　Competition
　　New products
　　Service requirements
　B. Traffic (transportation economics)
　　Present versus proposed site location or consolidation
　　Service advantages and disadvantages
　C. Location or consolidation objectives
II. Data development
　A. Distribution patterns of company
　　Indicate total annual volume to key markets under these headings:

| Cities (or states) | Annual volume Dollars, pounds |
|---|---|

| Percent of weight |
|---|
| Carload, truckload, LTL, other |

　　What percentage of total annual weight shipped to key markets, by product and shipping point, under these headings:

| Cities (or states) | Plant shipments Plant #1, plant #2 |
|---|---|

| Warehouse shipments |
|---|
| Warehouse A, warehouse B |

　　What pool car and stop-off arrangements?
　　What TOFC or COFC operations? Type of plan used; will these be extended at a new facility?
　　Location of public and/or private warehouses: Present facilities—warehouse, service territory, average inventory in pounds and dollars, average turnover of inventory
　B. Description of existing facilities
　　Location of production plant and/or warehousing
　　Products manufactured and/or stored at each facility
　　A breakdown of total floor space for receiving, storage of finished goods, picking, and packing and shipping.
　　Floor space for office or other distribution-related activities.

---

[31] "Benchmarks for Site Selection," *Distribution Magazine* 75, no. 12 (December 1976):36.

**TABLE 6-17** *(continued)*

    Is warehouse a single-story or multi-story facility?
    If multistory, what are floor load limitations, elevator capacity, etc.?
    What are internal work assignments in each department?
    Are goods processed or repackaged at warehouse?
    What is the service territory of plant and/or warehouse?
C. What transportation services available?
    Names of serving rail carriers
    Private siding capacity (number of cars)
    Is same siding used for inbound and outbound shipments?
    Is facility at car-level height?
    Names of for-hire motor carriers
    Platform capacity (number of vehicles)
    Is same platform used for inbound and outbound shipments?
    Is facility at truck-level height?
    Names of air-freight carriers
    Proximity of airport to site
    Carrier pick-up and delivery area and services
    Is there water transportation?
    Depth of channel
    Describe dock, bulkhead, transit shed, etc.
    Handling facilities from vessel to dock to warehouse
D. What are service characteristics of modes?
    Frequency of rail switching service
    Is warehouse within reciprocal switching limits?
    Does carrier provide TOFC or COFC service?
    Is warehouse or plant within LCL pickup and delivery zone?
    What is general quality of carload and LCL service?
    Is plant or warehouse within motor common carrier ICC commercial zone?
    Is facility within terminal zone of the over-the-road carrier?
    Do carriers park trailers at facility for convenience loading and unloading?
    Does product require special motor-carrier equipment?
    What is general quality of truckload and LTL service?
E. What other transportation services?
    Carloading (forwarder) companies, location of terminals and frequency of service.
III. Potential for change
    Does present layout restrict free flow of goods through facility?
    Is additional rail siding capacity feasible?
    Can truck platforms be extended?
    Is additional land (or floor space) available for expansion at this location?
    Can distribution points be effectively consolidated?
    Would more warehouses increase the use of volume transportation?
    Will automation economically increase the efficiency of any part of the operation?
    Can customer buying habits be changed to improve efficiency and lower costs?
    Will a change in material handling help efficiency and decrease costs?
    Would new facilities improve service to customers?
    Is time in transit an important factor in sales? (Weigh answer against trade-offs of being closer to the customer or source of raw material)
    Indicate weaknesses in present distribution system
    Indicate strengths of competitors' distribution methods.
    Will a *net* reduction in work force be attained by establishing new facility?
    How do labor costs at other sites compare with those in existing plant and/or warehouse?
IV. New site location
  A. Consider potential labor force
    Availability of manpower and skills associated with distribution
    Workers' attitude and turnover rate at other facilities in area
    Prevailing labor rates (don't forget to add in fringe benefits)

**TABLE 6-17** (*continued*)

      Unions and satisfactory disposition of labor disputes
      Labor problems of vendors and carriers who would serve new facility
      Service skills available, i.e. plumbing, carpenters
  B. Transportation services
      Rail lines serving site, switch service available
      Outbound routes, service, and transit time to customers.
      Inbound service routes and transit times from source of raw material or producing plants
      Damage experience of other companies in area—particularly related to local yards
      Car supply—assigned, free runners, seasonal fluctuations of car supply in area, history of embargoes such as result of dock strike
      Transit applications; average demurrage agreements
      Local rail management's attitude toward service and customers; rail's attitude in handling OS&Ds
      Attractiveness of inbound revenue to the line-haul carrier and switch carrier
      Participation of railroad in building trackage to site
      General financial and physical conditions of the railroad; security problems
      Rate economics and willingness of railroad to support rate requests
      Alternate rail service in case of storms or strikes
      Car size and weight restrictions
      Clearance between railcar and unloading dock requirements
      Piggyback and container service
      Motor common carriers available
      Opportunity for contract, irregular route, and private carriage
      Common carrier terminals
      Rates and charges; consolidation delivery opportunities
      Carriers' claims and financial history
      Availability of equipment and type
      Location of site within terminal area or commercial zone
      Security or labor problems
      Distance of site to good transportation arteries and interstate highways; service to highways in event of snow storm
      State highway limitation on size and weight of vehicles
      Physical height and weight restrictions related to access highway
      Air-passenger and freight service
      Air-freight rates
      Proximity of airport to site
      Carrier pick-up and delivery area and service
      Water service available
      Distance of site from port; carriers serving port; barge service
      Customs service at port; brokers and freight forwarders available; export packaging service
      Loading and unloading facilities; container service
      General shuttle operations and conveyor service from local plants
      Postal and other ground service
  C. Taxes—city, county, state
      Basis for assessed evaluation of real estate
      Real estate rate per $100 of assessed evaluation and per square foot
      Personal property tax
      Inventory tax restrictions, exemptions, rate basis, rate assessment date
      Payroll taxes
      Fuel taxes
      Projections on future tax increases
      Tax relief granted to attract new industry
  D. Site data
      Title; ownership
      Zoning of land and of adjacent land; present use of land and of adjacent land
      Acreage available; building coverage as a percent of total land
      Maximum slope; elevations—high and low
      Easements for pipelines, present and future roads, rail lines, power lines, sewers and ditches, and tax and utility boundary lines
      Soil load-bearing characteristics; subsoil characteristics

**TABLE 6-17** (*continued*)

- Depth to bedrock; depth to ground water
- Drainage—natural run-off
- Need for artificial drainage facilities
- Need for flood protection
- Cost of property, survey fees, unpaid assessments
- Fees for clearing old buildings and trees
- Grading and field cost
- Below-ground cost, piling, expand footings, etc.
- Road building; rail lines
- Climatic and natural conditions, i.e. precipitation (rain and snow)
- Average temperature by month and range within month
- Humidity; prevailing winds and hurricane protection; earthquake stressing
- Utility companies—water, gas, electrical, and sewer (storm and sanitation)
- Company names, rates, capacity of service
- Cost of extending to site, including connecting costs if applicable
- Cost of transformers and other electrical equipment
- Quality of fire protection service
- Nearest fire department service—volunteer or permanent
- Estimated time to respond to alarm
- Size of prime department and alternate units
- Location of fire hydrants
- Building restrictions as set forth in building code

E. Security
- Size of municipal police department; workload; reputation; scheduled patrols in area.
- Organized crime; known fencing operations, high-jacking
- Civil unrest
- Availability of private security protection services; kind, cost

F. Local factors
- Attitude of community and state toward new industry
- Willingness to support changes in zoning, etc.
- Willingness of utility companies to make concessions for new industry
- Willingness of state and community in getting concessions from PUC, public utility companies, and transportation companies
- Commitments on adequate police and fire service
- Effectiveness of local business organizations such as the chamber of commercial and industrial associations

G. Legal
- Review of state and local ordinances
- Review of abstract and title
- Preparations of leases, contracts, agreements, etc

V. Construction

A. Requirements of Building
- Storage layout and capacity
- Inventory turns
- Rail versus truck volume
- Material handling systems to be used
- Floor-load requirements per square foot
- Stacking height
- Fire and security protection levels
- Office space
- Sanitary facilities
- Docks and truck aprons
- Lighting level
- Environmental control and heating
- Rail docks

B. Design and Engineering
- Space design
- Architectural drawings
- Soil borings
- Structural, heating, electrical and plumbing, engineering
- Security fences and landscaping

C. Contractor Selection
- Bid package
- Contract awards
- Method of financing
- Construction timetable

VI. Pre-start-up

A. Material handling equipment
- Type, quantity and specification
- Capital documentation
- Purchasing

B. Service contractor selection
- Exterminator
- Heating and electrical contractors
- Janitorial and landscaping service
- Lift-truck maintenance service
- Disposal service

**TABLE 6-17** *(concluded)*

| | |
|---|---|
| Security and fire protection service | Start-up crew |
| Medical service | Employment screening |
| Salvage outlets | Physical examinations |
| C. Final inspection and sign-off on building | Hiring |
| | Training |
| D. Insurance | F. Building preparation |
| Fire and extended coverage | Sign up for utilities including telephone and protective service |
| a. Building and rail track | |
| b. Inventory | Safety equipment installation |
| Sprinklers | Office and lunchroom equipment |
| Boiler explosion | Clean and seal floors |
| Liability | Stripe floors |
| Fidelity bonds | Set up salvage area |
| Theft insurance | Install communications equipment |
| Workers compensation | G. Inventory |
| General liability | Schedule start-up stock |
| E. Employment | Stock house |
| Assign start-up management teams | H. Start-Up |
| Select and train operating managers | Fill-out crew as required |

Source: "Benchmarks for Site Selection," *Distribution Worldwide* 75, no. 12 (December 1976), pp. 36–39.

site-selection decision and highlight the importance that distribution management should place on making that decision. As stated by the director of planning, physical distribution division, International Paper Company:

> ... the warehouse is essentially a part of a total distribution system, and that all the factors that come to bear on that system, such as the transportation in and out, production runs, customer service requirements, have to be considered before you make a site decision.[32]

## SUMMARY

In this chapter you were shown how warehousing provides many distribution services, the most important being storage of inventories. A firm may utilize owned or leased facilities, called private warehousing, or rented facilities, called public warehousing.

Warehousing has two major functions: movement and storage. The movement function includes receiving, transfer, order selection, and shipping. The efficiency of a firm's warehousing network is affected by such factors as layout and design, the type of material handling system used, and the packaging characteristics of the products being stored.

An important decision facing the distribution executive is whether to employ public or private warehousing, or both. The factors considered in

---
[32] Jack W. Farrell, Lowell E. Perrine, and Stephen Tinghitella, eds., "A TM Seminar on Warehouse Management's Growing Role," *Physical Distribution Forum* (Boston: Cahners Books International, 1973), p. 253.

that decision are cost and/or service related. In order to achieve maximum efficiency from the warehousing activity, performance of the firm's public and private facilities must be measured and controlled. A number of financial approaches are possible including those which examine productivity, utilization, and performance. Warehouse site selection, public or private, can influence the effectiveness of the firm's marketing efforts. The decision is complex and involves consideration of a multitude of factors.

With this as background, you are ready to examine the role of inventory in the physical distribution network. The financial aspects of inventory and concepts of inventory management are the subjects of Chapters 7 and 8.

## Appendix A: Problem 1—Where Should In-Process Parts Be Stored for Minimum Travel Costs?

A mini-load AS/R system stores in-process parts for four production departments. Currently (see Present layout), the AS/RS is located near the receiving dock and reserve storage area, because of heavy lift-truck traffic between the three locations. Production people feel the AS/RS is too far from their operations, that their people spend too much time in travel to and from it. How do you determine where the AS/RS should be located?

*Step 1: Analyze moves.* Determine: number of trips to and from AS/RS by production people; travel time per unit of distance traveled; cost per unit of time of travel of each employee; and number of trips to and from the AS/RS by materials handling people, and the cost per unit of distance traveled for each trip.

*Step 2: Establish coordinates.* Set up X and Y coordinates on present layout and find centroids (center points) for each department, plus the entry/exit door at reserve storage and the receiving dock.

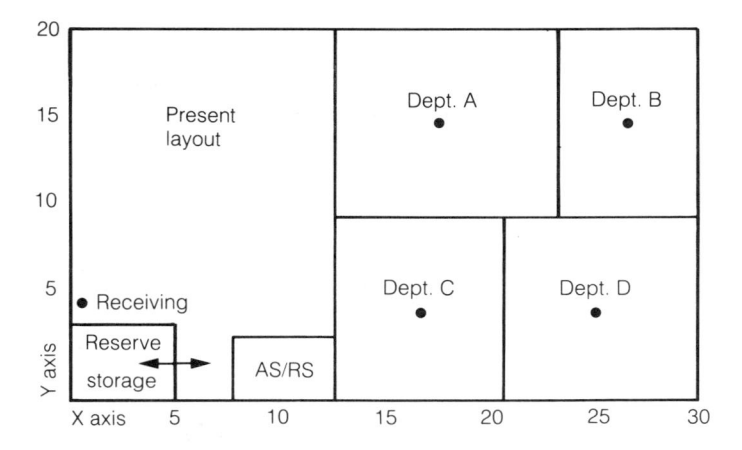

Source: James A. Tompkins and John A. White, "Location Analysis—More than Just Plant Layout," *Modern Materials Handling* 32, no. 9 (September 1977), p. 66. Copyright 1977 by Cahners Publishing Company, Division of Reed Holdings, Inc.

*Step 3: Weight each facility.* The weight for a production department is found by multiplying the number of trips per month to and from the AS/RS by the speed of the trips and by the cost per hour spent in travel. You get the weight for reserve storage and receiving by multiplying the number of trips per month to and from the AS/RS by the cost per unit of distance traveled, including handling equipment cost.

|  | Coordinates |  |  |
| --- | --- | --- | --- |
| Facility | X | Y | Weight |
| Receiving | 0 | 5 | 5 |
| Reserve storage | 4 | 2 | 10 |
| Department A | 17 | 15 | 22 |
| Department B | 26 | 15 | 18 |
| Department C | 16 | 5 | 12 |
| Department D | 25 | 5 | 14 |
| Total weight |  |  | 81 |
| One-half of total weight = 40.5 |  |  |  |

*Step 4: Make calculations.* The objective now is to find the point on both $X$ and $Y$ axes where not more than half the total weight lies to the left and no more than half lies to the right. To do this, look at the $X$ axis and look along it left to right and note down the facilities as you come to them as in the table below. You come to receiving, first, at coordinate 0; reserve storage second at X-4; Department C next, at X-16; and so on. You put in the weightings and then add the weightings cumulatively until they reach one half the total weight (40.5). As in the table, you can see that you reach this point at X-17. Now you go through the same process with the $Y$ coordinates. It's a little different with the $Y$ axis, because when you get to Y-5 there are three facilities and, therefore, three weightings. At Y-15, you find two facilities and two weightings. By adding the weightings on $Y$, you find one-half the total weight at Y-5.

| X Axis | Weight | Sum | Y Axis | Weight | Sum |
| --- | --- | --- | --- | --- | --- |
| 0 | 5 | 5 | 2 | 10 | 10 < 40.5 |
| 4 | 10 | 15 |  |  |  |
|  |  |  | 5 | 31 | 41 > 40.5 |
| 16 | 12 | 27 < 40.5 |  | (5 + 12 + 14) |  |
| 17 | 22 | 49 > 40.5 | 15 | 40 |  |
|  |  |  |  | (22 + 18) |  |
| 25 | 14 |  |  |  |  |
| 26 | 18 |  |  |  |  |

*Step 5: Plot contour lines.* Using the weightings, plot contour lines on the layout, with each point on a contour line having the same weighted distance value. This step will enable you to make a sounder decision regarding your mathematical results. The contour lines roughly indicate the area into which your AS/RS should be located.

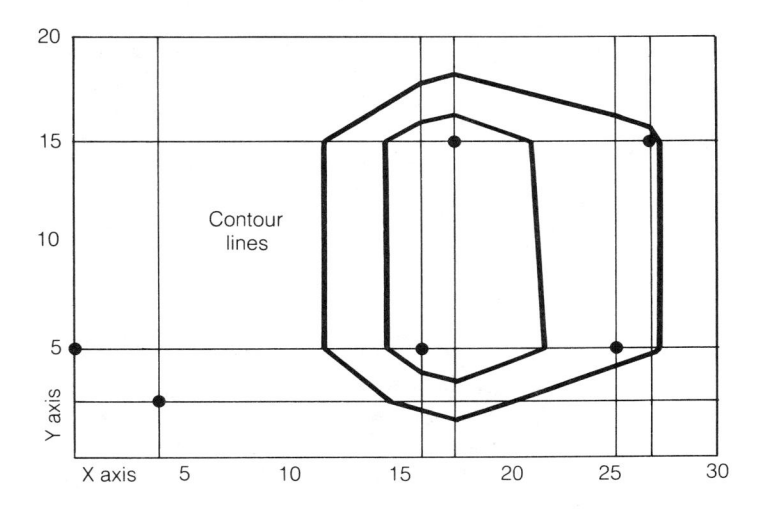

The mathematical solution puts the AS/RS in the heart of Department C, not a good idea. Within the contour lines, as plotted in step 5, the best location is along a main aisle between departments at Y-10. Relocation costs also favor the aisle. Thus judgment plays a part in locating the AS/RS as in the proposed layout. But it's judgment backed by solid knowledge of costs.

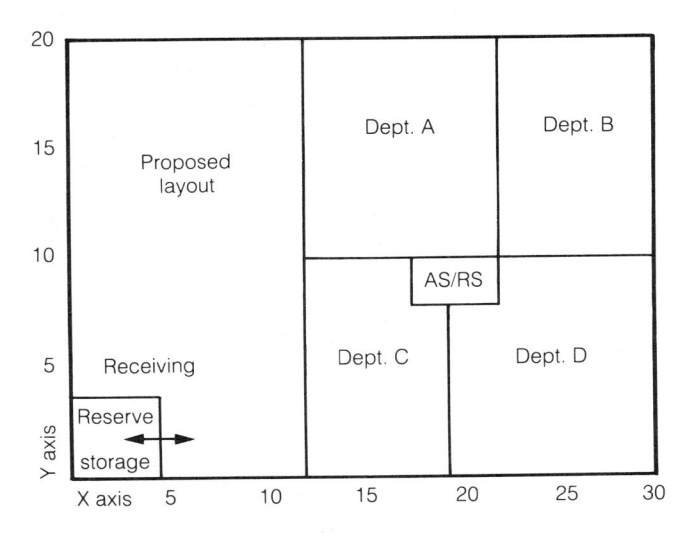

## Appendix B: Problem 2—How Do You Assign Storage Locations to Minimize Travel?

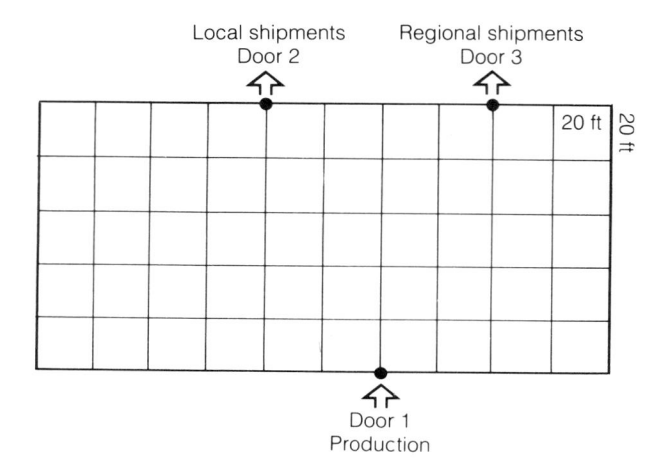

A warehouse has 50 bays, 20-foot square, in which we want to store two products which cannot share a bay. Product A needs 20 bays and Product B needs 30. In both cases this includes aisle space. Material enters through door 1. Local shipments, about 20 percent of the volume, leave by door 2. Regional shipments leave by door 3. Product A enters the warehouse at 600 loads a month; Product B enters at 1,000 loads a month. Flow is Fifo. How do we locate product in the warehouse to minimize the average distance traveled per month?

*Step 1: Compute distances.* Compute average distance from each bay to doors based on weights of 50 percent for door 1, 10 percent for door 2, and 40 percent for door 3.

| 172 | 152 | 132 | 112 | 94 | 78 | 72 | 76 | 88 | 108 |
|---|---|---|---|---|---|---|---|---|---|
| 172 | 152 | 132 | 112 | 94 | 78 | 72 | 76 | 88 | 108 |
| 172 | 152 | 132 | 112 | 94 | 78 | 72 | 76 | 88 | 108 |
| 172 | 152 | 132 | 112 | 94 | 78 | 72 | 76 | 88 | 108 |
| 172 | 152 | 132 | 112 | 94 | 78 | 72 | 76 | 88 | 108 |

*Step 2:* Rank products by handling rate (C) divided by storage area (A).

| Product | Handling Rate (C) | Storage Area (A) | C/A |
|---|---|---|---|
| A | 1,200 per month | 20 bays | 60 |
| B | 2,000 per month | 30 bays | 66.66 |

Source: James A. Tompkins and John A. White, "Location Analysis—More Than Just Plant Layout," *Modern Materials Handling* 32, no. 9 (September 1977), p. 68. Copyright 1977 by Cahners Publishing Company, Division of Reed Holdings, Inc.

*Step 3: Make first assignment.* The product with the greatest C/A ratio is assigned to the required number of bays with the lowest distance values. In this case product B goes in the 30 bays with smallest distance values, as shown.

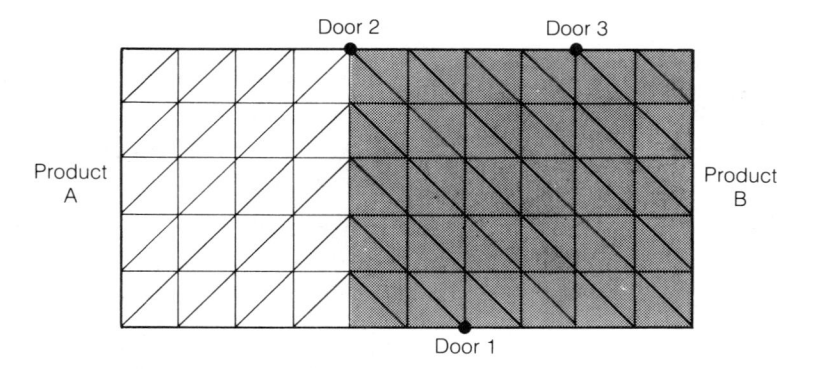

*Step 4: Make next assignment.* In this case, Product A goes into the remaining bays. If there are more products (hundreds or even thousands) the same process is repeated over and over again until all locations are assigned.

## QUESTIONS AND PROBLEMS

1. Warehousing is used for the storage of inventories during all phases of the distributive process. Why is it necessary for a firm to store inventories of any kind since inventory carrying costs can be very high?

2. Distinguish between *private* and *public* warehousing. What are the advantages and disadvantages of each type of warehousing?

3. Discuss what is meant by cost trade-off analysis within the context of warehousing. Give at least two examples of the cost trade-offs involved in a firm's decision to use a combination of public and private warehousing rather than public or private warehousing alone.

4. Briefly differentiate between *standard* and *automated* warehouse-handling systems. Comment upon how various handling systems can impact a firm's warehousing efficiency.

5. Packaging serves two basic functions: (1) marketing; and (2) distribution. Identify the role of packaging in each of these functional areas.

6. In general, the modern public warehouse provides many services in addition to storage. The role of the public warehouse has expanded considerably. Discuss some of the services being offered by today's public warehouse and identify the role it plays in a firm's physical distribution network.

7. Productivity has been defined as the ratio of real output to real input. In terms of the warehousing function, how could a firm measure the productivity level of its public and private facilities?

# 7 Financial Impact of Inventory

Introduction

**Financial Aspects of Inventory Strategy**
   Inventory and Corporate Profitability
   Inventory and Least Total Cost Physical Distribution

**Inventory Carrying Costs**
   Calculating Inventory Carrying Costs
      Capital Costs on Inventory Investment
      Inventory Service Costs
      Storage Space Costs
      Inventory Risk Costs
      Section Summary and Examples

The Impact of Inventory Turnover on Inventory Carrying Costs

**Summary**

**Appendixes**
A. Inventory Carrying Costs—Six Case Studies
B. Inventory Carrying Costs—Forms For Data Collection

**Objectives of this chapter:**

To show how inventory investment influences corporate profit performance

To show how inventory management contributes to least total cost physical distribution

To show how to calculate inventory carrying costs

## INTRODUCTION

Inventory represents the largest single investment in assets of most manufacturers, wholesalers, and retailers. The highly competitive markets of the past decade have led to a proliferation of products as companies attempted to satisfy the needs of diverse market segments. Also, in most industries, customers have become accustomed to high levels of product availability. For many firms the result has been higher inventory levels. For example, the inventory investment of manufacturers of consumer packaged goods can represent as much as one-third of their total assets (see Table 7–1).

**TABLE 7–1** Selected Financial Data for 10 Manufacturers of Consumer Packaged Goods ($ millions)

| Company | Fortune 500 Ranking | Sales | Net Profits | Total Assets | Inventory Investment | Inventories as a Percent of Assets |
|---|---|---|---|---|---|---|
| Borden | 82 | $ 4,595.8 | $ 147.8 | $2,643.3 | $ 506.0 | 19% |
| Bristol-Myers | 117 | 3,158.3 | 270.6 | 2,209.4 | 545.2 | 25 |
| Colgate-Palmolive | 64 | 5,130.4 | 173.2 | 2,578.1 | 769.7 | 30 |
| Consolidated Foods | 62 | 5,342.9 | 127.7 | 2,263.4 | 730.5 | 32 |
| General Foods | 55 | 6,012.0 | 255.8 | 2,978.5 | 1,003.0 | 34 |
| Johnson & Johnson | 74 | 4,837.4 | 400.7 | 3,342.5 | 848.8 | 25 |
| Procter & Gamble | 24 | 10,772.0 | 1,083.0 | 6,553.4 | 1,488.1 | 23 |
| Quaker Oats | 160 | 2,405.2 | 96.4 | 1,334.2 | 342.5 | 26 |
| Ralston Purina | 72 | 4,886.0 | 163.0 | 2,246.5 | 566.4 | 25 |
| Standard Brands | 128 | 3,018.5 | 104.4 | 1,608.4 | 555.9 | 35 |

Note: All figures are for 1980.

The fact that capital invested in inventories must compete with other investment opportunities available to the firm, combined with the out-of-pocket costs associated with holding inventory, makes inventory management an activity of significant importance.

The purpose of this chapter is to show you how inventory management contributes to least total cost physical distribution; and to show you how to calculate inventory carrying costs.

## FINANCIAL ASPECTS OF INVENTORY STRATEGY

The quality of inventory management and the inventory policies set by a firm can have a significant impact on corporate profitability and management's ability to implement least total cost physical distribution.

### Inventory and Corporate Profitability

*Excessive Inventories Can Lower Profitability*

Inventory represents a significant portion of the assets of a firm. Consequently, excessive inventory levels can lower corporate profitability in two ways: (1) net profit is reduced by the out-of-pocket costs associated with holding inventory such as insurance, taxes, storage, obsolescence, damage, and perhaps interest expense, if money is borrowed specifically to finance inventories; and (2) total assets are increased by the amount of the inventory and the result is lower return on investment.

For example, consider ABC Company whose financial data are presented in summary in Figure 7−1. As a result of poor forecasting, lack of attention to inventory management, and the absence of an integrated systems approach to the management of physical distribution, it was found that the company's inventory was $6 million too large. What would be the impact on profitability and return on investment of a change in management practice if: (1) the cash made available from the $6 million reduction in inventory was

**FIGURE 7−1** The Strategic Profit Model With Financial Data for ABC Company (all $ figures in millions)

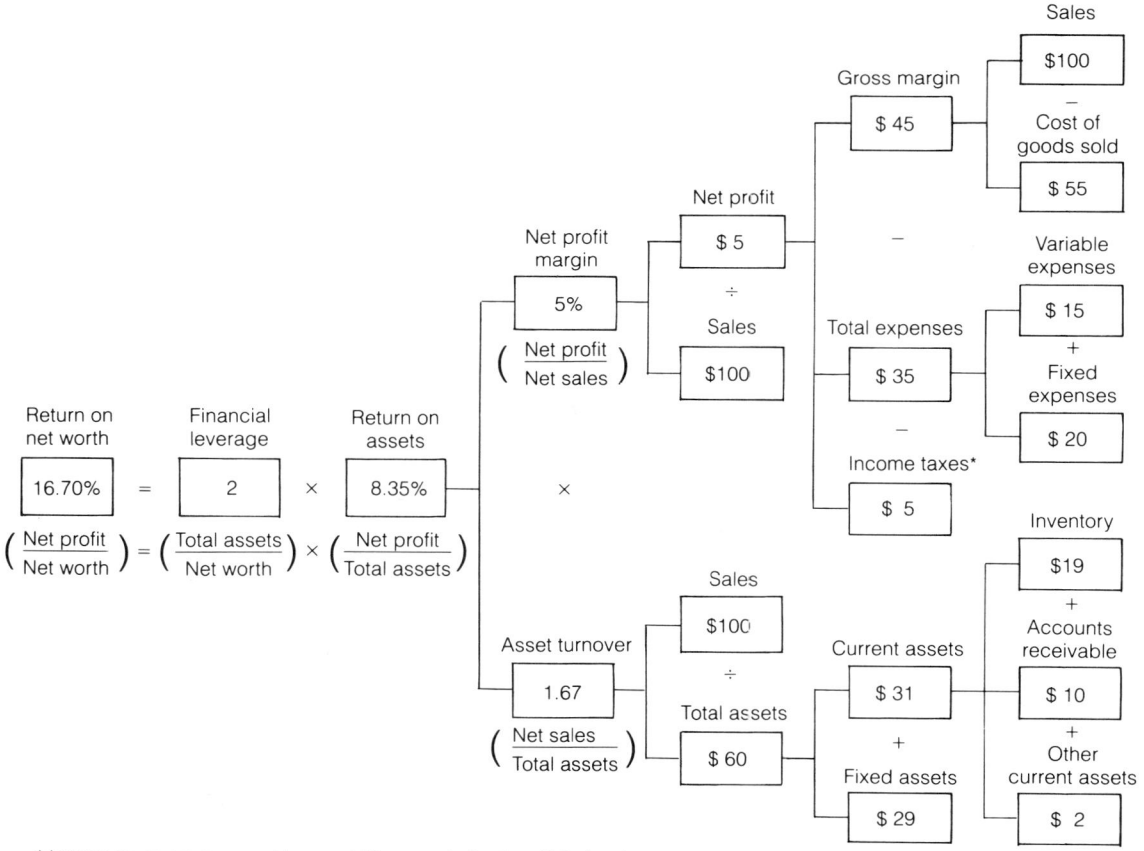

*Income taxes are assumed to equal 50 percent of net profit before taxes.

used to repay a bank loan at 15 percent interest; and (2) the total of the other out-of-pocket costs such as insurance, taxes, storage, obsolescence, and damage saved by the reduction in inventory equaled 5 percent of the inventory value? The answer is contained in Figure 7−2, which shows that: (1)

**FIGURE 7-2**  Impact of Inventory Reduction on ABC Company's Net Worth when Bank Loan is Repaid (all $ figures in millions)

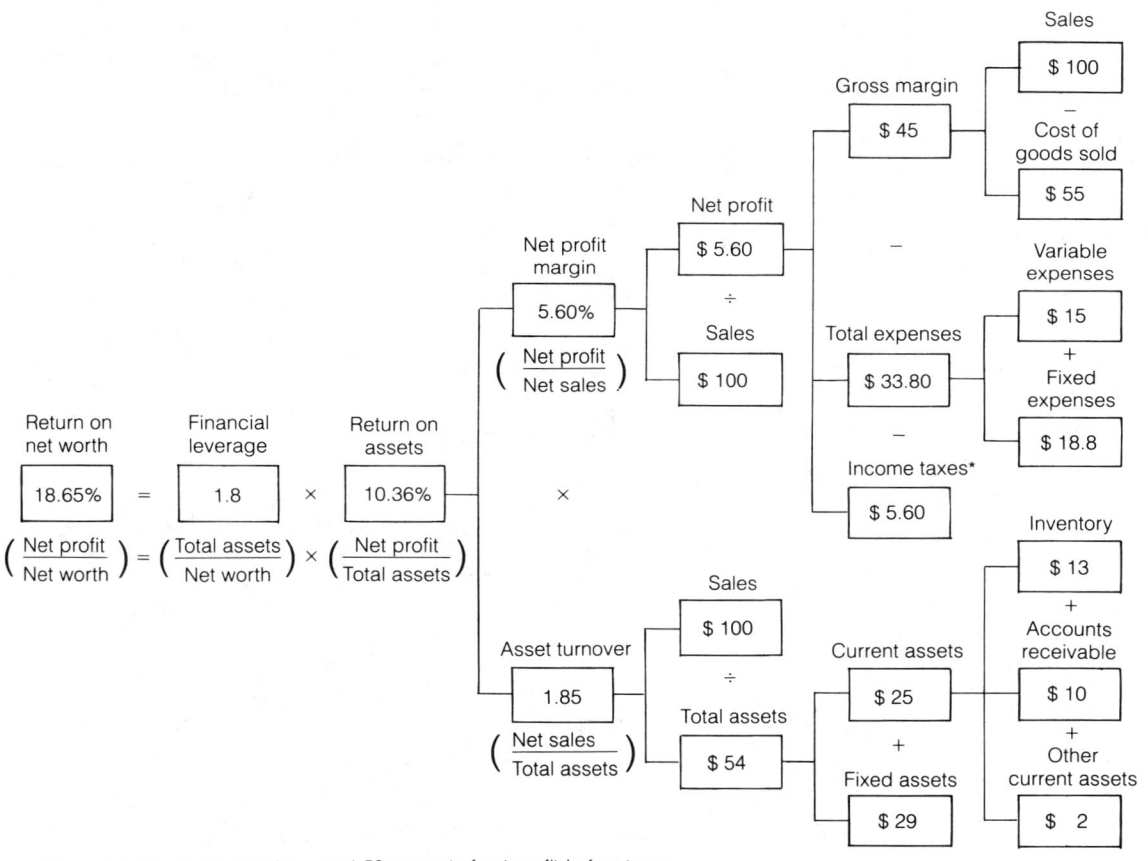

```
                                                                                                    Sales
                                                                                                    $ 100
                                                                                                      −
                                                                                  Gross margin    Cost of
                                                                                    $ 45          goods sold
                                                                                                    $ 55
                                                                 Net profit
                                                  Net profit      $ 5.60                          Variable
                                                   margin                                         expenses
                                                   5.60%            ÷                               $ 15
                                                                   Sales         Total expenses      +
                                                 ( Net profit  )                    $ 33.80       Fixed
                                                   Net sales       $ 100                          expenses
 Return on       Financial        Return on                                                         $ 18.8
 net worth       leverage          assets                                           −
                                                                                 Income taxes*
   18.65%   =      1.8      ×      10.36%             ×                             $ 5.60         Inventory
                                                                                                    $ 13
( Net profit ) ( Total assets ) ( Net profit  )                   Sales                              +
  Net worth  =   Net worth    ×   Total assets                    $ 100                           Accounts
                                                Asset turnover                    Current assets  receivable
                                                                    ÷                $ 25           $ 10
                                                    1.85        Total assets          +              +
                                                ( Net sales  )    $ 54                              Other
                                                  Total assets                    Fixed assets    current assets
                                                                                     $ 29           $ 2
```

*Income taxes are assumed to equal 50 percent of net profit before taxes.

assets and total assets are reduced by $6 million; (2) asset turnover increases from 1.67 times to 1.85 times; (3) total expenses are reduced by $1.2 million—$900,000 in fixed interest expense plus $300,000 in other fixed expenses; (4) net profit before taxes increases by $1.2 million but income taxes increase by $600,000 resulting in an increase in after tax net profit of $600,000; (5) net profit margin increases from 5 percent to 5.6 percent; (6) return on assets increases from 8.35 percent to 10.36 percent; (7) financial leverage declines from 2 to 1.8; and (8) return on net worth increases from 16.70 percent to 18.65 percent.

**236**   Part Two

**Capital Rationing Raises the Cost of Carrying Inventory**

However, if the company was experiencing capital rationing, that is, there was not enough money to invest in all of the new projects available to the firm, it would be necessary to determine where the money from the inventory reduction would be invested and at what rate of return. For example, if the money would be invested in plant modernization that would reduce manufacturing costs and yield a 20 percent aftertax return which equals 40 percent before tax, then this opportunity cost should be reflected in the analysis. Assuming that excluding the cost of capital, the costs associated with the inventory equal 5 percent of the inventory value, what would be the impact on return on net worth? The answer is contained in Figure 7−3

**FIGURE 7–3**   Impact of Inventory Reduction on ABC Company's Net Worth when Capital Rationing Exists ($ million)

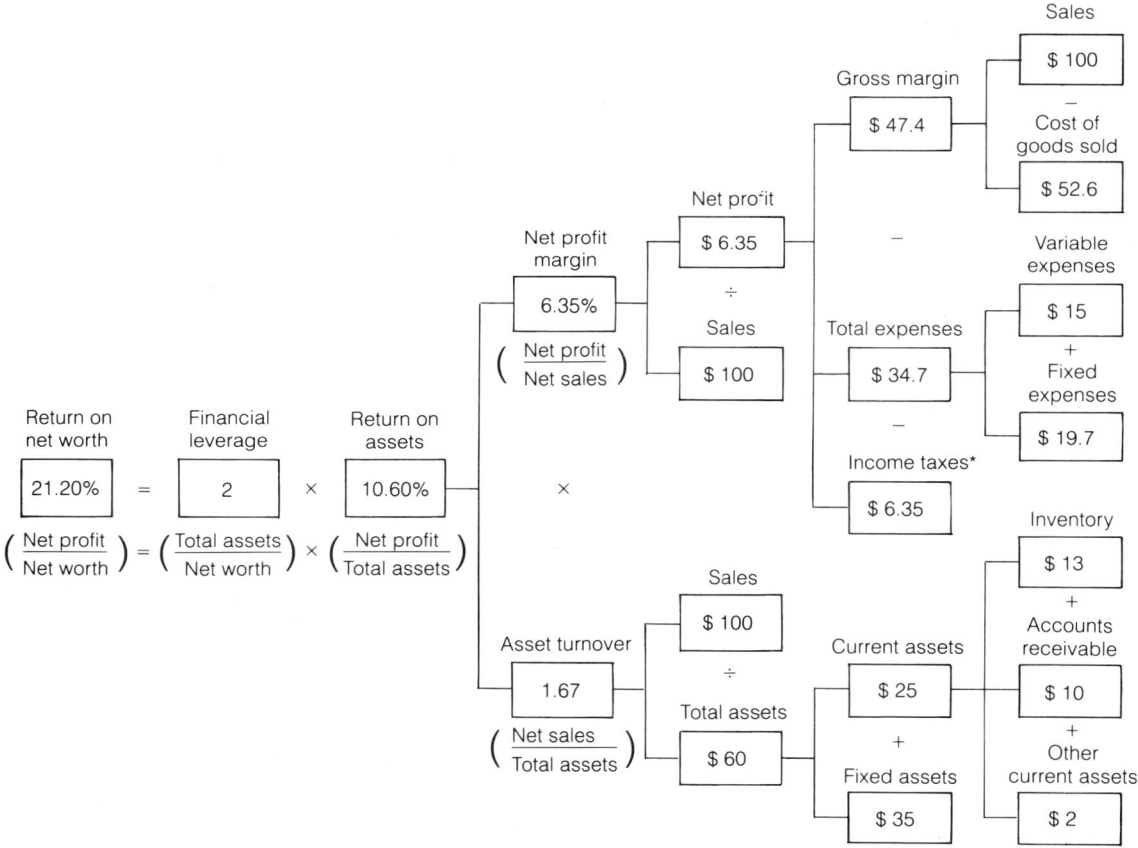

*Income taxes are assumed to equal 50 percent of net profit before taxes.

which shows that: (1) current assets are reduced by $6 million and fixed assets are increased by $6 million, the cost of the plant modernization; (2) total assets and asset turnover remain the same; (3) cost of goods sold is reduced by $2.4 million ($6 million × 40%) and gross margin increases from

$45 million to $47.4 million; (4) fixed expenses and total expenses are reduced by $300,000 in other expenses; (5) net profit before taxes increases by $2.7 million but income taxes increase by $1.35 million resulting in an increase in aftertax net profit of $1.35 million; (6) net profit margin increases from 5 percent to 6.35 percent; (7) return on assets increases from 8.35 percent to 10.60 percent; (8) financial leverage remains at 2; and (9) return on net worth increases from 16.70 percent to 21.20 percent.

In both examples it was shown that too much inventory can erode net profits and return on net worth. In order to establish the optimal inventory stocking strategy, it is necessary to think in terms of the cost trade-offs that are required in a physical distribution system.

**Inventory and Least Total Cost Physical Distribution**

Least total cost physical distribution is achieved by minimizing the total of the costs illustrated in Figure 7–4 for a specified level of customer service. However, successful implementation of cost trade-off analysis requires that adequate cost data be available to management. Inventory levels and inventory turnover policies should not be set arbitrarily but with full knowledge of inventory carrying costs and total system costs.

The cost of carrying inventory has a direct impact not only on the number of warehouses that a company maintains, but on all of the firm's distribution policies. Given the same customer service level, low inventory carrying costs lead to multiple warehouses and a slower mode of transportation such as railroads. High inventory carrying costs, on the other hand, result in a limited number of stock locations and require a faster means of transportation such as motor or air carriers in order to minimize total costs. Without an accurate assessment of the costs of carrying inventory, it is unlikely that a company would choose the distribution policies that would minimize costs.

In addition, knowledge of the cost of carrying inventory is also required to accurately determine economic manufacturing quantities, economic order quantities, and sales discounts, all of which are currently calculated on the basis of estimated costs in the majority of companies who use these formulas.[1]

## INVENTORY CARRYING COSTS

Inventory carrying costs, the costs that are associated with the quantity of inventory stored, include a number of different cost components and generally represent one of the highest costs in physical distribution.[2] The magnitude of these costs and the fact that inventory levels are influenced by the configuration of the physical distribution system demonstrate the need for an accurate assessment of inventory carrying costs if the appropriate

---

[1] These will be discussed in the inventory management section of this chapter.

[2] This section draws heavily from Douglas M. Lambert, *The Development of an Inventory Costing Methodology: A Study of the Costs Associated with Holding Inventory* (Chicago: National Council of Physical Distribution Management, 1976).

**FIGURE 7-4** Cost Trade-offs Required in a Physical Distribution System

*Marketing:* Product, Price, Promotion, Place-customer service levels (cost of lost sales)

*Physical distribution:* Inventory carrying costs, Transportation costs, Production lot quantity costs, Order processing and information costs, Warehousing costs (throughput costs not storage)

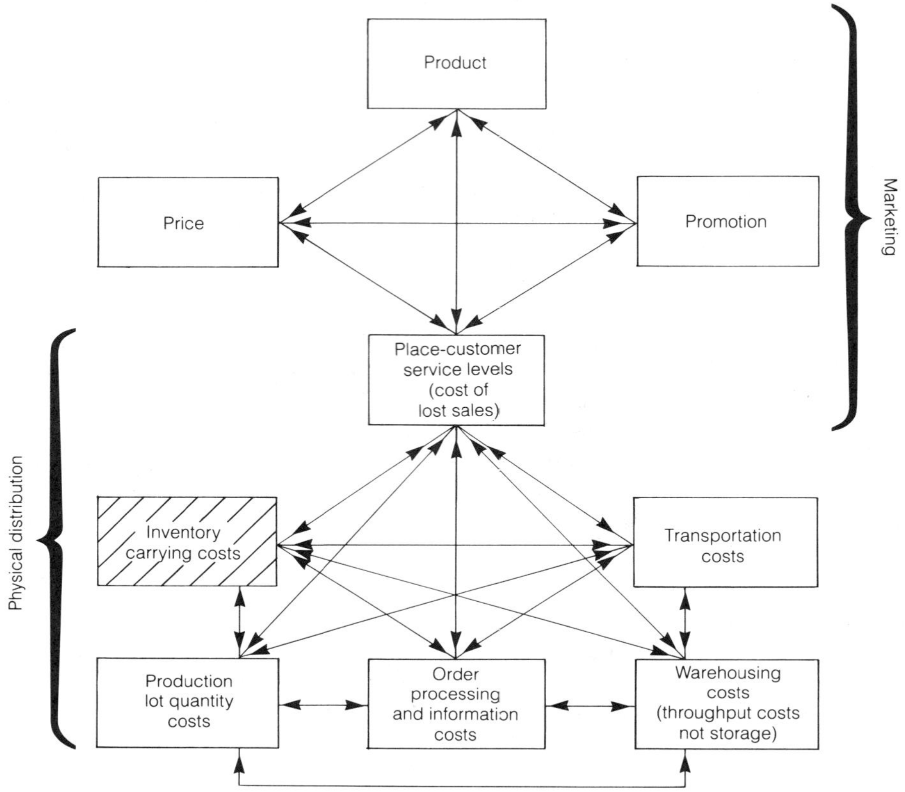

Objective: Minimize total costs

Total costs = Transportation costs + Warehousing costs
+ Order processing and Information costs + Production lot quantity costs
+ Inventory carrying costs + Cost of lost sales

Source: Adapted from Douglas M. Lambert, *The Development of an Inventory Costing Methodology: A Study of the Costs Associated with Holding Inventory* (Chicago: The National Council of Physical Distribution Management, 1976), p. 7.

---

trade-offs are to be made within the firm. Currently, most managers who consider the cost of holding inventory use estimates or traditional industry benchmarks. In fact, many corporations do not calculate inventory carrying costs even though these costs are both real and substantial.

We have shown how inventory levels can impact on corporate profit performance and established the need for assessment of inventory carrying costs in physical distribution system design. The next question might be, What inventory carrying cost percentages are managers currently using for physical distribution system design (cost trade-off analysis) and such things as determining economic order quantities and sales discounts?

**What is the Cost of Carrying Inventory?**

Unfortunately, in many companies inventory carrying costs have not been calculated. When they have been developed they include only the current interest rate plus such items as insurance and taxes. Also, many managers use traditional textbook percentages or industry averages. There are problems with all of these approaches.

First, there are only a few special circumstances where the current interest rate is the relevant cost of money and these will be explored in "Capital Costs on Inventory Investment" which follows. Traditional textbook percentages also are not without serious drawbacks. Table 7−2 contains a number of estimates of inventory carrying costs that are widely referenced in the physical distribution and inventory management literature.

The 12−34 percent range offered by George Aljian covers a range so large, that picking a number within the range almost would allow a manager

**TABLE 7-2** Estimates of Inventory Carrying Costs

| Author | Publication | Estimate of Carrying Costs as a Percent of Inventory Value |
|---|---|---|
| L. P. Alford and John R. Bangs (eds.) | *Production Handbook* (New York: Ronald Press, 1955) p. 397. | 25% |
| George W. Aljian | *Purchasing Handbook* (New York: McGraw-Hill, 1958) pp. 9–29. | 12–34 |
| Dean S. Ammer | *Materials Management* (Homewood, Ill.: Richard D. Irwin, 1962) p. 137. | 20–25 |
| Donald J. Bowersox | *Logistical Management* (New York: Macmillan, 1978) pp. 157–59. | 20* |
| J. J. Coyle and E. J. Bardi | *The Management of Business Logistics,* 2d ed. (St. Paul, Minn.: West Publishing, 1980) pp. 85–87. | 25–30 |
| Gordon T. Crook | "Inventory Management Takes Teamwork," *Purchasing,* March 26, 1962, p. 70. | 25 |
| Thomas W. Hall | "Inventory Carrying Costs: A Case Study" *Management Accounting,* January 1974, pp. 37–39. | 20.4 |
| J. L. Heskett, N. A. Glaskowsky, Jr., and R. M. Ivie | *Business Logistics,* 2d ed. (New York: Ronald Press, 1973), p. 20. | 28.7 |
| John F. Magee | "The Logistics of Distribution: *Harvard Business Review,* July–August 1960, p. 99. | 20–35 |
| Benjamin Melnisky | *Management of Industrial Inventory* (Conover-Mast Publication, 1951) p. 115. | 25 |
| W. Evert Welch | *Scientific Inventory Control* (Management Publishing Corporation, 1956) p. 63. | 25 |
| Thomson M. Whitlin | *The Theory of Inventory Management* (Princeton, N.J.: Princeton University Press, 1957) p. 220. | 25 |

* Not specified, although 20 percent was used in examples.

to cost-justify any inventory policy.[3] The 1960 *Harvard Business Review* article by John Magee has many of the same shortcomings as the Aljian publication.[4] In the 1974 *Management Accounting* article by Thomas Hall, the carrying cost was calculated to be 20.4 percent, but a review of the publication revealed that Hall had added an after tax cost of capital to the other components which were pretax numbers.[5] In addition, storage costs that were not variable with the quantity of inventory held were included in the calculations.

The time period covered by the publications listed in Table 7−2, covers the years from 1951 to 1980. However, most of the carrying costs percentages used during that period are near 25 percent. It would seem reasonable to ask the question: "If 25 percent was an accurate number in 1951, how could it be accurate in 1980, when during that period the prime interest rate has fluctuated between 3 percent and 20 percent?"

Finally, the question of using inventory carrying costs that are based on industry averages must be addressed. Business people, for the most part, seem to find comfort in such numbers but many problems are inherent with this practice. For example, if you are working for a manufacturer of cosmetics, do you want to compare your firm to Avon, a company which sells its products from door-to-door, Revlon, a company which sells its products through major department stores, or—even worse—use an average of the two companies? The latter, of course, represents a nonentity—no company at all. Even if two companies are very similar in terms of the manufacture and distribution of their products, the availability of capital may lead to two very different inventory strategies. That is, one firm may be experiencing shortages of capital, capital rationing, and the other may have an abundance of cash. The former has a cost of money for inventory decisions of 40 percent pretax and the latter has a cost of money of 10 percent pretax which is the current bank interest rate. Which of these companies is likely to have the most inventory? The company with the 10 percent cost of money will have the most inventory. Because of the lower cost of money, this company will increase inventory levels and move toward transporting carload and truckload quantities of its products. Each company may have what represents least total cost physical distribution and yet one may turn its inventories 6 times per year and the other 12 times. Transportation costs as a percent of sales may be significantly higher for the company with the 40 percent cost of money. However, if either company were to change any component of its physical distribution system in order to match the other's performance, total costs could increase and return on net worth could decrease.

---

[3] George W. Aljian, *Purchasing Handbook* (New York: McGraw-Hill, 1958), pp. 9−29.

[4] John F. Magee, "The Logistics of Distribution," *Harvard Business Review* July−August 1960, p. 99.

[5] Thomas W. Hall, "Inventory Carrying Costs: A Case Study," *Management Accounting* January 1974, pp. 37−39.

### Calculating Inventory Carrying Costs

Each company should determine its own distribution costs and strive to minimize the total of these costs. Inventory carrying costs should include only those costs that vary with the quantity of inventory and can be categorized into the following groups: (1) capital costs; (2) inventory service costs; (3) storage space costs; and (4) inventory risk costs.

*Capital costs on inventory investment.* Holding inventory ties up money that could be used for other types of investments. This reasoning holds for internally generated funds as well as capital obtained from sources external to the firm such as debt from banks and insurance companies or from the sale of common stock. Consequently, the company's opportunity cost of capital, the rate of return that could be realized from some other use of the money, should be used in order to reflect accurately the true cost involved. In companies experiencing capital rationing, which is the rule rather than the exception, the hurdle rate, which is the minimum rate of return on new investments, should be used as the cost of capital. Where capital rationing does not exist, the capital invested in inventory should reflect the alternative use of the money. That is, if the inventory investment was reduced, where would the capital be invested? If the money would be invested in marketable securities then that is the rate of return for inventory carrying cost purposes. If the money would be placed in a bank account or used to reduce some form of debt, then the appropriate interest rate applies.

Some companies may differentiate among projects by categorizing them according to risk and looking for rates of return that reflect the perceived level of risk. For example, management could group projects into high, medium, and low categories of risk. High-risk projects might include investments in new products, since market acceptance is difficult to predict, or new equipment for the plant, if technology is changing so rapidly that the equipment could be obsolete within a short period of time. The desired rate of return on high-risk projects might be 25 percent after tax. Medium-risk projects, on the other hand, may be required to obtain an 18 percent after-tax return. Low-risk projects which may include such investments as warehouses, private trucking, and inventory, might be expected to achieve an aftertax return of 10 percent. In this company, corporate aversion to risk would require that cash made available by a reduction in inventory be used for another low-risk category investment. Consequently, the cost of money for inventory carrying costs would be 10 percent after taxes which equals 20 percent before taxes. It should be emphasized that all inventory carrying cost components must be stated in before-tax numbers because all of the other costs in the trade-off analysis, such as transportation and warehousing, are reported in before-tax dollars. In some very special circumstances, such as the fruit-canning industry, short-term financing may be used to finance the seasonal buildup of inventories. The seasonal buildup of inventory is in contrast to the inventories determined by the strategic deployment of product to achieve least total cost physical distribution. In the latter case, any change in the quantity of inventory will cause other cost compo-

---

Four Major Components of Inventory Carrying Costs

nents of physical distribution to change. In the former situation, the actual cost of borrowing is the acceptable cost of money.

Once the cost of money has been established, it is necessary to determine the value of the inventory on which the inventory carrying cost is to be based. At this point, it is necessary to know which of the costing alternatives is being used. For example, is the company using direct costs in determining the inventory value or is it using some form of absorption costing?

**Direct versus Absorption Costing**

Direct costing is that method of cost accounting which is based upon the segregation of costs into fixed and variable components. For management planning and control purposes, the fixed-variable cost breakdown yields more information than that obtained from current financial statements designed for external reporting. Under direct costing, the fixed costs of production are excluded from inventory values. With absorption costing, otherwise known as full costing or full absorption costing, which is the traditional approach used by most companies, fixed manufacturing overhead is inventoried.

In addition to the direct costing versus absorption costing distinction, companies may value inventories based upon actual costs or standard costs. The following represents four distinct costing alternatives:

1. *Actual absorption costing* includes actual costs for direct material and direct labor plus predetermined variable and fixed manufacturing overhead.
2. *Standard absorption costing* includes predetermined direct material and direct labor costs plus predetermined variable and fixed overhead.
3. *Actual direct costing* includes actual costs for direct material and direct labor plus predetermined variable manufacturing overhead; excludes fixed manufacturing overhead.
4. *Standard direct costing* includes predetermined costs for direct material and direct labor plus predetermined variable manufacturing overhead; excludes fixed manufacturing overhead.

The preceding material on methods of inventory valuation supports the conclusion that using industry averages for inventory carrying costs is not a good policy. This is due to the fact that the various component percentages may not be calculated using comparable inventory valuation systems.

The situation may seem to be complicated even further if one considers the various *methods of accounting for inventory*. The American Institute of Certified Public Accountants makes the following statement concerning inventory valuation:

> Cost for inventory purposes may be determined under any one of several assumptions as to the flow of cost factors (such as first-in first-out, and last-in first-out). The major objective in selecting a method should be to choose the one which under the circumstances most clearly reflects periodic income. . . .
>
> Although selection of the method should be made on the basis of individual circumstances it is obvious that financial statements will be more useful if

uniform methods of inventory pricing are adopted by all companies within a given industry.[6]

Most companies use one of the following *three methods of accounting for inventory:*

**Methods of Accounting for Inventory**

1. *First-in, first-out (Fifo):* Stock acquired earliest is assumed to be sold first leaving stock acquired more recently in inventory.
2. *Last-in, first-out (Lifo):* Sales are made from the most recently acquired stock leaving items acquired in the earliest time period in inventory. This method attempts to match the most recent costs of acquiring inventory with sales. Lifo will result in lower inventory valuation and lower profits than the Fifo method in periods of rising prices. The converse is true when prices are declining.
3. *Average cost:* This method could be a moving average in which *each* new purchase is averaged with the remaining inventory to obtain a new average price or a weighted average in which the total cost of the opening inventory plus all purchases is divided by the total number of units.

Neither Fifo nor Lifo isolates and measures the effects of cost fluctuations as special managerial problems. However, when standard costing is used, the currently attainable standards automatically provide a measure of cost variance—gains or losses—that can be reported separately.[7]

For the purposes of calculating inventory carrying costs, it is immaterial whether the company uses Lifo, Fifo, or average cost for inventory valuation. The value of the inventory for calculating carrying costs is determined by multiplying the number of units of each product in inventory by the standard or actual variable costs associated with manufacturing the product and moving it to the storage location. The way that a manufacturer decreases its inventory investment is to sell a unit from inventory and not produce a replacement. Similarly, inventories are increased by manufacturing more product than is curently demanded. Consequently, in either case, it is the current manufacturing costs that are relevant for decision making, since these are the costs that will be saved if inventories are reduced and they are the costs that will be incurred if inventories are increased. Likewise, if products are held in field locations, the transporattion cost incurred to move them there plus the variable costs associated with moving them into storage are costs that are inventoried just as are direct labor costs, direct material costs, and the variable manufacturing overhead.

The implicit assumption is that a reduction in finished goods inventory will lead to a corresponding reduction in inventory throughout the system

---

[6]*Statement 4*, chap. 4 of *Accounting Research Bulletin No. 43* from "Accounting and Reporting Problems of the Accounting Profession," 3d ed. (Arthur Andersen & Co., 1969) p. 90.

[7] Charles T. Horngren, *Cost Accounting: A Managerial Emphasis*, 3d ed. (Englewood Cliffs, N.J.: Prentice-Hall, 1972), p. 558.

**FIGURE 7–5** Inventory Positions in the Physical Distribution System

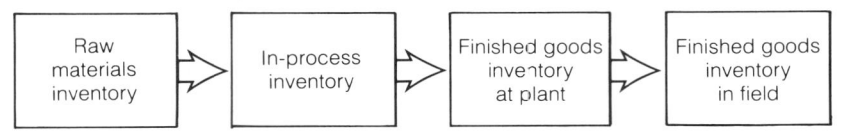

Raw materials inventory → In-process inventory → Finished goods inventory at plant → Finished goods inventory in field

Assumption: A one-time increase (decrease) in finished goods inventory results in a one-time increase (decrease) in raw materials purchased.

(see Figure 7–5). That is, a one-time reduction in finished goods inventory results in a one-time reduction in raw materials purchases as inventory is pushed back through the system. Similarly, a planned increase in finished goods inventory results in a one-time increase in the quantity of raw materials purchased and subsequently pushed through the system. When this one-time change in inventory value, a balance sheet account, is multiplied by the opportunity cost of money it becomes an annual cost, a profit and loss statement account. This is important because all other components of the inventory carrying cost are annual costs and impact the profit and loss statement as do the other cost categories such as transportation, warehousing, production lot quantity, and order processing.

In summary, many business people think that inventory is a relatively liquid and riskless investment. For this reason, they feel that a somewhat lower return can be justified on inventory investments. However, inventory requires capital that could be used for other corporate investments, and by having funds invested in inventory a company foregoes the rate of return that could be obtained in such investments. Therefore, the company's opportunity cost of capital should be applied to the investment in inventory. The cost of capital should be applied to the out-of-pocket investment in inventory. Although most manufacturers use some form of absorption costing for inventory, only variable manufacturing costs are relevant. That is, the cost of capital, the company's minimum acceptable rate of return, or the appropriate opportunity cost of money, should be applied to only the variable costs directly associated with the inventory.

Taxes and Insurance

*Inventory service costs.* Inventory service costs are comprised of taxes and insurance paid as a result of holding the inventory. *Taxes* vary depending on the state in which inventories are held. The tax rates can range from zero in states where inventories are exempt to 19.8 percent of the assessed value in Indiana.[8] In general, taxes vary directly with inventory levels. Although *insurance* rates are not strictly proportional to inventory levels, since insurance is usually purchased to cover a certain value of product for a specified time period, the policy will be revised periodically based on expected inventory policy changes. In some instances, policies can be issued where premiums are based on the monthly amounts insured. Insurance rates vary depending on the materials used in the construction of the

---

[8] "Inventory Taxes," *Transportation & Distribution Management*, July/August 1975, pp. 31–36.

storage building, its age, and considerations such as the type of fire prevention equipment installed.

For both insurance and taxes, the actual dollars spent on each of these expenses during the past year can be calculated as a percentage of that year's inventory value and added to the cost of money component of the carrying cost. If budgeted figures are available for the coming year, they can be used as a percentage of the inventory value based on the inventory plan, the forecasted inventory level, in order to provide a future-oriented carrying cost. In most cases, there will be few, if any, significant changes from year to year in the taxes and insurance components of the inventory carrying cost.

**Storage Costs**

*Storage space costs.* In general, there are four types of facilities that should be considered: (1) plant warehouses; (2) public warehouses; (3) rented (leased) warehouses; and, (4) privately owned warehouses.

The costs associated with *plant warehouses* are primarily fixed in nature. If any costs are variable, they are usually variable with the amount of product that moves through the facility, throughput, and not with the quantity of inventory stored. If there are some variable costs such as the cost of taking an inventory or any other expenses that would change with the level of inventory, they should be included in inventory carrying costs. Fixed charges and allocated costs are not relevant for inventory policy decisions. If the warehouse space could be rented or used for some other productive purpose, if not used for storing inventory, and the associated opportunity costs are not readily available to the manager, than it may make sense to substitute the appropriate fixed or allocated costs as surrogate measures.

*Public warehouse* charges usually are based on the amount of product that is handled and the amount of inventory held in storage. In some cases, the first month's storage must be paid when the products are moved into the facility. This in effect, makes the first month's storage a handling charge since it must be paid on every case of product regardless of how long it is held in storage.

The use of public warehouses is a policy decision made because it is the most economical way to provide the desired level of customer service without incurring excessive transportation costs. For this reason, the majority of costs related to the use of public warehouses, the handling charge, should be considered as throughput costs, and only charges for recurring storage that are explicitly included in the warehouse rates should be considered in inventory carrying costs.

In situations where a throughput rate is given based on the number of inventory turns, it will be necessary to estimate the storage cost component by considering how the throughput cost per case would change if the number of inventory turns changed. Of course, the public warehouse rates paid at the time that inventory is placed into field storage should be included when calculating the value of the inventory investment.

*Rented (leased) warehouse* space is normally contracted for, and the contract is in force for a specified period of time. The amount of space rented is based on the maximum storage required during the period covered by the contract. Thus, the rate of warehouse rental charges does not fluctuate from day-to-day with changes in the inventory level, although the rental rates can vary from month to month or year to year when a new contract is negotiated. Most costs, such as rent payment, the manager's salary, security costs, and maintenance expenses are fixed when related to time. However, some expenses such as warehouse labor and equipment operating costs, vary with throughput. During the contract very few, if any, costs will vary with the amount of inventory stored.

All of the costs could be eliminated by not renewing the contract and are therefore a relevant input for decision making. However, operating costs that are not variable with the quantity of inventory held should not be included in the carrying costs, but rather in the warehousing cost category of the cost trade-off analysis. The inclusion of fixed costs and those that are variable with throughput in inventory carrying costs has no conceptual basis. Such a practice is simply incorrect and will result in erroneous decisions.

The costs associated with *company-owned warehouses* are primarily fixed although some may be variable with throughput. All operating costs that could be eliminated by closing a company-owned warehouse or the net savings resulting from a change to public warehouses should be included in warehousing costs and not in inventory carrying costs. Only those costs that are variable with the quantity of inventory belong in inventory carrying costs.

## Risk Costs

***Inventory risk costs.*** Inventory risk costs vary from company to company, but typically will include charges for (1) obsolescence, (2) damage, (3) pilferage, and (4) relocation of inventory.

The cost of *obsolescence* is the cost of each unit which must be disposed of at a loss because it is no longer possible to sell it at regular price. It is the difference between the original cost of the unit and its salvage value or the original selling price and the reduced selling price, if the price is lowered to move the product to avoid obsolescence. This figure may or may not show up on the profit and loss statement as a separate item. Usually, obsolescence results in an overstatement of the costs of goods manufactured account or the cost of goods sold account. Consequently, some difficulty may be experienced in arriving at this figure.

The cost of *damage* should be included only for the portion of damage that is variable with the amount of inventory held. Damage incurred during shipping should be considered a throughput cost since it will continue regardless of inventory levels. Damage attributed to a public warehouse operation is usually charged to the warehouse operator if above some specified maximum amount. Often damage is identified as the net amount after claims.

*Shrinkage* has become an increasingly important problem for American businesses. Inventory theft in the view of many authorities is a more serious problem than cash embezzlement. It is far more common and involves far more employees, and is hard to control. However, this cost may be more closely related to company security measures than inventory levels even though it will definitely vary with the number of warehouse locations. Consequently, in many companies it may be more appropriate to assign some or all of the shrinkage costs to the warehousing cost category.

*Relocation costs* are incurred when inventory is transshipped from one warehouse location to another to avoid obsolescence. For example, products that are selling well in the Midwest may not be selling on the West coast. By shipping the products to the location where they will sell, the company avoids the obsolescence cost but incurs additional transportation costs. Often, these costs are not reported separately, but are simply included in transportation costs. In such cases, a managerial estimate or a statistical audit of freight bills can be used to isolate the transshipment costs. The frequency of these types of shipments will determine which approach is most practical in any given situation. That is, if such shipments are rare, the percentage component of the carrying cost will be very small and a managerial estimate should suffice.

In some cases, transshipment costs may be incurred as a result of inventory stocking policies. For example, if inventories are set too low in field locations, stock-outs may occur and may be rectified by shipping product(s) from the nearest warehouse location which has the item(s) in stock. Consequently, the costs are a result of decisions which involve trade-offs between or among transportation costs, warehousing costs, inventory carrying costs, and/or stock-out costs. They are transportation costs and should not be classified as inventory carrying costs.

Since it is not always known just how much of such costs as damage, shrinkage, and relocation costs are related to the amount of inventory held, it may be necessary to determine mathematically if a relationship does exist. For example, a cost for damage may be available, but how much of this cost is due to the volume of inventory may not be known. Damage can be a function of such factors as throughput, general housekeeping, the quality and training of management and labor, the type of product, the protective packaging used, the materials handling system, the number of times that the product is handled, and how it is handled. To say which of these factors is most important and how much damage each one accounts for is extremely difficult. Even an elaborate reporting system may not yield the desired results as employees may try to shift the blame for the damaged products. The quality of damage screening during the receiving function and the fact that higher inventories may hide damaged product until inventories are reduced may contribute to the level of damage reported, regardless of the cause.

Using Regression Analysis to Determine Inventory Related Costs

One method of determining the portion of a cost that is variable with inventory is to use regression analysis or to plot the data graphically.[9] Consider the damage rates and inventory levels shown in Table 7-3. Simple linear regression can be used as a tool for segregating the portion of a cost

---

[9] The interested reader may find the following sources to be informative: Morris Hamburg, *Statistical Analysis for Decision Making* (New York: Harcourt, Brace & World, 1970), pp. 459–507; William Mendenhall and Lyman Ott, *Understanding Statistics* (Belmont, Calif.: Duxbury Press, 1972), pp. 173–97; and, John E. Freund and Frank J. Williams, *Elementary Business Statistics: The Modern Approach*, 2d ed. (Englewood Cliffs, N.J.: Prentice-Hall, 1972), pp. 344–76.

**TABLE 7-3** Damage and Corresponding Inventory Levels at Various Points in Time

|  | Time Periods |  |  |  |  |  |  |
|---|---|---|---|---|---|---|---|
|  | 1 | 2 | 3 | 4 | 5 | 6 | 7 |
| Y, damage ($000) | 80 | 100 | 70 | 60 | 50 | 70 | 100 |
| Z, inventory ($ millions) | 11 | 15 | 13 | 10 | 7 | 9 | 13 |

component that is related to the level of inventory held. The principal objective in simple linear regression analysis is to establish a quantitative relationship between two related variables. In order to establish the relationship between two variables, X and Y, a number of paired observations similar to those in Table 7-3 must be obtained.

For example, we are able to obtain the total damage figure in dollars for a number of time periods, but we do not know how much of this damage is directly related to the level of inventory. The first pair of observations ($Y = 8$, $X = 11$) indicates that $80,000 worth of damage occurred in the period when inventory was $11 million.

Now the data can be plotted on graph paper with each pair of observations represented by a point on the chart (see Figure 7-6). A point is

**FIGURE 7-6** Graphing the Relationship between Damage and Inventory Levels

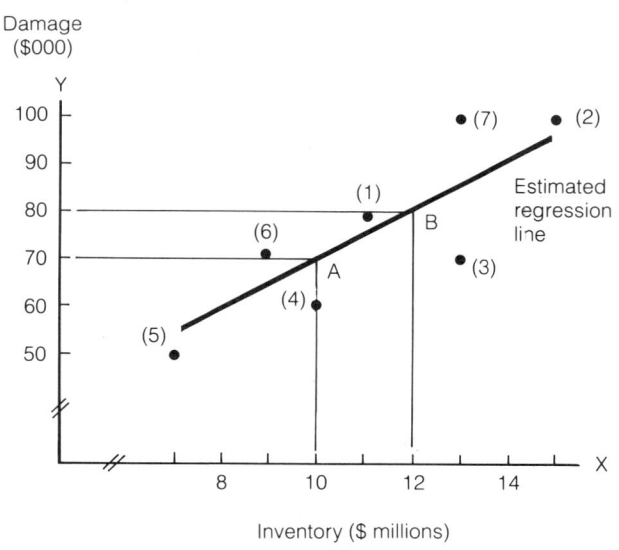

obtained by plotting the independent variable, X, along the horizontal axis and the dependent variable, Y, along the vertical axis. When all the pairs of observations have been plotted, a straight line is drawn that attempts to minimize the distance of all the points from the line (the statistical technique is referred to as least-squares regression).

**FIGURE 7-7** Examples of the Strength of Relationship between Two Variables

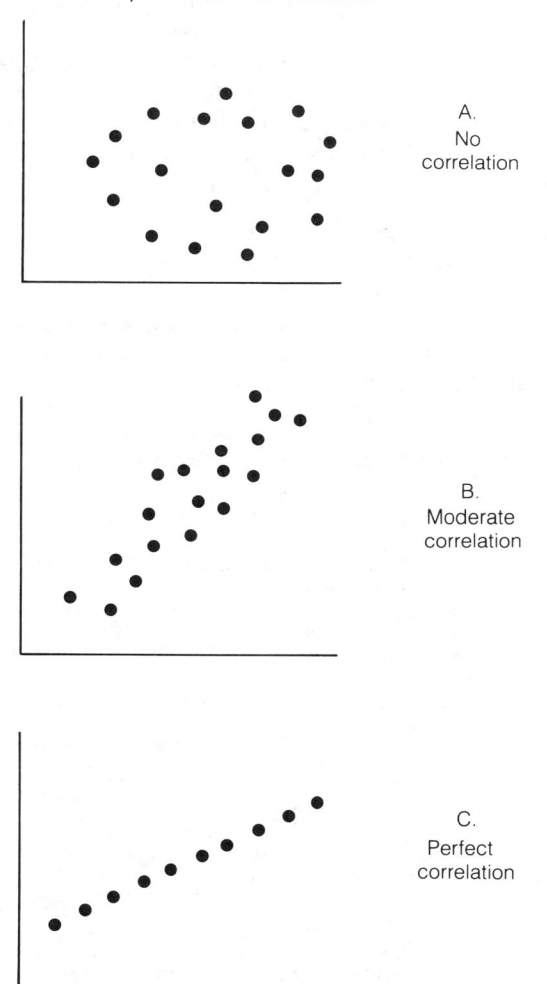

A. No correlation

B. Moderate correlation

C. Perfect correlation

Once this has been done, any two points, A and B, should be selected on the estimated regression line (see Figure 7–6). The increment in the damage from A to B and the change in the inventory from A to B should be expressed as a percentage:

$$(\Delta D/\Delta I) \times 100\%$$
$$= \frac{\$10,000}{\$2,000,000} \times 100\%$$
$$= 0.5\%$$

The 0.5 percent can be interpreted as the percentage of the inventory investment that is damaged because product is being held in inventory. This percentage can be added to the other cost components to determine the total carrying cost percentage. It should be noted that if damage does in fact increase with increased levels of inventory, then the estimated regression line must move upward to the right. A line that is vertical, horizontal, or sloping upward to the left, would indicate that such a relationship does not exist.

The ability to successfully fit a line through the plotted points will depend upon the strength of the relationship present, the degree of correlation. Figure 7–7 depicts three possibilities:

A. No correlation—points are scattered all over indicating that no relationship exists.
B. Moderate correlation—points are all situated relatively close to the estimated regression line indicating a moderate relationship.
C. Perfect correlation—all of the points fall on the line. This would be a correlation of 1.0. The closer the correlation is to 1.0, the stronger the relationship.

*Section summary and examples.* The methodology that should be used

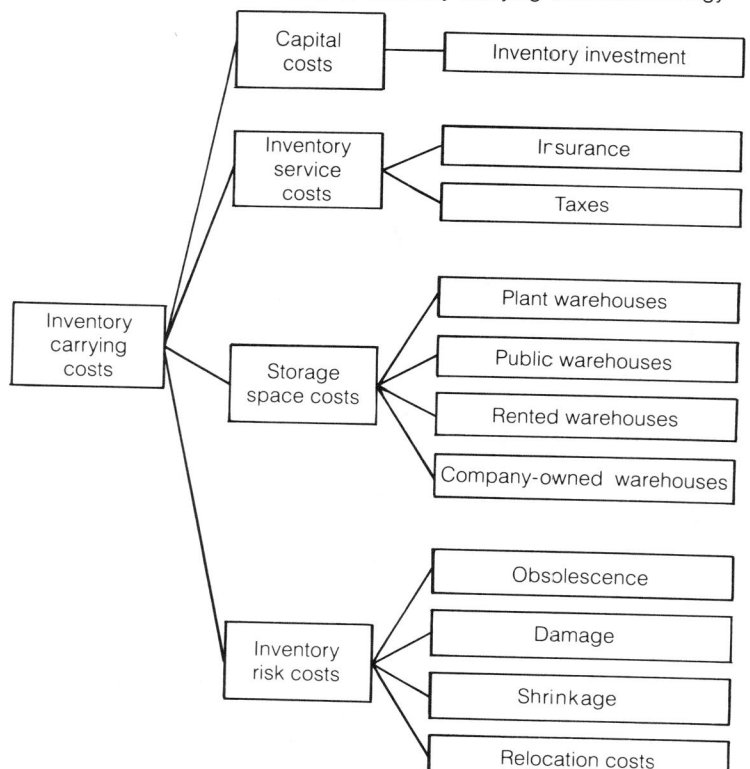

**FIGURE 7–8** Normative Model of Inventory Carrying Cost Methodology

Source: Douglas M. Lambert, *The Development of an Inventory Costing Methodology: A Study of the Costs Associated with Holding Inventory* (Chicago: NCPDM, 1976), p. 68.

to calculate inventory carrying costs is summarized in Figure 7−8. The model is referred to as being *normative* because using it will lead to a carrying cost which accurately reflects a firm's costs. An actual application of the methodology for a manufacturer of packaged goods will be illustrated next, followed by an example from the bulk chemicals industry.

### A CONSUMER PACKAGED GOODS INDUSTRY EXAMPLE

Using the methodology summarized in Figure 7−8, it is necessary to calculate costs for the following four basic categories: (1) capital costs, (2) inventory service costs, (3) storage space costs, and (4) inventory risk costs.

*Capital costs.* In order to establish the opportunity cost of capital, the minimum acceptable rate of return on new investments, an interview was conducted with the company's controller. Due to capital rationing, the current hurdle rate on new investments was 15 percent after taxes. The company conducted a post-audit of most projects in order to substantiate the rate of return. This was required by corporate policy and in the majority of cases the desired rate of return was achieved although there was considerable variability on individual marketing projects. The difficulty in estimating the rate of return on marketing projects was caused by the inability to forecast the market's acceptance of new products. Consequently, the cost of money used for inventory carrying costs was set at 30 percent before taxes or 15 percent after taxes.

The opportunity cost of capital should be applied to only the out-of-pocket investment in inventory. This is the direct variable expense incurred up to the point at which the inventory is held in storage. In other words, it was necessary to obtain the average variable cost of products, delivered to the warehouse location. Since the company used standard fully allocated manufacturing cost for valuing inventory, it was necessary to investigate the standard costs for each product in order to determine the variable manufactured cost per unit. Using the company's inventory plan for the coming year, it was possible to calculate the average inventory for each product. The average inventory of each product can be determined for each storage location or for the total system depending on the information available within the firm. In this case, the average inventory for the physical distribution system was used.

Next, the average transportation cost per case of product was added to the variable manufactured cost. This is necessary because the transportation cost must be paid just like the manufacturing labor and raw material costs. Finally, if any warehousing costs are incurred moving products into storage in field locations, these costs should be added on a per-case basis to the standard variable manufactured cost. When public warehousing is used, any charges paid at the time products are moved into the facility should be added on a per-case basis to all products held in inventory. In the case of corporate facilities, only variable out-of-pocket costs associated with moving the products into storage should be included.

The company had $10 million in average system inventory valued at full manufactured cost. Annual sales were $175 million or approximately $125 million at manufactured cost. The inventory value based on variable manufacturing costs and the forecasted product mix was $7 million. The $7 million was the average annual inventory held at plants and field locations in order to achieve least cost distribution. The variable costs associated with transporting the strategically deployed field inventory and moving it into public warehouses totalled $800,000. Therefore, the average system inventory was $7.8 million when valued at variable cost delivered to the storage location.

All of the remaining inventory carrying cost components should be calculated as a percentage of the variable delivered cost ($7.8 million) and added to the capital cost percentage. However, in some companies inventory reports may value products only at full standard manufactured cost and the cost or time involved in changing reporting practices may seem high relative to the benefits to be gained. If a firm faces this type of situation, the cost of money can be adjusted when the carrying cost is developed in order to reflect that it is being applied to a value larger than the cash generated by a reduction in inventory. Methods of adjusting the carrying cost calculation to represent only variable costs are shown in Table 7-4.

**TABLE 7-4** Adjusting the Cost of Money to Fit the Method of Inventory Valuation

| | | |
|---|---|---|
| Method A | | |
| Inventory at full cost | | $10,000,000 |
| Variable cost is 80 percent of full cost | × | 80% |
| Inventory at variable cost | | 8,000,000 |
| Cost of money before tax is 40% | × | 40% |
| Cost of money associated with the inventory investment | | $ 3,200,000 |
| Method B | | |
| Cost of money before tax | | 40% |
| Variable cost is 80 percent of full cost | × | 80% |
| Adjusted cost of money | | 32% |
| Inventory at full cost | | $10,000,000 |
| Adjusted cost of money | × | 32% |
| Cost of money associated with the inventory investment | | $ 3,200,000 |

The assumptions are that variable costs are 80 percent of full cost and that the cost of money is 40 percent pretax or 20 percent after taxes. If the inventory shown on management reports is valued at $10 million at full cost, a manager could take 80 percent of this number and then apply the 40 percent cost of money. This would yield a capital cost of $3.2 million. Another alternative is to adjust the cost of money at the time the inventory carrying cost is developed. By taking 80 percent of the 40 percent cost of money the adjusted cost of money, 32 percent, can be applied to the inventory value shown on the management reports. This method also yields a capital cost of $3.2 million. If full cost is used and the cost of money is appropriately adjusted, all remaining cost components should be calculated as a percentage of the full cost inventory value.

*Inventory service costs.* Return to the example of the manufacturer of packaged goods with system inventories of $7.8 million valued at variable cost delivered to the storage location. *Taxes* for the year 1979 were $90,948 which is 1.166 percent of the $7.8 million inventory value and this figure was added to the 30 percent capital cost (see Table 7-5).

*Insurance* costs covering inventory for the year were $4,524 which is 0.058 percent of the inventory value.

*Storage space costs.* The storage component of the *public warehousing* cost was $225,654 for 1979 which equals 2.893 percent of the inventory value. Variable storage costs in *plant warehouses* should include only those costs that are variable with the amount of inventory stored. The vast majority of plant warehousing expenses were fixed in nature. Those costs that were variable, fluctuated with the

**TABLE 7-5** Summary of Data Collection Procedure

| Step No. | Cost Category | Source | Explanation | Amount (current study) |
|---|---|---|---|---|
| 1. | Cost of money | Comptroller | This represents the cost of having money invested in inventory and the return should be comparable to other investment opportunities | 30% pretax |
| 2. | Average monthly inventory valued at variable costs delivered to the distribution center | 1. Standard cost data—comptroller's department  2. Freight rates and product specs are from distribution reports  3. Average monthly inventory in cases from printout received from sales forecasting | Only want variable costs since fixed costs go on regardless of the amount of product manufactured and stored—follow steps outlined in body of report | $7,800,000 valued at variable cost delivered to the DC (variable manufactured cost equaled 70% of full manufactured cost. Variable cost FOB the DC averaged 78% of full manufactured cost |
| 3. | Taxes | The comptroller's department | Personal property taxes paid on inventory | $90,948 which equals 1.1667% |
| 4. | Insurance | The comptroller's department | Insurance rate/$100 of inventory (at variable costs) | $4,524 which equals 0.058% |
| 5. | Recurring storage (public warehouse) | Distribution operations | This represents the portion of warehousing costs that are related to the volume of inventory stored. | $225,654 annually which equals 2.893% |
| 6. | Variable storage (plant warehouses) | Transportation services | Only those costs that are variable with the amount of inventory stored should be included. | Nil |
| 7. | Obsolescence | Distribution department reports | Cost of holding product inventory beyond its useful life | 0.800 percent of inventory |
| 8. | Shrinkage | Distribution department reports | Requires managerial judgment to determine the portion attributable to inventory storage. | $100,308 which equals 1.286% |
| 9. | Damage | Distribution department reports | Requires managerial judgment to determine the portion attributable to inventory storage. | |
| 10. | Relocation costs | Not available | Only relocation costs incurred to avoid obsolescence should be included. | Not available |
| 11. | Total carrying costs | Calculate the numbers generated in steps 3, 4, 5, 6, 8, 9, and 10 as a percentage of average inventory valued at variable cost delivered to the distribution center and add them to the cost of money (step 1). | | 36.203% |

amount of product moved into and out of the facility (throughput) and were not variable with inventory levels. Consequently, variable storage costs were negligible in plant warehouses.

*Inventory risk costs.* *Obsolescence* cost, which is the cost of holding products in inventory beyond their useful life, were being tracked in this company and for 1979 represented 0.800 percent of inventory.

*Shrinkage* and *damage* costs were not recorded separately. Regression analysis would have been a possible means of isolating the portion of these costs that were variable with inventories. However, management was confident that no more than 10 percent of the total shrinkage and damage, $100,308, was related to inventory levels. Therefore, a managerial estimate of 10 percent was used. This was equal to 1.286 percent of the inventory value of $7.8 million.

*Relocation costs*, those costs incurred transporting products from one location to another to avoid obsolescence, were not available. Management said that such costs were incurred *so infrequently* that they were not recorded separately from ordinary transportation costs. When totalled, the individual percentages gave an inventory carrying cost of 36.203 percent.

Up to this point, we have assumed that the company has a relatively homogeneous product line, that is, products can be manufactured at each plant location, products are shipped in mixed quantities, and products are stored in the same facilities. Consequently, if the company has a 12-month inventory plan and standard costs are available, a weighted-average inventory carrying cost can be used for all products and locations. This figure would require updating on an annual basis when the new inventory plan, updated standard costs, and the previous year's expenditures for insurance, taxes, storage, and inventory risk costs become available.

Management at General Mills, Inc., calculated an inventory carrying cost for each location where product was held and it was found that considerable variation existed.[10] Since the costs have to be collected by storage location minimal additional effort is required to "fine tune" the numbers for decisions regarding a specific location or type of inventory. If the differences are minimal, the weighted average inventory carrying cost will be sufficient.

However, in companies with heterogeneous products, inventory carrying costs should be calculated for each individual product. For example bulk chemical products cannot be shipped in mixed quantities or stored in the same tanks. For this reason, transportation and storage costs should be included on a specific product/location basis rather than using an average transportation and storage cost as is the case with homogeneous products.

The next section contains an industry example from the bulk chemicals industry which will clarify the distinction that have been made between homogeneous and heterogeneous products.

### A BULK CHEMICALS INDUSTRY EXAMPLE

Due to the vastly different nature of bulk chemical products in terms of storage requirements, shrinkage, and terminal locations, and because of the absence of

---

[10] William R. Steele, "Inventory Carrying Cost Identification and Accounting," *Proceedings of the Annual Conference of the National Council of Physical Distribution Management*, October 15–17, 1979, pp. 75–86.

an inventory forecast, it was necessary to determine an inventory carrying cost figure for each major product or class of products. There was an additional problem caused by the fact that the selling price per ton, the full manufactured cost, and variable costs per ton varied by plant and also varied within a plant throughout the year.

This example will focus on two products manufactured by the industrial-chemicals division. The one product was selected because it had a relatively low variable cost of production and the other was chosen because its variable cost of production represented a substantially higher percentage of the full manufactured cost. The two products were representative of the range of products manufactured by the company in terms of cost and shipping and storage requirements. Since the variable costs of transportation would be different for each stocking point, inventory carrying costs were calculated as a percentage of variable costs at the manufacturing location.

*Capital costs.* An interview with the controller revealed that a 20 percent return after taxes was required on new investments of over $500,000. As a result of this meeting, it was established that the opportunity cost of capital to be applied to inventory investment would be 20 percent after taxes or 40 percent before taxes. The latter made it comparable to the other expenses, such as transportation and terminal expenses, considered in the physical distribution cost trade-off analysis. The opportunity cost of capital should be applied only to the out-of-pocket investment in inventory. The first step in the analysis of these out-of-pocket costs was to determine the standard variable costs of each product and to express these costs as a percentage of full manufactured costs and average net back per ton which was the average selling price less the selling expenses per ton. Since all monthly physical distribution reports valued inventory at average net back, all components of inventory carrying costs were expressed as a percentage of average net back per ton as well as variable costs and full manufactured costs (see Tables 7 — 6 and 7 — 7). However, depending on where the inventory was held, the variable costs as a percentage of average net back per ton may change. This is because transportation costs should be added to field inventory.

*Inventory service costs.* The company was self-insured for $250,000 of finished-product inventory at each warehouse location, but for inventory over $250,000 at any specific location the insurance rate was $0.2648 per $100 of average inventory. Since the cost of the insurance on the first $250,000 of inventory was not readily available, the $0.2648 per $100 figure was used in the calculation of inventory carrying costs with the realization that it may be fractionally below or above the actual figure.

*Taxes* paid on inventory vary depending on the state and city in which the terminal is located. The actual tax rate payable for each location should be used when determining specific sites for the terminals. However, in preliminary studies it was recommended that the average tax figure for the preceding year be used. Based on average monthly inventory for 1973 and 1973 taxes this represented 0.207 percent of inventory valued at average net back. This figure was such a small portion of the total inventory carrying-cost percentage that it was unlikely that using the actual tax figure for a location would alter the decision.

*Storage space costs.* There were four types of warehouse facilities that required consideration, and the treatment was different for each one. The costs associated with *plant storage tanks* were fixed in nature and therefore not relevant for decisions related to increasing the level of inventory in any particular storage tank. If an increase in inventory required additional plant storage and the installation of new tanks, a capital budgeting decision would be required. Once

**TABLE 7-6** Inventory Carrying Costs for Product LMN

|  | Percentage Based on Average Net Back per Ton ($393) | Percentage Based on Budgeted Full Manufacturing Costs per Ton ($138.51) | Percentage Based on Variable Costs per Ton ($80.43) |
|---|---|---|---|
| Capital costs |  |  |  |
| Capital cost (minimum acceptable rate of return = 20% after taxes— 40% before taxes) | 8.188* | 23.227† | 40.000 |
| Inventory service costs |  |  |  |
| Insurance | 0.265 | 0.752 | 1.295 |
| Taxes (vary with location—average) | 0.274 | 0.777 | 1.338 |
| Storage space costs | —‡ | —‡ | —‡ |
| Inventory risk costs |  |  |  |
| Obsolescence |  |  |  |
| Shrinkage | 3.220 | 9.137§ | 15.735 |
| Damage |  |  |  |
| Relocation costs |  |  |  |
| Total (before taxes) | 11.947 | 33.893 | 58.358 |
| Inventory carrying costs (per ton) | $46.95 | $46.95 | $46.95 |

\* Based on variable costs of $80.43 per ton and average net back per ton of $393. Variable costs = 20.47% of average per ton net back. Therefore capital costs = 0.2047 × 40% = 8.188% of average net back per ton.

† Budgeted full manufacturing costs were $138.51. Variable costs as a percentage of full manufacturing costs = 58.068%. Therefore capital costs = .58068 × 40% = 23.227%.

‡ Fixed over the relevant range of inventory levels.

§ Calculated on the basis of tons of shrinkage as a percent of average inventory in tons. Applied to full manufacturing costs as a surrogate for variable manufacturing costs plus transportation and adjusted to corresponding percentage based on net back and variable costs per ton.

Source: Douglas M. Lambert, *The Development of an Inventory Costing Methodology: A Study of the Costs Associated with Holding Inventory* (Chicago: NCPDM, 1976), pp. 167-8.

an additional storage tank was built, changes in the level of product held in the tank would not affect the storage costs.

A similar argument held for *rented terminal space* since the cost of such space was fixed on an annual basis. The cost per gallon might decrease as larger quantities of storage space were contracted, but usually the total annual cost was insensitive to the quantity of product held within a given tank. Handling costs were related to sales (throughput) and not to the quantity of product held in storage. The manager of warehouse and terminal operations said that in some instances it was necessary to guarantee four turns of inventory per year. A logistics analyst confirmed that although terminal lease costs were required when making a decision to locate a terminal, once the terminal was on-stream the terminal costs were considered fixed when deciding if other customers should be routed through the terminal.

*Inventory risk costs.* These costs usually include obsolescence, damage, pilferage, and relocation costs. *Obsolescence* was not a factor since the company was experiencing a "seller's market" for its products due to product shortages in the chemical industry. However, in a "buyers market" the obsolescence costs should be measured.

*Damage* that resulted while the product was in the custody of a carrier was claimed, and was therefore not a significant cost. It is recognized that managing

**TABLE 7-7** Inventory Carrying Costs for Product XYZ

|  | Percentage Based on Average Net Back per Ton ($50.84) | Percentage Based on Budgeted Full Manufacturing Costs per Ton ($28.89) | Percentage Based on Variable Costs per Ton ($2.34) |
|---|---|---|---|
| Capital costs |  |  |  |
| Capital cost (minimum acceptable rate of return = 20% after taxes— 40% before taxes) | 1.841* | 3.240 | 40.000 |
| Inventory Service Costs |  |  |  |
| Insurance | 0.265 | 0.466 | 5.757† |
| Taxes (vary with location—average) | 0.2740 | 0.482 | 5.865† |
| Storage space costs | —‡ | —‡ | —‡ |
| Inventory risk costs |  |  |  |
| Obsolescence |  |  |  |
| Shrinkage | 0.730 | 1.284§ | 15.852 |
| Damage |  |  |  |
| Relocation costs |  |  |  |
| Total (before taxes) | 3.110 | 5.472 | 67.474 |
| Inventory carrying costs (per ton) | $1.58 | $1.58 | $1.58 |

*This depends on the percentage of average net back per ton that variable manufacturing costs plus variable transportation costs represent. For product held at the plant and based on $2.34 per ton variable cost and $50.84 average net back per ton. Variable cost = 4.602% of average per ton net back. Therefore capital costs = .04602 × 40% = 1.841%. For field inventory, transportation costs would be added before calculating the variable cost percentage.

† Based on variable costs of $2.34 per ton and average net back of $50.84. Variable manufacturing costs = 4.602% of average per ton net back. Consequently, 0.265% of $50.84 = 5.757% of $2.34 and 0.270% of $50.84 = 5.865% of $2.34. Full manufacturing costs were $28.89 per ton and percentages based on this figure were calculated in a manner similar to the percentages based on average net back per ton.

‡ Fixed over the relevant range of inventory levels.

§ Calculated on the basis of tons of shrinkage as a percent of average inventory in tons. Applied to full manufacturing costs as a surrogate for variable manufacturing costs plus transportation and adjusted to corresponding percentage based on net back and variable costs per ton.

Source: Douglas M. Lambert, *The Development of an Inventory Costing Methodology: A Study of the Costs Associated with Holding Inventory* (Chicago: NCPDM, 1976), pp. 165–6.

the claims function has costs attached to it, but the variable cost of making these claims against carriers should not be included in inventory carrying costs since the majority of these claims are related to throughput and not the amount of inventory held.

All other *shrinkage* costs amounted to 1.51 percent of the average inventory for all products (see Table 7–8). However, they varied substantially by product. The wide fluctuation in the price of each product, caused by such factors as the plant in which it was produced and the supply-demand relationship, made the dollar shrinkage figure as determined by management extremely tenuous. For this reason a weighted-average cost per ton was calculated for the two products being studied (Table 7–8). However, this problem could be avoided by just considering the shrinkage in tons as a percentage of average annual inventory in tons. This yields a percentage figure that is independent of dollars (Table 7–8).

*Relocation costs* which are the costs associated with the transshipment of inventory from one stocking location to another were believed to be negligible and were not included.

**258** Part Two

**TABLE 7–8** Terminal Inventory and Shrinkage for 19—

|  | Product XYZ ||| Product LMN ||| |
|  | Dollars | Tons | Dollars per Ton | Dollars | Tons | Dollars per Ton | Total |
|---|---|---|---|---|---|---|---|
| January |  |  |  |  |  |  |  |
| February |  |  |  |  |  |  |  |
| March |  |  |  |  |  |  |  |
| April |  |  |  |  |  |  |  |
| May |  |  |  |  |  |  |  |
| June |  |  |  |  |  |  |  |
| July |  |  |  |  |  |  |  |
| August |  |  |  |  |  |  |  |
| September |  |  |  |  |  |  |  |
| October |  |  |  |  |  |  |  |
| November |  |  |  |  |  |  |  |
| December |  |  |  |  |  |  |  |
| Monthly average |  |  |  |  |  |  |  |
| Annual shrinkage |  |  | * |  |  | * |  |
| Percent shrinkage |  |  |  |  |  |  |  |

* Best number to use since it is independent of the price per ton (since percentage can be applied to any value of inventory). However, this percentage should only be applied to out-of-pocket costs. Since variable manufacturing costs do not include transportation costs, it is recommended that this shrinkage percentage be applied to full manufacturing costs (surrogate measure for variable manufacturing cost plus transportation).

Source: From *Summary of Warehouse Valuation* report from Distribution Accounting.

*Total inventory carrying costs.* The total inventory carrying cost figure to be used for decision making was 58.36 percent of variable costs before taxes for product LMN and 67.47 percent of variable costs before taxes for product XYZ. These percentages may seem high, but they are applied only to the variable costs associated with the inventory and not to full manufacturing costs. For example, if these figures were calculated as percentages of the full manufactured costs they would be 33.89 percent and 5.47 percent, respectively. As percentages of the average net back per ton, they would be 11.95 percent from product LMN and 3.11 percent for product XYZ even though the inventory carrying costs expressed in dollars were $46.95 per ton for product LMN and $1.58 per ton for product XYZ (see Tables 7–6 and 7–7, respectively).

All of the percentages were calculated under the assumption that the inventory would be stored at the plant. However, if the inventory was located in field warehouses, the variable costs would include transportation costs plus any charges associated with moving the product into storage and would represent a higher percentage of full manufactured cost average net back per ton. Consequently, it was recommended that the percentage based on variable costs be used when calculating inventory carrying costs.

This chemical industry example should make it abundantly clear why it is a mistake to simply take an inventory carrying cost percentage that is an industry average or textbook percentage and apply it to inventory in your company. Not only were the inventory carrying costs significantly different for each of the products considered, but the carrying costs varied widely for each product depending on the method of inventory valuation used.

The previous example should have clarified the methodology and how it can be applied. You should be able at this point to calculate a carrying cost for a company if required to do so.

## THE IMPACT OF INVENTORY TURNOVER ON INVENTORY CARRYING COSTS

In Chapter 2 it was pointed out that in many firms management attempts to improve profitability by emphasizing the need to improve inventory turnover. However, pushing for increased inventory turnover without considering the impact on total physical distribution system costs may actually lead to decreased profitability. For example, Table 7–9 illustrates the im-

**TABLE 7-9** Relationship Between Inventory Turnover and Inventory Carrying Costs

| Inventory Turnover | Average Inventory | Carrying Cost at 35 Percent | Carrying Cost Savings |
|---|---|---|---|
| 1  | $30,000,000 | $10,500,000 | — |
| 2  | 15,000,000 | 5,250,000 | $5,250,000 |
| 3  | 10,000,000 | 3,500,000 | 1,750,000 |
| 4  | 7,500,000 | 2,625,000 | 875,000 |
| 5  | 6,000,000 | 2,100,000 | 525,000 |
| 6  | 5,000,000 | 1,750,000 | 350,000 |
| 7  | 4,286,000 | 1,500,000 | 250,000 |
| 8  | 3,750,000 | 1,312,500 | 187,500 |
| 9  | 3,333,000 | 1,166,550 | 145,950 |
| 10 | 3,000,000 | 1,050,000 | 116,550 |
| 11 | 2,728,000 | 954,800 | 95,200 |
| 12 | 2,500,000 | 875,000 | 79,800 |
| 13 | 2,308,000 | 807,800 | 67,200 |
| 14 | 2,143,000 | 750,000 | 57,800 |
| 15 | 2,000,000 | 700,000 | 50,000 |
| 16 | 1,875,000 | 656,250 | 43,750 |
| 17 | 1,765,000 | 617,750 | 38,500 |
| 18 | 1,667,000 | 583,450 | 34,300 |
| 19 | 1,579,000 | 553,650 | 29,800 |
| 20 | 1,500,000 | 525,000 | 28,650 |

pact that increasing inventory turnover has on total carrying costs. Improving turns from 6 times to 12 times results in an annual savings of $875,000; thus profits will increase. But many times management finds itself in the position where inventory turns are expected to increase each year. If the physical distribution system is currently efficient and the goal is to increase turnovers from 11 to 12, the annual savings in carrying costs would be $79,800. Care must be taken that transportation costs do not increase by more than this amount and/or that lower customer service levels do not result in lost profit contribution in excess of the carrying cost savings. Figure 7–9 illustrates graphically the relationship between inventory carry-

**FIGURE 7–9** Annual Inventory Carrying Costs per Unit Compared to Inventory Turnover

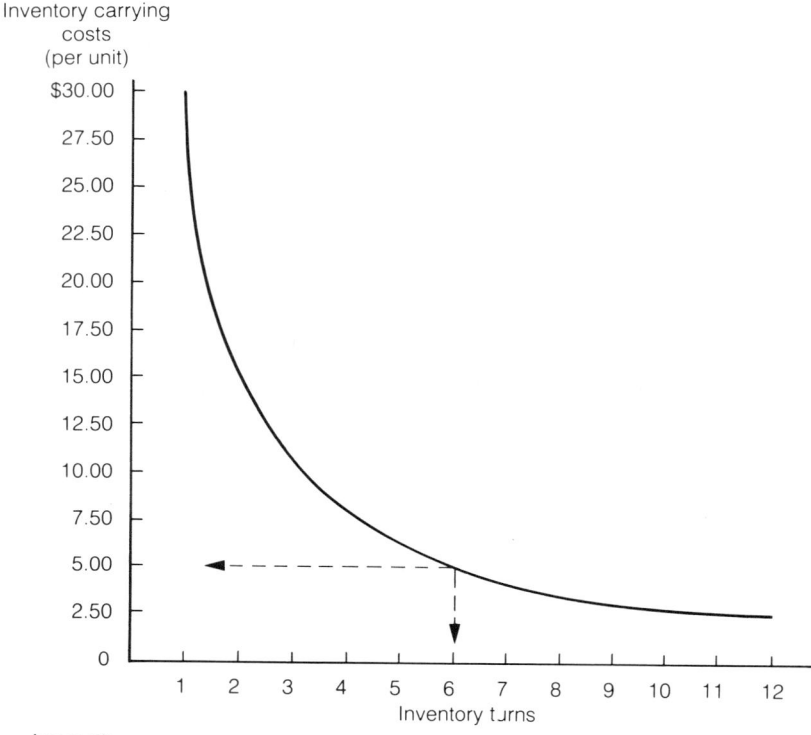

Assumptions:
1. The average value of one unit of product is $85.70.
2. The annual inventory carrying cost is 35 percent.
3. The annual inventory carrying cost per unit is $30.00.

Source: Jay Sterling, doctoral candidate, Graduate School of Business Administration, Michigan State University, 1981.

ing costs on a per unit basis and the number of inventory turns. The example shows that improvements in the number of inventory turnovers has the greatest impact if current inventory is turned over less than six times per year.

## SUMMARY

In this chapter you were shown how to determine the impact of inventory investment on a firm's corporate profit performance. Also, you were shown how inventory policy affects least total cost physical distribution and you were provided with a methodology that you can use to calculate inventory carrying costs. Finally, you were shown the relationship that exists between inventory turnover and inventory carrying costs.

Now that you are aware that inventory is a costly investment and you know how to determine inventory carrying costs, you are ready for Chapter 8 in which you will be shown: how the basic concepts of inventory management are applied; how to calculate safety stocks; how production policies influence inventory levels; how inventories and customer service levels are interrelated; how to recognize poor inventory management; how to improve inventory management; and how profit performance can be improved by systems that reduce inventories.

## Appendix A: Inventory Carrying Costs—Six Case Studies

In order to provide you with further knowledge regarding inventory carrying costs calculations, data from six case studies with manufacturers of packaged-goods products are presented. Most of their sales were in the household consumer market, although some of the companies had substantial institutional sales. All of the companies had sales of over $1 billion or were divisions of multinational corporations with sales volumes in excess of $1 billion annually. Every company had multiple products that were marketed in the United States.

Three of the firms used public warehouses to satisfy 100 percent of their field-warehousing requirements. One company used leased facilities exclusively and another used public warehouses and corporate-managed facilities on a 50–50 basis. The sixth company used private, leased, and public warehouses on a 10 percent, 40 percent, and 50 percent basis, respectively. In addition to plant warehouses, the number of field warehouses used by the respondents ranged from 5 to over 20 with two companies falling into the last category.

The data collected from the six companies are shown in Table 7A–1. The results supported the contention that each company should calculate its own figure since individual carrying cost percentages ranged from a low of 14 percent to a high of 43 percent before taxes. With few exceptions, the data were readily available in each of the companies; however a number of minor data-collection problems were experienced:

1. One company did not have a specific hurdle rate for new investments, and another company, although it used a hurdle rate of 20 percent, was required to pay its corporate head office only 8 percent for money that was invested in inventories or accounts receivable. Consequently, the 8 percent figure was used since it reflected the division's true cost.
2. Although the inventory investment data and the insurance and taxes on the inventory investment were readily available in most cases, in one company three days work was required to determine accurately a tax calculation of 0.460 percent of the inventory value. Since a small percentage error would have little impact on a carrying cost of 30 percent, it was recommended that in the future, the percentage of total inventory represented by each product group be applied to the total tax figure, a procedure which would require approximately 15 minutes.
3. The variable costs associated with the volume of inventory held were available in every company; however, the costs of damage and shrinkage, and to some extent the cost of obsolescence, required managerial estimates. In only one company were these costs not recorded.
4. Relocation costs, which are the costs associated with the transshipment of inventory from one stocking location to another in order to avoid obsolescence, were believed to be negligible.

---

Source: Douglas M. Lambert, *The Development of an Inventory Costing Methodology: A Study of the Costs Associated with Holding Inventory* (Chicago: NCPDM, 1976), pp. 80–103.

**TABLE 7A-1** Summary of Inventory Carrying Cost Data from Six Packaged Goods Companies

| | Company A | Company B | Company C | Company D | Company E | Company F |
|---|---|---|---|---|---|---|
| Inventory carrying cost components | | | | | | |
| Capital costs | 40.000% | 29.000% | 25.500% | 8.000% | 30.000% | 26.000% |
| Inventory service costs | | | | | | |
| Insurance | 0.091 | 0.210 | 1.689 | 0.126 | 0.023 | 4.546 |
| Taxes | 1.897 | 0.460 | 0.085 | 1.218 | 0.028 | 0.334 |
| Storage space costs | | | | | | |
| Recurring storage | 0.738 | — | 0.573 | 2.681 | 0.456 | 2.925 |
| Inventory risk costs | | | | | | |
| Obsolescence | — | — | — | 0.785 | 1.700 | n.a. |
| Damage | 0.233 | 0.398 | 0.500 | 1.393 | 0.124 | — |
| Shrinkage | — | — | — | — | 0.329 | — |
| Transshipment costs | — | — | — | n.a. | 0.302 | — |
| Total inventory carrying costs (before taxes)* | 42.959† | 30.068 | 28.347 | 14.203‡ | 32.962 | 33.805§ |
| Inventory carrying cost percentage used prior to this study | 9.5‖ | 15 | 20 | 8 | 25 | 15 |
| Average inventory of division or product group studied | $10,000,000 | $25,000,000 | $8,000,000 | $500,000 | $45,000,000 | $2,000,000 |
| Method of inventory valuation | Full manufactured cost | Variable cost delivered to the customer | Actual variable costs of production | Full manufactured cost | Variable cost delivered to D.C. | Full manufactured cost |
| Time required for data collection | 16 hours | 70 hours but only 20 hours per year required for update | 40 hours | 30 hours | 20 hours | 20 hours |
| Cost of data collection | $150 | $300 | $300 | $225 | $150 | $200 |

* As a percentage of the variable costs delivered to the distribution center (this allows a comparison to be made of all companies).
† Inventory carrying costs were 35.441 percent of the full manufactured cost.
‡ Inventory carrying costs were 14.100 percent of the full manufactured cost.
§ Inventory carrying costs were 27.321 percent of the full manufactured cost.
‖ Although 9.5 percent was the aftertax number, the company had been using it as a before tax figure in the cost trade-off analysis.

For all six companies, the cost of annually updating the carrying cost figure was estimated to be $300 or less with individual estimates ranging from $150 to $300. These estimates were based on the data-collection experience in the companies and the rate of pay of the person or persons responsible for the update. Although they are not out-of-pocket costs, they serve as a measure of the effort required to complete the carrying cost calculation.

Some caution should be exercised in viewing the data-collection expense as the absolute maximum. This is because the $150 to $300 range assumes a certain level of sophistication in terms of the corporate accounting system. In a less sophisticated company it is conceivable that substantial additional effort may be required in order to accurately trace some of the cost components. For example, in situations where inventory-risk costs represent a substantial proportion of the total inventory carrying costs, a managerial estimate of the proportion of these costs related to the level

**TABLE 7A-2** Summary of Data Collection Procedure Showing Source of Data

| Step No. | Cost Category | Explanation | Company A | Company B | Company C | Company D | Company E | Company F |
|---|---|---|---|---|---|---|---|---|
| 1. | Cost of money | This represents the cost of having money invested in inventory and the return should be comparable to other investment opportunities | Corporate controller | Divisional vice president and general managers | Vice president and controller | Vice president controller and treasurer | Manager, financial analysis | Vice president and controller |
| 2. | Average monthly inventory valued at variable costs delivered to the distribution center | Only want variable costs since fixed costs remain the same regardless of inventory levels | Standard costs from accounting Inventory plan from distribution Location of inventory and freight rates from distribution | Monthly computer print out | Director of distribution planning from monthly inventory print-out | Standard cost data from controller's dept. Freight rates and product space from distribution dept. reports Average monthly inventory in cases from sales forecasting | Inventory planning manager | From budget report |
| 3. | Taxes | Personal property taxes paid on finished goods inventory | Manager corporate taxes | Property tax representative | Director, corporate taxes | Controller's department | Manager, ad valorem taxes | From budget |
| 4. | Insurance | Insurance paid on inventory investment | Budgeted figures from accounting report | Manager, corporate insurance | Director, corporate insurance | Controller's department | Assistant treasurer | |

**TABLE 7A-2 (continued)**

| Step No. | Cost Category | Explanation | Company A | Company B | Company C | Company D | Company E | Company F |
|---|---|---|---|---|---|---|---|---|
| 5. | Variable storage | Only those costs that are variable with the amount of inventory stored should be included | Manager, materials management | Warehouse managers | Director, distribution center operations | Distribution operations analyst and transportation | Year end summary of monthly computer report | Distribution report |
| 6. | Obsolescence | Obsolescence due to holding inventory | Manager materials management planning and analysis | Manager claims shrinkage and damage | Not available | From distribution department reports | Reclamation expense report | Distribution reports or knowledge of manager |
| 7. | Shrinkage | Shrinkage related to volume of inventory | | | | | Reclamation expense report | |
| 8. | Damage | Damage that is directly attributable to the level of inventory hold | | | | | Manager, materials handling systems | |
| 9. | Relocation costs | Only relocation costs that result in order to avoid obsolescence | | Manager, distribution research | Not available | Not available | Inventory planning manager | |
| 10. | Total carrying costs percentage | Calculate the numbers generated in steps 3 to 9 as a percentage of average inventory and add to cost of money (step 1) | | | | | | |

of inventory held would not suffice. Consequently, it would be necessary to implement a reporting system that would accurately reflect these costs or to use regression analysis to determine the portion of these costs that were variable with the quantity of inventory.

Table 7A–2 contains a summary of where in each of the six organizations the individual carrying cost components were obtained. This table should be of substantial use to you as an indicator of where in a company you might look for specific inventory carrying components.

Finally, one minor problem was experienced in terms of using the inventory carrying cost percentage in economic order quantity (EOQ) analysis. If the quantity generated from this formula required that additional fixed storage space be added, then the EOQ should be recalculated including an estimated annual cost for any additional facilities that are necessary. Should the EOQ change appreciably, a number of additional recalculations would be necessary in order to find the best trade-off between order quantity and the additional capital costs.

## Appendix B: Inventory Carrying Costs — Forms for Data Collection

**TABLE 7B–1** Inventory Service Costs—198_

| Cost Category | Percentage or Dollar Amount | Source | Time Required to Obtain Data |
|---|---|---|---|
| Insurance | Inventory in Plant Warehouses Based on inventory (average monthly) of approximately $_____ = _____% of inventory values. | | |
| Taxes | Summary<br><br>Warehouses        Taxes<br><br>A ..........................  $<br>B ..........................<br>C ..........................<br>Public ....................<br>    Total ..................  $<br><br>Taxes as a percent of inventory = _____%. | | |
| Cost of capital | Cost of capital = $_____<br>Inventory at full factory cost = $_____.<br>Variable cost = _____% of full cost and the cost of capital should only be applied to the variable portion of inventory cost. | | |

Source: Douglas M. Lambert, *The Development of an Inventory Costing Methodology: A Study of the Costs Associated with Holding Inventory* (Chicago: NCPDM, 1976), pp. 133–46.

**TABLE 7B-2** Warehousing Costs (Finished Goods)

|  | (Warehouse Location) | Nature of Cost* |
|---|---|---|
| Payroll | | |
|   Labor—direct | | |
|   Overtime | | |
|   Shift premium | | |
|     Total payroll | | |
| Direct expenses | | |
|   Variable | | |
|   Fixed | | |
|   Total | | |
| Insurance | | |
|   Stock | | |
|   Fire Plant | | |
| Taxes | | |
| Depreciation | | |
|     Total insurance, taxes, and depreciation | | |
|     Total before allocations | | |
| Allocations† | | |
|   Supervision and benefits | | |
|   Plant administration | | |
|   Plant floor space | | |
|   Electricity | | |
|   Water | | |
|   Light | | |
|   Steam | | |
|   Compressed air | | |
|   Maintenance | | |
|     Total allocations | | |
| Total | | |

\* Fixed or variable.

† *Basis for allocation* (examples of possible bases): Labor hours, Square feet, Kw hours used, Water—gallons used, Pounds of steam, Pounds of compressed air, Maintenance labor hours used, Cost of taking inventory.

**TABLE 7B-3**  198_ Finished Goods Inventory Plan ($000 of factory cost)

| Products | January | February | March | April | May | June | July | August | September | October | November | December | Monthly Average |
|---|---|---|---|---|---|---|---|---|---|---|---|---|---|
| | | | | | | | | | | | | | |
| Total finished goods inventory/month | | | | | | | | | | | | | |

**TABLE 7B-4** 198_ Major Cost Breakdown by Product Class (standard costs in dollars per case)

| Products | Stock Code | Fixed: Labor and Overhead | Variable: Materials | Total Factory Cost | Variable Cost as a Percentage of Total Cost | Distribution Cost Including Plant Shipping and Storage Cost | Plant Shipping and Storage Only (fixed) | Total Distributed Cost | Variable Cost as a Percentage of Total Distributed Cost | Variable Cost of Distribution as a Percentage of Variable Factory Cost |
|---|---|---|---|---|---|---|---|---|---|---|
| | | | | | | | | | | |

**TABLE 7B-5** 198_ Average Monthly Finished Goods Inventory Plan ($000)

| Products | Average Monthly Inventory at Full Factory Cost | Percentage of Factory Costs that are Variable | Average Monthly Inventory at Variable Cost |
|---|---|---|---|
| | | | |
| Total Finished Goods Inventory/Month | A | | B |

Variable cost as a percentage of full factory cost = $A/B \times 100\%$ = _____%

**TABLE 7B-6** 198_ Average Monthly Finished Goods Inventory Plan (Public Warehouses Only $000)

| Products | Average Monthly Inventory in Public Warehouses (approximate percentage of column 3 in Table 7B-5) | Variable Cost of Distribution as a Percentage of Variable Factory Cost | Total Variable Cost of Distribution | Total Variable Distributed Cost |
|---|---|---|---|---|
|  |  |  |  |  |
| Total |  |  |  |  |

A. Total system inventory at total factory cost = $_____.
B. Inventory held at public warehouses = $_____ at factory cost [(A) × __%].
C. Distributed cost of (B) at variable cost = $_____.
D. Variable distributed cost as a percentage of total factory cost = $(C)/(B) \times 100\%$ = ___%.

**TABLE 7B-7** Calculation of Variable Costs Associated With System Inventory

| Segment | Approximate Percent of Total Inventory | Percent Variable Cost | Weighted Percentage (variable costs)* |
|---|---|---|---|
| Public warehouses<br>Plants released<br>Plants nonreleased<br>In-transit |  |  |  |

Therefore, of the approximately $_____ of system inventory, about _____% of that value represents direct variable costs tied up in inventory.

* Weighted average of variable costs associated with system inventory.

**TABLE 7B-8**

| Cost Component | Yes | No | With Modification —State Change | Estimated Cost |
|---|---|---|---|---|
| 1. Cost of capital (opportunity) | | | | |
| 2. Inventory investment | | | | |
| 3. Cost of assets (to support inventory) | | | | |
| 4. Taxes on inventory | | | | |
| 5. Insurance on inventory | | | | |
| 6. Cost of plant warehouses (variable storage) | | | | |
| 7. Cost of public warehouses (variable storage) | | | | |
| 8. Cost of rented warehouses | | | | |
| 9. Cost of private warehouses | | | | |
| 10. Obsolescence | | | | |
| 11. Damage | | | | |
| 12. Shrinkage | | | | |
| 13. Relocation costs | | | | |

**TABLE 7B-9**  Data Collection

| Data | Source | Time Required to Obtain Data Value ($) |
|---|---|---|
| 1. Insurance and taxes on inventory for the past year | | |
| 2. Breakdown of warehousing costs both fixed and variable by plant warehouses and field warehouses | | |
| 3. Inventory risk costs (expressed in dollars for the past year)<br>    Obsolescence<br>    Shrinkage<br>    Damage<br>    Relocation costs (if any) | | |
| 4. Standard manufacturing costs for each product | | |
| 5. Average monthly finished goods inventory for each product (either last year's actual or this year's projected) | | |
| 6. Average annual total finished-goods inventory for the past year | | |
| 7. Breakdown of where in the system inventory is held, for example:<br>    33%—Field warehouses<br>    45%—Plant warehouses<br>    22%—In transit | | |
| 8. Current inventory carrying cost and method of calculation (if used: also obtain explanation for costs included) | | |

## QUESTIONS AND PROBLEMS

1. Explain how excessive inventories can erode corporate profitability.

2. How should management determine the necessary quantity of finished goods inventory that should be held?

3. Many business people rely on industry averages or textbook percentages for the inventory carrying cost that they use when setting inventory levels. Why is this approach wrong?

4. Explain how you would determine the cost of capital that should be used in inventory decisions.

5. How would you determine the value of a manufacturer's finished goods inventory investment? How would this differ in the case of a wholesaler or retailer?

6. Explain how you would obtain the fixed and variable components of such costs as plant warehousing and damage.

7. Using the following data, determine the fixed and variable warehousing costs for the Columbus plant warehouse.

| Month | Number of Loads Shipped | Total Plant Warehousing Cost |
|---|---|---|
| January | 750 | $ 9,200 |
| February | 1,080 | 10,800 |
| March | 1,010 | 11,400 |
| April | 840 | 9,900 |
| May | 860 | 10,900 |
| June | 830 | 10,800 |
| July | 970 | 11,200 |
| August | 920 | 10,000 |
| September | 1,160 | 11,000 |
| October | 1,200 | 12,300 |
| November | 1,100 | 11,600 |
| December | 510 | 9,300 |

8. Calculate the inventory carrying cost percentage for ABC Company given the following information:

   a. Finished goods inventory is $28 million valued at full manufactured cost.

   b. Based on the inventory plan, the weighted-average variable manufactured cost per case is 65 percent of the full manufactured cost.

   c. The transportation cost incurred moving the field inventory to warehouse locations was $1,500,000.

   d. The variable cost of moving the field inventory into storage locations was calculated to be $300,000.

   e. The company is currently experiencing capital rationing and new investments are required to earn 20 percent after taxes.

   f. Personal property taxes paid on inventory were approximately $200,000.

g. Insurance to protect against loss of finished goods inventory was $50,000.
h. Storage charges at public warehouses totalled $450,000.
i. Variable plant storage was negligible.
j. Obsolescence was $90,000.
k. Shrinkage was $100,000.
l. Damage related to finished goods inventory levels was $9,800.
m. Relocation costs were $30,000.

9. Show the impact of a change from a mail-based order-processing system to a system where customers telephone in orders on ABC Company's before-tax return on investment given: (a) the financial data contained in Figure 7−1; (b) the annual cost of the new system is $250,000 greater than the cost of the existing system; (c) the inventory carrying cost is 48 percent which includes a cost of money of 40 percent; (d) the estimated reduction in inventories resulting from three-days increased planning time is $5,000,000; and (e) the variable delivered cost of inventory (to warehouse locations) is 60 percent of full manufactured costs.

10. Using your answer from question 9 what percentage increase in sales would be necessary in order to realize a similar impact on return on net worth?

# 8  Inventory Management

Introduction

Basic Inventory Concepts
   Why Hold Inventory?
      Economies of Scale
      Balancing Supply and Demand
      Specialization
      Protection from Uncertainties
   Inventory as a Buffer
   Types of Inventory
      Cycle Stock
      In-Transit Inventories
      Safety or Buffer Stocks
      Speculative Stocks
      Seasonal Stock
      Dead Stocks

Basic Inventory Management
   Inventory Management under Conditions of Certainty
      Economic Order Quantity
      Adjustments to the EOQ
   Inventory Management under Uncertainty
   Calculating Safety Stock Requirements
   Inventories and Customer Service
   Production Scheduling
   Symptoms of Poor Inventory Management

Improving Inventory Management
   ABC Analysis
   Forecasting
   Inventory Models
   Order Processing Systems

Impact of an Inventory Reduction on Corporate Profit Performance

Summary

**Objectives of this chapter:**

To show how the basic concepts of inventory management are applied

To show how to calculate safety stocks

To show how production policies influence inventory levels

To show how inventories and customer service levels are interrelated

To show how to recognize poor inventory management

To show how to improve inventory management

To show how profit performance can be improved by systems that reduce inventories


## INTRODUCTION

In the last chapter, you were shown that inventory is a large and costly investment. Better management of corporate inventories can result in improved cash flow and increased return on investment.

In this chapter you will be shown how the basic concepts of inventory management are applied; how to calculate safety stocks; how production policies influence inventory levels; how inventories and customer service are interrelated; how forecasting can be used to improve inventory management; and how profit performance can be improved by systems that reduce inventories.

## BASIC INVENTORY CONCEPTS

In this section, we will consider basic inventory concepts such as the reasons for holding inventory and the various types of inventory.

### Why Hold Inventory?

*Five Reasons for Having Inventory*

Formulation of an inventory policy requires an understanding of the role of inventory in manufacturing and marketing. Inventory serves five purposes within the firm: (1) it enables the firm to achieve economies of scale; (2) it balances supply and demand; (3) it enables specialization in manufacturing; (4) it provides protection from uncertainties in demand and order cycle; and (5) it acts as a buffer between critical interfaces.

*Economies of scale.* Inventory is required if a firm is to realize economies of scale in purchasing, transportation, and/or manufacturing. For example, raw materials inventory is necessary if the manufacturer is to take advantage of the per unit price reductions associated with volume purchases. Purchased materials will have a lower transportation cost per unit if ordered in larger volumes. This lower per unit cost results because truckload and full rail-car shipments receive lower transportation rates than smaller shipments of less than truckload (LTL) or less than carload (LCL) quantities.

The reasons for holding *finished goods inventory* are similar to those for holding raw-materials inventory. Transportation economies are possible with large-volume shipments but in order to take advantage of these more-economical rates, larger quantities of finished-goods inventory are required at manufacturing locations and at field warehouse locations, or at the customers' location.

Finished-goods inventory also makes it possible to realize manufacturing economies. Plant capacity is greater and per unit manufacturing costs are lower if long production runs with few line changes are scheduled. Producing small quantities leads to short production runs and high changeover costs.

However, the production of large quantities may require that some of the items be carried in inventory for a significant period of time before they can be sold. The cost of maintaining this inventory must be compared to the production savings realized. Although frequent production changeovers will reduce the quantity of inventory that must be carried, they require time that could be used for manufacturing a product. When a plant is operating at or near capacity, frequent line changes may mean that contribution to profit is lost because there is not enough product to meet demand. In such situations, the cost of lost sales plus the changeover costs must be compared to the increase in inventory carrying costs that would result from longer production runs.

*Balancing supply and demand.* Seasonal supply and/or demand may make it necessary for a firm to hold inventory. For example, a producer of a premium line of boxed chocolates experienced significant sales volume increases at Christmas, Valentine's Day, Easter, and Mother's Day. The cost of establishing production capacity to handle the volume at these peak periods was substantial. In addition, substantial idle capacity and wide fluctuations in the labor force would result if the company were to produce for demand. The decision to maintain a relatively stable work force and produce at a somewhat constant level throughout the year resulted in significant inventory buildup at various times during the year, but at a lower total cost to the firm. Seasonal inventories were held in a freezer warehouse that was built adjacent to the plant.

Also, demand for a product may be relatively stable throughout the year as in the case of canned fruits and vegetables, but raw materials may be available only at certain times during the year. This makes it necessary to manufacture finished products in excess of current demand and hold them in inventory.

*Specialization.* Inventory makes it possible for each of a firm's plants to specialize in the products that it manufactures. The finished products can be shipped to large mixing warehouses from which customer orders and products for field warehouses can be shipped. The economies that result from the longer production runs as well as savings in transportation costs more than offset the costs of additional handling. Whirlpool Corporation has found significant cost savings in the operation of consolidation warehouses that allow the firm to specialize manufacturing by plant location.

***Protection from uncertainties.*** Inventory is also held as protection from uncertainties. Raw materials inventories in excess of that required to support production can be the result of speculative purchases made because a future price increase is expected or future supply is in doubt. Other reasons include seasonal availability of supply such as in the case of fruits or vegetables for canning or in order to maintain a source of supply. Regardless of the reason for maintaining a raw materials inventory the costs of holding the inventory should be compared to the savings realized or costs avoided by holding the inventory.

Work-in-process inventory is often maintained between manufacturing operations within a plant to avoid a shut down if a critical piece of equipment were to break down. The stockpiling of work-in-process within the manufacturing complex permits maximum economies of production without work stoppage.

Inventory planning is critical to successful manufacturing operations since a shortage of raw materials can shut down the production line or lead to a modification of the production schedule which may increase expense and/or result in a shortage of finished product. However, while shortages of raw materials can disrupt normal manufacturing operations, excessive inventories can increase costs and reduce profitability by increasing inventory carrying costs.

Finally, finished goods inventory can be used as a means of improving customer service levels by reducing the likelihood of a stock-out due to unanticipated demand. Increased inventory investment, if the inventory is balanced, will enable the manufacturer to offer higher levels of product availability and less chance of a stock-out. A balanced inventory is one that contains items in proportion to expected demand.

**Inventory as a Buffer**

Inventory is held throughout the channel of distribution to act as a buffer for the following critical interfaces:

Supplier-procurement (purchasing).

Procurement-production.

Production-marketing.

Marketing-distribution.

Distribution-intermediary.

Intermediary-consumer/user.

Channel participants are separated geographically and the successful achievement of time and place utilities makes it necessary to hold inventory at several locations.

The typical inventory positions in a supplier-manufacturer-intermediary-consumer channel of distribution is shown in Figure 8—1. Raw materials must be moved from a source of supply to the manufacturing location where they will be input to the manufacturing process. In many cases this will require holding work-in-process inventory.

**FIGURE 8-1** Inventory Positions in a Channel of Distribution

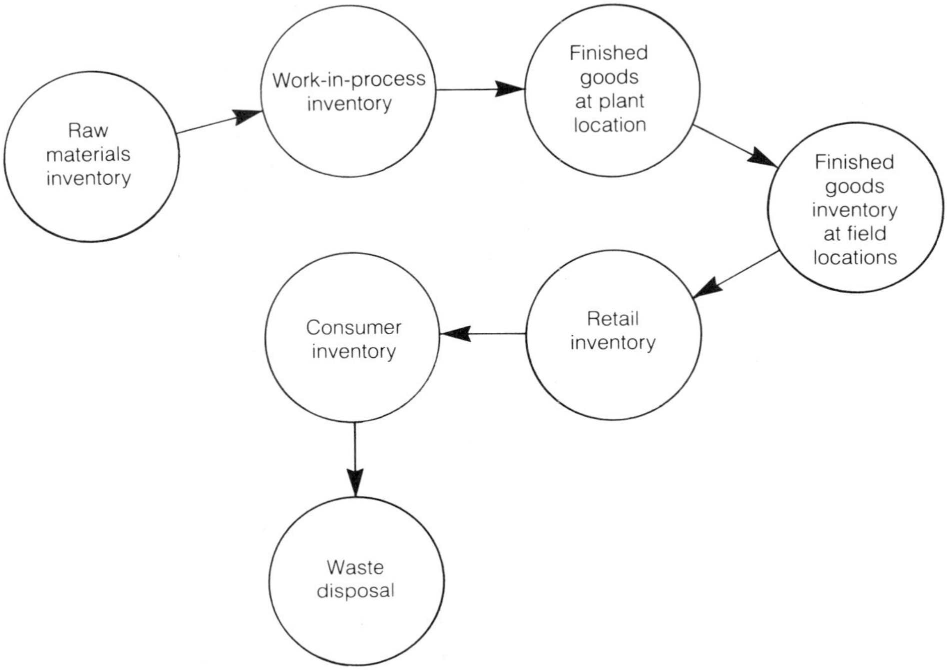

*[Diagram showing flow: Raw materials inventory → Work-in-process inventory → Finished goods at plant location → Finished goods inventory at field locations → Retail inventory → Consumer inventory → Waste disposal]*

Once the manufacturing process has been completed, product must be moved into finished-goods inventory at plant locations. The next step is the strategic deployment of finished goods inventory to field locations which may include corporate-owned or -leased distribution centers, public warehouses, wholesalers' warehouses, and/or retail chain distribution centers. Inventory is then positioned to enable consumer or customer purchase. Similarly, the consumer or customer maintains an inventory to support individual or institutional consumption.

The final phase which promises to become a bigger factor in the future is waste disposal. One specific example involves "bottle laws" such as those enacted in Michigan, Vermont, and Oregon. As rising sensitivities to packaging litter and concern over resource utilization increases, such laws most likely will be considered by environmentalists and concerned citizens in other states, if not nationally. To date, these laws have applied to only beer and soft-drink containers but it is conceivable that other packaging materials may become future targets.

### Types of Inventory

Six Types of Inventory

Inventories can be categorized into the following types which signify the reasons for which they are accumulated: cycle stock, in-transit inventories, safety or buffer stock, speculative stock, seasonal stock, and dead stock.

*Cycle stock.* Cycle stock is inventory that results from the replenishment process and is required in order to meet demand under conditions of certainty. That is, in situations in which we can predict demand and replenishment times (lead time) perfectly. For example if the rate of sales for a product was a constant 20 units per day and the lead time was always 10 days no inventory beyond the cycle stock would be required. While assumptions of constant demand and lead time remove the complexities involved in inventory management the example will be used to make clear the basic inventory principles. The example is illustrated in Figure 8–2 which shows three alternative reorder strategies. Since demand and lead

**FIGURE 8–2** The Effect of Reorder Quantity on Average Inventory Investment with Constant Demand and Lead Time

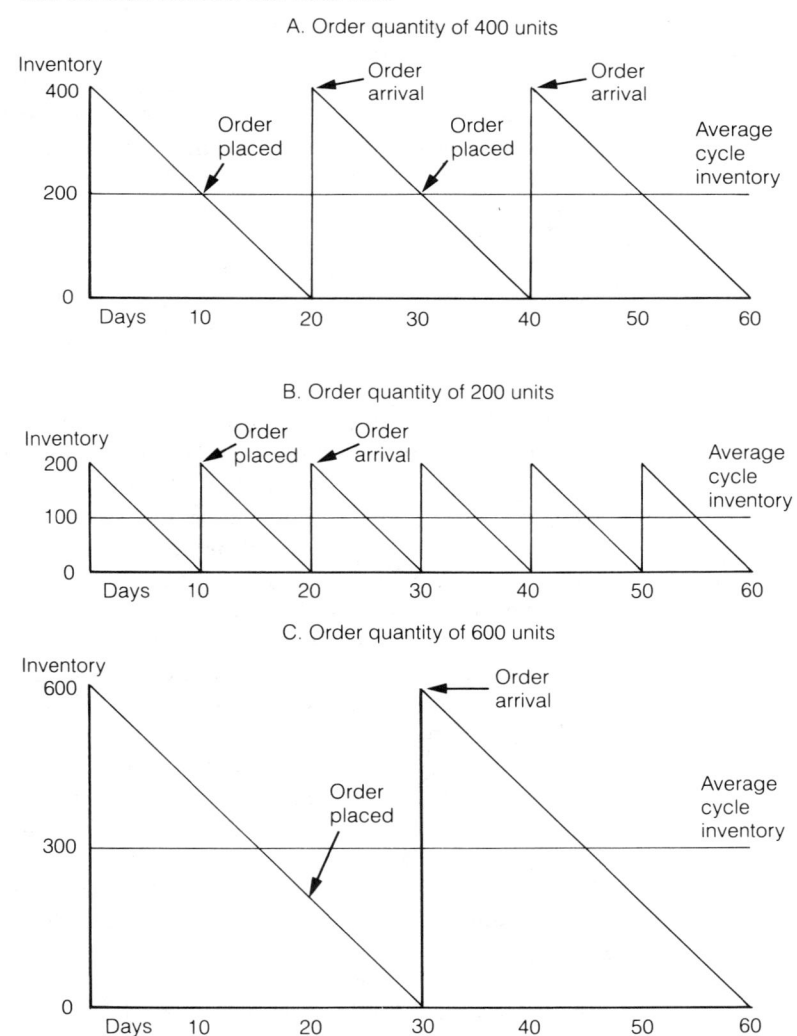

time are constant and known, orders are scheduled to arrive just as the last unit is sold. Thus no inventory beyond the average cycle stock is required. The average cycle stock in all three examples is equal to one half of the order quantity.

*In-transit inventories.* In-transit inventories are items that are en route from one location to another. They may be considered to be part of cycle stock even though they are not available for sale and/or shipment until after their arrival at the destination. For the calculation of inventory carrying costs, in-transit inventories should be considered as being inventory at the place of shipment origin since the transportation cost has not yet been incurred and the items are not available for sale and/or subsequent shipment.

*Safety or buffer stocks.* Safety or buffer stocks are held in excess of cycle stocks because of uncertainty in demand or lead time. The notion is that a portion of average inventory should be devoted to cover short-range variation in demand and lead time. Average inventory at a stock keeping location is equal to half the order quantity plus the safety stock. For example, in Figure 8 – 3 the average inventory would be 100 units if demand and lead time were constant. However, if demand was actually 25 units per day instead of the predicted 20 units per day with a 10-day lead time, inventory would be depleted by the 8th day (200/25). Since the next order (order was placed at day zero) would not arrive until the 10th day, the company would experience stock-outs for two days. At 25 units of demand per day, this would be a stock-out of 50 units in total. If management believed that the maximum variation in demand would be plus or minus five units, a safety stock of 50 units would prevent a stock-out due to variation in demand. This would require holding an average inventory of 150 units.

Now consider the case (Figure 8 – 3B) when demand is constant but lead time can vary by plus or minus two days. If the order arrives 2 days early the inventory on hand would be equal to a 12-day supply or 240 units since sales are at a rate of 20 units per day and 40 units would remain in inventory when the new order arrived. However, if the order arrived two days late, on day 12, which is the most likely occurrence, stock-outs would be experienced for a period of two days (40 units). If management believed that shipments would never arrive more than two days late, a safety stock of 40 units would insure that a stock-out due to variation in lead time would not occur if demand remained constant.

In most business situations management must be able to deal with variability in demand and lead time. Forecasting is rarely accurate enough to predict demand and demand is seldom if ever constant. In addition, transportation delays and supplier and production problems make lead time variability a fact of life. Consider Figure 8 – 3C, the case in which demand uncertainty (Figure 8 – 3A), and lead time uncertainty (Figure 8 – 3B) are combined. This is the worst of all possible worlds. In this case demand is above forecast by the maximum, 25 units instead of 20 units per day, and the incoming order arrives two days late. The result is a stock-out period of four days at 25 units per day. If management wanted to protect against the

**FIGURE 8-3** Average Inventory Investment under Conditions of Uncertainty

A. With variable demand

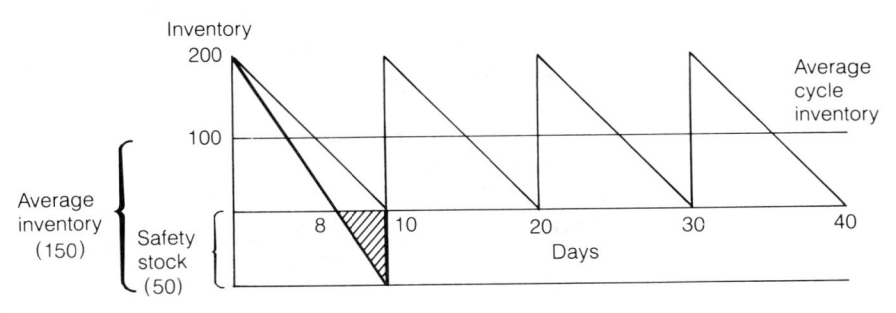

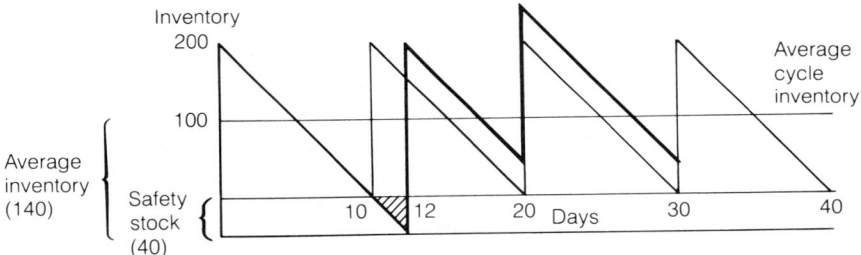

B. With variable leadtime

C. With variable demand and leadtime

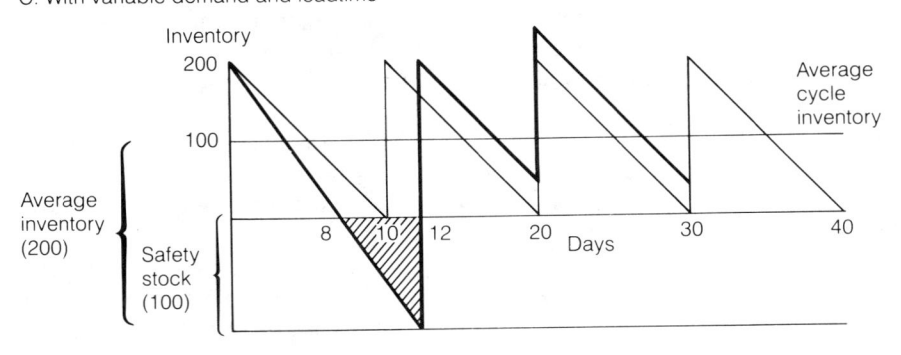

maximum variability in both demand and lead time a safety stock of 100 units would be required. This policy (no stock-outs) would result in an average inventory of 200 units.

*Speculative stocks.* Speculative stocks are inventories that are held for reasons other than satisfying current demand. For example, materials may be purchased in larger-than-required volumes in order to receive quantity discounts, because of a forecasted price increase or materials shortage, or to protect against the possibility of a strike. Also, production economics may lead to the manufacture of products other than when they are demanded. Finally, goods may be produced seasonally for consumption throughout the year, or at a constant level in anticipation of seasonal demand in order to maintain workload and a labor force.

*Seasonal stock.* Seasonal stock is a form of speculative stock which involves the accumulation of inventory before a season begins in order to maintain a stable labor force and stable production runs.

*Dead stocks.* Dead stocks are items for which no demand has been registered for some specified period of time. Such stock might be obsolete on a total company basis or just at one stock-keeping location. If it is the latter, the items may be transhipped to another location to avoid the obsolescence penalty.

## BASIC INVENTORY MANAGEMENT

*The Objectives of Inventory Management*

Inventory is a major use of capital and, for this reason, the objectives of inventory management are: to increase corporate profitability; to predict the impact of policies on inventory levels; and total cost integration.

Corporate profitability can be increased by increasing sales volume or reducing inventory costs. Increased sales are often possible if maintaining inventory at high levels leads to better in-stock availability and more consistent service levels. Some methods of decreasing inventory costs include such measures as reducing the number of back orders or expedited shipments. Also, transshipment of inventory between field warehouses and small-lot transfers can be reduced or eliminated by better inventory planning. Better inventory management can increase the ability to control and predict the reaction of inventory investment to changes in management policy. For example, how will a change in the corporate hurdle rate influence the quantity of inventory held?

Finally, total cost integration should be the goal of inventory planning. That is, it is necessary to determine the inventory level required to achieve least-total-cost physical distribution given the required customer service objectives.

Inventory managers must determine how much inventory to order and when to place the order. In order to illustrate the basic principles of reorder policy we will consider the case of inventory management under conditions of certainty. When this is accomplished we will consider inventory management under conditions of uncertainty, which is the rule rather than the exception.

### Inventory Management under Conditions of Certainty

*Ordering Costs Include Many Components*

Replenishment policy under conditions of certainty requires the balancing of ordering costs against inventory carrying costs. For example, a policy of ordering large quantities infrequently may result in inventory carrying costs in excess of the savings in ordering costs. Ordering costs for products purchased from an outside supplier typically include (1) the cost of transmitting the order, (2) the cost of receiving the product, (3) the cost of placing it in storage, and (4) the cost associated with processing the invoice for payment. In the case of restocking its own field warehouses, a company's ordering costs typically include (1) the cost of transmitting and processing the inventory transfer, (2) the cost of handling the product if it is in stock or the cost of setting-up production to produce it, and the handling cost if the product is not in stock, (3) the cost of receiving at the field location, and (4) the cost of associated documentation. It should be emphasized that only direct out-of-pocket expenses should be included. These costs will be explained in detail in Chapter 9, Order Processing and Information Systems.

*Economic order quantity.* The best ordering policy can be determined by minimizing the total of inventory carrying costs and ordering costs using the economic order quantity model (EOQ).

The EOQ Model

Referring to the example given in Figure 8–2, two questions seem appropriate:

1. Should we place orders for 200, 400, 600 units, or some other quantity?
2. What is the impact on inventory if orders are placed at 10-, 20-, 30-day intervals or some other time period? Assuming constant demand and lead time, sales of 20 units per day and 240 working days per year, annual sales will be 4,800 units. If orders are placed every 10 days, 24 orders of 200 units will be placed. With a 20-day order interval 12 orders of 400 units are required. If the 30-day order interval is selected, 8 orders of 600 units are necessary. The average inventory is 100, 200, and 300 units, respectively. Which of these policies would be best?

The cost trade-offs required to determine the most economical order quantity are shown graphically in Figure 8–4. By determining the EOQ and

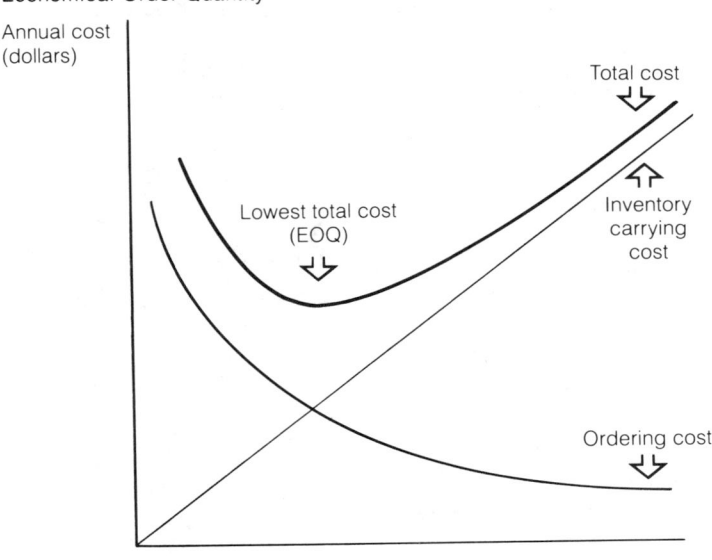

**FIGURE 8–4** Cost Trade-offs Required to Determine the Most Economical Order Quantity

dividing the annual demand by it, the frequency and size of the order that will minimize the two costs are identified.

The EOQ can be calculated using the following formula:

$$EOQ = \sqrt{\frac{2PD}{CV}}$$

where

$P$ = The ordering cost (dollars per order)
$D$ = Annual demand or usage of the product (number of units)
$C$ = Annual inventory carrying cost (as a percentage of product cost or value)
$V$ = Average cost or value of one unit of inventory.

The mathematical derivation of the EOQ model which was one of the first operations research applications is contained in Figure 8–5.

Now using the EOQ formula we will determine the best ordering policy for the situation described in Figure 8–2.

$V$ = $100 per unit
$C$ = 25%
$P$ = $40
$D$ = 4,800 units

$$EOQ = \sqrt{\frac{2(\$40)(4,800)}{(25\%)(100)}}$$
$$= \sqrt{\frac{384,000}{25}}$$
$$= 124 \text{ units}$$

If 20 units fit on a pallet, then the reorder quantity of 120 units would be established. This analysis is shown in tabular form in Table 8–1.

**TABLE 8–1** Cost Trade-offs Required to Determine the Most Economic Order Quantity

| Order Quantity | Number of Orders (D/Q) | Ordering Cost P × (D/Q) | Inventory Carrying Cost 1/2 Q × C × V | Total Cost |
|---|---|---|---|---|
| 40  | 120 | $4,800 | $  500 | $5,300 |
| 60  | 80  | 3,200  | 750    | 3,950  |
| 80  | 60  | 2,400  | 1,000  | 3,400  |
| 100 | 48  | 1,920  | 1,250  | 3,170  |
| 120 | 40  | 1,600  | 1,500  | 3,100  |
| 140 | 35  | 1,400  | 1,750  | 3,150  |
| 160 | 30  | 1,200  | 2,000  | 3,200  |
| 200 | 24  | 960    | 2,500  | 3,460  |
| 300 | 18  | 720    | 3,750  | 4,470  |
| 400 | 12  | 480    | 5,000  | 5,480  |

**FIGURE 8-5** Mathematical Derivation of the Economic Order Quantity Model

$$\text{Total annual cost } (TAC) = \left[\frac{1}{2}(Q) \times (V) \times (C)\right] + [(P) \times (D/Q)]$$

where

$Q$ = The average number of units in the economic order quantity during the order cycle.

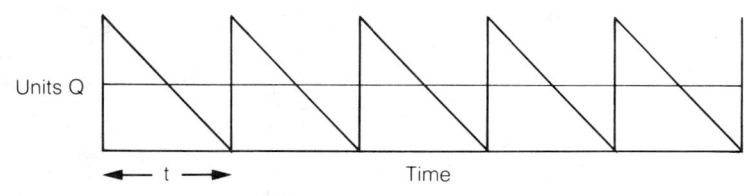

Units Q

← t →   Time

Mathematical solution

$$\frac{d\,TAC}{dQ} = \frac{VC}{2} - \frac{PD}{Q^2}$$

$$\text{Set} = \text{Zero}: \frac{VC}{2} - \frac{PD}{Q^2} = 0$$

$$\frac{VC}{2} = \frac{PD}{Q^2}$$

$$VCQ^2 = 2PD$$

$$Q^2 = \frac{2PD}{CV}$$

$$Q = \sqrt{\frac{2PD}{CV}}$$

The EOQ model has received significant attention and use in industry; however, it is not without its limitations. The simple EOQ model is based upon the following assumptions:

**Assumptions of the EOQ Model**

1. A continuous, constant, and known rate of demand.
2. A constant and known replenishment or lead time.
3. A constant price or cost which is independent of the order quantity or time.
4. The satisfaction of all demand (no stock-outs are permitted).
5. There is no inventory in-transit.
6. There is only one item in inventory or at least there is no interaction.
7. There is an infinite planning horizon.
8. There is no limit on capital availability.

It would be extremely rare to find a situation where demand is constant, lead time is constant, both are known with certainty, and costs are known precisely. However, simplifying assumptions are only of great concern if policy decisions will change as a result of the assumptions made. The EOQ solution is relatively insensitive to small changes in the input data. Referring to Figure 8–4, you can see that the EOQ curve is relatively flat around the solution point. This is born out in Table 8–1. Although the calculated EOQ was 124 units (rounded to 120), a variation about the EOQ of 20 units or even 40 units does not significantly change the total cost.

*Adjusting the EOQ for Volume Discounts*

***Adjustments to the EOQ.*** Typical refinements that must be made to the EOQ model include adjustments for volume transportation rates and for quantity discounts. The simple EOQ model did not consider the impact of these two factors. The following adjustment can be made to the EOQ so that it will consider the impact on total costs of quantity discounts and/or freight breaks:[1]

$$Q^1 = \frac{2rD}{C} + (1-r)Q^o$$

where:

$Q^1$ = The maximum quantity that can be economically ordered to qualify for a discount on unit cost
$r$ = The fraction of price reduction if a larger quantity is ordered
$D$ = The annual demand in units
$C$ = The inventory carrying cost percentage
$Q^o$ = The EOQ based on current price.

Another option to using the above formula would be to add a column to the analysis shown in Table 8–1 and include the annual transportation cost associated with each of the order quantities, adding this amount to the total costs. It is also possible to include purchase discounts by adding a column, annual product cost, and appropriately adjusting the inventory carrying cost. Once again, the desired EOQ would be the order quantity that resulted in the lowest total cost.

**Inventory Management under Uncertainty**

As was previously mentioned, rarely, if ever, will firms know for sure what demand to expect for their products. Also, order cycle times are not constant. Transit times will vary and it may take more time to assemble an order or wait for scheduled production on one occasion than another.

Consequently, a manufacturer has the option of maintaining additional inventory in the form of safety stocks (as was shown in Figure 8–3) or suffer a potential loss of sales revenue due to stock-outs at a distribution center. Hence an additional cost trade-off must be considered: inventory carrying costs versus stock-out costs.

The uncertainties associated with demand and lead time cause most managers to concentrate on when to order rather than the order quantity. The order quantity is important to the extent that it influences the number of orders and, consequently, the number of times that the company is

---

[1] See Robert G. Brown, *Decision Rules for Inventory Management* (New York: Holt, Rinehart & Winston, 1967), pp. 205–6.

**Fixed Order Point, Fixed Order Quantity Model**

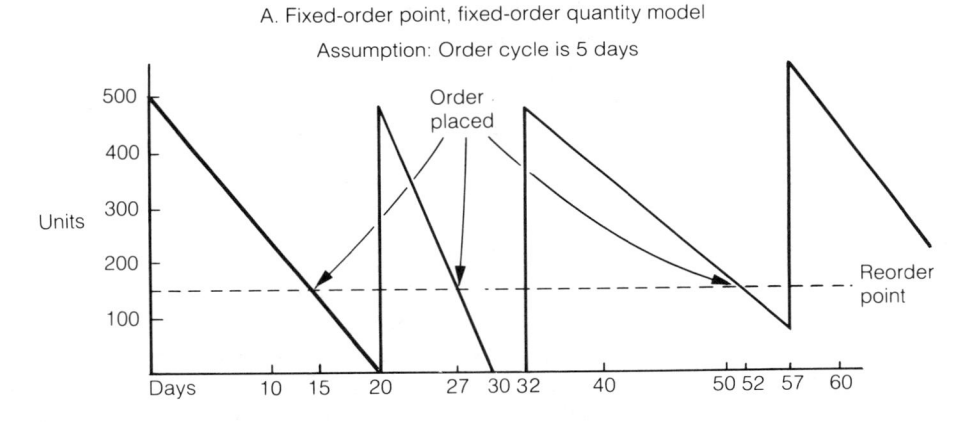

**Fixed Order Interval Model**

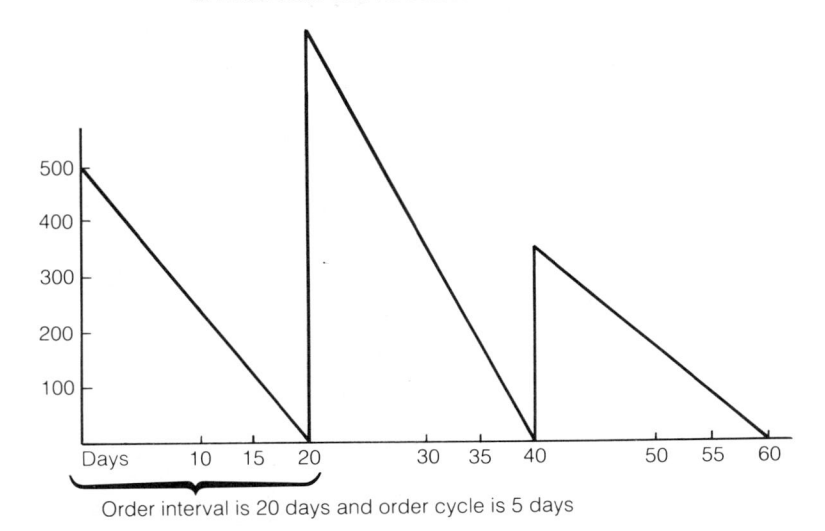

exposed to potential stock-out at the end of each order cycle. It is the point at which the order is placed that is the primary determinant of the future ability to fill demand while waiting for replenishment stock.

One method to approach inventory control under conditions of uncertainty is the *fixed order point, fixed order quantity model*. With this method an order will be placed when the inventory on hand and on order reaches a predetermined minimum level required to satisfy demand during the order cycle. The economic order quantity will be ordered whenever demand drops the inventory level to the reorder point.

In contrast, a *fixed order interval model* compares current inventory with forecasted demand and places an order for the necessary quantity at a regular, specified time. The two methods are illustrated in Figure 8–6.

**FIGURE 8–6** Inventory Management under Uncertainty

A. Fixed-order point, fixed-order quantity model
Assumption: Order cycle is 5 days

B. Fixed-order interval model

Order interval is 20 days and order cycle is 5 days

A review of Figure 8–6A shows that replenishment orders are placed on days 15, 27, and 52, respectively, for the fixed order point, fixed order quantity model. In contrast, when the fixed order interval model is used (see Figure 8–6B) orders are placed at 20-day intervals on days 15, 35, and 55, respectively. With the fixed order interval model it is necessary to forecast demand for days 20 through 40 on day 15, for days 40 through 60 on day 35, and so on. The fixed order interval system is more adaptive in that management is forced to consider changes in sales activity and make a forecast for every order interval.

### Calculating Safety Stock Requirements

*How to Determine the Amount of Safety Stock*

The amount of safety stock necessary to satisfy a given level of demand can be determined by computer simulation or by statistical techniques. This illustration will address the use of statistical techniques. In calculating safety-stock levels it is necessary to consider the joint impact of demand and replenishment cycle variability. This can be accomplished by gathering statistically valid samples of data on recent sales volumes and replenishment cycles. Once the data is gathered it's possible to determine safety stock requirements by using this formula:

$$\sigma c = \sqrt{\bar{R}\ \sigma S^2 + \bar{S}^2\ \sigma R^2}$$

where

$\sigma c$ = Units of safety stock needed to satisfy 68 percent of all probabilities (one standard deviation)
$\bar{R}$ = Average replenishment cycle
$\sigma R$ = Standard deivation of the replenishment cycle
$\bar{S}$ = Average daily sales
$\sigma S$ = Standard deviation of daily sales

Assume that the sales history contained in Table 8–2 has been developed for market area 1.

**TABLE 8–2** Sales History for Market Area 1

| Day | Sales in Cases | Day | Sales in Cases |
|---|---|---|---|
| 1 | 1,000 | 14 | 800 |
| 2 | 800 | 15 | 900 |
| 3 | 700 | 16 | 900 |
| 4 | 600 | 17 | 1,000 |
| 5 | 800 | 18 | 1,400 |
| 6 | 900 | 19 | 1,100 |
| 7 | 1,200 | 20 | 1,200 |
| 8 | 1,100 | 21 | 700 |
| 9 | 1,100 | 22 | 1,000 |
| 10 | 1,100 | 23 | 1,300 |
| 11 | 1,300 | 24 | 1,100 |
| 12 | 1,200 | 25 | 900 |
| 13 | 1,000 | | |

The next step is to calculate the standard deviation of daily sales as shown in Table 8–3.

**TABLE 8–3** Calculation of Standard Deviation of Sales

| Daily Sales in Cases | Frequency (f) | Deviation From Mean (d) | Deviation Squared ($d^2$) | $fd^2$ |
|---|---|---|---|---|
| 600 | 1 | −400 | 160,000 | 160,000 |
| 700 | 2 | −300 | 90,000 | 180,000 |
| 800 | 3 | −200 | 40,000 | 120,000 |
| 900 | 4 | −100 | 10,000 | 40,000 |
| 1,000 | 5 | 0 | 0 | 0 |
| 1,100 | 4 | +100 | 10,000 | 40,000 |
| 1,200 | 3 | +200 | 40,000 | 120,000 |
| 1,300 | 2 | +300 | 90,000 | 180,000 |
| 1,400 | 1 | +400 | 160,000 | 160,000 |
| $\bar{x} = 1,000$ | n = 25 | | | $\Sigma fd^2 = 1,000,000$ |

From this sample the standard deviation of sales can be calculated. The formula is:

$$\sigma S = \sqrt{\frac{\Sigma fd^2}{n-1}}$$

where

$\sigma S$ = Standard deviation (variance) of daily sales
$f$ = Frequency of event
$d$ = Deviation of event from mean
$n$ = Total observations
$\bar{x}$ = Mean

Applying this formula to the data yields a standard deviation of sales equal to 200 units:

$$\sigma S = \sqrt{\frac{1,000,000}{25-1}}$$
$$= 200 \text{ (rounded to the nearest 10)}$$

This means that 68 percent of the time, daily sales fall within 800 to 1,200 units (1,000 units ± 200 units). Two standard deviations protection or 400 units would protect against 95 percent of all events. However, in setting safety stock levels, it is important to consider only events which exceed the mean sales volume. Thus, a safety stock level of 400 units actually affords protection against almost 98 percent of all possible events.

The same procedure can be used to arrive at the mean and standard deviation of the replenishment cycle. Once this is accomplished, the formula shown previously can be used to determine safety stock requirements at a certain level of demand. For example, analysis of replenishment cycles might yield the results shown in Table 8–4.

**TABLE 8-4** Calculation of Standard Deviation of Replenishment Cycle

| Lead Time in Days | Frequency (f) | Deviation from Mean (d) | Deviation Squared ($d^2$) | $fd^2$ |
|---|---|---|---|---|
| 7 | 1 | −3 | 9 | 9 |
| 8 | 2 | −2 | 4 | 8 |
| 9 | 3 | −1 | 1 | 3 |
| 10 | 4 | 0 | 0 | 0 |
| 11 | 3 | +1 | 1 | 3 |
| 12 | 2 | +2 | 4 | 8 |
| 13 | 1 | +3 | 9 | 9 |
| x = 10 | n = 16 | | | Σfd = 40 |

The standard deviation of the replenishment cycle

$$(\sigma R) = \sqrt{\frac{\Sigma fd^2}{n-1}}$$

$$= \sqrt{2.67}$$
$$= 1.63$$

The average replenishment cycle

$$(\bar{R}) = 10$$

The combined safety stock required to cover variability in both demand and lead time can be found using the formula:

$$\sigma c = \sqrt{\bar{R}\ \sigma S^2 + \bar{S}^2\ \sigma R^2}$$
$$= \sqrt{10(200^2) + (1{,}000^2)(1.63)^2}$$
$$= \sqrt{400{,}000 + 2{,}670{,}000}$$
$$= \sqrt{3{,}070{,}000}$$
$$= 1{,}750 \text{ (rounded to the nearest 10)}$$

Thus, in a situation where daily sales vary from 600 cases to 1,400 cases and the inventory replenishment cycle varies from 7 to 13 days a safety stock of 1,750 cases will allow the manufacturer to satisfy 68 percent of all possible occurrences. To protect against 98 percent of all possibilities, 3,500 cases of safety stock are required. Table 8−5 shows alternative customer service levels and safety stock requirements.[2]

In order to establish the average inventory for various levels of customer service it is necessary to determine the EOQ. The projected yearly demand is found by multiplying the average daily demand by 250 working days

---
[2] Given a distribution of measurements that is approximately bell-shaped, the mean plus or minus one standard deviation will contain approximately 68 percent of the measurements. This leaves 16 percent in each of the tails which means that inventory sufficient to cover sales one standard deviation in excess of mean daily sales will actually provide an 84 percent customer service level. If the sample does not represent a normal distribution the reader should refer to a basic statistics book for an alternative treatment.

**TABLE 8-5** Summary of Alternative Service Levels and Safety Stock Requirements

| Service Level (percent) | Number of Standard Deviations ($\sigma c$) Needed | Safety Stock Requirements (cases) |
|---|---|---|
| 84.1 | 1.0 | 1,750 |
| 90.3 | 1.3 | 2,275 |
| 94.5 | 1.6 | 2,800 |
| 97.7 | 2.0 | 3,500 |
| 98.9 | 2.3 | 4,025 |
| 99.5 | 2.6 | 4,550 |
| 99.9 | 3.0 | 5,250 |

which equals 250,000 cases (250 × 1,000). The inventory carrying cost was calculated to be 40 percent, the average value of a case of product was $12 and the ordering cost was $18.

$$EOQ = \sqrt{\frac{2(\$18)(250,000)}{40\% \times 12}}$$
$$= 1,370 \text{ cases}$$

The average inventory required to satisfy each service level is shown in Table 8−6.

**TABLE 8-6** Summary of Average Inventory Levels Given Different Service Levels

| Service Levels (percent) | Average Cycle Stock (½ × EOQ) | Safety Stock (units) | Total Average Inventory (units) |
|---|---|---|---|
| 84.1 | 685 | 1,750 | 2,435 |
| 90.3 | 685 | 2,275 | 2,960 |
| 94.5 | 685 | 2,800 | 3,485 |
| 97.7 | 685 | 3,500 | 4,185 |
| 98.9 | 685 | 4,025 | 4,710 |
| 99.5 | 685 | 4,550 | 5,235 |
| 99.9 | 685 | 5,250 | 5,935 |

Note that the establishment of a safety stock commitment is really a customer service/inventory availability policy. And although we have demonstrated a quantitative method of calculating safety stock requirements there are several important qualitative factors to consider.

**Inventories and Customer Service**

The establishment of a service level, and thus, safety stock policy is really a matter of managerial judgment. Some additional factors that should be considered include customer relations and the ability of the firm to support continuous production.

In many companies customer service levels are improved simply by the addition of safety stock. This is due to the fact that the cost of carrying inventory has often not been calculated for the firm or has been set at an artificially low and arbitrary level. Figure 8–7 illustrates graphically the

**FIGURE 8-7** Relationship between Inventory Investment and Customer Service Levels

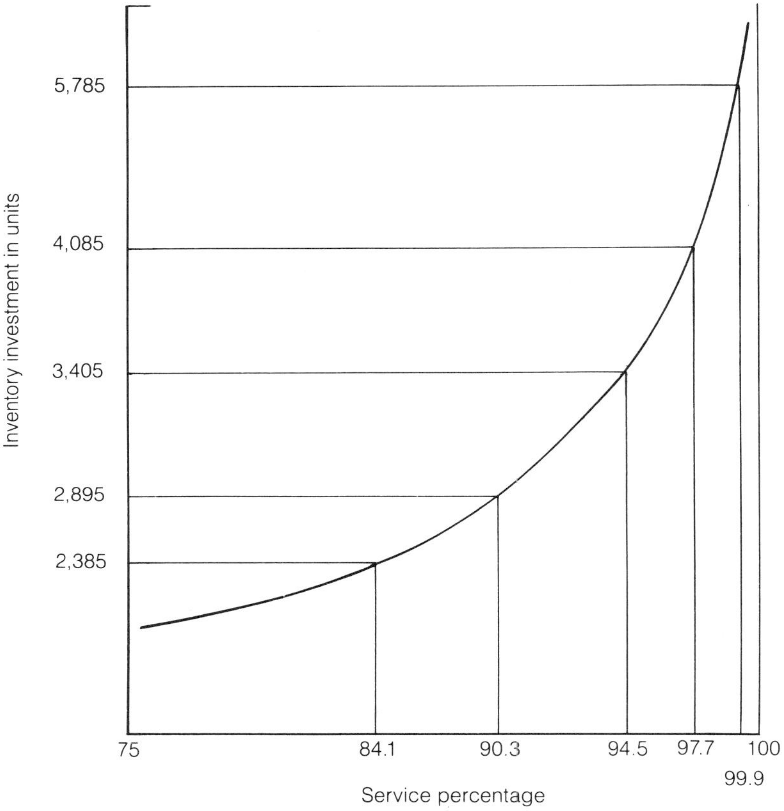

relationship between customer service levels and inventory investment shown in Table 8–6.

Although the inventory investment figures shown in the example will vary from situation to situation, similar relationships will hold. As customer service levels move toward 100 percent, inventory levels increase disproportionately. It becomes obvious that customer service levels should not be improved solely by the addition of inventory. The need to develop an accurate inventory carrying cost for the purpose of planning should be obvious.

One way of resolving this problem would be to substitute transportation costs for inventory carrying costs by using premium transportation to improve customer service. Another possibility would be to recognize the wide differences in demand levels and demand variation associated with each product. Many companies make the mistake of treating all products the same. Generally, a more economical policy is to stock the highest volume items at retail locations, high and moderate volume items at field warehouse locations, and maintain inventory of slow moving items at centralized locations. The centralized location may be a distribution center or a plant warehouse. This type of multiechelon stocking procedure is referred to as *ABC analysis* and will be discussed in a following section of this chapter.

**Production Scheduling**

Earlier in this chapter, it was discussed how inventory levels can be influenced by production policies. The reverse is also true. In many cases distribution policy changes, especially those that decrease inventory levels, can result in significant increases in total production costs which are out of the control of manufacturing management. For example, General Mills Incorporated has a production operations division that manufactures and distributes products for the various marketing divisions of the firm. Consequently, the physical distribution function receives a sales forecast from marketing and, given the divisions' inventory deployment policies and their objective to minimize total physical distribution costs, manufacturing is told how many units of each item to produce. Manufacturing then establishes a production schedule. The system was not without its problems. This was because manufacturing performance was judged on the basis of comparing actual production costs with the cost arrived at by multiplying the various units produced by the standard manufacturing cost for each product. The standard cost was a full cost standard comprised of:

1. Direct materials.
2. Direct labor.
3. Variable overhead.
4. Fixed overhead.

The overhead costs included production setup costs that were based on a projected number of setups for each product for the year divided by the estimated number of units produced during the year.

Physical distribution influenced the number of setups actually incurred by manufacturing but the standard cost was not changed during a year to reflect this. Since the number of setups incurred would influence manufacturing performance, policies that would change the projected number of setups were resisted by plant management. The solution was to maintain two separate standard costs for each product. One was a variable cost per unit excluding a setup component and the other was a standard setup cost for each product. Manufacturing performance was to be judged on the ability to manufacture a specified quantity efficiently. Physical distribution was charged with the responsibility of considering setup costs in the analysis when inventory policies were determined. An inventory policy decision that reduces physical distribution costs by less than the increase in production setup cost would result in lower overall profit performance for the company. For this reason, physical distribution managers must be aware of the impact of their decisions on the efficiency of manufacturing operations and consider associated changes in manufacturing costs when establishing distribution policies.

### Symptoms of Poor Inventory Management

*How to Recognize Poor Inventory Management*

The final portion of this section deals with how you can recognize those situations where inventories are not being managed properly. Recognition of problem areas is the first step in determining where opportunities exist for improving physical distribution performance.

The following symptoms may be associated with poor inventory management:

1. Increasing back-order status.
2. Increasing dollar investment in inventory with back orders remaining constant.
3. High customer turnover rate.
4. Increasing number of orders being cancelled.
5. Periodic lack of sufficient storage space.
6. Wide variance in inventory turnover among distribution centers and among major inventory items.
7. Deteriorating relationships with middlemen as typified by dealer cancellations and declining orders.

In many instances inventory levels can be reduced by one or more of the following:

*Ways to Reduce Inventory Levels*

1. Multiechelon inventory planning—ABC analysis is an example of such planning.
2. Lead-time analysis.
3. Delivery-time analysis—this may lead to a change in carriers or negotiation with existing carriers.
4. Elimination of low-turnover items.
5. Analysis of pack size and discount structure.
6. Examination of returned-goods procedures.

In many companies the best method of reducing inventory investment is by reducing order-cycle time using advanced order-processing systems. If the order cycle currently being offered to customers is satisfactory, the time saved in order transmittal, order entry, and order processing can be used for inventory planning. The result will be a significant reduction in inventory.

## IMPROVING INVENTORY MANAGEMENT

Inventory management can be improved by one or more of the following techniques: ABC analysis, forecasting, inventory models, and advanced order-processing systems.

### ABC Analysis

The logic behind ABC analysis is that a few customers and products account for the bulk of a manufacturer's sales and profits. A rule of thumb is that 20 percent of the customers or products account for 80 percent of the sales and perhaps an even larger percentage of profits. The first step in ABC analysis is to rank products by sales and preferably by contribution to corporate profitability if such data are available. The next step is to check for differences between high-volume and low-volume items that may suggest certain items should be treated differently.

Inventory levels increase with the number of stock-keeping locations. By stocking low-volume items at a number of distribution centers, the national demand for these products is divided by the number of locations. Safety stock must be maintained at each of these locations. The resulting total safety stock is greater than the safety stock that would be required if one centralized location had been used for these items. For example, if only one centralized warehouse is used and sales are forecast on a national basis, a sales increase in Los Angeles may cancel a sales decrease in New York. However, safety stock is required to protect against variability in demand and there is greater variability in demand when national demand is subdivided. The total system inventory will increase with the number of field-warehouse locations because the variability in demand must be covered at each location, that is, a sales increase in one market area will not be offset by a sales decrease in another market.

When slow-moving items are consolidated at a centralized location transportation costs often increase. However, these costs can be offset by lower inventory carrying costs and fewer stock-out penalties. Customer service can be improved through consolidation of low volume items by decreasing the probability of experiencing a stock-out. The ABC analysis is a method for deciding which items should be considered for centralized warehousing.

*The 80/20 Rule*

### Forecasting

Forecasting how much of each product is likely to be purchased is an important aspect of inventory management.

One forecasting method is to survey buyer intentions by mail questionnaires, telephone interviews, or personal interviews. These data can be used to develop a sales forecast. However, this approach is not without problems. It can be costly and the accuracy of the information may be questionable.

Another approach is to solicit the opinions of salespeople or known experts in the field. This method, termed a *judgment sample*, is relatively fast and inexpensive. However, the data are subject to the personal bias of the individual salespeople or experts.

Most companies simply project future sales based on past sales data. This is because most inventory systems require only a one- or two-month forecast and short-term forecasting is therefore acceptable. A number of techniques are available to aid the manager in developing a short-term sales forecast.[3] The most frequently used techniques will be discussed in Chapter 10, Materials Management, along with a description of each technique and its advantages and disadvantages.

**Inventory Models**

A number of computerized inventory-control systems are available including advanced versions of IBM's IMPACT[4] and COGS[5]. These systems have the ability to produce purchase orders, shipping orders, bills of lading, and invoices. The work flow and functions performed by a typical IMPACT system are illustrated in Figure 8–8. Many firms have made use of such systems with considerable success. For example, Jefferson G. Summers, director of management information systems, Sterling Drug, Inc., reported the following success story with IBM's COGS:

*Computerized Inventory Management Increased Profits at Sterling Drug*

A new approach to inventory management at Sterling Drug promises to roll back inventories at several divisions to levels of two years ago—even as normal sales growth continues.

Specifically, sales for our Glenbrook Division are expected to continue growing normally through 1973, but the dollar value of inventory at the end of that year should be at 1971 levels. Similarly, in the face of normal sales growth, we expect inventory value for the Winthrop Division at the end of 1974 will be at 1972 levels.

This represents a complete turnaround from the classic sales/inventory pattern in which increasing inventories are generally needed to support increasing sales. The expected turnaround at Sterling will result from implementation of a computer-based system employing a group of IBM programs known as COGS (Consumer Goods System). The system takes an advanced approach to the problems of forecasting sales demand, and allocating specific products to distribution centers to meet that demand.

The range of benefits from this system at Sterling Drug includes cost savings in seven figures and greatly improved production and distribution operations.

Some idea of the stakes for Sterling Drug can be seen in the world-wide sales figures for our divisions and subsidiaries. In 1971, they rose to $708,453,000, up from $643,873,000 in 1970, and double what they were in 1962. Sales and earnings records have been set for 21 consecutive years, and there is every expectation that this will continue.[6]

Other advantages of the system included:

J. D. Winig, Glenbrook Laboratories Division vice president—manufacturing, has expressed particular satisfaction that distribution and production managers are getting away from crisis-to-crisis operations.

"The harried phone calls at four o'clock in the evening have been sharply reduced," says Mr. Winig. "Although there are still differences of opinion, our

---

[3] For excellent in-depth coverage of various forecasting methods see: Steven C. Wheelwright and Spyros Makridakas, *Forecasting Methods for Management* (New York: John Wiley & Sons, 1973).

[4] "Inventory Management and Control Techniques (IMPACT)," IBM publication GE20-8105-1.

[5] "Consumer Goods System (COGS)," IBM publications DOS 5736-D31 and DOS 5736-D32.

[6] Jefferson G. Summers, "A System to Roll Back Inventory Levels," *Transportation and Distribution Management*, October 1973, p. 33.

**FIGURE 8–8** Workflow and Functions Performed in a Typical IMPACT System

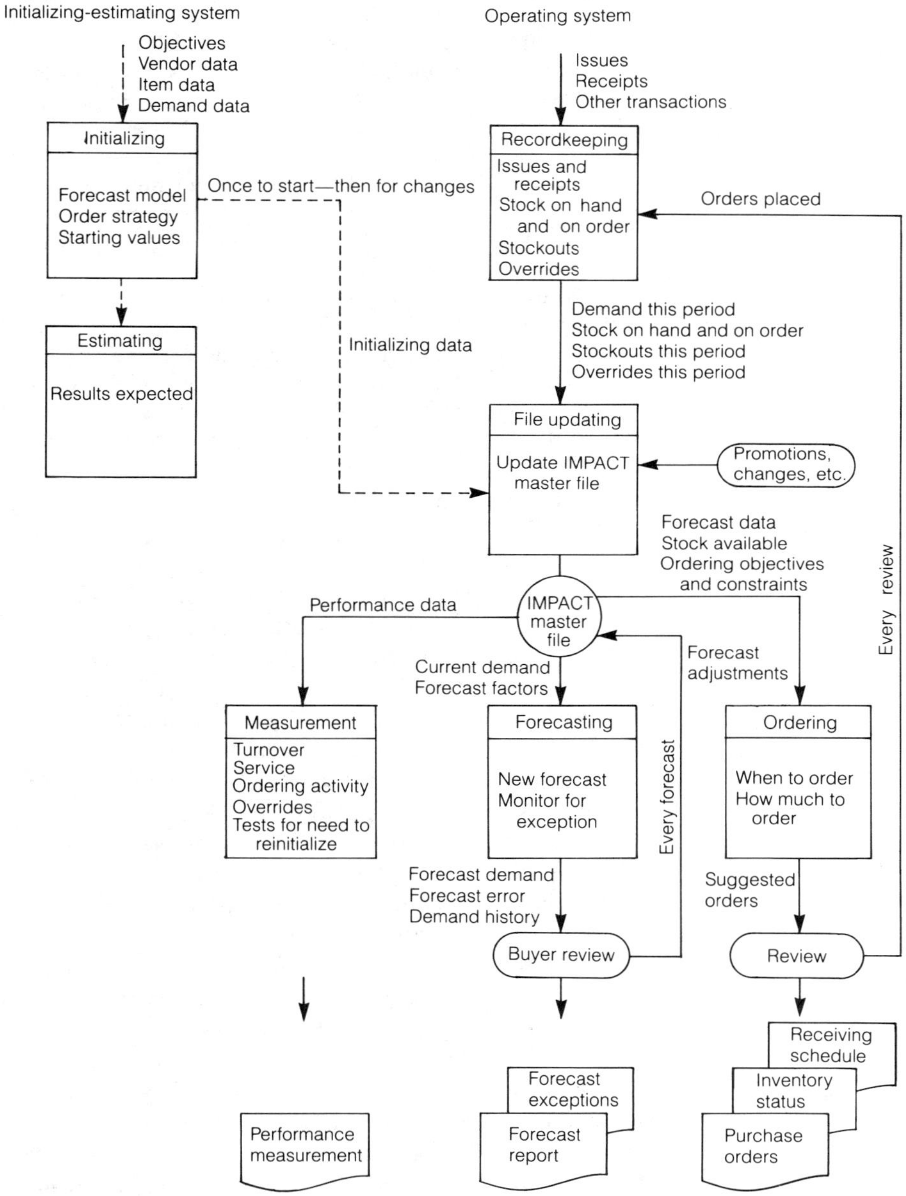

*Initializing-estimating system*

Objectives
Vendor data
Item data
Demand data
↓

**Initializing**
Forecast model
Order strategy
Starting values

Once to start—then for changes

**Estimating**
Results expected

*Operating system*

Issues
Receipts
Other transactions
↓

**Recordkeeping**
Issues and receipts
Stock on hand and on order
Stockouts
Overrides

Orders placed

Demand this period
Stock on hand and on order
Stockouts this period
Overrides this period

Initializing data

**File updating**
Update IMPACT master file

Promotions, changes, etc.

Forecast data
Stock available
Ordering objectives and constraints

IMPACT master file

Performance data

Current demand
Forecast factors

Forecast adjustments

Every review

**Measurement**
Turnover
Service
Ordering activity
Overrides
Tests for need to reinitialize

**Forecasting**
New forecast
Monitor for exception

Every forecast

**Ordering**
When to order
How much to order

Forecast demand
Forecast error
Demand history

Suggested orders

Buyer review

Review

Performance measurement

Forecast exceptions
Forecast report

Receiving schedule
Inventory status
Purchase orders

Source: "Introduction to IBM Wholesale IMPACT (Inventory Management Program and Control Techniques)," GE20–0278–0, International Business Machines Corporation, Data Processing Division, White Plains, N.Y. © by International Business Machines Corporation. Reprinted by permission.

people in the plant and in management information systems are talking the same language, developing a far better common understanding of problems, and this is bound to have positive effects. We're developing an excellent aid for production management, smoothing the peaks with a sane approach to the overall problem, and have every reason to expect we will be lowering inventories."

"The new system takes the hokus-pokus out of scheduling by giving us better information faster," says A. J. Freeman, Glenbrook Laboratories manager—production scheduling. "The plants and my office here in New York City now work with the same data, so that they are a party to the scheduling and adjustments made in New York. We can anticipate needs without heavy advance scheduling, and this should lead to reductions in warehouse inventories."

On the basis of experience to date, we have set a goal of rolling Glenbrook and Winthrop Division inventories back two years even as sales continue to expand. And we are confident we can do this without affecting service levels. This will mean reductions in inventory of millions of dollars. Further down the line is the potential for refining existing service levels by justifying them against experience with the new system and perhaps generating additional savings.[7]

**Order Processing Systems**

Many companies have not undertaken comprehensive and ongoing analysis and planning of inventory policy because of lack of time and lack of information.[8] Many times a poor communications system is a contributing factor. A primary goal of inventory management is to achieve an optimum balance between inventory carrying costs and customer service. The essential task of determining the proper balance requires continuous and comprehensive planning. It hinges on the availability of information. Communications makes information available. An automated and integrated order-processing system can reduce the time needed to perform certain elements of the order cycle-order entry (communications), order processing, and inventory update (replenishment). Time saved in the performance of these activities can be used for inventory planning, assuming the current order-cycle time is satisfactory to the manufacturer's customers. This can result in substantial cost savings to the firm by reducing safety-stock levels.

*Advanced Order Processing Systems Can Reduce Inventory Requirements*

In addition, an automated and integrated order-processing system can reduce message errors and unexpected time delays. This facilitates better decision making and improves internal coordination in the firm. Remote terminals linked to a central processing unit can handle the most complex communications flows. The terminals can make the right data available when and where it is needed. The result is reduced inventories and faster invoicing, which improve cash flow.

With full, up-to-the-minute information on orders, raw-materials inventory and production scheduling can be better managed. The distribution center can meet customer commitments without increasing inventories. Invoicing can prepare more accurate invoices, bill customers sooner, and receive payment more quickly with fewer reconciliations necessary. And

---

[7] Ibid., p. 35.

[8] Adapted from materials provided by Douglas E. Zemke, American Telephone and Telegraph Company, Business Marketing, Market Management Division.

reconciliations that do occur can be resolved much more quickly. Reduced inventories and faster invoicing improves cash flow. An advanced order-processing system can improve inventory management by placing vital information into the hands of the decision makers and by providing them with the necessary time to use this information in planning inventory strategies.

## IMPACT OF AN INVENTORY REDUCTION ON CORPORATE PROFIT PERFORMANCE

In order to illustrate the impact of an inventory reduction on corporate profit performance consider the case of XYZ Company, whose financial data are presented in summary in Figure 8–9.

The company has sales of $100 million less $60 million cost of goods sold yielding a gross margin of $40 million. When variable expenses of $18 mil-

**FIGURE 8–9** The Strategic Profit Model with Financial Data for XYZ Company—before System Change (financial data in $ millions)

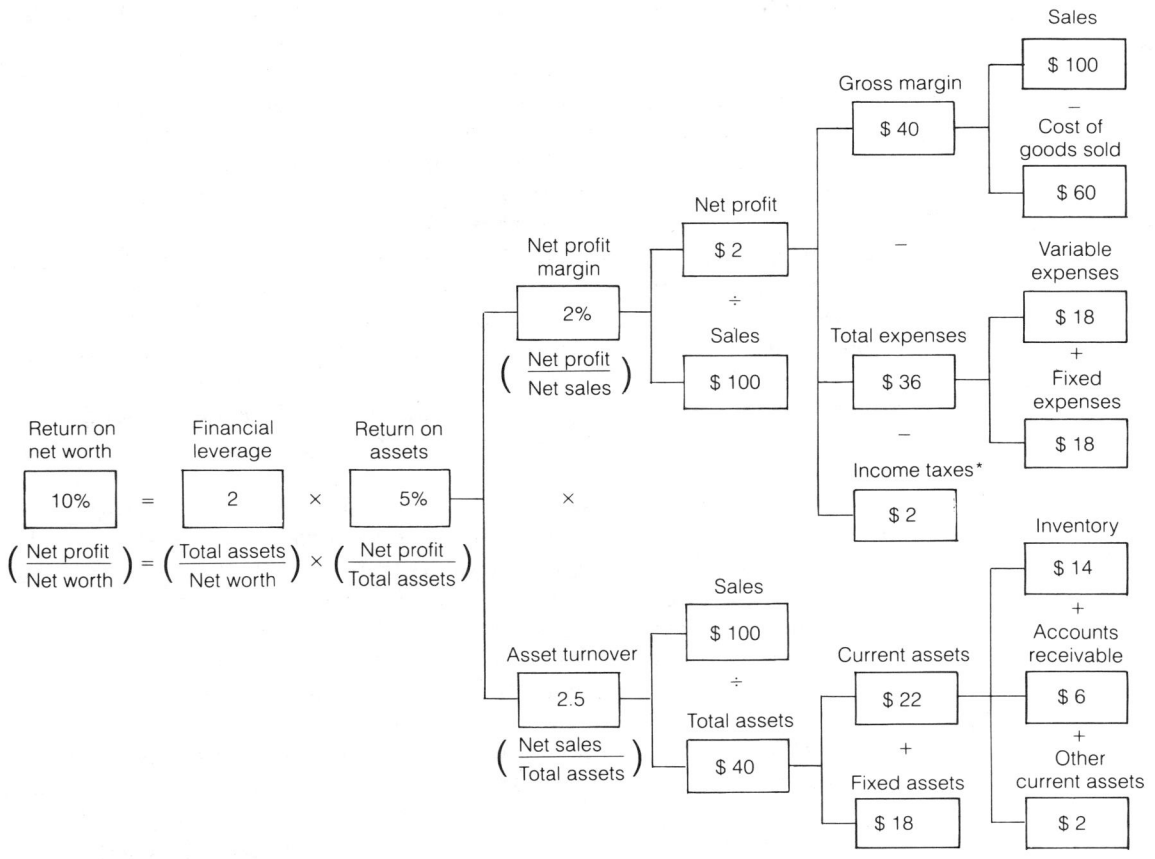

*Income taxes are assumed to equal 50 percent of net profit before taxes.

lion, fixed expenses of $18 million, and income taxes of $2 million are deducted, the net profit is $2 million, which gives a net profit margin of 2 percent of sales.

On the balance sheet portion of the model, current assets of $22 million are comprised of inventory of $14 million, accounts receivable of $6 million and other current assets of $2 million. The current assets plus $18 million of fixed assets result in total assets of $40 million and asset turnover of 2.5 times. The net profit of 2 percent multiplied by the asset turnover of 2.5 times equals a return on assets of 5 percent. The financial leverage of 2 to 1 boosts the return on net worth to 10 percent. The question for consideration is, How would a systems-change impact the performance of the physical distribution function and affect corporate return on net worth? In order to answer this question, the following information about the company is required:

1. Customers mail in orders to the company for processing and the order cycle is 10 days. That is, from the time the customer places the order in the mail until the product has been received by the customer, 10 days have elapsed plus or minus some margin of error (100 percent consistency would be unlikely). The company's customers are fully satisfied with the 10-day order cycle since that is what all of the major suppliers offer to the trade.

2. The company does not calculate inventory carrying costs, but if they did so, the noncost of money components of inventory carrying costs such as insurance, taxes, variable storage costs, obsolescence, shrinkage, and damage would be 5 percent of the average inventory value. The fact that the company does not specifically identify inventory carrying costs does not make these costs any less real. They are still incurred.

3. The company is experiencing capital rationing. That is, there is a shortage of capital for investment in new projects, and investments promising a return of 20 percent after taxes or 40 percent pretax cannot be undertaken. If the capital was available, the company could invest up to $5 million in modernization for the plant which would generate a return of 40 percent pretax. If such an investment was made, it would be depreciated on a straight line basis over a 10-year period ($500,000 per year if the investment was $5 million).

When the company's order processing system is subjected to further study it becomes apparent that an advanced order-entry system would shorten the order cycle by four days, as well as offer other benefits. For example, customers would telephone orders to customer-service representatives within the firm, who are equipped with CRTs. With this system, the customer service representative would enter the order on a real-time inventory control system, while the customer was still on the telephone. The inventory levels could be reduced by the amount of the purchase, thereby eliminating the problem of two customers being promised delivery of the same stock. If the desired product(s) was(were) not available, product substitution could be arranged or delivery scheduled based on future planned production. Consequently, the proposed system would contribute to improved customer service.

Since the company's customers are currently satisfied with the 10-day order cycle, this policy should be maintained. The four days eliminated at the front end of the order cycle can be used to plan production and stage field inventories resulting in a $5 million reduction in inventories on a company-wide basis. The $5 million obtained from the inventory reduction is now available for investment in the new plant equipment which was previously rejected due to the shortage of capital.

Finally, it is estimated that the annual cost of the proposed order-processing system will be $750,000. What is the financial impact of the proposed system on before-tax return on net worth? Refer to Figure 8–10 for the answer.

**FIGURE 8–10** The Strategic Profit Model with Financial Data for Company XYZ—after System Change (financial data in $ millions)

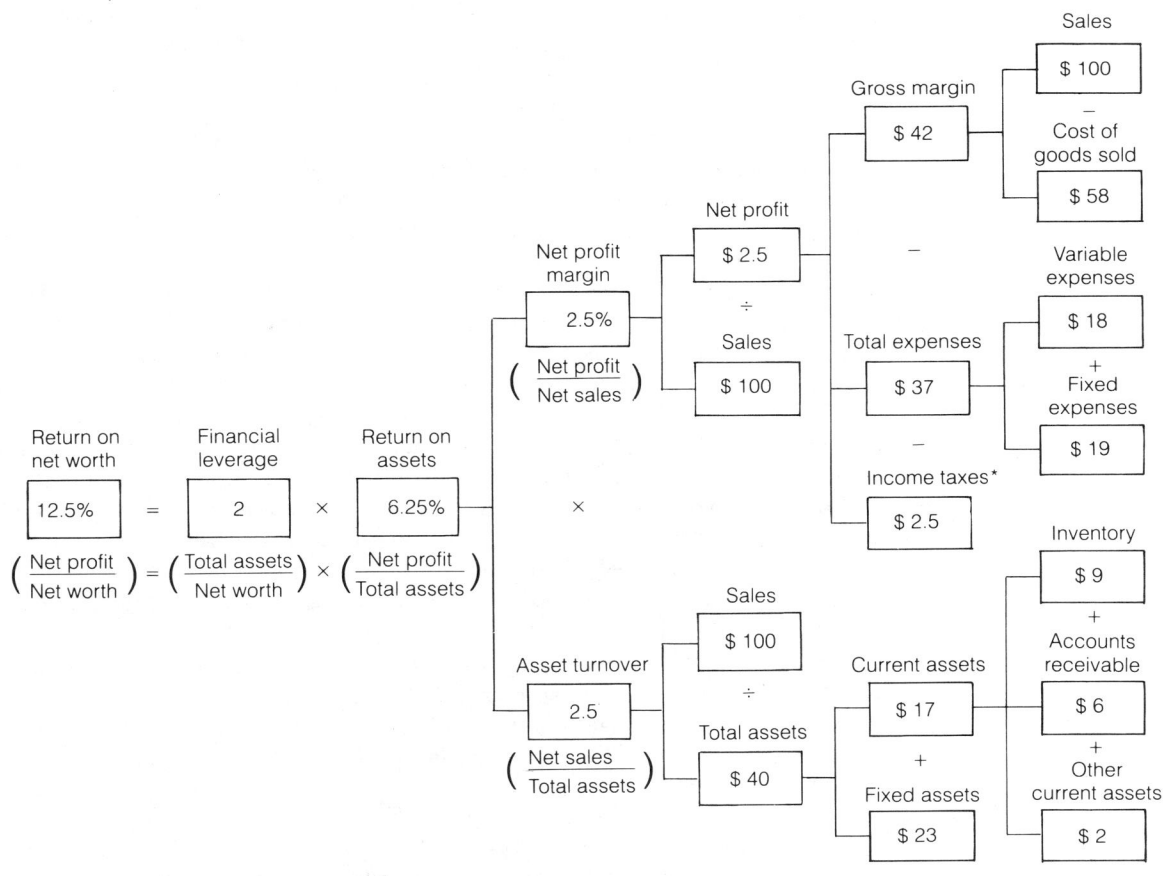

*Income taxes are assumed to equal 50 percent of net profit before taxes.

First, consider the impact on asset turnover. Inventory is reduced by $5 million from $14 million to $9 million, thereby reducing current assets to $17 million. However, total assets remain unchanged at $40 million because the capital from the inventory reduction is used to purchase $5 million of plant equipment which increases fixed assets by $5 million. So the asset is merely switched from a current asset to a fixed asset. Because sales and total assets are unchanged, asset turnover remains at 2.5 times.

A number of profit and loss statement accounts are affected by the proposed system. The new plant equipment will reduce production costs and generate a 20 percent aftertax return which is 40 percent before taxes of $2 million. As a result, cost of goods sold is reduced to $58 million from $60 million increasing the gross margin to $4 million. Expenses that are variable with sales remain the same, but those that are variable with inventory or the noncost of money out-of-pocket costs associated with the $5 million inventory reduction, lower fixed expenses by $250,000. However, the increased order-processing costs of $750,000 per year plus depreciation on the new plant equipment of $500,000 per year raise the fixed expenses by $1.25 million so that the fixed expenses increase to $19 million and total expenses to $37 million. New profit before taxes is increased from $4 million to $5 million resulting in income taxes of $2.5 million. Net profit after taxes is $2.5 million and the net profit margin is 2.5 percent. Consequently, return on assets are increased from 5 percent to 6.25 percent. Since corporate financing has not been affected, financial leverage stays at 2 to 1 and return on net worth increases from 10 percent to 12.5 percent.

The purpose of this exercise was twofold: (1) to illustrate how the strategic profit model can be used to identify the impact of a change in physical distribution operations on return, on assets, and return on net worth; and (2) to show that even though a firm may not calculate inventory carrying costs, the costs are indeed real. Also, the cost of money for inventory carrying cost purposes should reflect how the money would be used if it was not invested in inventory.

In the example, it was assumed that the money could be reinvested in a project that would yield 20 percent after taxes. Figure 8–11 shows what the return on net worth would be if the money was used to reduce bank loans by $5 million. It is assumed that the interest rate on the loan was at 10 percent. Of course, this is a pretax expense.

Since the money is being used to reduce debt, total assets decrease by $5 million to $35 million and asset turnover increases from 2.5 times to 2.86 times. In this example gross margin is unchanged. Fixed expenses are decreased by $750,000 which is comprised of a $250,000 reduction in noncost of money inventory-related expenses plus a $500,000 decrease in interest expense. However, the increase in order processing and communication costs of $750,000 negates the decrease in expenses and results in no change in the total. Net profit margin remains at 2.0 percent and return on assets becomes 5.72 percent. The reduction in debt lowers financial leverage from 2.0 ($40 million ÷ $20 million) to 1 to 1.75 ($35 million ÷ $20 million) to 1. The impact on return on net worth is to increase it marginally from 10 percent to 10.1 percent.

You have been shown how changes in inventory levels, which come about as a result of revisions in the physical distribution system, can influence corporate return on net worth.

**FIGURE 8-11** The Strategic Profit Model for Company XYZ—after System Change Assuming Repayment of Bank Loan (financial data in $ millions)

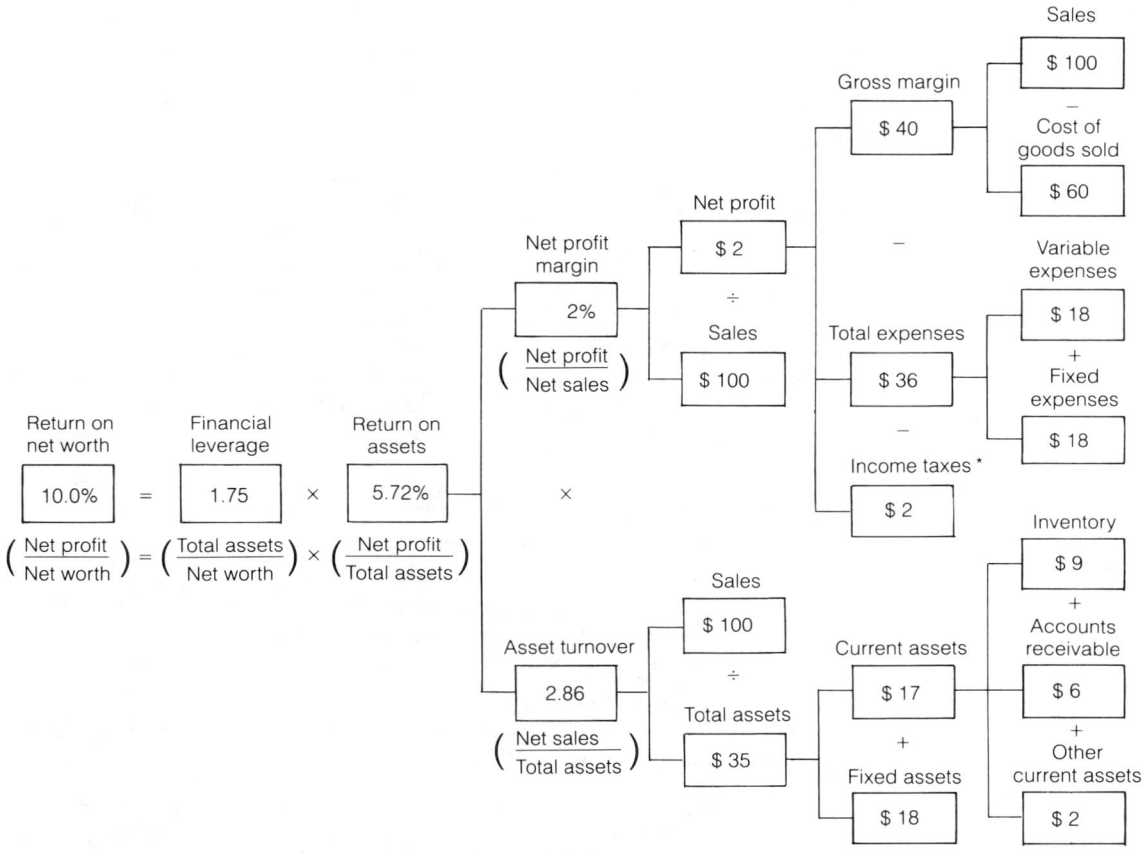

*Income taxes are assumed to equal 50 percent of net profit before taxes.

## SUMMARY

In this chapter, the basic concepts of inventory management were explained. The EOQ model was introduced and methods for adjusting it were suggested. In addition, demand and order cycle uncertainty were explained and you were shown a method for considering both types of uncertainty when calculating safety stock requirements. It was also shown that the traditional approach to improving customer service, increasing inventory investment, was shown to be costly and inefficient. The impacts of inventory investment on production scheduling were explained and you were shown how to recognize poor inventory models.

The chapter concluded with an explanation of techniques that can be used to improve inventory management and a method for determining the impact of an inventory reduction on corporate profit performance. In the next chapter, you will be shown how the order processing system can be used to improve physical distribution performance.

## QUESTIONS AND PROBLEMS

1. Why is inventory so important to the efficient and effective management of a firm?

2. How does uncertainty in demand and lead time impact inventory levels?

3. How does the economic order quantity model mathematically select the most economical order quantity?

4. One of the product lines carried by Farha Wholesale Foods was a line of canned vegetables manufactured by Vegetable Manufacturer's Inc. Mr. Jones, the canned-goods buyer knew that the company did not reorder from its suppliers in a systematic manner and wondered if the EOQ model might be appropriate. For example, 200 cases of canned corn were ordered each week and the annual volume was about 10,000 cases. The purchase price was $8.00 per case, the ordering cost was $15 per order and the inventory carrying cost was 35 percent. Vegetable Manufacturer's Inc. paid the transportation charges and there were no price breaks for ordering quantities in excess of 200 cases. Does the economic order quantity model apply in this situation? If so, calculate the economic order quantity.

5. How would the following information affect your solution to question 4?
   a. Farha Wholesale Foods pays the freight.
   b. The canned corn weighs 20 pounds per case.
   c. The freight rate is $5 per hundredweight on shipments of less than 15,000 pounds, $4.85 per hundredweight on 15,000 to 39,000 pounds and $4.55 per hundredweight for truckload quantities of 40,000 pounds or more.
   d. Orders are all shipped on pallets of 20 cases.

   Verify your answer using a tabular format similar to the one illustrated in Table 8–1. Be sure that you include the additional cost categories.

6. Explain the basic differences between a fixed order point, fixed order quantity model, and a fixed order interval inventory model. Which is likely to lead to the largest inventory levels?

7. Calculate the economic order quantity, the safety stock, and the average inventory necessary to achieve a 95 percent customer service level given the following information.
   a. The average daily demand for a 25-day period was found to be:

| Day | Units Demand | Day | Units Demand | Day | Units Demand |
| --- | --- | --- | --- | --- | --- |
| 1 | 8 | 11 | 7 | 21 | 7 |
| 2 | 5 | 12 | 8 | 22 | 6 |
| 3 | 4 | 13 | 12 | 23 | 8 |
| 4 | 6 | 14 | 9 | 24 | 10 |
| 5 | 9 | 15 | 10 | 25 | 11 |
| 6 | 8 | 16 | 5 | | |
| 7 | 9 | 17 | 8 | | |
| 8 | 10 | 18 | 11 | | |
| 9 | 7 | 19 | 9 | | |
| 10 | 6 | 20 | 7 | | |

b. There is no variability in order cycle.
   c. The ordering cost is $25 per order.
   d. The annual demand is 2,000.
   e. The cost is $100 per unit.
   f. The inventory carrying cost is 40 percent.
   g. The products are purchased FOB destination.

8. Recalculate your answer to question 7 given the following sample of replenishment cycles:

| Replenishment Cycle | Lead Time in Days |
|---|---|
| 1  | 10 |
| 2  | 12 |
| 3  | 11 |
| 4  | 10 |
| 5  | 10 |
| 6  | 9  |
| 7  | 8  |
| 8  | 12 |
| 9  | 11 |
| 10 | 9  |
| 11 | 8  |
| 12 | 10 |
| 13 | 11 |
| 14 | 9  |
| 15 | 9  |
| 16 | 10 |
| 17 | 11 |
| 18 | 10 |

9. What is the cost saving to the customer resulting from manufacturer's ability to reduce variability by two days given the following information:
   a. Average sales of 40 cases per day.
   b. Cost per case of product is $45.
   c. Transportation cost per case is $5.
   d. The order cycle is 10 days.
   e. Inventory carrying cost is 40 percent.

   How does this compare with the cost saving associated with a two-day reduction in the order cycle with no change in order cycle variability?

10. Using the financial data in Figure 8–8 show the impact of a $4,000,000 reduction in inventory given that:
    a. Inventory carrying costs are 45 percent which includes 5 percent for noncost of money components.
    b. The average variable cost of the inventory delivered to the storage location is 75 percent of full manufactured cost.
    c. The inventory reduction is accomplished by eliminating rail shipments, which represent 30 percent of all shipments, and shipping all products by truck. As a result, transportation costs would increase by $350,000.

# 9 Order Processing and Information Systems

Introduction

Customer Order Cycle
    How Do Customer Orders Enter the Firm's Order Processing Function?
    The Path of a Customer's Order

The Communications Function
    Advanced Order Processing Systems
    Integrating Order Processing and the Company's Physical Distribution
        Management Information System
    Basic Need for Information
    Designing the Information System

A Distribution Data Base for Decision Making

Financial Considerations

Summary

**Objectives of this chapter:**

To show how the order processing system can influence performance of the physical distribution function

To show how order processing systems can be used to improve customer communications and total order cycle time, and/or lead to substantial inventory reductions as well as transportation efficiencies

To show how the order processing system can form the basis of a physical distribution information system

To show how the physical distribution information system is used for both strategic and tactical planning of distribution operations

## INTRODUCTION

The order processing system is the nerve center of the physical distribution system. A customer order serves as the communications message that sets the physical distribution process in motion. The speed and quality of the information flow has direct impact on the cost and efficiency of the entire operation. Slow and erratic communications can lead to lost customers and/or excessive transportation, inventory, and warehousing costs as well as possible production inefficiencies caused by frequent line changes. The order processing and communications system forms the foundation for the physical distribution and corporate management information systems. It is an area that offers considerable potential for improving physical distribution performance.

In this chapter you will be shown how the order processing system can directly influence performance of the physical distribution function; how order processing systems can be used to improve customer communications and total order cycle time, and/or lead to substantial inventory reductions as well as transportation efficiencies; how the order processing system can form the basis of a physical distribution information system, and how the physical distribution information system is used for both strategic and tactical planning of distribution operations.

## CUSTOMER ORDER CYCLE

*Six Components of the Order Cycle*

The customer order cycle includes all of the elapsed time from order placement until the product is received and placed into the customer's inventory. The typical order cycle consists of the following components: (1) order preparation and transmittal, (2) order receipt and order entry, (3) order processing, (4) warehouse picking and packing, (5) order transportation, and (6) customer delivery and unloading.

Figure 9−1 illustrates the flow associated with the order cycle. In this example, the total order cycle is 10 days from the customer's point of view. However, many manufacturers make the mistake of measuring and controlling only that portion of the order cycle which is internal to the firm. That

**FIGURE 9-1** Total Order Cycle: A Customer's Perspective

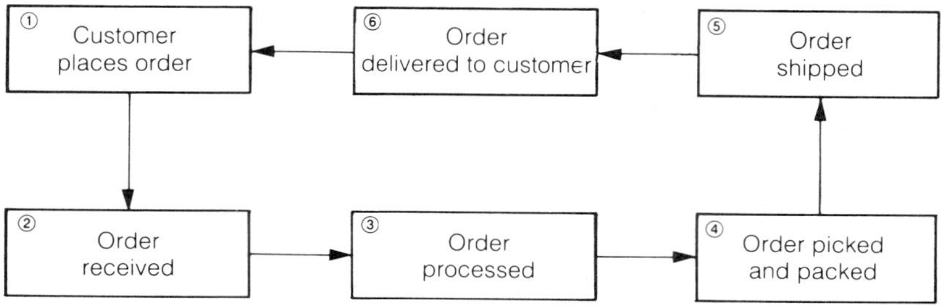

```
①Customer    ←  ⑥Order           ← ⑤Order
 places order    delivered to customer   shipped
      ↓                                    ↑
②Order      →  ③Order          → ④Order picked
 received       processed           and packed
```

Key:
1. Order preparation and transmittal (orders mailed) ...... 3 days
2. Order received and entered into system ............... 1
3. Order processing ..................................... 1
4. Warehouse picking and packing ........................ 1
5. Transit time ......................................... 3
6. Warehouse receiving and placing into storage ......... 1
   Total order cycle time .............................. 10 days

is, they only monitor the elapsed time from receipt of the customer order until it is shipped. The shortcomings of this approach should be obvious. In the example presented in Figure 9–1, the portion of the total order cycle that is internal to the manufacturer amounts to only 3 of the 10 days. This ratio would not be unusual for companies that did not have an automated order-entry and processing system. Improving the efficiency of the three-day portion of the order cycle that is "controlled" by the manufacturer may be extremely difficult and costly as compared to eliminating a day from the seven days not directly under the manufacturers control.

For example, it may be possible to reduce transit time as much as one day by monitoring carrier performance and switching business to those carriers with the fastest and most consistent transit times. A change in the method of order placement and order entry has the potential for the most significant reduction in order cycle time. An advanced order processing system could reduce the total order cycle by as much as four days, more than the active portion considered to be under the manufacturer's direct control.

A study sponsored by the National Council of Physical Distribution Management, supported the hypothesis that the largest portion of the total order cycle time for manufacturers occurs prior to the order being received and after the order has been shipped (see Table 9–1).[1] Also, it was found that the average order cycle for all manufacturing types was about 10 days.

---
[1] Bernard J. LaLonde and Paul H. Zinszer, *Customer Service: Meaning and Measurement* (Chicago: National Council of Physical Distribution Management, 1976).

**TABLE 9-1** Components of Order Cycle by Selected Industries (in days)

| Element | Manufacturing All | Manufacturing Chemical and Plastics | Manufacturing Food | Merchandising All | Merchandising Consumer | Merchandising Industrial |
|---|---|---|---|---|---|---|
| Order placement/order receipt | 1.9 | 1.2 | 2.0 | 1.0 | 0.8 | 0.8 |
| Order received/order processed | 2.1 | 0.8 | 1.5 | 1.1 | 1.0 | 1.0 |
| Order processed/order shipped | 2.2 | 1.7 | 0.8 | 1.6 | 0.9 | 1.5 |
| Order shipped/order received | 4.1 | 3.0 | 3.0 | 1.8 | 1.0 | 3.2 |
| Total order cycle time | 10.3 | 6.7 | 7.3 | 5.5 | 3.7 | 6.5 |

Source: Bernard J. LaLonde and Paul H. Zinszer, *Customer Service: Meaning and Measurement*, (Chicago, National Council of Physical Distribution Management, 1976), p. 119.

## Order Cycle Variability

In the examples used so far in this chapter, we have treated the performance of order cycle components as though no variability occurred. Figure 9–2 provides an illustration of the variability that is likely to occur for each component of the order cycle and for the total. Although for the purposes of this illustration, we have assumed that each of the variable time patterns was a normal statistical distribution, other statistical distributions may actually be experienced. In our example, the actual order cycle could range from a low of 5 days to as many as 25 days with the most likely being 15 days. Variability in cycle time is costly to the manufacturer's customer because safety stock must be carried to cover for possible delays or sales will be lost as a result of stock-outs.

Return to the example in Figure 9–2. If the average order cycle time is 15 days but can be as long as 25 days, the customer must maintain additional inventory equivalent to 10 days sales just to cover variability in lead time. If daily sales are equal to 20 units and the company's economic order quantity is 200 units, a 10-day supply, the average cycle stock is 100 units, one half the order quantity. The additional inventory required to cover the order cycle variability of 10 days is 200 units or twice the amount required under conditions of lead-time certainty. Excluding demand uncertainty, average inventory would increase from 100 units to 300 units due to the variability in the order cycle. Which would have the greatest impact on the customer's inventory: a five-day reduction in the order cycle; or a five-day reduction in order cycle variability? If the customer continued to order the economic order quantity of 200 units little or no impact would occur. The customer would simply wait five days longer before placing an order. On the other hand, if the customer ordered 100 units every time instead of 200, the average cycle stock would be 50 units rather than 100 units, but safety stock of 200 units would be required to cover the 10 days of variability. The total impact would be a reduction in total average inventory of 50 units from 300 to 250 units. However a five-day reduction in order cycle variability would

**FIGURE 9-2** Total Order Cycle with Variability

1. Order communication
Frequency:
3
Time range 1 to 5 days

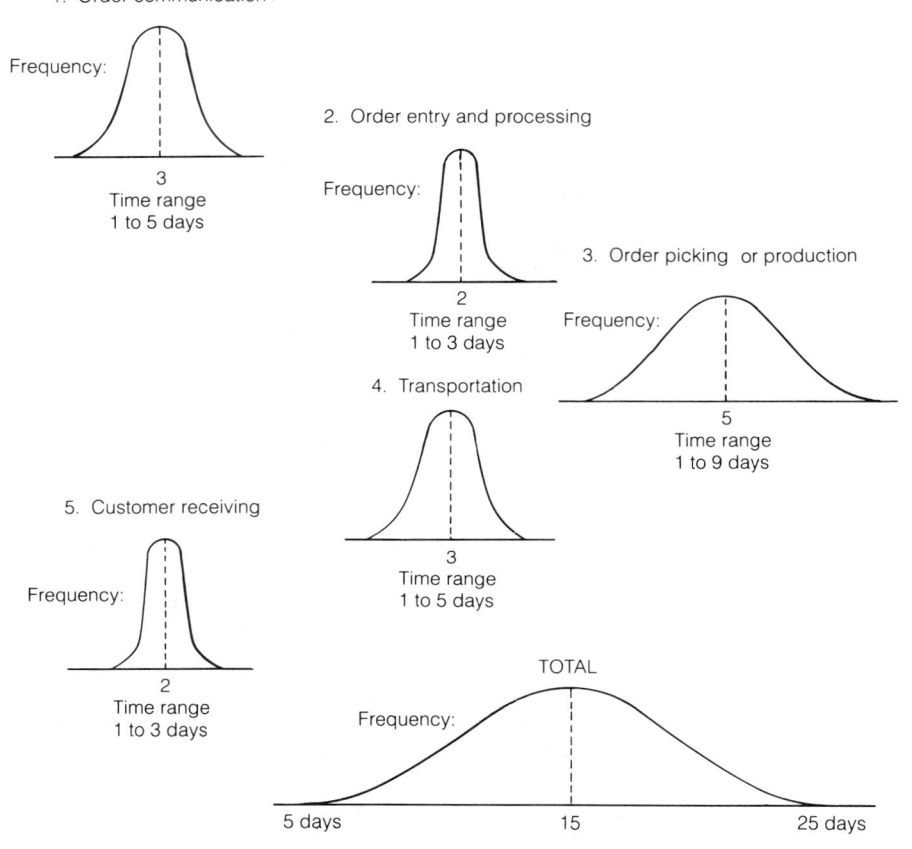

2. Order entry and processing
Frequency:
2
Time range 1 to 3 days

3. Order picking or production
Frequency:
5
Time range 1 to 9 days

4. Transportation
3
Time range 1 to 5 days

5. Customer receiving
Frequency:
2
Time range 1 to 3 days

TOTAL
Frequency:
5 days  15  25 days

reduce safety stocks by 100 units and result in an average inventory of 200 units. This example should make it clear why order cycle consistency is preferred to fast delivery.

In the next two sections we will look at how customer orders enter the order processing function and the typical path taken by a customer's order.

### How Do Customer Orders Enter the Firm's Order Processing Function?

Methods of Order Entry

There are a number of ways that a customer order can be placed, transmitted, and entered into a manufacturer's order processing function. Traditionally, orders were written and given to salespeople or mailed to the supplier. The next level of sophistication was telephoning the order to the manufacturer order clerk who wrote it up. An advanced system might have customers placing orders over the telephone with customer service representatives located at the manufacturer's headquarters and equipped with

CRTs. This type of system allows the customer-service representative to check to see if the ordered products are available in inventory. The items are then deducted from inventory so that they are not promised to another customer. If a stock-out occurs, product substitution can be arranged while the customer is still on the telephone or the customer can be informed as to when the product will be available. Shipping instructions and special handling also can be arranged. In effect, this type of system would eliminate the first four days of the order cycle described in Figure 9–1.

Electronic methods such as an electronic terminal with information transmitted by telephone lines, and computer-to-computer hookups are becoming more widely used in order to gain the maximum speed and accuracy of order transmittal and order entry. These types of systems will be discussed further in a following section of this chapter.

Generally, rapid forms of order transmittal are more costly. However, the physical distribution system cannot be set into motion until the order is entered at the processing point and an increase in order processing speed will make it possible to reduce inventories throughout the system while maintaining the desired customer service level. Also, time saved in order transmittal can be used to realize transportation consolidation opportunities. An alternative strategy would be to decrease the order cycle time offered to the customer which would allow the customer to hold less safety stock.

The direct cost trade-off between inventory carrying costs and communications costs is clear. It should be recognized, however, that the more sophisticated the communications system becomes, the more vulnerable the company becomes to any internal or external communications malfunction. This is due to the fact that with advanced order processing systems and inventory levels, safety stocks have been substantially reduced leaving the customer with minimal protection against stock-outs that result from any variability in the order-cycle time.

Table 9–2 summarizes the various methods by which customer orders can enter a firm's order processing system. A quick review of this table reveals that significant potential exists for using advanced order processing to improve physical distribution performance.

**TABLE 9–2**  How Do Customer Orders Enter the Firm's Order-Processing Functions?

| Groupings/Order Entry | Sales Staff | Phone | Mail | Electronic | Other |
|---|---|---|---|---|---|
| All manufacturing | 9% | 36% | 33% | 21% | 1% |
| Chemicals and plastics | 3 | 51 | 16 | 15 | 15 |
| Food | X | 25 | 27 | 48 | X |
| All other manufacturing | 12 | 28 | 38 | 22 | X |
| All merchandising | 18 | 28 | 46 | 8 | X |
| Consumer goods | 12 | 9 | 67 | 12 | X |
| Industrial goods | 25 | 51 | 24 | X | X |

Source: Bernard J. LaLonde, Riley Professor of Marketing and Logistics, The Ohio State University, 1976.

The Path of a Customer's Order

## The Path of a Customer's Order

When studying a firm's order-processing system, it is important to understand the information flow that begins when a customer places an order. Figure 9–3 represents one interpretation of the path that a customer's

**FIGURE 9-3**  The Path of a Customer's Order

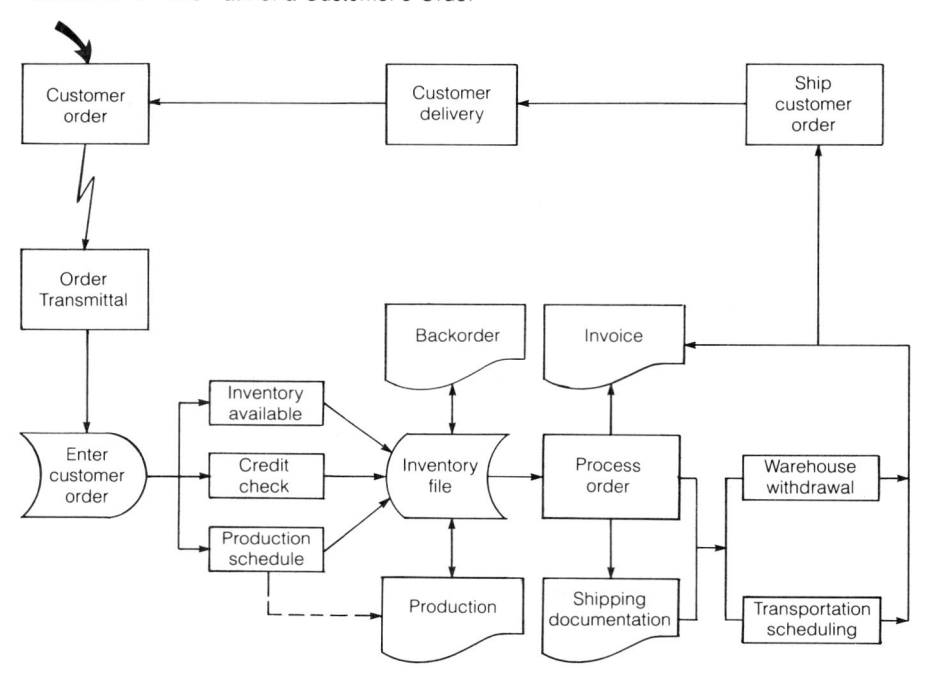

order might take. The first step is the customer recognizing the need for certain products and transmitting an order to the supplying manufacturer. Since the various methods of order transmittal already have been discussed, there is no need to elaborate on them at this time.

Once the order has been received and entered into the manufacturer's order processing system various checks must be made to determine (1) if the desired product is available in inventory in the quantities ordered, (2) if the customer's credit is satisfactory to accept the order, and (3) if the product is scheduled for production if not currently in inventory. Next the inventory file is updated, product back ordered if necessary, and production is issued a report showing the inventory balance. The information on daily sales is also used as an input to the company's sales-forecasting package. Order processing next provides: information to accounting for invoicing; acknowledgement of the order to send to the customer; picking and packing instructions to enable warehouse withdrawal of the product; and shipping documentation.

When the product has been pulled from warehouse inventory and transportation scheduled, documentation is sent to accounting so that invoicing may proceed.

## THE COMMUNICATIONS FUNCTION

The primary function of the order processing system is to provide a communication network that links the customer and the manufacturer. Various methods of order transmittal should be evaluated for consistency of message delivery. Usually, greater inconsistency is associated with slower methods of order transmittal. Also, manual methods of order transmittal require more handling by individuals and consequently there is greater chance of a communication error. Methods of order transmittal can be evaluated on the basis of speed, cost, consistency, and accuracy. Order transmittal should be as direct as possible and transmitted electronically rather than manually in order to minimize the risk of a human error.

In addition, the order processing system can communicate useful sales information to marketing, to finance for cash-flow planning, and to production for production scheduling (see Figure 9–4). Finally, the order processing system provides the communication network that provides information

**FIGURE 9-4**  Management Information Provided by an Advanced Order Processing System

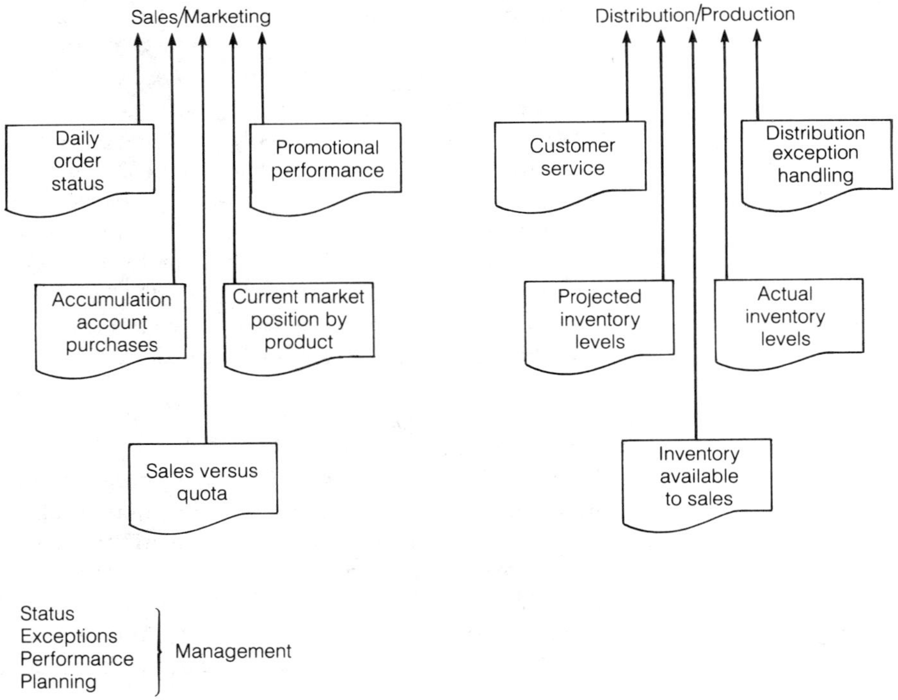

Source: American Telephone and Telegraph Company, *Business Marketing*, Market Management Division, 1981.

to those individuals who assign warehouses, clear customer credit, update inventory files, prepare warehouse picking instructions, and prepare shipping instructions and the associated documentation. Communication is extremely important because it sets the physical distribution system in motion.

**Advanced Order Processing Systems**

There is no component of the physical distribution function that has benefited more from the application of electronic and computer technology than order entry and processing. Some advanced systems are so sophisticated that the only human effort is to enter the order and monitor the results.

At one level of advanced order processing systems customers and salespeople transmit orders to distribution centers of corporate headquarters via a toll-free number. The order clerk is equipped with a data terminal and can both enter and access information on a real-time basis. As soon as the customer code is entered, the order format, including the customer's name, billing addresses, credit code, and shipping address is displayed on the screen. The clerk receives the rest of the order information verbally, enters it on the terminal, and it is displayed along with the header information. Deviations from standard such as products on promotion, special pricing arrangements, and allocations, may be highlighted on the cathode-ray tube (CRT) to ensure that they receive special attention from the order clerk. The system can match order quantity against a minimum-shipment-quantity list to ensure that the order meets the necessary specifications. The clerk may then read the order back to the originator. When the order meets all criteria for accuracy and completeness it is released for processing.

A major chemical company replaced a manual system with a system using CRT input similar to the one just described. Prior to the new order-entry system, orders were taken over the phone and recorded on a form. They were then transferred to another form for keypunching and finally were batch-processed into the system. CRT order entry was cost justified based on the savings over the manual system. As a result, sales increased by 23 percent with no increase in order processing costs. An additional benefit was that customer billing took place the day after the product was shipped rather than five days later which had been the case. The result was improved cash flow.

Sometimes order information is entered direct to the computer. Although not widely used, there is evidence of a trend developing in computer-to-computer ordering. The National Wholesale Druggist Association (NWDA) has implemented a CPU-to-CPU ordering system. In 1980, Arthur D. Little completed a study directed at evaluating the technical and economic feasibility of electronic data interchange in the industry.[2] The study was sponsored by the six major trade associations in the industry:

---

[2] Arthur D. Little, Inc., *Electronic Data Exchange for The Grocery Industry: Feasibility Report* (Washington, D.C.: Joint Committee For Grocery Industry Data Transmission, 1980).

**Order Processing at Eli Lilly Corporation**

Cooperative Food Distributors of America; Food Marketing Institute; Grocery Manufacturers of America; National American Wholesale Grocers' Association; National Association of Retail Grocers of the United States; and National Food Brokers Association.

The Eli Lilly Corporation is in the final stages of implementation of an advanced order entry and processing system for its pharmaceutical division.[3] The division makes use of five corporate distribution centers and distributes its products through 360 wholesalers. All products are manufactured at the company's Indianapolis plant. The company receives about 300,000 orders each year which total more than 6 million lines. The new system was initiated in 1972 for about 10 percent of the line items and Bergen Brunswig Corporation, a California-based drug wholesaler, was the first application. Prior to the new system Bergen Brunswig mailed orders to Indianapolis and orders were shipped from a distribution center in Fresno. The total order cycle was from 17 to 18 days. With the new computer-to-computer system, the order cycle was reduced to three days. By 1980, 90 percent of the pharmaceutical division's line items were ordered using the automated system. Fifty-three percent of the orders were transmitted computer to computer (core to core); 34 percent were transmitted by portable hand-held terminals and 13 percent were received by mail.

Management identified the following benefits of the system for its wholesalers: faster order cycle, reduced inventory, reduced errors, scheduled transmission of orders, and confirmed order receipt. The advantages to Eli Lilly were believed to include: by-passing the mail room, automated order edit, eliminated encoding of orders, work load leveling as a result of scheduled order transmissions, faster service to customers, and scheduled deliveries. This last point was important since Eli Lilly paid the freight.

**Advanced Order Processing at E. R. Squibb and Sons, Inc.**

E. R. Squibb and Sons, Inc., also has successfully implemented an advanced order processing system. In early 1978, the physical distribution department replaced its decentralized, batch-oriented order-entry system with an online distributed computer network called *SOLIDS* (Squibb on-line inventory and distribution system).[4]

> Video terminals are used as in computerized order entry, but inventory and information management are integrated in the same system. After more than a year's operation, SOLIDS' achievements have been significant. Same-day shipments increased more than 16 percent and cost savings on computer equipment and operation were substantial.
>
> Squibb's Physical Distribution Department distributes over 800 pharmaceutical products through nine distribution centers to more than 125,000 customers, predominantly pharmacies and hospitals. Before SOLIDS, the decentralized order entry system was based on nine batch-processing computers, one at each distribution center. The nine IBM Model 360/20 computers were linked to Squibb's Data Center in East Brunswick, N.J., which is equipped with IBM 370/155 and 370/138 mainframes.

---

[3] Robert A. Bruce and John J. Nevin, "Remote Entry at Eli Lilly and Company"; in *Proceedings of the Eighteenth Annual Conference of the National Council of Physical Distribution Management*, October 13–15, 1980, pp. 277–86.

[4] Squibb's New Order Entry System, *Distribution* 79, no. 3 (March 1980):67–70.

The order entry procedure resembled many other batch systems. Orders received through the mail or by telephone from customers and sales representatives were accumulated in groups of from 50 to 150. Order cards were punched and fed into the batch computer to price the products, sort the line items in optimum picking sequence, and print the customer invoices.

If the warehouse was out of stock on a particular item, it was automatically back-ordered by the computer and so recorded on the invoice. The day's shipments and inventory position were then transmitted to the Data Center in the evening. The main drawback of batch order entry was that only 59 percent of orders were shipped on the day of receipt.

The elapsed time between entering an order and having it ready for shipment ranged from two to five hours. Most of the time was consumed in accumulating orders and keypunching.

This portion of the cycle time was generally acceptable for mail orders, since the orders spent at least one day in the mail anyway. As mail service deteriorated, the proportion of telephone orders had gradually come to average well over half the total, and same-day shipments became far more important in maintaining good customer service.

Another problem with the batch system was that the inventory status of products was unknown at the time telephone orders were taken. As a result, customers didn't learn of out-of-stock products until they received their shipments.

Finally, data could only be transmitted from the distribution centers to the East Brunswick Data Center. Any information on customers or products that was maintained at the Data Center could not be sent to the distribution centers within the batch system and therefore had to be transmitted separately by mail, telex, or telephone.

The cost of the non-batch-type computers and keypunch personnel was extremely high, particularly for the distribution centers that handled small volumes. Also, the cost of change and expansion was simply too high. If volume rose substantially in a particular area, establishing a new distribution center would have required installing an additional computer and hiring additional people. If one distribution center temporarily shut down, there was no way the computer at another center could take over its order entry tasks.

In preparing for SOLIDS, Squibb's Planning and Systems Department ran feasibility studies on three concepts for order entry/inventory management/information management systems. The first was a decentralized system of independent batch machines (the existing concept for order entry alone). The second was a totally centralized system in which input/output terminals would be directly linked to the Data Center's mainframes. The third was an on-line distributed computer network.

Even if the batch computers were to be replaced with interactive systems at the distribution centers, the first alternative was relatively expensive and still lacked the desired communications capability.

With the second alternative, the dedicated telephone lines would have entailed extremely high communications cost (although hardware costs would have been substantially lower), and there would have been no local storage and control of distribution information. Also, a hardware malfunction would halt the distribution system nationally.[5]

---

[5] Ibid., pp. 67–68 and 70.

After one year of study the company selected alternative 3—a network of interactive minicomputers linked to the data center for two-way transmission using dial-up telephone lines.

Each satellite distribution center is a complete warehouse and shipping point. The procedure at the satellites is exactly the same as at the master distribution center even though the actual order processing is done by the master computer, which may be located as much as 1,500 miles away.

The disk drives controlled by the master computer store a number of data files, among them the Product Information File (including for each line item its name, package, size, inventory status, price and weight) and Customer Information File (including name, address, credit rating).

The Product Information File is common to all distribution centers; the Customer Information File at the master computer contains only customers served by the master center and its satellite (the satellite having no data files of its own).

The central product inventory and customer information files for the entire Squibb system—those that must be accessed by other data processing systems running on the mainframes—are maintained at the Data Center.

The on-line configuration of SOLIDS offers several major advantages over a batch system. Order data is verified on the CRT screen at the time of entry rather than after keypunching. Direct data entry reduces the possibility of transcription errors (in the batch system, the order information was first recorded on a paper form and then transposed by the keypunch operator).

Prompting from SOLIDS insures that all data necessary to complete an order are collected from customers while they are still on the phone. In the on-line mode, order and inventory transactions update files as they are entered and all information in files is immediately available for inquiry.

The master/satellite configuration offers identical SOLIDS service at nine locations with computers at only the five master centers. There can be as many as three satellites linked to each master, so that up to 11 or more distribution centers can be added to SOLIDS with additional investment in only the low-cost video and printing terminals and leased lines.

SOLIDS can then be easily and economically extended to new distribution centers to maintain or improve customer service as distribution patterns change. System backup has been increased, too. When a master computer temporarily shuts down, SOLIDS service can be switched over to another distribution center (downtime hasn't yet been long enough to make this necessary).[6]

The first year benefits of the new system include:

Increased same-day shipments—from 59 percent to 75 percent with all other nonback-ordered shipments leaving the following day.

Higher order entry productivity—order takers at the Metro distribution center, for example, now average one minute of video-terminal time per order.

Improved customer relations—telephone customers can be given prices, special offers, stock status, and other information over the telephone during their initial call.

---
[6] Ibid., p. 70.

More informative invoices—longer descriptions of line items, itemized calculation of figures, more data for sales representatives, reference to the terminal operator who entered the order, special offer information, and time entered. (Some of the additional information, of course is of more interest to Squibb than to its customers).

More accurate orders—through on-line verification and elimination of a transposition step.

Lower system operating cost—substantial savings have been achieved through consolidation of distribution sites and order entry positions, improved efficiency, and elimination of redundancy in order processing.[7]

## A New System at Johns-Manville Canada, Inc.

Another company that has successfully implemented an advanced order transmittal, order entry and order processing system is Johns-Manville Canada, Inc.[8] In 1978 Johns-Manville Canada, Inc., invested $750,000 in an on-line order entry, order processing and inventory control system which had paid for itself in less than two years.

Prior to the implementation of the new system, a customer would telephone an order for fiberglass home insulation, which is one of Johns-Manville's products, to one of three customer service clerks located in Toronto. One of these clerks was assigned to the telephone while the other two were kept busy writing orders. The telephone clerk received the order and passed it on to one of the others for processing. Information required to complete the order was obtained from different files in many locations and manually filled in on each order set.

When this process was completed, the order was sent to the order and billing department, where it was typed and sent to the shipping location. Once the order was shipped, the order form and a shipping document created at the shipping location were returned to the customer service clerks to be verified and forwarded to the billing department to be typed again.

The three customer service clerks could process an average of 12 orders per day, with overtime required during peak periods. This piecemeal method of handling customer orders created a considerable amount of pressure and resulted in a relatively high incidence of human error.

Now when a customer telephones an order to Johns-Manville Canada, the customer service clerk enters the name of the customer on a video display screen. At this point, all pertinent customer information is displayed on the screen and applied to the order. When the product is entered, all inventory, price, and other related information about that item is displayed and applied to the order.

When all items have been added to the order the total weights and percentages of a truckload shipment are calculated. If the order is for less than a truckload quantity the customer is told the cost of increasing the

---

[7] Ibid.

[8] This example was furnished by Donald J. Allison, Division Manager, Physical Distribution, Johns-Manville Canada, Inc., 1981.

order to truckload as well as the discount that would occur. This allows the customer service clerks to provide an inside sales function. The computer also calculates the total value of the order and compares this to the credit limit that has been established for that customer. If the securement amount is greater than the credit limit the order is placed on credit hold pending review by the credit manager.[9]

Once the order is completed, the shipping documents such as packing slips and bills of lading are printed at the shipping locations. At each shipping location the shipping date is automatically entered into a terminal along with such things as the quantity shipped, carrier, carrier number, and products substituted. At this point inventory files are automatically updated.

The customer service clerk reviews and verifies all information on the order and releases the order for billing. The billing is then printed out automatically by the computer in French and English and mailed to the customer. The computer also generates accounts receivable and sales detail reports. If required, a back order is created.

Benefits associated with the new system are numerous. Edits built into the system reduced billing errors by as much as 85 percent. With a 5 percent reasonability factor built into the system, it is able to detect errors made by the clerks as they are processing the order through its various stages. It has also streamlined Johns-Manville's Canadian organization by 19 customer-service people. Time and space-consuming typing and filing have been eliminated to a large degree. The level of customer service has been improved. In addition the cash flow of the company has been accelerated by several days because of the system's ability to generate customer billings the same day the shipment is made. Also, the system has been integrated with the company's inventory-management system.

As orders are placed and shipped, inventory backlogs are automatically updated. This feature provides accurate data for production scheduling and a great variety of other reports—marketing-securement and billing reports, exception reports showing beyond-normal transportation costs, and carrier-revenue reports.

Interfaces are also possible between similar systems that have been set up in the Toronto-, Montreal-, and Edmonton-based operations. This interface allows orders to be placed from any one region to any other region in the Canadian operation; and allows total control of the order by the customer service clerk who has responsibility for that customer regardless of where the order will be shipped within Canada.

The flow of an order through the Johns-Manville system is shown in Figure 9–5.

Generally, the more rapid a form of order transmittal, the more costly it is. Likewise, on-line order entry may be more costly when viewed as a stand-alone cost. However, the physical distribution system cannot be set

---

[9] The company referred to orders received as *securements*. As orders came in they were accumulated, measured, and reported on securement reports. Once the customer was billed, the order was counted as a sale.

**FIGURE 9-5** An Advanced Order Processing System Implemented at Johns-Manville Canada

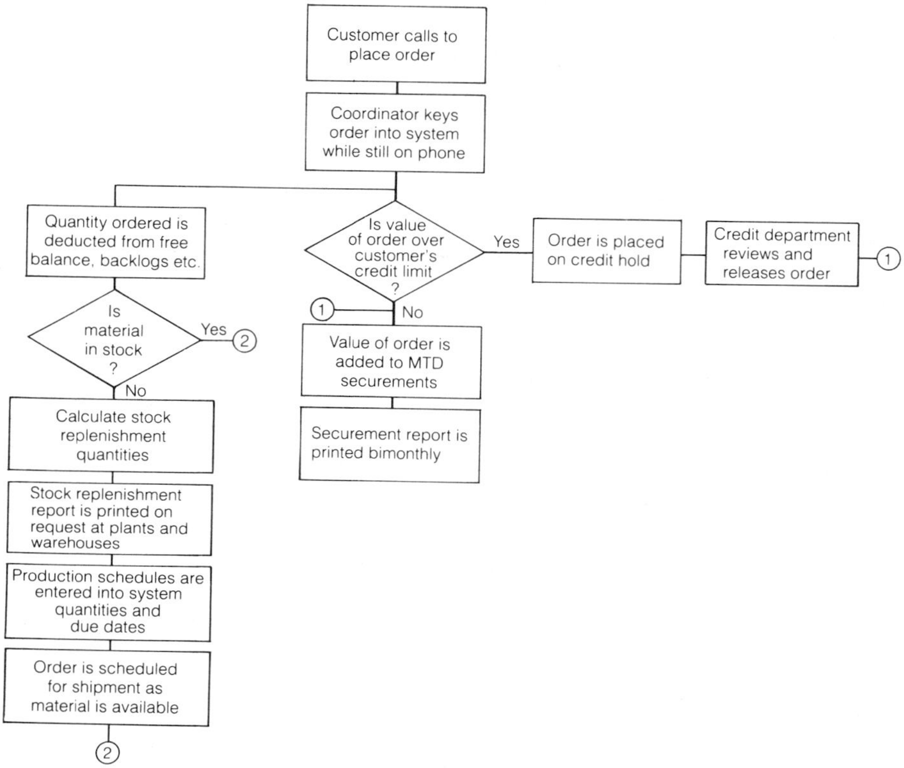

Source: Donald J. Allison, Division Manager Physical Distribution, Johns-Manville Canada, Inc., Products Division, 1981.

into motion until the order is entered at the processing point; an increase in order processing speed, accuracy, and consistency will make it possible to reduce inventories throughout the system while maintaining the desired customer service level. Also, time saved in order transmittal and entry can be used to realize transportation-consolidation opportunities. An alternative strategy would be for the manufacturer to decrease the order cycle time offered to the customer which would allow the customer to hold less safety stock. In addition a reduction in the order cycle time would result in lower in-transit inventories if the customer changed the order quantity. However, it has already been pointed out that most customers prefer a consistent order cycle to a shorter one. Therefore, the most likely result of an increase in lead time due to faster order transmittal and entry would be reduced costs for the manufacturer, lower inventory levels, and lower freight rates. The total reduction in the manufacturers costs will more than offset—*cost displace*—the increased communications expenditures.

**FIGURE 9-5** (continued)

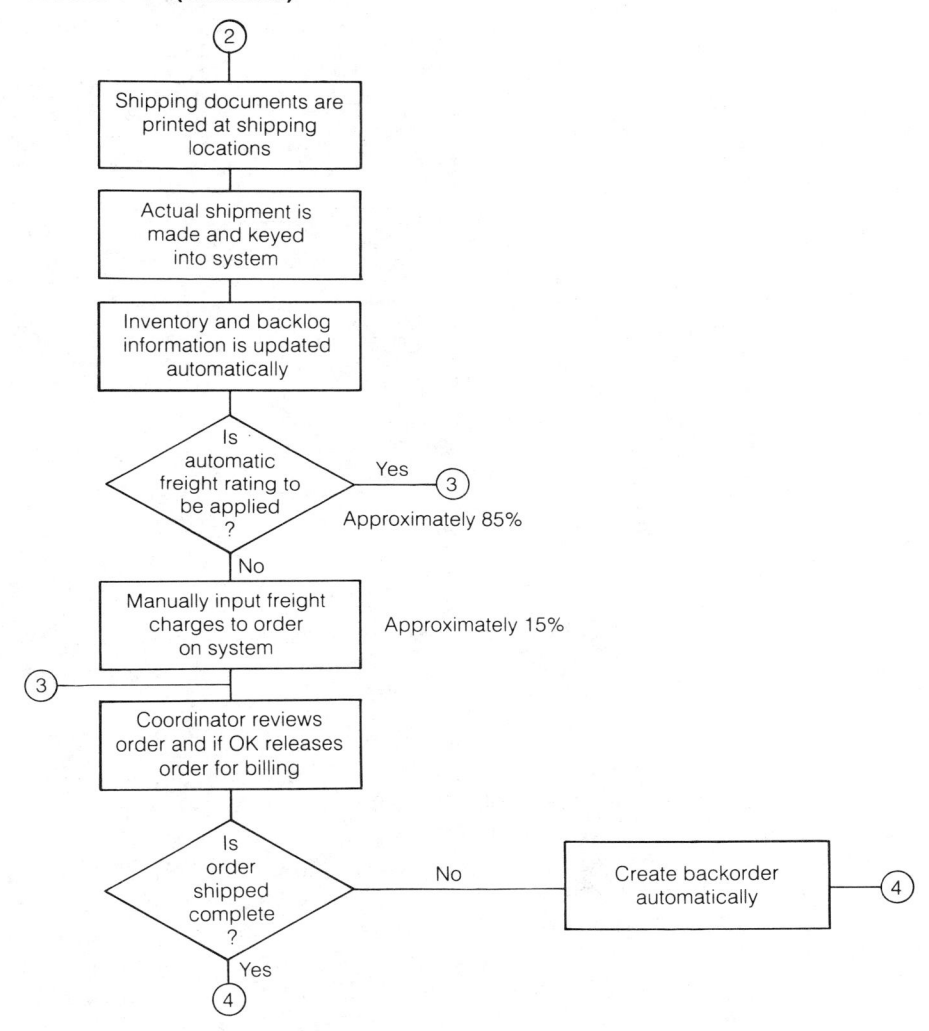

```
                    (2)
                     │
        ┌────────────────────────┐
        │ Shipping documents are │
        │  printed at shipping   │
        │       locations        │
        └────────────────────────┘
                     │
        ┌────────────────────────┐
        │   Actual shipment is   │
        │    made and keyed      │
        │      into system       │
        └────────────────────────┘
                     │
        ┌────────────────────────┐
        │ Inventory and backlog  │
        │ information is updated │
        │     automatically      │
        └────────────────────────┘
                     │
                  ╱     ╲
                 ╱   Is  ╲
                ╱automatic╲  Yes
               ╱ freight   ╲──────▶ (3)  Approximately 85%
               ╲ rating to ╱
                ╲be applied╱
                 ╲   ?    ╱
                  ╲      ╱
                     │ No
        ┌────────────────────────┐
        │ Manually input freight │
        │   charges to order     │   Approximately 15%
        │      on system         │
        └────────────────────────┘
                     │
       (3)───────────┤
                     │
        ┌────────────────────────┐
        │  Coordinator reviews   │
        │ order and if OK releases│
        │   order for billing    │
        └────────────────────────┘
                     │
                  ╱     ╲
                 ╱   Is  ╲                    ┌──────────────┐
                ╱  order  ╲  No               │Create backorder│
               ╱ shipped   ╲──────────────────▶│automatically  │──▶(4)
               ╲ complete  ╱                  └──────────────┘
                ╲    ?    ╱
                 ╲  Yes  ╱
                    │
                   (4)
```

### Integrating Order Processing and the Company's Physical Distribution Management Information System

The Order Processing System Initiates Many Activities

The order processing system initiates physical distribution activities such as:

1. Determining the transportation mode, carrier, and loading sequence.
2. Inventory assignment and preparing picking and packing lists.
3. Warehouse picking and packing.
4. Updating the inventory file, subtracting actual products picked.

**FIGURE 9-5** (*concluded*)

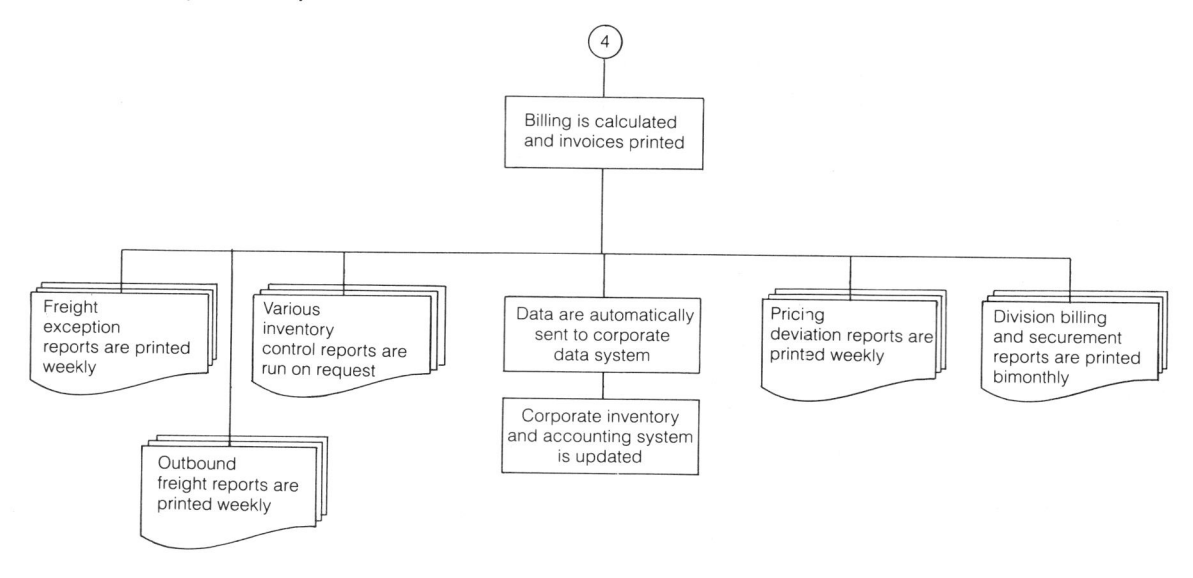

```
                              (4)
                               |
                    ┌──────────────────────┐
                    │ Billing is calculated │
                    │ and invoices printed  │
                    └──────────────────────┘
                               |
    ┌──────────┬───────────────┼───────────────┬──────────────┐
┌─────────┐ ┌─────────┐  ┌─────────────┐  ┌──────────┐  ┌──────────────┐
│Freight  │ │Various  │  │Data are     │  │Pricing   │  │Division      │
│exception│ │inventory│  │automatically│  │deviation │  │billing and   │
│reports  │ │control  │  │sent to      │  │reports   │  │securement    │
│are      │ │reports  │  │corporate    │  │are       │  │reports are   │
│printed  │ │are run  │  │data system  │  │printed   │  │printed       │
│weekly   │ │on request│ │             │  │weekly    │  │bimonthly     │
└─────────┘ └─────────┘  └─────────────┘  └──────────┘  └──────────────┘
                 |              |
         ┌──────────┐   ┌─────────────┐
         │Outbound  │   │Corporate    │
         │freight   │   │inventory and│
         │reports   │   │accounting   │
         │are       │   │system is    │
         │printed   │   │updated      │
         │weekly    │   │             │
         └──────────┘   └─────────────┘
```

5. Automatically printing replenishment lists.
6. Preparing shipping documents, a bill of lading if using a common carrier.
7. Shipping the product to the customer.

Other computerized order processing applications include maintaining inventory levels and preparing productivity reports, financial reports, and special management reports.

*Order Processing Provides Important Information to MIS*

Processing an order necessitates the flow of information from one department to another as well as the referencing or accessing of several files or data bases such as customer credit status, inventory availability, and transportation schedules. The information system may be fully automated or manual but most are somewhere in between. Depending upon the sophistication of the order processing system and the corporate management information system (MIS) the quality and speed of the information flow will vary, affecting the manufacturer's ability to achieve transportation consolidations and lowest possible inventory levels. Generally, manual systems are very slow and error prone. The expected time to elapse tends to be quite long and variable, and information delays occur with frequency. Such a system seriously restricts a company's ability to implement integrated physical distribution management; specifically to reduce total costs while maintaining or improving customer service. Some common problems include the inability to detect pricing errors, access timely credit information, and determine inventory availability. Negative impacts that occur as a result include invoice errors, payment delays, and inappropriate rejection of an order due to incorrect inventory information. Lost sales and higher costs combine to reduce the manufacturer's profitability.

Indeed, timely and accurate information has value. Information delays will hamper the completion of all activities that follow them in the process. Automating and integrating the order process frees up time and reduces the likelihood of information delays. Automation helps distribution managers integrate the physical distribution system and allows them to reduce costs through reductions in inventory and freight rates. Clearly, the communications network is a key factor in the achievement of least-total-cost distribution.

### Basic Need for Information

A physical distribution management information system is necessary in order to provide management with the knowledge to exploit new markets, to take advantage of innovative transportation systems, to make changes in packaging design, to choose between common carriage or private trucking, to increase or decrease inventories, to determine the profitability of customers, to establish profitable customer-service levels, to choose between public and private warehousing, and to determine the number of field warehouses and to what extent the order processing system should be automated. To make these strategic decisions requires knowledge of how costs and revenue will change given the alternatives being considered.

Once a decision has been reached, performance must be evaluated on a routine basis in order to determine: (1) if the system is operating in control and at a level consistent with original profit expectations; and (2) if current operating costs justify an examination of alternative systems. This is referred to as operational decision making. The order processing system can be a primary source of information for both strategic and operational decision making.

An advanced order processing system is capable of providing a wealth of information to various departments within the organization. Terminals for data access can be made available to physical distribution management, production management, and sales/marketing management. The system can provide a wide variety of reports on a regularly scheduled basis as well as status reports upon request. It also can accommodate requests for all current reports as well as a variety of data including customer order history, order status, and market and inventory position.

### Designing the Information System

*Knowing Customer Needs Is the First Step in System Design*

The design of a physical distribution management information system should begin with a survey of customer needs and the determination of standards of performance for meeting these needs. Next, customer needs must be matched with the current abilities of the firm and current operations must be surveyed to identify areas that will require monitoring. It is important at this stage to interview various levels of management in order to determine what strategic and operational decisions are made and what information is needed for decision making and in what form. Table 9–3 illustrates the various types of strategic and operational decisions that must

**TABLE 9-3** Typical Strategic and Operational Decisions by Physical Distribution Function

| Decision Type | Customer Service | Transportation | Warehousing | Order Processing | Inventory |
|---|---|---|---|---|---|
| Strategic | Setting customer service levels | Selecting transportation modes | Determination of number of warehouses and locations | Extent of mechanization | Replenishment systems |
| | | Freight consolidation programs | Extent of warehouse automation | Centralized or decentralized | Safety stock levels |
| | | Common carriers versus private trucking | Public versus private warehousing | | |
| Operational | Service level measurements | Rate freight bills | Picking | Order tracking | Forecasting |
| | | Freight bill auditing | Packing | Order validation | Inventory tracking |
| | | Claims administration | Stores measurement | Credit checking | Carrying-cost measurements |
| | | Vehicle scheduling | Warehouse stock transfer | Invoice reconciliation | Inventory turns |
| | | Rate negotiation | Staffing | Performance measurements | |
| | | Shipment planning | Warehouse layout and design | | |
| | | Rail-car management | Selection of materials handling equipment | | |
| | | Shipment routing and scheduling | Performance measurements | | |

**TABLE 9-3** (*continued*)

| Decision Type | Customer Service | Transportation | Warehousing | Order Processing | Inventory |
|---|---|---|---|---|---|
| | | Carrier selection | | | |
| | | Performance measurements | | | |

Source: American Telephone and Telegraph Company, *Business Marketing*, Market Management Division, 1981.

Need for a Common Data Base

be made by management within each of the functions of physical distribution.

The next stage is to survey current data-processing capabilities to determine what changes must be made. Finally, common data files must be created and management reports designed considering the costs and benefits of each. Figure 9–6 identifies the basic features of an integrated information system. A good system design must support the management uses previously described and must have the capability of moving information from locations where it is collected to the appropriate levels of management. Telephones, teletypewriters, personal conversations, and computer-to-computer linkups are just a few of the ways that information can be transferred. In addition to information processing, the computerized information system must have a storage capability in order to hold information until it is required for decision making.

Sources of Data

Data for a physical distribution management information system can come from many sources. The most significant sources of data for the common data base (see Figure 9–6) are (1) the order processing system, (2) company records, (3) industry data, and (4) management data.

The *order processing system* is capable of providing data such as customer locations, items demanded, revenue by customer and item, sales patterns (when items are ordered), order size, and salesperson.

*Company records* can be used to provide manufacturing and distribution cost information, cost of capital, amount spent on various items such as insurance, taxes, obsolescence and damage, and company resources.

*Industry data* can be obtained from trade and professional organizations. Statistics on competitors and their relative market shares can be purchased from firms such as Nielsen. Professional journals and trade publications may report on surveys of current practice as well as research projects and are, therefore, a useful source of data. Also statistics compiled by the federal government may be of significant value since they report on such things as population shifts, inventory levels, housing starts, and consumer-credit expenditures.

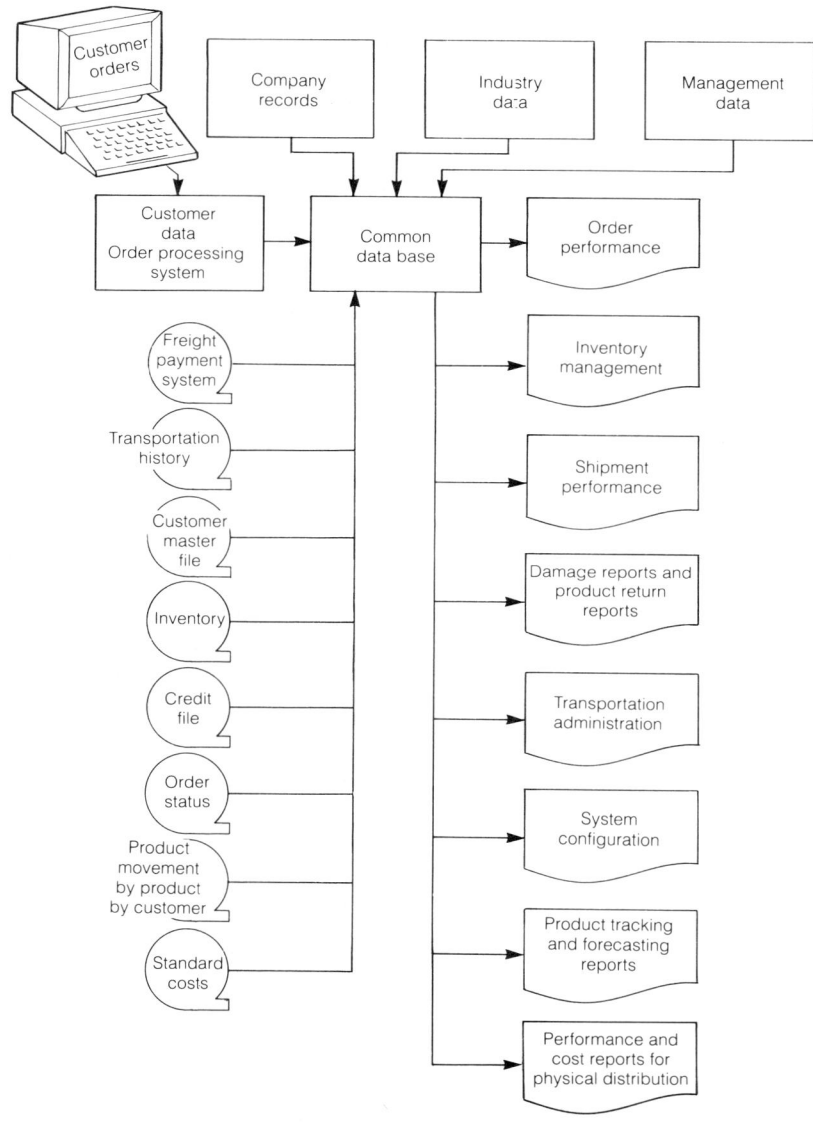

**FIGURE 9-6** A Physical Distribution Information System

Source: American Telephone and Telegraph Company, *Business Marketing*, Market Management Division, 1981.

*Management* also can provide the computerized data base with useful input such as likely competitive reactions, future trends in sales, government policy, availability of supplies, and the probable success of alternative strategies.

The data base usually will contain computerized data files such as the freight payment system, transportation history, inventory status, open or-

**Capabilities of a Computerized Information System**

ders, deleted orders, and standard costs for various physical distribution activities as well as for marketing and manufacturing.

The computerized information system must be capable of (1) data retrieval, (2) data processing, (3) data analysis, and (4) report generation.

*Data retrieval* is the capability of recalling data such as a freight rate, a standard warehousing cost, or the current status of a customer order. Basically, the data are still in their raw form and the computerized records allow fast and convenient access to the information.

*Data processing* is the capability to transform the data, by relatively simple and straightforward conversion to a more useful form. Examples of data processing capability include preparation of warehousing picking instructions, preparation of a bill of lading, and printing a purchase order.

*Data analysis* refers to taking the data from orders and providing management with information for strategic and operational decision making. A number of mathematical and statistical models are available to aid the firm's management including linear programming and simulation models. Linear programming is probably the most widely used strategic and operational planning tool in physical distribution management. It is an optimization technique that subjects various possible solutions to constraints that are identified by management. Simulation is a technique used to model a situation so that management can determine how the system's performance is likely to change if various alternative strategies are chosen. The model is tested using known facts. Although simulation does not provide an optimal solution the technique allows management to determine satisfactory or acceptable solutions from a range of alternatives. A number of simulation models are available for purchase if the firm does not have the resources to develop its own. One of the most popular canned packages is a version of the LREPS model, a dynamic multiecheloned simulation model, developed at Michigan State University in the early 1970s and funded by Johnson & Johnson and Whirlpool Corporation.

The last feature of an information system is *report generation*. Typical reports that can be generated from a physical distribution management information system include: order performance reports; inventory management reports; shipment performance reports; damage reports; transportation administration reports; system configuration reports which may contain the results of data analysis from mathematical and statistical models; and cost reports for physical distribution.

## A DISTRIBUTION DATA BASE FOR DECISION MAKING

**The Modular Data Base Concept**

One of the most promising data base systems for generating distribution cost information and profit contribution performance reports is the modular data base concept (see Figure 9–7).[10] This is a central storage system where source documents such as invoices, transportation bills, and other expenses and revenue items, are fed into a data base in coded form.

---

[10] See Frank H. Mossman, Paul M. Fischer, and W. J. E. Crissy, "New Approaches to Analyzing Marketing Profitability," *Journal of Marketing* 38 (April 1974): 43–48.

**FIGURE 9-7** A Modular Data-Base System for Reporting Cost and Revenue Flows

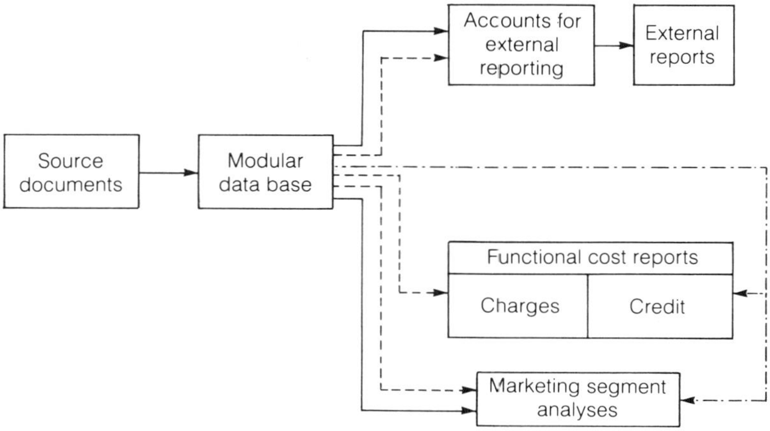

```
                                    ┌──────────┐   ┌──────────┐
                                ┌──→│Accounts for│──→│ External │
                                │   │ external  │   │ reports  │
                                │   │ reporting │   │          │
                                │   └──────────┘   └──────────┘
┌──────────┐    ┌──────────┐    │
│  Source  │───→│ Modular  │────┤
│documents │    │data base │    │
└──────────┘    └──────────┘    │   ┌─────────────────────────┐
                                │   │ Functional cost reports │
                                ├──→│  ┌────────┐┌────────┐   │←──
                                │   │  │Charges ││ Credit │   │
                                │   │  └────────┘└────────┘   │
                                │   └─────────────────────────┘
                                │   ┌──────────────┐
                                └──→│Marketing segment│←──
                                    │   analyses   │
                                    └──────────────┘
```

Revenue flow ——————
Actual recorded cost flow - - - - - -
Standard estimated cost applied to actual activity — · — · — · —

Source: Frank H. Mossman, Paul M. Fischer, and W. J. E. Crissy, "New Approaches to Analyzing Marketing Profitability," *Journal of Marketing* 38 (April 1974): 45.

Inputs can be coded at the lowest possible level of aggregation according to function, subfunction, territory, product, salesperson, channel of distribution, revenue, or expense just to name a few. For example, the information that may be recorded by customer order is shown in Table 9-4. The system is capable of filing large amounts of data and allows rapid aggregation and retrieval of various modules of information for decision making or external reporting. The modular data base combined with standard costs is capable of generating both functional cost reports and segment contribution reports. The system works by charging functions, such as warehousing and transportation, with actual costs which are then compared to predetermined standards. Individual segments such as customers or products are credited with segment revenues and charged the standard cost plus controllable variances.

The approach will be illustrated using a channels of distribution example.[11] In order to monitor the contribution from selling to department stores, grocery chains, drug stores, and discount stores, the accounting system must be able to provide revenue data by channel (which requires summing the revenues of all products sold per channel location) as well as the manufacturing, distribution, and marketing costs associated with the sales to the channel.

The first step is to determine the variable costs of goods manufactured. For those firms on a direct-costing system for internal reporting, this infor-

---

[11] This example is adapted from Douglas M. Lambert and Howard M. Armitage, "An Information System for Effective Channel Management," *MSU Business Topics*, Autumn 1979, pp. 13-22.

**TABLE 9-4** Information that May Be Recorded in the Modular Data Base by Customer Order

*Customer Order Data*
Customer number
Customer name
Order number
Previous order number
Customer order number
Customer billing address
Customer shipping address
Customer order date
Requested shipping date
Ship date
Date, time, and operator
Priority code
Salesperson number
Territory
Region
Partial ship back-order number
Credit limit
Credit outstanding
Prepaid/collect freight
Terms
Instruction—shipping—product substitution
Quantity—product number—price
Packing and shipping instructions
Carrier
Bill of lading number

mation is already available. For those which include all overhead costs (fixed and variable) as product costs, the fixed costs must be removed. The marketing and physical distribution cost associated with warehousing, transportation, order processing, inventory, accounts receivable, and sales commissions must be attached to each channel of distribution. Finally assignable nonvariable costs such as sales promotion, advertising, and bad debts are identified by the specific channel in which they were incurred. It should be emphasized that only those assignable nonvariable costs that would be incurred or eliminated by adding or dropping a channel should be included.

Referring to the specific example illustrated in Table 9-5, traditional accounting data might reveal that a profit of $2 million has been earned on sales of $43.5 million. While management knows that this profit is not adequate, traditional accounting leaves few, if any, clues with regard to the specific problem. However, profitability analysis by type of account using a contribution approach may be used to diagnose areas where performance is inadequate. In this example, sales to drugstores were the largest of the four channels used by the manufacturer, but the segment controllable margin-to-sales ratio was the lowest. The segment controllable margin-to-sales ratio was almost one half that of the third most profitable segment and less than one half that of the most profitable segment. Nevertheless, the

**TABLE 9–5** Profitability by Type of Account—a Contribution Approach ($000)

|  | Total Company | Department stores | Grocery chains | Drug stores | Discount stores |
|---|---|---|---|---|---|
| Sales | $43,500 | $6,500 | $11,000 | $20,000 | $6,000 |
| Less discounts, returns and allowances | 3,500 | 500 | 1,000 | 2,000 | — |
| Net sales | 40,000 | 6,000 | 10,000 | 18,000 | 6,000 |
| Cost of goods sold* | 20,000 | 3,000 | 5,000 | 9,000 | 3,000 |
| Manufacturing contribution | 20,000 | 3,000 | 5,000 | 9,000 | 3,000 |
| Variable selling and distribution costs: |  |  |  |  |  |
| Sales commissions | 800 | 120 | 200 | 360 | 120 |
| Transportation costs | 2,500 | 250 | 225 | 1,795 | 230 |
| Warehouse handling | 600 | 150 | — | 450 | — |
| Order processing costs | 400 | 60 | 25 | 280 | 35 |
| Charge for investment in accounts receivable | 700 | 20 | 50 | 615 | 15 |
| Contribution margin | 15,000 | 2,400 | 4,500 | 5,500 | 2,600 |
| Assignable nonvariable costs (costs incurred specifically for the segment during the period) |  |  |  |  |  |
| Sales promotion | 750 | 100 | 150 | 200 | 300 |
| Advertising | 500 | — | — | 500 | — |
| Bad debts | 300 | — | — | 300 | — |
| Display racks | 200 | — | — | 200 | — |
| Inventory carrying costs | 1,250 | 200 | 150 | 800 | 100 |
| Segment controllable margin | $12,000 | $2,100 | $4,200 | $ 3,500 | $2,200 |
| Segment controllable margin-to-sales ratio | 27.6% | 32.3% | 38.2% | 17.5% | 36.7% |

Note: This approach could be modified to include a charge for the assets employed by each of the segments as well as a deduction for the change in market value of these assets. The result would be referred to as the net segment margin (residual income).
* Variable manufacturing costs.

segment controllable margin at $3.5 million is still substantial and it is doubtful that elimination of drugstores would be a wise decision. For this reason a product-channel matrix might be generated to determine the impact of product mix on channel profitability. If this analysis showed that product mix was not the source of the problem, then a customer-channel matrix might reveal that small drugstore accounts are the least profitable, medium-sized drug accounts are moderately profitable, and drug chains have a segment controllable margin-to-sales ratio almost as large as that of department stores.

Using this information and cost trade-off analysis, management could determine potential channel profitability if small and medium drugstore accounts were served by either drug wholesalers or by strategically located field warehouses. The alternative that would lead to the greatest improvement in corporate profitability would be selected, resulting in the addition of a new channel of distribution. A framework for performing this analysis incorporating marketing cost trade-offs is illustrated in Table 9–6.

Poor performance by a channel does not necessarily mean the channel

**TABLE 9–6** How Manufacturers Can Calculate the Impact of Using a Wholesaler Costs Associated with Manufacturer Selling Direct to Retailers

| | | |
|---|---|---|
| Costs of direct selling versus using an intermediary .......... | | $_____ |
| Additional promotional expenses associated with direct sales ............................................. | | _____ |
| Customer service costs | | |
|    Cost of sales lost at retail level due to stockouts resulting from long and/or erratic lead time. .............. | $_____ | |
|    Return foregone on capital invested in accounts receivable. ............................................ | _____ | |
|    Credit losses associated with accounts receivable. ......... | _____ | _____ |
| Order filling costs | | |
|    Cost of dealing with many customers. .................... | $_____ | |
|    Cost of filling small orders. .............................. | _____ | |
|    Cost of filling frequent orders. ........................... | _____ | _____ |
| Inventory carrying costs | | |
|    Return foregone on capital invested in inventory. ........... | $_____ | |
|    Insurance paid on inventory. ............................. | _____ | |
|    Taxes paid on inventory. ................................ | _____ | |
|    Storage costs. .......................................... | _____ | |
|    Cost of obsolescence. .................................. | _____ | |
|    Cost of damaged product. ............................... | _____ | |
|    Cost of pilferage. ....................................... | _____ | |
|    Transshipment costs. ................................... | _____ | _____ |
| Warehousing costs | | |
|    Return foregone on capital invested in field warehouses (if owned). ........................................... | $_____ | |
|    Operating expenses associated with such warehouses. ..... | _____ | _____ |
| Transportation costs | | |
|    Cost of processing shipping documents (for many LTL shipments). ...................................... | $_____ | |
|    Cost of processing freight claims. ........................ | _____ | |
|    Excessive freight costs (associated with LTL shipments) .... | _____ | _____ |
| General and administrative | | |
|    Reduction in management costs associated with holding and supervising inventory. ...................... | | _____ |
| Total annual cost of direct selling ........................... | | $_____ |
|    Less volume discounts to wholesaler ..................... | | _____ |
| Total amount saved by using a wholesaler .................. | | $_____ |

Source: Adapted from Douglas M. Lambert and Bernard J. LaLonde, "The Economics of Using a Frozen Food Distributor," *Frozen Food Factbook, 1975* (Hershey, Pa.: National Frozen Food Association, 1974), p. 60.

should be eliminated. Factors such as the percentage of potential market being reached by the channel, the stage of the product life cycle of the products involved, and the stage in the life cycle of the institutions involved also deserve consideration. In addition, elimination of an unprofitable channel may not be the only viable solution for the firm striving to improve corporate profitability. Changing the physical distribution system or shifting some of the business to another channel, as in the previous example, may be the most desirable solution. Also, within a channel a customer-product contribution matrix may be used to isolate customers or products as candidates for elimination or revitalization.

In addition to being able to evaluate the profitability of individual customers, product lines, territories, and/or channels of distribution, the data base permits the user to simulate trade-off decisions and determine the effect of proposed system changes on total cost. The report generating capabilities of the modular data base are summarized in Figure 9–8. In

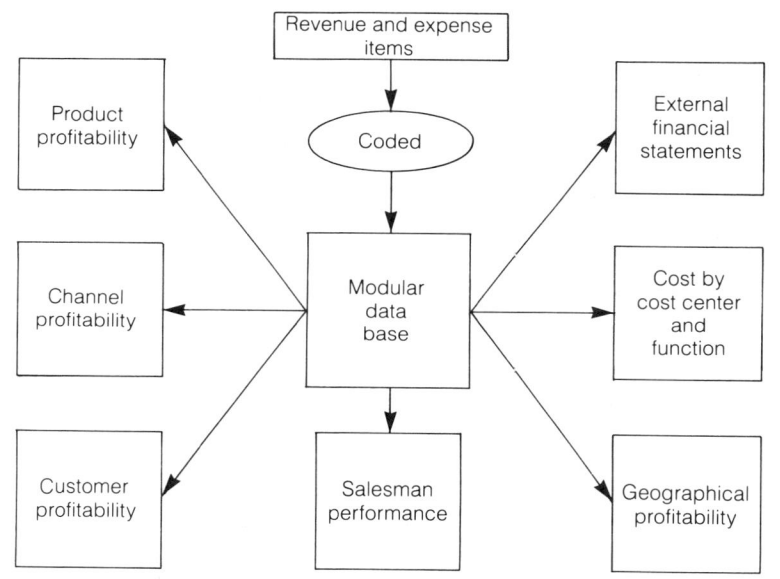

**FIGURE 9-8** Report Generating Capabilities of the Modular Data Base

order to implement the modular data base approach, it is necessary to collect the raw distribution cost data and break them down into fixed variable and direct-indirect components. In other words, the data must be sufficiently refined to permit the formulation of meaningful modules. Full implementation of the integrated physical distribution management concept and knowledgeable decision making in the areas of strategic and operational planning require a sophisticated management information system.

## FINANCIAL CONSIDERATIONS

Cost Justification for an Advanced Order Processing System

Of course it will be necessary to justify an advanced order processing system in terms of a cost/benefit analysis. The cost of developing the system, start-up costs, can be justified by discounting the improvement in cash flows associated with the new system and comparing them to the initial investment. In most cases, cash flow will improve by changing to an advanced order processing system, if the volume of orders processed is large. However, in smaller operations this may not be true if the proposed system is more than the company needs.

In any case, the difference in cash flows that result from the existing and proposed systems can be calculated using the framework shown in Figure 9–9. It is important, when the cash flow is calculated, to include in your analysis only those costs that will change with the system change. Usually, the most significant cost differences will occur in the order processing, inventory, transportation, and warehousing cost components.

Figure 9–10 illustrates how an advanced order processing system can

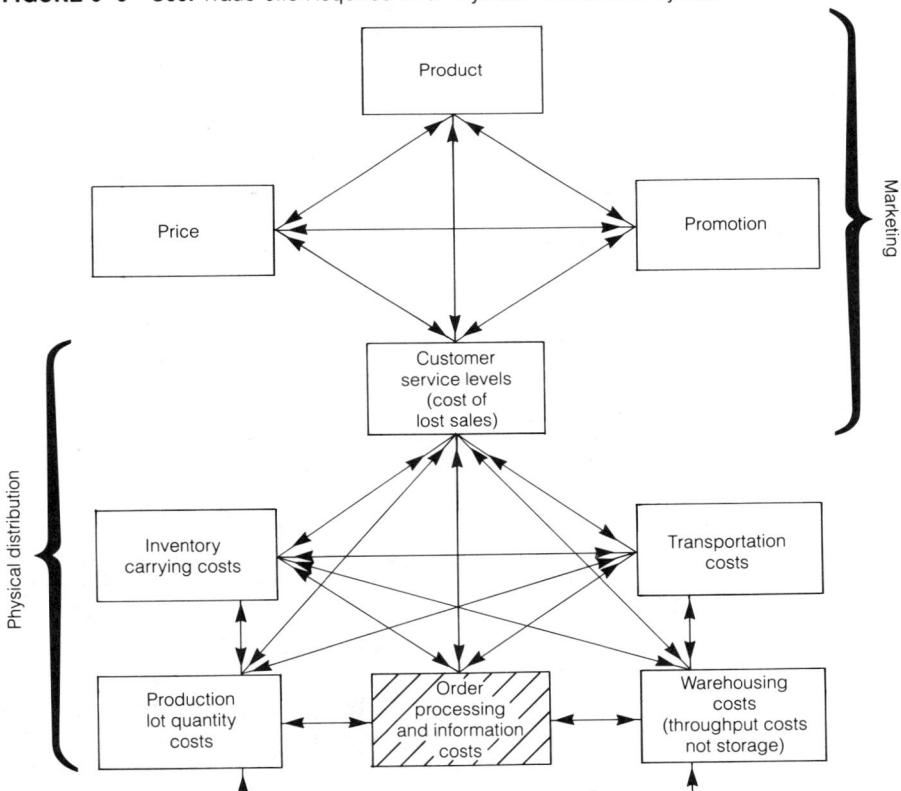

**FIGURE 9–9** Cost Trade-offs Required in a Physical Distribution System

Objective: Minimize total costs.

Total costs = Transportation costs + Warehousing costs
  + Order processing and information costs + Production lot quantity costs
  + Inventory carrying costs + Cost of lost sales

Source: Adapted from Douglas M. Lambert, *The Development of an Inventory Costing Methodology: A Study of the Costs Associated with Holding Inventory* (Chicago, The National Council of Physical Distribution Management, 1976), p. 7.

**FIGURE 9–10** Total Order Cycle with Variability Both before and after Implementing an Advanced Order Processing System

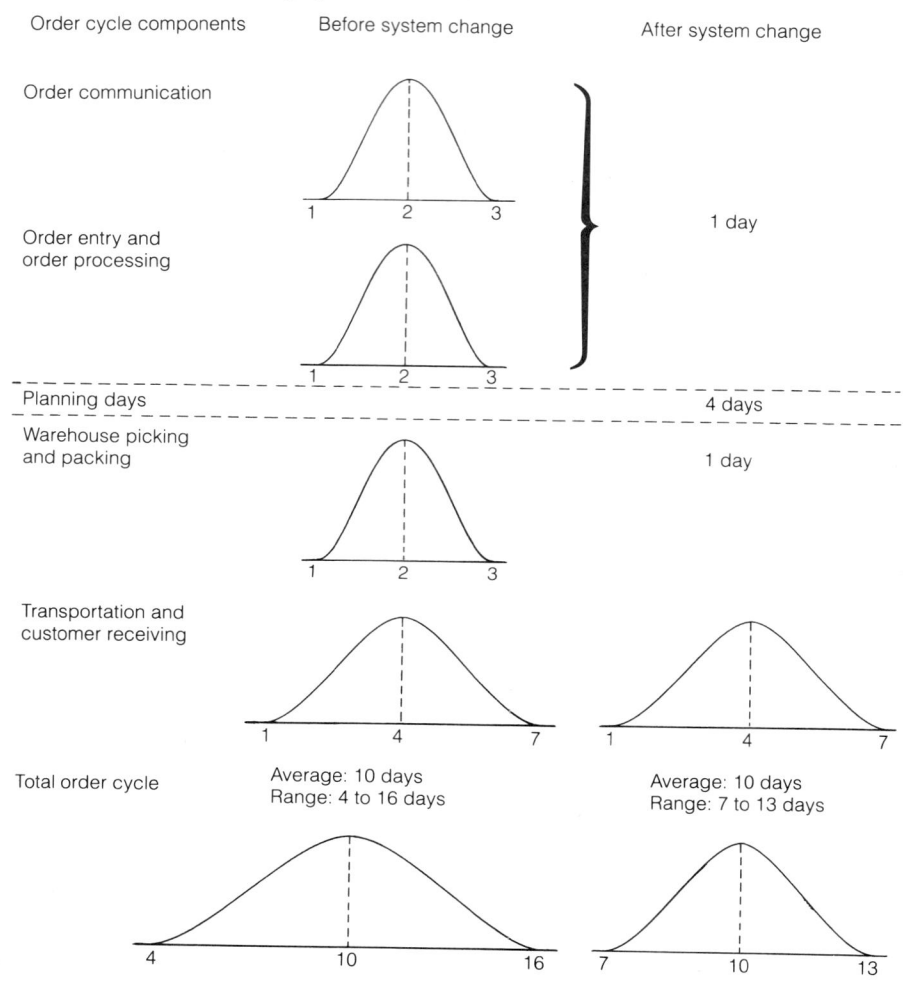

| Order cycle components | Before system change | After system change |
|---|---|---|
| Order communication | (distribution: 1, 2, 3) | 1 day |
| Order entry and order processing | (distribution: 1, 2, 3) | |
| Planning days | | 4 days |
| Warehouse picking and packing | (distribution: 1, 2, 3) | 1 day |
| Transportation and customer receiving | (distribution: 1, 4, 7) | (distribution: 1, 4, 7) |
| Total order cycle | Average: 10 days<br>Range: 4 to 16 days<br>(distribution: 4, 10, 16) | Average: 10 days<br>Range: 7 to 13 days<br>(distribution: 7, 10, 13) |

free up time for planning. By reducing order communication, order entry and order processing time from an average of four days to one day, on the average three days are made available for planning. This planning time means that sales forecasting and production scheduling receive sales information three days sooner, as do the managers of physical distribution activities such as warehousing, transportation, and inventory management. The advance notice at field warehouses allows the more productive allocation of orders to level volume. In any case it is possible to plan so that all orders are shipped from warehouse locations after the sixth day. In essence, then, four days in total are available for planning warehouse picking and packing, transportation consolidations, and reduced levels of safety stock.

This of course assumes that the manufacturer's customers find a 10-day order cycle acceptable and a reduction in order cycle is not given to them. If transportation and customer receiving is the only variability remaining in the order cycle, variability in the total order cycle to the customer can be reduced from 6 days, when the order cycle ranged from 4 to 16 days, to 3 days, with the order cycle ranging from 7 to 10 days. This improvement in order cycle consistency will allow the manufacturer's customers to cut their safety stocks by one half. Consequently, the entire channel of distribution will become more efficient and realize cost savings as a result of the advanced order processing application. In addition, the improved customer service may result in increased sales and market share for the manufacturer.

Generally, the fixed costs associated with an advanced order processing system will be higher than those incurred by a manual system. However, the variable costs per order will be significantly less with the advanced system. This type of cost analysis will be expanded in Chapter 11 which deals specifically with the calculation of physical distribution cost savings.

## SUMMARY

In this chapter you were shown how the order processing system can directly influence performance of the physical distribution function. You were also shown how order processing systems can be used to improve customer communications and total order-cycle time, and/or lead to substantial inventory reductions as well as transportation efficiencies. Information is vital for the planning and control of physical distribution systems and you were shown how the order processing system can form the basis of a physical distribution information system.

Modern computer technology and communication systems make it possible for management to have the information required for strategic and operational planning of the physical distribution function. You were shown how the order processing system can significantly improve the quality and quantity of distribution information for decision making. The next chapter will deal with the materials management function, its interrelationship with physical distribution management, and specific strategies and techniques for management of materials flow.

## QUESTIONS AND PROBLEMS

1. What do wholesalers and retailers perceive to be the order cycle provided to them by a manufacturer?

2. Explain the impact of order cycle variability on the inventory levels of wholesalers and retailers.

3. How is physical distribution performance affected by the order processing system used?

4. What are the primary advantages associated with the implementation of an integrated and automated order processing system?

5. How does the order processing system form the foundation of the physical distribution management information system?
6. How is the physical distribution information system used to support planning of distribution operations?
7. What are the primary advantages of the modular data base system?
8. Show the impact that implementation of an automated order processing system would have on a manufacturer's return on investment given the following information:
    a. After tax net profit is $2 million.
    b. Return on assets is currently 10 percent.
    c. With the current system customer orders are mailed, sales people collect them and either hand carry them to sales offices where they are telephoned or mailed to headquarters, or sales people telephone or mail orders directly to headquarters.
    d. With the proposed order processing system, customers will telephone orders to inside sales people (customer-service representatives) equipped with CRTs, who immediately input the order.
    e. The proposed order processing system will provide management with four additional planning days and eliminate two days of variability in the order cycle.
    f. The planning time made available by the proposed order processing system will enable management to: reduce inventories by $1,000,000; achieve $250,000 in transportation savings as a result of consolidations; and reduce handling charges in public warehouses by $50,000 as a result of direct plant-to-customer shipments.
    g. The proposed system will increase order processing costs by $125,000 per year.
    h. The noncost-of-money components of inventory carrying cost are 5 percent of the inventory value.
    i. The company is experiencing capital rationing and could achieve a 20 percent after-tax rate of return on additional capital if it was available.
9. Explain how the proposed order processing system described in question 8 would impact the customer service levels provided by the manufacturer.

# 10 Materials Management

Introduction

**Scope of Materials Management Activities**
   Purchasing and Procurement
      Supplier Selection and Evaluation
      Quality Control
      Forward Buying
   Production Control
   Inbound Traffic and Transportation
   Warehousing and Storage
   MIS Control
   Inventory Planning and Control
   Salvage and Scrap Disposal

**Administration and Control of Materials Management**
   Materials Requirements Planning (MRP)

**Summary**

   Appendix:   Evaluating Suppliers in a Typical Manufacturing Firm

**Objectives of this chapter:**

To show how materials management and physical distribution management are interrelated

To show how to effectively manage materials flow in a manufacturing environment

To examine specific management strategies and techniques for materials management

## INTRODUCTION

As defined in this book, physical distribution management is concerned with the efficient flow of raw materials, in-process inventory, and finished goods from point-of-origin to point-of-consumption. An integral part of that flow, referred to as materials management, encompasses the administration of raw materials and in-process inventory. In a formal sense, materials management can be defined as follows: "Materials management is the single-manager organization concept embracing the planning, organizing, motivating, and controlling of all those activities and personnel principally concerned with the flow of materials into an organization."[1]

The importance of materials management to the total physical distribution process cannot be overstressed. Although materials management does not directly interface with the final customer, the degree to which raw materials, component parts, and subassemblies are made available to the production process ultimately determines the availability of products to the customer. The decisions, good or bad, made in the materials management portion of the physical distribution process will have a direct effect on the level of customer service offered, the ability of the firm to compete with other companies, and the level of sales and profits achieved in the market.

It is the availability of finished products that enables the firm to undertake and complete distribution activities. Without efficient and effective management of inbound materials flow, the manufacturing process cannot produce products at the desired price and/or when they are required for distribution to the firm's customers. It is essential that the physical distribution manager understand the role of materials management and its impact on the company's cost/service mix. The role of materials management in physical distribution is shown in Figure 10–1. The left side of the figure represents the operational aspects of physical distribution and includes the materials management activity as well as goods-in-process transfers and final goods distribution. The solid arrows indicate product and materials flow from point-of-origin to point-of-consumption. The right side of Figure 10–1 illustrates the coordination aspect of physical distribution. Coordination is represented by the broken-lined arrows and are the information flows which take place within the distribution organization.[2]

---

[1] Harold E. Fearon, "Materials Management: A Synthesis and Current View," *Journal of Purchasing* 9, no. 1 (February 1973): 33.

[2] Donald F. Bowersox, *Logistical Management*, 2d ed. (New York: MacMillan, 1978), pp. 17–18.

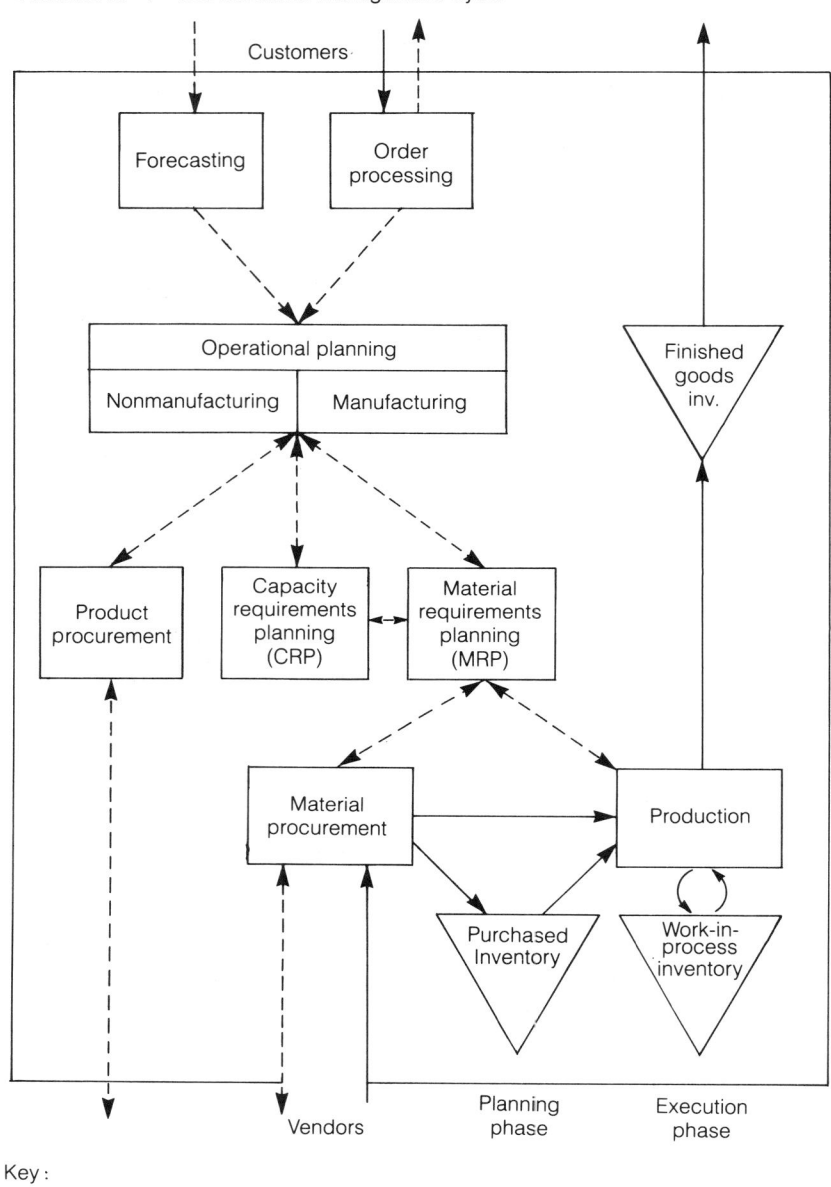

**FIGURE 10-1** The Materials Management Cycle

Source: Steven A. Melnyk, Graduate School of Business Administration, Michigan State University. Adapted with permission of Macmillan Publishing Company, Inc. from *Logistical Management*, 2d ed. by Donald J. Bowersox. Copyright © 1978 by Donald J. Bowersox.

In this chapter, the various components of materials management will be identified. You will be shown how to effectively manage materials flow within a manufacturing environment. Finally, we will examine specific management strategies and techniques used in the planning, implementation, and control of materials management.

## SCOPE OF MATERIALS MANAGEMENT ACTIVITIES

Typically, materials management is comprised of four basic activities:

*Four Basic Activities of Materials Management*

1. Anticipating materials requirements.
2. Sourcing and obtaining materials.
3. Introducing materials into the organization.
4. Monitoring the status of materials as a current asset.[3]

Figure 10−2 identifies some of the functions performed by materials managers.

**FIGURE 10-2**  Materials Managers Wear Many Hats

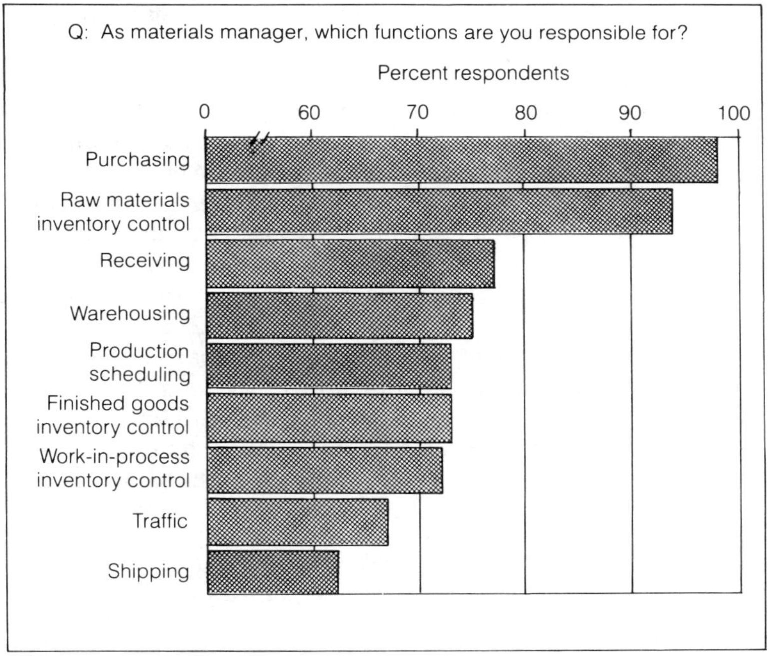

Q: As materials manager, which functions are you responsible for?

Percent respondents

- Purchasing
- Raw materials inventory control
- Receiving
- Warehousing
- Production scheduling
- Finished goods inventory control
- Work-in-process inventory control
- Traffic
- Shipping

Source: Rebecca Lipman, "Buyers' Goals Match Materials Managers'," *Purchasing*, August 8, 1979, p. 39. Reprinted with permission by *Purchasing Magazine*. Copyright © Cahners Publishing Co.

The definition of materials management used in this chapter views the activity as an organizational system with the various function as subsystems. "It recognizes that the individual subsystems are all interrelated and

---

[3] Fearon, "Materials Management: A Synthesis and Current View," p. 33.

interactive. The interfaces between the subsystems must be approached and regulated in view of overall materials (and firm) objectives, which might result in suboptimization for the firm as a whole."[4] This is nothing more than implementing the "integrated physical distribution management concept."

Materials management encompasses a variety of distribution activities. In a manner similar to the administration of finished-goods distribution, the materials manager must be concerned with inventory control, warehousing and storage, order processing, transportation, and almost every other distribution activity. The primary differences between the materials management process and the process which distributes finished goods are that the items being handled are now raw materials, component parts, and subassemblies, and the recipient of the distribution effort is the production or manufacturing group rather than the final customer.

Integral aspects of materials management include purchasing and procurement, production control, in-bound traffic and transportation, warehousing and storage, MIS control, inventory planning and control, and salvage and scrap disposal. Within the purchasing and procurement activity is included supplier selection and evaluation, quality control, and forward buying.

**Purchasing and Procurement**

The acquisition of materials has long been an important aspect of materials management and will continue to be in the future. "The rapidly changing supply scene, with cycles of abundance and shortages, varying prices, lead times, and availabilities, provides a continuing challenge to those organizations wishing to obtain a maximum contribution from this area."[5]

Purchasing and procurement are terms often used interchangeably although they do differ in scope. Purchasing generally refers to the actual buying of materials and those activities associated with the buying process. Procurement is broader in scope and includes purchasing, traffic, warehousing, and receiving inbound materials.

"The purchasing decision maker might be likened to a juggler, attempting to keep several balls in the air at the same time, for the purchaser must achieve several goals simultaneously. . . ."[6] The goals of purchasing are to:

Goals of Purchasing

1. Provide an uninterrupted flow of materials, supplies, and services required to operate the organization.
2. Keep inventory investment and loss at a minimum.
3. Maintain adequate quality standards.
4. Find or develop quality vendors.
5. Standardize, where possible, the items bought.

---
[4] Ibid.

[5] Michiel R. Leenders, Harold E. Fearon, and Wilbur B. England, *Purchasing and Materials Management*, 7th ed. (Homewood, Ill.: Richard D. Irwin, 1980), p. 1.

[6] Ibid., p. 27.

6. Purchase required items and services at lowest ultimate price.
7. Maintain the organization's competitive position.
8. Achieve harmonious, productive working relationships with other departments within the organization.
9. Accomplish the purchasing objectives at the lowest possible level of administrative costs.[7]

Among the primary purchasing activities which influence the ability of the firm to achieve its objectives are supplier selection and evaluation (sourcing), quality control, and forward buying.

*Supplier selection and evaluation.* In the acquisition process, perhaps the most important activity is selecting the best supplier from among a number of vendors that can supply the needed materials. The buying process is complex because of the variety of factors which must be considered when making such a decision. The process includes both decision makers and decision influencers, which combine together to form the decision-making unit (DMU). Also, the process is multistage and includes the following steps:

Selecting a Supplier

1. Identify needs.
2. Establish specifications.
3. Search for alternatives.
4. Establish contact.
5. Set purchase and usage criteria.
6. Evaluate alternative buying actions.
7. Determine budget availability.
8. Evaluate specific alternatives.
9. Negotiate with suppliers.
10. Buy.
11. Use.
12. Conduct postpurchase evaluation.[8]

A particular firm may not have to go through all 12 stages of the buying process unless the decision is a totally new one. If the decision has been made before (e.g., routine buying) then many of the steps can be bypassed.

In a study of purchasing managers, Philip White (1978) identified 16 variables which were involved in the purchasing decision. Six of the variables could be classified into one group because each was concerned with product characteristics:

1. Product reliability.
2. Ease of maintenance.
3. Ease of operation or use.
4. Price.
5. Technical specifications.
6. Training time required.

---

[7] Ibid., pp. 27–29.

[8] Yoram Wind, "The Boundaries of Buying Decision Centers," *Journal of Purchasing and Materials Management,* 14, no. 2 (Summer 1978), p. 24.

The remaining 10 variables related to supplier characteristics:

7. Confidence in the sales representative.
8. Convenience of placing the order.
9. Experience with the supplier in analogous situations.
10. Financing terms.
11. Overall reputation of the supplier.
12. Reliability of delivery date promised.
13. Sales service expected after date of purchase.
14. Supplier's flexibility in adjusting to the buying company's needs.
15. Technical service offered.
16. Training offered by the supplier.[9]

White further identified six major product categories which were purchased by most companies: (1) component parts, (2) raw materials, (3) process materials, (4) accessory equipment, (5) major equipment, and (6) operating supplies.[10] Each product category could be purchased in any of four buying situations:

*Four Types of Buying Situations*

1. *Routine order situations* —includes situations where the product has been purchased many times previously and where order routines or procedures are generally established.
2. *Procedural-problem situations* —includes purchases which are not routine and which may require that employees learn how to use the product.
3. *Performance-problem situations* —includes nonroutine purchases of products which are designed to be substitutes for current products but which must be tested for performance.
4. *Political-problem situations* —includes nonroutine purchases of products whose use would affect many departments of the company, thus, a number of individuals throughout the firm will be involved in the decision process.[11]

When White asked purchasing managers to rank each of the 16 evaluation criteria along the dimensions of product category and buying situation, the results shown in Table 10-1 were obtained. In general, the factors of quality, price, delivery, and service were consistently rated as important in almost every product category/buying situation combination. In most firms, the evaluation process probably takes place informally, although some companies have established formal, written procedures for the purchasing process.

The evaluation process must be a continuous purchasing task.

Some procurement executives have attempted to establish formal vendor rating procedures as an aid in selecting suppliers. Inasmuch as price can usually be

---

[9] Phillip D. White, "Decision Making in the Purchasing Process: A Report," *AMA Management Briefing* (New York: American Management Association, 1978), p. 12.

[10] Ibid., pp. 13-14.

[11] Reprinted by permission of the publisher from *Decision Making in the Purchasing Process: A Report*, An AMA Management Briefing, by Phillip D. White, © 1978 by AMACOM, a division of American Management Associations, pp. 15-17. All rights reserved.

**TABLE 10-1** A Matrix for Rating Product and Supplier Attributes by Buying Situation and Product Category

|  | Routine Order Situations | Procedural Problem Situations | Performance Problem Situations | Political Problem Situations |
|---|---|---|---|---|
| Component parts | 1. Reliability of delivery<br>2. Price<br>3. Past experience<br>4. Overall supplier reputation<br>5. Ease of operation or use<br>6. Ease of maintenance | 1. Ease of operation or use<br>2. Reliability of delivery<br>3. Training offered<br>4. Training time required<br>5. Technical service offered<br>6. Technical specifications | 1. Ordering convenience<br>2. Supplier flexibility<br>3. Ease of operation or use<br>4. Technical service offered<br>5. Training offered<br>6. Financing terms | 1. Sales Service<br>2. Overall supplier reputation<br>3. Reliability of delivery<br>4. Training offered<br>5. Ease of maintenance<br>6. Ordering convenience |
| Raw materials | 1. Reliability of delivery<br>2. Price<br>3. Product reliability<br>4. Past experience<br>5. Overall supplier reputation<br>6. Technical specifications | 1. Technical Service offered<br>2. Product reliability<br>3. Training offered<br>4. Technical specifications<br>5. Overall supplier reputation | 1. Technical Service offered<br>2. Product reliability<br>3. Ease of operation or use<br>4. Technical specifications<br>5. Reliability of delivery<br>6. Training offered | 1. Product reliability<br>2. Reliability of delivery<br>3. Technical specifications<br>4. Technical service offered<br>5. Price<br>6. Overall supplier reputation |
| Process materials | 1. Reliability of delivery<br>2. Price<br>3. Overall supplier reputation<br>4. Past experience<br>5. Product reliability<br>6. Ease of operation or use | 1. Training offered<br>2. Ease of operation or use<br>3. Technical service offered<br>4. Technical time required<br>5. Reliability of delivery<br>6. Technical specifications | 1. Ordering convenience<br>2. Ease of operation or use<br>3. Technical service offered<br>4. Supplier flexibility<br>5. Training offered<br>6. Financing terms | 1. Overall supplier reputation<br>2. Sales service<br>3. Training offered<br>4. Ease of maintenance<br>5. Ordering convenience<br>6. Reliability of delivery |
| Accessory equipment | 1. Reliability of delivery<br>2. Price<br>3. Ease of operation or use<br>4. Past experience<br>5. Overall supplier reputation<br>6. Ease of maintenance | 1. Training offered<br>2. Ease of operation or use<br>3. Training time required<br>4. Technical service<br>5. Reliability of delivery<br>6. Product reliability | 1. Supplier flexibility<br>2. Ordering convenience<br>3. Training offered<br>4. Technical specifications<br>5. Ease of operation or use<br>6. Financing terms | 1. Sales service<br>2. Training offered<br>3. Reliability of delivery<br>4. Overall supplier reputation<br>5. Ease of maintenance<br>6. Ordering convenience |
| Major equipment | 1. Reliability of delivery<br>2. Price<br>3. Overall supplier reputation<br>4. Past experience<br>5. Ease of maintenance<br>6. Sales service | 1. Technical service offered<br>2. Training offered<br>3. Overall supplier reputation<br>4. Ease of operation or use<br>5. Technical specifications<br>6. Product reliability | 1. Ease of operation or use<br>2. Technical service offered<br>3. Product reliability<br>4. Technical specifications<br>5. Ease of maintenance<br>6. Overall supplier reputation | 1. Technical service<br>2. Product reliability<br>3. Overall supplier reputation<br>4. Price<br>5. Technical specifications<br>6. Ease of maintenance and ease of operation or use |
| Operating supplies | 1. Reliability of delivery<br>2. Price<br>3. Past experience<br>4. Overall supplier reputation<br>5. Supplier flexibility<br>6. Ease of operation or use | 1. Training offered<br>2. Ease of operation or use<br>3. Technical service offered<br>4. Training time required<br>5. Ease of maintenance<br>6. Product reliability | 1. Product reliability<br>2. Technical service offered<br>3. Ease of operation or use<br>4. Technical specifications<br>5. Reliability of delivery<br>6. Ease of maintenance | 1. Reliability of delivery<br>2. Overall supplier reputation<br>3. Price<br>4. Product reliability<br>5. Ease of operation<br>6. Technical specifications |

Source: Adapted, by permission of the publisher, from *Decision Making in the Purchasing Process: A Report*, AMA Management Briefing, by Phillip D. White, © 1978 by AMACOM, a division of American Management Associations, pp. 20-47. All rights reserved.

determined objectively, if a way can be found to measure quality, delivery, and service, the attempt at rating is usually confined to these three factors.

One method which has been found effective in rating quality is to make a monthly tabulation of the invoices from each supplier and the value of the supplier's materials which were rejected during the month. The latter figure is then divided by the value of the materials shipped, and the resulting percentage indicates the rate of rejection.

Comparison of rejection rates among competing suppliers, or against an average of the rejection rates shows those suppliers who are providing the proper quality.[12]

Evaluating a Supplier

A variety of evaluation procedures are possible and there is no "best" method or approach. The important thing is to make certain that there are some types of procedures that are being used. An example of an evaluation procedure is presented in the Appendix. The materials manager or his/her designate would identify all potential suppliers for the item(s) being procured. The decision maker or evaluator would then develop a list of factors upon which to evaluate each supplier. These factors could be the 16 factors identified by White (and identified earlier) or some other list developed by the company or the evaluator. After determining the evaluation criteria, suppliers should be rated according to how well they are able to satisfy each factor, e.g., product reliability, price, ordering convenience. A five-point scale (1 = Worst rating; 5 = Highest rating) is used in the illustration, but any scale is appropriate. (Note: If more scale points are used, more precision is needed in the evaluation process. However, a large scale allows the decision maker to develop finer distinctions between suppliers.)

After rating suppliers on each factor, the evaluator would determine the importance of the factors to the firm. For example, if product reliability was of paramount importance to the firm, that factor would be given the highest importance rating. If price was important, but not as vital as product reliability, that factor would be assigned a lower importance rating. Any factor which was not important to the firm would be assigned a zero rating.[13]

The next step is to develop a composite measure of the supplier rating on each attribute or factor and the importance of the factors to the firm in the buying situation being undertaken. By multiplying the supplier rating by the factors' importance rating, a weighted score results which provides a measure of supplier/factor importance. The addition of the composite scores for each factor under each supplier provides the evaluation with an overall supplier rating which can be compared with other potential suppliers. The higher the composite score, the better the supplier meets the needs and specifications of the procuring company.

In principle, this kind of analysis is not completely new to purchasing managers. Many decisions involve balancing one type of variable or characteristic

---

[12] Leenders, Fearon, and England, *Materials Management*, p. 229.

[13] Some factors may be of no importance to the firm in one type of buying situation but of moderate or high importance at other times. Therefore, it is necessary that all potential factors be included in the rating form in order to eliminate the need for a new form in each buying situation.

against another. What is new and valuable about this approach, however, is that it makes the process of weighing variables explicit: because it forces us to formalize the important elements of the purchasing decision, it helps us bring our tacit assumptions to the surface and questions our intuitive or habitual priorities.[14]

**Sourcing of Materials in International Markets**

For firms involved in the sourcing of materials from international markets, the supplier-selection process is more difficult. A larger number of firms however, are securing their raw materials, components, and subassemblies from foreign sources primarily because of cost and availability factors. When a company utilizes foreign suppliers it is advantageous to have an understanding of some of the problems associated with international sourcing. Table 10−2 identifies some of the more common problems which a firm should consider *before* engaging in foreign sourcing.

**TABLE 10-2** Sourcing Problems in International Markets

1. Lack of local technological backup
2. License and foreign exchange difficulties
3. Poor service from indigenous supply sources (e.g., poor delivery-schedule performance, quality failure, limited variety)
4. Political instability or risk affecting investment (either with respect to the company itself or potential suppliers)
5. Tariffs and host-government pressure to buy within the country
6. Governmental pressures regarding their own purchasing from the company
7. Necessity for carrying higher inventories
8. Necessity for intensifying goods-inwards inspection activities
9. "Home" derived specifications not available from local supply markets
10. Quality inconsistency with certain imported components
11. Lack of trained local staff, affecting supply-department performance

Source: D. H. Farmer, "Source Decision-Making in the Multi-National Company Environment," *Journal of Purchasing* 8, no. 1 (February 1972): 34–35.

The rewards associated with the proper selection and evaluation of suppliers can be significant. As was seen in Chapter 1 (Figure 1−8), physical distribution can exercise substantial leverage on corporate profitability. Purchasing and materials management activities can have positive effects on the firm's profits. Figure 10−3 shows the dramatic profit leverage that is available from effective purchasing management. In addition, customer service improvements can result because the production or manufacturing process can operate smoothly, without slowdowns or shutdowns. Also, since effective purchasing management results in the acquisition of high-quality materials, there is less likelihood of customer return of finished goods due to product failure.

**Quality Control Is Important in Materials Acquisition**

*Quality control.* Although cost considerations are the most important aspects of materials acquisition, quality control is also vital. The initial pur-

---
[14] White, "Decision Making in the Purchasing Process," p. 11.

**FIGURE 10-3** Relationship of Purchasing to the Firm's Profitability

When purchasing is a high percent of controllable expenditures...

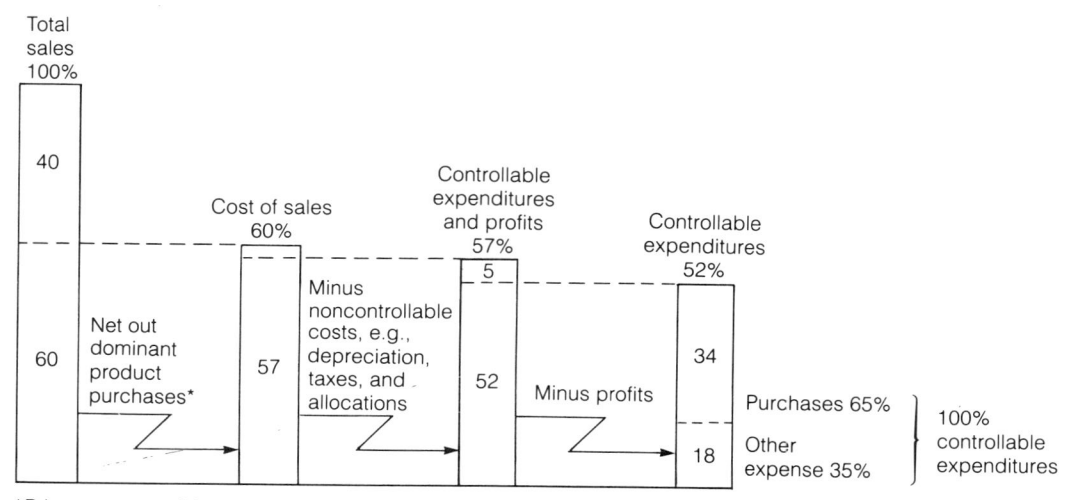

Total sales 100% | 40 / 60 Net out dominant product purchases* | Cost of sales 60% / 57 Minus noncontrollable costs, e.g., depreciation, taxes, and allocations | Controllable expenditures and profits 57% / 5 / 52 Minus profits | Controllable expenditures 52% / 34 / 18 | Purchases 65% / Other expense 35% } 100% controllable expenditures

*Primary commodities of oil, grain, wood products and metals companies are not usually procured by purchasing.

Dramatic profit leverage usually is available

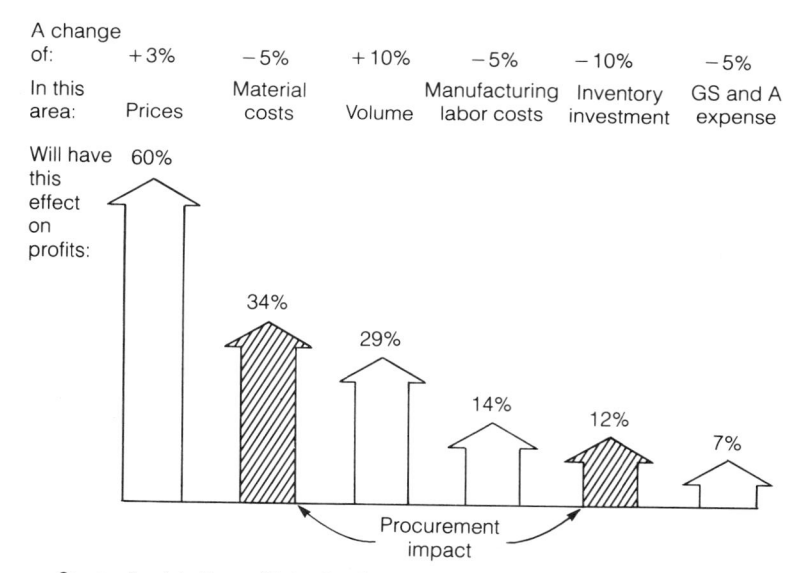

| A change of: | +3% | −5% | +10% | −5% | −10% | −5% |
| In this area: | Prices | Material costs | Volume | Manufacturing labor costs | Inventory investment | GS and A expense |
| Will have this effect on profits: | 60% | 34% | 29% | 14% | 12% | 7% |

Procurement impact

Source: Frank L. Bauer, "Better Purchasing: High Rewards at Low Risk," *Journal of Purchasing and Materials Management,* 12, no. 2 (Summer 1976): 4.

chase price of an item is only one element of the total cost. For example, some items are easier to work with than others and can save production costs. Materials of higher quality may require fewer fabrication processes or have longer life spans, thus resulting in lower overall product costs and/or higher prices for finished products. Some balance must be achieved between the components of the acquisition process; namely, price, cost, and value received.[15]

After the quality level has been determined, usually by manufacturing, it becomes purchasing's responsibility to secure the proper materials. Involved are the correct specifications of quality to suppliers and selection of the vendor which offers the best cost/quality package. Quality level can be specified to suppliers in a variety of ways including:

1. Market grades.
2. Brand or trade names.
3. Commercial standards.
4. Chemical or physical specifications.
5. Performance specifications.
6. Material and method-of-manufacture specifications.
7. Blueprints (engineering drawings).
8. Samples.
9. Quality products list.
10. Combination of above.[16]

It is important that the firm not pay higher prices to obtain materials with quality materials above those specified by manufacturing, unless there are justifiable marketing and/or distribution reasons for doing so. The purchase of materials which needlessly exceed quality specifications adds unnecessary costs to the ultimate cost of the product.

*Forward buying.* In theory, all purchasing activities, except those of an emergency nature, are forward buying because materials, component parts, and subassemblies need to be available in advance of the time when they are needed. Forward buying then, more accurately refers to purchasing materials in quantities exceeding current requirements well in advance of their need or use.

> For an organization to practice forward buying, it must be experiencing some unusual, changing, or unstable market condition. This kind of a purchase can be made because of a pending price increase, a potential supply shortage, or some unusual . . . condition. Effective forward buying can help maximize purchasing's contribution to profits.[17]

Reasons for Forward Buying

Essentially, there are two major reasons why a firm would engage in forward buying. First, forward buying minimizes the effects of rising material costs. At least for a time, until the materials are depleted from inventory,

---

[15] Lamar Lee, Jr., and Donald W. Dobler, *Purchasing and Materials Management*, 3d ed. (New York: McGraw-Hill, 1977), p. 36.

[16] Ibid., p. 37.

[17] Richard J. Tersine and Edward T. Grasso, "Forward Buying in Response to Announced Price Increases," *Journal of Purchasing and Materials Management* 14, no. 2 (Summer 1978): 20.

the firm is protected from price increases in the marketplace. Second, forward buying provides protection against future availability problems. As an example, firms which secured large quantities of gasoline and/or diesel fuel in anticipation of higher fuel costs and spot shortages after the 1973 oil embargo, were able to carry out near-normal operations while other companies had to curtail their activities. Forward buying is becoming more popular among firms as availability uncertainties occur with increasing regularity.

While there are benefits associated with forward buying, there are also disadvantages which the materials manager must keep in mind. Many forward purchases are made in anticipation of price increases. However, there are times when materials prices actually go down because of technological developments, competitive pressures, and other factors. Thus, there is a risk that the firm may purchase materials at prices higher than necessary due to future price reductions. Another disadvantage associated with forward buying, often overlooked by firms, is the increased inventory carrying cost that is incurred with holding excess inventory. The savings realized from forward buying must exceed the additional inventory carrying costs. Table 10–3 presents an example of the role of inventory carrying costs in the forward-buying decision. If the firm buys forward for a period of one month the average level of inventory would be $1,000 with a savings of $200 (10 percent of $2,000). The inventory carrying costs incurred would equal $25

**TABLE 10–3** Using Inventory Carrying Costs to Evaluate Forward Buying

| Number of Months Supply Purchased | Value | Average Inventory $(\frac{1}{2} \times \text{Order quantity})$ | Savings in Order Processing Costs From Fewer Orders Being Placed | Savings in Purchase Price | Inventory Carrying Costs $(30\% \times \text{Average inventory} \times \frac{\text{Number of months}}{12})$ | Inventory Carrying Costs for Remaining Months Assuming Purchases of $2,200 per Month | Net Saving from Forward Buying |
|---|---|---|---|---|---|---|---|
| 1 | $ 2,000 | $ 1,000 | — | $ 200 | $ 25 | $302.50 | $(127.50) |
| 2 | 4,000 | 2,000 | $ 20 | 400 | 100 | 275.00 | 45.00 |
| 3 | 6,000 | 3,000 | 40 | 600 | 225 | 247.50 | 167.50 |
| 4 | 8,000 | 4,000 | 60 | 800 | 400 | 220.00 | 240.00 |
| 5 | 10,000 | 5,000 | 80 | 1,000 | 625 | 192.50 | 262.50 |
| 6 | 12,000 | 6,000 | 100 | 1,200 | 900 | 165.00 | 235.00 |
| 7 | 14,000 | 7,000 | 120 | 1,400 | 1,225 | 137.50 | 157.50 |
| 8 | 16,000 | 8,000 | 140 | 1,600 | 1,600 | 110.00 | 30.00 |
| 9 | 18,000 | 9,000 | 160 | 1,800 | 2,025 | 82.50 | (147.50) |
| 10 | 20,000 | 10,000 | 180 | 2,000 | 2,500 | 55.00 | (375.00) |
| 11 | 22,000 | 11,000 | 200 | 2,200 | 3,025 | 27.50 | (652.50) |
| 12 | 24,000 | 12,000 | 220 | 2,400 | 3,600 | — | (980.00) |

*Assumptions*
1. Monthly usage = $2,000.
2. Expected price increase = 10 percent.
3. Inventory carrying cost = 30 percent.
4. Order processing cost = $20./order.

Source: Douglas M. Lambert, "Measuring Purchasing Performance," unpublished manuscript, 1981.

(30 percent of the average level of inventory for one month). To this amount, it is necessary to add the carrying costs associated with the average inventory for the remaining 11 months. The net saving resulting from forward buying for one month would be negative $127.50. This indicates that a larger quantity should be purchased. At some point the savings (from forward buying) exactly equals the additional inventory carrying costs. As shown in Table 10−3 the optimal forward buy would be a five-months supply, which would result in a net savings of $262.50. However, if the purchasing manager is judged solely on the per unit purchase price, a 12 month supply would be purchased. This example should make it clear that inventory carrying costs must be included in the forward buying decision.

Finally, another disadvantage is the reduction in the firm's working capital that results from forward buying. Funds expended for inventories are not available for other uses. Therefore, the firm should anticipate future working capital needs before engaging in forward buying.

**Production Control**

Production control is an activity traditionally positioned under manufacturing, although in a few firms, it is placed under physical distribution. Its position in the firm's organizational chart is probably not that crucial so long as both manufacturing and physical distribution have an input into the production-control activity.

The role of production or manufacturing in the physical distribution process is twofold. First, the production activity determines how much and what kinds of finished products are produced. This, in turn, influences when and how the products are distributed to the firm's customers. Second, production directly impacts the company's need for raw materials, subassemblies, and component parts that are used in the manufacturing process. Therefore, it is axiomatic that production control decisions be jointly shared by manufacturing and distribution.

**Inbound Traffic and Transportation**

Materials management is concerned with product flows into the firm. For the materials manager, his/her customer is the manufacturing or production department rather than intermediate or final customers in the marketplaces. Much like the firm's target markets, manufacturing requires certain levels of customer service which are dependent upon the ability of materials management to adequately administer a variety of distribution functions including traffic and transportation, warehousing and storage, and MIS control.

One of the most important activities administered by materials management is the inbound traffic and transportation function. Like his/her counterpart who is responsible for finished goods movement, the materials manager must be aware of the various modes and modal combinations available to the company; the regulations which impact upon the transportation carriers used by the firm; the private versus for-hire decision; leasing; evaluating mode/carrier performance; and the cost/service tradeoffs involved in the inbound movement of product.

There are basically only two major differences between the administration of inbound versus outbound transportation. First, the market demand which generates the need for outbound movement is generally considered to be uncertain and fluctuating. The demand of concern to the materials manager originates with the production activity and is much more predictable and stable. Therefore, transportation decisions made by the materials manager are not subject to the same types of problems encountered by his/her counterpart in making outbound traffic decisions. Second, the materials manager is more likely to be concerned with bulk movements of raw materials or large shipments of parts and subassemblies. In addition, raw materials and parts will have different handling loss and/or damage characteristics which will effect the entire mode/carrier selection and evaluation process.

### Warehousing and Storage

Raw materials, component parts, and subassemblies must be placed in storage until they are needed in the manufacturing process. Unlike the warehousing of finished goods, which often occurs in the field, items awaiting use in the production process are usually stored on-site, that is, at the point of manufacture. The materials manager is usually much more concerned with warehousing and inventory costs because they account for a larger percentage of product value. Generally, finished goods are valued significantly higher than goods-in-process, raw materials, parts, or subassemblies. As a result, warehousing and storage costs are not as important, on a comparative basis, as they would be to the materials manager.

In addition, the warehousing requirements for raw materials and other items, are usually quite different. For example, open or outside storage is possible with many raw materials such as iron ore, sand and gravel, coal, and other unprocessed materials. Also, damage and/or loss due to weather, spoilage, or theft is minimal with raw materials because of their unprocessed nature and/or low value per pound.

### MIS Control

The materials manager needs direct access to the firm's information system in order to effectively and efficiently administer materials flow into and within the organization. The types of information often needed by the materials manager include demand forecasts for production, names of suppliers and supplier characteristics, pricing data, inventory levels, production schedules, transportation routing and scheduling data, and various other financial and marketing facts. Additionally, materials management supplies input into the firm's MIS. Data on inventory levels for materials, delivery schedules, pricing, forward buys, and various supplier information, are examples of some of the input provided by materials management.

### Inventory Planning and Control

Inventory planning and control of raw materials, component parts, subassemblies, and goods-in-process are just as important as the management

**Forecasting and MRP Are Important Components of Inventory Planning and Control**

of finished goods inventory. Many of the concepts such as ABC analysis, inventory carrying costs, and EOQ, discussed in Chapters 7 and 8, are directly applicable to materials management.

Two aspects of inventory planning and control which require further emphasis within the context of materials management are (1) forecasting and (2) materials requirements planning (MRP). Effective and efficient materials management requires three types of forecasts:

*Demand forecast.* Investigation of the firm's demand for the item, to include current and projected demand, inventory status, and lead times. Also considered are competing demands, current and projected, by industry and end-product use.

*Supply forecast.* Collection of data about current producers and suppliers, the aggregate current projected supply situation, and technological and political trends that might affect supply.

*Price forecast.* Based on information gathered and analyzed about demand and supply, this forecast provides a prediction of short- and long-term prices and the underlying reasons for those trends.[18]

The firm may utilize a variety of forecasting techniques ranging from those based on general market information from suppliers, sales force, customers, and others, to those that are highly sophisticated computer algorithms. The specific technique or approach selected by a firm should be one that is appropriate for the unique characteristics of the company and its markets. As illustrations, Tables 10−4 and 10−5 identify some of the forecasting methods being utilized by business firms.[19]

Examples of some of the time series methods of forecasting include the moving average, exponential smoothing, and adaptive smoothing. The moving average technique is fairly simplistic and consists of taking a set of observed values, such as sales, volume, or inventory levels, for a prescribed period, and computing an average. The average is used as the forecast for the next time period. Exponential smoothing is similar to the moving average approach although instead of assigning equal weights to each prior time period, the most recent observations or periods are given more weight or importance. The rationale is that more recent periods are more reflective of what may happen in the future. Adaptive smoothing is an expansion of exponential smoothing and is applicable to large forecasting problems involving hundreds or thousands of items.

The remaining forecasting techniques presented in Table 10−5 represent more sophisticated variations of the time series methods shown in Table 10−4. Any firm seeking to utilize one or more of these forecasting methods should be aware of the advantages and disadvantages of each one and be familiar with the situations where they can be correctly applied.

Materials requirements planning (MRP) is a production/inventory planning system which can improve the efficiency of materials management.

---

[18] Leenders, Fearon, and England, *Materials Management*, p. 517.

[19] For an in-depth discussion of these and other forecasting techniques see Spyros Makridakis and Steven C. Wheelwright, *Forecasting: Methods and Applications* (Santa Barbara, Calif: John Wiley & Sons, 1978).

**TABLE 10-4** Time Series Analysis

| Method | Description | Advantages | Disadvantages |
|---|---|---|---|
| Moving average* | Average of past sales Assigns equal weight to each period | Simple | Equal weights to all past periods<br>Inability to pinpoint turning point<br>Unresponsive<br>Lag actual sales<br>Number of periods used is a judgment |
| Exponential smoothing† | Extension of moving average but assigns most importance to recent data<br>Trend and seasonality can be included (triple exponential smoothing) | "Average" responds more quickly to changes in the level of demand | Judgment still required (forecaster must set values of smoothing constants) |
| Adaptive smoothing‡ | Tracking signals are used to monitor the error term | It can give accurate forecasts for a much wider range of situations than exponential smoothing or moving averages | Manager must specify the value of $\alpha$<br>Manager must specify the number of weights |

\* Formula: $ES_t = \dfrac{S_{t-1} + S_{t-2} + \cdots + S_{t-N}}{N}$.
† Formula: $ES_t = \alpha S_{t-1} + (1 - \alpha)ES_{t-1}$.
‡ Formula: $\alpha = f(\text{forecasting error})$.

## MRP Defined

A material requirements planning (MRP) system, narrowly defined, consists of a set of logically related procedures, decision rules, and records (alternatively, records may be viewed as inputs to the system) designed to translate a master production schedule into time-phased *net requirements*, and the planned *coverage* of such requirements, for each component inventory item needed to implement this schedule. An MRP system replans net requirements and coverage as a result of changes in either the master production schedule, or inventory status, or product composition.[20]

In the process of planning, an MRP system allocates existing on-hand quantities to item *gross requirements* and reevaluates the validity of the timing of any outstanding (open) orders in determining net requirements. To cover net requirements, the system establishes a schedule of *planned orders* for each item, including orders, if any, to be released immediately plus orders scheduled for release at specified future dates. Planned-order quantities are computed according to one of several lot-sizing rules specified by the system user as applicable to the item in question. In its entirety, the information on item requirements and coverage that an MRP system generates is called the *material requirements plan*.

. . . material requirements planning is product-oriented . . . material requirements planning . . . ignores history in looking toward the future as defined

---
[20] The master production schedule is the specific timetable which states when and how much of an item will be produced or manufactured during a given time period, usually on a weekly basis.

**TABLE 10-5** Forecasting Techniques

| Technique | Description | Advantages | Disadvantages |
|---|---|---|---|
| Brown's* Technique | Basic exponential smoothing model Employs a tracking signal $$\text{Mean} = \frac{\text{Sum of errors}}{\text{Absolute Deviation}}$$ Where: Sum of errors = Previous sum of errors and latest error MAD = $(1 - \alpha)$ previous MAD and $\alpha$ latest MAD | Requires little input Easy to use | Contains no forecast error adaptability or provision for trend or cyclical variation Unchanging smoothing factor Management must select smoothing constant Not capable of pinpointing the turning point |
| Winter's exponentially-weighted moving averages† | Similar to Brown's but adds trend and seasonal variation Smoothing constant = $\alpha$ Seasonality constant = $\beta$ Trend constant = $Y$ | Incorporates level, trend, and seasonal components | Does not deal with sales forecast adaptability (i.e., will not automatically adjust values of any of the smoothing constants) |
| Trigg and Leach‡ | Incorporates a tracking signal that is a measure of forecast error Automatically adjusts Winter's level-smoothing constant | Adaptive tracking signal for forecast error (i.e., tracking signal approaches 1 as the error term increases) | No consideration of seasonality or trend |
| Roberts and Reed self-adaptive forecasting technique (SAFT) | Employs three smoothing constants Using historical data, the evolutionary operations technique (EVOP) determines the optimum values for each of the smoothing constants | Any radical change in the patterns of basic sales, trend, or seasonality which causes an increase in the forecast error is automatically accounted for by the determination of a new set of smoothing-constant values | Increased computer cost because of the number of iterations required |
| Box-Jenkins | One of the most sophisticated time series analysis projection techniques available The time series is fitted with a mathematical model that is optimal in the sense that it assigns smaller errors to history than any other model | Improved versatility over more automatic methods The model may be modified to meet the needs of the user No need to assume or specify an internal pattern in the series Supplies statistical analysis of forecast | One of the most time-consuming and expensive forecasting methods |

\* Employs exponential smoothing formula: Forecast = $\alpha$ (Actual sales) + $(1 - \alpha)$ (Old forecast).
† Employs exponential smoothing formula modified to provide for seasonal and trend variations:

$$\text{Forecast} = \alpha \frac{\text{Actual sales}}{\text{Seasonal factor}} + (1 - \alpha)(\text{Old forecast} + \text{Trend factor}).$$

‡ Employs exponential smoothing model: Forecast = $\alpha$ (Actual sales) + $(1 - \alpha)$ (Old forecast).

by the master production schedule and works with data specifying the relationship of components (the bill of material) that make up a product.[21]

**Salvage and Scrap Disposal**

One of the most important areas of materials management which is often overlooked or considered a minor activity of the firm is the disposal of scrap, surplus, or obsolete materials. Many firms view this activity more as a nuisance than a potential profit center. Of course, there are many items which are truly waste materials and must be disposed of in as efficient and expeditious manner as possible. In those instances the firm will have to incur some disposal costs.

However, there are many materials which can be salvaged and sold to other companies. Estimates of total annual sales of scrap and waste materials in the United States exceed $10 billion.[22] An illustration can highlight the potential. A film-processing firm had been selling the residual chemicals and materials that were by-products of its operations for a relatively small price. The firm invested in a machine which could separate the waste material into its components. While the company was still able to sell some of the components to the same salvage firm (the salvage firm had previously been performing the separation process), one of the residues which was produced was silver, which the company subsequently sold to a precious-metals dealer for a handsome profit. The company realized a payback period for the separator machine of less than two years.

Almost all firms will produce some type of surplus materials as a by-product of their operations. The existence of this material can result from ". . . overoptimism in the sales forecast; changes in design and specifications; errors in estimating mill usage; inevitable losses in processing; careless use of material by factory personnel; and overbuying resulting from attempts to avoid the threat of rising prices or to secure quantity discounts on large purchases."[23]

The responsibility for managing the disposal of surplus materials rightly belongs to the materials manager for several reasons. Among the more important are the following:

1. Knowledge of probable price trends.
2. Contact with salespeople is a good source of information as to possible users of the material.
3. Familiarity with the company's own needs may suggest possible uses for, and transfer of, the material within the organization.
4. Unless a specific department is established within the firm to handle this function, purchasing is probably the only logical choice.[24]

---

[21] Joseph Orlicky, *Material Requirements Planning* (New York: McGraw-Hill, 1975), pp. 21–22.

[22] Leenders, Fearon, and England, *Materials Management*, p. 415.

[23] Ibid., p. 417.

[24] Ibid., p. 421.

Like all of the functions of distribution, materials management activities must be properly administered and controlled.

## ADMINISTRATION AND CONTROL OF MATERIALS MANAGEMENT

Proper administration and control of materials management requires some methods to identify the level of performance achieved by the firm. Specifically, the firm must be able to *measure, report,* and *improve* upon performance.

**Measuring Materials Management Performance**

In measuring the performance of materials management a number of elements should be examined, including supplier service levels, inventory, prices paid for materials, quality levels, and operating costs.[25]

Service levels can be measured using any of a number of methods including the following:

Order cycle time for each supplier.

Order fill rate for each supplier.

Percentage of orders from each supplier that are overdue.

Percentage of production orders not filled on time.

Number of stock-outs resulting from late deliveries from suppliers.

Number of production delays caused by materials being out of stock.

Inventory is an important aspect of materials management and can be controlled using the following measures:

Amount of dead stock.

Comparison of actual inventory levels with targeted levels.

Comparison of inventory turnover rates with historical rates.

Percentage of stock-outs caused by improper purchasing decisions.

Number of production delays caused by improper purchasing decisions.

Materials price level measures would include:

Gains and losses resulting from forward buying.

Comparison of prices paid for major items over several time periods.

Comparison of actual prices paid for materials with targeted prices.

In the area of quality control, measures which can be used are:

Number of product failures caused by materials defects.

Percentage of materials rejected from each shipment from each supplier.

As an overall measure of performance, the firm can compare the actual budget consumed by materials management compared to the targeted budget allocated at the beginning of the operating period.

---

[25] For an in-depth discussion of materials management control procedures see Lee and Dobler, *Purchasing and Materials Management,* pp. 470–88.

## Major Materials Management Reports

Once performance measures have been established for each component of the materials management process, data must be collected and results reported to those executives in decision-making positions. The major operating reports that should be developed by materials management include (1) market and economic conditions and price performance, (2) inventory investment changes, (3) purchasing operations and effectiveness, and (4) operations affecting administration and financial activities. A summary of the reports needed are presented in Table 10−6.

**TABLE 10-6** Operating Reports that Should be Developed by the Purchasing and Materials Management Functions

1. Market and economic conditions and price performance
    a. Price trends and changes for the major materials and commodities purchased. Comparison with standard costs where such accounting methods are used.
    b. Changes in demand-supply conditions for the major items purchased. Effects of labor strikes or threatened strikes.
    c. Lead time expectations for major items.
2. Inventory investment changes
    a. Dollar investment in inventories, classified by major commodity and materials group.
    b. Days' or months' supply, and on order, for major commodity and materials group.
    c. Ratio of inventory-dollar investment to sales-dollar volume.
    d. Rates of inventory turnover for major items.
3. Purchasing operations and effectiveness
    a. Cost reductions resulting from purchase research and value analysis studies.
    b. Quality rejection rates for major items.
    c. Number of out-of-stock situations which caused interruption of scheduled production.
    d. Number of change orders issued, classified by cause.
    e. Number of requisitions received and processed.
    f. Number of purchase orders issued.
    g. Employee work load and productivity.
    h. Transportation cost analysis.
4. Operations affecting administration and financial activities
    a. Comparison of actual departmental operating costs to budget.
    b. Cash discounts earned and cash discounts lost.
    c. Commitments to purchase, classified by types of formal contracts and by purchase orders, aged by expected delivery dates.
    d. Changes in cash discounts allowed by suppliers.

Source: Michiel R. Leenders, Harold E. Fearon, and Wilbur B. England, *Purchasing and Materials Management*, 7th ed. (Homewood, Ill.: Richard D. Irwin, 1980), pp. 544–45.

Finally, after performance has been measured and reported, it must be improved upon whenever possible. An example from the purchasing area will demonstrate how performance can be improved.

Specific analysis of both routine and critical items are necessary to pinpoint procurement improvement opportunities. Commodity analysis can help translate top management's awareness that purchasing is not being done effectively into action for improving it. Even a small sample of individual commodity studies can provide an indication of how to rejuvenate the entire purchasing function.

Commodity analysis consists of taking a systematic and detailed look at the procurement of an item or a closely related group of items. Past buying practices and present organizational constraints are put aside in a creative search for the best way to procure the item.[26]

Table 10–7 identifies some guidelines for conducting a commodity analysis.

**TABLE 10–7** Guidelines for Making a Commodity Purchasing Study

The information resulting from a commodity study should:

1. Provide a basis for making sound procurement decisions.
2. Present purchasing management and top management with information concerning future supply and price of purchased items.

The completed commodity study should provide data and/or answers for each of the following points or questions. (The investigation should not be limited to these items; depending on the particular commodity under consideration, additional items may be very pertinent, and some of the listed items may not be important.)

A. *Current status*
   1. Description of commodity
   2. How and where commodity is used
   3. Requirements
   4. Suppliers
   5. How commodity is purchased
   6. How commodity is transported
   7. Current contracts and expiration dates
   8. Current price, terms, and annual expenditure
   9. Scheduling
   10. Receiving
   11. Inspection
   12. Expediting
   13. Packaging
   14. Storage capacity
B. *Production process*
   1. How is the item made?
   2. What materials are used in its manufacture?
      a. Supply/price status of these materials
   3. What labor is required?
      a. Current and future labor situation
   4. Are there alternative production processes?
   5. What changes are likely in the future?
   6. Possibility of making the item?
      a. Costs
      b. Time factor
      c. Problems

---

[26] Frank L. Bauer, "Better Purchasing: High Rewards at Low Risk," *Journal of Purchasing and Materials Management* 12, no. 2 (Summer 1976), p. 5.

**TABLE 10-7** *(continued)*

C. *Uses of the item*
   1. Primary use(s)
   2. Secondary use(s)
   3. Possible substitutes
      a. Economics of substitution
D. *Demand*
   1. Our requirements
      a. Current
      b. Projected into the future
      c. Inventory status
      d. Sources of forecast information
      e. Lead times
   2. Competing demand, current and projected
      a. By industry
      b. By end-product use
      c. By individual firms
E. *Supply*
   1. Current producers
      a. Location
      b. Reliability as a source
      c. Quality levels
      d. Labor situation
      e. Ownership
      f. Capacity
      g. Distribution channels used
      h. Sales strategy
      i. Expansion plans
      j. Warranties and guarantees
      k. Strengths and weaknesses of each suppler
   2. Total (aggregate) supply situations
      a. Current
      b. Projected
   3. Import potential and problems
   4. Pertinent government regulations and controls
   5. Potential new suppliers
   6. Technological change forecast
   7. Political trends
   8. Ecological problems
   9. Weather
   10. Capital investment per unit of output
F. *Price*
   1. Economic structure of producing industry
   2. Price history and explanation of significant changes
   3. Factors determining price
   4. Cost to produce and deliver
   5. Incremental costs
   6. Coproducts or byproducts
   7. Effect of materials and labor cost changes on prices
   8. Transportation cost element
   9. Tariff and import regulations
   10. Effect of changes in the business cycle
   11. Effect of quantity on price
   12. Seasonal trends
   13. Estimated profit margins of various vendors

**TABLE 10-7** *(concluded)*

   14. Price objective(s) of vendors
   15. Potential rock-bottom price
   16. Do prices vary among various industries using the item?
   17. Forecast of future price trend
   18. Specific pricing system used by various vendors
   19. Influence of actions of specific vendors on prices of others; that is, a price leader?
   20. Relation to prices of other products
   21. Foreign exchange problems
G. *Strategy to reduce cost*
   Considering forecast supply, usage, price, profitability, strengths, and weakness of suppliers, and our position in the market, what is our plan to lower cost?
   1. Make the item in our facility
   2. Short-term contract
   3. Long-term contract
   4. Acquire a producer
   5. Find a substitute
   6. Develop a new producer
   7. Import
   8. Exploit all methods to make maximum use of our purchasing power
   9. Detailed preplanning of negotiations
   10. Use of agents
   11. Hedging
   12. Toll contract
   13. Value engineering/analysis
   14. Handling of scrap
H. *Appendix*
   1. General information
      a. Specifications
      b. Quality control requirements and methods
      c. Freight rates and transportation costs
      d. Storage capacity
      e. Handling facilities
      f. Weather problems
      g. Raw material reserves
   2. Statistics
      a. Price trends
      b. Production trends
      c. Purchase trends

Source: Michiel R. Leenders, Harold E. Fearon, and Wilbur B. England, *Purchasing and Materials Management,* 7th ed. (Homewood, Ill.: Richard D. Irwin, 1980), pp. 518–20.

Another approach to improving materials management performance is through the use of a computer-based planning and control system. One such system presently gaining acceptance in many firms is materials requirements planning (MRP).

**Materials Requirements Planning (MRP)**

The MRP system differs from traditional inventory control systems in one fundamental way. "In a MRP operation the master production schedule (as updated each week) is the force that directly initiates and drives subsequent activities of the purchasing and manufacturing functions."[27] MRP systems are usually employed when one or more of the following conditions exist:

**When Are Conditions Right for MRP?**

1. When usage (demand) of the material is discontinuous or highly unstable during a firm's normal operating cycle. This situation is typified by an intermittent manufacturing or job-shop operation, as opposed to a continuous-processing or mass-production operation.
2. When demand for the material is directly dependent on the production of other specific inventory items or finished products. MRP can be thought of as primarily a component-fabrication planning system, in which the demand for all parts (materials) is dependent on the demand (production schedule) for the parent product. . . .
3. When the purchasing department and its suppliers, as well as the firm's own manufacturing units, possess the flexibility to handle order placements or delivery releases on a weekly basis.[28]

**Objectives of MRP**

The objectives of MRP are basically twofold. First, the system attempts to eliminate or minimize inventory levels. Second, MRP tries to have materials delivered to exactly meet the timing requirements of the production schedule. As a result, the major benefits arising from MRP are cost related. Use of an MRP system minimizes inventory carrying costs and reduces the amount of working capital tied up in inventory. An additional benefit or advantage of MRP is that the system is closely related to the production schedule and therefore more directly influenced by final customer demand than are other inventory control techniques.

MRP does have a number of drawbacks which should be examined by a firm considering adoption of the system. First, MRP does not tend to optimize materials acquisition costs. Because inventory levels are kept to a minimum, materials must be purchased more frequently and in smaller quantities. This results in increased ordering costs. Higher transportation bills and higher unit costs are also incurred because the firm is less likely to qualify for large-volume discounts. The company must trade off the anticipated savings from reduced inventory carrying costs against the greater acquisition cost resulting from MRP. Another disadvantage of MRP is the potential hazard of production shut-downs that may arise because of such things as unforeseen delivery problems and materials shortages.

The availability of safety stocks gives production some protection against stock-outs of essential materials. As safety stocks are reduced, this level of protection is lost. A final disadvantage of MRP arises from the use of standard computer software packages. "Because standardized computer programs are used, modifications to accomodate unique operating situations in a given firm become major factors that must be considered thoroughly and built into the system at the time it is designed. . . . Once the system is established, basic program changes cannot be made easily."[29]

---

[27] Lee and Dobler, *Purchasing and Materials Management*, p. 198.
[28] Ibid., pp. 198–99.
[29] Ibid., p. 223.

**FIGURE 10-4** The MRP System—Inputs and Outputs

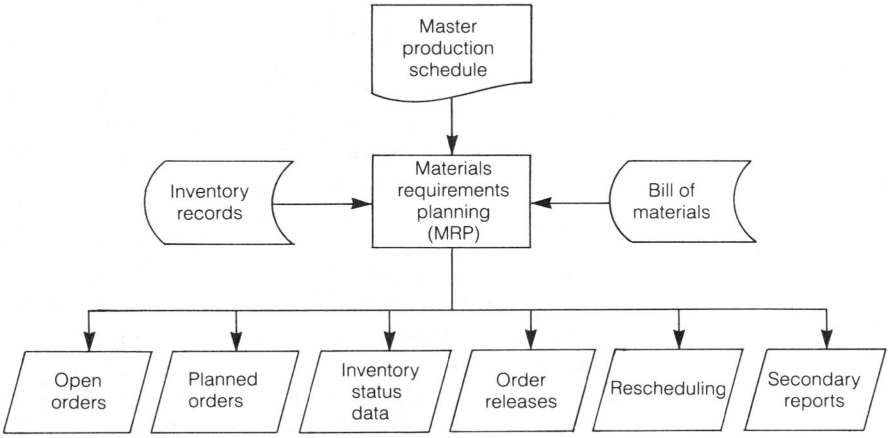

Figure 10-4 portrays the MRP system and the outputs of the program. The master production schedule serves as the major input into the MRP system. Other inputs include the bill of materials file and the inventory records file. The bill of materials file contains the component parts of the finished product identified by part number. The inventory records file maintains a record of all inventory on hand and on order. It also keeps track of due dates for all component parts as well as finished goods.

Leenders, Fearon, and England have identified two major types of output from an MRP program. The first type includes reports needed to undertake the production and purchasing functions:

Output from an MRP Program

1. Planned orders to be released at a future time.
2. Order release notices to execute the planned orders.
3. Changes in due dates of open orders due to rescheduling.
4. Cancellations or suspensions of open orders due to cancellation or suspension of orders on the master production schedule.
5. Inventory status data.[30]

Other types of additional reports which are more managerial in scope include the following:

1. Planning reports to be used, for example, in forecasting inventory and specifying requirements over some future time horizon.
2. Performance reports for purposes of pointing out inactive items and determining the agreement between actual and programmed item lead times and between actual and programmed quantity usages and costs.

---
[30] Leenders, Fearon, and England, *Materials Management*, p. 193.

3. Exception reports, which point out serious discrepancies such as errors, out-of-range situations, late or overdue orders, excessive scrap, or nonexistent parts.[31]

For many companies, MRP can prove to be very beneficial. It is an alternative method to inventory planning and control which can enhance the materials management performance level of many firms.

**SUMMARY**

Materials management is an important component of the physical distribution process of a firm. Although materials management activities do not directly interface with the final customer, they do influence the firm's cost/service mix.

In this chapter the relationship between materials management and physical distribution was discussed. Materials management is generally thought to include four basic activities: (1) anticipating materials requirements, (2) sourcing, (3) introducing materials into the company, and (4) monitoring the status of materials. Specifically the functions of materials management include purchasing and procurement, production control, in-bound traffic and transportation, warehousing and storage, management of components of the firm's information system, inventory planning and control, and salvage and scrap disposal.

Important aspects of the purchasing process are supplier selection and evaluation (sourcing), quality control, and forward buying. In the area of inventory planning and control, forecasting and materials requirements planning (MRP) were shown to be important aspects of the materials management process. Forecasting includes estimates of future demand, supply, and price. MRP utilizes the master production schedule to develop purchasing and manufacturing plans and can be a useful planning and control mechanism for many firms.

An additional materials management activity which is often overlooked is salvage and scrap disposal. Surplus materials offer significant profit potential if they are properly managed.

Proper administration and control of materials management requires that the firm measure, report, and improve upon the performance level of materials management activities. A number of approaches were examined which identified how a firm could improve its materials management process.

---

[31] Ibid., pp. 193 – 94.

# Appendix: Evaluating Suppliers in a Typical Manufacturing Firm

| Factor | Rating of supplier (1 = Worst rating; 5 = Highest rating) 1 2 3 4 5 | (×) | Importance of factor to your Firm (0 = No importance; 5 = Highest importance) 0 1 2 3 4 5 | (=) | Weighted Composite Rating (0 = Minimum; 25 = Maximum |
|---|---|---|---|---|---|
| Supplier A |  |  |  |  |  |
|   Product reliability |  |  |  |  |  |
|   Price |  |  |  |  |  |
|   Ordering convenience |  |  |  |  |  |
|   . |  |  |  |  |  |
|   . |  |  |  |  |  |
|   After-the-sale service |  |  |  |  |  |
|     Total for supplier A |  |  |  |  | _____ |
| Supplier B |  |  |  |  |  |
|   Product reliability |  |  |  |  |  |
|   Price |  |  |  |  |  |
|   Ordering convenience |  |  |  |  |  |
|   . |  |  |  |  |  |
|   . |  |  |  |  |  |
|   After-the-sale service |  |  |  |  |  |
|     Total for supplier B |  |  |  |  | _____ |
| Supplier C |  |  |  |  |  |
|   Product reliability |  |  |  |  |  |
|   Price |  |  |  |  |  |
|   Ordering convenience |  |  |  |  |  |
|   . |  |  |  |  |  |
|   . |  |  |  |  |  |
|   After-the-sale service |  |  |  |  |  |
|     Total for supplier C |  |  |  |  | _____ |

Decision rule: Select the supplier with highest composite rating.

## QUESTIONS AND PROBLEMS

1. Explain why "supplier selection and evaluation" is the most important activity in the purchasing and procurement function.

2. In a study by White published by the American Management Association, four buying or purchasing situations were discussed. Briefly identify and summarize the characteristics of each situation.

3. International sourcing of materials is a much more difficult process than domestic sourcing. What are some of the more significant problems in international sourcing which effect the physical distribution manager.

4. Explain the concept of *forward buying* and its relationship to *total cost trade-off* analysis.

5. Materials requirements planning (MRP) is a relatively recent systems innovation in materials management. Describe the types of situations where MRP can be useful in a firm and identify the advantages and disadvantages associated with a MRP system.

6. Briefly discuss the major inputs into a MRP system, specifically:
   a. Master production schedule.
   b. Inventory records.
   c. Bill of materials.

# Part Three

# 11 Financial Control of Distribution Performance

Introduction

The Importance of Accurate Cost Data
  Total-Cost Analysis
  Controlling Physical Distribution Activities
  Case Studies
    Case 1. The Effect of Freight Averages on Customer/Product Profitability
    Case 2. Inability to Distinguish between Fixed and Variable Costs
    Case 3. The Pitfalls of Allocation
    Case 4. Control Deficiencies

Solving the Problem of Insufficient Cost Data
  Standard Costs and Flexible Budgets
  Budgetary Practices
  Productivity Standards
  Physical Distribution Costs and the Corporate Management Information System
  The Role of the Order Processing System

Cost Justification of Physical Distribution System Changes

Summary

Appendixes
A. An Application of Standard Costs in Physical Distribution
B. Developing Standard Costs and Flexible Budgets for Warehousing

**Objectives of this chapter:**

To show how to use physical distribution costs for decision making

To show how to measure and control performance of the physical distribution function

To show how to cost justify changes in physical distribution structure

## INTRODUCTION

In Chapter 2 you were made aware of the fact that physical distribution costs can exceed 25 percent of the cost of doing business at the manufacturing level. For this reason, better management of the distribution function offers large potential savings which can contribute to improved corporate profitability. In an economy in which corporate profitability is continuously being eroded by high interest rates and inflation, it is necessary to look for ways to improve productivity.

In many firms physical distribution has not been managed as an integrated system and even in those firms that have accepted the integrated physical distribution management concept, evidence suggests that the required cost data are not available.[1] The accurate measurement and control of physical distribution costs offers significant potential for improving cash flow and corporate return on assets.

In this chapter you will be shown (1) how to use physical distribution costs for decision making; (2) how to measure and control performance of the physical distribution function; and (3) how to cost justify changes in physical distribution structure using the total-cost concept.

## THE IMPORTANCE OF ACCURATE COST DATA

Prior to 1960, physical distribution was viewed as a fragmented and often uncoordinated set of activities spread throughout various organizational functions. However, the notion that a firm's total physical distribution costs could be reduced, customer service improved, and interdepartmental conflicts substantially reduced by the coordination of distribution activities, has emerged as an important concept. The emergence of computers, operations-research techniques, and the systems approach brought high-speed processing and the logic of mathematics to the field of logistics and led not only to changes in transportation strategy, inventory-control techniques, warehousing-location policy, order-processing systems, and distribution communication, but also to the desire to manage the costs associated with these functions in an integrated format.

Today most of the early obstacles confronting full implementation of the integrated physical distribution management concept appear to be removed. However, the lack of adequate cost data has prevented its full poten-

---

[1] Douglas M. Lambert and John T. Mentzer, "Is Integrated Physical Distribution Management A Reality?" *Journal Of Business Logistics* 2, no. 1 (1980): 18–34.

tial from being reached. In general, accountants have not kept pace with developments in physical distribution and in fact, have shown relatively little interest in the area. Consequently, much of the necessary cost analysis has not been carried out.[2]

*Accurate Cost Data Required for Integrated PDM*

Accurate cost data are required for successful implementation of the integrated physical distribution management concept using total cost analysis. Also they are required for the management and control of physical distribution operations.

**Total-Cost Analysis**[3]

The key to managing the physical distribution function is total cost analysis, that is, at a given level of customer service, management should minimize total logistical cost rather than attempting to minimize the cost of individual activities. The major shortcoming of a nonintegrative approach to distribution cost analysis is that attempts to reduce specific costs within the distribution function may be suboptimal and lead to greater total costs.

Total distribution costs do not respond to cost-cutting techniques which are individually geared to warehouse, transportation, or inventory costs since reductions in one cost invariably give rise to increases in one or more of the others. For example, aggregating all finished-goods inventory into fewer distribution centers may minimize warehousing costs and increase inventory turnover but it will lead to increased transportation expense. Similarly, savings resulting from favorable purchase prices on large orders may be entirely offset by greater inventory carrying costs. Thus, to minimize total cost it is necessary to understand the effect of trade-offs within the distribution function.

Cost trade-offs between and among the various components of the physical distribution system are essential. Profit can be enhanced, for example, if the reduction in inventory carrying cost is less than the increase in the other functional costs (Figure 11–1) or if improved customer service yields greater overall profitability. However, if knowledgeable trade-offs are to be made, it is imperative that we be able to account for the costs associated with each component and to account for how changes in each cost contribute to total costs.

As the cost of physical distribution increases, the need for accurate accounting for the costs becomes increasingly critical. Since the physical distribution function is relatively more energy intensive and labor intensive than other areas of the firm, its ratio of costs to total company costs has been steadily increasing. The full potential of distribution cost trade-off analysis cannot be realized until the cost related to separate functional areas and their interaction can be fully determined.

The quality of the accounting data will influence managements ability to exploit new markets, take advantage of innovative transportation systems,

---

[2] Douglas M. Lambert and Howard M. Armitage, "Distribution Costs: The Challenge," *Management Accounting*, May 1979, p. 33.

[3] This section is adapted from Lambert and Armitage, "Distribution Costs: The Challenge," pp. 33–34.

**FIGURE 11–1** Cost Trade-offs Required in a Physical Distribution System

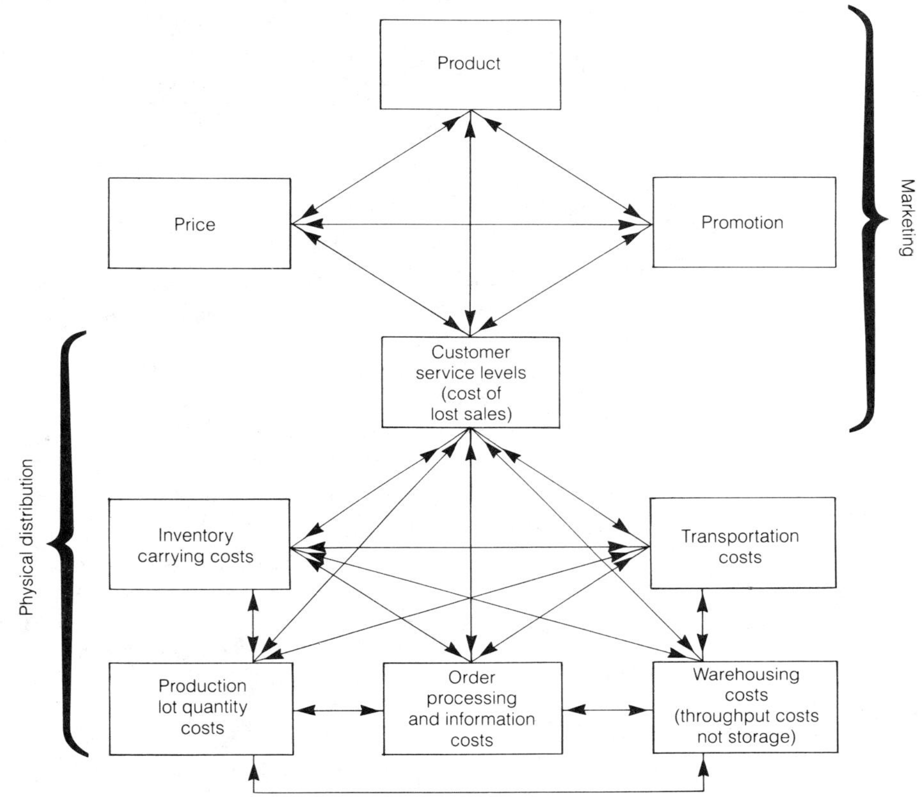

Objective: Minimize total costs.

Total costs = Transportation costs + Warehousing costs
+ Order processing and information costs
+ Production lot quantity costs + Inventory carrying costs
+ Cost of lost sales.

Source: Adapted From: Douglas M. Lambert, *The Development of an Inventory Costing Methodology: A Study of the Costs Associated with Holding Inventory* (Chicago: The National Council of Physical Distribution Management, 1976), p. 7.

make changes in packaging, choose between common carriers and private trucking, increase deliveries or increase inventories, and determine to what extent the order-processing system should be automated.

The accounting system must be capable of providing information to answer such questions as:

Many Management Decisions Require Good Cost Data

1. How do physical distribution costs impact contribution by product, by territory, by customer, and/or by salesperson?
2. What are the costs associated with providing additional levels of customer service? What trade-offs are necessary and what are the incremental benefits or losses?

3. What is the optimal amount of inventory? How sensitive is the inventory level to changes in warehousing patterns or to changes in customer service levels? How much does it cost to hold inventory?
4. What mix of transportation modes/carriers should be used?
5. How many field warehouses should be used and where should they be located?
6. How many production set-ups are required? Which plants will be used to produce each product?
7. To what extent should the order-processing system be automated?

To answer these and other questions requires knowledge of the cost and revenues that will change if the physical distribution system changes. That is, determination of a product's contribution should be based on how corporate revenues, expenses, and hence profitability would change if the product line were dropped. Any costs or revenues which are unaffected by this decision are irrelevant to the problem. For example, a relevant cost would be public warehouse handling charges associated with a product's sales, and a nonrelevant cost would be the overhead costs associated with the firm's private trucking fleet.

Implementation of this approach to decision making is severely hampered by the lack of availability or the inability to use the right accounting data when they are available. The best and most sophisticated of our models are only as good as the accounting input and a number of recent studies attest to the gross inadequacies of distribution-cost data.[4]

### Controlling Physical Distribution Activities

*Cost Data Are Essential for Control*

One of the major reasons for improving the availability of distribution cost data is to control and monitor physical distribution performance. Without accurate cost data, performance analysis is next to impossible. How for example, can a firm expect to control the cost of shipping a product to a customer if it does not know what the cost should be? How can management determine if distribution-center costs are high or low in the absence of performance measurements? What is good performance for the order-processing function? Are inventory levels satisfactory, too high or too low? The list is not all-inclusive, but it serves to illustrate the need for accurate cost data.

The importance of a good measurement program for the management and control of distribution performance was addressed by the National Council of Physical Distribution Management in a 1978 study:

> If no measurement program exists, the "natural" forces shaping the behavior of busy managers tend to place the emphasis on the negative. Issues only attract

---

[4] For example see: David Ray, "Distribution Costing and The Current State of the Art," *International Journal of Physical Distribution* 6, no. 2 (1975): 75–107 at p. 88; Michael Schiff, *Accounting and Control in Physical Distribution Management* (Chicago: National Council of Physical Distribution Management, 1971), pp. 4–21 (hereafter cited as NCPDM); R. E. Bream and R. Galer, *A National Survey of Physical Distribution Management*, Whitehead and Partners, 1974; Lambert and Mentzer, "Is Integrated Management a Reality?", pp. 18–34; and Douglas M. Lambert, *The Distribution Channels Decision* (New York: The National Association of Accountants, and Hamilton, Ontario: The Society of Management Accountants of Canada, 1978).

management attention when something is "wrong." In this type of situation, there is often little reinforcement of positive results. A *formal* measurement program helps focus attention on the positive and helps improve employee morale. ... Once a plan has been established, actual results can be measured and compared with the plan to identify variances requiring management attention. ...[5]

## Case Studies

As the cost of physical distribution continues to rise, the need for management to be able to account for the costs associated with each component becomes increasingly critical.[6] It is also necessary to know how changes in the costs of each component affect total costs and profits. Depending on the nature of the company, estimates of distribution costs ranging from 15 percent to 50 percent of total sales are not uncommon. However, these are at best only educated guesses since they are usually based on costs incorrectly computed by management. From a corporate standpoint, the inability to measure and manage physical distribution costs leads to missed opportunities and expensive mistakes. The following four actual examples will serve to highlight the problems associated with most distribution-accounting systems.

*Freight Averages Distort Segment Profitability*

*Case 1—The effect of freight averages on customer/product profitability.* Freight costs are a major expense in most companies, yet few attempt to track their actual freight costs by customer or by product. When management does attempt to determine these costs, they usually rely on the use of national averages. These averages, however, do not indicate the actual costs of moving each product to its destination and, hence, profitability calculations are erroneous.

To illustrate, company A used a national average freight rate when calculating customer and product profitability. It was determined by taking the total corporate transportation bill as a percentage of total sales revenue. The same cost, 4 percent of sales, was applied to products moving by common carrier from Chicago to New York and from Chicago to Los Angeles as was used on deliveries in the Chicago area where the company's own vehicles made the deliveries. Four percent was used for the transportation cost regardless of the product being shipped, the size of the shipment, or the distance involved.

The fallacy of this approach is threefold. First, management was unable to determine the profitability of individual products or customers. The averaging process hid the fact that delivery of small quantities and/or to distant customers may be highly unprofitable, thereby reducing the overall corporate rate of return. Second, using the same percentage rate for all products ignores the impact of product characteristics such as weight, cube, and distance on freight rates and consequently on product and cus-

---

[5] A. T. Kearney, *Measuring Productivity in Physical Distribution* (Chicago: NCPDM, 1978), pp. 18–19.

[6] This material is adapted from Douglas M. Lambert and Howard M. Armitage, "Managing Distribution Costs for Better Profit Performance," *Business,* September/October 1980, pp. 46–52. Reprinted by permission from *Business* Magazine.

tomer profitability. Finally, a trade-off analysis between the cost of the current system and the costs of an alternative system where carload shipments would go first to a regional warehouse on the West Coast and then on to the customers in that market is made more difficult if actual customer-delivery costs are not known. The result of simplifying the allocation of freight costs in this company led to erroneous profitability figures for customers and products and lower overall profit performance.

*Separating Fixed and Variable Costs Can Be a Problem*

*Case 2—Inability to distinguish between fixed and variable costs.* Company B utilized a product reporting statement which deducted manufacturing, distribution, and marketing costs from sales to arrive at a net income for each product. The profit statement was used for making decisions about the acceptability of product performance, the assignment of marketing support, and the deletion of products. The allocation of distribution costs to each product was carried out on an ABC basis, in which the A products were allocated a certain amount of distribution cost, the B products twice as much as A, and the C products three times as much as A. These allocations contained costs such as warehouse labor, supplies, and freight expense which varied with activity and costs such as corporate allocations, depreciation, and administration costs of the corporate fleet which remained fixed, irrespective of activity levels. Several of the company's products, including 1 which was among the company's top 10 in terms of sales performance, were showing negative profits and, hence, were candidates for being discontinued. An analysis revealed, however, that a large proportion of the total distribution cost, as well as approximately 30 percent of the manufacturing cost, was fixed and would not be saved if the products were eliminated. In fact, by discontinuing these products, total corporate profitability would decline, since all the revenues related to these products would disappear but all of the costs would not. Although the variable costs and the specifically identifiable fixed costs would be saved, the majority of fixed costs, which in this case were substantial, would continue to be incurred regardless of the product deletions that were being considered. If the products were discontinued, the existing fixed costs would be redistributed to the remaining products, leading to the very real possibility that even more products would appear to be unprofitable.

Furthermore, the ABC classification method was found to be subject to wide variations in accuracy. Category C products often took less time to store, pick from warehouse stock, and ship than did category A products, even though they were being allocated three times the distribution cost. In effect, because of the distribution-costing system, the company had inaccurate information about product profitability and hence total performance suffered.

*The Pitfalls of Allocation*

*Case 3—The pitfalls of allocation.* Most distribution-costing systems are in their infancy and rely heavily on allocations to determine the performance of segments such as products, customers, territories, divisions, or functions. Company C provides an example where such allocations led to erroneous decision making and loss of corporate dollars. The firm was a multidivision corporation that manufactured and sold high-margin pharmaceuticals as well as a number of lower-margin packaged-goods products. The company maintained a number of field-warehouse locations managed by corporate staff. These climate-controlled facilities were designed for the pharmaceutical business and required security and housekeeping practices which far exceeded those necessary for packaged goods. In order to fully utilize the facilities, however, the corporation encouraged nonpharmaceutical divisions to store their product in these distribution centers. The costs of operating the warehouses were primarily fixed although additional warehouse employees were necessary if the volume of product handled (throughput) increased. The corporate policy was to allocate costs to user divisions on the basis of the square-footage occupied. Due to the pharmaceutical warehousing requirements this charge was relatively high. Furthermore, the corporate divisions were managed on a decentralized profit-center basis. The vice president of physical distribution in one of the divisions realized that similar services could be obtained at lower cost to his division by using a public warehouse. For this reason, he withdrew the division's products from the corporate facilities and began to use public warehouses in these locations. Although the volume of product handled and stored in the corporate distribution centers decreased significantly, the cost savings were minimal in terms of the total costs incurred by these facilities. This was due to the high proportion of fixed costs. Consequently, approximately the same cost was allocated to fewer users which made it even more attractive for the other divisions to change to public warehouses in order to obtain lower rates. The result was higher, not lower, total company warehousing costs. The corporate warehousing costs were primarily fixed and whether the space was occupied or not would not significantly alter these costs. When the nonpharmaceutical divisions moved to public warehouses, the company continued to incur approximately the same total expense for the corporate owned and operated warehouses, as well as incurring the additional public-warehousing charges. In effect, the distribution-costing system motivated the divisional distribution managers to act in a manner which was not in the best interests of the company and total costs escalated.

*Case 4 – Control deficiencies.* Control of costs and motivation of key personnel is critical in every business activity. Physical distribution is no exception. However, the control concepts successfully utilized by other functional areas have not been widely adopted for physical-distribution activities. In some cases, the argument has been advanced that distribution is different from other disciplines and cannot be evaluated with the same tools. In most cases, however, the application has never been attempted. A particular case in point is the application of the flexible-budgeting concept.

Application of Control Techniques Lacking in PD

Company D maintained an annual budget for its branch warehousing costs. These costs consisted of variable and fixed expenses. Each month, the budget was divided by 12 and compared to the actual costs of that month. Differences from the budget were recorded as variances upon which management took action. However, the sales of company D were seasonal and some months were far more active than others. During peak periods, the variances were virtually always unfavorable, while during slow months, the variances were favorable. Productivity ratios, on the other hand, gave different results. During peak periods, productivity ratios were high and dropped during slower periods. In such a situation, neither cost control nor employee motivation is being adequately addressed. Dividing the budget by 12 and comparing it to actual costs means that management is trying to compare costs at two different levels of operation—the planned budget and actual. However, the costs should be the same only if actual activity is equal to one-twelfth of the planned activity. A far more acceptable approach is to recognize that a proportion of the costs are variable and should go up or down with the level of output. Flexing the budget to reflect what the costs should have been at the operating level experienced permits a true measure of efficiency and productivity and provides more meaningful evaluations of individual performance.

These examples are by no means unique. A recent survey of 300 North American firms by Douglas Lambert and John Mentzer revealed that the individual cost components such as inventory carrying costs; transportation cost by channel, product or customer; order processing costs; warehousing costs; and production-lot quantity costs necessary to implement distribution cost trade-off analysis were generally unavailable.[7] In fact, not a single firm reported the availability of all of the physical distribution cost components. This lack of cost data makes analysis extremely difficult. Not only does the distribution-costing system in the majority of firms not lend itself to effective physical distribution management, if effective physical distribution management can be defined as the ability to make the right operational and strategic choices, *but* it is difficult for management to obtain the data required to cost justify proposed systems changes.

## SOLVING THE PROBLEM OF INSUFFICIENT COST DATA

*PD Costs Are Often Grouped into Natural Accounts*

One of the difficulties in obtaining physical distribution costs is that they may be grouped under a series of natural accounts rather than by functions. Natural accounts are used to group costs for financial reporting on the firm's income statement and balance sheet. For example, all payments for salaries might be grouped into a salaries account, whether they are for production, marketing, physical distribution, or finance, and the total shown on the financial statements at the end of the reporting period.[8] Other examples of natural accounts might include rent, depreciation, selling expenses, general and administrative expenses, and interest expense. It is entirely possible that in a firm with a strong financial accounting orientation, physical distribution costs such as warehousing and transportation may not be given separate headings in the natural accounts. Instead they

---

[7] Douglas M. Lambert and John T. Mentzer, "Is Integrated Management a Reality," pp. 18–34.

[8] Wilbur S. Wayman, "Harnessing the Corporate Accounting System for Physical Distribution Cost Information," *Distribution System Costing: Concepts And Procedures*, Proceedings of the Fourth Annual James R. Riley Symposium on Business Logistics, (Columbus, Ohio: Transportation and Logistics Research Foundation, 1972), p. 35.

are lumped into such diverse catchalls as overhead, selling, or general expense. Further there has been a tendency, particularly in the case of freight, to abandon the accrual-accounting concept and match costs of one period with revenues of another period. These conditions make it difficult to determine distribution expenditures, control costs, or perform trade-off analysis.

The challenge is not so much to create new data, since much of it already exists in one form or another, but to tailor the existing data in the accounting system to meet the needs of the physical distribution function.[9] By improving the availability of physical distribution cost data, management will be in a better position to make both operational and strategic decisions. It stands to reason that abnormal levels of costs can be detected and controlled only if it is known what they ought to be for various levels of activity. As shown in Figure 11–2 physical distribution performance can be monitored by using standard costs, budgets, and/or productivity standards.[10]

**FIGURE 11–2** Controlling Physical Distribution Activities

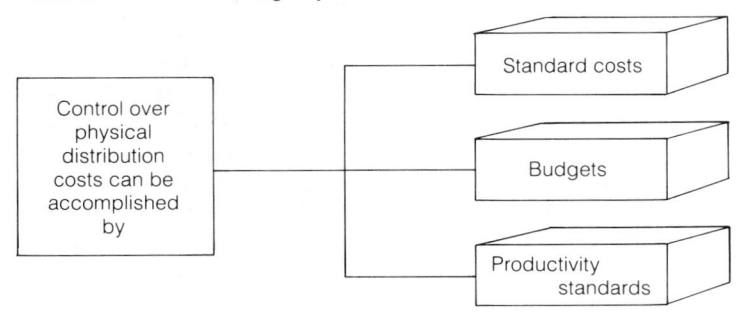

## Standard Costs and Flexible Budgets

Standard Costs and Flexible Budgets Improve Control

Control of costs through predetermined standards and flexible budgets is the most comprehensive type of control system available. The use of standard costs represents a frontal assault on the physical distribution costing problem because it attempts to determine what the costs should be rather than basing future cost predictions on past cost behavior.

A decision to use standard costs requires a systematic review of physical distribution operations in order to determine the most efficient means of achieving the desired output. Accounting, physical distribution, and engineering personnel must work together using regression analysis, time and motion studies, and efficiency studies so that a series of flexible budgets can be drawn up for various operating levels in different physical distribution cost centers. Standards can and have been set for such warehouse opera-

---

[9] A system for recording accounting data in the necessary format will be discussed later in this chapter.

[10] The following sections on standard costs, budgets, and productivity standards are adapted from Douglas M. Lambert and Howard M. Armitage, "Managing Distribution Costs for Better Profit Performance," *Business*, September–October 1980, pp. 50–51. Reprinted by permission from *Business* Magazine.

tions as stock picking, loading, receiving, replenishing, storing, and packing merchandise. In addition, they have been successfully utilized in order processing, transportation, and even clerical functions. However, the use of standards has not been widespread. In part, this is due to the belief that physical distribution costs are, by nature, quite different than those in other areas of the business. While there may be some merit to this argument, physical distribution activities are, by nature, repetitive operations, and such operations lend themselves to control by standards. A more compelling reason why standard costs have not achieved widespread acceptance is that few attempts have been made to install such systems, a phenomenon directly attributable to the fact that it is only recently that the importance of physical distribution cost control has been recognized. This is unfortunate because the management accountants and industrial engineers of most firms have a wealth of experience in installing standard costs in the production area, which, with some effort, could be expanded into physical distribution. However, developing standards for physical distribution may be more complex because the output measures can be considerably more diverse than in the case of production. For example, in developing a standard for the picking function, it is possible that the eventual control measure could be stated as a standard cost per order, a standard cost per order line, a standard cost per unit shipped, or a standard cost per shipment. Despite the added complexities, work measurement does appear to be increasing in physical distribution activities. One example of a successful application was given by Michael Schiff.[11] The firm used a computerized system with standard charges and routes for 25,000 routes and eight different methods of transportation. Up to 300,000 combinations were possible and the system was updated regularly. Clerks at any location could obtain from the computer the optimum method of shipment. A monthly computer printout listed the following information by customer:

*A Computerized System of Freight Standards*

a. Destination.
b. Standard freight cost to customer.
c. Actual freight paid for shipments to customer.
d. Standard freight to warehouse cost.
e. Total freight cost.
f. Origin of shipment.
g. Sales district office.
h. Method of shipment.
i. Container used.
j. Weight of shipment.
k. Variance in excess of a given amount per hundred weight.

Another monthly report listed the deviation from standard freight cost for each customer and the amount of the variance. This system obviously provided the firm with a measure of freight performance. Equally impor-

---

[11] Michael Schiff, *Accounting and Control in Physical Distribution Management* (Chicago: NCPDM, 1972) pp. 4–63 to 4–70.

tant, the standards provided the means for determining individual customer profitability and identification opportunities for physical distribution cost trade-offs. Because this firm used standards as an integral part of its management information system it would be relatively straightforward to determine the impact of a system change such as an improved, automated, order processing system on transportation costs.

The use of standards as a management control system is depicted in Figure 11–3. As the figure indicates, standards may result from either formal investigation, philosophy/intuition, or both.

**FIGURE 11–3**  The Use of Standards as a Management Control System

The Control System

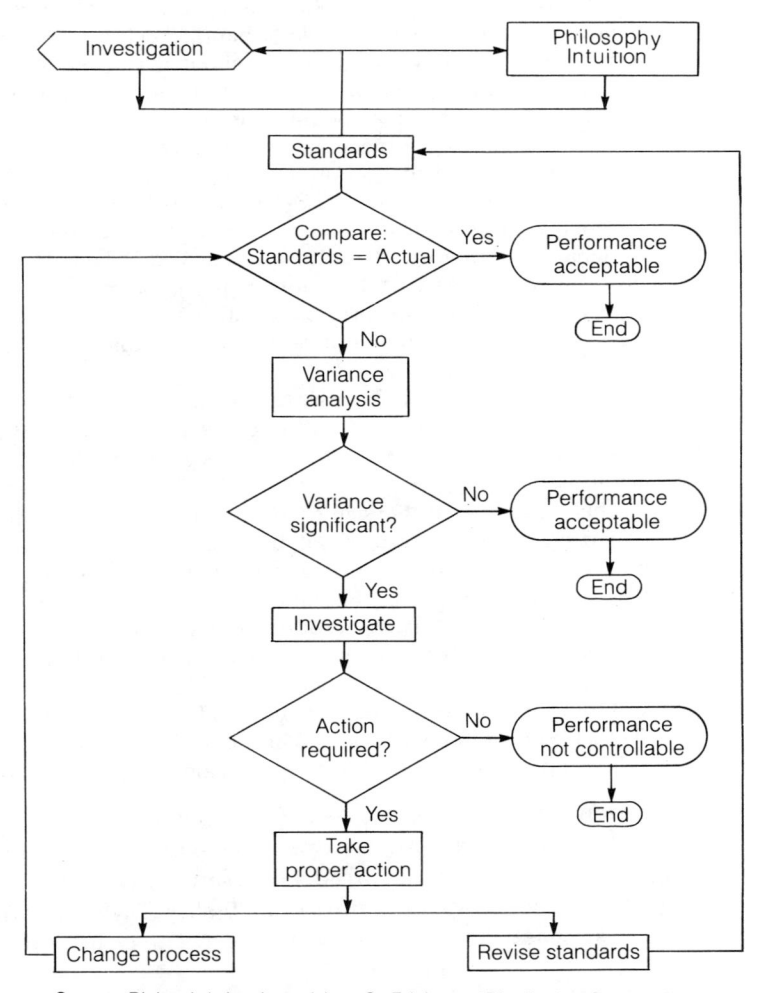

```
         Investigation ─────►─────◄───── Philosophy
                                         Intuition
              │                              │
              └──────────►  Standards  ◄─────┘◄──────────────┐
                                │                            │
                                ▼                            │
                        Compare:          Yes   Performance  │
                   Standards = Actual ──────►   acceptable   │
                                │                  │         │
                                │ No              End        │
                                ▼                            │
                           Variance                          │
                           analysis                          │
                                │                            │
                                ▼                            │
                          Variance     No    Performance     │
                         significant? ────►   acceptable     │
                                │                  │         │
                                │ Yes             End        │
                                ▼                            │
                          Investigate                        │
                                │                            │
                                ▼                            │
                           Action      No    Performance     │
                          required?  ────►  not controllable │
                                │                  │         │
                                │ Yes             End        │
                                ▼                            │
                            Take                             │
                        proper action                        │
                          │        │                         │
                          ▼        ▼                         │
                    Change      Revise standards ────────────┘
                    process
```

Source: Richard J. Lewis and Leo G. Erickson, "Distribution System Costing: An Overview," in John R. Grabner and William S. Sargent, eds., *Distribution System Costing: Concepts and Procedures* (Columbus, Ohio: Transportation and Logistics Research Foundation, 1972), p. 17A.

Once standards have been set the firm must compare actual performance with the particular standard to see if it is acceptable. If performance is acceptable the system is deemed to be under control and that is the end of the control process. Inherent in this notion is that management operates under the principle of exception, exerting no changes in the system so long as it operates satisfactorily; and the measure of "satisfactory" is found in the standard.

It is highly unlikely that performance will exactly equal standard. Where there is a departure, the procedure is to break the variance down into its component parts to try to ascertain its sources. For example, the standard may be a budgeted amount for transportation in a territory. If the actual exceeds the budget, management would like to see the variance analyzed into separate measures of volume and efficiency. It is impossible to know how to proceed unless the variance is analyzed into meaningful sources.

The next question is whether the observed variance is great enough to be deemed significant. It is possible to handle such a question in strictly statistical terms, setting quality control limits about the standard. This may be done in terms of standard deviations and an acceptable limit established on the down side only or the limit may be on either side of the standard. Thus, in the latter case, if performance exceeds standard, management may decide to raise the standard or reward the performer accordingly. Probably of greater concern are those departures in which performance is below standard.

Much of physical distribution lends itself to measures of statistical significance in departures from standard. However, as with demand obtaining activities, it is probably more meaningful to judge departures from standards in terms of their *practical* significance. A form of sensitivity analysis goes on here in which the question is raised of how critical is the departure in its effects on bottom line performance, net profit.

Regardless of how the assessment is made, the variance will be termed either significant or not significant. If it is not significant, performance is judged acceptable and the control process is ended. If significant, the next question is whether action is required.

The variance may be significant but, in analyzing it and explaining it, the departure from standard is not judged controllable. If so, no action may be indicated and the control process terminated. If action is indicated, it will be one of two broad kinds. Either the standard is held to be wrong and must be changed, or the process itself is not producing the results it should and thus must be changed. The feedbacks go up to the appropriate levels. If the process is changed and the standard is held, comparisons are again made. If the standard is changed and the process remains unchanged, the feedback is to the standard. It is possible that both would be changed. Thus, both feedbacks may result from the action phase and the system cycles through again.[12]

A standard tells management the expected cost of performing selected activities and allows comparisons to be made to determine whether operating inefficiencies have occurred. For example, Table 11–1 indicates a report which is useful at the operating level. It shows why the warehouse labor for the picking activity was $320 over budget. The costs of physical distribution

---

[12] Richard J. Lewis and Leo G. Erickson, "Distribution System Costing: An Overview," in John R. Grabner and William S. Sargent, ed., *Distribution System Costing: Concepts and Procedures* (Columbus, Ohio: Transportation and Logistics Research Foundation, 1972), pp. 18–20.

**TABLE 11–1** Summary of Warehouse Picking Operation Week of _____

| | |
|---|---|
| Items picked during week | 14,500 |
| Hours accumulated on picking activities | 330 |
| Standard hours allowed for picks performed based on 50 items per hour | 290 |
| Variation in hours | 40 |
| Standard cost per labor hour | $ 8 |
| Variation in cost due to inefficiency | $320* |

*The cost was $320 over budget because of 40 picking hours in excess of the standard number of hours allowed for efficient operation.

activities can be aggregated by department, division, function, or total, compared to their standard, and be included as part of a regular weekly or monthly performance report. One such level of aggregation which would be of interest to the president is shown in Table 11–2. This report allows the president to see at a glance why targeted net income has not been reached.

**TABLE 11–2** Segmental Analysis Using a Contribution Approach Explanation of Variation from Budget

| | Budget | Variance Due to Ineffectiveness ($000) | Standard Allowed for Output Level Achieved | Variance Due to Inefficiency | Actual Results |
|---|---|---|---|---|---|
| Net sales | $90,000 | $10,000 | $80,000 | — | $80,000 |
| Cost of goods sold (variable manufacturing cost) | 40,500 | 4,500 | 36,000 | — | 36,000 |
| Manufacturing contribution | $49,500 | $ 5,500 | $44,000 | — | $44,000 |
| Variable marketing and physical distribution costs (out-of-pocket costs that vary directly with sales to the segment)* | $22,500 | 2,500 | 20,000 | $1,400 | 21,400 |
| Segment contribution margin | $27,000 | $ 3,000 | $24,000 | $1,400 | $22,600 |
| Assignable nonvariable costs (costs incurred specifically for the segment during the period)† | 6,000 | — | 6,000 | — | 6,000 |
| Segment controllable margin | $21,000 | $ 3,000 | $18,000 | $1,400 | $16,600 |

Notes: Segments could be products, customers, geographic areas, or divisions.
Assumption: Actual sales revenue decreased, a result of lower volume. The average price paid per unit sold remained the same. (If the average price per unit changes then an additional variance—the marketing variance—can be computed.)
Difference in income = $4,400 ($21,000 − 16,600).
Explained by:
  a. Ineffectiveness—inability to reach target sales objective ...... $3,000
  b. Inefficiency at operating level achieved of $80,000 ........... 1,400
                                                                                           $4,400

* These costs might include: sales commissions, transportation costs, warehouse handling costs, order-processing costs, and inventory carrying costs.

† These costs might include: salaries, segment-related advertising, and bad debts. The fixed costs associated with corporate owned and operated facilities would be included if, and only if, the warehouse was solely for this segment of the business.

On the one hand, there is a $3 million difference due to ineffectiveness, which simply indicates the net income that the company has foregone because of its inability to meet its budgeted level of sales. On the other hand there is also an inefficiency factor of $1 million. This factor indicates that at the level of sales actually achieved, the segment-controllable margin should have been $18 million. The difference between $18 million and the actual outcome of $16 million is the variation due to inefficiencies within the marketing and physical distribution functions.

**Budgetary Practices**

Conceptually, there is little doubt regarding the general superiority of standard costs for control. However, there will be times when the use of standards is inappropriate. This is particularly true in situations which are essentially nonrepetitive tasks and for which work-unit measurements are difficult to establish. In these situations, control can still be achieved through budgetary practices. However, the extent to which the budget is successful depends on whether individual cost-behavior patterns can be predicted and whether the budget can be flexed to reflect changes in operating conditions.

Most physical distribution budgets are static. That is, they are a plan developed for a budgeted level of output. If actual activity happens to be the same as budgeted, a realistic comparison of costs can be made, and control will be effective. However, this is seldom the case. Seasonality or internal factors invariably will lead to different levels of activity, the efficiency of which can be determined only if the reporting system can compare the actual costs with what they should have been at the operating level achieved. In a warehousing example, for instance, the estimated or budgeted level of activity may be 1,000 line items per week. The actual level of activity, however, may be only 750.

Comparing the budgeted costs at 1,000 line items against the actual costs at 750 leads to the erroneous conclusion that the operation has been efficient since items such as overtime, temporary help, packing, postage, and order processing are less than budget. A flexible budget, on the other hand, indicates what the costs should have been at the 750 line items level of activity and a true dollar measure of efficiency results.

The key to successful implementation of a flexible budget lies in the analysis of cost behavior patterns. To date, little of this analysis has been carried out in the physical distribution function. The expertise of the management accountant and industrial engineer can be invaluable in applying tools such as scatter-diagram techniques and regression analysis to determine the fixed and variable components of costs. These techniques utilize previous cost data to determine a variable rate per unit of activity and a total fixed-cost component. Once accomplished, the flexible budget for control becomes a reality. However, unlike engineered standards, the techniques are based on past cost behavior patterns which undoubtedly contain inefficiencies. The predicted measure of cost, therefore, may not be a measure of what the activity should cost but an estimate of what it will cost based on the results of previous periods. Appendix B shows how to develop standard costs and flexible budgets for a warehouse operation.

### Productivity Standards

*Productivity Ratios*

Physical distribution costs also can be controlled by the use of productivity ratios. These ratios take the form of:

$$\text{Productivity} = \frac{\text{Measure of output}}{\text{Measure of input}}$$

For example, a warehouse operation might make use of such productivity ratios as:

$$\frac{\text{Number of orders shipped this period}}{\text{Number of orders received this period}}$$

$$\frac{\text{Number of orders shipped this period}}{\text{Average number of orders shipped per period}}$$

$$\frac{\text{Number of orders shipped this period}}{\text{Number of direct labor hours worked this period}}$$

Productivity ratios for transportation might include:[13]

$$\frac{\text{Ton-miles transported}}{\text{Total actual transportation cost}}$$

$$\frac{\text{Stops served}}{\text{Total actual transportation cost}}$$

$$\frac{\text{Shipments transported to destination}}{\text{Total actual transportation cost}}$$

The transportation resource inputs for which productivity ratios can be generated include: labor, equipment, energy, and cost. The specific relationships between these inputs and transportation activities are illustrated in Table 11–3. An X in a cell of the matrix denotes an activity/input combination which could be measured. Similar activity/input matrices for: warehousing; purchasing, inventory management, and production management; and, customer service (order processing/customer communications) are shown in Tables 11–4, 11–5 and 11–6, respectively.

Productivity measures of this type can and have been developed for most physical distribution activities. They are particularly useful in the absence of a standard costing system with flexible budgeting since they do provide some guidelines on operating efficiencies. Furthermore, they are measures that are easily understood by management and employees. However, productivity measures are not without their shortcomings:

*Shortcomings of Productivity Measures*

1. Productivity measures are expressed in terms of physical units and actual dollar losses due to inefficiencies, and predictions of future physical

---

[13] A. T. Kearney, Inc. *Measuring Productivity In Physical Distribution* (Chicago: NCPDM, 1978), p. 76.

**TABLE 11–3** Transportation Activity/Input Matrix

| Activities | Labor | Facilities | Equipment | Energy | Financial investment | Overall (cost) |
|---|---|---|---|---|---|---|
| Company-operated over-the-road trucking | | | | | | |
|   Loading | X | — | — | — | — | X |
|   Line-haul | X | — | — | X | — | X |
|   Unloading | X | — | — | — | — | X |
|   Overall | X | — | X | X | — | X |
| Company-operated pickup/delivery trucking | | | | | | |
|   Pretrip | X | — | — | — | — | X |
|   Stem driving | X | — | — | X | — | X |
|   On-route driving | X | — | — | X | — | X |
|   At-stop | X | — | — | — | — | X |
|   End-of-trip | X | — | — | — | — | X |
|   Overall | X | — | X | X | — | X |
| Outside transportation—all modes | | | | | | |
|   Loading | — | — | — | — | — | X |
|   Line-haul | — | — | — | — | — | X |
|   Unloading | — | — | — | — | — | X |
| Transportation/traffic management | | | | | | |
|   Company-operated | — | — | — | — | — | X |
|   Outside transportation | — | — | — | — | — | X |

Source: A. T. Kearney, Inc. *Measuring Productivity in Physical Distribution*, (Chicago: The National Council of Physical Distribution Management, 1978), p. 51.

**TABLE 11–4** Warehouse Activity/Input Matrix

| Activities | Labor | Facilities | Equipment | Energy | Financial | Overall |
|---|---|---|---|---|---|---|
| Company-operated warehousing | | | | | | |
|   Receiving | X | X | X | | | X |
|   Put-away | X | | X | | | X |
|   Storage | | X | | X | | X |
|   Replenishment | X | | X | | | X |
|   Order selection | X | | X | | | X |
|   Checking | X | | X | | | X |
|   Packing and marking | X | X | X | | | X |
|   Staging and order consolidation | X | X | X | | | X |
|   Shipping | X | X | X | | | X |
|   Clerical and administration | X | | X | | | X |
|   Overall | X | X | X | X | X | X |
| Purchased-outside warehousing | | | | | | |
|   Storage | | | | | | X |
|   Handling | | | | | | X |
|   Consolidation | | | | | | X |
|   Administration | | | | | | X |
|   Overall | | | | | | X |

Source: A. T. Kearney, Inc., *Measuring Productivity in Physical Distribution* (Chicago: The National Council of Physical Distribution Management, 1978), p. 101.

**TABLE 11-5** Purchasing, Inventory Management, and Production Management Activity/Input Matrix

|  | Inputs | | | |
|---|---|---|---|---|
| Functions/Activities | Labor | Equipment | Financial | Overall |
| Purchasing | | | | |
|    Sourcing | X | | | X |
|    Procurement | X | X | | X |
|    Cost Control | X | | | X |
|    Overall | | | | X |
| Inventory management | | | | |
|    Forecasting | X | X | | X |
|    Planning and budgeting | X | X | | X |
|    Execution and control | X | X | | X |
|    Overall | | | X | X |
| Production management | | | | |
|    Production planning | X | | | X |
|    Production control | X | | | X |
|    Scheduling and dispatching | X | X | | X |
|    Shop floor data collection | X | X | | X |
|    Overall | | | | X |

Source: A. T. Kearney, Inc., *Measuring Productivity in Physical Distribution* (Chicago: The National Council of Physical Distribution Management, 1978), p. 152.

**TABLE 11-6** Customer Service (order processing/customer communication) Activity/Input Matrix

|  | Inputs | | | |
|---|---|---|---|---|
| Activity | Labor | Facilities/ Equipment | Working Capital | Overall |
| Order processing | | | | |
|    Order entry/editing | X | X | X | X |
|    Scheduling | X | | | X |
|    Order/shipping set preparation | X | X | | X |
|    Invoicing | X | X | | X |
| Customer communication | | | | |
|    Order modification | X | X | | X |
|    Order status inquiries | X | X | | X |
|    Tracing and expediting | X | X | | X |
|    Error correction | X | | | X |
|    Product information requests | X | | | X |
| Credit and collection | | | | |
|    Credit checking | X | X | | X |
|    Accounts receivable processing/collecting | X | X | X | X |

Source: A. T. Kearney, Inc., *Measuring Productivity in Physical Distribution* (Chicago: The National Council of Physical Distribution Management, 1978), p. 191.

distribution cannot be made. This makes it extremely difficult to cost justify any system changes that will result in improved productivity.

2. The actual productivity measure calculated is seldom compared to a productivity standard. For example, a productivity measure may indicate the number of orders shipped this period to the number of direct labor hours worked this period but it does not indicate what the relationship ought to be. Without work measurement or some form of cost estimation it is impossible to know what the productivity standard should be at efficient operations.

3. Finally, changes in output levels may in some cases distort measures of productivity. This occurs because the fixed and variable elements are seldom delineated. Consequently, the productivity measure computes utilization and not efficiency. For example, if 100 orders shipped represents full labor utilization and 100 orders were received this period, then productivity as measured by

$$\frac{\text{Number of orders shipped this period}}{\text{Number of orders received this period}}$$

times 100 percent, which is 100 percent. However, if 150 orders had been received, and 100 orders shipped, productivity would have been 66.67 percent even though there was no real drop in either efficiency or productivity.

**Physical Distribution Costs and the Corporate Management Information System**

While substantial savings can be generated when management is able to compare its actual costs to a set of predetermined standards or budgets, even greater opportunities for profit improvement exist in the area of decision making. If management is to make informed decisions it must possess the ability to choose between such options as hiring additional common-carrier transportation or enlarging the company's private fleet, increasing deliveries or increasing inventories, expanding or consolidating field warehouses, and automating the order processing system. The addition or deletion of territories, salespeople, products, or customers requires knowledge of how well existing segments are currently performing and how revenues and costs will change with the alternatives under consideration. What is required is a data base capable of aggregating data so that routine information on individual segments such as customers, salespeople, products, territories, or channels of distribution can be obtained. Also the system must be able to store data by fixed and variable components so that the incremental revenues and costs associated with alternative strategies can be developed. One promising data base is the one introduced in Chapter 9 (Figure 9–7). It is a central storage system where source documents are fed into the data base in coded form. Inputs can be coded according to function, subfunction, territory, product, revenue or expense, channel, or a host of other possibilities. When combined with the computer, the system is capable of filing large amounts of data and allows rapid aggregation and retrieval of various modules of information for decision analysis.

With this information, management is in a position to evaluate the profitability of various segments. In addition, the data base permits the user to simulate trade-off situations and determine the effect of proposed system and strategic changes on total cost.

### The Role of the Order Processing System

*The Order Processing System Can Impact PD in Two Major Ways*

The order processing system can impact on the performance of the physical distribution function in two major ways. First, the system can improve the quality of the management information system by providing such data as customer names, locations of customers, items demanded by customer, revenue by customer, sales by customer, sales patterns (when items are ordered), order size, sales by salesperson, and sales data for the company's sales forecasting package.

Second, the customer order is the message that sets the physical distribution function in motion. The speed and quality of the information provided by the order processing system has direct impact on the cost and efficiency of the entire physical distribution process. Slow and erratic communications can lead to lost customers and/or excessive transportation, inventory, and warehousing costs as well as possible production inefficiencies caused by frequent line changes. Implementation of the latest technology in order processing and communications systems can lead to significant improvements in physical distribution performance.

## COST JUSTIFICATION OF PHYSICAL DISTRIBUTION SYSTEM CHANGES

*Cost Justifying Changes in the PD System*

In Chapter 2 it was emphasized that an integrated approach to the management and control of the physical distribution function could significantly improve a firm's profitability. However, successful implementation of integrated physical distribution management is dependent on total-cost analysis. That is, changes in physical distribution system structure must be cost justified by comparing total costs before and after the change. In order to illustrate how to perform this cost benefit we will build upon an example first introduced in Chapter 8. The following background on the company is provided:

1. Financial data for the current year which is presented in Figure 11–4.
2. Customers mailed orders to the company for processing and the order cycle was 10 days on the average. That is, from the time that a customer placed an order in the mail until the shipment was received by the customer an average of 10 days had elapsed. Customers were satisfied with the 10-day order cycle since all major suppliers offered the same terms. Although, the company's average order cycle was 10 days, the range was from 8 days to 12 days. Consequently, to avoid stock-outs customers were required to plan for the worst possible outcome—a 12-day order cycle.

**FIGURE 11-4** The Strategic Profit Model with Financial Data for Company XYZ—before System Change (financial data in $ millions)

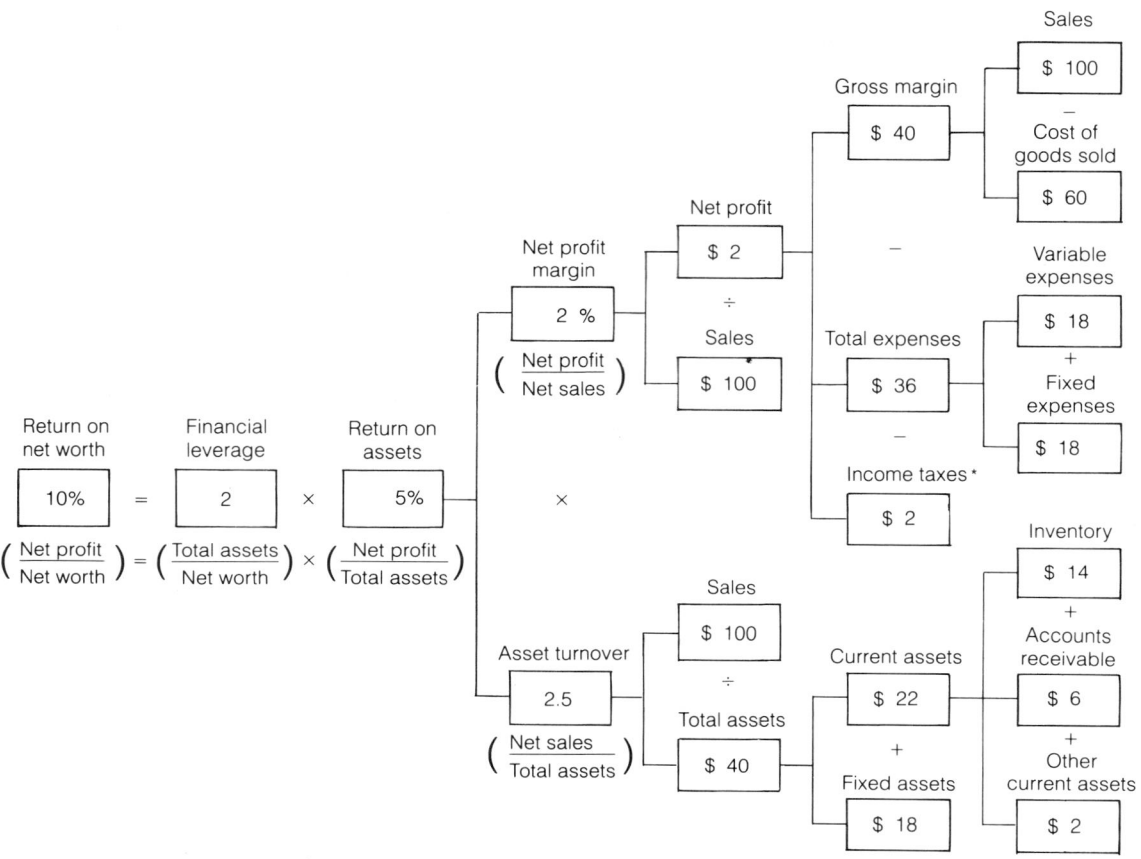

```
                                                                           Sales
                                                                          $ 100
                                                          Gross margin    −
                                                             $ 40         Cost of
                                                                          goods sold
                                                                          $ 60
                                            Net profit
                              Net profit       $ 2                        Variable
                              margin                                      expenses
                                                                          $ 18
                                2 %          ÷                            +
                              ( Net profit ) Sales        Total expenses  Fixed
                                Net sales    $ 100           $ 36         expenses
                                                                          $ 18
                                                          −
                                                          Income taxes*
                                                             $ 2
Return on      Financial      Return on                                   Inventory
net worth      leverage       assets                                      $ 14
  10%     =      2      ×       5%       ×                                +
( Net profit ) ( Total assets ) ( Net profit )            Sales           Accounts
  Net worth      Net worth       Total assets             $ 100           receivable
                              Asset turnover              ÷      Current assets  $ 6
                                 2.5                      Total assets  $ 22     +
                              ( Net sales )               $ 40                   Other
                                Total assets              +                      current assets
                                                          Fixed assets           $ 2
                                                          $ 18
```

* Income taxes are assumed to equal 50 percent of net profit before taxes.

3. The company calculated its inventory carrying costs to be 45 percent of the inventory valued at variable cost delivered to the field warehouse locations.
4. The company utilized 10 field warehouse locations for the distribution of its products. An example of one market area is shown in Figure 11−5. Products were shipped to a public warehouse by rail and the shipments to customers were by motor carrier.

A study of the company's order processing system revealed that an advanced order entry and processing system would shorten the total order cycle by four days. With the proposed system, customers would place their orders by telephone with customer service representatives equipped with CRTs. With this system, the customer service representative would enter the order on a real-time inventory control system while the customer was still

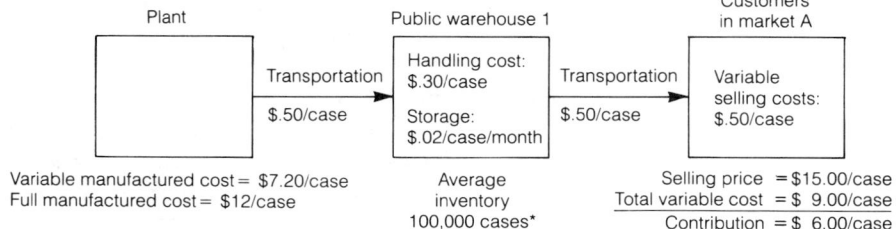

**FIGURE 11-5** Company XYZ's Physical Distribution System for Market A with Associated Costs

```
        Plant                          Public warehouse 1                    Customers
                                                                             in market A
                        Transportation   Handling cost:    Transportation    Variable
                                         $.30/case                           selling costs:
                        $.50/case        Storage:          $.50/case         $.50/case
                                         $.02/case/month
```

Variable manufactured cost = $7.20/case       Average              Selling price      = $15.00/case
Full manufactured cost = $12/case             inventory            Total variable cost = $ 9.00/case
                                              100,000 cases*       Contribution       = $ 6.00/case

*Average inventory valued at variable-cost delivered to the distribution center = ($7.20 + $0.50 + $0.30) × 100,000 = $800,000

on the telephone. The inventory levels would be reduced by the amount of the purchase thereby eliminating the problem of two customers being promised delivery of the same stock. In the event of a stock-out product substitution could be arranged or delivery scheduled based on planned production. Consequently, the proposed system would improve customer service by providing immediate information on inventory availability and making it possible to arrange for product substitution if a stock-out occurred. Also, target delivery dates could be communicated to the customer.

If the estimated annual cost of the proposed order processing system was $300,000 higher than the existing manual system, a cost-benefit analysis would be necessary in order to justify the increased cost.[14]

A number of possibilities exist for cost-benefit analysis but some are better than others. First, the four-day improvement in order cycle could be passed along to the company's customers by reducing the leadtime on orders from 10 to 6 days. The rationale would be that the manufacturer's market share and profitability would increase as a result of the improved customer service. Alternatively, customers of the manufacturer might be willing to pay for the increased service because it would make it possible for them to reduce their inventory levels. The problem with attempting to cost justify a proposed system change based on either of these outcomes is that it will be difficult to obtain the revenue data to support your analysis. Also, the outcomes described above may never be realized because of competitor reactions and other environmental factors.

The second alternative is for the manufacturer to use the four day reduction in order cycle time internally to improve efficiency of the physical distribution system and thereby reduce its costs. The cost savings can be used to perform a cost-benefit analysis for the new system. For example, if the company has annual sales of 1,200,000 cases of product in market A (see

---

[14] In companies where the order processing system is manual and the latest technology has not been applied it may be possible to cost justify the proposed system entirely by eliminating excessive costs associated with the current order processing system. Nevertheless, all of the cost savings should be documented in order to fully understand the financial impact of the proposed system.

Figure 11–5) and the additional four days are used for planning, inventory levels in the public warehouse can be decreased to 50,000 cases from 100,000 cases. Since the variable delivered cost of each case of product at the public warehouse is $8 ($7.20 variable manufactured cost plus 50 cents per case for transportation and 30 cents per case to move the product into the public warehouse), the reduction in inventory of 50,000 cases represents $400,000. With an inventory carrying cost of 45 percent, which includes a 40 percent pretax cost of money, the inventory reduction will result in an annual savings of $180,000 in inventory carrying costs in market A. Also, the four days will allow the manufacturer to consolidate some large orders to customers for direct truckload shipment with one or two stop-offs. This will allow the manufacturer to by-pass the public warehouse on approximately one third of its annual volume or 400,000 cases. If the truckload rate including stop-off charges was 85 cents per case, the transportation savings per year would be $60,000 [($1.00 − $0.85) × 400,000]. In addition, the 30 cents per case handling charge would be saved on the 400,000 cases resulting in a savings of $120,000 in public warehousing costs.

In summary, the annual cost savings in market A, the company's largest market, would be:

| | |
|---|---:|
| Reduced inventory carrying costs | $180,000 |
| Reduced transportation costs | 60,000 |
| Reduced warehousing costs | 120,000 |
| Total annual savings | $360,000 |

When this analysis was repeated for each of the manufacturer's 10 markets the following total annual savings were calculated:

| | |
|---|---:|
| Reduced inventory carrying costs | $ 936,000 |
| Reduced transportation costs | 175,000 |
| Reduced warehousing costs | 335,000 |
| Total annual savings | $1,446,000 |

From these savings it would be necessary to deduct the net annual cost of $300,000 associated with the new system. In addition, the freight-consolidation program would make it necessary to carry more inventory at plant locations to cover direct shipments to customers. The associated inventory carrying costs would be $250,000. Also, additional warehouse handling expenses of $96,000 would be incurred at plant locations. Therefore, the net savings associated with the new system would be $800,000 before taxes or $400,000 after income taxes. The $400,000 aftertax savings would increase profitability from $2 million to $2.4 million, thereby increasing return on assets from 5.0 percent to 6.0 percent and return on net worth from 10 percent to 12 percent.

In addition to the financial analysis, a number of qualitative, or less easily quantified, benefits can be presented to management. These should not be relied on to justify the system but rather as a supplement to the financial analysis—as icing on the cake. The additional benefits should include:

1. *Customer service improvements.* Customer service will be improved in basically two ways. First, the improved communication will allow the customer and the customer service representative to arrange for immediate substitution if a stock-out occurs or to provide the customer with a realistic estimated delivery date if it is necessary to wait for the product to be manufactured. Also, postorder inquiries regarding order status are facilitated by the new system.

Second, the improved communication should be able to reduce the variability associated with the order cycle time. Recall that the current order cycle of 10 days actually ranged from 8 days to 12 days—2 days variability. Reducing order cycle variability by 1 day to a range of 9 to 11 days will enable the customers to reduce their safety stocks.

2. *Improved cash flow.* The advanced order processing system will result in more accurate and timely invoicing of customers which will improve cash flow.

3. *Improved information.* The advanced order processing will improve information in two major ways. First, sales data will be captured sooner and more reliably, leading to more timely and better information for sales forecasting and production planning. Second, the advanced order processing system can be used as a source of valuable input for the physical distribution management information system.

A similar analysis can be used to determine the financial impact of purchasing a new forecasting model, inventory control package, or any other physical distribution system change.

With a well-thought-out financial analysis, you will be able to determine the probable profit impact of any proposed system. In the process you will contribute to improved productivity in physical distribution in the United States thereby raising the standard of living for all of us.

## SUMMARY

Accurate cost data are required if least-cost physical distribution is to be achieved. Successful implementation of the integrated physical distribution management is dependent upon full knowledge of the costs involved. Also cost data are required to manage physical distribution operations.

In this chapter you were shown how to use physical distribution costs for decision making and how erroneous decisions result when inaccurate costs are used. You were also shown how to measure and control physical distribution performance using: standard costs and flexible budgets; budgetary practices; and productivity standards. Finally, you were shown how to cost justify changes in physical distribution structure using the total cost concept.

In the next chapter you will be shown how management theory can apply to physical distribution organization structure, how to evaluate existing physical distribution organization structures, and how to develop an effective physical distribution organization.

## Appendix A: An Application of Standard Costs in Physical Distribution

The M company uses a system of standard variable costs for its distribution center activities. The purpose of this system is to:

1. Measure performance.
2. Aid in budgeting.
3. Develop appropriate costs to use in charging its users (branches).
4. Schedule work and plan laborpower.

A. The steps the company uses to develop its standards are as follows:
   I. Standard methods development
      A. Define the product
      B. Define the selling unit (each product)
         1. Case
         2. Carton
         3. Stock lengths
         4. Etc.
      C. Define the major functions (each selling unit)
         1. Unload and store
         2. Replenish
         3. Pick
         4. Assemble
         5. Etc.
      D. Develop all pertinent information relative to each function
         1. Product characteristics
         2. Material storage (rack design)
         3. Working conditions
         4. Product mix
         5. Material handling equipment
         6. Etc.
      E. Weigh all possible methods that could be used to perform each function (in order)
         1. Brain-storming approach
            a. The most ridiculous idea may have merit
            b. Never think a method is impossible
         2. Consider each in relation to optimum cost
         3. Arrive at the best method or methods
            a. A function may contain more than one method due to product mix
      F. Break the function down into job elements
      G. Determine the number of workers required to perform each element
      H. Determine the number of units to be handled for each element
   II. Standard time value development
      A. Develop time values for each job element, using a work measurement technique
         1. Simulation
         2. Standard engineering data
         3. Time study

---

Source: Howard M. Armitage, Associate Professor of Accounting, The University of Waterloo, adapted from Michael Schiff, *Accounting and Control in Physical Distribution Management* (Chicago: NCPDM, 1972).

B. Calculate labor-minutes per unit for each job element
C. Total the job element values—function cycle
D. Convert the time values for the function cycle to a common denominator
E. If a function cycle has more than one method due to a product mix, calculate a weighted average
F. Calculate the final labor-hour values for each product selling unit
G. Prepare an appropriate summary of all labor-hour values for accounting
H. Periodically update the standard values due to a change in
  1. Product mix
  2. Methods
  3. Packaging
  4. Storage system
  5. Equipment
  6. Etc.

A sample calculation of a standard cost with weighting for product mix follows:

*Location:* Distribution center 1

*Product:* "X"

*Selling unit:* Case

*Function:* Pick and load (four representative packs)

*Assumptions:*
  1. Load case on standard rack truck
  2. Equipment
  3. Case is picked and loaded on the night shift
  4. Average number of cases per order-pick run = 4 (2 workers), 1 (4 workers)
  5. Average number of cases loaded on each truck side rack = 7
  6. Average distance, storage area to truck = 200 feet.
  7. Average travel speed = 100 feet per minute

|  |  |  |  |  |  | Labor |
|---|---|---|---|---|---|---|
| *I. Elements (4 cases at 20 pounds):* | Workers | × Units | × Minutes | = | Minutes |
| A. Pick: | | | | | |
|   1. End pick to A-frame | 2 × | 4 × | 1.4 | = | 11.2 |
|   2. Move A-frame to truck | 2 × | 1 × | $\frac{200}{100}$ | = | 4.0 |
| B. Load: | | | | | |
|   1. Load truck | 2 × | 4 × | 0.4 | = | 3.2 |
|   2. Case protection | 2 × | 4 × | 0.3 | = | 2.4 |
|   3. Secure case | 2 × | 4 × | 0.3 | = | 2.4 |
|   4. Clerical | 2 × | 4 × | 0.1 | = | 0.8 |
|   5. Building factor (+ 10%) | | | | = | 0.9 |
| C. Miscellaneous: | | | | | |
|   1. Pick: | | | | | |
|     a. Assemble equipment | 2 × | 1 × | 3.0 | = | 6.0 |
|   2. Load: | | | | | |
|     a. Prepare truck | 2 × | 4 × | 0.5 | = | 4.0 |
|     b. Return equipment | 2 × | 1 × | 2.0 | = | 4.0 |
|     Total (4 cases) | | | | = | 38.9 |
|     Total (1 case) | | | | = | 9.7 |
| *II. Elements (4 cases at 40 pounds)* | | | | | |
| A. Pick: | | | | | |
|   1. End pick to A-frame | 2 × | 4 × | 1.7 | = | 13.6 |
|   2. Move A-frame to truck | 2 × | 1 × | $\frac{200}{100}$ | = | 4.0 |

II. *Elements (4 cases at 40 pounds) (continued)*
   B. Load:
      1. Load truck        2 × 4 × 0.7 = 5.6
      2. Case protection    2 × 4 × 0.6 = 4.8
      3. Secure case       2 × 4 × 0.6 = 4.8
      4. Clerical           2 × 4 × 0.1 = 0.8
      5. Building factor (+ 10%)            = 1.6
   C. Miscellaneous:
      1. Pick:
         *a.* Assemble equipment   2 × 1 × 3.0 = 6.0
      2. Load:
         *a.* Prepare truck       2 × 4 × 0.5 = 4.0
         *b.* Return equipment    2 × 1 × 2.0 = 4.0
             Total (4 cases)                  = 49.2
             Total (1 case)                   = 12.1

III. *Elements (4 cases at 60 pounds)*
   A. Pick:
      1. End pick to A-frame    2 × 4 × 2.2 = 17.6
      2. Move A-frame to truck   2 × 1 × $\frac{200}{100}$ = 4.0
   B. Load:
      1. Load truck        2 × 4 × 0.8 = 6.4
      2. Case protection    2 × 4 × 0.7 = 5.6
      3. Secure case       2 × 4 × 0.7 = 5.6
      4. Clerical           2 × 4 × 0.1 = 0.8
      5. Building factor (+ 10%)            = 1.8
   C. Miscellaneous:
      1. Pick:
         *a.* Assemble equipment   2 × 1 × 3.0 = 6.0
      2. Load:
         *a.* Prepare truck       2 × 4 × 0.5 = 4.0
         *b.* Return equipment    2 × 1 × 2.0 = 4.0
             Total (4 cases)                  = 55.8
             Total (1 case)                   = 14.0

IV. *Elements (1 case at 90 pounds)*
   A. Pick:
      1. End pick to dolly      4 × 1 × 1.3 = 5.2
      2. Move dolly to truck    4 × 1 × $\frac{200}{100}$ = 8.0
   B. Load:
      1. Load truck        4 × 1 × 1.0 = 4.0
      2. Case protection    4 × 1 × 0.8 = 3.2
      3. Secure cases      4 × 1 × 0.8 = 3.2
      4. Clerical           4 × 1 × 0.1 = 0.4
      5. Building factor (+ 10%)            = 1.1
   C. Miscellaneous:
      1. Pick:
         *a.* Assemble equipment   4 × 1 × 3.0 = 12.0
      2. Load:
         *a.* Prepare truck       2 × 1 × 0.5 = 1.0
         *b.* Return equipment    4 × 1 × 2.0 = 8.0
             Total (1 case)                   = 46.1

    The company uses a weighted-average standard cost which is calculated either in terms of labor-minutes per case or labor-minutes per pound.

1. L-M per case = $\dfrac{9.7 \text{ L-M}(20\%) + 12.1 \text{ L-M}(50\%) + 14.0 \text{ L-M}(20\%) + 46.1 \text{ L-M}(10\%)}{100\%}$

    = 15.4 L-M per case

2. L-M per pound =
    $\dfrac{20 \text{ pounds }(20\%) + 40 \text{ pounds }(50\%) + 60 \text{ pounds }(20\%) + 90 \text{ pounds }(10\%)}{100\%}$

    = 45.0 pounds per case

Therefore

$$\dfrac{15.4 \text{ L-M per case}}{45.0 \text{ pounds per case}} = 0.34 \text{ L-M per pound.}$$

### B. Relationship to Planned Volume

The standard costs just developed are related to the planned volume for each distribution center and a budget of variable and fixed costs is developed. This is illustrated below.

| Account Name | Number of Employees | Hours | Budget Variable Portion | Budget Fixed Portion | Total | Variable Rate Per Unit |
|---|---|---|---|---|---|---|
| Salaries | | | | | | |
| Wages—Class 1 | | | | | | |
| Wages—Class 2 | | | | | | |
| Wages—etc. | | | | | | |
| Overtime premium | | | | | | |
|     Total wages and salaries | | | | | | |
| Employee benefits | | | | | | |
| Travel | | | | | | |
| Dues and subscription | | | | | | |
|     Total expenses of employees | | | | | | |
| Repairs to office equipment | | | | | | |
| Telephone and telegraph | | | | | | |
| Depreciation furniture and equipment | | | | | | |
| Depreciation autos | | | | | | |
| Warehouse expense | | | | | | |
| Truck expense | | | | | | |
|     Total delivery and office expense | | | | | | |
| Other expense | | | | | | |
| Interest on investment | | | | | | |
| Corporate charges | | | | | | |
|     Total service charges | | | | | | |
| **Grand total** | | | | | | |

## C. Operations Report

|  | (A)<br>Hours<br>Operated | (B)<br>Throughput<br>(000 Pounds) | (C)<br>(B − A)<br>Productivity<br>Pounds per<br>Labor Hour | (D)<br>Productivity<br>Goal | (E)<br>(B − D)<br>Standard<br>Hours | (F)<br>(A − E)<br>Deviation<br>Hours |
|---|---|---|---|---|---|---|
| Operating Data |  |  |  |  |  |  |
| 1. D.C. receiving |  |  |  |  |  |  |
| 2. D.C. shipping |  |  |  |  |  |  |
| 3. Depot receiving |  |  |  |  |  |  |
| 4. Depot shipping |  |  |  |  |  |  |
| 5. Deliveries |  |  |  |  |  |  |
| 6. Total hours operated |  |  |  |  |  |  |
| Summary |  |  |  |  |  |  |
| 7. Total hours budgeted |  |  |  |  |  |  |
| 8. Deviation |  |  |  |  |  |  |
| 9. Overtime hours |  |  |  |  |  |  |
|     Warehouse |  |  |  |  |  |  |
|     Cartage |  |  |  |  |  |  |
|     Total |  |  |  |  |  |  |
| 10. Holiday and vacation hours |  |  |  |  |  |  |
|     Warehouse |  |  |  |  |  |  |
|     Cartage |  |  |  |  |  |  |
|     Total |  |  |  |  |  |  |
| 11. Number of late truck departures |  |  |  |  |  |  |
| 12. Number of orders delivered on time  =  % |  |  |  |  |  |  |
| 13. Billing status—Days behind |  |  |  |  |  |  |
| 14. Number of backorders |  |  |  |  |  |  |
| 15. Number of lost sales |  |  |  |  |  |  |

D. Variance Reporting

A monthly and year-to-data report is provided for each distribution center. For each item in the budget the following calculations are made.

| Account Name | Actual Expense | Allowed Expense | Variance from Standard | Rate Variance | Efficiency Variance |
|---|---|---|---|---|---|
| Salaries | | | | | |
| Wages—Class I | | | | | |
| Wages—Class II | | | | | |
| Wages—etc. | | | | | |
| Overtime premium | | | | | |
|     Total wages and salaries | | | | | |
| Employee benefits | | | | | |
| Travel | | | | | |
| Dues and subscription | | | | | |
|     Total expense of employees | | | | | |
| Repairs to office equipment | | | | | |
| Telephone and telegraph | | | | | |
| Depreciation furniture and equipment | | | | | |
| Depreciation autos | | | | | |
| Warehouse expense | | | | | |
| Truck expense | | | | | |
|     Total delivery and office expense | | | | | |
| Other expense | | | | | |
| Interest on investment | | | | | |
| Corporate charges | | | | | |
|     Total service charges | | | | | |
| **Grand total** | | | | | |

## Appendix B: Developing Standard Costs and Flexible Budgets for Warehousing

The first step is to define operating characteristics. Possible units of measure of activities in warehousing might be—order, case, shipment, SKU, line item, arrival, and/or overpacked carton. The basic elements of this warehouse operation consist of receiving (unloading and clerical), shipping (clerical and order consolidation), stock put away, stock replenishment, order picking, and overpacking. A description of the process is shown in Figure 11B−1.

All of the basic functions of warehousing are present. A 45-day sample was obtained and data was accumulated for the various important functions of the operation. The results of the sample are shown in Table 11B−1. Also included are the average number of occurrences observed and the standard deviation which is a

Source: This material is adapted from Howard M. Armitage and James F. Dickow, "Controlling Distribution with Standard Costs and Flexible Budgets," in *Proceedings of the Seventeenth Annual Conference of the National Council of Physical Distribution Management, October 15– 17, 1979*, pp. 116–20.

**FIGURE 11B-1** Operating Characteristics

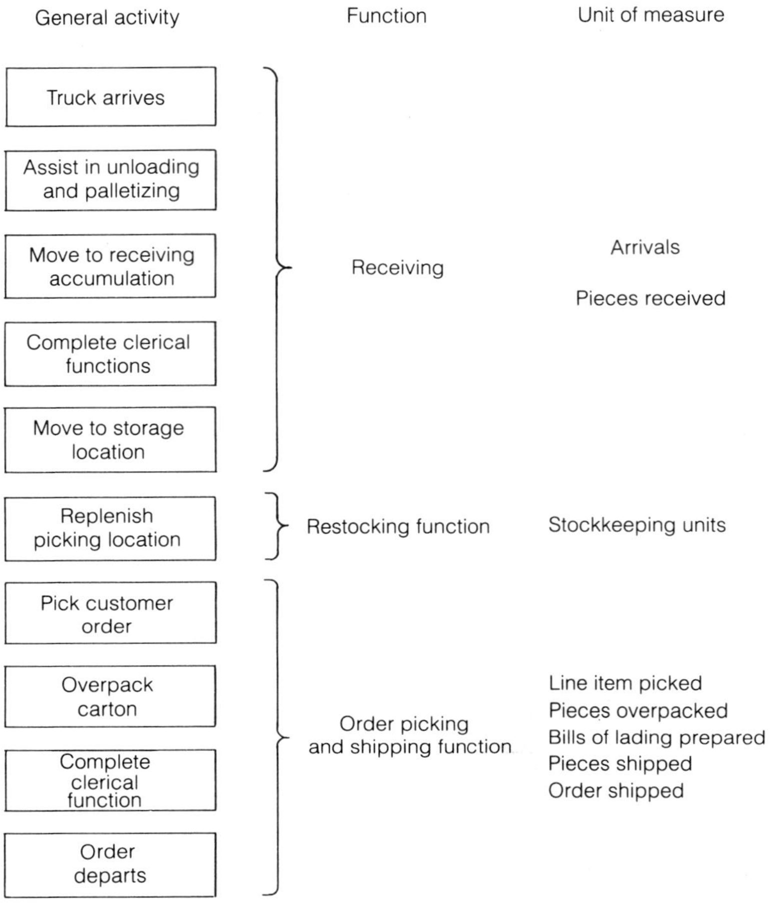

| General activity | Function | Unit of measure |
|---|---|---|
| Truck arrives | | |
| Assist in unloading and palletizing | | |
| Move to receiving accumulation | Receiving | Arrivals |
| Complete clerical functions | | Pieces received |
| Move to storage location | | |
| Replenish picking location | Restocking function | Stockkeeping units |
| Pick customer order | | Line item picked |
| Overpack carton | Order picking and shipping function | Pieces overpacked |
| Complete clerical function | | Bills of lading prepared |
| Order departs | | Pieces shipped |
| | | Order shipped |

**TABLE 11B-1** Activity Levels (45-day sample)

| Function | Unit of Measure | Average (units of measure per day) | Standard Deviation (units of measure per day) |
|---|---|---|---|
| Receiving functions: | | | |
|   Arrivals | Arrivals | 18 | 14 |
|   Unloaded | Pieces | 735 | 731 |
|   Stock put away | Pieces | 735 | 731 |
| Replenishment functions: | | | |
|   Volume | SKU | 200 | 0 |
| Shipping functions: | | | |
|   Order picking | Line items | 279 | 72 |
|   Overpacking | Pieces | 85 | 37 |
|   Orders | Orders | 113 | 31 |
|   Freight shipments | Bill of lading | 61 | 14 |
|   Small shipments | Pieces | 83 | 24 |
|   Load | Pieces | 863 | 198 |

measure of central tendency or variation around the average. The larger the standard deviation, the more variation there is in day-to-day activity. For instance, the receiving function has higher standard deviations than the order-picking function. This is logical, since receiving activities tend to fluctuate. Shipping, on the other hand, is more consistent and the standard deviation of the number of lines picked per day is small.

Now that the process has been described—its operating characteristics and activity levels known—the next step is to develop activity standards. These were developed using empirical standards. These standards could have been developed based upon industry standards, engineering studies, or historical data, but the empirical method of observing the operation and using judgement to develop estimates was thought to be the most appropriate in this case (see Table 11B−2).

**TABLE 11B−2**  Activity Standards—Empirical

| Operating Function | Unit of Measure (per labor-hour) | Time Standard (units of measure per labor-hour) |
|---|---|---|
| Warehouse: | | |
| Receiving | | |
|   Unload truck | Pieces | 250 |
|   Check receipts | Pieces | 167 |
|   Clerical function | Pieces | 500 |
|   Putaway stock | Pieces | 150 |
| Shipping | | |
|   Order picking | Line items | 30 |
|   Order packing | Pieces | 22.7 |
|   UPS/small shipment | Pieces | 100 |
|   Freight shipping | Bills of lading | 15 |
| Stockkeeping | | |
|   Bulk items | Skill | 70 |
|   QA and shelf items | Skill | 50 |

Now, that the daily activities, the approximate levels of activity, and knowledge of the process have been determined, this information is used to develop standard costs (see Table 11B−2).

The information in Table 11B−3, which includes the standard times and hourly wage rates allows an incremental cost per unit of measure to be calculated. The unit of measure for each one of the activities might be different—and in this case they are different, that is, piece, SKU, line item, and freight shipment. In some cases it is possible to lump activities together as they are in the receiving function, but this is not possible in every situation. The standard cost per unit of measure is obtained by dividing the labor costs per labor-hour by the estimated standard time.

If this warehousing operation were using flexible budgeting, the standard costs would be used to develop the flexible budget. An example is contained in Table 11B−4.

In this week, 4,200 cases were received, 1,000 stockkeeping units were replenished, etc. These activity levels, when multiplied by the standard costs per unit, gave the total standard costs for each activity. The actual costs incurred during the week also are shown, and variances—favorable or unfavorable—are calculated. For the activity levels achieved during the week, a net unfavorable variance of $125 was calculated.

**TABLE 11B-3** Standard Costs

| Function | Units of Measure | Daily Activity (units of measure) | Standard Time (units of measure per MH) | Hourly Rate ($ per MH) | Standard Cost ($ per unit of measure) |
|---|---|---|---|---|---|
| Receiving: | | | | | |
|   Unload truck | Pieces | 735 | 250 | 7.50 | 3.0¢/Piece |
|   Check receipts | Pieces | 735 | 167 | 7.50 | 4.5¢/Piece |
|   Clerical | Pieces | 735 | 500 | 7.50 | 1.5¢/Piece |
|   Putaway stock | Pieces | 735 | 150 | 7.50 | 5.0¢/Piece |
| | | | | | 14.0¢/Piece |
| Replenishment: | | | | | |
|   Replenish | SKU | 200 | 50 | 7.50 | 15.0¢/SKU |
| Shipping: | | | | | |
|   Order picking | Line item | 279 | 30 | 8.00 | 27.0¢/Line |
|   Overpacking | Pieces | 86 | 23 | 7.50 | 33.0¢/Piece |
|   Small shipping | Pieces | 83 | 100 | 8.00 | 8.0¢/Piece |
|   Freight shipping | Shipments | 61 | 15 | 8.25 | 55.0¢/Shipment |

**TABLE 11B-4** Application to a Flexible Budget

| | | | Weekly Summary | | | |
|---|---|---|---|---|---|---|
| Function | Unit of Measure (U/M) | Standard Cost ($/U/M) | Activity (U/M) | Std. Cost ($) | Actual Cost ($) | Variance ($) |
| Receiving | Piece | 0.14 | 4,200 | 588 | 800 | 212 U |
| Replenishment | SKU | 0.15 | 1,000 | 150 | 100 | 50 F |
| Shipping | | | | | | |
|   Order picking | Line item | 0.27 | 1,430 | 386 | 450 | 64 U |
|   Overpacking | Piece | 0.33 | 350 | 116 | 100 | 16 F |
|   Small shipping | Piece | 0.08 | 500 | 40 | 25 | 15 F |
|   Freight shipping | Shipments | 0.55 | 400 | 220 | 150 | 70 F |
| | | | | 1,500 | 1,625 | 125 U |

Since this activity level was significantly higher than the average level of activity, the unfavorable variance would have been larger had a fixed budget approach been used. Developing standard costs and using them to develop a flexible budget gives management a tool to *measure* the *performance* of individuals. The minimization of unfavorable variances is a goal that when achieved, will yield increased profits.

## QUESTIONS AND PROBLEMS

1. Why is it so important to have accurate cost data for management of the physical distribution function?

2. What problems are associated with the use of average cost data for decision making?

3. How does the inability to distinguish between fixed and variable costs hamper good management practice?
4. What are the problems associated with the arbitrary allocation of physical distribution costs?
5. How do accurate cost data contribute to the motivation of personnel?
6. Why is it difficult to obtain physical distribution cost data in many firms?
7. Explain the three methods that can be used for controlling physical distribution activities.
8. What are the limitations associated with the use of productivity standards for measuring physical distribution performance? What are the advantages of using productivity standards?
9. How can the order-processing system improve the equality of the physical distribution information system?
10. What is the impact on return on net worth of a new order-processing system given the following information about the Michigan Manufacturing Company:
    a. Sales of $200 million.
    b. Net profit of $8 million after taxes.
    c. Asset turnover of 2.5 times.
    d. Financial leverage of 2.
    e. Taxes are 50 percent of net income.
    f. The new system will provide management with four additional days for planning physical distribution operations.
    g. Inventories will be reduced by $2 million, valued at variable costs delivered to the storage location.
    h. The company's inventory carrying cost is 45 percent which is comprised of a pretax cost of money of 40 percent and noncost of money components of 5 percent of the inventory value.
    i. Transportation consolidations made possible by the additional planning time will reduce transportation costs by $500,000 per year.
    j. Warehousing costs of $50,000 will be eliminated.
    k. The new order-processing system will cost $300,000 per year more than the existing system.
    l. Software costs associated with the new system will increase the first-year costs by $100,000.

# 12 Physical Distribution Organizations

Introduction
   Importance of an Effective Physical Distribution Organization
   Types of Physical Distribution Organizational Structures

Decision-Making Strategies in Organizing for PDM
   Components of an Optimal Physical Distribution Organization
      Organizational Characteristics
      Environmental Characteristics
      Employee Characteristics
      Managerial Policies and Practices
   An Approach to Developing an Optimal Physical Distribution Organization
      Corporate Objectives
      Corporate Structure
      Functional Responsibilities
      Management Style
      Flexibility
      Support Systems
      Personnel Considerations
   Measuring the Effectiveness of the Physical Distribution Organization

Summary

**Objectives of this chapter:**

To show how management theory can apply to physical distribution organization structure

To show how to evaluate existing physical distribution organization structures

To show how to develop an effective physical distribution organization

## INTRODUCTION

A number of distribution futurists were questioned regarding their views on the future of physical distribution. The consensus of these academic and practitioner futurists was that "the projected demand for [physical distribution] services during the remainder of the 20th century is frightening. Even a conservative growth will push the existing [distribution] framework far beyond its demonstrated capability."[1]

Such a statement is not unrealistic. Distribution executives have seen their discipline develop over the past 20 years from infancy, when the logistics functions were dispersed throughout the organization, to a highly structured, computerized, and large-budget activity. The role of the physical distribution executive is far different today than it was 20 years ago and most probably different from what it will be 20 years hence. The next two decades promise challenges unparallelled in the past.

> Due to increased uncertainties in the forces that affect supply and demand for industrial and consumer products, a greater priority must be put on anticipating shifts and improving forecasting procedures regarding uncontrollable environmental trends. With a sounder focus on a futures orientation, the planning process can more effectively apply Management-by-Objectives as the corporate and logistical philosophy, instead of reacting to problems as exemplified by the Management-by-Crisis formula.[2]

The physical distribution manager has been beset with a multitude of problems including economic uncertainty, inflation, product and energy shortages, regulatory constraints, and rising customer demands and expectations. The distribution activity is becoming increasingly more difficult to manage effectively and efficiently. In this chapter the issues of how to organize physical distribution within the firm as well as how to measure its effectiveness, will be examined. You will be shown the importance of an effective physical distribution organization to a firm and the types of organizational structures which exist. Although no single "ideal" organization structure is appropriate for all companies, you will be shown how to evalu-

---

[1] Brian S. Moskal, "No Buck Rogers in Corporate Logistics," *Industry Week* 196, no. 4 (February 20, 1978): 86.

[2] Dennis R. McDermott and James R. Stock, "A Futures Perspective on Logistics Management: Applying the Project Delphi Technique," in Robert H. House, ed., *Proceedings of the Eighth Annual Transportation and Logistics Educators Conference*, October 15, 1978, p. 1.

ate various physical distribution organization structures and the methods which can be used to develop an effective organization for your firm.

### Importance of an Effective Physical Distribution Organization

In July 1976, Johnson & Johnson Baby Products Company committed itself to reducing its distribution costs by 45 percent.[3] As a result of the completion of a distribution system design project, the company was able to achieve a cost savings, partially due to organizational design efficiencies adjusted to 1976 costs and volumes, of 11 percent in 1978. By 1979 the cost savings were 47 percent and for 1980, the company projected a savings of 49 percent. The cost reductions were achieved through modifications of the firm's organization structure, customer service levels, storage facilities, and inventory policies.

*Companies Realize Savings through Reorganization*

Whirlpool Corporation reorganized its distribution activities in late 1971 and established a new position of vice president of distribution. The company estimated savings of more than $10 million a year in distribution costs.[4] The savings resulted from pulling together a number of distribution-related activities under a single organizational unit with a reporting relationship to marketing. In addition, two traditional marketing activities were placed under distribution's control: sales forecasting and order processing.

In 1975, Hooker Chemicals and Plastics Corporation combined its distribution and purchasing functions into a single unit and created a high-level executive position, director of materials management, to head it. The company has reported favorable results in the areas of cost reduction, improved levels of customer service, and higher profits.[5] Companies as diverse as Abbott Laboratories, Uniroyal, Incorporated, Eastman Kodak Company, Maremont Corporation, and Mead Johnson and Company have undergone similar changes and achieved much the same results as Johnson & Johnson, Whirlpool, and Hooker.

Traditionally, the various physical distribution functions were scattered throughout the organization, with no single executive, department, or division responsible for managing the entire distribution process. Such a situation is depicted in Figure 12−1.

Each element of distribution tends to get lost among the other activities of marketing, finance and accounting, and manufacturing. [Figure 12−1] also highlights the inevitable conflict of objectives that results from this organization pattern. Only the president really seeks maximum total company return on investment, and the individual objectives of executives in marketing, finance and

---

[3] This case example is based upon a presentation entitled "Assessing the Organizational Trade-Offs in the Distribution Strategic Planning Process," by Peter H. Soderberg, director—physical distribution and planning, Johnson & Johnson Baby Products Company, at the annual meeting of the National Council of Physical Distribution Management, Houston, Texas, in October 1979.

[4] Thomas J. Murray, "A Powerful New Voice in Management," *Dun's Review* 107, no. 4 (April 1976): 71.

[5] Ibid., p. 70.

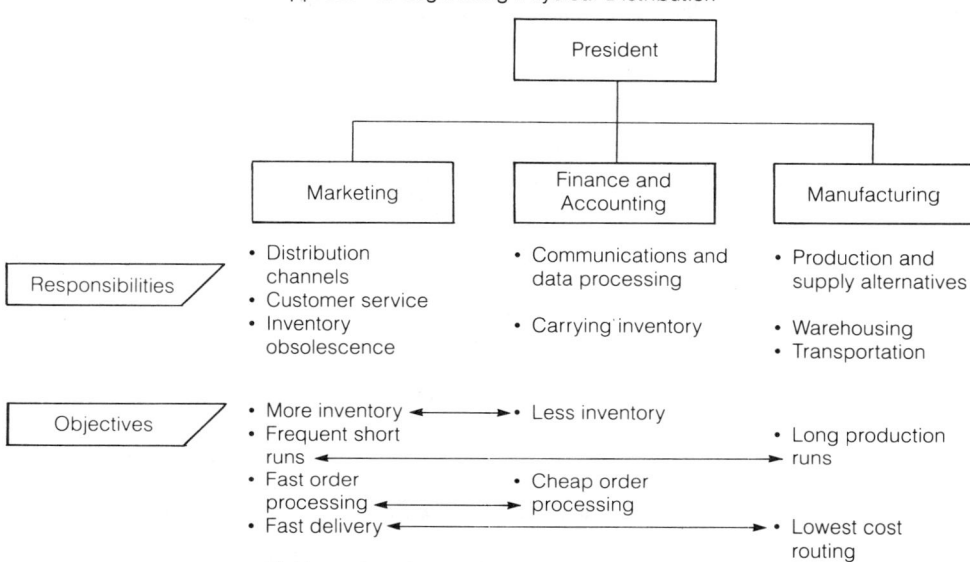

**FIGURE 12-1** Traditional Approach to Organizing Physical Distribution

```
                          President
            ┌────────────────┼────────────────┐
        Marketing      Finance and       Manufacturing
                        Accounting
```

**Responsibilities**
- Marketing:
  - Distribution channels
  - Customer service
  - Inventory obsolescence
- Finance and Accounting:
  - Communications and data processing
  - Carrying inventory
- Manufacturing:
  - Production and supply alternatives
  - Warehousing
  - Transportation

**Objectives**
- More inventory ←——→ Less inventory
- Frequent short runs ←————————————→ Long production runs
- Fast order processing ←——→ Cheap order processing
- Fast delivery ←————————————————→ Lowest cost routing
- Field warehousing ←——→ Less warehousing ←——→ Plant warehousing

Source: Reprinted by permission of the *Harvard Business Review*. Exhibited from "How to Manage Physical Distribution" by John F. Stolle (July–August 1967), p. 95. Copyright © 1967 by the President and Fellows of Harvard College; all rights reserved.

accounting, and manufacturing often conflict with this overall objective—and with each other (as the arrows denote).[6]

The lack of an organizational structure which combines the activities of physical distribution under a single, high level executive indicates a failure to adopt and implement the integrated physical distribution management concept (discussed in Chapter 2 of this book).

However, since the early 1960s, there has been a trend toward the integration of many distribution functions under one top-ranking corporate executive. Table 12 – 1 overviews the range of activities for which the distribution executive has had authority. There has been a continual expansion of the distribution executive's span of control to include transportation, warehousing, inventories, order processing, packaging, materials handling, forecasting and planning, and purchasing and procurement.

In a survey of the *Fortune* 1,000 largest industrial firms in the United States it was found that the percentage of respondent companies that had integrated their physical distribution activities under a single department or division had increased from 42 percent in 1971 to 50 percent in 1976.[7]

---

[6] John F. Stolle, "How to Manage Physical Distribution," *Harvard Business Review* 45, no. 4 (July–August 1967): 94.

[7] Douglas M. Lambert, James F. Robeson, and James R. Stock, "An Appraisal of the Integrated Physical Distribution Management Concept," *International Journal of Physical Distribution and Materials Management* 9, no. 1 (1978): 84.

**TABLE 12-1** Control Exercised by the PD Executive over Various Distribution Activities

|  |  |  |  | Percent of Reporting Companies |  |  |  |
|---|---|---|---|---|---|---|---|
| Activities | (A) 1962 | (B) 1966 | (C) 1972 | (D) 1976 | (E) 1978 | (F) 1979 | (G) 1981 |
| Transportation | 90% | 89% | 100% | 94% | 89% | 97% | 85% |
| Warehousing | 66 | 70 | 98 | 93 | 94 | 95 | 84 |
| Inventory control | 72 | 55 | 90 | 83 | 86 | 82 | 67 |
| Order processing | 12 | 43 | 88 | 76 | 84 | 81 | 64 |
| Packaging | 40 | 8 | 73 | 70 | 66 | 71 | 55 |
| Materials handling | 64 | 19 | * | * | * | 80 | 4 |
| Forecasting and planning | * | 26 | 40 | 42 | 49 | 45 | 33 |
| Purchasing and procurement | * | 15 | * | 58 | 64 | 42 | 42 |
| Number of reporting companies | 50 | 47 | Not available | 180 | 122 | 101 | 118 |

\* = Data not collected in study.
Sources:
(A) Warren Blanding, "Profile of PDM," *Transportation and Distribution Management* 2, no. 6 (June 1962): 13–17.
(B) John F. Spencer, "Physical Distribution Management Finds Its Level," *Handling and Shipping* 7, no. 11 (November 1966): 67–69.
(C) Herbert W. Davis, "Organization and Management of the Logistics Function in Industry," *Logistics Spectrum*, Fall 1972, pp. 9–13.
(D) Bernard J. LaLonde and James F. Robeson, "Profile of the Physical Distribution Executive," in *Proceedings of the Fourteenth Annual Conference of The National Council of Physical Distribution Management*, October 13–15, 1976, pp. 1–23.
(E) Bernard J. LaLonde and Jerome J. Cronin, "Profile of the Physical Distribution Manager," in *Proceedings of the Sixteenth Annual Conference of The National Council of Physical Distribution Management*, October 16–18, 1978, pp. 33–57.
(F) James R. Stock, "Measuring Distribution Organizational Effectiveness," in Bernard J. LaLonde, ed., *Proceedings of the Tenth Annual Transportation and Logistics Educators Conference*, October 12, 1980, pp. 15–25.
(G) Bernard J. LaLonde and Martha Cooper, "Career Patterns in Distribution—Profile 1981," in *Proceedings of the Nineteenth Annual Conference of The National Council of Physical Distribution Management*, October 18–21, 1981.

Coordination of the various distribution activities is crucial to the well being of a firm. In the next section, the various organizational types found in business firms are presented and discussed.

### Types of Physical Distribution Organizational Structures

Distribution management has been defined as:

> . . . that phase of administration responsible for the effective functioning of the overall distribution process. Organizationally, distribution management consists of:
>
> 1. The top physical distribution executive in the business unit.
> 2. Functional managers and their respective staffs.
> 3. The physical distribution project services groups.
> 4. Field operations management personnel and their respective line and staff organizations.[8]

Most distribution strategists would agree that for organizations of all sizes, coordination of the various PD activities is essential. This would be true irrespective of the organizational structure.

---
[8] A. T. Kearney, Inc., *Measuring Productivity in Physical Distribution* (Chicago: National Council of Physical Distribution Management, 1978), p. 215, (hereafter cited as NCPDM).

**Basic PD Organizational Structures**

The real issue concerns the extent to which distribution activities need to be coordinated—and the extent to which this coordination should be achieved through a formal distribution organization rather than through formalized procedures and operating practices in a traditional organization pattern.[9]

Coordination of the various PD activities can be achieved in several ways. The basic distribution organizational systems are generally structured utilizing a combination of the following:

1. Strategic versus operational.
2. Centralized versus decentralized.
3. Line versus staff.

Strategic versus operational refers to the level at which PD activities are positioned within the firm. Strategically, it is important to determine PD's position in the corporate hierarchy relative to other activities such as marketing, manufacturing, and finance/accounting. Equally important however, is the operational structuring of the various PD activities—warehousing, inventories, order processing, transportation, and others—under the senior distribution executive.

Centralized distribution can refer to the fact that PD activities are administered at a central location, typically a corporate headquarters, or to a system where operating authority is controlled under a single department or individual. In firms where products or markets are homogeneous, centralized organizational structures usually exist. Centrally programming activities such as order processing, traffic, inventories, and others can result in significant cost savings due to economies of scale. On the other hand, decentralization of PD activities can be effective for firms with diverse products or markets. Some argue, with justification, that decentralizing distribution activities often leads to higher levels of customer service.

"Traditional organization theory suggests the use of line and staff functions within the structure to achieve overall efficiency through specialization of labor in the hierarchical structuring. . . . In essence, the staff function is a delegation of authority laterally, not the vertical or hierarchical relationship encompassed in the line authority."[10] In the typical staff approach to distribution organization, PD finds itself in primarily an advisory role. In line organizations PD responsibilities are operational, that is, they deal with the management of day-to-day activities. Combinations of line and staff organizations are possible and most companies are structured in that fashion.

Three types of organizational structures can be identified: line, staff, or a combination of line and staff.[11] "Many companies are grouping line distribution activities only, thus forming another line function comparable to sales and production. When this is done, one individual is made responsible for

---

[9] Stolle, "How to Manage Physical Distribution," p. 94.

[10] John J. Coyle and Edward J. Bardi, *The Management of Business Logistics*, 2d ed. (St. Paul, Minn.: West Publishing, 1980), pp. 391–92.

[11] Stolle, "How to Manage Physical Distribution," pp. 96–98.

'doing' the distribution job."[12] In the staff organization, the line activities such as order processing, traffic, and warehousing are housed under production, marketing or, finance/accounting. The various staff activities assist and coordinate the line functions. The combination of line and staff activities combines the two previous organizational structures so as to eliminate the shortcomings inherent in systems where line and staff activities are not coordinated.

> Combination of line and staff functions provides the logistics department with the analytical skills to design, plan, and analyze existing and proposed logistics systems and with the authority to exercise control over the administration of these staff decisions to the day-to-day operations. Such an organizational structuring eliminates the subordinate role of [physical distribution].[13]

Other organizational structures are possible. Examples include physical distribution as a function; physical distribution as a program; and matrix organization.[14] In Figure 12–2, the organizational design for physical dis-

**FIGURE 12–2** Organization Design for Physical Distribution as a Function

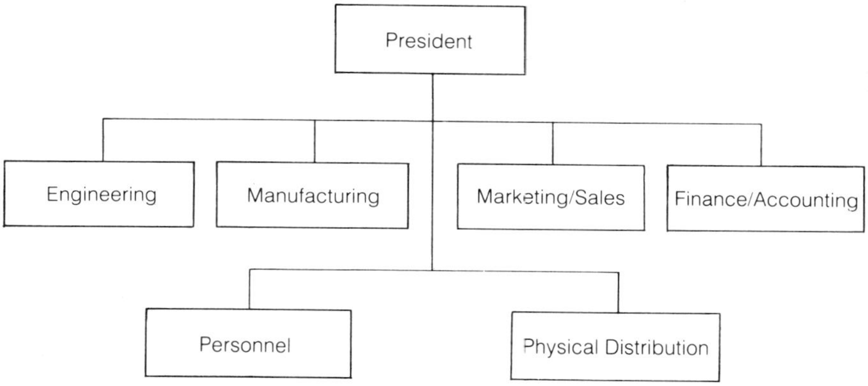

```
                          President
    ┌──────────┬──────────┼──────────┬──────────────────┐
 Engineering  Manufacturing  Marketing/Sales   Finance/Accounting
                   │
            ┌──────┴──────┐
        Personnel    Physical Distribution
```

tribution as a function is shown. The authors argue that if distribution is treated as a functional area, without regard to other activities of the firm, suboptimization will be the end result. Physical distribution is cross-functional and therefore requires a different organizational structure. The functional approach can be considered the antithesis of the systems approach in that:

*PD as a Function*

> The traditional functional view of organizations isolates physical mechanisms, material components, psychosocial effects, political-legal elements, economic constructs, and environmental constraints. Traditionally, each of these elements was optimized, often ignoring the interrelationships among them. But as organi-

---

[12] Ibid., p. 96.
[13] Coyle and Bardi, *Business Logistics*, p. 394.
[14] Daniel W. DeHayes, Jr., and Robert L. Taylor, "Making 'Logistics' Work in a Firm," *Business Horizons* 15, no. 3 (June 1972): 41–44.

PD as a Program

zations developed, complex interdependencies evolved, and a holistic approach became necessary to cope with the problems of the organization.[15]

When physical distribution is organized as a program (see Figure 12 – 3), the distribution activity assumes the role of a program in which the total

**FIGURE 12-3** Organization Design for Physical Distribution as a Program

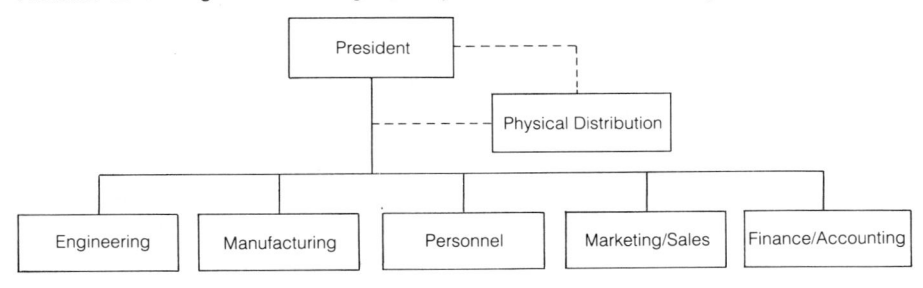

```
                    President
                   /        \
                  /     Physical Distribution
    ┌──────┬──────┬──────┬──────┐
Engineering Manufacturing Personnel Marketing/Sales Finance/Accounting
```

company participates. Functional areas are subordinate to the program. "[Physical distribution] considerations are given paramount importance, and systems cost minimization is equated with organization profit maximization. Demand generation and production processes are considered only in respect to how they contribute to the logistics system."[16]

It can be argued that the optimal distribution organization lies between the two extremes represented by the functional and program approaches. The middle approach has been termed the *matrix organization* and is shown in Figure 12 – 4.

Matrix Management

This type of structure is built around specific programs represented by the horizontal emphasis. Each program manager, such as the [physical distribution] program manager, is responsible for his program within established time, cost, quantity, and quality constraints. The line organization (the vertical emphasis) develops from the programs but is now a supporting relationship. . . . Instead of a line-and-staff relationship, there is a web of relationships, all acting and reacting in harmony. The [physical distribution] manager can assume his intended role; he becomes the overall coordinator among a whole series of functions.[17]

The matrix management approach requires the coordination of activities across unit lines in the organization, therefore it is essential that top-level management wholeheartedly support the physical distribution executive. Even with high-level support however, the coordination complexities are difficult to master. For example, any time there are multiple reporting responsibilities, as is common in matrix organizations, problems may arise. "The distribution manager might report to a vice president of distribution but also be responsible to the vice president of marketing where [he/she]

---

[15] Ibid., p. 40.
[16] Ibid., pp. 42 – 43.
[17] Ibid., pp. 43 – 44.

**FIGURE 12-4** Physical Distribution in a Matrix Organization

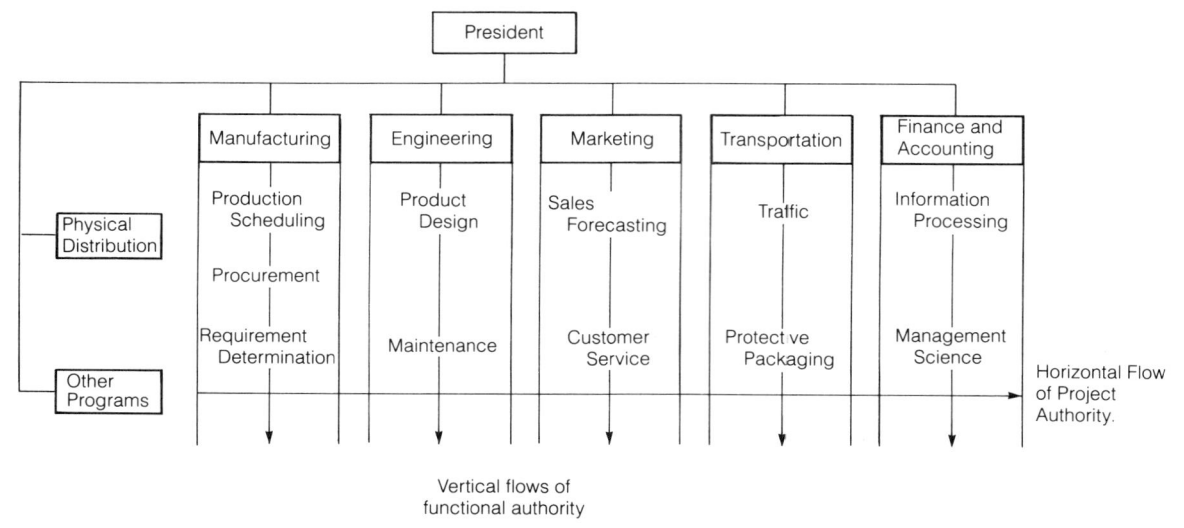

```
                              President
                                 │
        ┌────────┬───────────┬───────────┬────────────┬──────────────┐
        │        │           │           │            │              │
   Manufacturing Engineering Marketing Transportation Finance and
                                                      Accounting
        │        │           │           │            │
   Production  Product    Sales        Traffic     Information
   Scheduling  Design     Forecasting              Processing
        │
   Procurement
        │
   Requirement Maintenance Customer    Protective  Management
   Determination           Service     Packaging   Science
```

Physical Distribution

Other Programs

Horizontal Flow of Project Authority.

Vertical flows of functional authority

Source: Adapted from Daniel W. DeHayes, Jr., and Robert L. Taylor, "Making 'Logistics' Work in a Firm," *Business Horizons* 15, no. 3 (June 1972): 44.

contributes to market strategies. It's a teamwork organization."[18] Unfortunately, unless closely supervised, teamwork organization can tend to break down or disintegrate as spheres of authority and responsibility overlap and come into conflict with one another. In general, matrix organization ". . . results in a larger corporate staff, more regional offices, and more constraints on local managers."[19] For some industries matrix organization can be very effective. High technology firms are especially suited to organizing in a matrix structure because of the high incidence of task- or project-oriented activities which overlap several functional areas.

*What is the Ideal Organizational Structure?*

A review of the multitude of distribution organizational types found in companies would reveal a variety of structural forms. Firms can be very successful utilizing one or more organizational structures. Which form, however, is optimal for any given company? That is an immensely difficult question to answer. Rather than examine various distribution organizational structures of several companies and conjecture some "ideal" or "optimal" system, some empirical measures need to be employed to correlate organizational structure and efficiency/productivity. Obviously, the optimal system for a company would be one that maximizes its efficiency and productivity. Diagnostically, the distribution executive must not only determine the firm's organizational structure but also evaluate its performance or effectiveness.

---

[18] James P. Falk, "Organizing for Effective Distribution," in *Proceedings of the Eighteenth Annual Conference of the National Council of Physical Distribution Management, October 13–15, 1980*, p. 185.

[19] Ibid.

## DECISION-MAKING STRATEGIES IN ORGANIZING FOR PDM

As distribution executives face new challenges in the decades ahead, it will become even more important that distribution systems operate more efficiently. In the face of higher costs of operation and increasing pressures from customers for better service levels, the PD organization must evolve and change to meet the challenge. An understanding of the factors which make organizations effective and a knowledge of how those factors interrelate are the first steps toward developing the "optimal distribution system" for the firm's customers.

### Components of an Optimal Physical Distribution Organization

*Many Factors Influence Organizational Effectiveness*

Many factors can influence the effectiveness of a PD organization. A multiplicity of variables individually and/or jointly impact on a firm's organizational effectiveness. In general, the factors contributing to organizational effectiveness can be summarized as (1) organizational characteristics, (2) environmental characteristics, (3) employee characteristics, and (4) managerial policies and practices.[20] In Table 12−2 some illustrative items within each category are presented.

**TABLE 12-2** Factors Contributing to Organizational Effectiveness

| Organizational Characteristics | Environmental Characteristics | Employee Characteristics | Managerial Policies and Practices |
|---|---|---|---|
| Structure<br>  Decentralization<br>  Specialization<br>  Formalization<br>  Span of control<br>  Organization size<br>  Work-unit size<br>Technology<br>  Operations<br>  Materials<br>  Knowledge | External<br>  Complexity<br>  Stability<br>  Uncertainty<br>Internal (climate)<br>  Achievement orientation<br>  Employee centeredness<br>  Reward-punishment orientation<br>  Security versus risk<br>  Openness versus defensiveness | Organizational attachment<br>  Attraction<br>  Retention<br>  Committment<br>Job performance<br>  Motives, goals, and needs<br>  Abilities<br>  Role clarity | Strategic goal setting<br>Resource acquisition and utilization<br>Creating a performance environment<br>Communication processes<br>Leadership and decision making<br>Organizational adaptation and innovation |

Source: Richard M. Steers, *Organizational Effectivess: A Behavioral View* (Santa Monica, Calif.: Goodyear, 1977), p. 8.

***Organizational characteristics.*** Structure and technology are the major components of a firm's organizational characteristics. Structure refers to the relationships that exist between various functional areas—interfunctional (marketing, finance, operations, manufacturing, distribution) or intrafunctional (warehousing, traffic, purchasing, customer service)—and are most often represented by a company's organization chart. Examples of struc-

---
[20] Richard M. Steers, *Organizational Effectiveness: A Behavioral View* (Santa Monica, Calif.: Goodyear, 1977), p. 7.

tural variables are decentralization, specialization, formalization, span of control, organization size, and work-unit size. Technology "refers to the mechanisms used by an organization to transform raw inputs into finished outputs. Technology can take several forms, including variations in the materials used, and variations in the technical knowledge brought to bear on goal-directed activities."[21]

*Environmental characteristics.* The effectiveness of the PD organization is influenced by factors internal and external to the firm. Internal factors, which are basically controllable by the distribution executive, are known as *organizational climate*. Organizational climate can be defined as follows:

**Organizational Climate Defined**

> The idea of "organizational climate" appears to refer to an attribute or set of attributes, of the work environment. The idea of a "perceived organizational climate" seems ambiguous; one can not be sure whether it implies an attribute of the organization or of the perceiving individual. If it refers to the organization, then measures of perceived organizational climate should be evaluated in terms of the accuracy of the perceptions. If it refers to the individual, then perceived organizational climate may simply be a different name for job satisfaction or employee attitudes.[22]

It has been shown that organizational climate is related to organizational effectiveness. This is particularly evident when effectiveness is measured on an individual level (e.g., job attitudes, performance, satisfaction, involvement).[23]

External factors, sometimes referred to as uncontrollable elements, include the political and legal environment, economic environment, cultural and social environment, and competitive environment.

*Employee characteristics.* The keys to effective PD organizations are the employees which "fill the boxes" on the organization chart. The ability of individuals to carry out their respective job responsibilities ultimately determines the overall effectiveness of the organization.

**People Are Important in PD**

> Different employees possess different outlooks, goals, needs, and abilities. These human variations often cause people to behave differently from one another, even when placed in the same work environment. Moreover, these individual differences can have a direct bearing on two important organizational processes that can have a marked impact on effectiveness. These are "organizational attachment," or the extent to which employees identify with their employer, and individual "job performance." Without attachment and performance, effectiveness becomes all but impossible.[24]

*Managerial policies and practices.* Policies at the macro level (entire company) determine the overall goal structure of the firm. Policies at the micro level (departmental) influence the subgoals of the various corporate

---

[21] Ibid., pp. 7–9.

[22] R. M. Guion, "A Note on Organizational Climate," *Organizational Behavior and Human Performance* 9, no. 1 (February 1973): 120.

[23] See W. R. LaFollette and H. P. Sims, Jr., "Is Satisfaction Redundant with Organizational Climate?" *Organizational Behavior and Human Performance* 13, no. 2 (April 1975): 257–78; G. Litwin and R. Stringer, *Motivation and Organizational Climate* (Cambridge: Harvard University Press, 1968): and R. Pritchard and B. Karasick, "The Effects of Organizational Behavior and Human Performance 19, no. 1 (February 1973): 126–46.

[24] Steers, *Organizational Effectiveness*, p. 9.

functions, such as warehousing, traffic, order processing, customer service, and others. Macro and micro policies in turn effect the procedures and practices of the organization. The planning, coordinating, and facilitating of goal-directed activities—which determines organizational effectiveness—depend upon the policies and practices adopted by the firm at the macro and micro levels.

A number of factors have been identified which can aid the distribution executive in improving the effectiveness of the organization. Six of the more important factors which have been identified include:

Six Factors that Influence Organizational Effectiveness

1. Strategic goal setting.
2. Resource acquisition and utilization.
3. Performance environment.
4. Communication processes.
5. Leadership and decision making.
6. Organizational adaptation and innovation.[25]

*Strategic goal setting* involves the establishment of two clearly defined sets of goals: the overall organization goal(s); and individual employee goals. Both sets of goals must be compatible and aimed at maximizing company/employee effectiveness. For example, the company may have an overall goal to reduce order cycle time by 10 percent, but it is the collective actions of each employee attempting to improve their component of the order cycle that brings about achievement of the goal of 10 percent. These involve individual goals which reduce the time necessary for employees to complete the order processing, transportation, and other order cycle activities.

*Resource acquisition and utilization* includes the utilization of human and financial resources, as well as technology, to maximize the achievement of corporate goals and objectives. This would involve such things as having properly trained and experienced persons operating the firm's private truck fleet, the proper storage and retrieval system for the company's warehouses, and the necessary capital to take advantage of forward-buying opportunities, massing of inventories, and other capital projects.

The *performance environment* is concerned with having the proper organizational climate which motivates employees to maximize their effectiveness, and subsequently the effectiveness of the overall distribution function. An Opinion Research Corporation survey found that a majority of U.S. employees felt they could easily be more productive if they desired; however, many saw no reason to do so.[26] "The implications of these findings for organizational effectiveness are clear: if the majority of employees are not motivated to maximize their contribution to organizational goals, then organization-wide performance and effectiveness will suffer considerably."[27] Strategies which can be utilized to develop a goal-directed performance environment include (1) proper employee selection and placement, (2) training and development programs, (3) task design, and (4) per-

---

[25] Ibid., p. 136.

[26] Opinion Research Corporation, "America's Growing Anti-Business Mood," *Business Week*, no. 2233 (June 17, 1972), p. 101.

[27] Steers, *Organizational Effectiveness*, pp. 141–42.

formance evaluation combined with a reward structure which promotes goal-oriented behavior.[28]

**Strategies for Improving Communication**

In any organization, one of the most important factors influencing distribution effectiveness is the *communication process*. Without good communication, distribution policies and procedures cannot be effectively transmitted throughout the firm, and the feedback of information concerning the success or failure of those policies and procedures can not take place. Communication flows within the physical distribution area can be downward (boss → employee), upward (employee → boss), or horizontal (boss ↔ boss or employee ↔ employee). There are a number of ways that communication effectiveness can be improved. Table 12–3 identifies some of the most effective strategies.

Comparable to the importance of effective communications in a PD organization is the quality of *leadership and decision-making* expertise exercised by the distribution executive(s). In many companies the distribution department or division is a mirror image of the top PD executive. If the top executive is a highly capable and respected individual and one who makes thoughtful, logical, and consistent decisions, then the distribution organization which reports to him/her will most likely be highly effective. Conversely, a distribution organization led by an executive who lacks the necessary leadership and decision-making skills, usually will not be as efficient.

Finally, *organizational adaptation and innovation* is an important attribute of effective distribution organizations. The environment which surrounds the physical distribution activity requires constant monitoring. As conditions change, the distribution activity must adapt and innovate so as to continue to provide an optimal service—cost mix to the firm and its markets. Examples of fluctuating environmental conditions include changes in transportation regulations, service requirements of customers, or degree of competition in the firm's target markets; economic and/or financial shifts in the marketplace; and technological advances in the distribution sector. It is important however, that adaptation and innovation

**Effective Organizations Exhibit Stability and Continuity**

not be haphazard and unplanned. An effective distribution organization must also exhibit stability and continuity.

> Management is charged with the responsibility for maintaining a dynamic equilibrium by diagnosing situations and designing adjustments that are most appropriate for coping with current conditions. A dynamic equilibrium for an organization would include the following dimensions:
>
> 1. Enough stability to facilitate achievement of current goals.
> 2. Enough continuity to ensure orderly change in either ends or means.
> 3. Enough adaptability to react appropriately to external opportunities and demands as well as changing internal conditions.
> 4. Enough innovativeness to allow the organization to be proactive (initiate changes) when conditions warrant.[29]

---

[28] Ibid., p. 142.

[29] F. E. Kast and J. E. Rosenzweig, *Organization and Management: A Systems Approach*, 2d ed. (New York: McGraw-Hill, 1974), pp. 574–75.

**TABLE 12-3**  Strategies for Improving Communication Effectiveness

Downward communications
1. Job instructions can be presented clearly to employees so they understand more precisely what is expected.
2. Efforts can be made to explain the rationale behind the required tasks to employees so they understand why they are being asked to do something.
3. Management can provide greater feedback concerning the nature and quality of performance, thereby keeping employees "on target."
4. Multiple communication channels can be used to increase the chances that the message is properly received.
5. Important messages can be repeated to insure penetration.
6. In some cases, it is desirable to bypass formal communication channels and go directly to the intended receiver with the message.

Upward communications
1. Upward messages can be screened so only the more relevant aspects are received by top management.
2. Managers can attempt to change the organizational climate so subordinates feel freer to transmit negative as well as positive messages without fear of retribution.
3. Managers can sensitize themselves so they are better able to detect bias and distorted messages from their subordinates.
4. Sometimes it is possible to utilize "distortion-proof" messages, such as providing subordinates with report forms requiring quantified or standardized data.
5. Social distance and status barriers between employees on various levels can be reduced so messages will be more spontaneous.

Horizontal communications
1. Efforts can be made to develop interpersonal skills between group members and departments so greater openness and trust exist.
2. Reward systems can be utilized which reward interdepartmental cooperation and minimize "zero-sum game" situations.
3. Interdepartmental meetings can be used to share information concerning what other departments are involved in.
4. In some cases, the actual design of the organization itself can be changed to provide greater opportunities for interdepartmental contacts (e.g., shifting from a traditional to a matrix organization design).

Source: Richard M. Steers, *Organizational Effectiveness: A Behavioral View* (Santa Monica, Calif.: Goodyear, 1977), p. 151.

Earlier in this chapter it was reported that Johnson & Johnson Baby Products Company was able to achieve almost 50 percent cost savings in their distribution operations. Figure 12–5 identifies the procedure used by Johnson & Johnson to obtain the savings. As shown in the figure, three components of the firm's distribution system were analyzed: organization, service, and facilities including inventories. In the area of organization, the company developed a structure which was a combination of centralized and decentralized operations. Although other firms might develop different

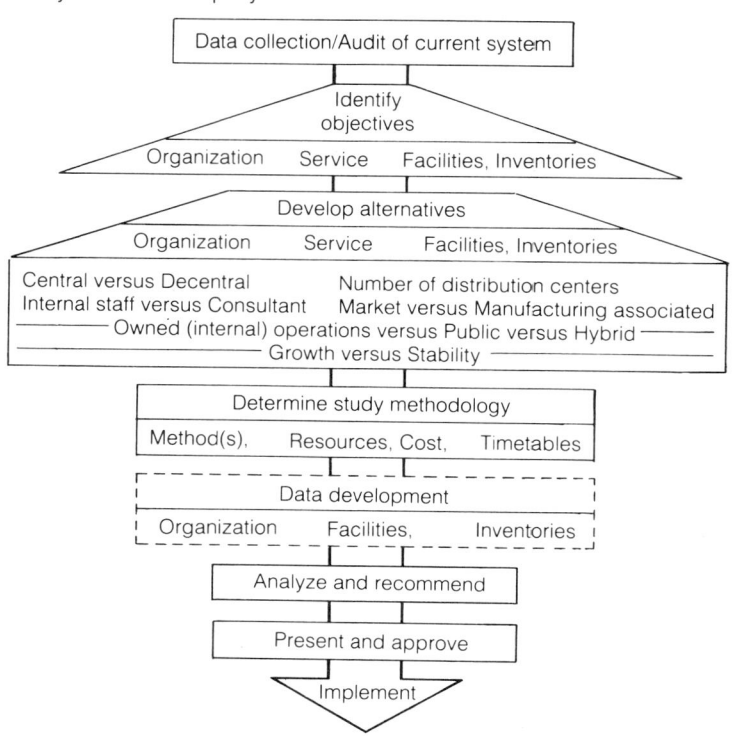

**FIGURE 12-5** Distribution System Design Project—Johnson & Johnson Baby Products Company

```
                    Data collection/Audit of current system
                              Identify
                              objectives
              Organization    Service    Facilities, Inventories
                          Develop alternatives
              Organization    Service    Facilities, Inventories
        Central versus Decentral      Number of distribution centers
        Internal staff versus Consultant   Market versus Manufacturing associated
              Owned (internal) operations versus Public versus Hybrid
                         Growth versus Stability
                    Determine study methodology
              Method(s),    Resources, Cost,    Timetables
                         Data development
              Organization    Facilities,    Inventories
                       Analyze and recommend
                        Present and approve
                             Implement
```

Source: This diagram was based on a presentation entitled "Assessing the Organizational Trade-Offs in the Distribution Strategic Planning Process," by Peter H. Soderberg, director—physical distribution and planning, Johnson & Johnson Baby Products Company, at the annual meeting of the National Council of Physical Distribution Management, Houston, Texas, in October 1979.

organizational forms, the approach used by Johnson & Johnson serves as an illustration of how the problem of organizational design can be approached.

### An Approach to Developing an Optimal Physical Distribution Organization[30]

In an address before a group of distribution executives at the 1980 Annual Conference of the National Council of Physical Distribution Management, James P. Falk, director—domestic transportation for Kaiser Aluminum and Chemical Corporation, stated:

> I think it's a fair observation that most physical distribution management organizations, or any others for that matter, *evolve*. The structure is not developed in final form on a piece of paper, then successfully practiced. The distribu-

---

[30] Much of the material in this section has been developed and adapted from Falk, "Organizing for Effective Distribution," pp. 181–99.

tion manager cannot afford to respond to the special demands of [his/her] interests alone. [He/she] is effective only to the extent that [his/her] energy is directed toward company goals and strategies.[31]

Falk identified a rather important organizational truth which was stated earlier in this chapter. Organizations evolve and change, that is, there is probably a variety of good organizational designs for a firm and over time, a design or structure may have to be modified to reflect environmental or corporate changes which have taken place. As a firm attempts to structure a new physical distribution organizational unit, or perhaps restructure an existing one, the following steps or stages should be followed:

*Seven Steps to Restructuring an Organization*

1. Research corporate strategy and objectives.
2. Organize your functions in a manner compatible with the corporate structure.
3. Define the functions for which you are accountable.
4. Know your management style.
5. Organize your flexibility.
6. Know your support systems.
7. Understand and plan for human resource allocation so that you compliment both the individual and organization objectives.[32]

*Corporate objectives.* Overall corporate strategy and objectives provide the distribution activity with long-term direction. They provide the underlying foundation and guiding light for each functional component of the firm—finance, marketing, production, and physical distribution. The distribution structure must support the overall corporate strategy and objectives. Therefore, it is imperative that the distribution executive completely understand the role his/her activity will play in carrying out corporate strategy. Furthermore, the distribution organizational structure must be compatible with the primary objectives of the firm.

*Corporate structure.* The specific organizational structure of the physical distribution activity will be affected by the overall corporate structure. For example, in a highly decentralized organization, it is likely that the distribution activity will be structured in a similar fashion. Similarly, if the firm is centralized, then distribution will usually be centralized. There are exceptions, but that is basically what they are . . . exceptions. The distribution component of the firm usually closely resembles the overall corporate organization structure. The primary reason for the similarity stems largely from the inherent advantages—administrative, financial, personnel—which result from organizational uniformity within a firm. Other aspects of overall corporate structure which will influence the distribution organization include:

1. Line—staff—coordinating responsibility.
2. Reporting relationships.
3. Span of control.

---

[31] Ibid., p. 186.
[32] Ibid., p. 195.

In the area of reporting relationships, physical distribution will typically report to the marketing group if the firm is a consumer-goods company, and will report to manufacturing/operations/administration if the firm is primarily an industrial-goods producer. In many firms with a combination of consumer- and industrial-goods customers, physical distribution is often a separate organizational activity reporting directly to the CEO/president.

*Functional responsibilities.* "The question causing more conflicts and problems than any other is a clear definition of the *function* of the physical distribution organization, especially if it is being restructured from other sub-structures having a traditional responsibility."[33] It is important to have all or most, physical distribution subfunctions housed under a single division or department. Such an organizational structure with full functional responsibility allows the firm to implement the concepts of integrated physical distribution management and total cost trade-offs. Illustrative of many of the functional responsibilities of the distribution organization are those shown in Table 12 — 1.

*Management style.* Almost as important as the formal structure of the physical distribution organization is the management style of the senior distribution executive. Many firms have undergone significant changes in the areas of personnel, employee morale, productivity, etc., as a result of a change in top management. Organizational restructuring does not necessarily have to occur. The style or personality of the senior distribution executive, and to a lesser degree, his/her lower-level managers, has an influence on employee attitudes, motivation, work ethic, and productivity at all levels of the organization. The element of management style is one of those intangibles that can make two companies with identical organizational structures, perform at significantly different levels of efficiency, productivity, and profitability. Management style is a vital ingredient to the success or failure of a firm's physical distribution mission and is one of the primary reasons that many different organizational structures can be equally effective.

*Flexibility.* "An organization must not be so parochially centered around physical distribution that it cannot react to changes around it. It must be able to accommodate business-cycle adjustments, sales-volume variations, and organizational changes."[34] Any physical distribution organization must be adaptive to changes which inevitably occur. Unresponsive and nonadaptable organizations typically lose their effectiveness after a period of time. While it may be difficult to anticipate future changes in the marketplace or the firm, the distribution organization must be receptive to those changes and able to respond to them in ways beneficial to the firm.

*Support systems.* Due to the nature of the physical distribution activity, the presence of support systems are essential. The distribution organization cannot exist on its own. There must be a variety of support services as well

---

[33] Ibid., p. 188.
[34] Ibid., p. 189.

as support specialists available to aid the physical distribution department or division. As was shown in Chapter 9, a good MIS system, manual or automated, is an important facet of an effective distribution network. Other support services or systems which can be used by physical distribution include:

1. Legal services.
2. Computer systems.
3. Administrative services.
4. Financial/accounting services.

*Personnel considerations.* Perhaps the most important component of an effective physical distribution organization is people. It is the people that fill the boxes of the firm's organization chart that ultimately determine how well the company operates. Therefore, it is vital that employee skills and abilities, pay scales, training programs, selection and retention procedures, and other employee-related policies be considered in the structuring or restructuring of a physical distribution organization. However, other employee aspects must also be considered. As stated by Falk:

> But we must design our organization so we consider not only *people development*, but individual personalities as well. Show me the theorist who says, "Don't compromise the optimum organization for people consideration" . . . and I'll show you a person who I would like to have managing our competition! We *have* to consider the strengths and weaknesses of our people, and use them where they can contribute most. This is not to say we organize around people . . . the basic organization should *not* be prostituted. It's important, however, to balance organizational structure with strengths and weaknesses of our human resources.[35]

While there will be no one "best" organizational form for a firm's physical distribution activity, there are benefits to be obtained from examining the organizational structures of successful companies. First, from a purely graphical representation, an organization chart allows a person to view how the many functional areas of the firm relate together and how the distribution subfunctions are coordinated. Second, viewing several organization charts of companies in a variety of industries illustrates the fact that there is no single ideal structure. Third, because of the commonality of the distribution activities across industry types, there will be marked similarities in the various organization charts. Companies have found through experience that certain distribution functions should be structured or organized in certain ways.

Representative organization charts from four industry groups—food, paper, pharmaceutical, and wholesale/retail—are shown in Figures 12–6 through 12–9. The companies represented are considered by their peers within their industries to have "good" physical distribution organizations.

---
[35] Ibid., p. 190.

**FIGURE 12-6** Nalley's Fine Foods—Materiel and Customer Service

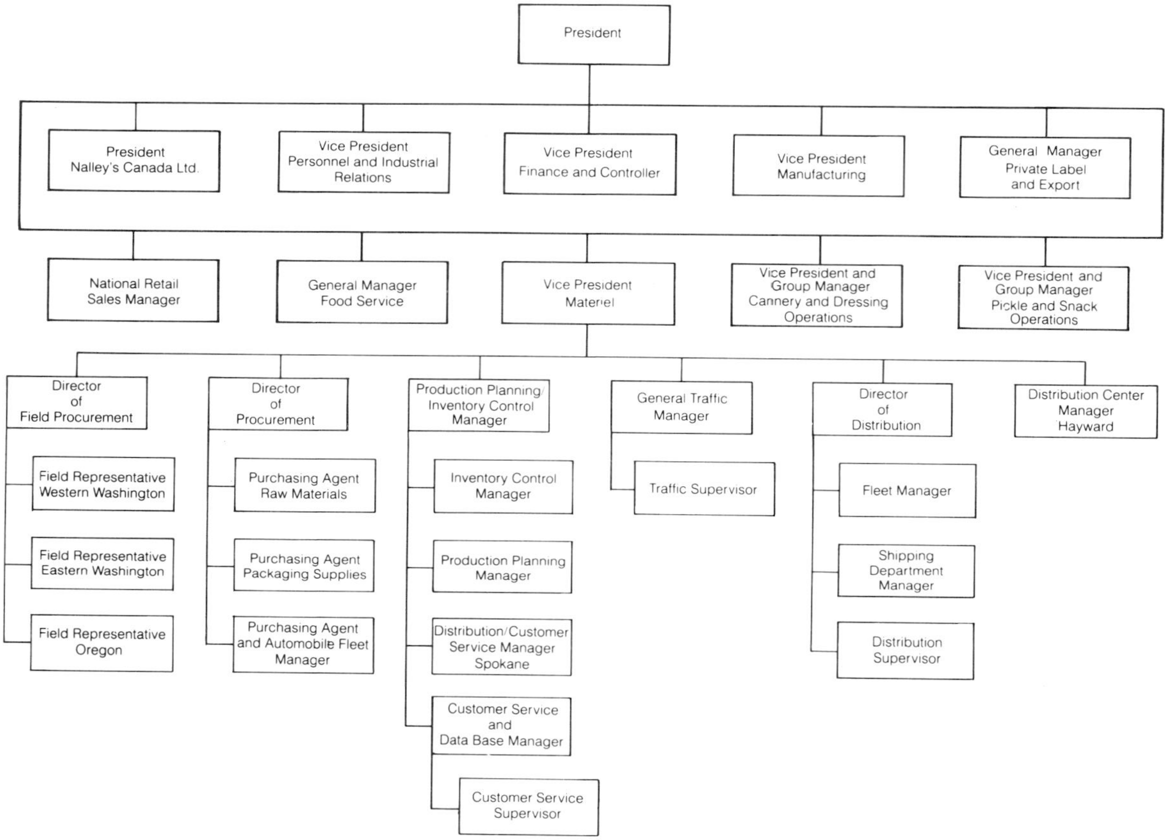

### Measuring the Effectiveness of the Physical Distribution Organization

The effectiveness or performance of a distribution organization can be measured along many dimensions. Examples of the multitude of performance dimensions include the following:

*There Are Many Dimensions of Effectiveness*

1. Flexibility—willingness to tackle unusual problems, try out new ideas.
2. Development—personnel participate in training and development.
3. Cohesion—lack of complaints, grievances, conflict.
4. Democratic supervision—subordinate participation in work decisions.
5. Reliability—completion of assignments without checking.
6. Delegation—delegation of responsibility by supervisors.
7. Bargaining—negotiation with other units for favors, cooperation.
8. Results emphasis—results, not procedures, emphasized.

**FIGURE 12-7** Sweetheart Cup Corporation (division of Maryland Cup Corporation)

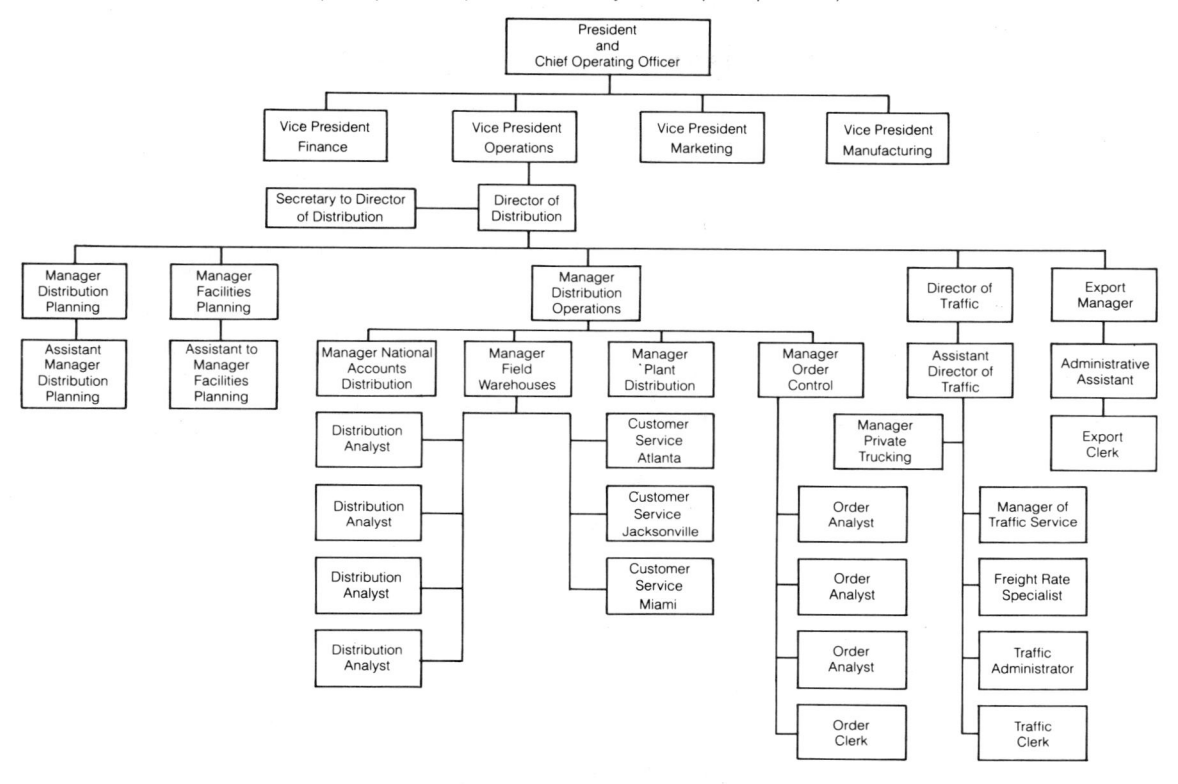

**FIGURE 12-8** E. R. Squibb & Sons, Inc.—Distribution Organization

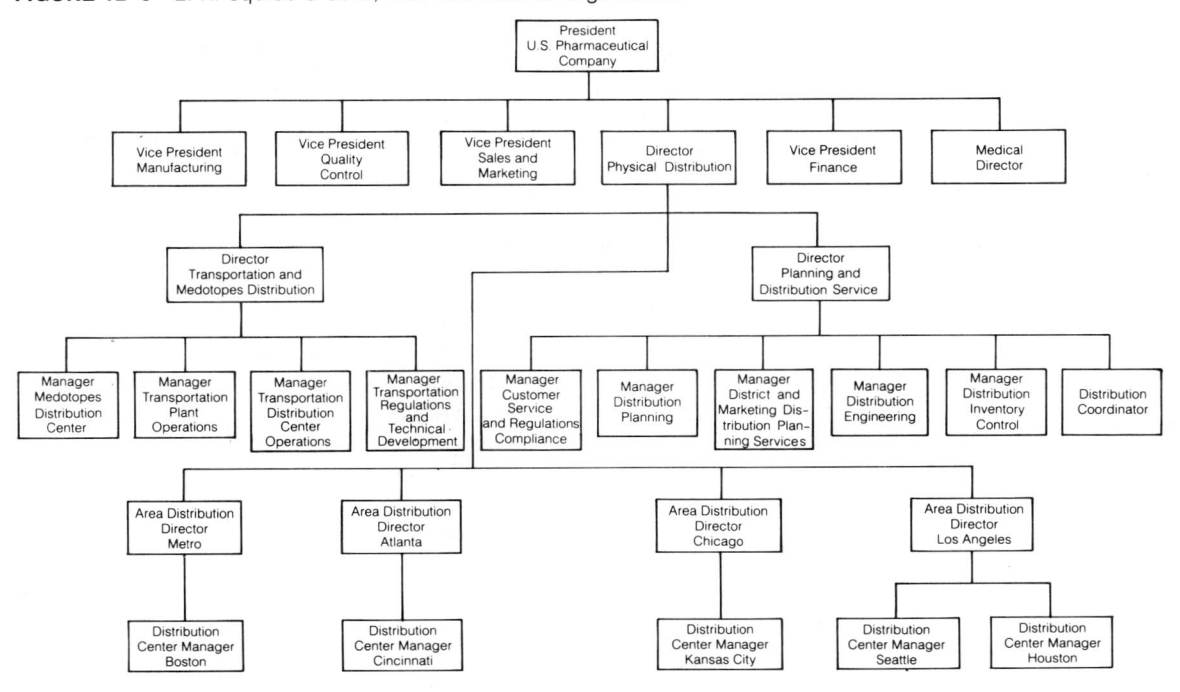

**FIGURE 12–9** Child World

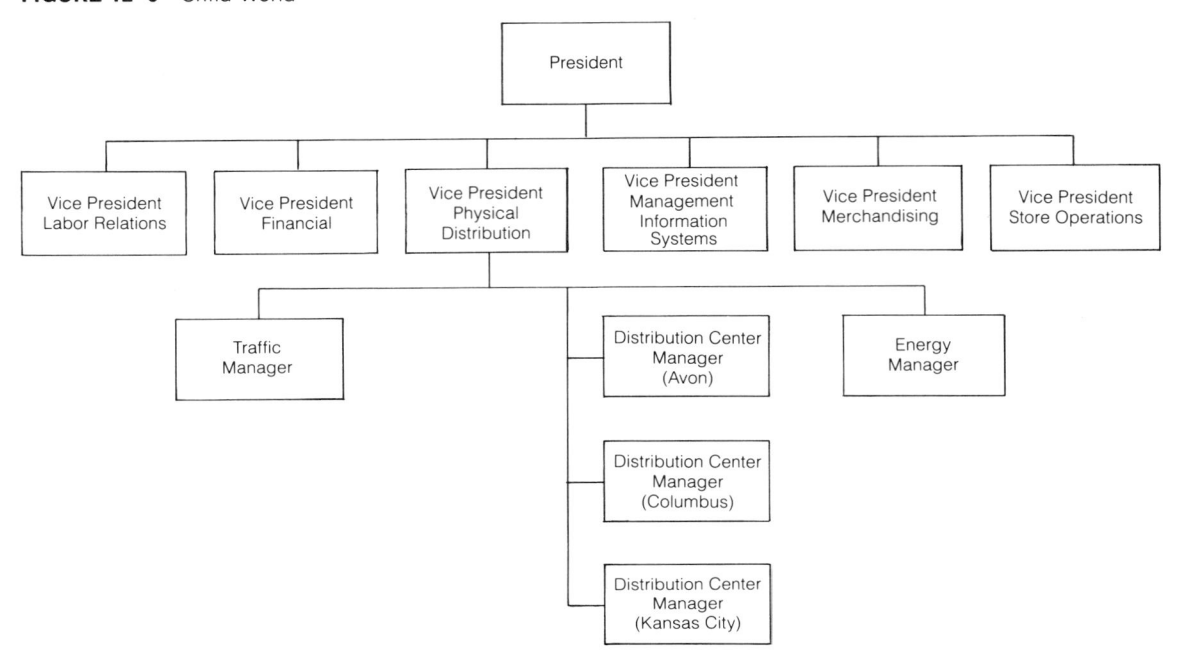

```
                                    President
                                        |
   ┌─────────────┬─────────────┬────────┼────────────┬─────────────┬─────────────┐
Vice President  Vice President  Vice President  Vice President  Vice President  Vice President
Labor Relations  Financial      Physical        Management       Merchandising   Store Operations
                                Distribution    Information
                                     |          Systems
         ┌───────────────┬───────────┴────┬────────────────┐
    Traffic         Distribution Center              Energy
    Manager         Manager (Avon)                   Manager
                         |
                    Distribution Center
                    Manager (Columbus)
                         |
                    Distribution Center
                    Manager (Kansas City)
```

9. Staffing—personnel flexibility among jobs, backups available.
10. Cooperation—responsibilities met and work coordinated with other units.
11. Decentralization—work decisions made at low levels.
12. Conflict—conflict with other units over responsibility and authority.
13. Supervisory backing—supervisors back up subordinates.
14. Planning—waste time avoided through planning and scheduling.
15. Productivity—efficiency of performance within unit.
16. Support—mutual support of supervisors and subordinates.
17. Communication—flow of work information.
18. Initiation—initiate improvements in work methods.
19. Supervisory control—supervisors in control of work progress.[36]

Of course, it is not enough to merely identify the dimensions of distribution organizational effectiveness, although it is a necessary first step. The second step is to prioritize the various effectiveness or performance categories and to develop specific measuring devices to evaluate the level of effectiveness achieved by the distribution organization. It is vital that a firm identify the measures of organizational effectiveness it wishes to utilize and prioritize them. It is impractical in most instances to employ every effec-

---

[36] William Weitzel, Thomas A. Mahoney, and Norman F. Crandall, "A Supervisory View of Unit Effectiveness," *California Management Review* 13, no. 4 (Summer 1971): p. 39; © 1971 by the Regents of the University of California. Reprinted from *California Management Review*, XIII, no. 4, p. 39, by permission of the Regents.

tiveness measure in the evaluation process. Time and monetary constraints impede the collection and monitoring of all the data needed for such evaluation. Also, it is usually sufficient to examine only a portion of the available measures because patterns or trends are often exhibited very early in the evaluation process. The selection of particular effectiveness measures to be used by a company as it evaluates its distribution organization must be dependent on its particular characteristics and needs. Perhaps the much more difficult process is developing the techniques or procedures needed to measure the effectiveness criteria. In this regard, a number of alternatives exist.

**TABLE 12-4** Distribution Management Evaluation Measures

1. Distribution cost as a percent of sales
    a. Compared internally (e.g., among divisions)
    b. Compared externally (between similar companies)

2. Cost of specific distribution functions as a percent of sales or of distribution cost
    a. Compared internally (e.g., among divisions)
    b. Compared externally (between similar companies)

3. Performance
    a. Budget versus actual expressed in terms of:
       Dollars, manhours, headcount or other appropriate measures
    b. Productivity, output compared to input in appropriate terms
    c. Service provided:
       Time (order cycle, invoice cycle)
       On-time dependability
       Customer complaint level
       Errors (invoice, shipping)
    d. Project management within:
       Time constraints
       Dollar limitations
       Benefits projected (dollar savings, productivity improvement, etc.)

Source: A. T. Kearney, Inc., *Measuring Productivity in Physical Distribution* (Chicago: National Council of Physical Distribution Management, 1978), p. 221.

As shown in Table 12−4, effectiveness measures fall into three categories:

*Effectiveness Measures Fall into Three Categories*

1. Cost-to-sales ratios.
2. Cost-to-total cost ratios.
3. Performance measures, including:
    a. Budgets.
    b. Productivity.
    c. Service.
    d. Project management effectiveness.[37]

---

[37] A. T. Kearney, Inc., *Measuring Productivity*, p. 219.

Cost-to-sales ratios are used extensively by business firms to evaluate distribution organizational effectiveness. As with any measure used by a company, problems exist, especially with regard to which costs to include under the distribution activity. For example: "Were net or gross sales used? What distribution functions were included in the cost total? Were management salaries included? Was inventory carrying cost included? Has there been a change in order mix or service levels?"[38] There are no simple answers to these questions except to say that all costs that are rightfully distribution's, should be included. If the firm computing cost-effectiveness measures has adopted and implemented the integrated physical distribution management concept there is a greater likelihood that all relevant costs will be included.

Every measure identified in Table 12—4 must be evaluated against some predetermined standard. The standard may be internally generated, that is, developed within the firm so as to be compatible with corporate hurdle rates, return-on-investment percentages, and other financial-performance measures. In some instances, distribution performance standards may be "externally generated." Many companies believe that their standards should be based upon other firms within the same industry or the "leaders" in other industries with similar characteristics. The arguments in favor of this approach are many, but the major one states that a firm should be most concerned with its position relative to its competition and, therefore, the competition should influence the way in which you evaluate the effectiveness of your company. After all, in the marketplace customers are indirectly evaluating a firm's level of effectiveness or performance through their day-to-day buying decisions. A limitation of this approach which must be considered is that each competitor will have a different marketing mix and perhaps, slightly different target markets. One firm may spend substantially more on physical distribution than another firm yet realize higher profits and sales. Therefore, direct comparisons between competitors must be approached cautiously.

## An Approach to Measuring Organizational Effectiveness

An approach to measuring the effectiveness of distribution organizations was employed in a 1979 survey of NCPDM member firms.[39] A multivariate model of organizational effectiveness developed by Rensis Likert was used to examine over 100 manufacturing, retailing, and service firms.[40] Likert identified four management organization systems: exploitative-authoritative (System 1); benevolent-authoritative (System 2); consultative (System 3); and participative group (System 4). Each system has its own particular characteristics which are measurable. Likert's multivariate model has been successfully employed, from a general management perspective, in a variety of companies including Aluminum Company of Canada, Detroit Edison, Dow

---

[38] Ibid., p. 220.

[39] James R. Stock, "Measuring Distribution Organizational Effectiveness," in Bernard J. LaLonde, ed., *Proceedings of the Tenth Annual Transportation and Logistics Educators Conference, October 12, 1980*, pp. 15—25.

[40] See Rensis Likert, *New Patterns in Management* (New York: McGraw-Hill, 1961) and Rensis Likert, *The Human Organization: Its Management and Value* (New York: McGraw-Hill, 1967).

Chemical, General Electric, Genesco, IBM, Lever Brothers, Sun Oil, and Union Carbide.[41]

In the study of NCPDM firms, companies evaluated their distribution organizations by providing data on operating characteristics. The operating characteristics were classified into categories: leadership; motivation; communication; decisions; and goals. The profiles developed from the study are shown in Figure 12−10. Likert has suggested that the profiles be interpreted as follows:

> Research findings support the perceptions of managers that management systems more to the right, i.e., toward System 4, are more productive and have lower costs and more favorable attitudes than do systems falling more to the left toward System 1. Those firms . . . where System 4 is used show high productivity . . . low costs, favorable attitudes, and excellent labor relations. The converse tends to be the case for companies or departments whose management system is well toward System 1. Corresponding relationships are also found with regard to any shifts in the management system. Shifts toward System 4 are accompanied by long-range improvement in productivity, labor relations, costs, and earnings. The long-range consequences of shifts toward System 1 are unfavorable.[42]

The study suggested the possibility of developing effectiveness profiles for companies, based upon industry type, company size, location of the firm, and other factors. The result would be an ability of a firm to compare itself with other similar firms and to make improvements where necessary.

In the same study of NCPDM firms, the distribution literature was reviewed and a total of 15 factors were developed which characterized effective organizations. Some of the most widely recognized items included cost efficiency, flexibility, management orientation, employee turnover and morale, communication, coordination, and conflict within the organization.[43] In a fashion similar to the Likert model, a profile of organizational effectiveness was developed for firms. Profiles to the right in Figure 12−11 were considered to be more effective.

An additional use of the Likert approach to measuring organizational effectiveness is in a comparison of how various management levels within the company perceive the physical distribution organization. Ideally, all managers (top, middle, and lower levels) should have similar perceptions of the distribution organization. Generally, when perceptions are similar among and between various management and employee groups, the organization tends to be more efficient because of the unified spirit and direction taken by the firm. When perceptions differ, management groups may be operating counter-productively, resulting in less efficiency. It can prove extremely beneficial to a company to determine if perceptual differences exist within the firm. If they do, corrective action or education of the employees is probably in order.

---

[41] Likert, *The Human Organization*, p. 26.
[42] Ibid., p. 46.
[43] Stock, "Measuring Distribution Organizational Effectiveness," p. 17.

**FIGURE 12-10** Likert Model of Organizational Effectiveness

| Operating characteristics | System 1 Exploitive-authoritative | System 2 Benevolent-authoritative | System 3 Consultative | System 4 Participative group |
|---|---|---|---|---|

**Leadership**
How much confidence is shown in subordinates?
How free do they feel to talk to superiors about their job?
Are subordinates' ideas sought and used, if worthy?

**Motivation**
Is predominant use made of 1-fear, 2-threats, 3-punishment, 4-rewards, 5-involvement?
Where is responsibility felt for achieving organization's goals?

**Communication**
How much communication is aimed at achieving organization's objectives?
What is the direction of information flow?
How is downward communication accepted?
How accurate is upward communication?
How well do superiors know problems faced by subordinates?

**Decisions**
At what level are decisions formally made?
What is the origin of technical and professional knowledge used in decision making?
Are subordinates involved in decisions related to their work?
What does decision-making process contribute to motivation?

**Goals**
How are organizational goals established?
How much covert resistance to goals is present?
Is there an informal organization resisting the formal one?
What are cost, productivity, and other control data used for?

Key: Food ———
Chemical ·············
Automobile – – – –
Pharmaceuticals – · – · –

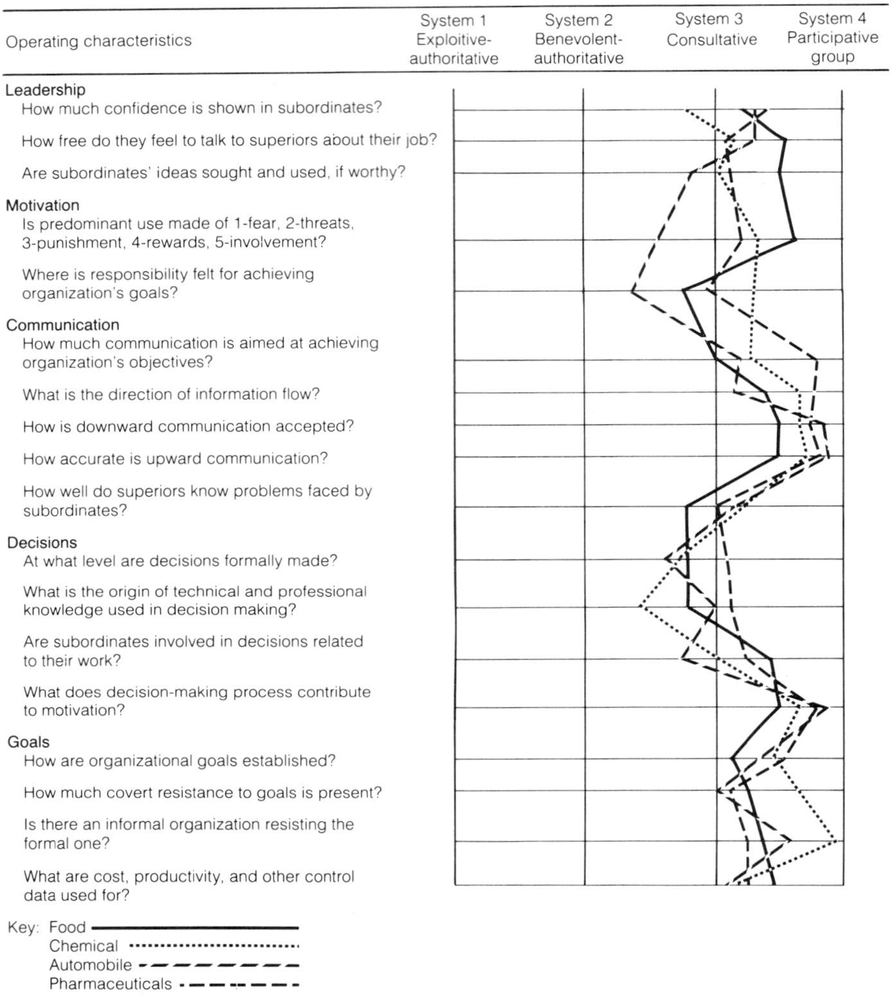

Source: James R. Stock, "Measuring Distribution Organizational Effectiveness," in Bernard J. LaLonde, ed., *Proceedings of the Tenth Annual Transportation and Logistics Educators Conference*, October 12, 1980, p. 22; List of operating characteristics in figure were adapted from *New Patterns in Management* by Rensis Likert. Copyright © 1961, McGraw-Hill Book Company. Used with the permission of McGraw-Hill Book Company.

If a firm is to measure its distribution organizational effectiveness it must employ a variety of factors. In addition, the factors must be measurable and standards of performance need to be established. Finally, the firm should compare itself with others in its industry. There is most likely no single ideal organizational structure which could be adopted by every company. The most logical approach to the problem of how a company should organize its distribution activities so as to maximize its effectiveness is to understand

**FIGURE 12-11** Profile of PD Organizational Effectiveness

| Left descriptor | Rating 1–5 | Right descriptor |
|---|---|---|
| Cost Inefficient | | Cost Efficient |
| Very inflexible | | Very flexible |
| Long lead times required to get things done | | Short lead times required to get things done |
| Management-by-crisis orientation | | Management-by-objectives orientation |
| Promotions based on seniority and loyalty | | Promotions based on results |
| Individual management responsibilities and authority not well understood | | Individual management responsibilities and authority well understood |
| Nonintegrated functions | | Integrated functions |
| Need for strong supervision of employees | | Employees left alone |
| Low organizational stability | | High organizational stability |
| Low productivity | | High productivity |
| High employee turnover | | Low employee turnover |
| Low degree of employee morale | | High degree of employee morale |
| Ineffective communication | | Effective communication |
| Poor coordination | | Good coordination |
| Substantial conflict between people | | People work well together |

Key: Food ———
Chemical ···········
Automobile – – – – –
Pharmaceuticals — — —

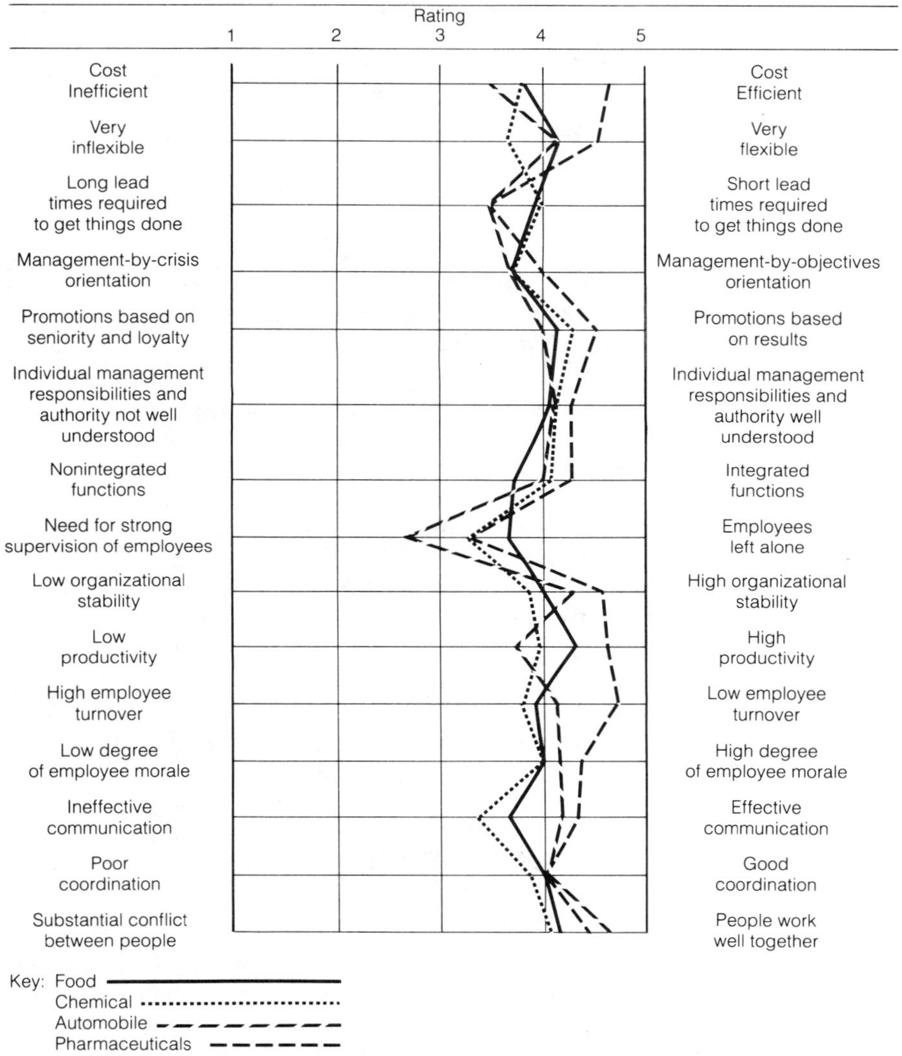

Source: James R. Stock, "Measuring Distribution Organizational Effectiveness," in Bernard J. LaLonde, ed., *Proceedings of the Tenth Annual Transportation and Logistics Educators Conference*, October 12, 1980, p. 24.

those factors which contribute to organizational performance and include them in the planning, implementation, and control of the organization.

## SUMMARY

Physical distribution organizations must, of necessity, become more cost and service efficient in the future as the business environment (domestic and international) becomes more uncertain and difficult to manage. An understanding of those factors which affect a firm's distribution organizational effectiveness coupled with strategies to improve those factors which exhibit weaknesses or deficiencies, can result in more efficient distribution systems. Organizational changes form the basis for procedural modifications that can reduce costs or improve service.

In this chapter the importance of an effective distribution organization to a firm was presented. Many firms have shown significant improvements in their cost/service mix as a result of organizational improvements. The most important ingredient in successful PD management is integration of all of the distribution activities under a single individual, department, and/or division.

You were shown that distribution organizations are generally structured along the following lines: strategic versus operational; centralized versus decentralized; and line versus staff in various combinations. There is probably no single ideal organizational structure. However, there are important elements which comprise an effective organization. In general, the factors contributing to organizational effectiveness can be categorized as: organizational characteristics, environmental characteristics, employee characteristics, and managerial policies and practices.

There are a number of approaches which can be taken to measure the effectiveness of the distribution organization. Each approach requires the company to identify the elements which impact on distribution effectiveness and then to prioritize them based upon some management scheme. Next, the elements must be measured and evaluated. Evaluation requires that standards of performance be established.

With this and the other preceding chapters as background, you are now ready to apply the concepts and principles you have learned to physical distribution in international markets. This is the subject of Chapter 13, International Physical Distribution.

## QUESTIONS AND PROBLEMS

1. Discuss the relationship between a firm's organizational structure and the integrated physical distribution management concept.

2. Coordination of the various physical distribution activities can be achieved in a variety of ways. Within the context of distribution organizational structure explain each of the following:
   a. Strategic versus operational.
   b. Centralized versus decentralized.
   c. Line versus staff.

3. It has been frequently stated that "There is no single ideal or optimal distribution organizational structure." Do you think that statement is accurate? Briefly present the arguments which support and reject such a statement.

4. How do personnel (i.e., people) impact on the degree of organizational effectiveness and/or productivity of the physical distribution activity of the firm?

5. Identify the role that the communication process has in influencing distribution effectiveness. Discuss several strategies which can be followed to improve downward, upward, and horizontal communications within a firm.

6. Identify how a firm's physical distribution management can be evaluated on each of the following factors:
    a. Total distribution cost.
    b. Cost of specific distribution functions.
    c. Performance.

# 13 International Physical Distribution

Introduction

International Distribution Channel Strategies
   Exporting
   Licensing
   Joint Ventures
   Ownership

Management of the Export Shipment
   Export Facilitators
      Export Distributor
      Customshouse Broker
      Foreign-Freight Forwarder
   Documentation
   Terms of Trade
   Free-Trade Zones

The International Marketplace
   Uncontrollable Elements
   Controllable Elements—Strategic
      Customer Service Strategies
      Inventory Strategies
      Transportation Strategies
   Controllable Elements—Managerial
      Packaging
      Warehousing and Storage
      Other Activities

Financial Aspects of International Physical Distribution

Managing International Physical Distribution Activities

Summary

**Objectives of this chapter:**

To identify key similarities and differences in the management of physical distribution in domestic and foreign environments

To show how to assess the physical distribution environment in international markets

To show how to develop an effective international physical distribution strategy

## INTRODUCTION

"World business, multinational company, and world enterprise are all terms being used with more frequency as a significantly larger number of businesses become international both in philosophy and in scope of operations. For a continually growing number of firms, the entire world is considered a marketplace for their products."[1] Table 13—1 shows the interna-

**TABLE 13-1** World Market Important to U.S. Multinationals—1977

|  | Percentage of Net Earnings | Percentage of Sales | Percentage of Assets |
|---|---|---|---|
| American Standard | 43.7 | 45.8 | 39.7 |
| IBM | 55.0 | 50.0 | 35.8 |
| NCR | 49.9 | 49.0 | 46.8 |
| Coca-Cola | 55.0 | 44.0 | 37.0 |
| H. J. Heinz | 34.2 | 40.7 | 36.3 |
| Johnson & Johnson | 47.7 | 30.8 | 33.0 |
| Scholl, Inc. | 49.3 | 47.5 | 48.0 |
| American Cyanamid | 41.0 | 35.0 | 36.9 |
| Dow | 41.8 | 45.6 | 36.4 |
| Standard Oil of California | 47.6 | 59.1 | 43.3 |
| Black & Decker | 63.0 | 55.1 | 38.6 |
| International Systems & Controls | 112.0 | 63.1 | 63.1 |
| ITT | 39.0 | 49.0 | 36.0 |
| J. W. Thompson | 58.7 | 43.8 | 33.8 |
| F. W. Woolworth | 58.9 | 34.7 | 37.6 |
| Avon | 30.6 | 38.3 | 27.9 |
| Gillette | 43.0 | 51.2 | 60.6 |
| Mattel | 45.1 | 19.7 | 41.3 |

Source: Philip R. Cateora and John M. Hess, *International Marketing*, 4th ed. (Homewood, Ill.: Richard D. Irwin, 1979), p. 48. © 1979 Richard D. Irwin, Inc.

tional involvement of many well known companies with worldwide markets. In some instances, a firm's international markets may produce more sales or profits than their domestic markets. To support nondomestic markets a company must have a distribution system or network that satisfies the particular requirements of those markets. For example, the distribution

---

[1] Philip R. Cateora and John M. Hess, *International Marketing*, 4th ed. (Homewood, Ill.: Richard D. Irwin, 1979), p. 3.

systems in the developing countries of Africa, South America, or Asia, are characterized by a large number of intermediaries (middlemen) supplying an even larger number of small retailers, inadequate transportation and storage facilities, a labor market comprised mainly of unskilled workers, and an absence of physical distribution support systems. In more highly developed countries, such as Japan, Canada, the United States, and most of Western Europe, the distribution systems are highly sophisticated. A firm entering these countries will find distribution networks which have good transportation systems, high technology warehousing, a skilled labor force, and the availability of a variety of distribution support systems.

In this chapter some of the similarities and differences in the management of physical distribution in domestic and international environments will be discussed. You will be shown how to assess the international physical distribution environment and to develop meaningful distribution strategies in that environment.

## INTERNATIONAL DISTRIBUTION CHANNEL STRATEGIES

There are many factors that would influence a company to enter into international markets. They include:

*Why Does a Firm Enter International Markets?*

1. A product can be near the end of its life cycle in the domestic market at the same time it experiences a growth market abroad.
2. In some product lines, competition in foreign markets may be less intense than domestically.
3. If the firm has excess capacity, it can produce for foreign markets at a favorable marginal cost per unit.
4. Geographical diversification, that is, going international, may be a more desirable alternative than product-line diversification.
5. Perhaps the most obvious reason to consider world markets is the potential they offer.[2]

An additional reason for a firm to enter international markets is sourcing of raw materials, component parts, or assemblies. For example, certain raw materials such as petroleum, bauxite, uranium, certain foodstuffs, and other items, are limited geographically in their availability. A firm may locate a facility and/or import an item for domestic use and thereby become international in scope.

Companies which enter into the international marketplace have four principle channel strategies available to them:

*Four Channel Strategies*

Exporting.
Licensing.
Joint Ventures.
Ownership.

---

[2] From *International Marketing*, Second Edition, by Vern Terpstra. Copyright © 1978 by The Dryden Press, a division of Holt, Rinehart and Winston, Publishers. Reprinted by permission of Holt, Rinehart and Winston.

**FIGURE 13-1** Selected International Channels of Distribution

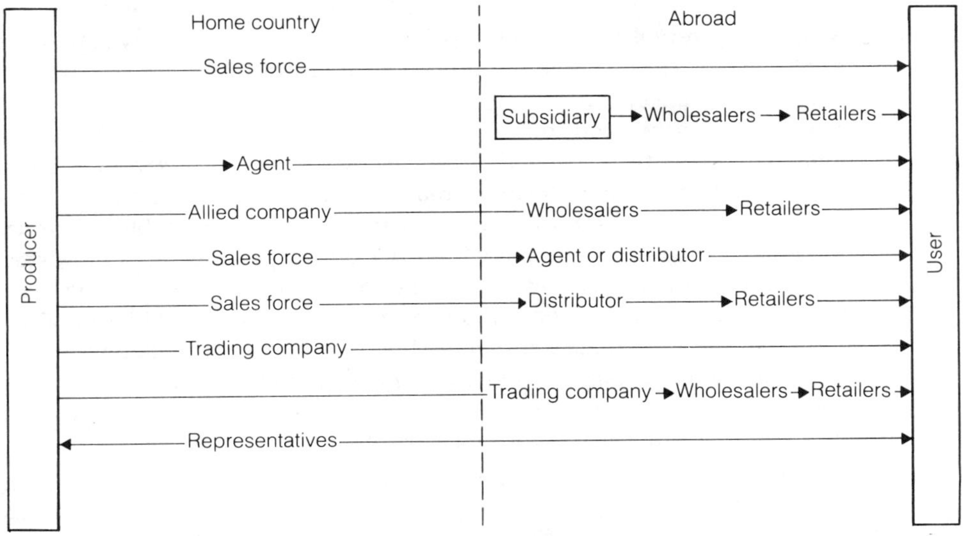

```
Producer ──Sales force──────────────────────────────────► User
                              │ Subsidiary │──►Wholesalers──►Retailers──►
         ──►Agent─────────────────────────────────────────►
         ──Allied company─────┬──Wholesalers──────►Retailers──►
         ──Sales force────────┼──►Agent or distributor──────►
         ──Sales force────────┼──►Distributor──────►Retailers──►
         ──Trading company────┤
                              ├──Trading company──►Wholesalers──►Retailers──►
         ◄──Representatives───┤
```

Home country | Abroad

Source: Ruel Kahler and Roland L. Kramer, *International Marketing*, 4th ed. (Cincinnati: South-Western Publishing, 1977), p. 169.

Within each channel strategy, several options are also available. Figure 13–1 identifies some of the distribution channels utilized by international firms.

**Exporting**

The most common form of distribution for firms entering international markets is exporting. Exporting requires the least amount of knowledge about foreign markets because the domestic firm allows an international freight forwarder, distributor, customshouse broker, trading company, or some other organization to carry out the distribution functions.

*Advantages of Exporting*

There are many advantages associated with exporting. Typically the company which exports is able to be more flexible. Additionally, exporting involves less risk than other international distribution strategies. For example, no additional production facilities or other fixed assets need to be committed to the foreign market because the firm produces the product domestically and allows the exporting intermediary to handle distribution of the product abroad. Also, no investment is required to establish a physical distribution network abroad.

Another advantage of exporting is the minimal exposure to the political uncertainties of some foreign environments. Without the presence of direct foreign investment the firm is not concerned with the host country nationalizing its operations. Also, if the foreign market does not meet the firm's profit and/or sales expectations it is not difficult to withdraw from the market.

Perhaps one of the major advantages of exporting is the experience that is gained by the domestic firm. "Private companies may favor exporting either as an initial entry strategy or as the most effective means of continuous servicing. Numerous . . . firms began by exporting, but now they operate their own production and marketing operations abroad. They tested the market by exporting and then employed other strategies to hold or expand it."[3]

**Disadvantages of Exporting**

Exporting is not without disadvantages. It can sometimes be difficult to compete with other firms located in the foreign market. For example, tariffs, taxes assessed on goods entering a market; import quotas, limitations on the amount of goods which can enter a market; or unfavorable currency exchange rates may adversely affect the price and/or availability of imported goods. Additionally, the domestic firm has very little control over the pricing, promotion, or distribution of its product when exporting is used. Success in the international markets served by the export firms is dependent to a large degree on the capability of the exporting intermediaries.

It is also important for the domestic firm to recognize that the export process is not as simplistic as it first appears.

> The export process begins long before the first carton leaves the warehouse. There is market planning, package design, sales negotiation, financial monitoring, banking, insurance, and consular documentation, just to name a few. These preliminary activities are the framework on which an export program hangs, and the distribution department should be involved in all of them. Without distribution's participation in various marketing and financial plans, the company risks serious problems.
>
> For instance, if a promised delivery time cannot be met, the company risks a costly default under many standard methods of export financing. Or if insufficient margin has been allowed for an export sales because certain costs were overlooked, the company needlessly takes a loss.[4]

When a firm is involved in exporting there are a number of middlemen or intermediaries which are available and which provide a variety of exporting services.

## Licensing

"Licensing is a method of foreign operation whereby a firm in one country (the licensor) agrees to permit a company in another country (the licensee) to use the manufacturing, processing, trademark, know-how, technical assistance, merchandising knowledge, or some other skill provided by the licensor."[5] Unlike exporting, licensing allows the domestic firm more control over how the product is distributed because distribution strategy is usually part of the prelicensing discussions. The specific physical distribution functions are carried out by the licensee using the established distribution systems of the foreign country.

**Licensing Does Not Require Large Capital Outlays**

Licensing does not require large capital outlays, which makes it similar to exporting in that it is less risky and provides more flexibility than other forms of international marketing. It is a strategy frequently used by small

---

[3] Ruel Kahler and Roland L. Kramer, *International Marketing*, 4th ed. (Cincinnati: South-Western Publishing, 1977), p. 80.

[4] Thomas A. Foster, "Anatomy of an Export," *Distribution* 79, no. 10 (October 1980): 76.

[5] Kahler and Kramer, *International Marketing*, p. 86.

and medium-sized businesses and can be an excellent approach if the foreign market has high tariff barriers and/or strict import quotas. The licensor is usually paid a royalty or a percent of sales by the licensee.

Licensing is not without disadvantages. Although licensing does provide the domestic firm with flexibility, it does not mean that licensing agreements can be terminated quickly. Although the agreement with the licensee may include termination or cancellation provisions there is usually a time lag between the decision to terminate and the actual date of termination. The time lag would usually be longer than that in an exporting situation. Another drawback, and perhaps the most serious, is that the licensee has the potential of becoming a competitor. As licensees develop their own know-how and capability they may end the licensing agreement and compete with the licensor.

> One way of avoiding the danger of strengthening a competitor through a licensing agreement is to ensure that all licensing agreements provide for a cross-technology exchange between licensor and licensee.
>
> For companies who do decide to license, agreements should anticipate the possibility of extending market participation and, insofar as is possible, keep options and paths open for expanded market participation.[6]

### Joint Ventures

*Joint Ventures Allow the Firm Greater Control in Foreign Markets*

A firm may wish to exercise more control over the foreign firm than is available in a licensing agreement. On the other hand, the firm may not desire to establish a free-standing manufacturing plant or other facility in the foreign market. If so, the joint venture offers a compromise.

The risk is higher and the flexibility lower to the domestic firm because an equity position is established in the foreign firm. However, the domestic firm is able to provide substantial management input into the channel and distribution strategies of the foreign company due to its financial partnership. This increased management voice does place additional burdens on the domestic firm, namely, it requires a greater knowledge of the international markets it is trying to serve.

> There are many reasons a joint venture would be attractive to an international marketer: (1) when it may enable a company to utilize the specialized skills of a local partner; (2) when it allows the marketer to gain access to a partner's local distribution system; (3) when a company seeks to enter a market where wholly owned activities are prohibited; and (4) when the firm lacks the capital or personnel capabilities to expand its international activities otherwise.[7]

The joint venture may be the only method of market entry if the firm wishes to exercise significant control over the distribution of its products. This would be especially true if wholly owned subsidiaries are prohibited by the foreign government. Such restrictions occur frequently in lesser developed countries (LDCs) where they are attempting to promote internal industrial or retail development.

---

[6] Warren J. Keegan, *Multinational Marketing Management*, 2d ed. (Englewood Cliffs, N.J.: Prentice-Hall, 1980), pp. 243–44.

[7] Cateora and Hess, *International Marketing*, p. 15.

### Ownership

*Foreign Ownership Requires Total Responsibility for Marketing and Distribution*

Complete ownership of a foreign subsidiary offers the domestic firm the highest degree of control of its international marketing and distribution strategies. Ownership can occur through acquisition or expansion. Acquisition of a foreign facility can be advantageous because it minimizes the start-up costs associated with locating and building facilities, hiring employees, and establishing distribution-channel relationships.

Ownership of a foreign subsidiary requires the most knowledge of the international market by the domestic firm. The firm is totally responsible for marketing and distributing its product and cannot have the exporter, licensee, or joint venture assume the responsibility for it.

Direct ownership in the foreign market allows the company to compete more effectively on a price basis due to the elimination of transportation costs incurred in shipments from domestic plants to foreign points-of-entry. Also, customs duties and other import taxes are eliminated.

There are drawbacks associated with direct ownership. Flexibility is lost because the firm has a long-term commitment to the foreign market. Fixed facilities and equipment cannot be disposed of quickly should the firm decide to withdraw from the market due to sales or profit declines, increased levels of competition, or other adversities.

Another drawback with ownership, especially in politically unstable countries, is the possibility of government nationalization of foreign-owned businesses. History is replete with examples of companies which have lost millions of dollars in assets as a result of their foreign operations being nationalized. Fortunately, such events do not occur frequently. It is a possibility, however, that should be considered when entering some international markets.

In general, firms will follow more than one market-entry strategy. Markets, product lines, economic conditions, and political environments change over time so it stands to reason that the optimal market-entry strategy may also change. Also, a good market-entry strategy in one country may not be so good in another. The following example illustrates the changing nature of market entry strategy.

> A large European chemical company had a five-stage strategy in its approach to foreign markets.
>
> *Stage 1.* Limited sales, a form of market testing, through trading companies or independent distributors who bought for their own account.
>
> *Stage 2.* Where markets looked promising, the company sent field representatives to aid the distributor. This was done in Nigeria and East Africa, for example.
>
> *Stage 3.* Where the field representatives reported strong sales possibilities in a sizeable market, the company moved to establish its own sales organizations.
>
> *Stage 4.* If the company sales subsidiary developed the market to a highly profitable degree, the company considered plant investment. The first step was a compounding or assembly plant to mix and package ingredients imported from Europe. Two examples of this are Brazil and Mexico.
>
> *Stage 5.* The final step is a complete manufacturing plant. Such a plant might

produce only a few of the many products of the firm depending on local raw material supply and markets. The company has such a plant in India.[8]

**A Procedure for Comparing Methods of Market Entry**

For the domestic firm considering the various market-entry methods—exporting, licensing, joint ventures, ownership—a formal procedure should be established for evaluating each alternative. Table 13–2 shows one approach to the market-entry decision. Each market-entry strategy can be evaluated based upon a set of management-determined criteria. Every functional area of the firm, e.g., accounting, manufacturing, marketing, physical distribution, must be involved in the establishment of the criteria and their evaluation. Only after a complete analysis of each market-entry method takes place should the firm decide on a method of international involvement.

**TABLE 13–2** Matrix for Comparing Alternative Methods of Market Entry

| Evaluation Criteria | Entry Methods ||||
| --- | --- | --- | --- | --- |
| | Exporting | Licensing | Joint Ventures | Ownership |
| 1. Number of markets | | | | |
| 2. Market penetration | | | | |
| 3. Market feedback | | | | |
| 4. International marketing learning | | | | |
| 5. Control | | | | |
| 6. Marketing costs | | | | |
| 7. Profits | | | | |
| 8. Investment | | | | |
| 9. Administration | | | | |
| 10. Foreign Problems | | | | |
| 11. Flexibility | | | | |
| 12. Risk | | | | |

Source: Adapted from Vern Terpstra, *International Marketing*, 2d ed. (Hinsdale, Ill.: Dryden Press, 1978), p. 310. From *International Marketing*, Second Edition, by Vern Terpstra. Copyright © 1978 by the Dryden Press, a division of Holt, Rinehart and Winston, Publishers. Reprinted by permission of Holt, Rinehart and Winston.

## MANAGEMENT OF THE EXPORT SHIPMENT

There are many facilitators or organizations which are involved in the exporting activity. Examples of such organizations include:

**Types of Export Facilitators**

1. Export distributor.
2. Customshouse broker.
3. Foreign-freight forwarder.
4. Export broker.
5. Export merchant.
6. Combination export manager.

---
[8] Terpstra, *International Marketing*, p. 343. From International Marketing, Second Edition, by Vern Terpstra. Copyright © 1978 by The Dryden Press, a division of Holt, Rinehart and Winston, Publishers. Reprinted by permission of Holt, Rinehart and Winston.

7. Cooperative exporter.
8. Trading company.
9. Foreign purchasing agent.[9]

**Export Facilitators**

For a firm becoming involved in exporting for the first time, the export distributor, customshouse broker, and/or foreign freight forwarder will most probably be used.

*Export distributor.* Often, a company involved in international markets will utilize the services of an export distributor. An export distributor will have the following characteristics: (1) be located in the foreign market; (2) buy on his/her own account; (3) be responsible for the sale of the product; and (4) have a continuing contractual relationship with the domestic firm.[10]

The distributor frequently:

*Functions of an Export Distributor*

1. Is granted exclusive rights to a set territory.
2. Refrains from handling the products of competing manufacturers.
3. Sells goods of other manufacturers to the same outlets.

The following functions are often performed by the distributor alone:

1. Obtaining and maintaining agreed-on levels of channel and sales effort.
2. Obtaining import business and handling the arrangements for customs clearance.
3. Obtaining the necessary foreign exchange for payment to the supplier.
4. Maintaining necessary government relations over time.
5. Maintaining inventories.
6. Providing warehousing facilities.
7. Performing, or overseeing, the inland-freight and delivery functions.
8. The performing of break-bulk operations.

To the above can be added an additional number of functions which the distributor alone, or in various degrees of cooperation with the supplier, may perform.

1. The extending of credit to channel intermediaries and final customers.
2. The gathering and transmitting of market information.
3. The planning and operating of advertising and sales promotions programs.
4. The maintaining of stocks of parts, etc., and providing postsale servicing.[11]

---

[9] A number of textbooks examine the many types of exporting organizations. For an in-depth review of each type see Keegan, *Multinational Marketing Management;* Cateora and Hess, *International Marketing;* Terpstra, *International Marketing;* and Kahler and Kramer, *International Marketing.*

[10] Randolph E. Ross, "Selection of the Overseas Distributor: An Empirical Framework," *International Journal of Physical Distribution* 3 (Autumn 1972): 83.

[11] Ibid., pp. 83–84.

Not only is it important to understand the functions which an export distributor performs, the factors which influence distributor selection must be understood as well. In a study of a broad spectrum of American firms, 25 factors were found to influence distributor selection. The factors were classified into two categories: factors internal to the firm; and factors external to the firm. Table 13-3 identifies the factors a firm uses in the selection of a distributor.

*Customshouse broker.* The customshouse broker performs two critical functions: (1) facilitation of product movement through customs; and (2) handling of the necessary documentation that must accompany international shipments.

The Customshouse Broker Is a Documentation Specialist

For many firms, the task of handling the myriad of documents and forms which must accompany an international shipment can be overwhelming. Coupled with the variety of customs procedures, restrictions, and requirements that differ in each foreign country, the job of facilitating export shipments across international borders requires a specialist—the customshouse broker. In general, if a company is exporting to a number of countries with different import requirements, and/or the company has a large number of items in its product line, e.g., automotive parts, electronic components, food products, a customshouse broker should be a part of the firm's international distribution network. The importance of the customshouse broker to firms involved in exporting was shown in a survey of traffic and distribution professionals conducted by *Distribution* magazine. Of those firms surveyed, 93.6 percent said that they used a customshouse broker in their import/export operations.[12]

*Foreign-freight forwarder.* Foreign or international freight forwarders serve an important role in the export distribution strategies of most firms. They ". . . are in business to provide coordination and assistance in all phases of shipments from the exporter's plant to final overseas destinations."[13] The primary services foreign-freight forwarders provide are as follows:

Services Provided by Foreign-Freight Forwarders

1. Prepare government-required export declarations.
2. Make cargo-space bookings.
3. Provide for transportation from the exporter to final destination.
4. Prepare and process air waybills and bills of lading.
5. Prepare consular documents in the languages of the countries to which the goods are shipped, and provide for certification.
6. Provide for warehouse storage when necessary.
7. Arrange for insurance upon request.
8. Prepare and send shipping notices to banks, shippers, or consignees as required.

[12] Thomas A. Foster, "Freight Forwarders: The Export Experts," *Distribution* 79, no. 3 (March 1980): 38.

[13] F. R. Lineaweaver, Jr., "The Role of the Export Traffic Manager," *Distribution Worldwide* 72, no. 10 (October 1973): 46.

**TABLE 13-3** Factors Which Influence the Selection of an International Distributor

**Factors internal to the firm**

*The competitive position of the exporting firm* (e.g., its financial resources, price of its products, existence of any valuable patents or trademarks, level and "surplus" of managerial expertise, etc.).

These strengths will partially determine what functions the exporter will need from the channel, the extent and type of support he will be able to offer the distributor, and to what extent his resources will permit him to exercise the degree of channel control he desires.

*The relative (long-run) importance that the top management of the supplier firm has assigned to the market.*

This will partially determine the extent to which the firm is willing to commit its resources to both the development of the market and the distributor (i.e., the lower the commitment, the more a self-sufficient distributor is wanted).

*The production capacity which the supplier firm plans to make available to serve the market (now and in the future).*

Importance of the capacity variable depends on the market's potential sales volume and the supplier firm's ability to meet both significant growth of, and fluctuations in, the sales volume. This will influence such distributor functions as maintaining inventories to meet demand fluctuations, the degree of sales and channel effort which is desired, and the extent to which the exporter should build up the distributor's anticipation of future profits.

*The amount of auxiliary services that the product(s) will require* (e.g., adjustments needed to fit customer requirements, special supplies for operation, after-sales servicing, and operator training).

Such service demands tend to increase as one moves from consumer to industrial types of products, for the service sector as opposed to manufacturing, and as the degree of technological sophistication increases.

*The expected replacement rate of frequency of consumer purchase of the product(s).*

This tends to influence the exporter's needs in such areas as sales-force size, size and location of inventories, warehousing, facilities, credit extension, and logistical support.

*The design of the product(s)* (e.g., whether the product is custom-made or of a standard design).

This influences the type of selling required (e.g., personal selling versus mass advertising), the inventories to be carried, size and type of credit, servicing needs, level of sophistication on the part of channel intermediaries, etc.

*The primary market(s) for the product(s).*

Markets may be grouped into three broad classes—industrial, institutional, and consumer. Since different channels and methods of selling may be required to serve each of these markets, the exporter must determine which markets he wishes to serve in order to determine the channels that the distributor candidate must be able to serve and the type of marketing operation which he must have an expertise in.

*The "normal" price of the product at various points in the distribution channel.*

Whatever method of pricing and margin setting is used, the volume-price-margin-service relationship should be understood by the exporter in order to judge what he can reasonably expect from any distributor candidate.

*The type of storage and handling that the product(s) require.*

The environmentally-imposed constraints . . . must be considered when evaluating the warehousing, inventory, and distribution needs of the supplier vis-à-vis the capacities of the candidate.

**TABLE 13-3** *(continued)*

*The type and degree of advertising, sales promotion, and personal selling "normally" used with the product.*

Two specific areas are of concern: The exporter's needs as regards these elements of the marketing mix for the particular country in question. The nature and extent of principal-distributor cooperation in these areas.

*The probability that the firm will introduce new products into the market in the future.*

Possible introduction of new products means that areas such as the distributor's (and channel's) willingness and potential ability to carry increasing volumes and varieties of products, service new markets and types of customers, and provide the additional and possibly different post-sale servicing need to be fully analysed.

**Factors external to the firm**

*The potential size of the market—now and in the future.*

Analysis of market potentials requires the exporter to consider the potential productivity of various individual distributor and channel alternatives in realizing the estimates. The greater the market potential, the more time, money, etc., the exporter should make available in selecting and developing the distributor with the most potential.

*The relevant trading areas for the product(s).*

Where the areas are located, the size of the area, the sales potential of each, the subdivision of these areas by product lines, etc., need to be reviewed. These can have significant implications for such decision criteria as: The size of salesforce the distributor must be able to provide. The number, size, and location of the stocks of inventory which he must be able and prepared to handle. The number of branches which any candidate may have to maintain. The number of distributors the exporter will need to adequately cover the entire country.

*The "newness" of the product type or brand to the market.*

The point of concern is the marketing problems surrounding the "developing" of a demand for a new product or the introduction of a new brand into a market. This will influence such marketing factors as pricing policies, advertising and promotional programs, acceptable order quantities (initially smaller), and the stature required of the distributor (for a new product type or brand the supplier is likely to need a well-known distributor, probably selling several leading products of other manufacturers, to do a good job).

*The existence of the necessary facilitating institutions* (e.g., available media, advertising agencies, credit information services, financing agencies, etc.)

The extent to which these institutions exist will indicate the extent to which the distributor and his channel will have to provide, or help provide, these services themselves.

The geographical aspects of the foreign country (e.g., size of the nation, population, densities and the distances between population centres, physical features of the terrain and topography, climatic conditions, etc.).

The geographical aspects will tend to influence the exporter's inventory and storage needs, the number of distributors and channels needed to effectively reach the trading areas, and the types of post-sale servicing problems he will face.

*The types and capacity of transportation facilities to the trading areas.*

The desired geographical location and number of distributors, and the size and location of their inventories will be dependent on the available logistical support.

*The strength of the major competitors.*

The decisions resulting from an analysis of the competition will influence the entire set of distributor characteristics and functions since the exporter's choice must be capable of meeting or exceeding the strengths of the competition.

**TABLE 13-3** *(concluded)*

*The availability of channels to the market.*

There is a dominant group of channels for most lines of merchandise and the exporter must establish the relationship of any distributor candidate with this dominant group.

The marketing services provided by the channels can differ significantly from one country to another and thus require considerable attention during the selection because of their significance in determining the nature of the channel and sales effort required or possible.

*The nature of the retailing system* (e.g., number and sizes of outlets, role of independents, existence of multi-store organisations, etc.).

It is most important that the exporter whose product is sold through retailers review these factors in order to understand and weigh correctly the relative importance of the various types of retailing in the distribution of his products and review the distributor candidate's operations in the light of these local practices.

*The ordering characteristics for the product(s).*

The following need to be considered: the influence of the dollar amount on the average sales order, the relative frequency of ordering, the regularity with which orders are placed, the number of separate product items in each order, the extent to which solicitation by salesmen may or may not be necessary for repeat sales, and the relative bargaining power of the various channel members. These factors will influence the exporter's needs with regards to the size and location of inventories, the types of logistical support, and the level of sales effort and credit extension required.

*The country's laws which may influence the exporter's activities* (e.g., laws regarding price controls, promotional methods, exclusive territory agreements, contract law, product quality, labour laws, patents, trademarks, antitrust laws, restrictions on entry, and legislation affecting particular trades).

The exporter requires a distributor who is familiar with both the written and unwritten aspects of these laws, who can reason effectively with the government about the laws, and must take the various laws into account when designing the actual contract.

*The role that government plays in the organisation of trade and distribution for the type of product(s)* (e.g., marketing boards, government backed cooperatives, government overseeing of various sectors of the economy, and monitoring the pricing activities of the various middlemen).

The government can influence most of the distributor's activities and therefore the exporter needs to evaluate any distributor candidate's political "connections" and past ability to work effectively with such government agencies.

*The role that the government plays in licensing imports, enforcing exchange controls and other restrictions on the free flow of goods into the country.*

The exporter must be concerned with restrictions on imports from his "home" country in general, and, specifically, for his type of product(s).

The government's policies will undoubtedly influence the distributor's ability to import and pay for the goods. Therefore, the type of government relations the candidate is able to maintain will be most important during selection.

*The nation's formal or informal membership in trade groupings.*

The influence of this variable is primarily indirect. It may influence the relevant laws, the licensing of imports, the availability of foreign exchange, the potential size of the market, and the trading areas that must be served.

Source: Randolph E. Ross, "Selection of the Overseas Distributor: An Empirical Framework," *International Journal of Physical Distribution* 3 (Autumn 1972): 84–86.

9. Complete shipping documents and send them to shippers, banks, or consignees as directed.
10. Provide general assistance on export-traffic matters.[14]

Nearly every international company will utilize the services of a foreign-freight forwarder. "Even in large companies, with active export departments capable of handling documentation, a forwarder is usually involved in coordination duties at the port or at the destination."[15]

**Documentation**

"To most distribution managers, exporting means international transportation. In reality, the most important part of exporting is the planning, negotiating, and paperwork that takes place before the first pound of freight is shipped. The distribution manager has to know this side of exporting as well. . . ."[16] International documentation is much more complex than domestic documentation because each foreign country has its own specifications and requirements. Absolute accuracy is required inasmuch as errors may result in delayed shipments or penalties. It is beyond the scope of this chapter to examine in detail the multitude of export documents which exist: however, some of the more widely used items include:

Examples of Export Documents

1. Pro forma invoice—Quotes prices, delivery terms, dates, etc., to importer. Opens negotiations for payment terms.
2. Export declaration—Proves export license is issued and provides census data. It must provide merchandise data.
3. Shipper's letter of instruction—Provides all data needed for ocean bill of lading to be prepared.
4. Commercial invoice—Content determined by import country. Usually includes name and address of shipper, seller, consignee, or other principals, and any reference numbers; order date, shipping date, mode, delivery and payment terms; description of goods, prices, quantities, discounts; origin of goods and export marks; and any bank credit or advice numbers.
5. Certificate of origin—Required by some countries in addition to commercial invoice, usually to determine preferential duties.
6. Packing list—Itemizes material in each package; indicates type of package; net, legal, tare and gross weights for each package; any markings and shipper/buyer reference number.
7. Consular invoices—Only required by some countries (mostly Latin America). Exact format and data required by each country.
8. Inspection certificate—Sometimes requested by buyer to insure quality, quantity, and conformity of goods. Issued by independent surveyor.
9. Domestic bill of lading—For U.S. portion of transportation. Goods consigned to shipper or forwarder.

---

[14] Ibid.
[15] Foster, "Freight Forwarders," p. 38.
[16] Foster, "Anatomy of an Export," p. 75.

10. Air waybill—Usually single document for complete domestic and international movement. Special IATA form usually used and prepared by carrier or forwarder.
11. Ocean bill of lading—Two types: Nonnegotiable (straight) and negotiable (shipper's order). "Order" BLs used for most types of credit sales. Endorsements and numbers of originals stipulated by letter of credit or credit arrangement. The BL is "clean" when carrier accepts the goods and finds no damage, shortage, etc.
12. Dock/warehouse receipt—Used when terms of sale based on U.S. point, such as a port. Receipt shows goods were tendered as specified.
13. Certificate of manufacture—For advance purchase prior to manufacture. When goods are ready for shipment, certificate is sent to buyer with invoice and packing list. Requests payment and shipping instructions.
14. Insurance certificates—When terms of sale require seller to provide marine insurance, certificate indicates type and amount of insurance required.[17]

**Terms of Trade**

Closely related to the actual documents used in the export process are the terms of shipment or terms of trade. The terms of shipment are much more important to the international shipper because of the uncertainties and control problems that accompany foreign traffic movements. "For this reason, negotiating the final terms of sale is probably the most important part of an export deal. These terms of sale determine who is responsible for the various stages of delivery, who bears what risks, and who pays for the various elements of transportation."[18] A summary of the most commonly used terms of shipment in exporting from the United States is shown below. Foreign-based exports would have the same or similar terminology associated with them.

*Ex origin:* Origin should be identified as factory, plant, etc. Seller bears costs and risks until buyer is obligated to take delivery. Buyer pays for documents, must take delivery when specified and must pay for any export taxes.

*FOB (free on board) inland carrier:* Seller arranges for loading on railcars, truck, etc. Seller provides a clean bill of lading and is responsible for loss or damage until goods have been placed on inland vehicle.

*FOB vessel U.S. port:* The price quoted covers all expenses involved in delivery of goods upon the vessel designated at the port named. Buyer must give seller adequate notice of sailing date, name of ship, berth, etc. Buyer bears additional costs resulting from vessel being late or absent.

*FAS (free along side) vessel U.S. port:* Similar to FOB vessel, but certain

---
[17] Foster, "Anatomy of an Export," pp. 78–79.
[18] Ibid., p. 76.

additional port charges for the seller such as heavy lift may apply. The buyer is responsible for loss or damage while goods are on a lighter (small barge) or within reach of the loading device. Loading costs are also the responsibility of the buyer.

*FOB vessel foreign port:* The price quoted includes all transportation costs to the point goods are off-loaded in the destination country. Seller is responsible for insurance to this point. The buyer assumes risk as soon as the vessel is at the foreign port.

*FOB inland destination:* The price quoted includes all costs involved in getting the goods to the named inland point in the country of importation.

*C&F (cost and freight):* The price quoted includes all transportation to the point of destination. Seller also pays export taxes or similar fees. The buyer pays the cost of certificates of origin, consular invoices, or other documents required for importation to the buyer's country. The seller must provide these, but at the buyer's expense. The buyer is responsible for all insurance from the point of vessel loading.

*CIF (cost, insurance, and freight):* The price quoted under these terms includes the cost of goods, transportation, and marine insurance. The seller pays all taxes or fees, as well as marine and war risk insurance. Buyer pays for any certificates or consular documents required for importation. Although the seller pays for insurance, buyer assumes all risk after seller has delivered the goods to the carrier.[19]

### Free-Trade Zones

Free-trade zones (FTZs), sometimes referred to as foreign-trade zones, are areas where companies may ship products to postpone or reduce customs duties or taxes. Products remaining in the FTZ are not subject to duties or taxes until they are reshipped out of the zone into the country in which the FTZ is located. Within the FTZ firms often may process, assemble, sort, and repackage the product before reshipment. To the firm which is considering the use of FTZs, several advantages are possible.

Why Use a Free-Trade Zone?

1. They permit the firm to realize the economies of *bulk shipping* to a country without having to bear the burden of customs duties. Duties need to be paid only when the goods are released on a *small lot* basis from the zone or bonded warehouse.
2. They permit manufacturers to carry a local inventory at less cost than in facilities they own, because in their own facilities they must pay the duty as soon as the goods enter the country. If duties are high, the financial burden of covering the duty on goods in inventory is significant.
3. American exporters can use U.S. free-trade zones to bring in low-cost foreign ingredients and avoid duty payments on products reexported. Ormont Drug & Chemical Company makes antibiotics in the New York foreign-trade zone. Its raw materials, especially isoniazid, are pur-

---

[19] Ibid., pp. 76–77.

chased from overseas suppliers at prices 25 percent or more below domestic rates. They are imported duty free, but the completed products are exported immediately. There are extra savings from not having to ship through customs.

4. The ability to engage in local processing, assembly, repacking, and similar operations can mean savings to the international firm. It can ship to the market in bulk . . . for advantageous freight rates. Then it can process, assemble, or repack locally for local distribution. For many American and European firms, the local labor costs will be less than those at home. The free zones in Panama and Colombia have been popular with many European and American firms, for example, Ronson, Goodyear, Eastman Kodak, Ericson, and Celanese.[20]

Locations of some of the major free-trade zones throughout the world are shown in Table 13–4. As evidenced by the large number of FTZs in existence, there are few major world markets not directly served by, or within easy reach of, a free-trade zone.

## THE INTERNATIONAL MARKETPLACE

All forms of market entry into the international environment require an awareness of the variables which can impact the firm's distribution system. Some of these factors can be controlled by the physical distribution executive. Others, unhappily, are not subject to control but must be addressed and dealt with in any international marketing undertaking. Figure 13–2 shows the environment in which the physical distribution manager must operate.

### Uncontrollable Elements

Anything which effects the distribution strategy of the international firm yet is not under the direct control and authority of the physical distribution manager is an uncontrollable element. The major uncontrollable elements or environments include the political and legal systems of the foreign markets, economic conditions, degree of competition in each market, level of distribution technology available or accessible, the geographical structure of the foreign market, and the social and cultural norms of the various target markets.

The distribution executive also faces uncertainties in the economic, competitive, and other environments in the international marketplace. However, "a business operating in the home country undoubtedly feels comfortable in forecasting the business climate and adjusting business decisions to these elements . . . the process of evaluating the uncontrollable elements in an international marketing program often involves substantial doses of cultural, political, and economic shock."[21]

---

[20] Terpstra, *International Marketing*, pp. 381–82. From *International Marketing*, Second Edition, by Vern Terpstra. Copyright © 1978 by The Dryden Press, a division of Holt, Rinehart and Winston, Publishers. Reprinted by permission of Holt, Rinehart and Winston.

[21] Cateora and Hess, *International Marketing*, p. 9.

**TABLE 13-4** Free-Trade Zones around the World

*Europe*
  *Austria:* Graz, Linz, Solbad Hall, Vienna; *Belgium:* major ports and airports; *Denmark:* Copenhagen; *Finland:* Hanko, Helsinki, Lappeenranta, Turku; *West Germany:* Bremen, Bremerhaven, Cuxhaven, Emden, Hamburg, Kiel; *Gibraltar; Greece:* Piraeus, Thessalonika; *Ireland:* Shannon Airport; *Italy:* Trieste, Vienna, special facilities in Bari, Genoa, Imperia, Leghorn, Naples, Palermo; *The Netherlands:* major ports and airports; *Spain:* Barcelona, Cadiz, Vigo, Canary Islands, Ceuta, Melilla, special facilities in Algeciras, Alicante, Bilbao, Huelva, La Coruna, Las Palmas, Malaga, Pasajes, Santander, Seville, Valencia; *Sweden:* Gothenburg, Malmo, Stockholm; *Switzerland:* major cities; *Yugoslavia:* Belgrade, Koper, Novi Sad, Rijeka, Split.

*Latin America, the Caribbean, Bermuda*
  *Argentina:* (transit zones) Barranqueras, Buenos Aires, Concordia, Empedrado, Jujuy, La Quiaca, Mendoza, Monte Caseros, Paso de los Libres, Pocitos, Rosario, Salta, San Juan, Tierra del Fuego; *Bahama Islands:* Freeport; *Bermuda:* Ireland Island; *Brazil:* Manaus, (transit zones) Belem, Corumba, Paranagua, Porto Velho, Santos; *Chile:* (transit zones) Arica, Antofagasta; *Columbia:* Barranquilla, San Andres Island, Providencia Island, Amazonas; *Dominican Republic:* La Romana; *Mexico:* Coatzacoalcos, Salina Cruz, Baja California, Sonora, Quintana Roo; *Netherlands Antilles:* Aruba, Curacao; *Panama:* Colon; *Paraguay:* (transit zones) Concepcion, Encarnacion, Asuncion, Villeta; *Peru:* Amazon Region, Matarani, Mollendo; *Uruguay:* Colonia, Neuva Palmira.

*Asia*
  *Bahrain:* Mina Sulman; *Hong Kong; India:* Kandla, Calcutta; *Iran:* Bandar Shahpur, Khorramshahr; *Japan:* major ports and cities; *Lebanon:* Beirut, Tripoli; *Malaysia:* Labuan and Penang islands; *Pakistan:* Karachi; *Ryukyu Islands:* Naha; *Singapore; South Korea:* Masan; *South Yemen:* Aden; *Taiwan:* Kaohsiung; *Thailand:* Bangkok.

*Africa*
  *Angola:* Lobito; *French Territory:* Afars and Issas; *Ivory Coast:* Abidjan; *Liberia:* Monrovia; *Libya:* Tripoli; *Morocco:* Tangier; *Mozambique:* Beira, Lourenco Marques; *Senegal:* Dakar; *Tanzania:* Dar es Salaam; *Togo:* Lome.

*United States*
  *Arizona:* Tucson; *Arkansas:* Little Rock; *California:* San Francisco, San Jose; *Florida:* Miami, Orlando, Port Everglades; *Georgia:* Shenandoah; *Hawaii:* Honolulu; *Illinois:* Chicago, Granite City; *Kansas:* Kansas City; *Kentucky:* Louisville, Wilder; *Louisiana:* New Orleans; *Massachusetts:* Boston, New Bedford; *Michigan:* Battle Creek, Bay County, Sault Ste. Marie; *Nebraska:* Omaha; *New Jersey:* Newark, Newark/Elizabeth; *New York:* Brooklyn, Buffalo, Lockport, Newburgh; *Ohio:* Cincinnati, Cleveland, Columbus, Evandale, Toledo; *Oregon:* Portland; *Pennsylvania:* Harrisburg, Philadelphia, Pittsburgh, Pittston; *South Carolina:* Spartanburg, Summerville; *Texas:* Dallas/Ft. Worth, Galveston, McAllen; *Utah:* Salt Lake City; *Virginia:* Portsmouth; *Washington:* Seattle; *Wisconsin:* Milwaukee; *Puerto Rico:* Mayaguez.

Source: Adapted from Tom Dulaney, "Foreign Trade Zones: What's in It for the Shipper," *Distribution* 79, no. 3 (March 1980): 44, and "The Uses of Foreign Trade Zones," *Transportation and Distribution Management* 13, no. 6 (June 1973): 30.

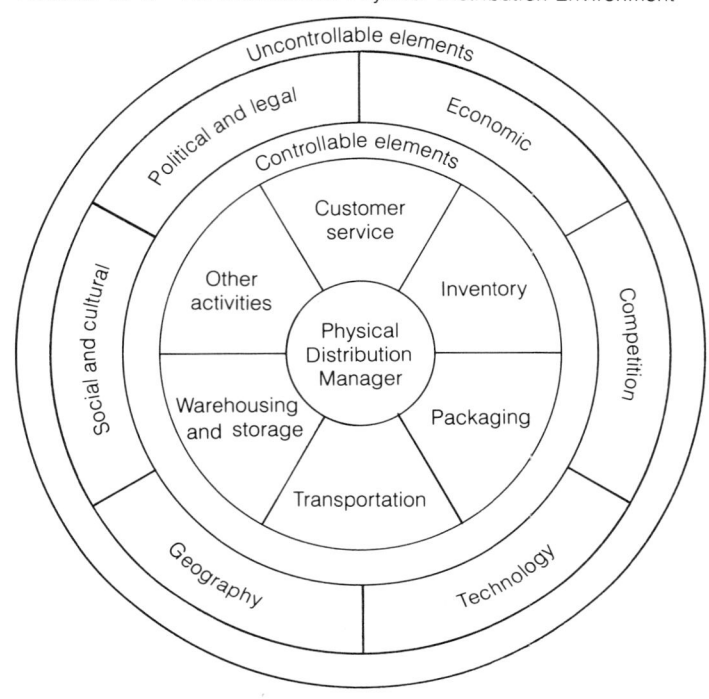

**FIGURE 13-2** The International Physical Distribution Environment

*[Diagram: Concentric circle diagram. Outer ring labeled "Uncontrollable elements" containing: Political and legal, Economic, Competition, Technology, Geography, Social and cultural. Inner ring labeled "Controllable elements" surrounding "Physical Distribution Manager" at center, with segments: Customer service, Inventory, Packaging, Transportation, Warehousing and storage, Other activities.]*

It is beyond the scope of this chapter to examine the various international uncontrollable elements in detail. A number of international marketing textbooks are available which address these elements.[22] It is sufficient to say that the uncontrollable elements affect the actions of the physical distribution executive and must be considered in the planning, implementation, and control of the firm's international physical distribution network.

### Controllable Elements—Strategic

When a firm becomes involved in international operations, the scope of the physical distribution manager's responsibilities often expands to include international distribution activities. In a survey of NCPDM members it was found that the relative frequency of distribution executives with full international distribution responsibility had increased from 9.5 percent in 1974 to 30.5 percent in 1980.[23] The trend will no doubt continue as companies expand into global markets.

---

[22] See footnote 9.

[23] Bernard J. LaLonde and Martha Cooper, "Career Patterns in Distribution: Profile 1980," *Proceedings of the Eighteenth Annual Conference of The National Council of Physical Distribution Management*, October 13–15, 1980, p. 15.

A firm involved in international distribution must still be concerned with administering the physical distribution components so as to minimize cost and provide an acceptable level of service to its customers. However, a firm's cost/service mix will vary in international markets. For example, distribution costs as a percentage of sales are much higher in Japan and the United States than in Australia or the United Kingdom. Table 13–5 shows some of

**TABLE 13-5**  Distribution Costs as a Percentage of Sales

| Country | U.S. | U.K. | Japan | Australia |
|---|---|---|---|---|
| Transportation | 6.4% | 5.5% | 13.5% | 2.5% |
| Receiving and dispatch | 1.7 | 2.5 |  | 1.4 |
| Warehousing | 3.7 |  |  | 1.8 |
| Packaging and storage | 2.6 | 2.0 | 13.0 | 1.7 |
| Inventory | 3.8 | 3.0 |  | 3.6 |
| Order processing | 1.2 | 1.0 |  | 2.1 |
| Administration | 2.4 | 2.0 |  | 1.0 |
| Total | 21.8 | 16.0 | 26.5 | 14.1 |

Source: Peter Gilmour and Peter J. Rimmer, "Business Logistics in the Pacific Basin," *Columbia Journal of World Business* 2, no. 1 (Spring 1976): 65.

the cost differences which exist among countries. Firms operating in these countries, or exporting to them, may have to follow different distribution strategies because of the varying cost structures they find. Companies involved in international distribution, and especially those which own foreign subsidiaries, should be aware of the variety of differences that exist between the administration of domestic versus foreign physical distribution activities.

*Customer service strategies.* In general, the level of service that a firm can provide to its domestic customers is higher than to its foreign customers if the company is involved in exporting. This is primarily due to the longer length of haul and delay in customs. Also, the consistency of service which the firm is able to provide its domestic customers probably can not be achieved internationally. Because international transportation movements tend to be longer and can involve several different types of carriers, multiple transfers and handlings, and the crossing of a number of international boundaries, there is a greater probability that time-in-transit can vary significantly from one shipment to the next.

Customer Service Is Viewed Differently in International Markets

Conversely, customer service levels may be higher in some international markets. This would especially be true if the firm had a facility in the foreign market. For example, in Japan, the order cycle time is generally shorter than in the United States. Because of the geographical differences between the two countries, the physical facilities of many wholesalers and retailers, and financial considerations, more than 80 percent of all consumer-goods orders are delivered in 24 hours or less. In no instance does it take longer than 48 hours if the product is available at the wholesale level of the channel of distribution.[24] For that reason, many international firms operate owned facilities in the foreign markets in order to compete effectively on a customer service basis.

The cost to provide a specified level of customer service may vary between countries. As shown in Table 13–5 distribution costs are higher in Japan and the United States than in Australia and the United Kingdom. In general, if a firm is serving those markets and is attempting to provide a uniform service level to each market, the cost of providing that service will be higher in those areas where distribution costs are highest. A company must examine the service requirements of customers in each foreign market and develop a distribution mix which best serves each area. Because of competition, specific customer needs, or other factors, a firm may have to incur higher distribution costs. Necessarily, this will result in lower profits for the firm. Such a decision requires a complete analysis of the situation by top management.

*It Costs More to Carry Foreign Inventories*

***Inventory strategies.*** Inventory control is particularly important to the international company. Firms involved in exporting have to be concerned with *pipeline* or *in-transit* inventories. Depending upon the length of transit and delays which can occur in international product movements, a firm may have to supply its distributors or other foreign middlemen with higher-than-normal levels of inventory. For high-value products the inventory carrying costs as well as the amount of accounts receivable outstanding can be extremely high.

> Inventory carrying costs are often overlooked and therefore not analyzed when designing a multinational distribution system. These costs include working capital tied up in inventory, obsolescence, shrinkage, damage, taxes, insurance, and warehousing. To optimize the total system, there must be a trade-off between inventory carrying costs and other distribution costs such as transportation and protective packaging.
>
> Example: a large multinational firm with facilities and customers the world over was shipping parts out of its midwest plant to one of its plants in the Orient via the east coast ports of the United States. It used a water-route around the Cape of Good Hope in Africa, the voyage taking 14 weeks, yet being cheaper than any other transport service. But delays, unreliable service, and faulty tracing caused the firm to make emergency air shipments to keep production lines in the Orient going. Air shipments became 70 percent of the total transport bill and additional substantial stock was stored in the Orient to guard against waterborne delivery uncertainties.
>
> Analysis determined that the parts could be trucked across the United States to west coast ports, then shipped by sea to reduce transit time and to increase reliability. The new procedure allowed an annual saving of more than $60,000 in transportation and inventory carrying costs.[25]

---

[24] Mikio Ikeda, "The Progress of PD in Japan," *Transportation and Distribution Management* 14, no. 1 (January/February 1974): 41.

[25] Lynn E. Gill, "Beware of Booby Traps in Multinational Distribution," *Handling and Shipping* 17, no. 3 (March 1976): 45.

In markets where the firm's products are sold at the retail level the shopping patterns of the population can be very important to determining inventory strategies.

> There are more wholesalers and retailers in Japan than in all of the United States. . . . Purchases of wholesalers or retailers are characterized by very small amounts per order. Most of the shops are small and display space is also very small—about 20 to 40 square meters. Wholesalers do not have enough space for stocks because of high land prices. Therefore, they order small lots nearly every day, though the order items differ from day to day.[26]

Within the countries of Europe retailing patterns differ greatly. Table 13–6 shows variations in European distribution channels by product and country. Different distribution channels necessitate different inventory policies and control procedures.

Companies in the United States can usually exercise greater control over their inventories because they can influence the amount of product ordered by their customers through discounts. This may not be a viable strategy in some international markets.

> In the United States, goods change in price according to the size of the lots ordered, but this is not the case in Japan. Instead, the Japanese manufacturers change the unit price considering the average amount of the customers' monthly purchases; or they pay rebates once or twice a year taking the annual amount of orders into consideration.[27]

Since conditions may vary in foreign markets it is important for the firm to develop inventory policies and control procedures that are appropriate for each market area.

*Transportation strategies.* International transportation of goods can involve any of the five basic modes of transportation although air and water carriage are perhaps the most important in international movements. Motor, rail, and water carriage are most important in the intranational freight movement.

There can be significant differences between the transportation infrastructures found in nations throughout the world. For example, the transportation environments of the United States and the Common Market countries differ markedly. The differences in Common Market countries include:

**International Traffic Management Is Different**

*Different shipper traffic structures:* Only a few of the largest companies maintain clearly identified in-house traffic units.

*Different transport pricing methods:* Tariffs and classifications are simpler and smaller as well as fewer in number, but negotiated rates are the rule rather than the exception.

*Different modal services:* In routes, in equipment, and in the specific services they provide, carriers of Common Market freight are unlike their U.S. counterparts. Generally, their role is to provide basic transportation—paperwork,

---

[26] Ikeda, "PD in Japan," p. 42.
[27] Ibid.

**TABLE 13-6** Variations in European Distribution Channels by Product and Country (percent of sales in each channel)

|  | Furniture | | Domestic appliances | | Books and stationery | | Textiles | | Footwear | | Clothing | |
|---|---|---|---|---|---|---|---|---|---|---|---|---|
|  | France | UK | Germany | Netherlands | Belgium | Netherlands | Belgium | UK | Germany | UK | France | UK |
| Department and variety stores | 8.3% | 13.2% | 15.6% | 11.1% | 25.1% | 5.3% | 6.2% | 10.2% | 23.8% | 14.5% | 17.4% | 20.6% |
| Multiple chain stores | 4.8 | 26.9 | 16.8 | 22.6 | 9.1 | 33.4 | 7.2 | 16.0 | 16.0 | 48.5 | 4.1 | 50.7 |
| Mail order | 3.1 | 12.8 | 24.9 | 1.5 | 6.3 | 3.9 | 2.5 | 12.0 | 0.7 | 14.0 | 3.2 | 10.3 |
| Cooperatives | 2.2 | 7.8 | 2.3 | 0.3 | 0.1 | 0.3 | 0.8 | 3.6 | 0.2 | 3.6 | 1.2 | 2.8 |
| Independents and street trade | 81.6 | 39.2 | 40.3 | 64.5 | 59.4 | 57.1 | 83.3 | 58.2 | 59.1 | 19.4 | 74.1 | 15.6 |

Source: Vern Terpstra, *International Marketing*, 2d ed. (Hinsdale, Ill.: Dryden Press, 1978), p. 363. From *International Marketing*, Second Edition, by Vern Terpstra. Copyright © 1978 by The Dryden Press, a division of Holt, Rinehart and Winston, Publishers. Reprinted by permission of Holt, Rinehart and Winston.

consolidation, and other services not part of actual physical movement are performed for the shipper by others.

*Different forwarder duties:* Most of the work performed by shipper and carrier traffic departments in North America is handled instead by freight forwarders in Common Market countries and in all of Europe. Shippers only work directly with carriers where volume shipments move regularly; even these tend to be forwarder-processed when international through movement and consequent paperwork is involved.[28]

Any firm involved in international markets must be aware of the different transport services, costs, and modal availabilities in the countries in which they market their products. The differences that exist between nations can be due to taxes, subsidies, regulations, government ownership of carriers, and other factors. Rail service in Europe is usually much better than in the United States because equipment, track, and facilities are in better condition due to government ownership and/or subsidies of the rail system.

Japan and Europe utilize water carriage to a much larger degree than the United States or Canada. Due to the length and favorable characteristics of coastlines and inland waterways, water transport is a viable alternative for many shippers. For many companies shipping between or within the borders of foreign countries, a thorough reevaluation of the transport alternatives, costs, and services is needed. As an example, air and surface transportation directly compete for transoceanic shipments. Many factors must be considered when a firm compares the two alternatives. Table 13–7 iden-

**TABLE 13–7** Factors to Consider when Comparing International Surface Transportation with Air Distribution

1. Packing: Cost of material and labor for ocean-freight shipments compared with air-freight requirements
2. Inland freight and storage costs
3. Wharfage fees
4. Freight-forwarding charges
5. Minimum charges on bills of lading
6. Freight charges
7. Cost of in-transit damage and/or pilferage
8. Insurance
9. Reforwarding charges from port of unloading to inland points of final destination
10. Inland transportation costs
11. Cost of inventory carried in-transit between factory and destination
12. Custom duties
13. Local investments in in-house inventories and storage costs required for surface transportation lead times, compared with air shipments
14. Local taxes on in-house inventories

Source: F. R. Lineaweaver, Jr., "The Role of the Export Traffic Manager," *Distribution Worldwide* 72, no. 10 (October 1973): 47–48.

---

[28] Jack W. Farrell, "Common Market Transport: An Overview for U.S. Shippers," *Traffic Management* 16, no. 3 (March 1977): 36.

tifies some of the more important cost factors which effect the choice between air and surface transport. An example showing actual cost differentials between air and surface transport is presented in Table 13-8. It should be noted that each international shipment must be evaluated separately in order to ascertain the cost differential between air and surface transport.

**TABLE 13-8** Cost Comparison of International Surface Transportation with Air Distribution—A Case History

Product: Scroll-cutting line used in can-producing firm
Weight: 56 tons
Origin: Chicago, Illinois, U.S.A.
Destination: Denmark
Cost of machine down time: $2,000 per day

Comparative shipping and handling costs:

*Surface*
| | |
|---|---|
| $14,000 | Crating for export (five workers, three weeks, 5,000 feet of lumber) |
| 2,000 | Land transportation to port |
| 782 | Dock charges (truck to pier charge, heavy-lift charge) |
| 8,000 | Ocean freight |
| 600 | Overseas dock charge |
| 700 | Land transportation to factory |
| 2,500 | Uncrating, getting rid of 5,000 ft. of broken lumber, wiping off cosmolene |
| $28,582 | |

*Air*
| | |
|---|---|
| $ 300 | Cost of applying thin coat of oil, wrapping units in vinyl film |
| 200 | Pallets |
| 500 | Truck to airport |
| 28,195 | Air freight |
| 500 | Truck to factory |
| 500 | Take units off pallets, unwrap vinyl film, wipe |
| $30,195 | |

Loss in production time:

*Surface*
| | |
|---|---|
| 24 | Days to crate for export |
| 7 | Days to truck to port |
| 14 | Days on the ocean |
| 14 | Days in customs storage |
| 3 | Days from port to factory |
| 12 | Days to uncrate |
| 4 | Days to wipe off the cosmolene |
| 78 | Days × $2,000 = $156,000 |

*Air*
| | |
|---|---|
| 1½ | Days to apply thin coat of oil, wrap in vinyl film and palletize |
| ½ | Day to truck to airport |
| 3 | Days to load and fly two plane loads overseas |
| 3 | Days to truck to factory |
| 2 | Days to unload, unwrap, wipe off |
| 10 | Days × $2,000 = $20,000 |

Total cost for surface and air distribution:

*Surface*
| | |
|---|---|
| $ 28,582 | Shipping and handling |
| 156,000 | Loss in production time |
| $184,582 | total cost |

*Air*
| | |
|---|---|
| $30,195 | Shipping and handling |
| 20,000 | Loss in production time |
| $50,195 | total cost |

Source: Adapted from advertisement entitled "They Exploded the Myth that Heavy Equipment was too Damned Expensive to Ship by Air," in *The Wall Street Journal,* February 23, 1971, p. 10.

In addition, there are service factors which must be considered when a firm selects between air and surface transportation. General Motors Corporation is heavily involved in international distribution with 48 major overseas operations with plants in 60 cities. Increasing fuel prices and fuel shortages have caused the firm to reexamine the cost/service mix provided by air and ocean transport.

In addition to paying fuel-inflated transportation rates, ocean shippers have had to measure the impact of increased ocean transit times upon inventories, contractual obligations, and customer satisfaction. Lengthened voyages are the result of slow steaming practices adopted by carriers as a fuel conservation measure.[29]

Other service factors which may also effect a firm's mode choice include variability in transit time, loss and/or damage rates, and on-time pickup and delivery.

In making traffic and transportation decisions, the physical distribution manager must consider the differences which exist between the domestic and international markets. Modal availability, rates, regulatory restrictions, service levels, and other aspects of the transportation mix may vary significantly from one market to another. It is vital that the differences be known and understood so that an optimal transportation network can be established for each international market.

### Controllable Elements—Managerial

*Packaging.* "Among the major factors involved in designing the package are transportation and handling, climate, pilferage, freight rates, customs duties, and most importantly, the customer's requirements. It is well known that the greater number of handlings to which goods are subjected, the greater is the possibility of damage. International trade may require several such handlings."[30] In general, the rate of damage and/or loss in international traffic movements is higher than in domestic movements. Therefore, the international shipper must be much more concerned with the protective aspects of the package than his/her domestic counterpart.

In addition, the international shipper must take into account the handling characteristics of the product. The following example reveals the protective and handling aspects which must be considered when distributing internationally.

> Example: a major importer from Japan saved over $1 million in annual freight costs by redesigning its package. The original protection did a good job, but was not designed with the total distribution system in mind. The packaged product stacked well on typical Japanese flatbed trucks at origin point. But, in the intermodal container aboard ship and in the U.S. highway trailer heading for destination, the packaging allowed for only 50 percent of the capacity of those vehicles to be utilized.
>
> A redesign of the protective packaging brought 90 percent of all transport equipment utilization. A secondary benefit resulting allowed for the higher density use of the intermodal container for minibridge service across the United States to the east coast destination from Japan. This reduced overall transit time by more than two weeks.[31]

In order to facilitate product handling and to protect the product during movement and storage, many firms have turned to the use of containers.

---

[29] Rex R. Williams, "International Physical Distribution Management," *Survey of Business* 15, no. 3 (Spring 1980): 29.

[30] Kahler and Kramer, *International Marketing*, p. 204.

[31] Gill, "Booby Traps in Multinational Distribution," p. 45.

Containers are widely used in international distribution, especially when and/or water movements are part of the transport network. Many companies have adopted standard container sizes (8' × 8' × 10', 20', 30', or 40') which allow for intermodal movements as well as the use of standardized materials-handling equipment.

The advantages of containerization are numerous.

**Containers Facilitate International Shipments**

1. Costs due to loss and/or damage are reduced because of the protective nature of the container.
2. Labor costs in freight handling are reduced due to the increased use of automated materials-handling equipment.
3. Containers are more easily stored and transported than other types of shipments which results in lower warehousing and transportation costs.
4. Containers are available in a variety of sizes, many of which are standardized for intermodal use.
5. Containers are able to serve as temporary storage facilities at ports and terminals where warehousing space may be limited.

On the other hand, containerization is not without disadvantages. The major problem with the use of containers is that container ports or terminals may not be available in certain parts of the world. Also, even when such facilities exist, they may be so overburdened with inbound and outbound cargo that long delays occur. The next major problem associated with containerization is the large capital expenditure required to initiate a container-based transportation network. Significant capital outlays for port and terminal facilities, materials-handling equipment, specialized transport equipment, plus the containers themselves, are necessary before a firm can utilize containerization.

Related to the packaging component of international distribution is labeling.

> Labeling . . . has its own particular parameters. The major elements are language, government regulations, and consumer information. Even if labels were standardized in format and message content from country to country, still the language would probably vary in each market. If the label contains an important verbal communication for consumers, usually it must be in their language, which means different language labels for most foreign markets. The resulting economic loss is slight, since only printing diseconomies are involved, rather than the greater diseconomies associated with the higher production costs of package or product modification. Occasionally, however, firms try to avoid even this cost. One way is through the use of multilingual labels; for example, one label would carry information in French, German, and Italian for a product serving all three markets.[32]

From a cost standpoint, labeling is a relatively minor aspect of international distribution. However, accurate labeling is essential to the timely and efficient movement of products across international borders.

---

[32] Terpstra, *International Marketing*, p. 236. From *International Marketing*, Second Edition, by Vern Terpstra. Copyright © 1978 by The Dryden Press, a division of Holt, Rinehart and Winston, Publishers. Reprinted by permission of Holt, Rinehart and Winston.

***Warehousing and storage.*** Irrespective of the location of the target market, products must be stored at some point prior to their final consumption. Depending upon the particular conditions in effect in each foreign market, products may be stored at different points within the channel of distribution.

If the firm is involved in exporting, items may be stored domestically and shipped only after orders are received. Thus, no foreign storage is necessary. However, if distributors or other types of intermediaries are used, inventories will have to be stored or warehoused at other locations within the channel. The ability of the manufacturer or supplier to push the inventory down the channel of distribution will vary by each market depending upon the size of the channel intermediaries, customer inventory policies, demand for the product by final consumers, storage costs, and customer-service levels necessary to serve each market. As mentioned above, in Japan and most European countries, the retail network is composed of a great number of very small shops, each having little capacity for storage of inventories. As a result, they order frequently from distributors, manufacturers, or other channel intermediaries. The burden of storage is carried by the manufacturer or other channel member rather than the retailer. In the United States, because there are fewer retail stores of greater size, the storage function is more easily shifted away from the channel intermediaries directly to the retailer.

When warehousing facilities are needed in a foreign market, the international firm may find an abundance of sophisticated, modern warehouses in some industrialized nations. In Japan there is increasing use of high-cube automated warehousing.

> The first high cube automated warehouse was established by Fuji Heavy Industries in 1969. There are 10 aisles and 20 rows of racks, and the number of storage openings is 10,800, that is, 54 bins by 10 tiers by 20 rows. An on-line computer controls storage and retrieval by stacker cranes, and the transfer of materials from stack to conveyor system; the computer also stops and starts the conveyors, monitors pallet locations or moves, etc. Machines and equipment in this warehouse were supplied by Ishikawajimi Harima Heavy Industries and the computer by Fujitsu. There are not many automated warehouses yet, but their number will increase with the lowered price of computers in the near future.[33]

**The Quality and Availability of Foreign Warehousing Varies Widely**

On the other hand, in many lesser developed countries storage facilities may be nonexistent or very limited in availability or sophistication. In the latter instance the product package or shipping container may have to serve the warehousing purpose.

Public warehouses in many foreign markets may also provide services in addition to storage. In the United States many public warehouses provide services such as consolidation and break-bulk, customer billing, traffic management, packaging and labeling, etc. Other countries offer similar examples.

---

[33] Ikeda, "PD in Japan," p. 44.

One Dutch firm . . . in addition to warehousing offers customers brokerage, freight forwarding, packaging, insurance, and transportation service to all of Europe and the Middle East. In a product introduction for an American appliance manufacturer it also coordinated promotional material to assure that promotional packets and displays were available for the firm's marketing teams in the target cities.[34]

Like all physical distribution activities, the warehousing and storage activity must be administered differently in each foreign market. It is the responsibility of the distribution executive to recognize how the storage activity differs and adjust the firm's distribution strategy accordingly.

*Other activities.* Each of the activities or functions of physical distribution must be performed in the international market. The difference that exists between the domestic and foreign market is not whether the distribution activity is to be performed, rather, it is how each activity is to be carried out. It is in the execution of the various distribution functions that differences occur.

The concepts of *integrated physical distribution management* and *cost trade-off analysis* are still very important in international physical distribution. However, the relative importance of each distribution component may vary from market to market as may the costs incurred in carrying out each activity. This results in different cost/service equations for each international market.

The best advice for the company entering into international distribution for the first time is to obtain as much information about business conditions and operating procedures in each market from as many data sources as possible. Examples of selected information sources are shown in Table 13–9.

## FINANCIAL ASPECTS OF INTERNATIONAL PHYSICAL DISTRIBUTION

The firm that is involved in international distribution faces a financial environment quite different from that of a strictly domestic firm. Whether the company is involved in exporting, licensing, joint ventures, or owns a foreign subsidiary, there are concerns over currency exchange rates, costs of capital, the effects of inflation on distribution decisions and operations, tax structures, and other financial aspects of performing the physical distribution activity in foreign markets.

*Financing Is More Critical in International Distribution*

International distribution activities require financing for (1) working capital, (2) inventory, (3) credit, (4) capital investment, and (5) accomodation of merchandise adjustments which may be necessary.[35]

Working-capital considerations are very important to the international firm.

Time lags caused by distance and crossing international borders add cost elements to international marketing, making cash flow planning especially im-

---
[34] Kahler and Kramer, *International Marketing*, p. 216.
[35] Cateora and Hess, *International Marketing*, p. 666.

**TABLE 13-9** Items and Sources for Starting or Expanding Your Export/Import (international distribution) Activities

Guide to Sources of Foreign Trade Regulations: published by the International Trade Center, UNCTAD/GATT, Geneva, Switzerland.
Trade, tariff, other restrictions including quotas, licenses, exchange permits for various countries: published by the International Customs Tariff Bureau in Belgium. Available at most U.S. Commerce Department field offices.
*An Exporters Encyclopedia:* published by Dun & Bradstreet, 90 Church St., New York.
Carnet data: contact the International Chamber of Commerce, 1212 Avenue of the Americas, New York.
*Foreign Commerce Handbook:* contact the Chamber of Commerce of the United States, Washington, D.C.
International banking: check with your local bank, many have international banking sections.
Export packing information from two sources: The Containerization Institute, 15 E 40th St., New York; and, The Packaging Institute, 342 Madison Avenue, New York.
Foreign Freight Forwarding (air/surface) information from: National Customs Brokers Association of America, 26 Beaver St., New York; and The Air Freight Forwarders Association, 1730 Rhode Island Ave. N.W., Washington, D.C.

Information from the U.S. Commerce Department in Washington, D.C., or at many of its field offices . . .

| | |
|---|---|
| *Combination Export Management (CEM)* | FICA—9th Floor |
| *Commerce Today* magazine | One World Trade Center |
| *Commerce Business Daily* publication | New York |
| *A Foreign Traders Index* | |
| *Introductory Guide to Exporting* | Private Export Funding |
| *A Basic Guide to Exporting* | 40 Wall Street |
| *Trade Mission* information | New York |
| National Foreign Trade Council | Eximbank |
| 10 Rockefeller Plaza | 811 Vermont Ave., N.W. |
| New York | Washington, D.C. |

Source: Howard Grossman, "Almost Everything . . . You Should Know about International Distribution," *Handling and Shipping* 17, no. 3 (March 1976): 43.

portant. Even in a relatively simple transaction, money may be tied up for months while goods are being shipped from one part of the world to another; then customs clearance may add days, weeks, or months; payment then may be held up while the international payment documents are being transferred from one nation to another; and breakage, commercial dispute, or governmental restrictions may add still further delay.

The business may be profitable, but the companies may learn that the profit is all on the books, and that the slower cash flow of the international operation demands significant injections of funds to maintain cash position.[36]

Typically, foreign operations require larger amounts of working capital than domestic operations.

Inventories are also an important aspect of international distribution. "Adequate servicing of overseas markets may require goods to be inventoried in several locations; one company which uses two factory warehouses for the entire United States needed six foreign distribution

[36] Ibid., pp. 665–66.

points, which together handled less merchandise than either U.S. outlet."[37] In general, higher levels of inventory are needed to service foreign markets because of longer transit times, greater variability in transit times, port delays, customs delays, and other factors.

Additionally, inventories can have a substantial impact on the international firm due to the rapid inflation that exists in some countries of the world. In inflationary economies it is very important to use the proper inventory accounting procedure because of its impact on company profits. The Lifo (last in-first out) method is probably a more appropriate strategy because the cost of sales is valued closer to the current cost of replacement.[38] On the other hand, the Fifo (first in-first out) method gives a larger profit figure than Lifo because old costs are matched with current revenues. Fifo " . . . fails to correct the data for the depreciation in currency value. Fifo, therefore, gives management a false sense of gain and also an excessive tax liability."[39]

An international firm must also weigh the cost trade-offs involved in the buildup of inventories in anticipation of higher costs due to inflation or other factors. The trade-off is between accumulating excess inventory and their associated inventory carrying costs versus the reduced carrying costs of less inventory but higher acquisition costs at a later date.

When a firm is considering direct investment in facilities and distribution networks in the foreign market the capital budgeting aspect of financial planning becomes important.

> An international capital budget . . . would show the estimated size of the investment in each country or world region, the cost of the capital required, the anticipated revenues, and the risks peculiar to each country. . . . To arrive at these data, capital budgeting requires the following information:
>
> 1. An assessment of political uncertainties.
> 2. An economic forecast including the possibilities of inflation.
> 3. An analysis of the differences in financial costs and risks with particular reference to
>    a. Currency controls.
>    b. Exchange rates.
>    c. Character of money and capital markets of each country involved.
> 4. A projection of the impact which any particular investment will have on the cash flows of the firm.
> 5. A measurement of capital availability under different alternatives.
> 6. Methods to compute the cost of capital on the basis of capital-availability estimates.
> 7. A method for reducing the items in different currencies to a common denominator reflective of the real values involved.[40]

---

[37] Ibid., p. 667.

[38] At the same time, in periods of inflation, products in inventory will be carried at a much lower value than their current replacement cost.

[39] Endel J. Kolde, *International Business Enterprise*, 2d ed. (Englewood Cliffs, N.J.: Prentice-Hall, 1973), p. 387.

[40] Ibid., p. 366.

## 13 / International Physical Distribution 461

**Currency Fluctuations Make Planning Difficult**

One aspect of the capital budgeting process that deserves particular mention is the effect of currency exchange fluctuations on distribution operations in exporting. As is the case in domestic operations, customers in the international sector do not tender payment to the shipper until the product is delivered. As previously mentioned, many factors can cause the foreign shipment to take longer to be delivered than a comparable domestic shipment. The exporter must therefore be concerned with exchange rate fluctuations that may occur between the time when the product is shipped, delivered to the consignee, and finally paid for by the customer. "When the price is quoted in the foreign currency, the exporter accepts the risk of exchange fluctuation. Unless steps are taken to protect expected profits, a decline in exchange rates may reduce them or even convert them into a loss."[41] Table 13–10 identifies some of the factors which a firm can use to forecast currency value changes.

**TABLE 13–10**  Elements in Forecasting Currency Value Changes

Economic Factors
    1. Balance of payments
    2. Monetary reserves of the government
    3. Extent of foreign indebtedness and willingness of foreigners to retain it
    4. Present and anticipated economic strength of trading partners
    5. Monetary and fiscal policies of the government
    6. Trade, exchange, capital controls/incentives

Relational Factors
    7. Domestic inflation relative to world average rate of inflation
    8. Importance of currency
    9. Importance of country in total world commerce or certain items of trade
   10. Elasticities of supply/demand for goods, services, and capital

Political Factors
   11. History of past changes
   12. Personal philosophies of government officials
   13. Party philosophies
   14. Proximity of elections

Expectational Factors
   15. Opinions of bankers and businessmen and government officials and experts
   16. Forward market rates/black market

Significance of factors:
    I. Factors 1–4 determine whether a currency ought to devalue under existing conditions.
   II. Factors 5 and 6 determine the possibility of relieving pressure on the currency through policy measures. Will it be effective?
  III. Factors 8–10 determine results of currency value change on balance of payments. How much should it be?
  IV. Factors 11–14 are political considerations for estimating government intentions. These factors are less important with floating rates. With fixed rates, they are critical for estimating timing and amounts of devaluations/revaluations.
   V. Factors 15–16 can be seen as leading indicators.

Source: Warren J. Keegan, *Multinational Marketing Management*, 2d ed., © 1980, p. 172. Reprinted by permission of Prentice-Hall, Inc., Englewood Cliffs, N.J.

---

[41] Kahler and Kramer, *International Marketing*, p. 61.

## MANAGING INTERNATIONAL PHYSICAL DISTRIBUTION ACTIVITIES

Management of an international distribution system is much more complex than a purely domestic network. The firm must properly analyze the international environment, plan for it, and develop the correct control procedures to monitor the success or failure of the foreign distribution system. Figure 13–3 identifies some of the questions which the international physical distribution manager must ask—and answer—about the firm's foreign distribution program. The questions can be classified into five categories:

*Key Questions for Analysis, Planning, and Control in Foreign Markets*

**FIGURE 13–3** The International Physical Distribution Management Process

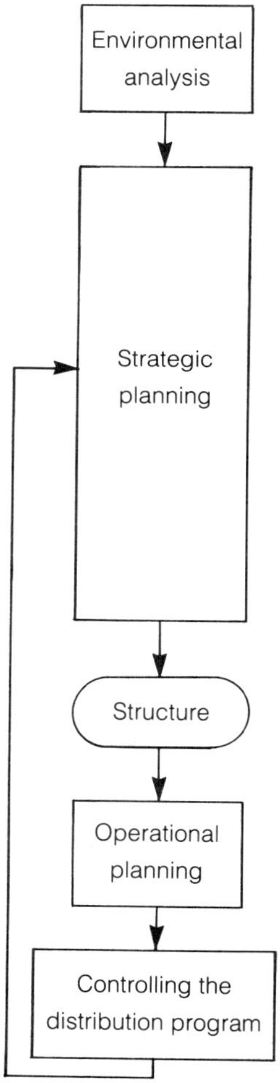

KEY QUESTIONS FOR ANALYSIS, PLANNING AND CONTROL

Environmental analysis

1. What are the unique characteristics of each national market? What characteristics does each market have in common with other national markets?
2. Should the firm cluster national markets for physical distribution operating and/or planning purposes?

Planning

3. Who should make distribution decisions?
4. What are our major assumptions about target markets? Are they valid?
5. What are the customer service needs of the target markets?
6. What are the characteristics of the physical distribution systems available to our firm in each target market?
7. What are our firm's major strengths and weaknesses relative to existing and potential competition in each target market?
8. What are our objectives, given the physical distribution alternatives open to us and our assessment of opportunity, risk, and company capability?
9. What is the balance of payments and currency situation in target markets? What will be their impact(s) on our firm's physical distribution system?

Structure

10. How do we structure our distribution organization to optimally achieve our objectives, given our skills and resources? What is the responsibility of each organizational level?

Plan implementation

11. Given our objectives, structure, and our assessment of the market environment, how do we develop effective operational distribution plans? Specifically, what transportation, inventory, packaging, warehousing, and customer service strategies do we have for each target market?

Controlling the distribution program

12. How do we measure and monitor plan performance? What steps should be taken to bring actual and desired results together?

Source: Adapted from Warren J. Keegan, *Multinational Marketing Management*, 2d ed., © 1980, p. 25. Reprinted by permission of Prentice-Hall, Inc., Englewood Cliffs, N.J.

(1) environmental analysis, (2) planning, (3) structure, (4) plan implementation, and (5) controlling the distribution program.[42]

The overall objective of the process diagrammed in Figure 13–3 is to develop the optimal distribution system for each international target market. It involves examining the various characteristics of the foreign market and developing a set of distribution alternatives or strategies that will fulfill the company's objectives. Given a set of objectives or strategies, the firm defines the proper organizational and channel structure. Once specific organizational structures are established the firm implements the distribution system. The final step is to measure and evaluate the performance of the system and provide feedback to the strategic-planning process for purposes of adjustment or modification of the system.

## SUMMARY

More and more companies are expanding their operations into the international sector. As customer markets are located and serviced in foreign countries, distribution systems must be established to provide the products and services demanded. While the components of an international distribution system may be the same as in a domestic system, the management and administration of the foreign network can be vastly different.

In this chapter, some of the reasons for firms expanding internationally were identified. Companies which expand into the international marketplace have four principal strategies available: exporting, licensing, joint ventures, and ownership. As part of the exporting process the specific roles of the export distributor, customshouse broker and foreign freight forwarder were discussed. Additionally, the importance of documentation and the use of free-trade zones were identified.

The international physical distribution manager must administer the various distribution components in a marketplace characterized by a number of uncontrollable elements—political and legal, economic, competition, technology, geography, and social and cultural. Within the uncontrollable environment, the manager attempts to optimize the firm's distribution cost/service mix. Some of the differences which exist between countries in administering each distribution component were presented.

Finally, the financial aspects of international physical distribution were examined. Inasmuch as distribution management is concerned with the costs associated with supplying a given level of service to foreign customers, it is important to recognize the factors which influence the costs of carrying out the physical distribution process.

With the first 13 chapters as background, you are now ready to develop the overall strategic physical distribution plan for the firm. This is the topic of the final chapter of this book, Chapter 14.

---

[42] Keegan, *Multinational Marketing Management*, p. 25.

## QUESTIONS AND PROBLEMS

1. An increasing number of firms are becoming involved in international marketing. Discuss the factors that would influence a company to enter international markets.

2. Companies which enter into the international marketplace have four principal channel strategies available to them including (a) exporting, (b) licensing, (c) joint ventures, and (d) ownership. Briefly discuss each strategy and include the advantages/disadvantages of each alternative.

3. Explain the role that each of the following exporting organizations has in international distribution:
   a. Export distributor.
   b. Customs house broker.
   c. Foreign-freight forwarder.

4. Discuss the uses of foreign-trade zones (free-trade zones) in international distribution.

5. Explain how it is usually more difficult for a firm to provide the same level of customer service in its foreign markets that it provides in its domestic markets.

6. Identify the factors which make the packaging component of the physical distribution process so much more important in international distribution as opposed to domestic distribution.

7. Discuss the relative importance of inventories in domestic versus international distribution. In your response, consider the financial impact of inventory decisions on the strategic position of the firm.

8. Although the transportation and warehousing activities are components of both domestic and international distribution, their relative importance, degree of use, cost, and services offered, differ widely. Briefly identify the differences which exist in transportation and warehousing in domestic versus international marketing.

# 14 The Strategic Physical Distribution Plan

Introduction

Developing a Strategic Physical Distribution Plan
   Formulating the Channel Strategy
   Formulating the Physical Distribution Plan
      The Physical Distribution Strategic Planning Process
      The Strategic Physical Distribution Plan
   Evaluation and Selection of Individual Physical Distribution Channel Members
   Performance Evaluation and Channel Modification

Future Challenges
   Distribution Accounting
   A Need for Broader-Based Management Skills
   Energy/Ecological Issues
   Regulatory Trends
   International Physical Distribution
   Consumerism
      Product Availability
      Product Quality
      Product Costs
      Environmental Concern
      Implications for Distribution Management
      Overview and Concluding Note

Conclusions

Appendix: Transportation Planning—An Overview

**Objectives of this chapter:**

To show how the marketing and physical distribution audit can be used to formulate physical distribution objectives

To show how to develop a strategic physical distribution plan

To identify future environmental forces that will affect physical distribution

## INTRODUCTION

A number of factors promise to make the next decade a period of both challenge and opportunity for the physical distribution professional. Increasingly higher-cost OPEC oil and deregulation of domestic petroleum will lead to substantial increases in transportation costs. Declining productivity growth rates will have a significant impact on distribution which tends to be labor intensive. Energy costs, declining productivity growth rates, and government spending will make inflation an ever-present threat and high interest rates will result in continued pressure to minimize investment in inventories. Government policies with regard to regulation of business and specifically the deregulation of transportation will have considerable impact on physical distribution. Maintaining the desired growth rates in corporate profitability and return on investment exclusively by increasing sales volume and market share will not be possible for most firms. Rather, the emphasis will shift to the development of profitable business segments and a premium will be placed on planning. An important component of the overall corporate plan is the physical distribution plan.

In this chapter you will be shown how to develop a strategic physical distribution plan. In addition, future environmental forces that will affect the physical distribution executive will be explored.

## DEVELOPING A STRATEGIC PHYSICAL DISTRIBUTION PLAN

The formulation of a physical distribution plan along with its continued evaluation and modification is essential to long-run profitable business development. The degree of change that is taking place in the business environment increases the risk of business failure for firms in which management has neglected to consider alternative future scenarios. In the absence of planning, managers must spend a disproportionate amount of their time in the role of fire fighter—reacting to crises.

*Strategic Planning Minimizes Risk in a Changing Environment*

There are basically two types of plans: the operating plan which covers a period of one or two years, and the long-range plan which covers a period of five or more years. "A long-range plan can be thought of as a set of guideposts which keep the operating plan on the path to meeting objectives. It is the operating plan which must be programmed in fine detail to demonstrate how the objectives will be reached and to justify the expenditures of the . . . budget."[1]

---

[1] Mark E. Stern, *Marketing Planning: A Systems Approach* (New York: McGraw-Hill, 1966), pp. 2–3.

Planning requires that managers evaluate the probability of various scenarios taking place and anticipate possible problems. In the process there is a shift in management posture from crisis management or reacting to changes in the environment, to planning for change. By doing so, capital requirements can be anticipated and, when necessary, financing arranged.

A major advantage of planning is that benchmarks can be set enabling progress to be measured and corrective action taken. "Thus, the plan provides a management philosophy, a day-to-day operating guide, and a basis for measuring both individual and total company performance."[2]

### Formulating the Channel Strategy

*Planning Facilitates Performance Measurement*

As was pointed out in Chapters 1 and 2, marketing and physical distribution must be closely coordinated. The physical distribution plan is deeply rooted in the marketing plan which must be based upon corporate objectives and strategy. Figure 14–1, "A Model for Design, Evaluation, and Modification of a Distribution Channel," provides a useful framework for visualizing physical distribution planning within the context of the channel of distribution, the firm, and its environment. It illustrates that all planning must take place within the following constraints:

The political and legal environment.
The social and economic environment.
The technological environment.
The competitive environment.

*Marketing and PD Must Be Closely Coordinated*

All businesses, if they are to be successful in the long run, must satisfy the needs of a large enough segment of customers to be able to generate the desired rate of return. The first step in the planning process is to define meaningful customer groups or segments so that the following questions can be answered:

1. Who buys or will buy?
2. Why do customers buy?
3. When do customers buy?
4. Where do customers buy?
5. What services do they require?
6. How do they buy?
7. What is the competitive environment in each of these segments?

*Selecting Target Markets*

Then target markets must be selected giving full consideration to company strengths and weaknesses such as production capabilities, marketing strengths, and financial resources; corporate objectives and strategy; marketing objectives and strategy; environmental considerations; and the marketing mix required for successful market development. Selection of target markets requires a preliminary profitability analysis of the type shown in Table 14–1. Basically, it is a form of segment performance measurement

---

[2] Ibid., p. 4.

**FIGURE 14–1** A Model for Design, Evaluation, and Modification of a Distribution Channel

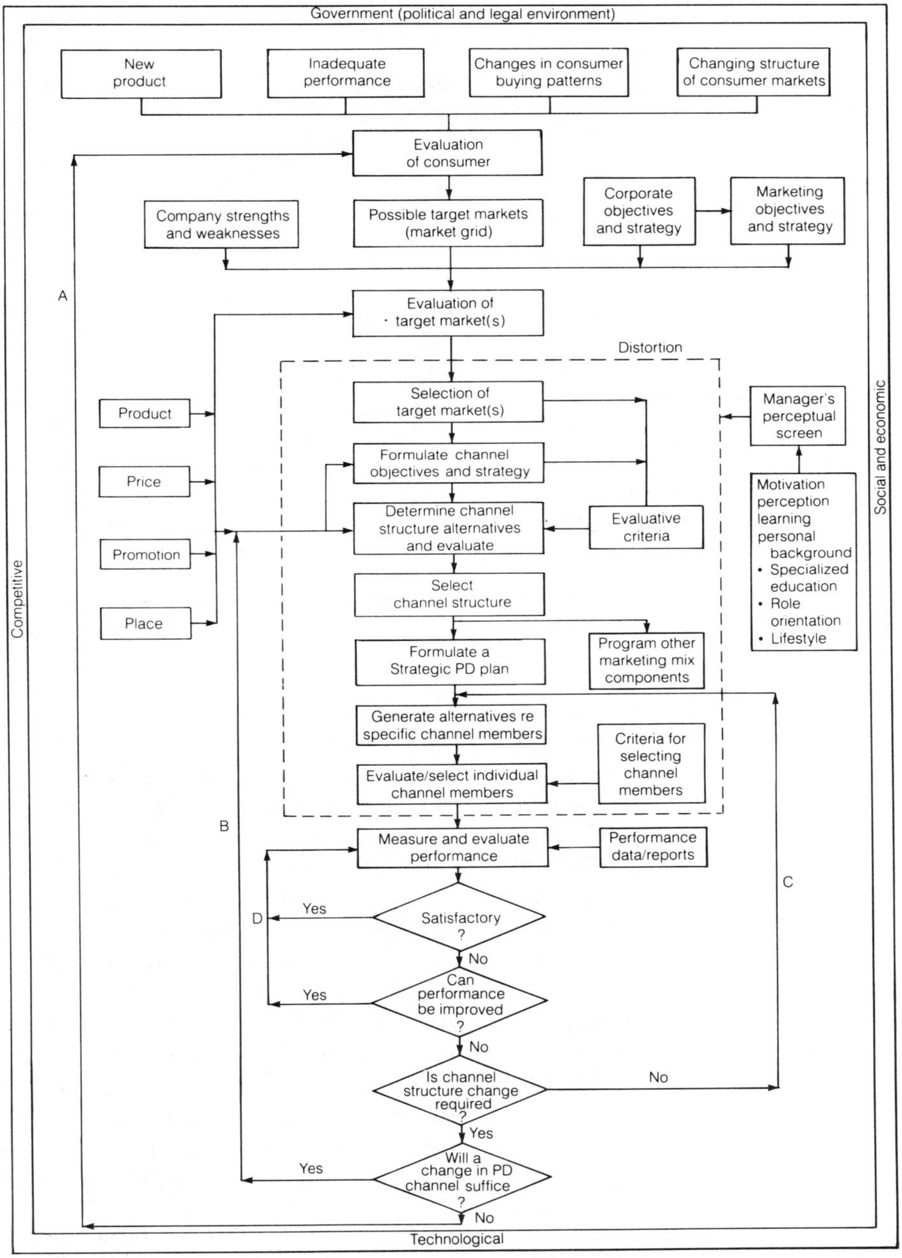

Source: Adapted from Douglas M. Lambert, *The Distribution Channels Decision* (New York: National Association of Accountants; and Hamilton, Ontario: The Society of Management Accountants of Canada, 1978), pp. 44–45 and 112–13.

**TABLE 14-1** Segment Profitability Analysis—Contribution Approach with a Charge for Assets Employed

|  | Total Company | Segment A | Segment B | Segment C |
|---|---|---|---|---|
| Net sales | | | | |
| Cost of goods sold (variable manufacturing cost) manufacturing contribution | _____ | _____ | _____ | _____ |
| Marketing and physical distribution costs | _____ | _____ | _____ | _____ |
| Variable: | | | | |
|   Sales commissions | | | | |
|   Transportation | | | | |
|   Warehousing (handling in and out) | | | | |
|   Order processing | | | | |
|   Charge for investment in accounts receivable segment contribution margin | _____ | _____ | _____ | _____ |
| Assignable nonvariable costs (costs incurred specifically for the segment during the period) | _____ | _____ | _____ | _____ |
|   Salaries | | | | |
|   Segment related advertising | | | | |
|   Bad debts | | | | |
|   Inventory carrying costs | _____ | _____ | _____ | _____ |
|   Segment controllable margin | _____ | _____ | _____ | _____ |
| Charge for assets used by segment | _____ | _____ | _____ | _____ |
| Net segment margin | _____ | _____ | _____ | _____ |

that recently has been advocated by a number of authors.[3] The analysis is based on the cost trade-off framework that has been used throughout this text and is illustrated once again in Figure 14–2. The total dollars committed to the marketing mix, that is, for product development, promotion, price, and place, will influence the ultimate market share, sales volume, and profitability. The total dollars spent on physical distribution are equal to the place expenditure, and the goal of management should be to allocate dollars of marketing effort in a way that will improve marketing effectiveness and efficiency, and result in greater corporate profitability. For example the decision to use wholesalers to reach retail accounts may lower advertising, selling, and physical distribution expenditures but the manufacturer will receive a lower price per unit for its products. The channel of distribution selected by the firm will have a significant impact on its profitability.

A channel of distribution can be defined as the collection or organization units, either internal or external to the manufacturer, which perform the functions involved in product marketing. These functions are pervasive and

---

[3] See W. J. E. Crissy, Paul M. Fischer, and Frank H. Mossman, "Segmental Analysis: Key to Marketing Profitability," *MSU Business Topics* 21 (Spring 1973): 42–49; V. H. Kirpalani and Stanley S. Shapiro, "Financial Dimensions of Marketing Management," *Journal of Marketing* 37 (July 1973): 40–47; Leland L. Beik and Stephen L. Buzby, "Profitability Analysis by Market Segments," *Journal of Marketing* 37 (July 1973): 48–53; Frank H. Mossman, Paul M. Fischer, and W. J. E. Crissy, "New Approaches to Analyzing Marketing Profitability," *Journal of Marketing* 38 (April 1974): 43–48; and Patrick M. Dunne and Harry I. Wolk, "Marketing Cost Analysis: A Modularized Contribution Approach," *Journal of Marketing* 41 (July 1977): 83–94.

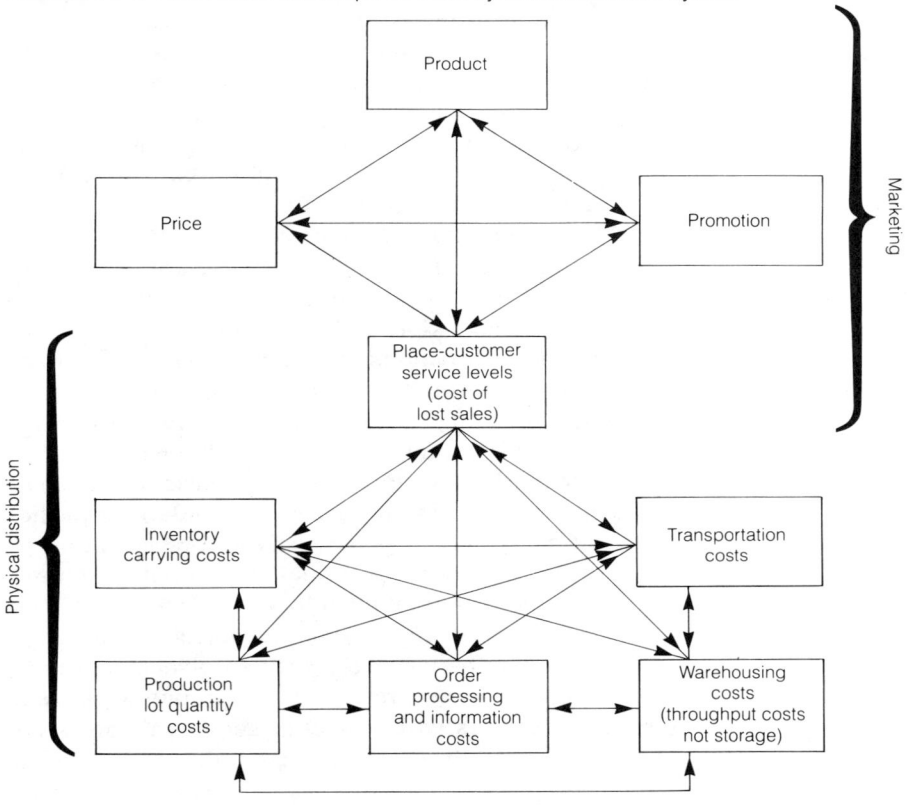

**FIGURE 14–2** Cost Trade-offs Required in a Physical Distribution System

Objective: Minimize total costs

Total costs = Transportation costs + Warehousing costs
+ Order processing and Information costs
+ Production lot quantity costs
+ Inventory carrying costs + Cost of lost sales

Source: Douglas M. Lambert, *The Development of an Inventory Costing Methodology: A Study of the Costs Associated with Holding Inventory* (Chicago: National Council of Physical Distribution Management, 1976), p. 7.

include buying, selling, transporting, storing, grading, financing, market risk bearing, and providing marketing information.[4] A firm that performs one or more of the marketing functions for the manufacturer becomes a member of the distribution channel.

Formulating Channel Objectives and Strategies

With the target markets selected, the next step is to formulate channel objectives and strategy. Channel objectives will flow from the firm's marketing objectives. Specific marketing objectives would include market-coverage objectives and customer-service objectives at the retail level which give full

---
[4] Fred E. Clark, *Principles of Marketing* (New York: Macmillan, 1923), p. 11; and Robert Bartels, *Marketing Theory and Metatheory* (Homewood, Ill.: Richard D. Irwin, 1970) pp. 166–75.

consideration to product characteristics that may limit channel alternatives. Channel strategy is the specific plan that the company will use to achieve its objectives. For example, consumer advertising could be used to pull the product through the channel of distribution or discounts could be offered in order to encourage wholesalers and retailers to push the product to consumers. In addition, a number of potential strategies are available in terms of the functions that the firm may perform internally or spin-off to external channel members.

The nature of the channel structure affects (1) speed and consistency of delivery and communications, (2) control of the performance of the functions, and (3) cost of operations. In selecting a channel or channels of distribution for its products, a manufacturer may choose to perform all of the marketing functions internally or may choose to have one or more of the functions performed by external channel members. A number of alternatives are presumed to be available to the manufacturer; however, in most cases not all channel alternatives are known or available when the decisions must be made. Consequently, the decisions may be less than optimal. Even if the optimal channel decision is made at a particular time, unforeseen environmental changes may lead to a reevaluation of the decision.

At this point various alternative channel structures must be evaluated in detail using the format introduced in Table 14−1. The alternatives that best satisfy corporate and marketing objectives should be selected. Multiple channels may be used to satisfy an objective of national coverage. This is because in some geographic areas the volume of business may permit direct sales to retailers while in other geographic areas corporate return on investment objectives can be met only when wholesalers/distributors are utilized.

Finally, the various components of the marketing mix must be programmed. It is at this point that the strategic physical distribution plan is formulated.

### Formulating the Physical Distribution Plan

The formulation of an effective physical distribution plan is dependent upon the following key inputs:[5]

*Five Inputs to the PD Plan*

1. The marketing plan.
2. The sales volume plan.
3. The manufacturing plan.
4. The financial plan.
5. The customer service plan.

The *marketing plan* must describe marketing's approach to the business in terms of new products to be introduced, existing products to be phased out, types and levels of promotional activity, and the long-term marketing strategy. In addition the plan should contain specific information with re-

---

[5] The following discussion is based on Robert E. Murray, "Strategic Distribution Planning: Structuring the Plan," *Proceedings of the Eighteenth Annual Conference of the National Council of Physical Distribution Management*, October 13−15, 1980, pp. 210−11.

gard to expected *sales volume* by product group and specific geographic area including seasonality and variation of product within given sales periods. It should define the type of customers by class and the method by which the sales force will service these customers. Also required are the method of processing orders and the desired order cycle time.

The *manufacturing plan* should describe the locations for the production of each product including product volume, production cycle, and capacity for each product group. When products can be produced at more than one production site, it should also include a definition of manufacturing trade-offs and the requirements for stock transfers between various production locations.

The *financial plan* should describe in detail the costs associated with the manufacturing, selling, and marketing of the respective product groups including the manufacturing cost by product for each of the production sites, as well as the costs to market the individual products and the selling costs related to channels of distribution.

Finally, the *customer service plan* should outline the basic requirements for servicing customers including the order cycle time as described in the marketing plan, as well as customer service objectives in terms of delivery and order fill. This plan must differentiate customers by trade class, geography, and size.

> As part of this planning process, the physical distribution function must provide information which describes the existing physical distribution network in terms of product storage locations at plant sites as well as in the field, transportation linkages between plants and distribution points, and distribution points and customers, and the operating characteristics of the field distribution locations in terms of size, volume, product mix, etc. In addition, costs related to each of the aspects of product distribution must be identified. This would include costs for plant warehousing, stock transportation, distribution center operations—including handling and storage and customer transportation.[6]

In many companies the collection of this information may be a difficult process. It is here that the marketing and physical distribution audit described in Chapter 2 can be of significant benefit.

***The physical distribution strategic planning process.***[7]   The physical distribution planning process must evaluate basic alternatives and recommend the physical distribution system configuration that satisfies the customer-service requirements at lowest total cost. Consequently the process must begin with the identification and documentation of customer service goals and strategies. For companies unable to determine the cost of lost sales associated with various customer service strategies, a customer-service survey can be used to determine the specific need and requirements.[8] These can be supplemented by face-to-face interviews. The plan must consider the specific requirements of the customers relative to cus-

---

[6] Ibid., p. 212.
[7] This section is based on Murray, "Strategic Distribution Planning" pp. 213–19.
[8] See Chapter 3, Appendix C.

tomer desires, competitive levels, and the degree of service that the company is willing to offer to support customer objectives.

The definition of customer service goals and strategies provides a specific input for: inventory goals and deployment strategies which will determine investment levels of inventory and the deployment of those inventories; the warehouse strategies and programs including the type and location of facilities; transportation strategies and programs which will determine the investment in transportation equipment and facilities; and order processing strategies and programs which will dictate MIS requirements and the related investment (see Figure 14–3).

**FIGURE 14–3** The Physical Distribution Strategic Planning Process

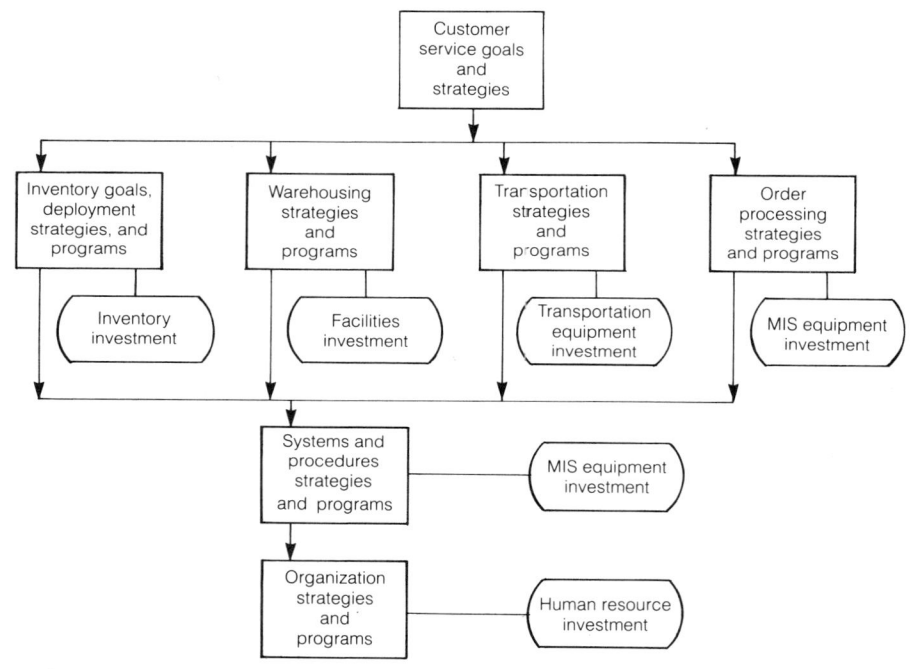

Source: Adapted from Robert E. Murray, Booz, Allen and Hamilton, Inc., from a presentation to the 18th Annual Conference of the National Council of Physical Distribution Management in Atlanta, Georgia, October 13–15, 1980.

Based upon the physical flow of the product and the flow of orders, the systems and procedures strategies will be developed. This will lead to the level of investment in MIS equipment necessary to process and transmit the orders to the various distribution locations. Finally it will be necessary to determine the organization strategy in terms of the human resources investment requirements for the corporation.

The planning process includes the evaluation of strategic operating alternatives to determine the most cost/service-effective plan for product distribution. Operating objectives and deployment objectives must be developed for each potential operating strategy. They will be used to develop the preferred operating strategy and lead to a plan for execution.

The factors that must be evaluated to determine the most cost-effective distribution service include: cost, service, and inventory. The cost considerations include the number and location of warehouses, shipment size and modes, freight consolidation opportunities, and material handling methods. The service considerations include inventory availability, delivery reliability, use of a private fleet versus common carrier, order cycle times, use of in-bound WATS service, and freight consolidation. The inventory considerations include customer service requirements, variability of demand, frequency of stock replenishments, shipping and receiving costs, and transit times.

The strategic distribution planning process involves three key and interrelated areas:

1. Developing a thorough understanding and appreciation of business strategies and marketing plans. This understanding is essential for providing sound strategic planning recommendations and for moving toward a distribution system that balances cost and service effectiveness.
2. Evaluating customer service requirements to determine what elements of service are viewed as key—how service is measured, and what levels of performance are expected, and how the business measures up against its competition.
3. Analyzing the distribution system and total costs of product distribution to identify the lowest cost network that meets business marketing and customer requirements.[9]

The planning process outlined is based on two fundamental considerations:

1. The belief that product distribution must be an integrated part of the corporation and the business product strategy, and should function as part of the dynamic business unit interfacing with marketing, sales, production, and finance.
2. The need to determine the most cost/service-effective system for the distribution of products to various customer classes considering distribution center locations, inventory deployment, transportation, and information and communications support.[10]

Murray described the planning process in terms of the following 11 major steps:

**Eleven Steps in the Planning Process**

1. *Initiate and plan the process.* This first step is a key to initiating the planning process, and must include a meeting with selected key management personnel, the establishment of data requirements, and the initiation of the preparation of a time-phased activity plan.
2. *Evaluate the current distribution activities.* This evaluation will serve to gain a thorough understanding of the current distribution practices and procedures and establish a base point for further evaluation. This workstep would

---

[9] Murray, "Strategic Distribution Planning", p. 216.
[10] Ibid.

include defining organizational responsibilities, understanding relevant systems of operations, physical examination of existing facilities, identification of key product groupings, the profiling of customer mix by products, and the analysis of cost and service performance. This step should finalize the collection of data that will be required during the course of this planning process.

3. *The identification of product manufacturing requirements.* Manufacturing requirements must be defined in order to determine the factors affecting the deployment of inventories maintained in field distribution center locations. This step will determine the source points of products by plant location, evaluate the inventory effect of key product manufacturing points, and identify alternative distribution channels and sources of products that should be considered in the planning process.

4. *Determine the impact of business growth.* Based on the previous step, product marketing plans must be reviewed in terms of major product groupings, resulting in a determination of seasonality patterns within product groups; the examination of key factors, such as shifts in regional demand and product line changes; and the determination of product volume projections over future time records.

5. *Develop a profile of competitive distribution networks.* A profile of competitive distribution networks will provide the identification of companies that market and distribute products similar to the business. It will further determine the characteristics of their physical distribution process, and develop a profile of the physical distribution system for each of the competitive companies. The result of this step will be a comparison of the competitive elements and functions of the distribution networks, and identification and rationalization of any major differences.

6. *Determine customer service requirements.* Marketing and service requirements must be based on the measurement of current customer-service levels and the determination of the need of present and future customers. This step should include the quantification of current customer service levels provided by major product groups, the selection and interviewing of certain marketing personnel and key customers to determine required service levels by product and class of customer, the identification of specific product characteristics that affect both inventory policy and customer service, the development of inventory customer service relationship curves, and the selection and review of alternative customer service strategies.

7. *Rationalize the physical distribution network.* This step will evaluate and determine the most cost/service-effective planned network for the distribution of product. It will include the analysis of cost/service characteristics of the present system, the development of alternative network configurations that will improve elements of cost and service, the identification of costs and benefits of alternative network configurations, and the selection and rationalization of the most cost/service-effective distribution network, in terms of number, size, location, and type of facility, inventory levels by product groups, transportation linkages, and order processing and information requirements.

8. *Review and recommend improvements to the functional relationships.* Functional relationships between related business components and product distribution within the business organization should be identified and reviewed in order to identify and assess functional relationships necessary to support physical distribution activities, determine the required linkages between organizational elements, and recommend necessary changes to improve exist-

ing operations and procedures in order to ensure maximum coordination and control.

9. *Formulate performance measurements and service levels.* Based on the results of this analysis and recommendation, performance measurements and service levels can be formulated, including identification of key factors related to distributon performance and customer-service levels, the development of specific performance measures necessary to monitor and report, and the development of a conceptual design for the processing of information to track and report these measures by product group and customer class.

10. *Review and recommend steps to improve organizational responsibilities.* From this process and analysis, recommendations should include the identification of functional organizational responsibilities required to support physical distribution activities, recommendation of the necessary functional interfaces required to accomplish product distribution, and recommendations of necessary steps required to improve functional support.

11. *Document the strategy plan and prepare an implementation plan.* As the final step in this process, the strategic plan should be documented in sufficient detail to provide the basis for planned implementation. A specific implementation plan should be prepared, including the sequence of steps and time required to physically implement the strategy.[11]

*Components of the Strategic PD Plan*

***The strategic physical distribution plan.*** The strategic physical distribution plan should consist of the following:[12]

1. A *management overview,* describing the distribution strategy in general terms and its relationship to the other major business functions.
2. A *statement of the distribution objectives* related to cost and service for both products and customers.
3. A *description of the individual inventory, customer service, and transportation strategies* necessary to support the overall plan.[13] For example, the transportation strategy may include the use of a private fleet.
4. An *outline of the major distribution programs or operational plans* that have resulted from the evaluation of various alternatives described in sufficient detail to document plans, related costs, timing, and their business impact.
5. A *forecast* of the necessary workforce requirements.
6. A *distribution financial statement* detailing physical distribution operating costs, capital requirements, and cash flow.
7. A description of the *business impact of the physical distribution strategy* in terms of corporate profits, customer service performance, and the impact of physical distribution on other business functions.

### Evaluation and Selection of Individual Physical Distribution Channel Members

Once the strategic physical distribution plan has been established, it will be necessary to develop operational procedures or methods for carrying

---

[11] Ibid., pp. 216–19.

[12] Adapted from Murray, "Strategic Distribution Planning," pp. 220–21.

[13] See Appendix for an example of the transportation planning process.

out the plans. It is at this stage that alternatives must be generated with respect to individual channel members such as carriers and warehouseman. They must be evaluated and those that satisfy the evaluative criteria selected. Table 14–2 contains a sample of criteria that may be used for the selection of wholesalers, carriers, pool-car operators/freight consolidators, public warehouses/terminals, and corporate owned or leased facilities.

**TABLE 14–2** Criteria for the Selection of Individual Channel Members

| Channel Member | Possible Selection Criteria | |
|---|---|---|
| Wholesalers | Services provided to our market segment<br>Market coverage<br>Marketing organization<br>Sales strength<br>Are they willing to spend money to sell our product<br>Reputation<br>Existing product lines | Warehouse capability<br>Ability to handle and move our product<br>Growth potential<br>Historical performance<br>Regulatory guidelines<br>Capitalization/financial strength<br>Must be truly in business as a wholesaler |
| Carriers | Service<br>Consistency/reliability<br>Damage<br>Cost<br>Equipment<br>Location of terminals<br>Authority to serve market<br>Pick-up time (past record)<br>Sanitation<br>Reputation<br>Form of ownership (i.e., contract) | Ability to grow<br>Reciprocity<br>Past experience with carrier<br>Run-through service (rail only)<br>Door-to-door delivery<br>Cooperativeness of drivers and dispatchers<br>Nondelivery<br>Theft<br>Financial strength<br>Chosen by public warehousemen<br>Chosen by customer |
| Pool car operators/<br>freight consolidators | Quality of service<br>Quality of pick-up and delivery | Damage<br>Rates |
| Public warehouses/<br>terminals | Cost<br>Facilities<br>Outbound freight (i.e., ability to consolidate)<br>Other accounts using facility<br>Service<br>Experience with our type of business<br>Can our carrier service<br>Sanitation<br>Rating of the organization (AWA member, D&B rating)<br>Warehouse operations (i.e., handling equipment) | Office procedures (i.e., billing procedure)<br>Employee turnover<br>Hours of operation<br>Field inspection<br>Financial strength<br>Reputation<br>Communications<br>Proximity to market<br>Damage<br>Taxes (income taxes)<br>Ability to meet our service levels |
| Corporate owned (leased) warehouses | Location criteria:<br>  Availability<br>  Cost<br>  Service time | Carrier services<br>Volume<br>Production points<br>Labor climate |

Source: Douglas M. Lambert, *The Distribution Channels Decision* (New York: The National Association of Accountants, and Hamilton, Ontario: The Society of Management Accountants of Canada, 1978), pp. 76–81.

### Performance Evaluation and Channel Modification

Successful implementation of the strategic physical distribution plan requires that performance be measured on a timely basis and changes made when performance is not satisfactory. Table 14–3 contains a number of

**TABLE 14–3** Data or Reports that May Be Used for Performance Measurement

| Channel Member | Possible Performance Measure | |
|---|---|---|
| Wholesalers | Sales reports<br>Gross margin<br>Net profit<br>Market coverage<br>Service reports<br>Evaluation reports | Performance objectives<br>Ability to receive account lists for follow-up<br>Attitude toward our company<br>Inventory (weeks of supply)<br>Credit department tracks payments |
| Common carriers | Damage reports/claims report<br>Postcard surveys<br>Cost<br>Transit time<br>Customer complaints<br>On time performance | Utilization (rail fleet)<br>Data from freight payment system<br>Reliability<br>Form letter to retail outlets re performance<br>Equipment supply—monthly report<br>Sanitation |
| Private trucking | Cost savings/cost per mile<br>Transit time | Customer service level |
| Freight consolidators | Cost savings<br>Customer complaints | Delivery times |
| Public warehousers | Annual warehouse inspection reports<br>Costs<br>Costs measured against standard<br>Inventory report | Performance report<br>Customer complaints<br>Safety and environmental factors |
| Company owned (leased) distribution centers | Performance reports<br>Cost reports by product against budget<br>Total costs | Inventory report<br>In-stock availability |
| Total channel system | Profit Impact<br>Sales<br>Customer complaints | Performance reports<br>Order-cycle time |

Source: Douglas M. Lambert, *The Distribution Channels Decision* (New York: The National Association of Accountants, and Hamilton, Ontario: The Society of Management Accountants of Canada, 1978), pp. 82–86.

data or reports that can be used to measure the performance of individual channel members and for the channels of distribution in total. Total channel performance should be measured using the profitability analysis framework shown in Table 14–1.

When performance is not satisfactory, the first thing that must be determined is whether performance can be improved with existing channel members. If it can, the necessary improvements should be made and performance should continue to be monitored (see loop D in Figure 14–1). If performance cannot be improved with the existing channel participants and a structural change is not required, alternative channel members should be considered and a replacement(s) selected (see Loop C in Figure 14–1). If a replacement is not available or a change in the physical distribution channel structure is required, channel objectives and strategy must be reviewed, and the planning process repeated at that point (see Loop B in Figure 14–1). However if a change in the physical distribution structure does not yield the necessary level of performance, the entire planning process must be repeated (see Loop A in Figure 14–1). In any case, the strategic physical distribution plan should be reevaluated each year to accommodate changes in consumer needs, market strategy, economic environment, competitive situations, governmental regulation, and available corporate resources. Such changes represent future challenges that will place an additional burden upon the physical distribution professional in the years ahead. Consequently, the remainder of this chapter will be devoted to a discussion of these future challenges.

## FUTURE CHALLENGES

The challenges that face the physical distribution professional in the next decade include: a need for improved distribution accounting systems; a need for broader-based management skills; issues relating to energy and ecology; government regulation and deregulation; the importance of international physical distribution; and consumerism.

### Distribution Accounting

*The Challenge to Improve Accounting Systems*

Integrated physical distribution management is based on total cost analysis. That is, at a given customer service level management should minimize total physical distribution cost rather than attempt to minimize the cost of individual activities.

In general, accountants have not kept pace with developments in physical distribution and have shown relatively little interest in the area. Consequently, the necessary cost data have not been made available and the lack of adequate cost data has prevented firms from achieving least-total cost physical distribution.

Developing a sound base for producing distribution cost information for decision making and control is one of the most critical areas facing management. Consequently, the availability of distribution cost information should be a primary concern.

Full implementation of integrated physical distribution is based on total cost analysis, and the true potential will not be reached until the required cost information is made available to decision makers. As was shown in Chapter 11, a considerable gap exists between the required level of cost availability and current industry practice. Overcoming these limitations represents a significant challenge. The future potential of the integrated distribution management concept depends upon the ability to obtain the necessary accounting information.[14]

### A Need for Broader-Based Management Skills

**PD Professionals Will Need to Broaden Their Skills**

As rising costs increase the percentage of each sales dollar that firms spend for physical distribution activities, the physical distribution function will continue to gain visibility within the organization. In fact, in a 1980 survey of senior distribution executives who were members of the National Council of Physical Distribution Management, Bernard LaLonde found that over three quarters of the executives reported to a president, senior/group vice president, or a functional vice president.[15] The reported salaries of these executives, shown in Table 14—4, also support the conclusion that

**TABLE 14–4** Average Compensation for Physical Distribution Professionals—1980

|  | Manager | Director | Vice President |
|---|---|---|---|
| Top quarter | $49,000 | $66,900 | $95,400 |
| Second quarter | 39,700 | 51,600 | 65,600 |
| Third quarter | 33,000 | 42,600 | 58,800 |
| Lowest quarter | 26,300 | 36,400 | 47,400 |
| Average | $36,800 | $49,400 | $67,400 |

Source: Bernard J. LaLonde and Martha Cooper, "Career Patterns in Distribution: Profile 1980," *Proceedings of the Eighteenth Annual Conference of the National Council of Physical Distribution Management*, October 13–15, 1980, p. 19.

the physical distribution executive has gained a position of substantial importance within the firm.

LaLonde's 1980 study also revealed broad ranges of responsibility. Managers spent approximately 30 percent of their time, and directors and vice presidents spent 40 percent of their time, outside the distribution function. Almost two thirds of the time spent outside of the function was spent in interacting with either the marketing or the production area.[16] With this responsibility has come the need for academic training in finance and accounting, general management, physical distribution management/logistics, distribution planning and models, marketing, and data processing (see Table 14—5). In a related study, David Herron (1979) asked distribution executives to indicate the subject areas they felt most important for their continuing PD education, and the format in which they felt each subject

---

[14] Douglas M. Lambert and Howard M. Armitage, "Distribution Costs: The Challenge," *Management Accounting*, May 1979, pp. 33—37 and 45.

[15] Bernard J. LaLonde and Martha Cooper, "Career Patterns in Distribution: Profile 1980", *Proceedings of the Eighteenth Annual Conference of the National Council of Physical Distribution Management*, October 13—15, 1980, pp. 1—30.

[16] Ibid.

**TABLE 14–5** Perceived Educational Needs—1980

| Area | First Choice | Second Choice |
|---|---|---|
| Finance | 37% | 21% |
| General management | 10 | 6 |
| Physical distribution management/logistics | 9 | 1 |
| Distribution planning plus models | 8 | 9 |
| Marketing | 6 | 10 |
| Data processing | 6 | 6 |

Note: Executives were asked: "If you were offered an opportunity to return to school in the near future for three months and could take a custom-designed curriculum of your choosing, what kinds of things would you study?"

Source: Adapted from Bernard J. LaLonde and Martha Cooper, "Career Patterns in Distribution: Profile 1980," *Proceedings of the Eighteenth Annual Conference of the National Council of Physical Distribution Management, October 13–15, 1980,* p. 21.

could most usefully be presented.[17] Five subject areas—transportation, financial control, quantitative analysis techniques, inventory management, and computer systems—received the greatest number of responses. A complete listing of the educational subjects mentioned most frequently, together with the preferred format for receiving further education in each subject, is shown in Table 14–6. For example, there were 700 respondents

**TABLE 14–6** Frequency of No. 1 Rankings of Desired Subjects for Further PDM Education

| Subject Area | Frequency | Preferred Format |
|---|---|---|
| Transportation | 137 | National professional meeting |
| Financial control | 125 | University seminar |
| Quantitative analysis techniques | 86 | University seminar |
| Inventory management | 85 | Professional educational organization |
| Computer systems | 78 | Company in-house training program |
| Warehousing | 62 | National professional meeting |
| Marketing | 54 | University seminar |

Source: David P. Herron "The Educational Needs of Physical Distribution Managers," *Proceedings of the Seventeenth Annual Conference of the National Council of Physical Distribution Management, October 15–17, 1979,* p. 50.

in this study and 137 of them, approximately 20 percent, chose transportation as their number one ranking for desired subjects for further physical distribution management education. The desired format for receiving this education was a national professional meeting. Financial control received a number one ranking from 125 executives and the preferred format for study was a university seminar.

---

[17] David P. Herron, "The Educational Needs Of Physical Distribution Managers", *Proceedings of the Seventeenth Annual Conference of the National Council of Physical Distribution Management, October 15–17, 1979,* pp. 45–52.

In LaLonde's 1980 survey respondents also were asked to: "Identify the two major factors which will, in your judgement, influence the growth and development of the corporate distribution function during the next decade." Sixty-one percent of the executives named distribution costs as their first or second choice. LaLonde concluded that "the most significant change from previous years' responses was the new importance of *Energy availability/cost, Economy,* and *Regulation* in the list of important factors. This suggests that increasingly the concerns of the distribution executive are for those factors which are external to the firm."[18] The complete responses are summarized in Table 14–7.

**TABLE 14–7** Factors Shaping the Future Distribution Environment, 1980–1985

| Factor | Most Important | Second-most Important |
|---|---|---|
| Distribution costs | 40% | 21% |
| Energy availability/cost | 13 | 11 |
| Regulation | 11 | 13 |
| Customer service | 7 | 11 |
| Economy | 4 | 9 |
| Top management's view of physical distribution | 4 | 5 |

Source: Bernard J. LaLonde and Martha Cooper, "Career Patterns in Distribution: Profile 1980," *Proceedings of the Eighteenth Annual Conference of the National Council of Physical Distribution Management,* October 13–15, 1980, p. 22.

### Energy/Ecological Issues

*Higher Prices and/or Shortages Will Lead to Distribution System Changes*

Worldwide, shippers and carriers have experienced an energy environment characterized by rapidly escalating prices and spot shortages. In recent years, the price of energy has outpaced cost increases for most other components of the physical distribution process. As a result, energy has become a more significant variable in the distribution cost equation. It is unlikely that the upward spiral of the cost of energy will end, at least in the short run. Therefore, energy management within the context of physical distribution will become increasingly more important.

Spot shortages of energy, as well as other items such as packaging materials, equipment, etc., will continue to occur. This will require managers to develop contingency plans for such eventualities. Such contingency planning would include consideration of alternative mode/carrier usage, relocation or redistribution of warehouses or inventories, modifications in customer-service policies, and many other distribution-related changes. These plans would be anticipatory rather than reactionary, and would be updated frequently.

Because of ecological concerns, it is likely that "reverse distribution," recycling, hazardous materials storage and transport, waste disposal, and

---

[18] LaLonde and Cooper, "Career Patterns," p. 5.

the use of clean burning fuels in distribution activities, will become more important distribution concerns in the future.

Illustrative of some of the more likely outcomes of the energy/ecological environment include the following:

1. Lengthening of lead times to customers.
2. Realignment of present modal shipping patterns (e.g., more waterway movements utilizing containers in international distribution; increased use of rail if service/equipment problems can be reduced; higher use of COFC and TOFC).
3. Increased consolidation of inbound and outbound shipments.
4. Increased management awareness and emphasis on frequent evaluation and updating of physical distribution plans due to changes in energy cost or availability.
5. Package redesign for full cube utilization in transportation and warehousing.
6. Intercorporate computer compatibility.
7. Increasing usage of freight forwarders and consolidators by small shippers.
8. Higher number of TL and CL shipments to conserve fuel and hold down costs.
9. Increase in the average shipping weight due to higher minimum requirements placed on customer orders.
10. Greater use of multiechelon customer service programs.
11. Increasing regulation of hazardous materials as they are stored or transported domestically or internationally.
12. Improvements in computer routing and scheduling algorithms.
13. Technological advancements in the area of loading/unloading techniques.
14. Improved energy efficiency of major pieces of transportation equipment due to technology.

The major issue facing the distribution executive is not "Will energy/ecology issues effect my firm?" Rather, it is "To what degree and in what areas of the distribution process will energy/ecology issues effect my company?"

**Regulatory Trends**

A number of important developments are likely to occur in the area of transportation regulation. For example proposed legislation would give railroads broad freedom to set rates by:

*Deregulation Will Change Distribution Patterns*

1. Relying on market forces for ICC policy.
2. Setting rates at market-determined levels.
3. Sanctioning shipper-carrier contracts.
4. Eliminating ICC suspension power.

5. Eliminating port equalization.
6. Repealing the long- and short-haul clause.[19]

In addition, more cost-oriented rate making will occur for motor carriers. The Motor Carrier Act of 1980 removed the following restrictions on ICC certificates:

1. Entry restriction if the proposed service is consistent with public convenience and necessity.
2. Prohibitions on intermediate stops.
3. Gateway restrictions.
4. Commodity restrictions.[20]

In addition, the Motor Carrier Act of 1980 permits intercorporate hauling for compensation, if the subsidiaries are wholly owned and a list of participating subsidiaries is given to the ICC. Informed sources believe that restrictions also will be lifted on less-than-truckload quantities and multimodal ownership. The implications are significant. Under the 1980 regulation, the rates charged on truckload quantities by common carriers are excessive and support the disproportionately low rates on LTL shipments. In other words, LTL shipments are subsidized by truckload shipments which is one reason why so many companies have found it to be profitable to engage in private trucking. Consequently, with deregulation of motor carriers, a significant increase in LTL rates can be expected. Also, more choices will be available to manufacturers for truckload shipments and competitive forces should result in substantial price competition.

Deregulation also will have an impact on the manufacturers that use railroads. A number of packaged goods manufacturers may face higher rail rates for low weight, high cube products. In fact, many shippers believe that a significant portion of the railcar shortage is due to railroads simply removing boxcars from service because the railroads believe that the revenues received do not cover the costs incurred.

Finally, multimodal ownership may be allowed. This would permit regulated carriers to own competing models of transportation and to contract with a manufacturer to handle all of its transportation and/or distribution needs. This would reduce paper flow and improve equipment utilization. The implications of these changes on manufacturers are substantial. First, it will be necessary to reevaluate each company's physical distribution system giving full consideration to the private versus common-carrier issue as well as the mix of modes, warehouse locations, and inventory levels. Second, with intercorporate hauling it will be necessary to integrate the data bases of subsidiaries to enable the efficient scheduling of vehicles and the tracing of shipments. Finally, better communications systems between the pur-

---

[19] Ronald S. Potter, "Transportation Planning: An Overview, 1980," *Proceedings of the Eighteenth Annual Conference of the National Council of Physical Distribution Management, October 13–15, 1980,* p. 230.

[20] "Section-by-Section Summary of New Motor Carrier Act," *Transport Topics,* July 7, 1980, pp. 20–21.

chasers and users of transportation services will be necessary for tracing of shipments.

In terms of energy and environmental regulations the following are likely to occur:

1. 55 MPH speed limit will continue and enforcement may be more strict.
2. Increased noise and emission standards are likely.
3. Gasoline tax uncertain, but prospects are diminishing.
4. Voluntary energy conservation measures will prevail.
5. Railroads less adversely impacted than motor carriers.[21]

**International Physical Distribution**

An increasing number of companies are becoming involved in international markets through exporting, licensing, joint ventures, and ownership. This trend will most likely continue. Coupled with this expansion into global marketing comes a need to develop worldwide distribution networks. The distribution executive must necessarily acquire a wide range of skills not needed in domestic distribution, e.g., international finance, documentation, political science, and foreign business practices and customs. As the firm expands internationally, the concepts of integrated physical distribution management and total cost trade-off analysis become even more complex and difficult to manage.

*More Firms Enter International Markets*

In the future several trends or events are expected to occur which will impact upon those firms already involved in international distribution or those companies anticipating such involvement. These items include:

1. Increasing number of physical distribution executives with international responsibility and authority.
2. Expansion of the number and size of foreign-trade zones.
3. Reduction in the amount and increased standardization of international paperwork and documentation, especially the bill-of-lading.
4. Increasing utilization of foreign warehousing, owned and controlled by the exporting firm.
5. Increasing number of smaller firms engaging in exporting with larger firms utilizing licensing, joint ventures, or direct ownership in lieu of exporting to foreign markets.
6. Domestically, especially in the United States, there will be a trend towards foreign ownership of distribution-service firms, e.g., public warehousing and transportation carriers.
7. Increasing vertical integration of the channel of distribution, but including channel members from several different countries (especially in the acquisition of foreign sources of supply for certain raw materials).

As customer markets are identified and developed in foreign countries, distribution systems must be established to provide the products and ser-

---

[21] Potter, "Transportation Planning," p. 233.

vices demanded. The single most significant development in international distribution will be the increasing sophistication and expertise of global physical distribution executives and departments.

### Consumerism

*Consumerism Will Impact Physical Distribution in Many Ways*

There are a number of factors which strongly indicate that the consumer movement will be an important force in the future and one about which physical distribution management must be concerned.[22]

1. As the world and national economies continue to expand there will be increased institutionalization of the marketing process and a corresponding increase in potential for lack of trust by the consumer for members of the marketing channel.

2. Inflation is a problem that may be with us for years to come, a fact that will foster economic discontent in the consumer.

3. Consumers, as they grow more affluent and have their more basic needs satisfied, will become more critical as their concern shifts to more altruistic motives and to quality of life versus quantity of things.

4. As products become more complex it will become increasingly difficult for consumers to make a choice when they purchase a product. This will put greater pressure on the marketing function to deliver the promised package of benefits.

5. As recession and inflation continue to reduce consumer purchasing power, greater emphasis will be placed on product quality at reasonable prices. Marketing must be equal to the task.

6. As consumers reach higher levels of education their increased awareness of rights and power will lead to less tolerance of marketing abuses.[23]

Marketing originally was conceived as the distribution of economic goods and services. Over the years, as the body of marketing thought has evolved, theory and practice have become concerned with demand creation. The consumer movement promises to force a reconsideration of the importance of physical supply as a component of the marketing process. Because consumerism has had a direct impact on marketing, it follows that the elements of the marketing process—product, price, promotion, distribution—also must be subject to the pressure of consumerism. This can be seen in the areas of product availability, product quality, product costs, and environmental concern.

*Product availability.* In the area of product availability, consumers demand products when and where they want them and in sufficient quantities to satisfy their needs. This requires that firms develop efficient distribution systems, able to service diverse consumer markets with products

---

[22] This material is taken from Douglas M. Lambert and James R. Stock, "Physical Distribution and Consumer Demands," *MSU Business Topics*, Spring 1978, pp. 49–56. Reprinted by permission of the publisher, Division of Research, Graduate School of Business Administration, Michigan State University.

[23] See "U.S. Consumer Groups: Livelier than Ever," *U.S. News and World Report*, December 6, 1976, pp. 90–91; "The Cries of Angry Consumers—What They're Telling Officials Now," *U.S. News and World Report*, April 18, 1977, pp. 61–62; and "America's Angry Consumers—What They're Telling Officials Now," *U.S. News and World Report*, May 10, 1976, pp. 56–58.

desired by consumers. Items especially important to the firm are customer service, routing and scheduling, warehousing, and inventories.

*Product quality.* The manufacturing area of the firm is primarily responsible for maintaining acceptable product quality. However, once the product is produced, it is the responsibility of the physical distribution system to maintain that level of quality from the point of production to the point of consumption. The distribution network must attempt to minimize product mishandling, poor routing and scheduling, and delays in transit. In addition, when products fail to perform and must be returned through the channel of distribution, it is the responsibility of distribution management to see that these returns are handled in the most efficient manner.

*Product costs.* Higher prices are generally criticized by consumerists, especially if the rise in price is not associated with a commensurate benefit to the buyer. The costs for movement, handling, and storage have a direct impact on consumer prices. Inefficiencies in physical distribution result in higher costs throughout the channel of distribution. Typically, these inefficiencies will take the form of small orders, less than truckload versus truckload movements, and failure to use pallets. It can be speculated that consumers, their real incomes reduced by inflation, are becoming intolerant of system inefficiencies and shortcomings since they are being forced to pay for these faults at the retail level.

*Environmental concern.* In addition to intolerance of increased costs due to system inefficiencies consumerists have doubts about intangible costs in the areas of energy, ecology, and urban congestion. Individuals, businesses, and governments are demanding efficient and productive distribution systems which move products with a minimum of pollution, the maximum in energy efficiency, and a minimum of system delays such as those caused by transportation congestion. It is imperative, then, that the distribution system operate in the most efficient and productive manner from a macro (societal) and a micro (the firm) perspective.

Related issues are recycling and reuse of containers. Oregon, Vermont, and Michigan laws banning nonreturnable containers are evidence that some consumers will accept the associated higher costs (in price or convenience).[24] Therefore, the distribution system has a responsibility to provide the most effective network possible to handle movement and storage of these containers.

*Implications for distribution management.* Specific implications for dealing with consumer demands on the physical distribution function can be categorized in terms of general management, customer service, transportation, inventory management, order processing and information control, warehousing, and packaging and material handling.

*Management* must orient itself toward a total systems approach in order to minimize interdepartmental conflict and the resulting inefficiencies. This

---

[24] Pat Murphy, "A Cost/Benefit Analysis of the Oregon Bottle Bill," *1974 Combined Proceedings of the American Marketing Association*, 1975, pp. 347–50.

will require new and better forms of distribution cost information and new standards by which to judge performance.

More efficiency in all areas of distribution may be necessary to reduce costs and reach the best cost-benefit ratio possible. All activities of physical distribution, including transportation, inventory management, order processing, storage, and materials handling, should be viewed as interrelated and integrated. Successful management of these activities should result in synergistic results for the firm and its customers.

In addition, management must develop improved costing systems so that distribution cost trade-offs can be implemented. Also, the cost trade-offs that are made must be communicated to the consumer. Too often, the costs associated with consumer legislation are not made known to consumers. Many times, business has not adequately presented its case.[25] In other situations the lack of adequate accounting information may have resulted in the evolution of inefficient channels of distribution.[26]

The *customer service area* represents the distribution system's most visible contact with the consumer. The Oregon and Michigan bottle laws initially placed heavy demands on the distribution networks of beer and soft drink distributors and bottlers. The existing distribution channel had to be modified so that the return of containers would have minimal effect on the consumer in terms of product cost. It was estimated that in Oregon the legislation would cause a $12 million hardship for beverage marketers in that state over the first 10 years.[27] Business must react to these hardships in a positive manner. One method might be for the industry to establish a standard bottle or bottles so that individual brand labels could be glued on and washed off. This would reduce the return problems associated with multiple bottle shapes and sizes. Other methods might include the use of machines at the retail level to compress returned aluminum containers for easy storage and transportation. Creative responses are required.

Better management of the corporate *transportation* can be realized by improving the use of existing equipment and using more efficient forms of transportation in terms of energy consumption and pollution. The former could be accomplished by making better use of railcar space by consolidating shipments, and the latter could take the form of increased use of rail or water transport, or changing to diesel-powered vehicles.

In addition, firms can ensure that key customers are monitored regularly by special personnel and are provided higher levels of service. This may require the use of premium transportation, for example, air freight. The company can ensure that its transportation carriers are competent, effi-

---

[25] Douglas M. Lambert and Jeffrey G. Towle, "A Theory of Return for Deposit: Economic and Logistical Implications of Return for Deposit Legislation," *California Management Review* 22, no. 4 (Summer 1980): 65 – 73.

[26] Douglas M. Lambert, *The Distribution Channels Decision* (New York: National Association of Accountants, and Hamilton, Ontario: The Society of Management Accountants of Canada, 1978).

[27] Murphy, "Oregon Bottle Bill," p. 351.

cient, and dynamic. Specifically, firms should require, at a minimum, certain services from its carriers (thus ensuring higher levels of service to its customers):

1. Manual or computer systems should be used to trace, reroute, and expedite shipments efficiently and to provide accurate rating and billing of accounts.
2. The firm and its customers should obtain reports of all inbound and outbound freight being shipped/received during a specific period.
3. Carriers should work with the firm and its customers on claims prevention through carrier sales people or claims representatives.
4. Carriers should work with the firm and its customers on the development of new services such as automatic billing and auditing, shipment tracing, and new equipment. For example, Spector-Redball Motor Freight has developed a system whereby a shipper's distribution personnel have direct access to the carrier's computer for the purposes of shipment tracing.

Improved routing and scheduling procedures may result in a reduced in-transit loss of perishables. These steps, plus any equipment improvements that would decrease the amount of loss and damage in transit, would ultimately reduce the cost to the consumer.

The area of *inventory management* holds significant potential for cost reduction. It is conceivable that pressure to increase inventory levels will occur as corporations attempt to satisfy increasingly divergent consumer markets. The ABC method of providing customer service levels is one way to reduce inventory. Other inventory control systems such as IBM's IMPACT (for wholesale operations) and COGS (for consumer goods manufacturers) could be used to satisfy service requirements at a reasonable cost.

*Order processing* constitutes a significant portion of the time, and some cases the cost, required in a logistics system ". . . a day saved in order-processing time may be as significant in reducing necessary inventories as a day saved in material handling or transportation. And it may be much less costly to accomplish time savings in information as opposed to physical flows."[28]

The adoption of online order-processing systems can be used to ensure prompt delivery and to eliminate late deliveries and stock-outs. Systems that can provide a timely and direct linkage with the customer (and hence the ultimate consumer) should be adopted in order to provide fast response time to shifts in consumer demand and to provide information about problems in the field.

The *warehousing function* has been affected by the proliferation of product offerings and shortened product life cycles which have resulted in

---

[28] James L. Heskett, Nicholas A. Glaskowsky, Jr., and Robert M. Ivie, *Business Logistics*, 2d ed. (New York: Ronald Press, 1973), p. 514.

increased stockkeeping units. This, combined with changing consumer demands, points to the major advantage of public warehousing over private or leased facilities—flexibility. With public warehousing facilities, the user can adapt to changes in buying patterns by adding or deleting storage space or storage locations at low cost.

The use of automated warehousing facilities offers the potential for creating true distribution centers as compared to storage locations. Automated warehouses could improve inventory turnover and lower inventory carrying costs.

Shared warehouses and consolidation terminals also represent opportunities for improved efficiency and reduced costs. Urban freight consolidation terminals have the added feature of reducing urban congestion and pollution.[29]

Improved *packaging* can reduce damage and increase the efficiency of material handling. Efficient material handling equipment, pallets, standardized pallet sizes, and containerization all offer potential cost savings to the firm and its customers.

It should be noted that the area of packaging and materials handling is becoming more difficult to manage, particularly for manufacturers of hazardous materials. This is due primarily to increased government regulation of such materials. One distribution executive in the chemical industry foresees the day when he will be unable to fill some customers' orders because (1) they will want a quantity (for example, 20 gallons) of a particular product that cannot be delivered safely in that size container, or (2) they will not possess the necessary equipment to handle and store the product safely once it has been received.

If this projection is valid, much effort will be required by industry to strike a reasonable balance between consumer/employee protection and the levels of service, availability, and cost demanded in the marketplace. Failure to deal effectively with this problem will cut corporate profits and could result in more government regulation. Failure to comply with government regulation has even greater risk—possible fines or jail terms for the managers involved.[30]

*Overview and concluding note.* As consumerism becomes more widespread in the United States and throughout the world, the demands on physical distribution will increase. Consumerism will not disappear. Since physical distribution is an essential element in a firm's product offering, and a significant contributor to the marketing concept, distribution strategy necessarily must adapt and change to meet the growing needs of consumers. Firms must increasingly become aware of their responsibilities in the physical supply of consumer demand. Consumerism promises to affect all

---

[29] For a detailed report on the potential of urban consolidation terminals, see James R. Robeson and Dennis R. McDermott, *The Economic Feasibility and Social Desirability of an Urban Consolidation Terminal* (Washington D.C.: U.S. Department of Transportation, July 1974).

[30] Tony McAdams and Robert C. Miljus, "Growing Criminal Liability of Executives, *"Harvard Business Review"* 56 (March–April 1977): 36–40.

aspects of the physical distribution process. Consequently, it deserves the attention of the physical distribution manager.

Consumerists will demand higher levels of customer service from business in the years ahead. Physical distribution is ideally situated within the corporate system; it offers the unique advantage of being able to increase efficiency without substantial expenditure. In fact, in some instances, it may be possible to improve customer service levels at no additional cost. Integrating physical distribution activities so as to achieve synergistic results provides the firm with a straightforward approach to satisfying the increasing demands of consumerism.

## CONCLUSIONS

Two decades have elapsed since the integrated physical distribution management concept was recognized and the first courses were offered in the area. The emphasis in the years ahead will be on the profitable development of business segments, and the high cost of energy and capital promise to make the physical distribution function a focal point within North American firms. The challenges and opportunities for the physical distribution professional have never been greater. The rewards for accepting these challenges and finding creative solutions will be significant. It is our hope that we have presented the material in this text in a manner that will encourage bright young men and women to seek careers within the profession and provide present practitioners with a reference source that will help them in their day-to-day management activities.

## Appendix:  Transportation Planning—an Overview

## Transportation Planning

In Chapter 14, we examined the elements which have a direct bearing on planning the distribution function as a segment of the total business plan. The transportation plan becomes an element of the total strategic plan when it is interactive with other functions of the business and affects the basic nature of the business. The plan could include such decisions as changes in channels of distribution, markets to be developed or harvested, production facility locations and missions, and marketing methods which may be based on transportation costs or service breakthrough.

### The Procedure

In terms of the transportation-traffic function, there are three phases of the planning procedure as indicated in Figure 14A—1 which can be defined:

*Phase I—Strategy.* In planning the transportation strategy, we should define how to best use the resources of the company, its basic patterns and volumes to

---

Source: Ronald S. Potter, "Transportation Planning an Overview, 1980", *Proceedings of the Eighteenth Annual Conference of the National Council of Physical Distribution Management, October 13–15, 1980,* pp. 223–27.

**FIGURE 14A-1** The Procedure

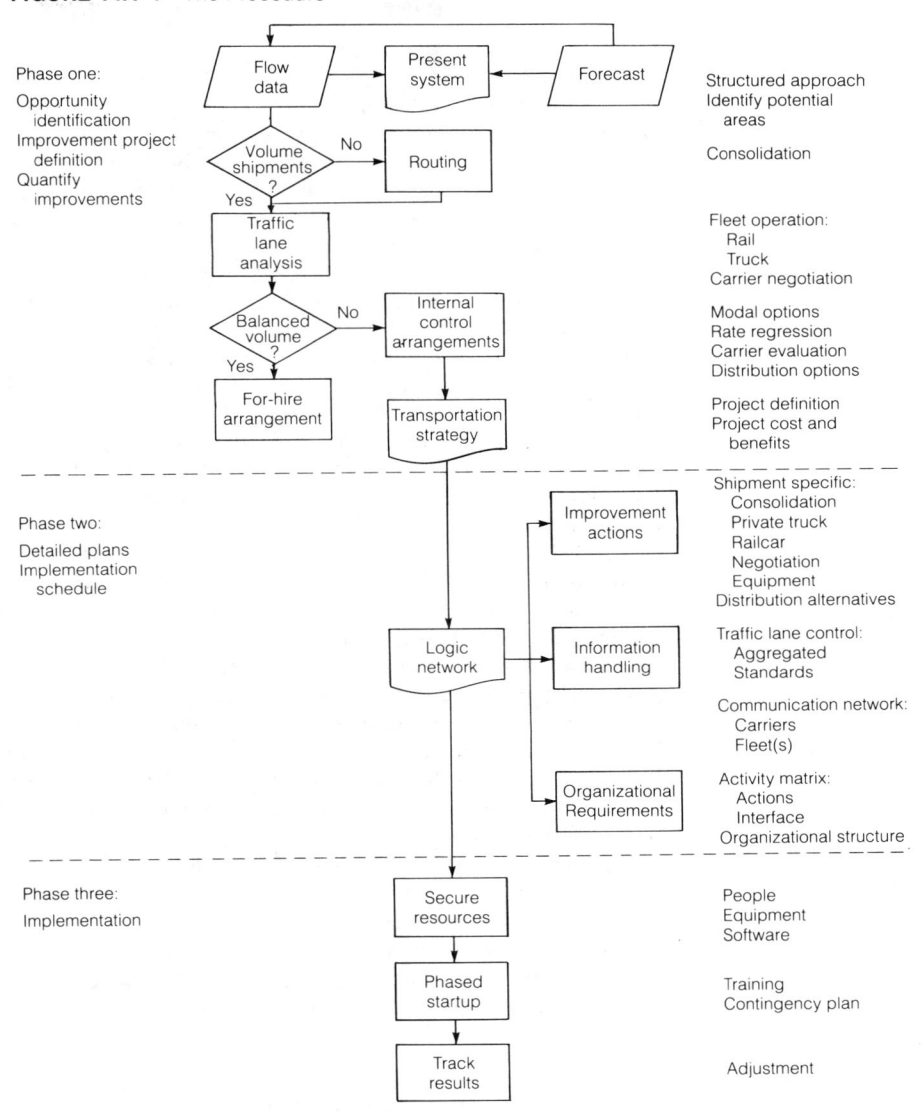

Phase one:
Opportunity identification
Improvement project definition
Quantify improvements

- Structured approach
- Identify potential areas
- Consolidation
- Fleet operation:
  - Rail
  - Truck
  - Carrier negotiation
- Modal options
- Rate regression
- Carrier evaluation
- Distribution options
- Project definition
- Project cost and benefits

Phase two:
Detailed plans
Implementation schedule

- Shipment specific:
  - Consolidation
  - Private truck
  - Railcar
  - Negotiation
  - Equipment
  - Distribution alternatives
- Traffic lane control:
  - Aggregated
  - Standards
- Communication network:
  - Carriers
  - Fleet(s)
- Activity matrix:
  - Actions
  - Interface
  - Organizational structure

Phase three:
Implementation

- People
- Equipment
- Software
- Training
- Contingency plan
- Adjustment

identify potential breakthroughs and basic improvements. The end product should be a development plan, described in project form, based upon the priorities established. Phase I develops a transportation strategy. The procedure includes:

*Define the present system.* In initial analysis use *flow data*. This is aggregated transportation information by general origin and destination points and is relatively easy to manipulate for analysis. The analytical procedure should also take into account forecasts of the future and the plans and strategies of marketing and manufacturing.

*Consolidation potential.* Examine patterns to determine where there are potentials for consolidation, either at origin/destination, or at intermediate terminals. This traffic is then routed.

*Traffic-lane analysis.* The routed consolidation traffic and volume shipment described in terms of origin and destination is the subject of traffic-lane analysis which has two major segments. Where there is balanced volume, examine how balance can be used for improvement, either with private trucks or with some other form of dedicated carriage. Review unbalanced movements for improvement potentials.

*Review options.* The traffic-lane information is subject to evaluation for changes in modes or rate-negotiation options.

The end product then of Phase I is a transportation strategy quantified and defined in terms of projects, their benefits, costs, and priorities, along with a development plan for Phase II.

*Phase II—Tactical plans.* The specific operating plans are based upon detailed analyses of the opportunity areas identified in Phase I. There are three major segments:

*Improvement actions.* The Phase I study was done with flow-type aggregated data. In Phase II the plans must be defined with shipment-specific information including all of the options such as consolidation, private-truck operation, railcar control and policy, negotiation, and equipment commitments, as well as alternative types of distribution arrangements.

*Information handling.* Advanced traffic management is an on-going activity. With the changes which are occurring at a rapid rate most major companies are planning or have developed formal transportation-information systems. These are based upon identification of movements by traffic lane where actual performance is compared to standards so that problem areas can be quickly identified and the work of the traffic organization directed. By access into the shipment-specific data base the information for solving problems identified and doing the creative work of traffic management is readily available on demand. The information handling also includes the communications network which is interactive with the carriers and with the private fleets.

*Organization.* The operation with an information system and with improved techniques has organizational implications in terms of the skills and type of activity which should be conducted.

*Phase III—Implementation.* Having defined the systems and the resources needed, implement them on a phased basis, including contingency plans. This phase must include the ability to track results.

## QUESTIONS AND PROBLEMS

1. Why is planning likely to be an important activity for physical distribution managers in the years ahead?

2. What is the role of the marketing plan in the development of a strategic physical distribution plan?

3. What do you believe to be the most important elements of the strategic planning process for physical distribution? Why?

4. Explain the importance of measuring and evaluating the performance of individual channel members.

5. Which of the challenges that face the physical distribution profession in the coming years do you believe to be the most significant? Why?

6. What is your evaluation of this text and course? Be sure to point out what you believe to be the major strengths and weaknesses. What changes, if any, would you suggest?

# Cases

1. The Dow Chemical Company
2. Smith Chemical Company
3. Acme Office Products, Inc.
4. Favored Blend Coffee Company
5. McGraw-Hill Book Company (A)
6. Giles Laboratories
7. Western Plywood Corporation
8. Riverview Distributing Company, Incorporated (B)
9. Ferle Foods, Inc.

## 1. THE DOW CHEMICAL COMPANY

### DISTRIBUTION OF DRY-CLEANING CHEMICALS

Located in Midland, Michigan, The Dow Chemical Company was a large, diversified producer of chemicals, metals, plastics, packaging, agricultural, pharmaceutical, and consumer products. The Dry-cleaning Chemicals Sales Group was responsible for sales of Dow Chemicals to the dry-cleaning industry. In 1934, Dow pioneered the use of perchloroethylene as a dry-cleaning solvent. Since then Dow has been one of the largest sellers of synthetic dry-cleaning solvents in the United States.

**Products**

The Dow Chemical Company manufactured Dow-Per, Dow-Clor 811, and Dow-Per C-S, for sale to the dry-cleaning industry. Dow-Per was Dow's registered trade name for synthetic perchloroethylene. This was the basic product in Dow's line of dry-cleaning solvents. After it was introduced in 1934, perchloroethylene gradually replaced naphtha and similar petroleum-based products to become the most widely used dry-cleaning solvent. Dow-Per was by far the leading selling product in Dow's line of dry-cleaning solvents.

Dow-Clor 811 was first introduced in the market in 1964 under the name Norge-Clor 811. It had been developed specifically for use in Norge coin-operated dry-cleaning machines which Norge had introduced into the market in 1960. In contrast to perchloroethylene, which required the addition of detergents and sweeteners in the dry-cleaning plant, Norge-Clor 811 already included these additives, thus making it a safe and simple product for use in coin-operated machines. In 1969, Dow changed the name of this product to Dow-Clor 811 in order to more closely identify it with the Dow Chemical Company and with the Dow distributor and service network. It was not changed physically and was still intended only for use in Norge equipment. At about this same time, another chemical producer introduced a competing product for this same market. Previously, Dow had had no direct competition on Dow-Clor 811.

Dow-Per C-S was introduced in 1967. Like Dow-Clor 811, it was a combination product that already included detergents and sweeteners. Unlike Dow-Clor 811, it was aimed at a much broader market. It was intended for use in both professional and coin-operated machines (except Norge). It offered several advantages to conventional dry-cleaners. Because detergents and sweeteners were preadded the dry cleaner did not have to perform this function. It also eliminated the need to periodically test the detergent concentration in the solvent system. It reduced the transfer of lint between garments. Like Dow-Clor 811, it was simple and easy for amateurs to use in coin-operated machines.

---

Written by Stewart H. Rewoldt, Professor of Marketing, Graduate School of Business Administration, The University of Michigan.

## Distribution

Within the dry-cleaning industry there were over 30,000 dry cleaners using perchloroethylene. Some of these dry cleaners were large, but the vast majority was quite small. To reach this dispersed market of many small dry cleaners, Dow sold through 140 distributors. Again, some of these were relatively large with multiple locations, but most distributors were smaller, single-location operators. Some were broad-line chemical-products distributors, but most specialized in selling dry-cleaning equipment and supplies to the dry-cleaning industry.

Distributors of Dow dry-cleaning solvents had been carefully chosen and were, as a group, the best in the industry. Distributors did not have exclusive territories, but the number of distributors authorized to sell Dow dry-cleaning solvents was limited to the number the available market would support. Dow wanted a sufficient number of distributors to assure access to 100 percent of the dry-cleaning market.

Dow salesmen called only on distributors who had been authorized to sell Dow products and did not attempt to sell Dow dry-cleaning solvents to distributors who represented competing suppliers of perchloroethylene. It wanted to retain the loyalty of its distributors and did not feel it could do so if it sold to every distributor who was willing to purchase Dow products. In return for this protection against unlimited competition in the sale of Dow solvents, Dow expected its authorized distributors to concentrate their purchases of dry-cleaning solvents with Dow.

Delivery of Dow-Per to dry cleaners was usually by tank truck, much as fuel oil is delivered to consumers. Thus there was no brand identification of the product when received by dry cleaners. The dry cleaner knew he was receiving Dow-Per, rather than a competitive brand of perchloroethylene, only because he had placed his order with an authorized Dow distributor.

Dow provided extensive technical services to its distributors, helping them solve dry-cleaning problems of their customers. It provided more extensive services than any other supplier of perchloroethylene.

## The Competitive Situation

Dow was the largest of nine domestic suppliers of perchloroethylene to the dry-cleaning industry, with over 25 percent of the available market. The next two largest producers each had sales about one half those of Dow. The other suppliers had smaller market shares, some of them with only 2 to 4 percent of the market.

In the 1930s, there were only two producers of perchloroethylene. As time passed, other firms entered the market and fought to establish distribution. The latest company entered the market only in recent years. As a consequence of the increased number of competitors, Dow's market share gradually fell to less than 30 percent, from a high of over 50 percent. Because of the growing use of perchloroethylene, however, absolute sales continued to gradually increase.

Because of the nature of the dry-cleaning market, all suppliers of perchloroethylene sold through distributors. Because the number of distributors, particularly the better ones, was limited, this created strong competition among suppliers for distributor representation. As the number of suppliers increased, this competition became intense.

Price competition on perchloroethylene was severe. No supplier could command a price premium without risking serious loss of market share. The price of perchloroethylene varied by geographical regions depending on the competitive situation. On the East Coast, for example, the price was substantially lower than elsewhere in the United States because of the competition that existed from lower-priced imports of perchloroethylene. This, and other competitive forces, caused price differences among other regions as well. Within a given region, Dow attempted to maintain a uniform price structure. However, when a distributor representing another supplier offered a price concession to a dry cleaner who had previously purchased from a Dow distributor, Dow might, depending on the situation, make a price concession to its distributor to enable him to hold that account.

**Encroachment by Competitors on Dow Distributors**

As noted above, Dow had the strongest distributor organization in the dry-cleaning industry. Because dry-cleaners tended to choose, and then stay with, a particular distributor, this was a source of marketing strength for Dow. To preserve this advantage, Dow tried to build distributor loyalty by: (1) not selling to any distributors other than authorized Dow distributors; (2) providing extensive services to distributors and their customers.

Other suppliers of perchloroethylene did not follow the same policy. Salesmen from other suppliers continued to call on Dow distributors, attempting to sell them at least a portion of their needs for perchloroethylene. Such efforts were particularly strong by those suppliers who were relatively new to the marketing of dry-cleaning solvents and were trying to build distribution. With most of the better distributors already taken by Dow and others, this appeared to them to be a sound course to follow. To the extent competitive suppliers were successful in selling other brands of perchloroethylene to Dow distributors, Dow could expect to lose sales and market share. Unfortunately, many Dow distributors did begin to buy a portion of their dry-cleaning solvents from these other suppliers.

Dow distributors offered a number of reasons for buying a portion of their needs from other sources. They said that they "wanted to know if Dow's price was right," or that "they wanted to keep Dow honest." Purchase from other sources gave them a basis for price comparison. In some cases, competitors would offer a special price on "just one truckload" in order to get a portion of the Dow distributor's business. Competitors' salesmen would call on dry cleaners, obtain orders for their brand of perchloroethylene, and then turn these over to distributors to be filled. Some suppliers threatened a distributor that they were determined to sell in his market. If he wouldn't give them a portion of his business, they would establish a competing distributor who would probably take away some share of his sales. Some distributors explained their purchases from other suppliers by saying that they wanted an alternative source of supply in case their supply from Dow was cut off by a labor strike.

In addition to the obvious threat to Dow's market position posed by these distributor purchases from competing suppliers, certain other problems were also created. When a dry cleaner purchased perchloroethylene from an authorized Dow distributor, he automatically assumed he was getting Dow-Per. Because his order was delivered by tank truck there was no brand identification, and he did not know he was receiving the product of another supplier. If he had any trouble with the product, he blamed Dow. Also, because he thought he was buying Dow-Per, he continued to expect Dow to provide him with technical and business service. Distributors likewise expected Dow to continue to provide them with full services, even though they bought a portion of their needs from other suppliers.

This situation posed a serious problem for Louis Brown, manager of dry-cleaning chemicals sales for Dow. He wanted to find a way to halt this invasion of Dow distributors by other producers of perchloroethylene but was uncertain about what course of action to take. He wondered whether Dow's policy of having its salesmen call only on authorized Dow distributors should be changed. Dow could call on distributors respresenting other suppliers and probably obtain some portion of their business. This would compensate for the loss of Dow distributor volume to competitors. On the other hand, this would probably further threaten the loyalty of Dow distributors and cause them to increase their purchases from other sources. Dow might lose some of its distributors entirely to its competitors. With the strongest distributor network in the industry, this would be a great risk to take. To do nothing, however, would invite further erosion of Dow's market share.

**Question**
*Should the Dow Chemical Company change its distribution policy for dry-cleaning chemicals? If so, how?*

---

## 2. SMITH CHEMICAL COMPANY

This case involves an evaluation of the customer service and cost of an agricultural chemical physical distribution system. Because of the industry's highly competitive nature, management decided to review its existing physical distribution system structure and operating practices.

Exhibit 1 outlines the existing Smith Chemical Company physical distribution system. Three types of facilities make up the system: (1) two continuous-process manufacturing plants. (2) six in-transit warehouses, and (3) 23 full-line distribution centers. For the review, management has excluded any relocation of the manufacturing plants and associated mate-

Source: Donald J. Bowersox, M. Bixby Cooper, Douglas M. Lambert, and Donald A. Taylor, *Management in Marketing Channels* (New York: McGraw-Hill Book Company, 1980) pp. 217–21. Copyright © 1980 by McGraw-Hill, Inc. Used with the permission of McGraw-Hill Book Company.

**EXHIBIT 1** Smith Chemical Company Existing Physical Distribution System

```
         Manufacturing plants
                 (2)
            ↙    ↓    ↘
  In-transit          Full-line
  warehouses  →      distribution
     (6)              centers (23)
      ↓  ↑             ↕
      ↓  ↑          Delivery and
      ↓  ↑          customer pickup
         Dealers
```

rial management operations. The review's scope is limited to the physical distribution of packaged dry and liquid chemicals.

Smith distributes 94 different products, or stock-keeping units (SKUs), on a national basis. For distribution considerations, the products can be grouped into two categories. Category A consists of 10 SKUs of a product called *Prevention*. The sales of Prevention are highly seasonal and account for 75 percent of Smith's total revenue. The 84-category B products (called *Support*) sell throughout the year but also have a seasonal pattern similar to that of Prevention's sales. Although the sales volume of category B is only 25 percent of Smith's total revenue, this group of products contributes approximately 40 percent of total before-tax profits. The typical end user of Smith's products buys a variety of both A and B products. In many cases, the products are used jointly in agricultural applications.

Smith's total product line is marketed through a network of agricultural dealers. Smith sells to the dealers, who resell products to farmers. The typical dealer provides farmers with a broad line of products, including those that are directly competitive with Smith products. Farmers tend to purchase both Prevention and Support products one to two weeks before field application. Application occurs at different times in different parts of the country and is directly related to the intensity of rainfall. Thus, Smith's products must be available when the farmers need them. Likewise, the quantity needed per acre varies depending on the rainfall an area receives. Therefore, although Smith produces Prevention and Support all year, sales to farmers take place during a very short time period. Farmers' requirements vary in time and duration of use throughout the country.

To even out physical distribution across the year to dealers, Smith offers an early-order program. For those dealers who purchase at least 90 days in advance of estimated application dates, Smith offers a warehouse allowance. The allowance is based on two features. First, the earlier the dealer commitment before the 90-day cut-off, the larger the discount. Second, the larger the quantity of the early order, the greater the discount. The application date is forecast by Smith's planning department. Even though the date has not been historically accurate, its specification has not caused conflicts between Smith and its dealers. In past years, the size of early-order discounts has ranged from 2 to 10 percent off normal dealer prices. The early-order program accounts for 65 to 75 percent of the total annual sales of Prevention and Support.

For the dealer, placing an early order means taking an inventory position on Prevention in advance of farmer purchases. However, since both Prevention and Support products are available, in effect the early-order warehouse allowance means a special discount on the Support products that sell all year. To avoid abuse of the program, Smith requires that at least 50 percent of each order consist of Prevention products. Smith also agrees to accept returns up to 15 percent of the total quantity of early-ordered Prevention products. The return policy is a refund of the full purchase price providing dealers prepay the return freight to a Smith warehouse.

In actual operation, the early-order program uses two physical distribution patterns. First, early-order shipments are scheduled at Smith's convenience to achieve the lowest possible transportation cost, which usually means full carload or truckload shipments direct to dealers. Second, the early-order program offers an added incentive to dealers to use their own transportation equipment to pick up early orders. These dealers are given an additional discount which is less than the transportation paid by Smith. Thus, to some degree, both parties benefit from dealer pickup. Analysis of past early-order programs indicates that approximately 30 percent of the dealers participate in the early-order program. Because of their desire to obtain both Prevention and Support products, dealers are allowed pickups only at the 23 full-line distribution centers.

Dealer sales not included in the early-order program—that is, those within 90 days of estimated application dates—are referred to as *seasonal sales*. Most seasonal sales to dealers occur within a few days of field application. Thus, to a significant degree, the quantity of seasonal sales depends on Smith's ability to deliver products rapidly. During the seasonal period, dealers expect Prevention and Support to be available for pickup at distribution centers within a few hours of the time of order. During this period, approximately 50 percent of the dealers pick up products. If transportation is arranged by Smith, dealers expect overnight delivery. Although the service level required during the seasonal period is high, these sales are very profitable for the dealers because the farmers who purchase the products are willing to pay the full dealer price. The capability to provide products during the application period is one of the most important criteria dealers use when selecting the chemical firms they will do business with.

Historically, sales have concentrated in 10 midwestern states that account for 70 percent of annual revenue. A summary of 1978 sales data is presented in Exhibit 2.

The existing Smith distribution pattern is as follows. The two manufacturing plants are located in Houston and in New Orleans. The Houston facility produces Prevention, and all Support products are processed at New Orleans. Both facilities are continuous-process plants, and their location at deep-water ports facilitates economical inbound raw material movement.

**EXHIBIT 2** Annual Sales, 1978

| | |
|---|---|
| Dollars | $338,511,000 |
| Weight (lbs.) | 300,274,000 |
| Cu. Ft. | 17,331,000 |
| Cases | 4,880,000 |
| Lines | 51,000 |
| Orders | 27,000 |

The six in-transit warehouses are utilized because the manufacturing plants have only enough storage space for two or three days' production. Exhibit 3 lists the in-transit facility locations and the Smith products stored at each.

**EXHIBIT 3** In-transit Warehouse Locations

| Location | Product |
|---|---|
| Baton Rouge, Louisiana | Prevention |
| Houston, Texas | Prevention |
| Lake Charles, Louisiana | Support |
| Mobile, Alabama | Prevention and Support |
| New Orleans, Louisiana | Support |
| Shreveport, Louisiana | Prevention |

In terms of the total system, the in-transit warehouses have three functions: (1) storage is provided until forward shipments are required, (2) the close proximity of the in-transit warehouses to manufacturing plants postpones the risk of advance shipment, and (3) the use of in-transit warehouses provides a combination of transportation rates that is lower to field distribution centers than the sum of published rates into and out of the in-transit warehouse. In a sense, the in-transit warehouses are economically supported by special transportation rates. All warehouses and distribution centers in the Smith system are public facilities. Therefore, Smith's costs are based on volume throughput and duration of storage.

The 23 full-line distribution centers are the primary facilities from which dealers are served. Although some early orders are shipped directly from plants and in-transit warehouses to dealers, those orders are limited to either Prevention or Support products, because the plants and in-transit warehouses lack full-line availability. The only in-transit warehouse that can make mixed shipments directly to customers is the one in Mobile. In total, less than 10 percent of the annual tonnage is shipped directly to dealers from plants or in-transit warehouses. Thus, 90 percent of all tonnage is either shipped from or picked up by dealers at the full-line distribution centers. Exhibit 4 provides a list of distribution center locations. Replenishment of distribution-center inventories is primarily on an allocation (push) basis controlled by central inventory planning.

**EXHIBIT 4** Full-line Field Distribution Center Locations

| | |
|---|---|
| Baltimore, Maryland | Little Rock, Arkansas |
| Boise, Idaho | Louisville, Kentucky |
| Chicago, Illinois | Minneapolis, Minnesota |
| Columbus, Ohio | Morgantown, West Virginia |
| Dallas, Texas | Omaha, Nebraska |
| Des Moines, Iowa | Portland, Oregon |
| Fort Wayne, Indiana | Reno, Nevada |
| Grand Rapids, Michigan | Riverside, California |
| Greensboro, North Carolina | St. Louis, Missouri |
| Indianapolis, Indiana | San Jose, California |
| Iowa City, Iowa | Syracuse, New York |
| | Tulsa, Oklahoma |

All orders are processed on a daily batch basis at the central office after they are received over a telecommunication network. The elapsed time from order entry to shipment release from the distribution center is less than 24 hours. During the early-order period this rapid processing is important, because it provides maximum time to consolidate dealer orders and realize transportation savings. During the seasonal application period, the system speed of order processing can be increased by short-interval order batching. During busy periods, two or three order batches are often processed in a single day. Usually, early orders that are picked up by dealers are processed using the normal system. However, during the application period, the distribution centers can release products on the telephone to dealers who want a same-day pickup. In these situations, confirmation about the released quantity is transmitted from the distribution center to central order processing following the dealer pickup.

The primary method of shipment from plants to in-transit warehouses and distribution centers is rail carload. Shipment from in-transit warehouses to distribution centers is also normally by rail. However, when inventory is needed quickly, the in-transit opportunity is bypassed and distribution-center replenishment is made by common carrier truck. Dealer shipments from distribution centers are made by truck. Transportation accounts for approximately 51 percent of total distribution cost.

A primary objective of the physical distribution system review is to evaluate the cost and service of the existing program in comparison with alternative methods of operation. Despite relatively smooth operations, the fact remains that at the end of each application season, many dealer requirements have not been satisfied, while other dealers have returned inventory. Thus, sales are lost that could have been enjoyed if products had been available to the dealers in need. A critical element of customer service is forward inventory availability to accommodate customer pickup.

Before deciding to undertake the study, management asked the accounting department to provide standard costs. The following standards were developed:

1. Order processing at a standard fixed cost per month with a variable cost per order.
2. Inventory at before-tax cost of 18 percent per annum of average inventory per distribution-center.
3. Handling and storage at actual local cost for each existing and potential facility. Appropriate storage rate applicable at in-transit warehouses.
4. Inbound transportation from plants and in-transit warehouses to distribution centers based on point-to-point rates.
5. Transportation rates to customers based on a combination of point-to-point and regression equation rates.

The costs for the reference year of 1978 are contained in Exhibit 5.

**EXHIBIT 5** Annual Distribution Costs, 1978

| | | |
|---|---:|---:|
| Transportation to warehouses | $6,868,000 | |
| Transportation transfers between distribution centers | 2,107,000 | |
| Transportation to dealers | 6,801,000 | |
| Total transportation | | $15,776,000 |
| Storage | | 2,863,000 |
| Handling | | 1,010,000 |
| Ordering | | 843,000 |
| Inventory | | 10,301,000 |
| Total | | $30,793,000 |

## Questions

1. To what extent does the existing design of Smith's physical distribution system incorporate the concept of structural separation?

2. The existing physical distribution system has 23 full-line distribution centers. If these distribution centers are reduced in number, management expects that total distribution costs will be reduced. (a) Do you agree? (b) Why or why not? (c) Assuming the above expectation is correct, how could customer service be improved by reducing the number of distribution centers, rather than having all benefits realized in the form of total cost reduction?

3. If Smith were to reduce its number of total distribution centers, do you feel conflict would develop regarding reduced availability of dealer pickup opportunities? If so, how would you suggest Smith prevent the development of such conflict?

4. Do you see justification for the development of an exclusive distribution system by Smith?

### 3. ACME OFFICE PRODUCTS, INC.

Herb Townsend had just returned to his office following the quarterly sales meeting of all airfreight sales people in the midwest region, Peerless Airlines. Herb had been told by his sales manager that Peerless, a national carrier, was embarking on an ambitious five-year plan that would expand the firm's lift capacity by 150 percent (with the addition of 28 wide-bodied jet aircraft). The increased capacity meant that Herb, as well as the rest of the Peerless airfreight sales team, would have to generate more revenues from their present customers or from new business. For some time Herb had been exploring the idea of trying to entice nonairline shippers into using the services of air freight. More specifically, Herb felt that many of the LTL shippers using motor carriers, who had been adversely affected by rising carrier rates in recent months, might be willing to consider Peerless's airfreight container rates. When container rates were first introduced to the sales force several months previously, one of the selling points was that they would directly compare with motor carrier LTL (less-than-truckload) rates on some product shipments and over some routes.

In the weeks that followed the sales meeting Herb investigated a number of industries that shipped primarily by LTL and he was able to identify several likely prospects for Peerless. One industry which seemed to offer substantial potential in terms of volume and growth was office products. Further analysis revealed that airfreight had been used in the past by companies in this industry only for emergency shipment of products. LTL shipments were the dominant method of transport in the industry, especially for small and medium sized companies.

Through a local library and chamber of commerce, Herb was able to develop a listing of office products firms in his sales territory. He decided that he would schedule a visit with one of the firms on the list early in the following week. As he examined the companies on the list, he saw that one firm, Acme Office Products, Inc., was located in the same general area as his regular sales calls. Herb obtained as much information as he could on the company and set up an appointment with the firm's traffic manager for early in the week.

### COMPANY BACKGROUND

Acme Office Products Company is one of five prominent U.S. manufacturers of electric pencil sharpeners/letter openers. The company has shown continued growth over the past 10 years of approximately 5 percent per year. Return on investment has averaged approximately 10 percent per year over this same period. Acme has had the reputation of producing a quality product at a modest price. This has been the major objective of corporate management since the company's inception. All aggregate planning decisions are made with this philosophy in mind.

---

This case was prepared by James R. Stock of the University of Oklahoma for the purpose of classroom discussion.

The company has one manufacturing facility which is located in Chicago, Illinois. Inventories of Acme's products are distributed through independent wholesalers in New York City, Dallas, and Los Angeles. The company uses public warehousing space in Denver, Minneapolis, and Atlanta. Additionally, the company owns a warehouse located adjacent to the plant. Essentially, the company produces only two models of pencil sharpeners—the basic model, retailing for $6.95, which is an electric pencil sharpener with no attachments; and the deluxe model, retailing for $19.95, which is both an electric pencil sharpener and a letter opener. The basic model is quite popular because of its low cost and also because of its superior quality in relation to competing electric pencil sharpeners at comparable prices.

The company services seven major markets: Chicago, Atlanta, Dallas, Denver, Los Angeles, Minneapolis, and New York City. In cities where Acme deals through wholesalers, the wholesalers are responsible for distribution of the product to retail stores. In those locations where the company uses public warehouses, and in Chicago where the company-owned warehouse is located, Acme must assume the costs for delivering its product to the retail outlets.

Acme is beginning to face severe competition from foreign manufacturers, especially in the Los Angeles market. These competitors have increased their combined market share from 5 percent to 28 percent in the Los Angeles market. While competition from these foreign manufacturers is not as critical in other markets, Acme management believes that these competitors will pose a serious threat to these markets within the next 1–3 years.

## SITUATION ANALYSIS

In August 1981, Herb Townsend called on Ron Simmons, traffic manager for Acme Office Products. Simmons was a bit surprised to see an airfreight salesman since in his 20 years on the job he had really not considered airfreight as a possible means of moving his goods. On several occasions Simmons had arranged to move an emergency shipment by air through his local freight forwarder. These emergencies usually occurred around the Christmas season and he was well satisfied with this emergency service. However, the idea of using airfreight to move all of his products to market did not really seem feasible from an economic point of view.

In their initial meeting, Townsend explained that new capacity, new rate structures, and new services provided by the airlines were increasingly attractive to LTL surface shippers. At this point, Townsend asked Simmons a series of screening questions about the product. These included questions about:

1. Size of shipment.
2. Origin and destination of shipments.
3. Weight/value of shipment.
4. Seasonal patterns of shipment.

5. Present shipping costs.
6. Public warehouse costs.
7. Company warehouse costs.
8. Production patterns.
9. Customer requirements.
10. Inventory policy.

Simmons did not have all of this information readily available but promised to send the information to Townsend as soon as it could be collected. On his part, Townsend promised to respond with a specific proposal for Simmons as soon as he received the information. The information supplied by Simmons is presented in Appendix A.

Herb Townsend also requested some information from his staff support group. This information is presented in Appendix B.

## PRODUCTION, INVENTORY, AND DELIVERY REQUIREMENTS

The company presently operates a single shift of eight hours. There are five work days per week and a total of 250 available work days per year (the company is shut down for two weeks each year for remodeling, repair and maintenance of machines, employee vacations, etc.) The production of the basic and deluxe models of sharpeners/letter openers is performed using work stations. Both models share the same facilities. At each work station, a different portion of the product is assembled and/or tested. Parts are moved through the facility on a conveyor-belt system. The casings for each model are manufactured on premises using an automatic molding machine. The packaging of each model is also completely automated. The manufacturing cycle is fairly long and completed models go into inventory continuously as production progresses.

Demand for the basic and deluxe models is seasonal with peak demand being November–December. Exhibit 3 shows orders received by month for the past four years. Sales volume of basic models is approximately two to one over the deluxe model.

Production lots are determined by the production superintendent. No systems of annual production budgets or monthly production goals exist, and therefore, production is scheduled on an intuitive basis (based only on the superintendent's past experience). Production figures for each model are provided in Exhibit 4.

Delivery is a very important concern of the company. Acme's competitors have been providing almost immediate delivery and some Acme salespeople have reported that some customers (wholesalers and retailers) cited delivery problems as the reason for selection of a competitor's product. This was especially true when the wholesalers or retailers were experiencing storage and/or demand problems. In such instances, they would select against those companies with longer and/or less consistent delivery times. The wholesalers with which Acme dealt were in very strong positions and management felt that the policies of the wholesalers had to be followed.

These wholesalers were considered by the industry to be the best available even with some of their restrictive policies. The retailers were also valued highly because of their past success in selling Acme's products. Most of the difficulties with retailers had been with the newer firms (department and variety stores) rather than with the older more traditional firms (stationary and office-supply stores). The older stores tended to be more lenient with respect to inconsistency in delivery.

Acme has been using a major motor carrier for the past 15 years in its shipment of goods to its major markets. Service had generally been satisfactory although on a few occasions shipments had arrived somewhat later than promised at various points. One example occurred about six months ago when a shipment was about six days late. The order was returned to Acme by the wholesaler because it had obtained a competitor's shipment the previous day. The wholesaler in Los Angeles, as well as the one in New York City, has a habit of refusing shipments that are several days late. Otherwise, service had been satisfactory. Shipment times did, however, vary somewhat, depending on the point serviced. For example, shipment time between Chicago and Los Angeles varied between three days and ten days, with most shipments requiring four to six days. See Exhibit 5 for shipment times between points and their respective probabilities. The probabilities had been obtained by examining shipping records over a one (1) year period. Shipment times were recorded and then arrayed on a graph to obtain a distribution of transit times. Probabilities were then obtained from these graphs. Loss due to theft and damage was normal for the carrier used and the commodity carried, although reimbursement for lost, stolen, or damaged items generally took six months or longer. The company had compared rates between rail and motor carriage for its LTL shipments several years before and had found that the LTL motor-carriage rate was lower. The company had not compared rates between various modes in recent years.

As mentioned previously, there are seven major distribution points. Of these seven points the company owns or rents public warehousing space at four of them. Inventories are carried at each of these locations in amounts sufficient to handle two-months' average demand before stock-outs occur. The largest part of the inventory is comprised of the basic model of pencil sharpeners. The values of inventory at the company owned and public warehouses are shown in Exhibit 1.

Inventory is valued at retail selling price for insurance purposes. Additionally, the company ships approximately 1,260 units per month to each wholesaler in New York City, Dallas, and Los Angeles. The other distribution

**EXHIBIT 1** Value of Inventory on Hand as of 12/31/80

|  | Basic Model | Deluxe Model |
|---|---|---|
| Denver | $15,679 | $ 23,940 |
| Minneapolis | 11,509 | 3,885 |
| Chicago | 84,095 | 143,640 |
| Atlanta | 16,680 | 26,613 |

points are shipped units as needed when the inventory on hand at any location falls below the level representing the total of two-months' average demand. Inventory in all warehouses is comprised of the two models of pencil sharpeners.

Few raw materials are carried in inventory at the manufacturing facility inasmuch as all parts not manufactured by Acme are availabile from sources within the Chicago area and delivery times for these items always average less than two days from time of order to receipt of shipment. At the Chicago warehouse a computerized inventory system is employed and management is provided with a computer printout of stock on hand at the end of each week. A clerk then determines whether the inventories have fallen below the specified levels. If so, the clerk sends an operation job ticket to the production superintendent. The superintendent usually holds these order tickets until there are enough to constitute a lot. At such time, production of the needed models is begun. With this batching of orders, lead time is reduced to one week.

An important consideration, as mentioned previously, is consistency in shipment time. Simmons has estimated that whenever a shipment exceeds its normal time in transit by a significant amount (i.e., when shipments that average two days or less take four or more days; when shipments that average more than two days but less than five days take six or more days; when shipments that average five days but less than six days take eight days or more; and when shipments that average six days to eight days take more than nine days) or whenever a stock-out occurs at either a public warehouse or wholesaler, the result is a lost sale—either because of unfilled demand in the case of a stock-out or returned orders in the case of the wholesaler.

## THE AIR FREIGHT PROPOSAL

Herb Townsend told Mr. Simmons that shipping by air would reduce inventories and improve customer service. He stated that he could improve consistency of service and make this improvement at competitive transportation charges.

Simmons has provided information about current shipping methods, cost, service levels, and other aspects of company policy.

### Questions

*Assume that you are Herb Townsend and are required to respond to his proposal.*

1. Prepare a proposal for submission to Simmons. Include in your proposal a consideration of:
    a. *Alternative shipping methods.*
    b. *Recommended shipping methods.*
    c. *Relative cost analysis—present system versus airfreight system.*

2. *How would you present the proposal to Simmons? What points would you stress? How would you handle the assumptions underlying your proposal?*

## Appendix A: Information Provided by Mr. Simmons, Traffic Manager, Acme Office Products Company

### Cost Information

Mr. Simmons has contacted the production superintendent, Mr. Boyd, in order to obtain an accurate and up-to-date listing of cost estimates. The total costs as provided by Mr. Boyd for the basic model averaged $4, and for the deluxe model, $14. These costs did not, however, include transportation charges from point of manufacture to point of distribution. Transportation charges are presented in Exhibit 6. Wholesalers are charged $5.50 per unit for the basic model and $16 per unit for the deluxe model. This includes delivery. With this mark-up, the company realizes a modest profit on each unit sold to wholesalers. Costs of warehousing are indicated below:

**EXHIBIT 2**

| | |
|---|---|
| Chicago | |
| Initial construction costs* | $75,000 |
| Operating costs per year: | |
| Taxes | 1,100 |
| Insurance | 800 |
| Heat | 2,000 |
| Electricity | 700 |
| Labor | 10,000 |

\* Does not include depreciation of building and fixtures on a straight-line basis over a 20-year period.

At Denver, Atlanta, and Minneapolis, where public warehousing is utilized, costs are as follows:

> Storage: 8 cents per carton per month.
> Handling: 22.5 cents per carton per month.

Delivery costs from the warehouse to the retail outlet are comparable to the rates as shown in Exhibit 7. The delivery rate per carton is the same as the minimum charge (i.e., in Atlanta, $3.30 per carton). Mr. Boyd has estimated that inventory carrying costs average 25 percent at each location where inventory is stored.

Other data which has been collected by Mr. Boyd includes the following:

| | |
|---|---|
| Merchandise value per pound | |
| Basic model | $1.75 |
| Deluxe model | $4.00 |
| Weight per item (per pound, including package) | |
| Basic model | 4.0 |
| Deluxe model | 5.0 |
| Turnover rate at all warehouses (per year) | |
| Basic model | 4.0 |
| Deluxe model | 2.5 |

Electric pencil sharpeners are packaged individually and then in cartons of 12 each. Dimensions of cartons containing either basic or deluxe models are 24″ × 18″ × 12″.

Ending inventories as of 12/31/80 at each owned or public warehouse are:

| Location | Units Basic Model | Deluxe Model |
|---|---|---|
| Chicago | 12,100 | 7,200 |
| Atlanta | 2,400 | 1,344 |
| Denver | 2,256 | 1,200 |
| Minneapolis | 1,656 | 696 |

**EXHIBIT 3** Orders Received (000 units)

|  | 1977 Basic | 1977 Deluxe | 1978 Basic | 1978 Deluxe | 1979 Basic | 1979 Deluxe | 1980 Basic | 1980 Deluxe |
|---|---|---|---|---|---|---|---|---|
| Jan. | 4.8 | 2.4 | 4.7 | 2.4 | 4.9 | 2.4 | 5.4 | 2.8 |
| Feb. | 5.0 | 2.7 | 4.5 | 2.6 | 5.2 | 2.8 | 5.3 | 3.0 |
| Mar. | 4.7 | 2.6 | 5.0 | 2.6 | 4.8 | 2.7 | 5.2 | 3.1 |
| Apr. | 4.7 | 3.0 | 5.0 | 2.8 | 5.5 | 3.1 | 5.5 | 2.9 |
| May | 4.6 | 2.7 | 5.2 | 3.2 | 4.9 | 2.8 | 5.3 | 3.4 |
| Jun. | 4.8 | 3.0 | 4.9 | 3.3 | 5.3 | 3.2 | 5.5 | 3.3 |
| Jul. | 4.9 | 2.8 | 4.9 | 3.2 | 5.1 | 3.4 | 5.3 | 3.2 |
| Aug. | 4.7 | 2.7 | 5.2 | 3.0 | 4.8 | 3.2 | 5.4 | 3.4 |
| Sept. | 5.0 | 2.8 | 5.3 | 2.7 | 5.0 | 3.2 | 5.2 | 3.0 |
| Oct. | 4.8 | 3.2 | 5.0 | 2.8 | 5.2 | 3.1 | 5.9 | 3.4 |
| Nov. | 5.8 | 4.0 | 6.0 | 4.0 | 6.4 | 3.8 | 6.8 | 4.2 |
| Dec. | 6.2 | 4.2 | 6.3 | 4.6 | 6.8 | 4.8 | 7.2 | 4.8 |
| Total | 60.0 | 36.1 | 62.0 | 37.2 | 63.9 | 38.5 | 68.0 | 40.5 |

**EXHIBIT 4** Electric Pencil Sharpener Production (000 units)

|  | 1977 Basic | 1977 Deluxe | 1978 Basic | 1978 Deluxe | 1979 Basic | 1979 Deluxe | 1980 Basic | 1980 Deluxe |
|---|---|---|---|---|---|---|---|---|
| Jan. | 5.2 | 2.9 | 5.7 | 2.8 | 5.4 | 3.0 | 5.3 | 3.2 |
| Feb. | 5.4 | 2.9 | 5.7 | 3.0 | 5.3 | 3.1 | 5.1 | 3.4 |
| Mar. | 4.8 | 2.8 | 5.6 | 3.1 | 5.7 | 3.0 | 5.1 | 3.5 |
| Apr. | 4.7 | 3.1 | 5.9 | 2.9 | 6.0 | 2.7 | 4.8 | 3.6 |
| May | 5.8 | 3.2 | 5.2 | 3.1 | 6.0 | 2.7 | 5.2 | 3.7 |
| Jun. | 6.0 | 3.1 | 6.1 | 3.2 | 5.7 | 3.0 | 5.1 | 3.6 |
| Jul. | 5.7 | 3.0 | 5.3 | 2.6 | 5.9 | 3.1 | 5.4 | 3.2 |
| Aug. | 5.9 | 3.2 | 5.2 | 3.1 | 5.1 | 2.9 | 6.0 | 3.2 |
| Sept. | 5.2 | 2.9 | 5.7 | 3.0 | 5.0 | 3.6 | 5.6 | 3.5 |
| Oct. | 5.0 | 3.0 | 5.0 | 3.2 | 5.1 | 3.4 | 5.3 | 3.3 |
| Nov. | 5.2 | 2.9 | 5.1 | 3.1 | 5.4 | 3.2 | 5.1 | 3.4 |
| Dec. | 5.7 | 2.8 | 5.8 | 3.2 | 5.4 | 2.9 | 5.6 | 3.2 |
| Total | 64.6 | 35.8 | 66.3 | 36.3 | 66.0 | 36.6 | 63.6 | 40.8 |

**EXHIBIT 5**  LTL Motor Transit Time

| | Days in Transit | Probabilities | Average |
|---|---|---|---|
| Chicago–New York City | 2–6 | P(2) = .05<br>P(3) = .20<br>P(4) = .50<br>P(5) = .20<br>P(6) = .05 | 4 days |
| Chicago–Atlanta | 2–6 | P(2) = .30<br>P(3) = .55<br>P(4) = .05<br>P(5) = .05<br>P(6) = .05 | 3 days |
| Chicago–Dallas | 2–6 | P(2) = .05<br>P(3) = .20<br>P(4) = .50<br>P(5) = .20<br>P(6) = .05 | 4 days |
| Chicago–Denver | 2–8 | P(2) = .05<br>P(3) = .10<br>P(4) = .20<br>P(5) = .30<br>P(6) = .15<br>P(7) = .15<br>P(8) = .05 | 5 days |
| Chicago–Minneapolis | 1–4 | P(1) = .40<br>P(2) = .30<br>P(3) = .20<br>P(4) = .10 | 2 days |
| Chicago–Los Angeles | 3–10 | P(3) = .05<br>P(4) = .15<br>P(5) = .20<br>P(6) = .25<br>P(7) = .15<br>P(8) = .10<br>P(9) = .05<br>P(10) = .05 | 6 days |

Rates apply to electric pencil sharpeners, Item No. 1265/ONMSCA13.

Cases  515

**EXHIBIT 6**  LTL Motor Carriage Rates (includes pick-up and delivery)

*Rates per CWT Minimum Weight (in pounds)*

|  | Minimum Charge | Up to 500 | 500–1,000 | 1,000–2,000 | 2,000–5,000 | 5,000 or over |
|---|---|---|---|---|---|---|
| Chicago–New York | 11.92 | 8.67 | 8.33 | 7.37 | 6.84 | 5.79 |
| Chicago–Minneapolis | 10.15 | 7.15 | 6.33 | 5.48 | 5.18 | 4.38 |
| Chicago–Atlanta | 10.40 | 7.70 | 7.62 | 6.51 | 5.93 | 5.12 |
| Chicago–Los Angeles | 14.80 | 14.80 | 9.21 | 8.27 | 7.82 | 7.37 |

|  | Minimum Charge | Up to 1,500 | 1,500–5,000 | 5,000 or Over |
|---|---|---|---|---|
| Chicago–Dallas | 13.40 | 8.54 | 7.82 | 6.98 |

*Minimum Charges*

|  | 0–100 lbs. | 100–150 | 150–200 | 200–250 | 250–300 | Over 300 |
|---|---|---|---|---|---|---|
| Chicago–Denver | 10.42 | 10.69 | 11.88 | 13.09 | 14.23 | 15.83 |

*Rates per CWT*

|  | Less than 1,000 lbs. | 1,000–2,000 | 2,000–5,000 | Over 5,000 |
|---|---|---|---|---|
| Chicago–Denver | 8.32 | 7.72 | 7.15 | 6.75 |

Rates apply to electric pencil sharpeners, Item No. 126510NMSCA13.

## Appendix B: Rate Information Provided by Peerless Airlines Staff Support Group

**EXHIBIT 7**  Pick-up Delivery Rates (airfreight shipments only: not applicable to containerized shipments)

*Rates per CWT Minimum Weight (in pounds)*

|  | Minimum Charge | 100 | 1,000 | 2,000 | 3,000 | 5,000 | 10,000 |
|---|---|---|---|---|---|---|---|
| Pick-up |  |  |  |  |  |  |  |
| Chicago | $5.00 | $2.05 | $1.70 | $1.30 | $1.15 | $1.00 | $0.75 |
| Delivery |  |  |  |  |  |  |  |
| Atlanta | 3.30 | 1.25 | 1.20 | 1.15 | 1.10 | 1.10 | 0.85 |
| Dallas | 2.80 | 1.30 | 1.20 | 1.05 | 1.00 | 0.75 | 0.65 |
| Los Angeles | 4.30 | 2.10 | 1.75 | 1.50 | 1.10 | 0.90 | 0.65 |
| New York | 6.95 | 3.45 | 3.15 | 3.00 | 2.70 | 2.05 | 1.50 |
| Minneapolis | 3.40 | 1.35 | 1.25 | 1.00 | 0.90 | 0.75 | 0.65 |
| Denver | 3.35 | 1.60 | 1.50 | 1.30 | 1.00 | 0.65 | 0.55 |

* All pick-ups and deliveries within Zone A.

**EXHIBIT 8** General Commodity Rates (airport to airport)

|  | Minimum Charge | Rates (per pounds) |  |  |  |  |
|---|---|---|---|---|---|---|
|  |  | 1 | 100* | 1,000† | 2,000 | 3,000 |
| Chicago–Atlanta | $10.00 | $0.16 | $12.45 | $11.40 | $10.75 | $ 9.70 |
| Chicago–Dallas | 10.00 | 0.18 | 13.15 | 11.40 | 11.40 | 10.80 |
| Chicago–Los Angeles | 12.00 | 0.32 | 23.50 | 21.15 | 20.45 | 19.70 |
| Chicago–New York | 10.00 | 0.17 | 12.45 | 11.40 | 10.75 | 9.35 |
| Chicago–Minneapolis | 10.00 | 0.12 | 7.90 | 7.15 | 6.80 | 6.30 |
| Chicago–Denver | 10.00 | 0.19 | 14.40 | 13.00 | 12.00 | 10.25 |

* Rate per 100 pounds for shipments weighing up to 999 pounds.
† Rate per 100 pounds for shipments weighing 1,000 pounds to 1,999 pounds.

**EXHIBIT 9** Pick-up and Delivery Rates (airfreight shipments only: applicable only to containerized shipments)

|  | Type A–1* | LD–3† | LD–N‡ |
|---|---|---|---|
| Pick-up |  |  |  |
| Chicago | $34.00 | $19.00 | $17.00 |
| Delivery |  |  |  |
| Atlanta | 27.00 | 11.00 | 9.00 |
| Dallas | 30.00 | 13.00 | 11.50 |
| Los Angeles | 44.00 | 30.00 | 30.00 |
| New York | 81.00 | 34.00 | 29.00 |
| Minneapolis | 22.00 | 11.00 | 10.00 |
| Denver | 27.00 | 15.00 | 13.50 |
| Breakbulk costs per container | 18.00 | 6.00 | 5.00 |

Note: Containers are carrier-owned.
* Type A–1 container (up to 425 cubic feet)—maximum gross weight, 10,000 lbs.; empty weight, 200 lbs.
† Type LD–3 container (166 cubic feet)—maximum gross weight, 3,500 lbs.; empty weight, 100 lbs.
‡ Type LD–N container (110 cubic feet)—maximum gross weight, 3,100 lbs.; empty weight, 100 lbs.

**EXHIBIT 10** Container Rates

|  | Chicago–Atlanta | Chicago–Minneapolis | Chicago–Dallas | Chicago–Los Angeles | Chicago–New York | Chicago–Denver |
|---|---|---|---|---|---|---|
| Type A–1 containers with net weight of 3,200 lbs. or over |  |  |  |  |  |  |
| Charge per container for net weight up to 3,200 lbs. | $219.00 | $153.00 | $297.00 | $555.00 | $257.00 | $321.00 |
| Rate per 100 lbs. for net weight over 3,200 lbs. | 4.80 | 2.75 | 7.25 | 12.55 | 5.95 | 7.85 |
| LD–3 containers |  |  |  |  |  |  |
| Charge per container | 76.00 | 57.00 | 105.00 | 201.00 | 89.00 | 122.00 |
| LD–N containers | 41.00 | n.a. | 87.00 | 144.00 | 75.00 | 86.00 |

n.a. = Not available.

**EXHIBIT 11**  Containers*

Type A–1 container (up to 425 cubic feet)
Max. gross weight 10,000 lbs.
Empty weight—Varies (usually about 200 lbs.)
Usable internal cubic capacity—390 cubic feet

Type LD–3 container (166 cubic feet)
Max. weight 3500 lbs.
Empty weight 100 lbs.
Usable internal cubic capacity 150 cubic feet

Type LD–N container (110 cubic feet)
Max. gross weight 3100 lbs.
Empty weight 100 lbs.
Usable internal cubic capacity 90 cubic feet

* Type A–1 and LD–3 containers are carrier owned. LD–N container is shipper owned.

## 4. FAVORED BLEND COFFEE COMPANY

### CASE BACKGROUND

The Favored Blend Coffee Company is a prominent manufacturer of coffee sold on a nationwide basis to food wholesalers and institutional markets. Sales are achieved primarily through wholesalers, under the brand name Favored Blend. Sales to the institutional market are achieved by direct account coverage and by the efforts of brokers under the brand name Best Blend. With the exception of packaging size and style, the two product lines are identical. Both Favored Blend and Best Blend offer ground and instant coffee in a variety of packages. Both brands are manufactured and distributed in the same production plants and through the same physical distribution system.

Until 1975 the Favored Blend Coffee Company prospered and expanded. Sales growth averaged 5 percent annually. Profits, while not increasing in the same proportion as sales, reflected a favorable growth. At the year-end management meeting in 1975, the management group was optimistic about continued growth in both sales and profits. By mid-1977 this optimism had given way to a serious situation. While the sales of Favored Blend's two product lines continued to grow, profits dropped sharply in 1976, and for the first quarter of 1977 a loss was experienced for the first time since 1929. Analysis of the operating figures clearly indicated that increased costs in physical distribution constituted the major reason for the profit decline. Transportation cost had increased by 12 percent in 1976 as compared to 1975 and warehousing costs were up by 7 percent. Despite a rigorous cost-

---

This case was provided by Donald J. Bowersox of the Graduate School of Business Administration, Michigan State University. All rights reserved to the contributor. Paul H. Zinszer of the University of Oklahoma provided modifications to the case which included considerations of warehouse location in the distribution process.

control program instituted in the last half of 1976, the cost trend had not been reversed during the first quarter of 1978. Year-end finished-goods inventory in 1977 was 8 percent higher than 1976. By the end of the first quarter of 1978 inventory had been forced in line as the result of a reduced production schedule.

In April 1978, Mr. Smith, president and chief executive officer of Favored Blend, called a general management meeting. While the entire group was aware of the fact that a physical distribution problem existed, the problem had reached a new climax when Big Food Wholesaler Inc. dropped Favored Blend Coffee from its product line. Mr. Smith had been informed by Big Food's chief executive officer that the company was forced into the decision by alleged poor inventory availability and erratic delivery of orders placed with Favored Blend Coffee. Based upon the apparent inability of Favored Blend's management group to correct the adverse situation, Smith decided, with the advice of his board of directors, to call in an independent consultant to study and analyze the company and its distribution structure.

At the April meeting Smith presented his decision to retain the services of Able Management Consultants—a firm of physical distribution specialists. The marketing vice president was in full agreement with the decision. The director of distribution services and the financial vice president were opposed. In their opinion the problem could be corrected if proper marketing and customer service policies were implemented on a corporate-wide basis. They questioned if a so-called high powered specialist would in fact have sufficient knowledge of food-product distribution to conduct a meaningful investigation. At one point in a heated discussion the vice president of manufacturing added to the general argument with the comment that "the last thing we need is some more theory—the last group of so-called experts spent three weeks here and then told us things we already knew and had told them. We need action, not research." After about two hours discussion Smith concluded the meeting with the following comment:

> Some of you may be right about consultants, but frankly I feel you're defensive and the figures just don't support standing by while the situation further deteriorates. I am going to call the head of Able, give him the facts as I know them and see what he would do if we gave him the job.

## CASE SITUATION

You are the head of Able Management Consultants. Mr. Smith has reviewed the background of Favored Blend's problem and provided you with the briefing contained in the next section of the case and Exhibits 1–4. Your immediate assignment is to answer questions as instructed in the last section of this case.

## BRIEFING: SMITH TO HEAD OF ABLE MANAGEMENT CONSULTANTS

In serving its nationwide market, Favored Blend Company operates processing facilities at Philadelphia, New Orleans, and Los Angeles. Each plant

**EXHIBIT 1** Market Areas Map and Listings

supplies a relatively fixed geographical portion of the United States. Operations at each of these fully integrated plants consist of receiving shipments of green coffee from overseas, and blending, roasting, grinding, processing, and packaging the product for shipment to company warehouses. As the packaging process is completed, the coffee moves into a shipping and storage area. Here it is consolidated into large-order lots for shipment either directly to institutional customers, or to warehouses throughout the territory of distribution. The production process consists of running a single-size package until estimated weekly requirements are satisfied and then processing other packs in scheduled sequence.

The space devoted to storage and shipping at each plant is small, having been whittled down in recent years by the expansion of space devoted to production facilities for instant coffee. A continuing search for additional space in the plants, on plant property, or on property contiguous to the plants has proven fruitless. As an expedient for making space, the distribution services department has come to favor rail shipments, principally because they find empty box cars can be used as auxiliary storehouses while being loaded. This added storage space is provided at moderate cost by reason of 48-hour free-time provisions in the demurrage tariff coupled with the fact that switching is performed at 8 A.M. at all plants. As a result, almost three days' loading time is provided on free time before demurrage accrues. H. J. Speedy, director of distribution services of Favored Blend Coffee Company is very proud of his accomplishment in this area and has presented the concept several times at industry meetings.

**EXHIBIT 2** Cost for Various Warehouse Configurations

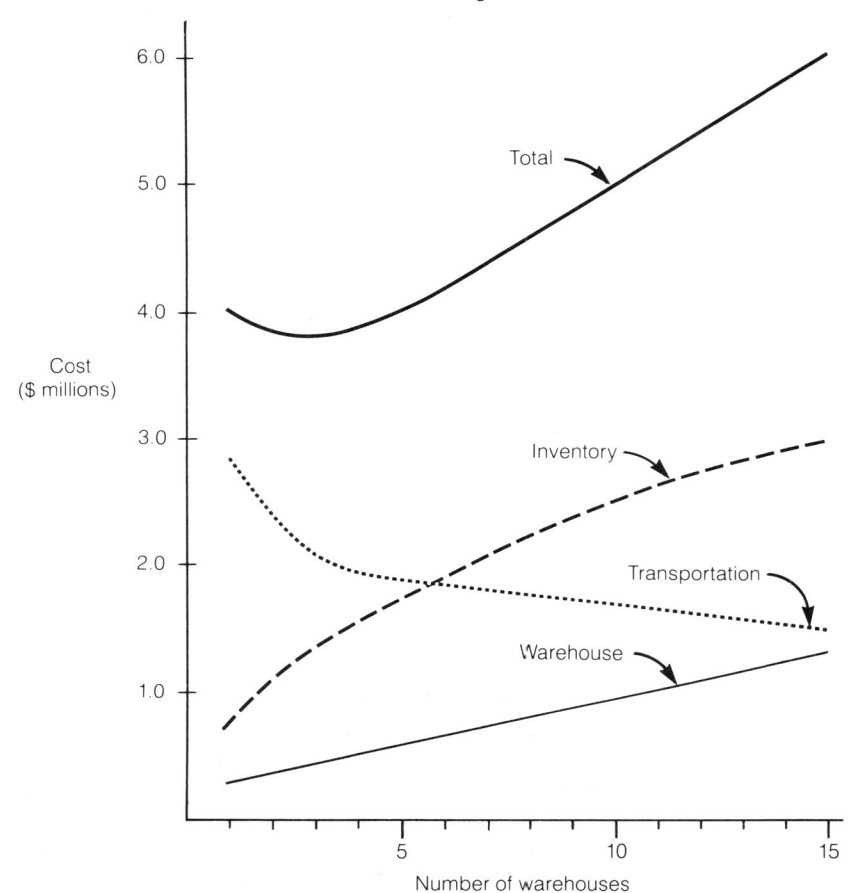

[Graph showing cost curves for Total, Inventory, Transportation, and Warehouse costs versus number of warehouses (1-15), with Cost in $ millions on the y-axis (0 to 6.0). Total cost curve reaches minimum around 3 warehouses at ~$3.8 million.]

Though coffee consumption in general is fairly predictable, orders from customers tend to be sporadic, so that shipments both direct from the plant and from the warehouses are rather irregular. Attempts have been made at predicting orders; however, the results have not been particularly accurate. The distribution services department has tended to utilize warehouses as the storage problem has become burdensome at the plant. In total, six warehouses are utilized by the firm for distribution—Philadelphia, New Orleans, Los Angeles, Chicago, San Antonio, Denver.

Consequently, though there is a planned supply program, some warehouses have tended to become greatly overstocked, others considerably understocked. The mixture of Favored Blend and Best Blend products at any single time at any single warehouse often lacks the proper combination of package sizes and grinds. Frequently, cross-hauling be-

**EXHIBIT 3** Service for Various Warehouse Configurations

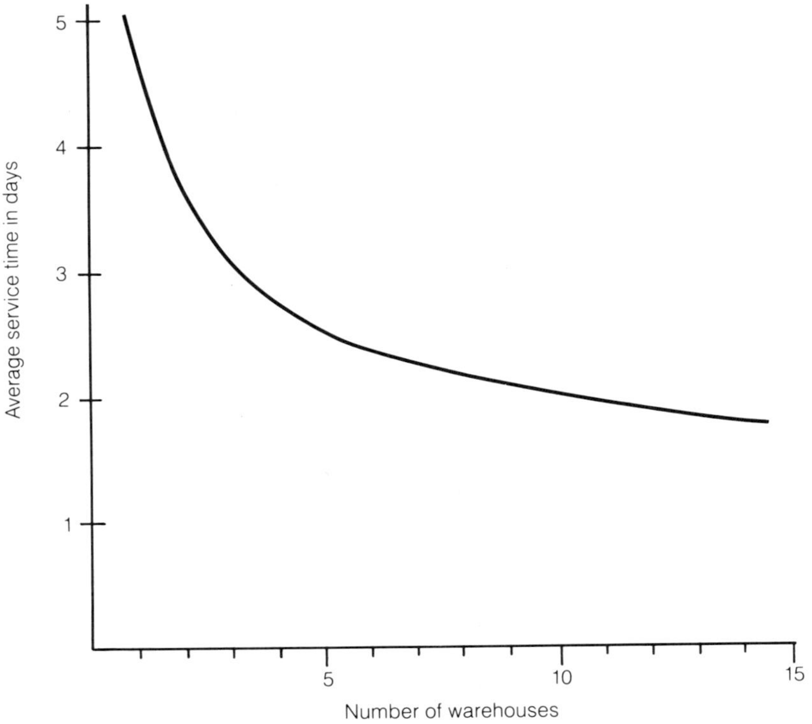

[Graph: Average service time in days (y-axis) vs. Number of warehouses (x-axis, 0 to 15). Curve decreases from about 5 days at 1 warehouse to under 2 days at 15 warehouses.]

tween warehouses and emergency shipments from plants have been necessary in order to fill customer orders.

The physical pattern of distribution has been a source of friction between the marketing and distribution services departments for a number of years. In general it consists of two principal methods: (1) direct shipments from the plants to the six company warehouses in carload quantities, and (2) shipments in LTL quantities to wholesalers, and to institutional customers located in the market area.

Quantity shipments direct from the plant to food wholesalers and institutional customers were at one time of considerable significance and are, in general, the lowest-cost and most desirable from the distribution services department's standpoint. However, in line with a general trend in business philosophy in recent years toward lower inventory levels, all customers have been hesitant to purchase in large enough quantities to warrant delivery in carload and truckload lots. The distribution services department has confronted an increasing demand on the part of customers to order in small lots on an immediate delivery basis, with requested truck delivery. The degree to which this trend has progressed is illustrated by tonnage reports

**EXHIBIT 4** Thirty Top Metropolitan Areas—Alternative Warehouse Locations

| Number | Zip Name | Population (000) |
|---|---|---|
| 1. | 100 New York | 25,815 |
| 2. | 606 Chicago | 13,000 |
| 3. | 900 Los Angeles | 10,993 |
| 4. | 191 Philadelphia | 8,654 |
| 5. | 482 Detroit | 9,248 |
| 6. | 770 Houston | 3,314 |
| 7. | 212 Baltimore | 2,509 |
| 8. | 752 Dallas | 5,992 |
| 9. | 200 Wash DC | 3,373 |
| 10. | 441 Cleveland | 4,693 |
| 11. | 532 Milwaukee | 3,850 |
| 12. | 941 San Francisco | 7,988 |
| 13. | 782 San Antonio | 2,040 |
| 14. | 921 San Diego | 1,433 |
| 15. | 631 St Louis | 4,322 |
| 16. | 701 New Orleans | 2,956 |
| 17. | 021 Boston | 8,370 |
| 18. | 641 Kansas City | 2,860 |
| 19. | 981 Seattle | 2,820 |
| 20. | 381 Memphis | 3,213 |
| 21. | 432 Columbus | 1,794 |
| 22. | 152 Pittsburgh | 4,841 |
| 23. | 303 Atlanta | 4,981 |
| 24. | 850 Phoenix | 1,714 |
| 25. | 462 Indianapolis | 2,484 |
| 26. | 452 Cincinnati | 3,220 |
| 27. | 332 Jacksonville | 2,368 |
| 28. | 802 Denver | 3,168 |
| 29. | 142 Buffalo | 2,898 |
| 30. | 554 Minneapolis | 5,428 |
|  | Total | 160,339 |

for 1976 in comparison to 1972. In 1972, 70 percent of all coffee from all locations combined was shipped to customers by rail and 30 percent by truck. By 1976 these figures had reversed.

Considerable time has been spent with the distribution services and marketing departments in attempting to solve the problem of increasing costs. In general the distribution services department feels that marketing has not instituted realistic price incentives to encourage quantity purchasing and that salesmen allowed customers to unduly dictate terms and routing of shipments. The marketing department in contrast points to increased competition from private as well as other national-branded coffee as the source of the problem. "Competitors provide the service desired by customers and we have little choice but to try to meet this service if we want the business."

Some significant facts:

| | |
|---|---|
| Annual sales | $160,000,000 |
| Market zones | Sales offices in each of the 30 largest cities in the United States. Sales are distributed proportionally with population at the rate of $1 of sales to each person annually. |
| Shipment characteristics | Product value is $1 per lb. All shipments are LTL. Average shipment is 1,000 lbs. |
| Inventory value | 50 percent of selling price. 12 turns on finished goods. 12 percent interest cost. |

Significant factors for the distribution system are:

| | |
|---|---|
| Warehouse costs | $80,000 fixed cost for management, controls, etc. $1.50 per hundredweight throughput for handling. |
| Inventory level | Varies as the square root of the number of warehouses. |

## Questions

1. What principles of physical distribution system design will be helpful to guide Able in approaching a revamping of Favored Blend's operation if they get the assignment? Be specific.

2. Is there sufficient similarity among physical distribution systems in general to support Mr. Smith's feeling that Able Management Consultants should be capable of handling a food-industry assignment? What factors, principles, or general reasons would you, as the president of Able, present to the management group of Favored Blend to help get the assignment?

3. In order to meet the needs of the food wholesalers (such as Big Food Wholesalers Inc.) it has been determined that enough warehouses must be used in the distribution system to achieve an average annual distribution time of two and one-half days (one day order entry and processing and one and one-half days transit) the maximum distance which would allow this is approximately the distance between Denver and Oklahoma City. Which warehouse locations would you select? What procedures did you use? Why? Should considerations for the location of satellite warehouse facilities be comparable to or different than this procedure?

## 5. McGRAW-HILL BOOK COMPANY (A): LOCATION OF WESTERN REGION WAREHOUSE

### THE COMPANY

The McGraw-Hill Book Company was a wholly owned subsidiary of the McGraw-Hill Publishing Company. Its sales were about $40 million per year. They represented approximately one-third of the gross revenues of the parent organization, the balance being derived from some 35 periodicals and trade journals which circulated widely in the business world. Included among these were such publications as *Business Week*, *Chemical Week*, *Aviation Week*, and *Coal Age*. Magazine publication was a separate operation, not connected with the operations of the book company.

McGraw-Hill Book Company consisted of 10 operating and marketing departments which handled nearly 4,000 titles. It was one of the four largest book publishers in the United States.

Each department specialized in a particular type of books. The College Department handled the wide range of college textbooks. The Blakiston Division handled professional books in medicine, dentistry, and related subjects. The School Division published academic texts for grades 7 to 12, while the Gregg Division produced a business education series. The Trade Division managed all books of a general nature, including fiction, while the Industrial and Business Book Division distributed reference books for engineers, scientists, and businessmen. Through these channels, McGraw-Hill was able to penetrate the market effectively with highly specialized books and books of general interest.

McGraw-Hill served a highly diversified group of customers in 1959. A special report celebrating the 50th anniversary of the company described them as follows:

> The customers are as diverse as, and more numerous than the books that they buy. Some 45,000 schools, colleges, libraries, and booksellers and more than 200,000 individual mail-order customers are regular recipients of book orders that may vary from one to several thousand copies of a title, all the way to 3,000 titles—one copy each!

The company employed a staff of some 160 representatives who made more than 220,000 calls per year. Each representative was connected with a particular book department and concentrated on a specific category of customers. Some books, however, were sold simultaneously through the channels of more than one division.

Marketing problems were further complicated by the fact that as few as 1,500 copies might be sold of some highly technical book, while such best-

---

© 1971 Karl M. Ruppenthal, Faculty of Commerce and Business Administration, The University of British Columbia, Vancouver, Canada. Reproduced by permission of the copyright holder.

sellers as Samuelson's *Economics* might account for 100,000 copies in a single year.

## DISTRIBUTION

The main distribution center for books was located at Hightstown, New Jersey, midway between New York and Philadelphia. This modern warehouse served customers in the eastern part of the United States. It also sent shipments to the other McGraw-Hill warehouses.

The company had field service offices (sales and accounting) and warehouses in San Francisco, Chicago, Toronto, Canada, and London, England. Each of these warehouses received inventory shipments from Hightstown.

McGraw-Hill maintained field warehouses primarily to provide fast service to any place in the United States. In the words of one company official, "book service and speed of delivery are of paramount importance in this business."

While some large orders and college bookstore preschool orders were shipped from Hightstown, most West Coast shipments were made from the warehouse in San Francisco. There a stock of nearly all current titles was maintained in order to give quick service to customers in the West.

The San Francisco facility was primarily concerned with fill-in orders for college textbooks. The large orders for college books, which were usually received in July and November, were shipped directly from Hightstown. Although direct shipments to large West Coast customers from Hightstown required more time, they made possible some savings in transportation costs. Furthermore, it was the opinion of McGraw-Hill management that college book prices were too competitive to support the expense of maintaining large field inventories at company warehouses. As a result of this policy the San Francisco warehouse was responsible only for the fill-in orders which came in when a prime order at a campus bookstore proved to be insufficient. These additional orders were usually for a small number of books. Shipments from San Francisco could be made quickly.

Several modes of transportation were used to dispatch shipments from the warehouse, but most of the bulky shipments were sent by truck. Smaller shipments were sent by parcel post at book rates. Shipments were made FOB warehouse, the customer paying the shipping charges. Selection of transportation mode and carrier was normally made by the McGraw-Hill shipping department (on the basis of cost, speed of delivery, and size of shipment). Exhibit 1 shows the relationship between selected truck rates and parcel post rates.

## HIGHTSTOWN DISTRIBUTION CENTER

In 1958, McGraw-Hill consolidated its East Coast shipping activities in Hightstown, New Jersey. Previously, shipments had been made from six

**EXHIBIT 1**  McGraw-Hill Book Company
Rate break point for motor truck and parcel post from San Francisco to selected destinations. Parcel post rates were less than motor truck rates for shipments smaller than those listed below. On larger shipments, truck rates were less than parcel post rates.

|  | Salt Lake City | Los Angeles | Port-land | Seattle | Phoenix | San Francisco |
|---|---|---|---|---|---|---|
| Salt Lake City | — | 67* | 79 | 82 | 55 | 67 |
| Los Angeles | 67 | — | 73 | 77 | 42 | 52 |
| Portland | 79 | 73 | — | 26 | 103 | 53 |
| Palo Alto (including Stanford University) | 67 | 52 | 56 | 59 | 66 | 38 |
| San Francisco (East Bay, including Berkeley) | 97 | 52 | 53 | 56 | 66 | — |
| Marin County | 67 | 57 | 58 | 61 | 83 | 38 |

Truck rates were based on a minimum charge for 100 pounds or less. Parcel post book rates were 5 cents per pound plus 4 cents per shipment. Thus the parcel post rate for a book shipment of five pounds (any U.S. destination) would be 29 cents.

* Weight in pounds.

different locations in New York City. The company described the Hightstown facility as follows:

> The Distribution Center, which occupies five acres of a 38-acre site, is all on one level, except for a two-story area given over to the office and recreation rooms. This area contains the only windows in the entire construction which is built of prestressed concrete panels, each with a pocket of insulating material.
>
> In addition to the several million books held ready for shipment, the center accommodates films and filmstrips and promotion materials.
>
> When a truck arrives at our new distribution center at Hightstown, the driver stops at a speaker box and reports what his vehicle is carrying. A traffic dispatcher inside the warehouse office tells him, through the same speaker, the number of the portal through which he should drive. The dispatcher presses a button to raise the portal door. The portal closes while the truck is inside so that loading and unloading are undisturbed by the weather. Eleven trucks of the largest size allowed on the highways can be accommodated simultaneously.
>
> Each title is packaged by the bindery in cartons which conform to the United States Post Office weight restrictions. Rather than handle books, we handle cartons. Each carton bears a code number based on the author's name—thus avoiding possible confusion among authors of the same name. Shipping orders are prepared in numerical code sequence so that the order can be assembled, item by item, on the conveyors which lead to the postage machine or the freight dock.
>
> A continuous belt conveyor takes the books to the packing machines, scales, and stamping machines and finally to the post office within the building if parcel post is to be used.
>
> In addition to its direct dispatches to customers in the United States and aboard, Hightstown feeds the company's five other distribution centers. From a crossroads which is near enough to headquarters to ensure rapid communication but far enough away to avoid the congestion of New York City, the new center is ideally placed both to assemble and store McGraw-Hill books and to speed them on their way to customers throughout the world.

## CALIFORNIA WAREHOUSE AND FIELD OFFICE

In 1958 the company considered duplicating the highly successful Hightstown facility (on a smaller scale) at its several branch locations. Particular attention was focused on the San Francisco warehouse which was grossly overcrowded because of rapid growth in West Coast sales.

Management believed that the San Francisco distribution branch had several problems which should be considered in the construction of new facility. Some of those considerations were:

1. The San Francisco warehouse, with an area of 14,000 square feet, was literally bursting at the seams. At least 40,000 square feet was needed for an efficient operation. The San Francisco location had no room for expansion.
2. The multistory facility was not nearly so efficient as a single-story operation. This had been demonstrated at Hightstown.
3. Because the San Francisco warehouse facility was so crowded, the executive and sales offices were housed in different quarters—more than 10 blocks from the warehouse. One of the officers felt that this created a "bad management situation" which could be corrected if both facilities were under one roof.
4. There was considerable congestion and traffic in the area where the warehouse was located.
5. Some of the company officials felt that taxes in San Francisco were not consistently administered and stated that the company "never knew where it stood" in the question of property taxes. They felt that tax assessments and administration might be more businesslike in another location.
6. There were industrial relations implications in a move. While the company would still deal with the same union, it would deal with a different local. There were sound reasons to believe that some industrial relations problems would be easier to handle in some other areas.

## ALTERNATIVE LOCATIONS

McGraw-Hill executives thought that there were several feasible alternatives: The facility could be located in Los Angeles, Portland, or Salt Lake City. Or it could be located somewhere in the San Francisco bay area (*a*) north of the Golden Gate Bridge in Marin County; (*b*) in the east bay area in Berkeley or in Oakland; (*c*) or south of San Francisco in San Mateo or Santa Clara County (possibly in the Stanford Industrial Park located on Stanford University property in Santa Clara County).

The sales department believed that in locating the new facility, adequate consideration should be given to the fact that the whole coast area was growing rapidly and that the new facility should be strategically located to give the best possible service to an important market.

Exhibit 2 recapitulates shipments from the San Francisco warehouse during a single week in January.

**EXHIBIT 2** Destinations of All Shipments From the San Francisco Warehouse for One Week in January, 1958*

| Destinations | Weight pounds | Total |
|---|---|---|
| Southern California | | |
|   Los Angeles | 5,640 | |
|   Los Angeles County | 2,820 | |
|   San Diego County | 1,110 | |
|   Fresno | 1,100 | |
|   Santa Barbara | 850 | |
|   Other | 1,530 | |
|     Sub total | | 13,050 |
| Northern California | | |
|   Berkeley | 1,850 | |
|   San Francisco | 2,000 | |
|   Other | 1,530 | |
|     Sub total | | 5,380 |
| Other Western States | | |
|   Washington | 4,300 | |
|   Oregon | 2,100 | |
|   Idaho | 1,965 | |
|   Arizona | 945 | |
|   Nevada | 865 | |
|   New Mexico | 465 | |
|   Utah | 400 | |
|   Montana | 365 | |
|     Sub total | | 11,405 |
| Miscellaneous (includes Hawaii and Alaska and return shipments to the east) | | 2,000 |
| | | 31,835 |

*The shipping clerk regarded this as a fairly typical week. He stated that shipments were much heavier in July, August, and September and that shipments in those months might be twice as large as in the other months of the year.

## ANALYZING THE MARKET

In 1958 the San Francisco warehouse served nine western states (California, Oregon, Washington, Idaho, Montana, Nevada, Utah, Arizona, New Mexico), plus Hawaii and Alaska. While sales in each of these areas varied from year to year, California accounted for approximately 50 percent of the total, followed by Washington and Oregon. Company officials estimated that about 50 percent of the California sales came from the greater Los Angeles area. Exhibit 3 shows the location of all state-supported colleges and universities in California in 1958.

**EXHIBIT 3**  Present and Projected Locations of State Supported California Colleges in 1970 (as of 1958)

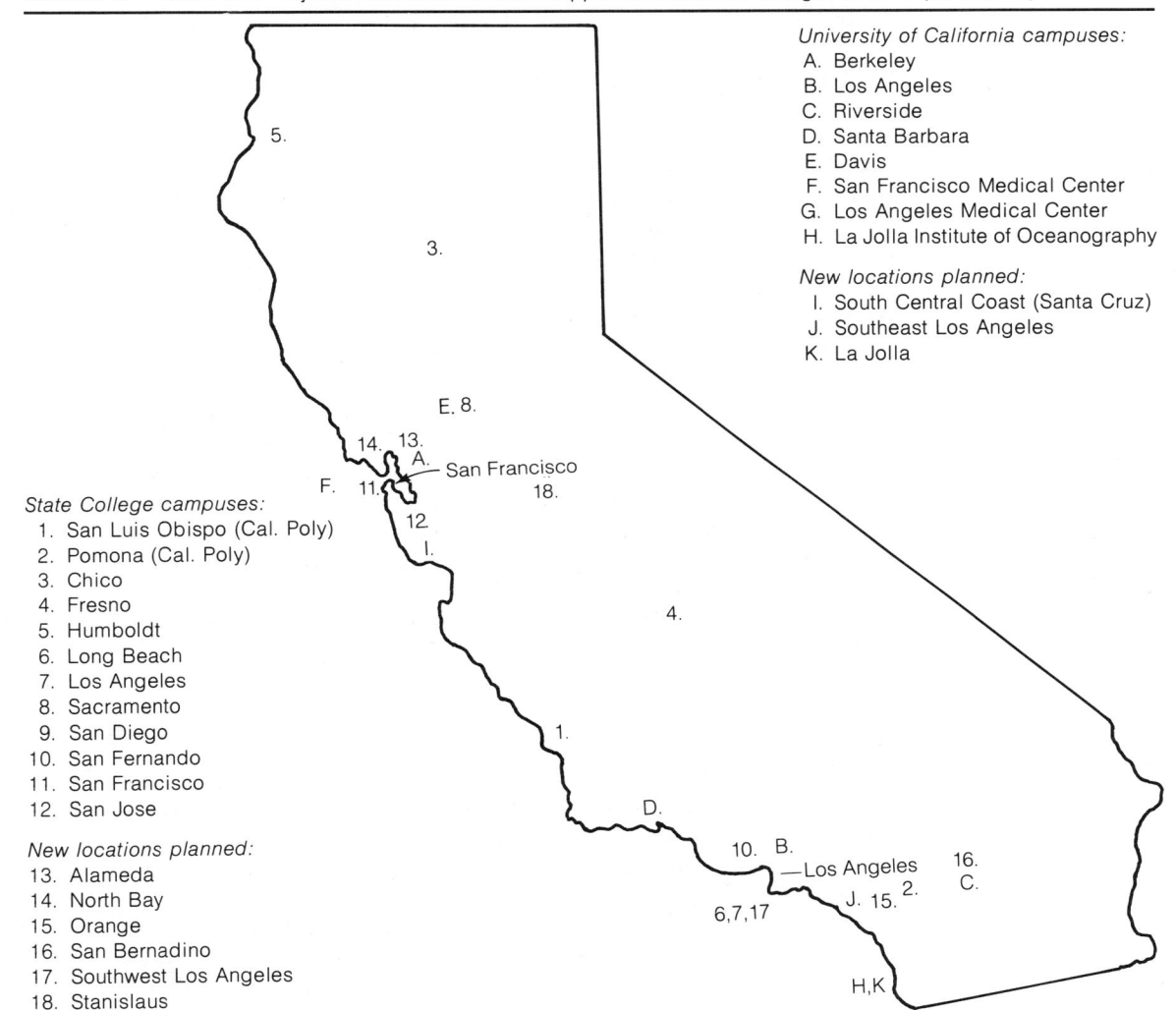

*University of California campuses:*
A. Berkeley
B. Los Angeles
C. Riverside
D. Santa Barbara
E. Davis
F. San Francisco Medical Center
G. Los Angeles Medical Center
H. La Jolla Institute of Oceanography

*New locations planned:*
I. South Central Coast (Santa Cruz)
J. Southeast Los Angeles
K. La Jolla

*State College campuses:*
1. San Luis Obispo (Cal. Poly)
2. Pomona (Cal. Poly)
3. Chico
4. Fresno
5. Humboldt
6. Long Beach
7. Los Angeles
8. Sacramento
9. San Diego
10. San Fernando
11. San Francisco
12. San Jose

*New locations planned:*
13. Alameda
14. North Bay
15. Orange
16. San Bernadino
17. Southwest Los Angeles
18. Stanislaus

## INBOUND SHIPMENTS

Nearly all of the inbound shipments to the San Francisco warehouse came by trust from Hightstown. A few books came directly from the binderies, and the company planned to ship more books directly to the West Coast warehouse without routing them through Hightstown.

Most binderies were located on the East Coast with a few in various other cities. All of the books for the Gregg Division were printed in Crawfordsville, Indiana. About 15 percent of the Gregg sales were made on the West Coast.

Since most of the books came from the east, mention was made of the fact that if the facility were located in Salt Lake City, there would be no back haul in shipping books to Nevada, Utah, and Arizona. Shipments from a West Coast facility to those states would necessarily involve a back haul.

## DELIVERY SPEED

The company believed that prompt delivery was vital in the book business and that the ability to give rush delivery to book stores and to industrial customers was an important sales tool. Some sales would be lost if customers were required to wait too long for their books. Repeat business would be particularly affected.

A college professor might be reluctant to use a textbook in his course, if he could not get extra books quickly when class enrollment exceeded expectations. In the case of industrial customers, the selection of a particular book might depend on the speed with which it could be obtained. An electronics firm might order the engineering book which could be delivered one day sooner than a competitive book that might be equally satisfactory. A retail bookstore could sell books only as fast as it could replenish its stock. While many orders had no delivery deadlines, the reputation of a publisher depended heavily on its ability to fill rush orders quickly.

Exhibit 4 shows the time required for delivery from several possible warehouse locations.

## PARCEL POST

If the new facility were located in Northern California the company felt that careful attention should be given to the matter of postal system routings. All Parcel Post to the north and east was routed through the Oakland postal terminal. If the facility were located in Palo Alto (or in the Stanford Industrial Park), shipments to the east and to the north would be taken by truck to the Oakland terminal. Southbound shipments would be loaded directly into trains at the Palo Alto station. All parcel post from Marin County and from the East Bay was routed through the Oakland terminal. While the post offices in some of the cities in the San Francisco Bay area had direct dispatches to the Oakland terminal, others did not. Parcels mailed in some of the smaller towns might require an additional day to reach the Oakland terminal.

There was no similar problem in Salt Lake City, Los Angeles, or Portland. The Post Office Department indicated that the specific location selected in any of these areas would not be a factor in delivery time.

McGraw-Hill also hoped that a postal substation might be located inside the new warehouse. The Hightstown facility had its own postal station. One post office employee worked inside the Hightstown warehouse where he sorted and processed mail. It was then dispatched by truck to a central postal terminal. This procedure cut as much as a full day from the transit time. The company hoped that the new West Coast facility might incorpo-

**EXHIBIT 4** Normal Transit Time (in days) Between Selected Cities

|  | Salt Lake City | Los Angeles | Portland | Seattle | Phoenix | San Francisco |
|---|---|---|---|---|---|---|
| Parcel post* |  |  |  |  |  |  |
| Salt Lake City | 1 | 3 | 3 | 3 | 4 | 3 |
| Los Angeles | 3 | 1 | 3 | 3 | 3 | 2 |
| Portland | 3 | 3 | 1 | 2 | 3 | 2 |
| Palo Alto | 3 | 2 | 2 | 3 | 3 | 1 |
| San Francisco (East Bay) | 3 | 2 | 2 | 3 | 3 | 1 |
| Marin County | 3 | 2 | 2 | 3 | 3 | 1 |
| Truck |  |  |  |  |  |  |
| Salt Lake City | 1 | 3 | 3 | 3 | 3 | 3 |
| Los Angeles | 3 | 1 | 3 | 3 | 2 | 2 |
| Portland | 3 | 3 | 1 | 2 | 5 | 3 |
| Palo Alto (including the Stanford Industrial Park) | 3 | 2 | 3 | 3 | 3 | 1 |
| San Francisco (East Bay, including Berkeley and Oakland) | 3 | 2 | 3 | 3 | 3 | 1 |
| Marin County (including San Rafael) | 3 | 2 | 3 | 3 | 3 | 1 |

* Special Handling might reduce parcel post times by approximately one day. Regular parcel post contemplated delivery within 24 hours after a parcel arrived at the destination post office. Special handling reduced this to three hours. Special handling charges were as follows:

Under two pounds ............ 25¢
2 pounds—10 pounds ........ 35
Over 10 pounds ............. 50

The Post Office did not guarantee any delivery time.

rate such a substation, the physical facilities being provided by the company, but staffed by post office employees.

The requirements for establishing a substation were generally uniform in all cities. The most important criteria were the volume of mail involved and whether such a facility would make for economies for the post office department. These decisions frequently turned on the status of the local post office. The department was more likely to authorize a substation in Palo Alto, for instance, where the post office was saturated than it would in an area where the post office had unused capacity.

The Post Office Department made no firm commitment at any of the proposed locations. However, the San Rafael post office in Marin County, was almost saturated, and there were indications that a unit substation would be approved in that locality. None of the book publishers that were already located in the Palo Alto-Stanford area had a substation, but there was no indication that any of these companies had seriously sought one. Prospects were not good for a unit substation in the East Bay, and the company had not explored the question in Portland, Salt Lake City or, Los Angeles.

## TRUCK SERVICE

Trucking service from the various locations was important since about half of all outbound shipments went by truck. Exhibit 5 lists truck rates from six possible locations to several important markets.

Service was at least as important as rates. Exhibit 6 lists several trucking companies serving each of the suggested locations. McGraw-Hill officials believed that service was generally better when there was competition.

## OTHER CONSIDERATIONS

The availability of land was also important. In the Stanford Industrial Park, all land was owned by Stanford University. Under the terms of the original grant by Leland Stanford, this land could not be sold. It was available only for lease for 99 years. The idea of leasing was not attractive to McGraw-Hill management, which had a policy of long standing that the company should own its own properties. Outside Stanford Industrial Park, no property on the peninsula was considered, as management felt that the cost was excessive. Further, McGraw-Hill's traffic manager stated that in his opinion the peninsula was planning "the world's biggest traffic jam."

Los Angeles had available land in locations somewhat similar to the Stanford Industrial Park area, which was primarily residential with limited zoning for light industry. Much of this land, however, was relatively remote and in areas where truck and postal facilities were not easily accessible.

Traffic in Oakland and Berkeley was congested. Several officials felt that they should locate in a less congested area. Land costs in Oakland were relatively high, and there were few sites available that would permit the construction of a 50,000-square-foot one-story building.

Marin County showed some attraction from the point of view of land availability. It had some new industrial areas, suitably zoned, about five miles north of the Golden Gate Bridge. This property was close to downtown San Francisco, but was relatively uncongested.

No detailed investigation of Salt Lake City or Portland real estate had been made, but a competent real estate agency stated that suitable land was available approximately at the prices listed in Exhibit 7. The company felt that it should purchase about five acres.

Exhibit 8 shows wage rates in various areas. A high-caliber work force was probably available in each of these areas, but a move from the San Francisco Bay Area might risk the loss of many clerical and warehouse employees. One officer stated, "A move to Los Angeles would mean starting all over again on the West Coast in terms of having to hire a new work force of hourly employees." Most of the employees lived in San Francisco and did not favor a move even as far as Palo Alto.

**EXHIBIT 5** LTL Rates for Book Shipments by Truck Between Selected Cities (1958)

*Rate (per hundredweight)*

From: Salt Lake City (local rate $1.10)
  To:
    Los Angeles .................................................. $3.39
                                                       2.36 (10,000 lbs. or more)
    Phoenix ......................................................... 2.77
                                                       1.58 (30,000 lbs. or more)
    Portland ......................................................... 3.98
                                                       2.28 (30,000 lbs. or more)
    Seattle ......................................................... 4.15
                                                       2.37 (30,000 lbs. or more)
    San Francisco ............................................... 3.39
                                                       2.36 (10,000 lbs. or more)

From: Los Angeles (local rate $1.20)
  To:
    Phoenix ......................................................... 2.07
                                                       1.86 ( 5,000 lbs. or more)
    Portland ......................................................... 3.69
                                                       3.56 (10,000 lbs. or more)
    Seattle ......................................................... 3.85
                                                       3.74 (10,000 lbs. or more)
    Salt Lake City ............................................... 3.39
                                                       2.02 (30,000 lbs. or more)
    San Francisco ............................................... 2.61
                                                       1.59 ( 4,000 lbs. or more)

From: Portland (local rate $1.10)
  To:
    Los Angeles .................................................. 3.69
                                                       3.65 (10,000 lbs. or more)
    Phoenix ......................................................... 5.16
                                                       2.95 (30,000 lbs. or more)
    Seattle ......................................................... 1.34
                                                       1.22 ( 5,000 lbs. or more)
    Salt Lake City ............................................... 3.98
                                                       2.28 (30,000 lbs. or more)
    San Francisco ............................................... 2.66
                                                       2.58 ( 5,000 lbs. or more)

From: San Francisco-Oakland Area (including Berkeley);
  (local rate $1.20)*
  To:
    Los Angeles .................................................. 2.61
                                                       1.59 ( 4,000 lbs. or more)
    Phoenix ......................................................... 3.34
                                                       1.88 (30,000 lbs. or more)
    Seattle ......................................................... 2.80
                                                       2.74 ( 5,000 lbs. or more)
    Salt Lake City ............................................... 3.39
                                                       2.02 (30,000 lbs. or more)
    Portland ......................................................... 2.66
                                                       2.58 ( 5,000 lbs. or more)

**EXHIBIT 5** *(continued)*

|  | *Rate (per hundredweight)* |
|---|---|
| From: Palo Alto-Stanford Area (local rate $1.20)* | |
| To: | |
| Los Angeles | $2.61 |
| | 1.59 ( 4,000 lbs. or more) |
| Phoenix | 3.34 |
| | 1.88 (30,000 lbs. or more) |
| Portland | 2.81 |
| | 2.74 ( 5,000 lbs. or more) |
| Seattle | 2.96 |
| | 2.90 ( 5,000 lbs. or more) |
| Salt Lake City | 3.39 |
| | 2.02 (30,000 lbs. or more) |
| San Francisco | 1.94 |
| | 1.23 ( 2,000 lbs. or more) |
| From: San Rafael (local rate $1.20)* | |
| To: | |
| Los Angeles | 2.88 |
| | 1.88 ( 4,000 lbs. or more) |
| Phoenix | Apply Phoenix-Berkeley rates plus the following arbitraries: |
| | 0.83 |
| | 0.67 ( 5,000 lbs. or more) |
| Portland | 2.90 |
| | 2.00 (30,000 lbs. or more) |
| Seattle | 3.06 |
| | 2.18 (30,000 lbs. or more) |
| Salt Lake City | 2.02 (30,000 lbs. or more) |
| | On quantities less than 30,000 lbs. apply Salt Lake City-Berkeley rates plus following arbitraries: |
| | 1.51 |
| | 0.98 ( 2,000 lbs. or more) |
| | 0.73 ( 4,000 lbs. or more) |
| | 0.43 (10,000 lbs. or more) |
| San Francisco | 1.92 |

* The local rate applied to all of San Francisco, Marin San Mateo, Santa Clara, and Alameda counties, including Berkeley and Oakland.

**EXHIBIT 6** Major Trucking Companies Serving Selected Cities With Nearby Terminals

Los Angeles:
   Alabama Freight Lines
   Asbury Transportation Company
   California Cartage Company
   Consolidated Copperstate Lines
   Desert Express Company
   Dependable Motor Truck
   Freight Transport Company
   Marr Freight Transit
   Signal Truck Service
   Star Truck Service
   Transcon Lines
   Western Truck Lines
   Navajo Freight Lines

Portland:
   Bend-Portland Truck Service
   Consolidated Freightways
   Home Transfer
   Nehalem Valley Motor Freight
   Pierce Freight Lines
   Risberg's Truck Lines
   St. John's Motor Express
   Sites Silver Wheel Freight Lines
   Tualatin Valley Transport Company
   Willamette Valley Transfer Company
   Pacific Motor Trucking Company

San Rafael:
   San Rafael had no truck terminals, but was served by most of the trucking companies that served San Francisco

San Francisco:
   Associated Freight Company
   Consolidated Motor Express
   Consolidated Motor Transport
   Merchants Express
   Pacific Motor Trucking Company
   Willig Freight Lines
   Pacific Intermountain Express Company

Oakland:
   Pacific Intermountain Express Company
   Pacific Motor Trucking Company
   Watson Transport

Palo Alto:
   Oregon-Nevada-California Fast Freight Company
   Southern California (SoCal) Freight Lines
   Pacific Motor Trucking Company

Salt Lake City:
   Belnap Freight Lines
   Browning Freight Lines
   Carbon Motorways, Inc.
   Interstate Motor Lines
   Magna Garfield Truck Lines
   Milne Truck Lines
   Salt Lake-Kanab Freight, Inc.
   Utah Arizona Freight Lines
   Wasatch Fast Freight
   Pacific Intermountain Express Company

This listing prepared by McGraw-Hill staff. For details on carriers and their terminals see latest issue of *National Highway and Airway Carriers and Routes,* published by National Highway Carriers Directory, Inc., 925 West Jackson Boulevard, Chicago, Illinois.

**EXHIBIT 7** Selected Comparisons

| | Average Cost of Land (per acre) | Present Tax Rates (percent of land costs per year) | Relative Cost of Construction* |
|---|---|---|---|
| Los Angeles | $70,000 | 02% | 100 |
| Salt Lake City | 20,000 | 03 | 85 |
| Portland | 25,000 | 03 | 90 |
| Marin County (including San Rafael and other areas north of San Francisco) | 30,000 | 01 | 110 |
| East Bay (including Berkeley and Oakland) | 60,000 | 02 | 110 |
| San Mateo and Santa Clara counties, including Stanford Industrial Park† | 40,000 | 02 | 110 |

* Based on Los Angeles as the standard.

† Land in the Stanford Industrial Park could not be purchased but could be leased on a 99 year lease for a total lease cost of $40,000 per acre.

**EXHIBIT 8** Labor Wage Rates for Alternative Locations

| Location | Clerical* | Ware-housemen* |
|---|---|---|
| Salt Lake City | $56.00 | $ 82.80 |
| Portland | 77.00 | 94.40 |
| Los Angeles | 88.00 | 94.80 |
| San Francisco, (Greater Bay Area, includes San Rafael, Palo Alto, and Berkeley) | 89.00 | 106.40 |

McGraw-Hill employed in excess of 20 clerical people and about 12 warehouse workers in the San Francisco office.

* All rates are per week.

Source: Office of the U.S. Bureau of Labor Statistics, San Francisco.

**Question**

1. *Where should McGraw-Hill locate the new West Coast Facility? Why?*

## 6. GILES LABORATORIES

Paul McNaughton, director of distribution services for Giles Laboratories, a wholly-owned subsidiary of the world-wide Thurber Pharmaceutical group of companies, was under strong pressure from top management to cut down on the number of field warehouses that the company maintained throughout the United States. Top management believed that the company could manage on fewer distribution facilities without hurting sales operations. They were concerned about Giles having more warehouses than the parent company even though the parent carried more products at a higher unit-sales volume. They were also disturbed by the fact that Giles's main competitor had fewer warehouses giving the same national market coverage.

At the beginning of 1982, Giles Laboratories had 37 field warehouses of which 33 were public. Four warehouses were owned by the parent company, but contractual arrangements with them paralleled those with public

---

This case was made possible by the cooperation of a business firm which remains anonymous; however, the essential quantitative relationships remain the same. It was written by Albert M. Ladores under the direction of Bernard J. LaLonde of the faculty of Marketing and Logistics, The Ohio State University, as the basis for classroom discussion rather than to illustrate good or bad administrative management.

Revised 1981 by Douglas M. Lambert.

warehouses. In addition to the 37 field warehouses, Giles owned four plant warehouses which served the field warehouses and customers located in areas where these plant warehouses were situated.

By March 1982, McNaughton was faced with the decision to phase out the public warehouse at Columbus, Ohio, and serve the customers in the area directly from the main plant warehouse at Indianapolis, Indiana. This meant extending the service area of the Indianapolis facility beyond Dayton, Ohio. The contract with the Columbus warehouse was up for renewal in mid-April.

## THURBER PHARMACEUTICALS

Giles was part of a group of companies that was controlled by Thurber Pharmaceuticals. Although the parent corporation specialized in a variety of prescription drugs, the products of the subsidiary companies ranged from food items to consumer sundries.

Each subsidiary operated as an autonomous corporate entity with its own set of executive officers and was relatively free to set its own policies in marketing, research, and manufacturing activities. Control by Thurber took the form of broad intercorporate policies and close monitoring of significant investment decisions. With the exception of the products of one of the subsidiary companies, an international division supervised the manufacture and marketing of all products in foreign countries.

## DATA ON GILES LABORATORIES

### Product Lines

Giles and its major competitor enjoyed about 75 percent of the nutrient and dietary-food market, with Giles' share of the total market approximately 40 percent.

The company manufactured 35 variations of one basic mixture of raw materials and product differences were determined primarily by the addition of additives and calorie content. Finished products came in both a liquid concentrate and a powder packed in cans of various sizes. The Indianapolis plant, which was the largest and oldest of the company's four plants, produced 25 of the product line. Each of the other plants manufactured as many of 12 of the products.

### Sales Operations

Approximately 90 percent of the company's sales were derived from consumer outlets, the most significant of which were department stores, wholesale drug houses, drug chains, and supermarket chains. The balance was sold directly to hospitals for patient use while recovering from illness. Demand for the company's products was not subject to seasonal variations.

Salesmen concentrated their selling efforts on medical practitioners, hospitals, and the major retail outlets. Their function was to promote product awareness by improving the sales distribution of the product lines and to assist retailers in merchandising. With minor exceptions, they did not act as order takers.

**Distribution Organization**

Mr. McNaughton, as the company's director of distribution services, reported to the vice president of operations and shared the same rank and status as the comptroller and the director of manufacturing. He had four major areas: distribution, operations planning, purchasing, and product planning, each headed by a manager reporting directly to him. The director had control over most of the logistics functions with the exception of plant shipping and receiving, which were the responsibility of each plant manager, who reported to the director of manufacturing.

All of the distribution personnel were located at the company's central headquarters in Indianapolis. The coordination of receiving and shipping activities at the plants was accomplished by the plant manager.

**Distribution Policies and Practices**

Giles Laboratories followed their traditional practice of distributing all products through public warehouses, which was in direct contrast to the parent company's system of ownership and control of warehouses. However, efforts had been initiated by Giles to determine the utility of continuing with its system of dealing exclusively with public warehouses.

Giles currently owned four plant warehouses, dealt with four warehouses owned by the parent company, and, as mentioned, maintained 33 public warehouses specializing in grocery products and servicing other companies in the grocery trade. In no instance did Giles totally occupy the leased space of a specific field warehouse and individual field-warehouse allocation ranged from 3,000 to 100,000 hundredweight. Except in the case of the four warehouses that were owned by the parent company, Giles did not share a public warehouse with any of its sister companies.

Most public warehouse rates were negotiated at least every 12 months and rarely did a contract extend beyond two years. In all cases, a one-shot billing system applied whereby a composite rate for storage and handling was set for every 100 pounds delivered to a warehouse. Accessorial charges for such things as damaged products and telephone expenses were billed separately. The public warehouses would assess a small penalty charge for every hundredweight in excess of the stipulated storage level per month. In plant warehouses, the rule of thumb was to assess storage and handling cost at 1.5 percent of the manufactured cost of average monthly inventory which was valued at the full cost of production. Full cost included allocations of overhead and other fixed charges in addition to the direct variable cost of manufacturing which at Giles represented 70 percent of the full cost.

Top management felt that it was necessary to maintain a 100 percent service level with respect to hospitals. This was a reflection of their belief that hospitals in general had poor inventory management. In actual experience, the achieved customer-service level was about 98 percent. Consumer products enjoyed a 96 percent service level which compared favorably to the target of 98 percent. The distribution manager said that studies were being conducted to determine the optimum service levels considering distribution costs (including the inventory holding costs) and actual service requirements. He explained that prior to 1982, the company did not have a documented inventory carrying cost figure and although a number had been used in plant expansion proposals he was not sure how it had been arrived at. ("Perhaps it was the cost of money at that time applied to the full manufactured cost of the inventory.") However, a study has just been completed by a distribution analyst who had recently completed his M.B.A. degree in the evenings while working at Giles. (A memo outlining the results of this study is given as Exhibit 1.)

**EXHIBIT 1**

GILES LABORATORIES
INTEROFFICE MEMO

Date: January 30, 1982

To: Mr. Paul McNaughton, Director of Distribution Services

From: Wesley Scott, Distribution Analyst

Subject: A Documented Inventory Carrying Cost

The following four basic cost categories must be considered when calculating inventory carrying costs: (1) capital costs, (2) inventory service costs, (3) storage space costs, and (4) inventory risk costs.

The money invested in inventory has a very real cost attached to it. Holding inventory ties up money that could be used for other types of investments. This reasoning holds for internally generated funds as well as those obtained from outside sources. Consequently, the company's opportunity cost of capital should be used in order to accurately reflect the true cost involved.

In order to establish the opportunity cost of capital (the minimum acceptable rate of return on new investments) for Giles Laboratories, an interview was scheduled with the comptroller, Mr. John Munroe. The corporate cost of capital was the charge paid to the parent company, Thurber Pharmaceuticals, and it approximated the prime rate. Currently, this rate is 16 percent before taxes. However, due to capital rationing the current hurdle rate on new investments was 40 percent before taxes (20 percent after taxes). The company conducted a postaudit of most projects in order to substantiate the rate of return. This was required by corporate policy and in the majority of cases the desired return was achieved. Occasionally a 50 percent hurdle rate was employed to ensure that the required corporate rate of 40 percent would be realized.

**EXHIBIT 1** *(continued)*

Although it would seem that the 40 percent hurdle rate also should be applied to inventory since in times of capital rationing an investment in inventory precludes other investments at the 40 percent rate, Thurber Pharmaceuticals only required a 16 percent return on inventory investments. Consequently, 16 percent before taxes is used as the cost of money in this study. However, this is an issue that must be resolved at the top management level.

Generally speaking, there are two types of capital cost that should be considered: (1) inventory investment, and (2) investment in assets.

The opportunity cost of capital should only be applied to the out-of-pocket investment in inventory. This is the direct variable expense incurred up to the point at which the inventory is stored. In other words, it was necessary to obtain the average variable cost of products, FOB the distribution center. The individual cost components and the final carrying cost percentages are shown below.

Inventory Carrying Costs

| Cost Component | Percentage of Inventory Value |
|---|---|
| Capital costs | 16.000 |
| Inventory service costs | |
|    Taxes | 1.366 |
|    Insurance | 0.256 |
| Warehousing costs | |
|    Public warehouses (recurring storage only) | 2.939 |
|    Plant warehouses | nil |
| Inventory risk costs | |
|    Obsolescence | 0.695 |
|    Shrinkage | 0.875 |
|    Damage | 0.430 |
|    Relocation (transshipment) costs | n.a.* |
| Total | 22.561† |

\* Not available.
† Inventory is valued at variable cost FOB the distribution center.

Approximately 90 percent of the shipments to field warehouses were consigned to rail carriers with the remainder shipped by motor carriers. By policy, the optimum weight per shipment was 100,000 pounds. No minimum was defined, but it was common practice to avoid shipping less than 40,000 pounds unless it was extremely necessary. Plant shipments weighing 80,000 pounds and above were shipped by rail and those below 80,000 pounds were shipped by motor carrier. All plant shipments represented a consolidation of most products and case packs were closely standardized by size and weight for ease of handling. The rail service from each plant warehouse to public-warehouse destination constituted direct point-to-point hauling and warehouses serving the company had railroad service.

The distribution analyst commented that rail service involved long transit time (a ratio of 8-to-1 time periods versus motor carrier) and a heavy damage toll. However, rail rates for shipments weighing 80,000 pounds and above were in total more favorable than public-trucking rates, and the savings more than offset the higher carrying costs and damaged burden connected with predominant rail service. Around 80 percent of the plant shipments were in the 100,000-pound category.

Shipments from field warehouses to customers were carried by motor carriers at prevailing cartage rates or negotiated-contract carrier rates with the exception of a few of the field warehouses which operated their own truck fleets. These customer deliveries were FOB destination. No orders below 15 cases were accepted, and truckload orders (40,000 pounds) were referred to the head office by field warehouse personnel for possible direct service from the nearest plant warehouse. Unit-sales prices for the company's products were quoted at two price break ranges: at 15 to 49 cases, and at 50 cases and over.

Shipping schedules from plant warehouses to field warehouses were initiated from central headquarters. Supervisors who reported to the distribution manager analyzed warehouse delivery receipts, in-transit stock levels, and bill-of-lading figures that indicated deliveries to customers, in order to initiate corrective action if required. Stocking requirements were determined according to normal usage levels (versus inventory levels) for each field warehouse and were reviewed periodically and changed if required.

Although most communication with public warehouses was by telephone or mail the company had begun to install direct data-transmission connections with warehouses located at major market areas.

The lead time for processing and consolidating orders was targeted at three days for consumer outlets, but an actual average of five days was experienced. For hospital deliveries, the usual experience was two days compared to a target of one day.

**Columbus Warehouse Facts and Data**

The Columbus field warehouse was serving the metropolitan area and neighboring municipalities within a 30-mile radius. The outlying areas were being serviced by wholesalers that drew stock from Columbus. The distribution manager estimated that shipments to Columbus would average in excess of 15,000 cases per month for the next year.[1] One third of the present shipments came from the Michigan plant and were consolidated at 80,000 pounds for shipment at a freight rate of 40 cents per cubic hundredweight. The rest of the shipments were sent out of the Indianapolis plant warehouse in truckload quantities (40,000 pounds) by public motor carrier

---

[1] A case of Giles products averaged 20 pounds and had a manufactured value of about $5. The selling price to wholesalers and chain accounts was $6.90 per case.

at a rate of 36 cents per cubic hundredweight. In this case, motor-carrier rates were more favorable than railroad rates. Shipments from Michigan represented products that were not manufactured in Indianapolis.

Mr. McNaughton was reviewing a plan that would phase out the Columbus public warehouse. Michigan shipments would be diverted to Indianapolis and could be expected to be transported at the same freight rate. Indianapolis would then serve Columbus customers directly by motor carrier under new rates and according to the following schedule:

| Percent of Total Weight | Cost per Hundredweight |
|---|---|
| 40 | $0.38 |
| 35 | 0.80 (LTL) |
| 25 | 1.05 (LTL) |

Under the new plan another trucking firm would be contracted to serve Columbus customers. This company was willing to offer better rates for LTL shipments and cartage (intracity) rates. Moreover, it had suggested allocating 100 sq. ft. of space at its Columbus terminal for transit storage at no additional expense to Giles Laboratories. The lower cartage rates would result in a small saving to the company.

If the contract with the Columbus warehouse was renegotiated, it was estimated that the throughput rate could be fixed at 50 cents per hundred pounds plus a storage penalty when inventory turns fell below 12 times per annum.

While reviewing the proposal, Mr. McNaughton became aware that total system inventory would decrease in value by $37,500 per annum with the elimination of the Columbus facility. Although this figure represented an intuitive estimate, he felt somewhat encouraged by the fact that it was the consensus among members of his department who had been dealing with distribution since the company started operations.

The phase-out possibility was not without its uncertainties. It was not clear whether additional personnel would be needed to process the orders emanating from the Columbus area. It appeared that the existing system was operating at capacity. There was also the matter of convincing the sales department to lengthen the service time from one day to two or three days. The main competitor was serving Columbus out of Pittsburgh which is 190 miles northeast of Columbus while the distance from Indianapolis is 171 miles. Mr. McNaughton has been advised by the president to attempt to phase out at least five field facilities within the year and the Columbus warehouse was the first to come up for lease renewal.

## 7. WESTERN PLYWOOD CORPORATION: LOGISTICS PROBLEMS OF A SOFTWOOD PLYWOOD PRODUCER

Alan Mann was on the phone.

Yes, Charlie, I realize that this is the third late car to your warehouse this month. I know how you rely on on-time deliveries, but you must appreciate our problems, too! Can't you see far enough ahead to consolidate into larger lots some of the items you order? These "grocery store" orders with a lift of this and a lift of that really kill the plywood plants—they just can't afford to produce in those small quantities and in order to get a longer production run, they accumulate several small orders before running a particular item.

Yes, I know that you only sell in small quantities, but you do have a warehouse that's designed to permit you to order in larger lots. If you could only lump some of your small weekly orders into a couple of larger biweekly orders it would sure help in expediting your stock. I can't see anyone else in the organization that is in a better position to forecast demand than you, the warehouse manager, Charlie.

Okay, I'll check with the mill to see when they expect to get that car out and I'll let you know by teletype. So long, Charlie, and good luck with the customer!

Mann hung up the phone and leaned back in his chair, rested his feet on the bottom drawer of his desk, and cast his mind back over the conversation. This was the second call he had received that morning from an irate branch-warehouse manager complaining about late shipments. Why was coordination of production and orders becoming such a problem and what could be done about it? Mann, manager of Western Plywood Corporation's production coordination and acquisition department, was responsible for solving these problems.

### COMPANY BACKGROUND

Western Plywood started out as a distributor of western softwood plywood. It purchased its sales requirements from western mills and sold these through its own outlets to retail dealers and to wholesale customers. As an aggressive sales force increased sales, new market areas were entered and new distribution outlets established.

With the rapid expansion in plywood consumption back in the early 1930s, it became apparent to the company that in order to assure itself future supplies of plywood of good quality at reasonable prices the company would have to get into the plywood manufacturing business. At first, only part interests were bought in independent producers, in order to minimize expense and to gain some measure of control.

As the demand for plywood continued to increase, these joint ventures were purchased outright and other producing plants acquired. The late 1950s witnessed a tremendous increase in plant acquisitions, and by 1959, the company was producing 33 percent of its total softwood sales volume.

---

This case is produced with the permission of its author Stuart U. Rich, Professor of Marketing and Director, Forest Industries Management Center, College of Business Administration, University of Oregon, Eugene, Oregon.

The proportion of softwood plywood sales produced in company-owned facilities had increased to 55 percent by 1962 and had remained at this level since then. As the number of company-owned plywood plants increased, manufacturing divisions were formed to consolidate control and coordinate the production patterns of the mills in a particular region.

In order to minimize investment in plant capacity and to maximize control over its sources of supply, Western Plywood contracted with independent mills to supply a stated quantity of plywood each year. These "contract partners" produced a fairly constant 20 percent of total sales. The contract partners were chosen because their production capabilities complemented the product mix of company mills and rounded out the assured supply of products required by Western Plywood's large distribution system. Firm contracts were drawn up in which Western Plywood guaranteed to sell set amounts of various plywood items which these mills were particularly suited to produce.

Western Plywood had established a policy of only committing itself to produce 75 percent of its total sales. The remaining 25 percent was purchased from outside producers, who also acted as a cushion in case of a slump in demand.

By 1965, Western Plywood had become one of the largest plywood sales organizations in the United States and among the largest softwood plywood producers. It had over 120 warehouses and sales offices throughout the United States, and 13 softwood plywood plants, located principally in Oregon, with some plants in Washington and northern California.

Sales had grown to an all-time high of 1.4 billion square feet ($3/8''$ basis) of softwood plywood in 1964 and the 1965 sales figure was expected to be over 20 percent higher. All softwood plywood sales were handled by the company-owned distribution centers and all company production was sold through these channels. Each distribution center had a warehouse and a sales office, and served as a plywood wholesaler, selling to retail lumber yards and large industrial customers. In addition to the warehouse and sales-office staff, each distribution center employed a number of outside salesmen who visited the various accounts and concentrated on obtaining orders for direct mill shipments.[1] Two thirds of the total plywood sales of the Western Plywood sales organization were from warehouse inventory, the average sales invoice being $150. The remaining one third of sales were direct mill shipments. No orders were accepted from outside buyers except through the company-owned distribution system.

As the company had grown, it had developed a very loose sales organization. Each distribution center manager was "Mr. Western Plywood" in his sales area and enjoyed a high degree of autonomy. He was responsible for a minimum return on investment, and his salary increased with the center's sales. Providing the warehouse exceeded a minimum turnover standard

---

[1] Direct mill shipments are shipments made directly to the customer from a particular mill. These shipments are generally in carload quantities.

established by the company, the manager was pretty well left alone to run his operation as he saw fit.

The turnover standards for the warehouses were set on a dollar standard basis. For fir plywood the average dollar value of inventory at cost price was to be turned over at least once every 1.8 months. The standard for the total warehouse stock was set at 2.5 months. Other products carried, besides fir plywood, included hardwood paneling, doors, mouldings, particle board, and hardboard.

Because of the company's long-standing concern with sales, customer service was a very important part of Western Plywood's policy. It liked to think that it enjoyed the highest degree of customer satisfaction in the industry, and placed great importance on maintaining this position. This meant delivering what the customer wanted, when and where he wanted it.

## PLYWOOD PRODUCTION COORDINATION AND ACQUISITION

Alan Mann was manager of the Plywood production coordination and acquisition department (PCA) of Western Plywood Corporation. PCA was responsible for coordinating the production and shipment of all orders coming in from the company distribution outlets. The orders were given to the company and contract mills in such a manner as to optimize the production capabilities and raw material utilization for each order. Orders that could not be conveniently produced in company or contract mills were purchased from any one of up to 100 independent plywood producers.

As the size of the company grew, so did the importance of PCA. In 1958, PCA had been established close to the center of the plywood production area in Oregon. It had originally been set up for the sole purpose of acting as a focal point for the collection of orders and the redistribution of these to the various mills; but since the company policy was to purchase a certain portion of its requirements from outside mills, this outside buying also became a function of PCA.

As contract partners were acquired, the PCA manager seemed to be the natural person to take charge of further acquisition of partners. From his vantage point he could see what the order mix requirements were and what type of mill was needed to complement the present capabilities of company mills and existing contract partners to produce this mix.

The PCA manager was also appointed softwood plywood merchandising manager, whose duty it was to see that all softwood plywood was produced and delivered on time, in the quantities desired by the sales organization, and at a profit to the company. These responsibilities strengthened the position of the manager and greatly expanded his authority. Between 1958 and 1965, sales of Western Plywood had nearly doubled and yet in this period the internal workings of PCA had changed very little. PCA and its activities had increased in physical size, but the ordering system and handling of the orders remained very much the same.

Under the present scheme, the distribution centers mailed carload quantity orders into PCA. Each center kept track of its floor inventory on a Kardex file.[2] When a particular item reached a level at which experience had shown that replenishment was required, the clerk in charge of the file would make a note to reorder. The reorder quantity was also determined by experience. If the item moved quickly, a large quantity would be ordered. When the quantity of items requiring re-ordering reached the point of a carload lot, then the distribution center would mail in an order to PCA containing a list of the items and the quantities of each required.

In addition to replenishment requirements for the warehouse, special orders for customers were also included when these amounted to less than a carload lot and the order was received far enough ahead of the required delivery date to be ordered from a mill rather than being filled out of warehouse inventory. This system had worked fairly well when the firm was relatively small and shipment dates for each carload could be negotiated with whichever mill would accept the full carload. The time necessary to produce these orders depended heavily on the order backlog of the particular mill and the stock it had in inventory at the time. Generally one to four weeks was necessary, but occasionally, for orders containing a variety of items in small quantities, shipment took even longer and stock-outs occurred at the distribution center before replenishment stock arrived, resulting in bad feeling all around.

As the volume of orders grew, this system became increasingly more complicated and less workable. The phone calls received by Mann were the result of the system's bogging down. The plywood plants had grown in size and were being pushed for production. They could not readily produce small quantities for an order since short runs, necessitating frequent change-overs and resulting in lost time, drastically reduced production, and increased unit costs. In order to avoid these high costs, the mills would put off production of an item until they had accumulated enough back orders for that item to warrant a reasonable press run.[3] This practice resulted in increased order-in-process inventories at the mills as shipment of an order would be held up waiting for the production of one or two items necessary to complete the order. The delay in shipment would result in stock-outs at the warehouse because of late delivery. In an effort to placate the customer, substitutions would be made, usually with a higher grade stock at the same price.

Recent advances in operations research in the plywood industry were working to force a change in the order procedure. Linear programming was being used in several company mills to evaluate all the factors affecting plywood production. By evaluating all these factors, the mill production control staff could arrive at an optimum order mix that was uniquely suited

---

[2] Kardex file: Under this system a file card is kept on each item carried by the warehouse. As stock is received it is added to the stock already in inventory as recorded on the card. As stock is sold, each sale is deducted from the total on the card.

[3] Press run: Each time a different item is produced the press and associated equipment have to be set up to handle it. The length of time between changes is a press run.

to the raw material and profitability factors affecting the production of that particular mill. By consulting this mix, a mill manager could determine exactly how profitable the production of any particular item would be in relation to producing any other. This knowledge permitted PCA to place orders with the mill best suited to handle them, but was resulting in more and more dividing up of orders into segments best suited to two or several mills. With the volume of orders handled, it was becoming more complicated for PCA to decide whether to schedule all of an order at one mill that was not best suited for certain items on the order, or to split up the order and incur charges for transporting the various parts of the order to a central point for consolidation and shipping.

As softwood plywood merchandising manager, Mann was responsible for trying to overcome these increasingly complex problems of order coordination, production control, and traffic management in order to avoid lost sales of his product. In view of the unique situation that Western Plywood was in—selling all its production only through its own outlets—Mann felt that an order control system could be initiated that would exercise much tighter control over the procedure than was possible with most of Western Plywood's competitors, who, in addition to serving their captive outlets, also accepted orders from independent wholesale distributors.

## ALTERNATIVES TO THE PRESENT ORDERING SYSTEM

Alan Mann had given considerable thought to possible alternatives to the present ordering system and had come up with only two choices. Basically, these were *fixed-order interval* and *fixed re-order point* systems. Whichever system was ultimately initiated, it would involve a lot of cooperation on the part of both production and sales.

### Fixed-Order Interval

In order to overcome the problem of fluctuations in the frequencies of orders from the warehouses, and to force the warehouses to consolidate their orders, one of the alternatives considered by Mann was the institution of a fixed order interval. By forcing the warehouses to order only at fixed intervals, the flow of orders could be regulated, thus resulting in consolidated, larger orders. PCA would be able to break these larger orders down into convenient carload lots in such a way that each carload could be assigned to the mill that was most suited to producing that particular mix. By assigning larger orders for each item, longer press runs would result and the shipment of orders would be expedited. This, in turn, would result in lower in-process inventories at the mills.

Mann had not decided on an optimum order interval. The controller of the largest manufacturing division, who was very much in favor of the institution of this method, suggested a four-week interval. His plan was to divide the sales outlets up into eight divisions of roughly equal sales volume, then have two of these divisions place their orders each week. From the manufacturer's point of view this system would be ideal, but Mann felt that the warehouse sales managers would oppose such a plan because it would require projections of demand for the forthcoming month and limit their feeling of autonomy.

In order to make the fixed-order interval into a workable system, extensive work would have to be done with each sales outlet to develop a forecasting system designed for each warehouse. Past sales data, present market expectations, and seasonal swings in demand would have to be considered, and a minimum safety stock allowance established. Mr. Mann felt that the objections to the system could be overcome by developing a mathematical formula which would allow the warehouse to order its requirements four weeks in advance. This formula would have to allow for the judgment of the warehouse manager in regard to special factors that should be considered.

Mann felt that one of the first objections to this method would be that there would be a tendency for the warehouses to initiate an inventory build-up to avoid stock-outs toward the end of the four-week period. He felt that if PCA broke the orders down correctly and scheduled their shipment from the mills at regular, controlled intervals throughout the four-week period, then a steady stream of stock could be supplied to the warehouses. Any need to increase inventories above the present levels would thus be avoided.

**Fixed Reorder Point**

Institution of a fixed reorder point system was the only other method Alan Mann could see to be practical. This method would consist of establishing a minimum economical order quantity. This quantity would vary for different items, and perhaps could be varied for different warehouses, depending on the volume of a particular item that a particular warehouse sold. In many ways the fixed reorder point system would be similar to the present system, but the minimum order quantities would be established in consultation with the company and contract mills. Operations research would have to be carried out to determine what a realistic minimum order lot size would be. Above this minimum it would be desirable to determine an economical order size. The cost of ordering would be constant, whatever size the order, but the size of the order would affect the frequency of orders and the average size of inventory.

In order to assure that the fixed reorder point system would operate smoothly, a perpetual inventory system would be required. The simplest system would be the method presently used — a Kardex file. It would also be necessary to determine a minimum re-order point. This point would be determined by the time required between the placing of an order with PCA and the receipt of the ordered stock at the warehouse, the volume of sales normally expected during that time, and a safety stock to allow for unusual fluctuations in demand. The reorder point would vary with different items and the safety stock would have to be determined from studies of past sales patterns for each item and the probable stock-out frequency that would be acceptable for a minimum level of customer service. It would be necessary for the clerk who updated the Kardex file to be constantly checking the balance of each item and comparing this to the minimum reorder point.

Mann felt that one of the advantages of this system would be that demand forecasting would not be so critical. Reordering would respond automatically to changes in demand. If actual demand consistently differed from the demand used to calculate the reorder point, then an adjustment would be necessary.

## THE PROBLEM OF RETAINING FLEXIBILITY

Mr. Mann knew that of the two methods, the sales managers would prefer the latter. He knew that sales forecasting was a tricky and time-consuming task, and the less the managers became involved in it the happier they would be. It was difficult enough to get them to submit an annual sales forecast. He could imagine what the reaction to a monthly forecast would be! Mr. Mann felt that the system using a fixed reorder point would require a minimum of forecasting, could be developed with more automatic controls for fluctuations in demand, and would allow the manager to feel that he was operating in a more flexible environment.

Mr. Mann felt that flexibility could be built into either system. In the fixed order interval system, assuming that a four-week interval was used, allowances could be made for the warehouses to add orders if required. The order files that PCA maintained for each mill could be purposely left with openings for additional items. The open order files would be maintained until just prior to production. If a sales office received a special order and wished to add this to a previous car load, PCA would schedule this for shipment as soon as possible, either from a company mill or from an outside producer if necessary. There were a number of items carried by the warehouses that would not require ordering at the designated time. These consisted of items, not produced by company mills, that could be readily purchased outside for immediate shipment, or items that were ordered sporadically, but moved in large volumes when they did sell. Non-waterproof interior sheathing was not produced at any company mill; hence, carloads could be ordered as required. Plyform, used for concrete forms, moved in large volumes, but sales were sporadic. There were a number of outside mills that specialized in Plyform, so orders could be placed with them at any time. Mann felt that the flexibility of the sales offices would not be affected as much as the managers might fear.

Either system would involve trade-offs.[4] The fixed interval system would require more forecasting on the part of the sales outlets, while the fixed reorder point might not entirely overcome the fluctuations in the frequency of orders, but it would cause the least upset to the distribution centers and permit the manufacturers, particularly company mills who did not have a steady market for specific items of production, to produce in a more efficient manner than at present.

---

[4] Trade-offs: Simply, cost increases in one sector are traded for cost decreases in another when a net gain results to the firm for instituting the change.

## TRAFFIC CONTROL

A traffic manager, whose office was located in the same building as PCA and who reported to the traffic department at corporate headquarters, worked closely with the manager of PCA. Since he was mainly concerned with rail shipments, his work largely involved establishing new routings as required, checking on existing or alternate rate structures, or following up on damage claim investigations when necessary. A great deal of his time was spent working on the problem of car supply. It was his responsibility to see that Western Plywood mills received their share of cars during periods of car shortage.

Most of what were considered day-to-day traffic management activities, however, were left to PCA. The majority of company orders were shipped by rail, and about twelve railroad companies were used on a regular basis. These same twelve railroads also accounted for a significant proportion of company softwood plywood sales. This plywood was used for car decking and car lining, and included special sizes and lengths for which a premium price was realized. The use of heavy panels, three-fourths inch to one inch in thickness, enabled the company to get rid of some of its lower quality veneer sheets which were used as interior core stock in the thick panels, with the higher quality veneer on the outside faces. The PCA manager kept careful track of these sales and tried to divide up the freight business which he gave to the various railroads in proportion to the volume of plywood purchases which they made from Western Plywood. Mann found himself getting more and more requests from the various company distribution centers to ship by the particular railroads which gave business to these various centers.

Once routings were established from a particular mill to a company sales outlet, these routes tended to become standard. Once the order forms had been made up in the PCA office, if a question arose as to routing a carrier, the clerk simply looked up the routing used on a previous order from the same distribution center to a given mill and used this as a guide. Since the warehouse purchased the order FOB mill, the routing or carrier was not too important to the mill and was rarely questioned.[5] The mills requested changes in routing only if cars from a certain line were not available and cars from an alternate line had to be used. At the other end of the system, complaints from warehouses about routings were not common except in cases of frequent damage by one carrier or unusually long delivery periods. If these cases were serious, either PCA or the traffic manager investigated. If difficulty was experienced in collecting on damage claims, shipments with that carrier were curtailed.

In case of shipments of stock requiring some intermediate processing between the original producer and the warehouse, PCA set up a special routing. Plywood of a certain type would be produced in one plant, then shipped to another plant where it was specially coated, tongue-and-

---

[5] When a purchase is made FOB (free on board) mill, the buyer purchases the goods loaded at the point of origin. The buyer is responsible for paying freight charges.

grooved, or treated in some way before being forwarded to its purchaser. These cars were subject to a special milling-in-transit rate (MIT).[6] Unless application was made to the railway for each of these cars, normal freight rates were applied. This resulted in charges for two short hauls, from the producer to the intermediary and from the intermediary to the final destination. A great deal of skill and experience was required for the firm to benefit fully from the various rates available and routings possible. At PCA, the MIT work was handled by clerks. These people became familiar with the routings established, and there had been few problems in this area until recently.

Cost studies carried out by the operations research people in the company mills had indicated that certain processes could be performed at lesser cost if one plant specialized in these processes. The institution of this policy resulted in an increase in the number of MIT shipments handled. Because of the sudden increase, new routings were not established immediately and full advantage was not taken of the best rates available.

Stop-off cars were another special problem handled by PCA.[7] When a complete order could not be produced at one plant, it was necessary to divide the order between two or three plants. As linear programming of the production schedules for the mills resulted in the development of optimum product mixes, an increasing number of stop-off cars were being required in order that the mills might optimize their production capabilities. Mann felt that whichever order control system were instituted, the stop-off cars could not be eliminated. When only a few such cars were encountered each week, PCA could control the routing and coordinate the loading of these cars. However, as the number of mills increased and consequently the number of stop-offs required increased, PCA lost its close contact with the mills, and keeping track of all the stop-off cars became an almost impossible task. If a partially loaded car arrived at a mill for completion and the stock required had not yet been produced, delays resulted and extra charges for holding the car were incurred.

Recently Western Plywood had purchased several resin tanker trucks designed expressly for hauling plywood when they were not hauling resin. The trucks were designed like a regular flat deck semi-trailer, with the resin tanks slung below the deck. The idea behind the purchase of these trucks had been that they could haul resin out to the various mills for use in waterproof glues, then transport plywood back to a central point, thus avoiding the need for a stop-off car. Up to the present time, however, full use had not been made of the capabilities of this innovation for there was no one in PCA who always knew when a truck would be at any one mill.

---

[6] Under a milling-in-transit rate, the through freight rate for whichever plant is furthest from the destination is charged plus a small charge for stop-over. It is used frequently in the forest products industry.

[7] A stop-off car is a boxcar that is partially loaded at one mill, then shipped to another mill for completion. The through freight rate from the mill furthest from the car's destination is charged, plus a small stop-off charge.

## INVENTORY CONTROL

Alan Mann felt that the present dollar standard turnover system had a serious weakness. Because Western Plywood purchased roughly 50 percent of its sales from noncompany owned mills, when the market prices of plywood rose, so did the cost price to the warehouses. These periods of high prices occurred during periods of peak demand. Due to the nature of the dollar value standard, as prices rose the pressure was on the warehouse to reduce its total inventory in order to maintain a constant dollar value. Mann felt that this standard resulted in an undue amount of confusion since the intuitive reaction to a rise in demand is to increase inventory to take advantage of the rise. Mann was aware that the other plywood wholesalers used a volume turnover standard rather than a dollar value standard. For profitable distributors the standards generally accepted were a sales volume (in $3/8''$ square feet equivalent) turnover of 45 days for fir plywood and a turnover of total warehouse volume every 90 days. This system had the advantage of being independent of price changes.

## WHAT RECOMMENDATIONS?

As manager of PCA and plywood merchandising manager, Alan Mann was faced with making constructive suggestions to his superiors on the problems that he saw arising in his sphere of responsibility. His major problem at present was which order system would be the most suitable. He knew that the firm was considering acquiring a computer. Would this have any effect on which system would be preferable?

How about inventory control—was the present system adequate? Were his ideas on the shortcomings of the dollar value standard really valid, and if so, what would be an alternative?

Was PCA really equipped to handle the variety of traffic problems that it presently dealt with? Could some of the stop-off coordination be placed with the mills, or should all traffic problems be handled by the traffic department?

Mann knew that as soon as he suggested any changes he would be asked to write up a report giving his preliminary recommendations, and as he mulled over the problem, he was trying to formulate that report.

## 8. RIVERVIEW DISTRIBUTING COMPANY, INCORPORATED (B)

In January 1978 David Rose, president and owner of Riverview Distributing Company, began to wonder if sales to certain types of retail outlets were more profitable to his firm than others. As a rack jobber of housewares, batteries, light bulbs, and home entertainment equipment based in Lansing, Michigan, Rose felt opportunities for continued sales growth in his current lines were very limited. He was planning a sales meeting in late January and was not sure which type of account offered the most profit potential for new business development or which of the company's existing accounts deserved the most attention from the sales force.

## BACKGROUND

Rose opened Riverview Distributing Company in 1965 when he realized that his earning potential as a ski instructor was low. The first product lines handled by his firm were light bulbs and electrical hardware equipment. His initial success appeared to be due to development of specialized display equipment which presented to customers many different bulbs and hardware items in one place. Previously, most retailers had purchased these products from cash-and-carry wholesalers, but Rose was successful in placing his display units in variety, drug, and grocery stores on a consignment basis. Although Riverview's prices were slightly higher than other wholesalers, the display units and the service provided by his firm were attractive to many retailers. The stores which used Riverview's display units greatly increased their sales in those products.

As the firm continued to grow, several new product lines were added. Because of its success with light bulbs, the firm added a photolamp product line which ultimately led to the inclusion of batteries for the photography market. The tremendous growth of transistorized radios and tape recorders further increased demand for batteries. The firm also expanded into the household products field. Kitchen utensils and supplies provided a steady, but not spectacular, source of income.

During 1973 and 1974 Rose decided his firm could distribute radios and tape recorders since it was currently selling batteries for those products. These two products were successful and other home entertainment equipment was added. By 1977 Riverview's product lines in the home entertainment field included radios, tape recorders, tape players, and stereo components such as speakers, amplifiers, and tuners. The addition of these "brown goods" brought about some changes in the firm's operations. Although each sale had a higher per-unit value than other products, customer financing was required for a longer period of time. Since this merchandise represented the company's fastest growing product line, accounts receivable tripled between 1974 and 1976.

The gross profit margins for products distributed by Rose varied consid-

---

Source: Donald J. Bowersox, M. Bixby Cooper, Douglas M. Lambert, and Donald A. Taylor, *Management in Marketing Channels* (New York: McGraw-Hill Book Company, 1980), pp. 326–32. Copyright © 1980 by McGraw-Hill, Inc. Used with the permission of McGraw-Hill Book Company.

erably. Although houseware items carried only a 16 percent margin, batteries and related items contributed a much higher margin of about 40 percent. Rose believed that with increases in sales his profit margins would also increase because his firm would qualify for volume discounts from suppliers. An examination of Riverview's income statements, shown in Exhibit 1, shows that gross margins in 1974, 1975, and 1976 were 27 percent, 27 percent, and 19 percent. Exhibit 2 contains balance sheets for the three most recent years.

**EXHIBIT 1**

RIVERVIEW DISTRIBUTING COMPANY, INC.
Statement of Income and Retained Earnings
For the Years Ending December 31, 1975–1977

|  | 1975 | 1976 | 1977 |
|---|---|---|---|
| Sales | $195,702 | $298,683 | $385,070 |
| Cost of sales: |  |  |  |
| Opening inventory | 48,713 | 76,186 | 125,600 |
| Purchases | 170,500 | 266,159 | 352,400 |
|  | 219,213 | 342,345 | 478,000 |
| Closing inventory | 76,186 | 125,600 | 165,537 |
| Total sales | 143,027 | 216,745 | 312,463 |
| Gross margin | 52,675 | 81,938 | 72,607 |
| Operating expenses: |  |  |  |
| Advertising, travel, and promotion | 2,375 | 4,450 | 6,158 |
| Truck expenses | 4,121 | 4,587 | 7,201 |
| Bad and doubtful accounts | 249 | 272 | 1,892 |
| Bank charges and interest | 1,035 | 1,418 | 2,406 |
| Depreciation | 4,083 | 4,097 | 5,510 |
| Insurance | 105 | 770 | 966 |
| Legal and audit | 620 | 791 | 2,702 |
| Light, heat, and power | 923 | 1,069 | 1,254 |
| Municipal taxes | 1,300 | 1,628 | 2,102 |
| Office supplies | 1,221 | 2,292 | 4,156 |
| Repairs | 551 | 895 | 406 |
| Salaries—Executive | 10,500 | 10,500 | 10,500 |
| —Other | 12,940 | 22,840 | 35,496 |
| Telephone | 639 | 672 | 1,058 |
|  | 40,662 | 56,281 | 81,807 |
|  | 12,013 | 25,657 | (9,200) |
| Cash discounts earned | 1,098 | 3,215 | 3,686 |
| Net income before taxes | 13,101 | 28,872 | (5,514) |
| Income taxes | 3,275 | 7,218 | — |
| Net income | 9,826 | 21,654 | (5,514) |
| Retained earnings, beginning of year | 28,850 | 38,676 | 60,330 |
| Retained earnings, end of year | $ 38,678 | $ 60,330 | $ 54,816 |

## SALES REPRESENTATIVES AND CUSTOMERS

Riverview operated in three sales territories, each covered by a single sales representative. The three territories were designated North, West, and

**EXHIBIT 2**

RIVERVIEW DISTRIBUTING COMPANY, INC.
Comparative Balance Sheets
For the Years Ending December 31, 1975–1977

|  | 1975 | 1976 | 1977 |
|---|---|---|---|
| *Assets* | | | |
| **Current assets:** | | | |
| Cash | $ 300 | $ 4,300 | $ 200 |
| Accounts receivable, less allowance for doubtful accounts | 16,876 | 33,706 | 58,405 |
| Inventory, valued at the lower of cost or market | 76,186 | 125,600 | 165,537 |
| Total current assets | 93,362 | 163,606 | 224,142 |
| **Fixed assets:** | | | |
| Display racks, building improvements, automotive and office equipment, at cost less accumulated depreciation | 28,506 | 28,553 | 34,330 |
| Total assets | $121,868 | $192,159 | $258,472 |
| *Liabilities* | | | |
| **Current liabilities:** | | | |
| Bank loans, secured | $ 5,000 | $ 10,000 | $ 15,000 |
| Accounts payable and accrued | 31,224 | 70,608 | 139,052 |
| Income and other taxes payable | 1,252 | 2,607 | 990 |
| Total current liabilities | 37,476 | 83,215 | 155,042 |
| **Long-term liabilities:** | | | |
| Loans due to directors | 44,716 | 47,614 | 47,614 |
| **Shareholders' equity:** | | | |
| Capital stock: Authorized—3,600 7% redeemable preference shares, par value $10 each; 4,000 common shares without par value; issued—1,000 common shares | 1,000 | 1,000 | 1,000 |
| Retained earnings | 38,676 | 60,330 | 54,816 |
| Total liabilities | $121,868 | $192,159 | $258,472 |

South, with the major cities in each being Lansing, Grand Rapids, and Jackson. Each sales representative had full responsibility for maintaining established accounts and opening new accounts in these territories. The sales representatives carried merchandise in a truck, made sales calls, and replenished stock on the spot. They were also responsible for inventory control in the trucks and for accounts receivable. Sales representatives replenished their inventories from Riverview's office-warehouse location in Lansing. They were compensated on a straight commission basis, 7.5 percent of their net collected sales.

Sales representatives were given complete discretion to call on accounts they felt would be potential customers. Informal meetings were held periodically in which Rose discussed the company's plans and encouraged the sales force to discuss problems they had with products and/or customers. Through such meetings and with many sales contests, he emphasized the importance of increased sales volume.

An analysis of the company's active customers by type and by route is shown in Exhibit 3. Exhibit 4 shows the sales breakdown by type of account.

## COMPANY GROWTH

Rose and his wife initially assumed all management responsibility for the firm. Mrs. Rose handled office duties until the job became so complex that another person was hired to handle all record keeping. The firm had moved

**EXHIBIT 3** Analysis of Active Accounts by Type and by Route

| Type of Account | South Route | West Route | North Route (includes Lansing) | All Accounts |
|---|---|---|---|---|
| Variety stores | 62 accounts<br>21 with sales of over $1,000<br>1 with sales of less than $100 | 41 accounts<br>10 with sales of over $1,000<br>4 with sales of less than $100 | 93 accounts<br>26 with sales of over $1,000<br>6 with sales of less than $100 | 195 accounts<br>57 with sales of over $1,000<br>11 with sales of less than $100 |
| Grocery stores | 18<br>6 over $1,000 | 12 | 20 | 50<br>6 over $1,000 |
| Drugstores | 10<br>8 over $1,000 | 7<br>2 over $1,000 | 8<br>1 over $1,000 | 25<br>9 over $1,000 |
| Hardware stores | 4 | 1 | 13<br>1 over $1,000 | 18<br>1 over $1,000 |
| Discount stores | 1 | 8<br>5 over $1,000 | 10<br>7 over $1,000 | 19<br>12 over $1,000 |
| Camera shops | 9<br>7 over $1,000* | 4<br>2 over $1,000 | 6<br>5 over $1,000† | 19<br>14 over $1,000 |
| Department stores | 5 | 5<br>1 over $1,000 | 4 | 14 |
| Radio/TV/appliance | 10<br>5 over $1,000 | 14<br>3 over $1,000 | 19<br>6 over $1,000 | 43<br>14 over $1,000 |
| Gas stations/auto supply | 9<br>2 over $1,000 | 10<br>4 over $1,000 | 34<br>4 over $1,000 | 53<br>10 over $1,000 |
| Miscellaneous | 14<br>3 over $1,000<br>4 less than $100 | 16<br>5 over $1,000<br>5 less than $100 | 35<br>1 over $1,000<br>8 less than $100 | 65<br>9 over $1,000<br>17 less than $100 |
| Total accounts | 142 | 118 | 242 | 502 |
| Sales | $99,058 | $107,852 | $110,110 | $317,220 |
| Sales/account | $699 | $914 | $455 | $632 |
| New accounts (1978) | 35 | 1 | 72 | 108 |
| Sales (1978) | $113,825 | $148,155 | $138,160 | $400,140 |
| Sales/account (1978) | $725 | $1,245 | $440 | $656 |

* Includes company's second largest account—$5,575.
† Includes company's largest account—$5,653.

**EXHIBIT 4** Analysis of Accounts by Type of Account for the Year Ended December 30, 1976

|  | All Routes | | |
|---|---|---|---|
| Type of Account | Number of Accounts | Cumulative Sales | Percent of Total Sales |
| Variety stores | 6 | $ 22,040 | 5.0 |
|  | 13 | 39,206 | 10.0 |
|  | 24 | 58,068 | 15.0 |
|  | 38 | 77,416 | 20.0 |
|  | 54 | 96,578 | 25.0 |
|  | 77 | 116,217 | 30.0 |
|  | 107 | 134,870 | 35.0 |
|  | 163 | 154,144 | 40.0 |
|  | 195 | 158,050 | 41.0 |
| Grocery stores | 25 | 19,379 | 5.03 |
|  | 50 | 22,520 | 5.8 |
| Drugstores | 18 | 19,465 | 5.05 |
|  | 25 | 20,584 | 5.34 |
| Hardware stores | 18 | 8,100 | 2.10 |
| Discount stores | 8 | 20,320 | 5.27 |
|  | 19 | 31,033 | 8.04 |
| Camera shops | 4 | 18,235 | 4.90 |
|  | 19 | 38,464 | 9.98 |
| Department stores | 14 | 9,403 | 2.44 |
| Radio/TV/appliance | 8 | 19,198 | 4.98 |
|  | 43 | 36,560 | 9.49 |
| Gas stations/auto supply | 13 | 19,798 | 5.14 |
|  | 53 | 32,009 | 8.31 |
| Miscellaneous | 7 | 18,842 | 5.01 |
|  | 65 | 28,347 | 7.36 |

from the basement of the Rose home to an office-warehouse location in Lansing in 1970. As product lines and sales volume grew, Rose hired a warehouse manager who also did some selling in the company's showroom attached to the office.

## OBJECTIVES

Rose wanted to increase sales because he wanted the firm to make more money. Until 1965 he had been interested primarily in skiing and enjoying life. But, after Rose married, his father-in-law began to pressure him to build a career. The other members of Mrs. Rose's family had successful professional careers, and Rose was determined to show his father-in-law that he could be just as successful. His objective for Riverview Distributing Company was to achieve a sales volume of $1 million by 1980.

**EXHIBIT 5**  Assorted Data by Product Line

| Product | Lead Time | Terms | Riverview's Margin | Estimated Average Accounts Receivable | Approximate Average Inventory |
|---|---|---|---|---|---|
| Batteries | 7–10 days | Net 60 days | 25% | $ 4,000 | $ 20,000 |
| Electrical hardware | 2–4 weeks | Net 30 days | 28 | 500 | 4,500 |
| Kitchen utensils | 5 days | 2% 10/net 30 | 16 | 500 | 15,000 |
| Light bulbs | 4–10 days | Net 90 days | 18 | 500 | 9,500 |
| Photo bulbs | 4 days | Net 90 days | 21 | 2,500 | 8,000 |
| Stereo components | Up to 6 months | Net 60 days | 22 | 50,000 | 124,000 |
| Transistors | Majority 7–10 days | Net 60 days | 18 | 25,000 | 35,000 |
| Tapes | 10 days | Net 30 days | 10.5 | 18,000 | 34,000 |

**EXHIBIT 6**  Sales by Account and Product Category

*Percentage Sales by Product categories*

| Type of Account | Batteries | Electrical Hardware | Kitchen Utensils | Light Bulbs | Photo Bulbs | Stereo Components | Transistors | Tapes | Total |
|---|---|---|---|---|---|---|---|---|---|
| Variety stores | 20 | 10 | 5 | 5 | 10 | 10 | 20 | 20 | 100 |
| Grocery stores | 35 | 5 | 35 | 15 | 10 | — | — | — | 100 |
| Drugstores | 10 | 5 | 5 | 5 | 5 | 10 | 35 | 25 | 100 |
| Discount stores | 10 | — | 15 | 15 | 30 | — | — | 30 | 100 |
| Camera shops | 45 | — | — | — | 55 | — | — | — | 100 |
| Department stores | 10 | 5 | 5 | 10 | 15 | 10 | 15 | 30 | 100 |
| Radio/TV/appliance | 5 | — | — | — | — | 35 | 40 | 20 | 100 |
| Gas station/auto supply | — | — | — | — | — | 20 | 30 | 50 | 100 |
| Miscellaneous* | 5 | — | 5 | 5 | 5 | 25 | 30 | 25 | 100 |

* Includes hardware stores

## THE CURRENT SITUATION

During 1978 accounts receivable had risen to almost $100,000 and although the year-end inventory count had not yet been made, the book value of inventories was in excess of $250,000. Rose compiled the data in Exhibits 5 and 6 and felt that he was now ready to begin his analysis.

### Questions

1. Which segments of Riverview's business are contributing the most toward corporate profitability?
2. What additional information would be useful for the analysis referred to in question 1?
3. What action should Rose take in order to achieve profitable future growth?

## 9. FERLE FOODS, INC.

It was 7:35 A.M. on November 16, 1981, and the American Airlines 727 had just taken off from New York's LaGuardia airport enroute to Chicago. In seat 17C was Charlie Sims, AT&T Long Lines' national account manager on the XYZ Industries account. Charlie found it difficult to contain his excitement. He had been directing a major order-processing system study at Ferle Foods, Inc., a subsidiary of XYZ Industries, for the past four months and the study was now drawing to a close. Bill Ward, the account executive on the Ferle Foods account had called Charlie on Friday with the news that the automated order-processing system that the Bell System account team was planning to recommend to management would result in an annual savings of more than $69,000 over the company's existing system. In addition, the proposed system would lead to inventory reductions, transportation consolidations, warehousing-cost savings and customer service improvements. However, dollar amounts still had to be attached to these benefits and Charlie wanted to assist in these calculations. He hoped that the savings would be large, in excess of $1 million, so that management at XYZ Industries would want similar studies in its other divisions.

### XYZ INDUSTRIES

Ferle Foods was a wholly-owned subsidiary of XYZ Industries, a Fortune 500 corporation which manufactured and sold a variety of package goods products ranging from food items to consumer sundries. Products of the subsidiary companies included food, beverages, toys, clothing, and specialty chemicals.

Each subsidiary operated as a separate corporate entity with its own management team which set policies. However, corporate approval was required for investment decisions involving more than $25,000. Corporate headquarters was placing the subsidiaries under increasing pressure to improve cash flow and return on investment.

Ferle Foods was the most recent acquisition made by XYZ Industries and although its sales volume was larger than most of the company's other subsidiaries, its net profit and return on investment were the lowest.

### BACKGROUND: FERLE FOODS, INC.

Ferle Foods manufactured and distributed nationally a full line of canned vegetables, fruits, condiments, and specialty items. The company had manufacturing facilities in Indianapolis, Indiana; Anaheim, California; and Griffin, Georgia. Each plant manufactured some of the product line but no plant manufactured the complete line.

---

This case was adapted by Douglas M. Lambert from material provided by the American Telephone and Telegraph Company, Business Marketing, Market Management Division. It was prepared to illustrate the type of situation the Bell System account executive is likely to face and any similarity with actual individuals or companies is purely coincidental. Used with permission of American Telephone and Telegraph Company.

The Indianapolis plant, which was the largest and oldest, produced 75 percent of the products in the product line, the Anaheim plant produced 50 percent of the product line and the Griffin plant manufactured about 35 percent of the products.

Ferle Foods had a sales volume of $200 million and a profit of $2 million in its most recent year of operations. The company's financial data are summarized in a strategic-profit-model format in Exhibit 1.

**EXHIBIT 1**  The Strategic Profit Model (financial data in $ million)

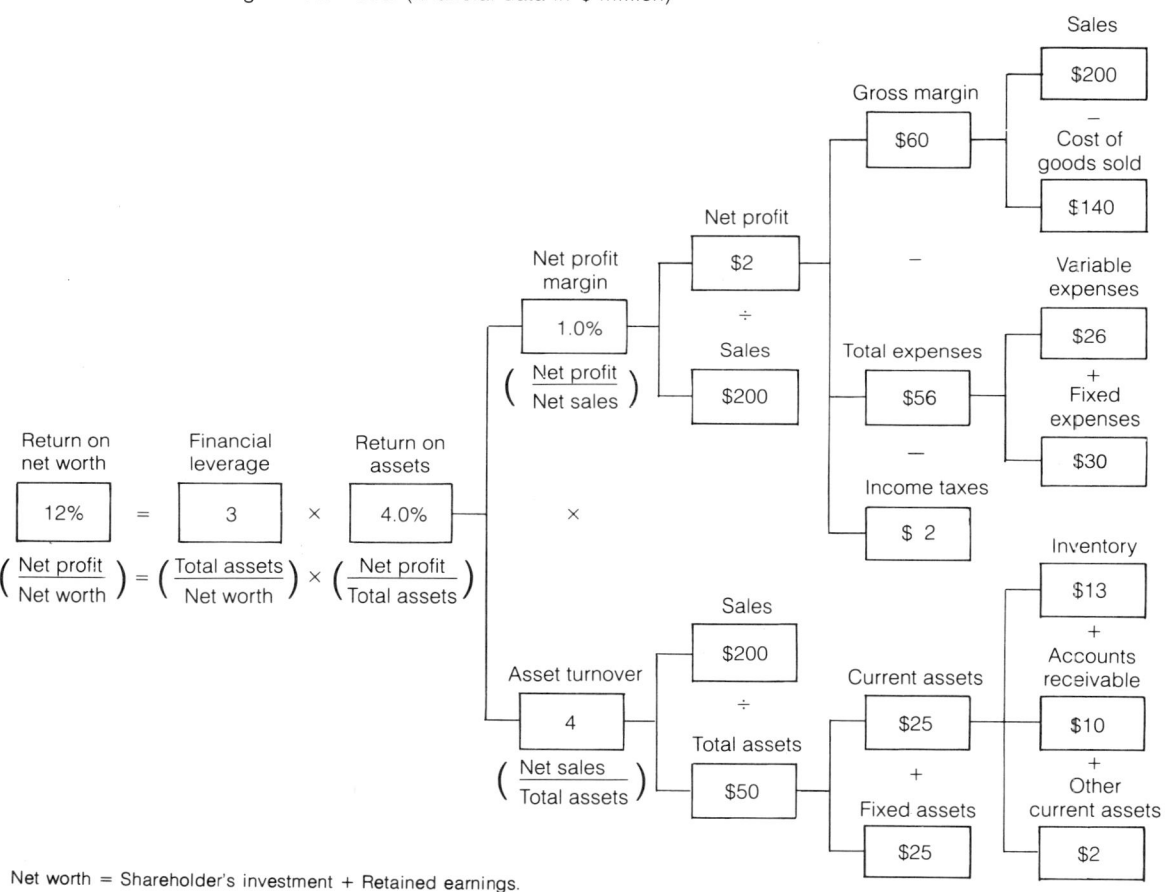

Return on net worth: 12%

$$\left(\frac{\text{Net profit}}{\text{Net worth}}\right) = \left(\frac{\text{Total assets}}{\text{Net worth}}\right) \times \left(\frac{\text{Net profit}}{\text{Total assets}}\right)$$

Financial leverage: 3

Return on assets: 4.0%

Net profit margin: 1.0% $\left(\frac{\text{Net profit}}{\text{Net sales}}\right)$

Net profit: $2 ÷ Sales: $200

Total expenses: $56

Gross margin: $60

Sales: $200 − Cost of goods sold: $140

Variable expenses: $26 + Fixed expenses: $30

Income taxes: $2

Asset turnover: 4 $\left(\frac{\text{Net sales}}{\text{Total assets}}\right)$

Sales: $200 ÷ Total assets: $50

Current assets: $25 + Fixed assets: $25

Inventory: $13 + Accounts receivable: $10 + Other current assets: $2

Net worth = Shareholder's investment + Retained earnings.

Approximately 90 percent of the company's sales were derived from wholesale grocers and supermarket chains. The balance was sold to institutional accounts. The company marketed its products under the Ferle brand name and also private labeled for major supermarket chains. About 10 percent of the annual sales volume was private label business but this was increasing.

The company handled between 2,000 and 2,200 orders per month. Ferle brand items, which comprised about 98 percent of the orders were sold to more than 1,000 customers. However, fewer than 50 of these customers represented 75 percent of the business. There were only 40 private label customers, primarily the large supermarket chains, which accounted for almost one half of the Ferle brand business and all of the private label sales.

Price was the single most important method of competing for private label sales followed by customer service. The private label market was characterized by a large number of small competitors. No advertising was undertaken and minimal sales effort was required. Generally customers wanted fast deliveries of these items because stock-outs on the private label resulted in lost retail sales. When stock-outs occurred on a national brand item, another national brand was usually given the shelf space.

National brands, on the other hand, were a different story. A few large companies dominated this market. Large sales forces and considerable mass advertising and promotional expenditures were the major means of meeting competition. Price was a much less important factor with nationally advertised brands. Ferle Foods employed a sales force of 83 for its nationally advertised Ferle brand products and 1 for the private label business.

Orders for Ferle brand products were filled from inventory and private label products were manufactured upon receipt of orders.

### Physical Distribution at Ferle Foods

The company's manager of physical distribution reported to the vice president of operations and shared the same rank and status as the manufacturing manager (see Exhibit 2). His areas of responsibilities included warehousing, distribution system design, inventory management, and transportation. All of the distribution personnel were located at the company's central headquarters in Chicago.

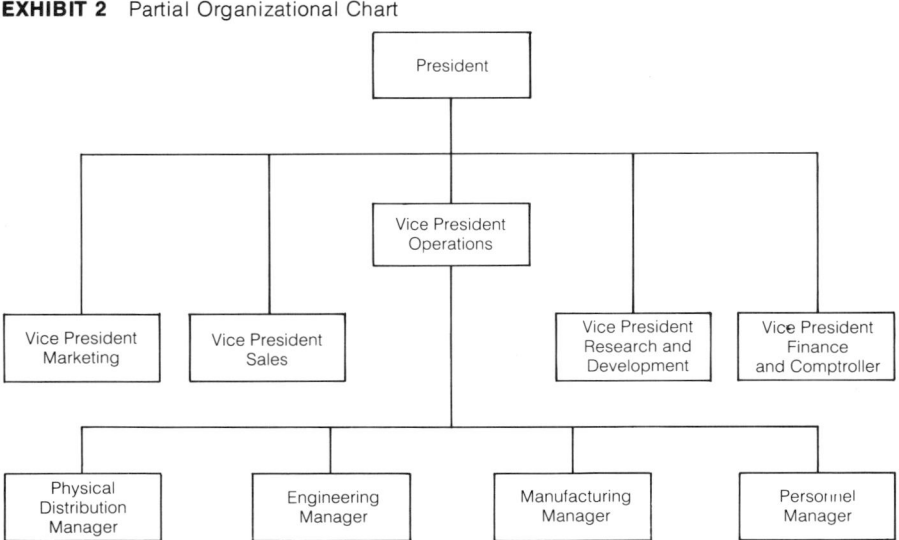

**EXHIBIT 2** Partial Organizational Chart

Ferle currently owned three plant warehouses which in addition to serving as distribution centers (DCs) in their respective market areas restocked field distribution centers. Ferle also used four warehouses owned by the company, and maintained three public warehouses specializing in grocery products and servicing other companies in the grocery trade. Customer service levels were set at 95 percent in stock availability but the company was currently achieving about 90 percent. The locations of the various facilities are summarized in Exhibit 3.

**EXHIBIT 3** Ferle Food Locations

Headquarters:
   Chicago, Illinois
Plants/distribution centers
   Indianapolis, Indiana
   Anaheim, California
   Griffin, Georgia
Distribution centers:
   Elizabeth, New Jersey
   Richmond, Virginia*
   Kansas City, Missouri*
   Dallas, Texas
   Denver, Colorado
   San Francisco, California
   Portland, Oregon*
Sales offices:
   Atlanta, Georgia
   Hartford, Connecticut
   Detroit, Michigan
   Chicago, Illinois
   Dallas, Texas
   Denver, Colorado
   San Francisco, California
   Long Beach, California
   Kansas City, Kansas
   Baltimore, Maryland
   Seattle, Washington
   New York, New York

* Public warehouses.

Rail carriers handled approximately 60 percent of the shipments to field warehouses and motor carriers handled the rest. All customer shipments were FOB destination. Truckload and carload orders received direct service from the nearest plant warehouse.

Restocking of field warehouses was based on normal usage levels for each location, which were reviewed periodically and changed if required. This enabled the company to react more quickly to changes in the market place than would be possible if an order were placed for the economic order quantity whenever the inventory on hand and on order reached a predetermined minimum level (fixed order point, fixed order quantity model). With the current system, orders were placed for inventory transfer when the normal usage indicated that the remaining cycle-inventory was equal to the expected demand during the replenishment cycle.

Communication with field warehouses was by telephone, teletype, or mail. Effective communications had been a problem with some of the public warehouses because their teletype terminals were not compatible with Ferle's system. In each case the warehouse operator solved the problem by adding an additional terminal.

**Order Processing**

All incoming orders were received by the sales/service department in Chicago from the field sales offices. The customer service representatives within sales/service answered customer inquiries about order status and solved customer problems related to damaged merchandise, incorrect shipments, or billing errors. Normally, the sales/service department received 100 orders per day but this volume could reach 350 per day in peak periods. An organization chart for this department is presented in Exhibit 4.

**EXHIBIT 4** Organization Chart—Sales/Service Department

```
                    Sales/Service
                      Manager        $1,800/monthly salary
                         |
        ┌────────────────┼────────────────┐
    Customer                          Customer
    Service                           Service        $1,100-1,400/monthly salary
    Representative                    Representative
                                         |
                                      Senior
                                      Order         $900-1,200/monthly salary
                                      Clerk
                                         |
                                                              $800-1,000/monthly salary
   ┌────────┬────────┬────────┬────────┬────────┬────────┐
  Order    Order    Order    Order    Order    Order    Order
  Writing  Writing  Writing  Writing  Writing  Writing  Writing
  Clerk    Clerk    Clerk    Clerk    Clerk    Clerk    Clerk
```

Approximate salary figures for different positions are also indicated on this chart.

The procedure for processing orders was as follows:

1. The sales people either met with or called their customers on a weekly or biweekly basis to get the orders. Then they called or mailed the orders to the district sales office. When orders were called in, a written order was still sent to the sales office. Orders were transmitted to the company's headquarters via teletype.

2. At the headquarters office, orders were given to clerical personnel who manually looked up all necessary information in the customer's file. The order-writing clerks filled out standard order forms, transcribing directly onto these forms the customers' requested shipping or delivery dates as the dates which would be met by the company.

3. Customer orders were then directed to the sales/service manager who compiled a log of the number of orders for branded products by truck/rail route and total tonnage by route, distribution center, and total company. The log also indicated the volume of private label ordered by plant location. Often, manufacturing managers from plants would call the sales/service manager to get a general idea of the volume of private label product being ordered on a given day. Likewise, distribution center managers called to get the jump on equipment needs, that is, the number of trucks/railcars required. Sometimes transportation needed to urge sales to sell more volume on a particular route to avoid shipping at less-than-truckload (LTL) rates. After entering the order in the log the orders were directed to the appropriate customer service representatives.

4. The customer service representatives noted the orders in their records and passed them back to the order-writing clerks. The customer service representatives spent about one third of their time actually processing orders and two thirds tracing late orders and resolving customer problems.

5. When the order-writing clerks received the orders, they keypunched them on an IBM key-to-diskette unit.

6. The orders were then batch loaded into the computer which generated the final order documents.

7. The computer generated picking documents and shipping information which were sent by teletype to each distribution center. Sales orders for private label products were transmitted to the appropriate plant location for production scheduling.

8. The teletypewriters at the field warehouse locations received and printed four-part picking and shipping documents. The orders were filled and a copy of the packing list was mailed to the Chicago headquarters for keypunching. From the packing list, customer invoices were prepared. Bills of lading were prepared at the field warehouses.

A simplified flowchart of the order-processing system as described above is presented in Exhibit 5. The order cycle from the customer's point of view is summarized in Exhibit 6. The customer's order-cycle time, that is, the time from order placement to receipt of merchandise ranged from 6 to 22 days and averaged 14 days. However, when order levels increased greatly prior to price changes, the average order-cycle time increased. Sometimes individual orders were lost in high-volume periods and did not reappear until after the customer complained about not receiving the shipment. Some of the confusion was due to the high turnover of order clerks and some was caused by the order clerks processing the less complicated orders first.

When the district sales offices were busy, orders often would not be transmitted to the Chicago headquarters until written confirmation had

**EXHIBIT 5** Flowchart of Existing Order-Processing System for Ferle Brand Sales

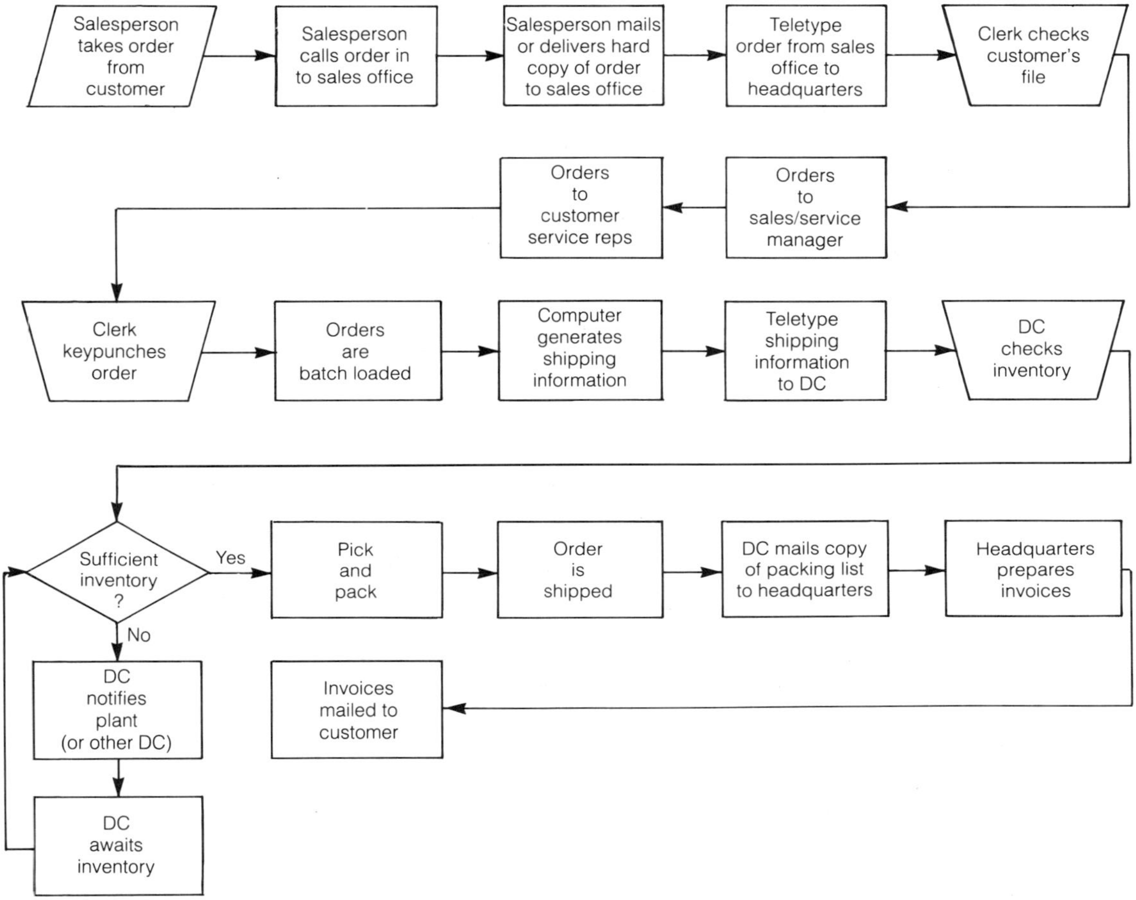

been received from the salesperson. The cutoff for the batch processing of orders was 3 P.M. each day and sometimes salespeople would attempt to override the system by telephoning late orders directly to the order-writing clerks for keypunching.

Salespeople did not receive notifications that an order had been entered into the system. Nor did they receive notice of product substitutions, shorts, order cancellations, or shipping delays. The changes in individual product pricing were updated monthly, and were sent out to the field on Thursdays. Promotions were updated on Thursday also, but did not take effect until the following Monday. Consequently, customers could be quoted incorrect prices or promotion information and were unaware of the discrepancy in prices until their copy of the invoice was received. However, the problem that annoyed the customers most was inconsistent delivery times. Two practices that contributed to this problem were (1) when a stock-out oc-

**EXHIBIT 6**  Customer's Order Cycle

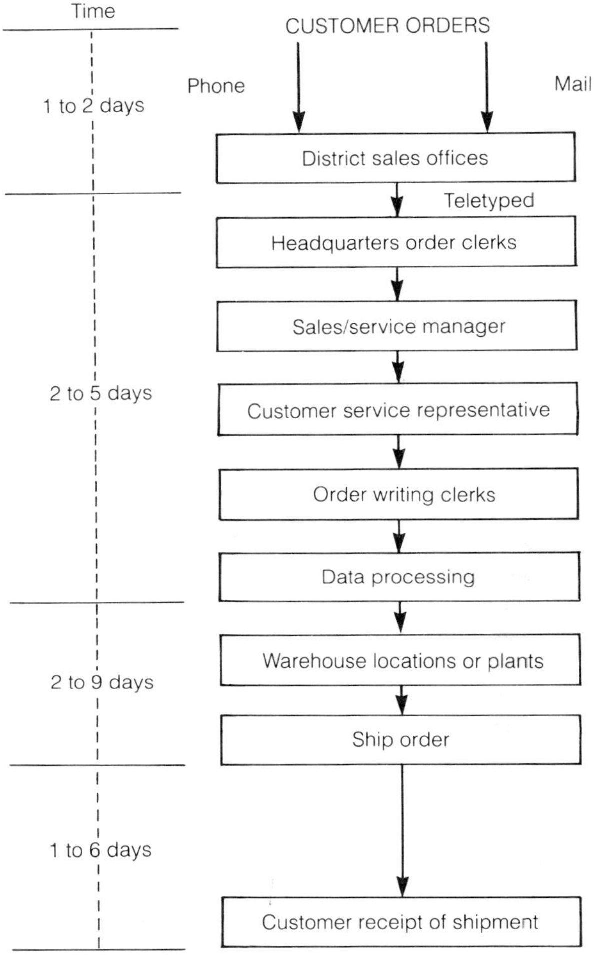

| Time | |
|---|---|
| 1 to 2 days | District sales offices ← Phone/Mail CUSTOMER ORDERS |
| 2 to 5 days | Headquarters order clerks (Teletyped) → Sales/service manager → Customer service representative → Order writing clerks → Data processing |
| 2 to 9 days | Warehouse locations or plants → Ship order |
| 1 to 6 days | Customer receipt of shipment |

Notes:
1. The order cycle ranged from 6 to 23 days.
2. The average order cycle was 14 days.

curred, orders were held at the distribution center or plant until the product was available; (2) the shipping department often held up shipments until a full truckload could be arranged.

Stock-outs at the distribution centers occurred in part because there was no system for tracking customer usage by product and, therefore, no established basic-inventory levels by product. When an order reached the distribution center, it was discovered that there was not enough inventory to fill the order. As a result, the order was held until the needed inventory arrived. There was no notification to either the customer or the salesperson that the order was waiting to be filled. When inventory was low, the order was shipped short or held for 100 percent fill, which could delay the order for as long as a week.

Complaint calls usually were made to the district sales offices, but some of the calls were routed to the customer service representatives and also to field warehouses. When customers were really annoyed, they would call the vice president of sales.

## THE BELL SYSTEM STUDY

During the flight Charlie Sims reviewed the major findings of the Bell System account team. A good deal of information had been collected and he wanted to be prepared for his meeting in Chicago.

*Excerpt from an interview with a Distribution-Center Manager:*

There are really many reasons for delivery dates being missed, and not all originate here in the distribution center. Sometimes we do let orders sit because we don't have sufficient inventory to fill them. When that happens, we end up having to fill an inordinate amount of orders in a short period of time, because we are filling the back orders as well as those new orders that are coming in.

*Excerpt from an interview with a Salesperson:*

The price figures we get are mailed from headquarters. They arrive on a weekly basis, usually on Tuesday, but they're effective beginning Monday. Unfortunately, we're frequently not in the office on Tuesday because we're out calling on customers. So we don't see the new price figures until at least Tuesday night and that means that what we've quoted for two days has been wrong. Therefore orders have to wait to be corrected by the shipping department or the clerks or someone. At any rate, the corrections really are out of our hands. But we hear about errors every day from the customers. They receive their bills and call to tell us we misquoted the price. Another recent problem involves consumer complaints. We hear about these problems through our customers. Ferle prints an address on packages so that consumers can write to the company with complaints.

*Excerpt from an interview with an Accounts-Receivable Clerk:*

Each of the five accounts-receivable clerks is assigned to a certain region, and we are in charge of making sure that the accounts are paid on time and that they are invoiced correctly. The job includes cutting the original invoice.

We have to correct any errors that are noted on remittances and then check every other item on the order individually to make sure that it's correct. Essentially, it means redoing the entire order. Let me tell you, it's a time-consuming job. Do you realize each price and promotion has to be looked up by hand? Sometimes, because the invoices are weeks old, we have to go back and check through three or four weeks of summaries to find the applicable unit price or promotion. It can be a slow process. The customers sure let us know when we've made a mistake, too. That is, the customers complain when the price on the invoice is higher than the one originally quoted. I have no idea how many errors are made in the customers' favor; I receive very few inquiries when the price on the invoice is less than the one originally quoted. An invoice can be processed in ten minutes if everything is straightforward. However, if there are questions and errors, it could take as long as two hours. On the average, it takes 45 minutes to reconcile an invoice. About 2 percent of all invoices require reconciliation.

*Excerpt from an interview with the Vice President of Sales:*

Consumer inquiries and complaints are handled by our customer service group at headquarters. We receive about 100 letters a month. Consumers today are getting very demanding. They want to know as much about the product as we do! We try to satisfy their curiosity but it's difficult. Often, we don't even have the information they want.

**Safety Stock Calculations**

The safety stock required to achieve the desired 95 percent product availability at the Elizabeth, New Jersey, distribution center was calculated by statistically sampling product movement for a representative 25-day period (10 percent sample):

| Day | Cases Demanded | Day | Cases Demanded |
|-----|----------------|-----|----------------|
| 1   | 900            | 14  | 1,200          |
| 2   | 1,100          | 15  | 1,300          |
| 3   | 1,300          | 16  | 1,100          |
| 4   | 1,000          | 17  | 1,000          |
| 5   | 700            | 18  | 1,100          |
| 6   | 1,200          | 19  | 1,200          |
| 7   | 1,100          | 20  | 900            |
| 8   | 1,400          | 21  | 800            |
| 9   | 1,000          | 22  | 600            |
| 10  | 900            | 23  | 700            |
| 11  | 900            | 24  | 800            |
| 12  | 800            | 25  | 1,000          |
| 13  | 1,000          |     |                |

Since the safety-stock calculation must consider lead time variability as well, a sample of 16 replenishment cycles for the Elizabeth facility was taken:

| Lead Time in Days | Frequency |
|-------------------|-----------|
| 3                 | 1         |
| 4                 | 2         |
| 5                 | 3         |
| 6                 | 4         |
| 7                 | 3         |
| 8                 | 2         |
| 9                 | 1         |

Because field and plant warehouses were restocked on the basis of the central inventory file at headquarters, shipments were not authorized until two or three days after the inventory level at the warehouse indicated a need for more stock. It was believed that a distribution information system could reduce the average replenishment cycle to the Elizabeth distribution center from six days to five days and would eliminate two days of variability in the replenishment cycle.

The safety stock levels for the company's other six distribution centers before and after the proposed system change are summarized below:

| Distribution Center | Current Safety Stock | Estimated Safety Stock |
|---|---|---|
| Richmond, Virginia | 1,875 | 1,150 |
| Kansas City, Missouri | 1,640 | 1,250 |
| Dallas, Texas | 2,400 | 1,350 |
| Denver, Colorado | 1,800 | 1,000 |
| San Francisco, California | 3,850 | 1,700 |
| Portland, Oregon | 2,400 | 1,400 |
| Totals | 13,965 | 7,850 |

In addition, it was estimated that inventories at plant warehouse locations could be reduced by approximately 10,000 cases of products.

### Inventory Investment Costs

The average variable cost per case of a product delivered to the distribution center had to be calculated for each location. The company used a full standard costing system and, based on the inventory plan, a weighted-average cost per case was $60.00. The weighted-average variable manufactured cost was 70 percent of the full cost. The transportation cost associated with replenishing the Elizabeth distribution center was approximately $845,000 for the most recent year. Warehouse handling charges for the same period were $125,000. The business year was comprised of 250 days.

Average variable cost figures for the other six field distribution centers used by the company were:

| Distribution Center | Average Variable Cost* |
|---|---|
| Richmond, Virginia | $46 |
| Kansas City, Missouri | 49 |
| Dallas, Texas | 44 |
| Denver, Colorado | 45 |
| San Francisco, California | 44 |
| Portland, Oregon | 45 |

*Per case of product delivered to location.

The inventory carrying cost data collected by the study team are summarized in Exhibit 7.

### Transportation Consolidations

The company's annual transportation bill was almost $16 million. The transportation manager believed that a distribution information system such as the one described by the study team could enable him to consoli-

**EXHIBIT 7** Inventory Carrying Costs—Summary of Data Collection Procedure

| Cost Category | Source | Explanation | Amount (current study) |
|---|---|---|---|
| 1. Cost of money | Comptroller | This represents the cost of having money invested in inventory and the return should be comparable to other investment opportunities | 40 percent pretax |
| 2. Average monthly inventory valued at variable costs delivered to the distribution center | Standard cost data—comptrollers department Freight rates, and product specs are from distribution department reports Average monthly inventory in cases from printout received from sales forecasting | Only wants variable costs since fixed costs go on regardless of the amount of products manufactured and stored | $10,140,000 valued at variable cost delivered to the DC. (Variable manufactured cost equaled 70% of full manufactured cost. Variable cost FOB the DC averaged 78 percent of full manufactured cost.) |
| 3. Taxes | Bill Johnson of the comptroller's department | Personal property taxes paid on inventory | $116,000 |
| 4. Insurance | Bill Johnson | Insurance rate per $100 of inventory (at variable costs) | $5,000 |
| 5. Recurring storage (public warehouse and corporate warehouses) | Frank Gardner, distribution operations analyst | This represents the portion of warehousing costs that are related to the volume of inventory stored | $289,000 annually |
| 6. Variable storage (plant warehouses) | Manager, transportation services | Only those costs that are variable with the amount of inventory stored should be included | nil |
| 7. Obsolescence | From distribution department reports | Cost of holding product in inventory beyond its useful life | 0.8 percent of inventory |
| 8. Shrinkage | Frank Gardner, from distribution department reports | Requires managerial judgment to determine portion attributable to inventory storage | 128,000 |
| 9. Damage | Frank Gardner, from distribution department reports | Requires managerial judgment to determine the portion attributable to inventory storage | |
| 10. Relocation costs | Not available | Only relocation costs incurred to avoid obsolescence should be included | Not available |
| 11. Total carrying costs percentage | Calculate the numbers generated in steps 3, 4, 5, 6, 8, 9, and 10 as a percentage of average inventory and add them to the cost of money (step 1). | | |

date 5 percent of the company's shipments for each day of planning made available by the system. Freight consolidations would lead to a 10 percent reduction in transportation costs for those shipments moving direct to customers from plants.[1] This would result in savings in distribution center handling costs of approximately $25,000 for each 5 percent of the shipments that were consolidated on a plant-to-customer basis.

**Current Communication and Data Equipment**

The cost of the company's current communication and data-processing equipment and the Bell System proposal are summarized in Exhibits 8–14. Other pertinent information is contained in Exhibit 15.

**EXHIBIT 8** Annual Savings in Order-Processing Costs Associated with the Proposed Order-Entry and Order-Processing System

| Activity | Annual Cost Existing System | Annual Cost Proposed System | Savings Associated with Proposed System |
|---|---|---|---|
| Order processing | | | |
| Headquarters | $152,416.50* | $179,455.00† | ($ 30,398.50) |
| Sales office | 149,832.00‡ | 159,480.00§ | (9,648.00) |
| Distribution centers | 246,277.00‖ | 138,250.00# | 108,027.00 |
| Total | $548,525.50 | $477,185.00 | $ 70,340.50 |

\* From Exhibit 9.
† From Exhibit 10.
‡ From Exhibit 11.
§ From Exhibit 12.
‖ From Exhibit 13.
# From Exhibit 14.

---

[1] For example, if $1 million worth of shipments were consolidated it would result in a $100,000 savings.

**EXHIBIT 9** Headquarters Costs—Existing System

| Activity | Annual Cost | |
|---|---:|---:|
| Order receipt (equipment costs) | | |
| $103 × 12 months | | $ 1,236.00 |
| Order-processing costs | | |
| Six order clerks | | |
| 100 orders at 30 minutes per order | | |
| = 50 hours which is 50 hours ÷ 6 clerks | | |
| = 8.33 hours per clerk per day at $6.40* | | |
| = $53.31 a clerk per day × 250 days | | |
| = $13,328 per year per clerk × 6 clerks | $79,968.00 | |
| Two customer-service reps. | | |
| 2.5 hours × $8.96 per hour† | | |
| = $22.40 × 250 days | | |
| = $5,600 per year × 2 people | 11,200.00 | |
| Sales/service manager at $21,600‡ | | |
| 75% time reviewing/logging orders | | |
| 25% time answering calls | 21,600.00 | |
| Senior order clerk at $14,400§ | | |
| Job undefined (assume back up) | 14,400.00 | 127,168.00 |
| Paper costs | | |
| Order forms | | |
| 100 order forms per day × $0.05 per page × 250 days | $ 1,250.00 | |
| Logs—sales/service manager | | |
| 3 pages per day × $0.05 per page × 250 days | 37.50 | |
| Customer-service reps | | |
| 2 × 9 pages per day × $0.05 per page × 250 days | 225.00 | 1,512.50 |
| Transmission costs | | |
| Distribution centers | | |
| 15 minutes × 10 DCs × $0.05 per minute × 250 days | $18,750.00 | |
| Plants | | |
| 10 minutes × 3 plants × $0.05 per minute × 250 days | 3,750.00 | $ 22,500.00 |
| Total headquarters cost—existing system | | $152,416.50 |

\* 6 order clerks at $12,000 per year = $6.40 per hour (usually only 6 of the 7 order clerk positions were filled).

† 2 customer-service reps. at $16,800 = $8.96 per hour.

‡ 1 sales/service manager at $21,600 = $11.52 per hour.

§ 1 senior clerk at $14,400 = $7.68 per hour.

**EXHIBIT 10**  Headquarters Costs—Proposed System

*Number of Lines Required*

    100 orders per day
×   18%
     18
×   6 minutes per order
    108 minutes per busy hour
×0.06 ccs factor‡
    64.8 ÷ 21.6 effective = 3 lines

| Equipment | | Annual Cost |
|---|---|---|
| 800 service | | |
| Three 800 numbers at $244 (average cost) = | | |
| $732 × 12 months ............................ | | $ 8,784 |
| (6 minutes × 100 orders per day × 250 days − 150,000 | | |
| minutes ÷ 60 = 2,500 − (30 hours × 12 months) = 2,140 | | |
| Cost = 2,140 hours × $18.30 per hour ........................ | | 39,162 |
| CRT terminal/printer | | |
| Three CRTs required: | | |
| $325 × 3 × 12 months ......................... | | 11,700 |
| MUX unit (one required per cluster of four CRT terminals)* | | |
| $170 × 12 months ............................. | | 2,040 |
| MODEM and local private line† | | |
| Two MODEMs and local private line: | | |
| $65 × 2 × 12 months .......................... | | 1,560 |
| Total for headquarters equipment ................................. | | $ 63,246 |
| Labor—Three order clerks at $14,400 ............................. | | 43,200 |
| Supervision—One sales/service manager at $21,600 ............... | | 21,600 |
| Transmission to DCs/plants | | |
| $2,250 × 10% ................................................... | | 225 |
| Total headquarters cost—proposed system .................. | | $128,721 |
| Plus | | |
| Three order clerks not totally eliminated by the new system ....... | $39,984 | |
| Two customer-service representatives .......................... | 11,200 | $ 51,184 |
| Adjusted cost—proposed system ........................... | | $179,455 |

\* MUX—An interface between the CRT terminals and the CPU (central processing unit).

† MODEM—A device which converts a machine readable signal into one that is compatible with the existing telephone network.

‡ Call seconds.

**EXHIBIT 11** Sales Office Costs—Existing System

| Activity | Annual Cost |
|---|---|
| Labor (clerk time) | |
|    One clerk is required for each office at $10,000 each | $120,000 |
| Transmission | |
|    100 orders per day × 1 minute each × $0.50 × 250 days | 12,500 |
| Paper | |
|    100 orders per day × 2 (salespersons' forms plus clerks' forms) × $0.05 per form × 250 days | 2,500 |
| Costs for 12 sales offices | $135,000 |
| Teletype rental ($103 × 12 months × 12) | 14,832 |
|    Total sales office costs | $149,832 |

Note: Salesperson expense for DDD (direct distance dialing) to call in orders was not calculated. Also, it was assumed that there was no change in salesperson call time.

**EXHIBIT 12** Sales Office Costs—Proposed System

| Equipment | Annual Cost |
|---|---|
| Teleprinters | |
|    One teleprinter (order status and price changes) for each sales office $120 per month × 12 months × 12 sales offices | $ 17,280 |
| Dataset and business lines | |
|    $50 per month × 12 months × 12 sales offices | 7,200 |
|    Assume average usage is 10 minutes per day at $0.50 per minute × 250 days × 12 sales offices | 15,000 |
| Labor | |
|    Clerk time per office at $10,000 each | 120,000 |
|    Total sales office costs | $159,480 |

**EXHIBIT 13** Distribution Center—Existing System

| Cost Category | Annual Cost |
|---|---|
| Labor | |
|   Clerks | |
|     One clerk is required at each DC at $15,000 each | $105,000 |
|   Clerks (inventory—assume full time) | |
|     Physical inventory inbound and outbound records, transhipments, etc. Total salary at $15,000 × 7 DCs | 105,000 |
| Paper | |
|    10 order forms per day × $0.05 per form × 250 days × 7 DCs | 875 |
| Mail (assumes mailing two envelopes per day) | |
|    Accounts Receivable mail 2.50 per day × 250 × 7 DCs | 4,375 |
|    Inventory mail 2.50 per day × 250 × 7 DCs | 4,375 |
| Teletype machine | |
|    $103 per month × 12 months × 7 DCs | 8,652 |
| Telephone | |
|   Inter-DC/plant calls (stock-outs, etc.) | |
|    200 calls per month × 15 minutes × $.50 per minutes × 12 months | 18,000 |
|    Total cost for seven distribution centers | $246,277 |

Assumption: Four company-owned DCs and three public warehouses were treated the same under the assumption that all expenses were billed to the manufacturer either under contract or by separate billing.

**EXHIBIT 14** Distribution Center Costs—Proposed System

| Equipment | Annual Cost |
|---|---:|
| Labor | |
|   One clerk per distribution center = 7 × $15,000 ........................ | $105,000 |
| CRT terminal/printers | |
|   One CRT for each DC = $325 per month × 12 months × 7 DCs .......... | 27,300 |
| Dataset and local business line | |
|   One for each DC = $50 per month × 12 months × 7 DCs ............... | 4,200 |
| Transmission costs | |
|   Ten orders per day at 2 minutes total to headquarters at $0.50 per minute × 250 days × 7 DCs ......................................... | 1,750 |
|     Total distribution center costs ..................................... | $138,250 |

**EXHIBIT 15** Other Pertinent Information

1. Order forms were purchased in large quantities because Ferle received the best price this way: 20,000 forms cost $1,000. These are four-part forms and are used by salespeople, sales clerks and order-writing clerks at headquarters. Each one fills out a form for every order. The salesperson fills out the form at the customer's place of business and gives one copy to the customer, keeps one, mails one to the sales office and throws the last copy away. If the order is called in the sales clerk fills out a form during and after the call. One copy is filed, the others thrown away after the order is teletyped to headquarters. The order-writing clerk at headquarters fills out a form, gives a copy to the sales-service manager and throws two copies away.
2. Order-writing clerks spent 30 minutes writing, editing, referencing files, and key punching one order. Order-writing clerks reference customer credit files, price lists, and promotional lists.
3. The sales-service manager spent 75 percent of his time reviewing and logging orders. The other 25 percent was spent responding to telephone calls from plant and DC managers. Some managers called twice daily while others never called.
4. The headquarters transmitted picking and shipping information on branded goods to 10 DCs daily at 5 P.M. It took 15 minutes per transmission.
5. At the DCs picking was carried out in a batch format; that is, all the cases of a given product were picked at one time and brought to a staging area. Here orders were assembled and loaded onto trucks or rail cars.
6. Headquarters had to send several documents to each DC: (1) picking lists—one for each storage area; (2) order information for use in staging, sequencing, and loading trucks and rail cars. All documents were sent to a warehouse clerk who sorted them, made copies when necessary, and delivered them to the appropriate personnel. In addition, sales offices teletyped special instructions and product allocation rules to the DCs.
    Following is a description of how these documents were distributed:
    a. Four-part picking lists—taken to the foreman who filed one copy, gave two copies to three picking supervisors (different picking lists) and threw one copy out. At the end of the night one copy of each of the picking lists was mailed to headquarters, where they were keypunched and entered into the computer to update the inventory file. This file was used to determine replenishment of the DCs and plant warehouses. As mentioned in the text, this caused delays and variability in replenishment cycles and contributed to large safety-stock levels and stock-outs.
    b. Assembly copies of orders—four-part document, one for each order—the clerk takes these to the transportation office for sequencing. A transportation clerk writes a sequence number on each one and makes a log of the orders by sequence and by route.

**EXHIBIT 15** *(continued)*

The clerk takes the assembly documents to the foreman, who gives them to the two assemblers. As an order is assembled this person records on the form shorts, substitutions, and weight of product being shipped. At the end of the night one copy is sent back to the transportation office where the bills of lading (BOLs) are prepared (they require tonnage data). The BOLs are sent to the dock and given to truck drivers. The remaining three copies are:
  (1) Sent with the order to the customer.
  (2) Mailed to headquarters for invoice preparation.
  (3) Filed at the CD.

  c. Special instructions and product allocation instructions were first copied by the clerk and then distributed to the foreman, who gave a copy to picking supervisors, inventory clerk, assemblers, and two or three men loading the trucks and rail cars, and sent to the transportation department.

7. The cost to mail picking and packing papers was $2.50 per day. Key punching was accomplished the same day the assembly and picking document arrived at headquarters.
8. Because stock-outs occurred often at DCs, they tended to circumvent headquarters by calling direct to plants or other DCs to locate product needed to fill orders. Telephone calls between DCs and plants usually lasted 15 minutes. About 200 calls per month were made for this reason. Ten calls could be placed in just one instance of a stock-out. Transhipments did come about as a result, which cost Ferle $500,000 annually in transportation costs alone.
9. The company works 22 days per month. (250 days per year).
10. Salaries at the distribution centers:
    a. Foreman—$25,000 per year.
    b. Picking supervisor—$22,000 per year.
    c. Transportation manager—$28,000 per year.
    d. Clerks—$15,000 per year.
    e. Assemblers and dock workers—$20,000 per year.
11. Customer service is defined as order fill rate, that is, the number of orders shipped versus the number of orders received (not line-item fill).

## Questions

1. Develop a proposal for the Ferle Foods account.
2. Demonstrate the cost justification for the new order-processing system.
3. Based upon the information given and upon your proposal what is the next area that you will pursue with this account?

# Author Index

## A

*Accounting Research Bulletin, No. 43*, 243
Aljian, George W., 240
Allison, Donald J., 318–19
American Telephone and Telegraph Co., 76–77, 298, 313, 325–26, 559
American Trucking Association, 106, 118, 135
Appleby, Harrison H., 26
Armitage, Howard M., 78, 370, 373, 377, 392, 397
Association of American Railroads, 116–17

## B

Bardi, Edward J., 7, 114, 407–8
Bauer, Frank L., 348, 359
Becker, H. G., Jr., 120, 159–60, 162
Beik, Leland L., 470
Bennion, Marcus Lyndsay, 71–72
Blanding, Warren, 78
Booz, Allen and Hamilton, Inc., 114–16
Borsodi, Ralph, 21
Bowersox, Donald J., 21, 65, 187, 339–40, 501, 517, 553
Bream, R. E., 372
Brown, Robert G., 286
Bruce, Robert A., 315
*Business Week*, 413
Buzby, Stephen L., 470

## C

Campbell, John H., 16, 18
Carrara, Earl A., 204
Cateora, Philip R., 431, 435, 438, 446, 458–60
Citicorp Industrial Credit, Inc., 167
Clark, Fred E., 21, 471
Cooper, M. Bixby, 65, 501, 553
Cooper, Martha, 31, 448, 481, 483
Coyle, John J., 7, 114, 407–8
Crandall, Norman F., 422
Crissy, W. J. E., 327–28, 470
Crowell, John F., 20
Culliton, James W., 21

## D

DeHayes, Daniel W., Jr., 408–9
Dickow, James F., 397
*Distribution Worldwide*, 17, 117, 222, 226
Dobler, Donald W., 349, 357, 362
Drake, Sheahan/Stewart Dougall, Inc., 123, 125
Drucker, Peter F., 11
Dulaney, Tom, 447
Dunne, Patrick M., 470

## E–F

England, Wilbur B., 342–43, 346, 353, 356, 358, 361, 363–64
Erickson, Leo G., 379–80
Falk, James P., 410, 416–19
Farrell, Jack W., 226, 453
Farris, Martin T., 106, 111–12
Fearon, Harold E., 339, 341–43, 346, 353, 356, 358, 361, 363–64
Fischer, Paul M., 327–28, 470
Flaks, Marvin, 36
Foster, Thomas A., 434, 439, 443–44
Frederick, John H., 186
Freund, John E., 247
Friedman, Walter F., 192, 195, 198, 200
Fulchino, Paul E., 121–22, 124–25, 155–58

## G

Galer, R., 372
Gecowets, George A., 9, 11
Gepfert, Alan H., 31–32
Gill, Lynn E., 450, 455
Gilmour, Peter, 58, 73, 449
Grabner, John R., 12, 25, 31, 33
Grasso, Edward T., 349
Guion, R. M., 412
Gustafson, John F., 56

## H

Hall, Thomas W., 240
Hamburg, Morris, 247
*Handling & Shipping*, 164
Harper, Donald V., 103
Hennessey, Dennis J., 12
Herron, David P., 482
Heschel, Michael, 146–47
Heskett, James L., 56, 490
Hess, John M., 431, 435, 446, 448, 458–60
Hoover, Edgar M., 221
Horngren, Charles T., 243
*The Howard Way Letter*, 1, 188
Hutchinson, William H., Jr., 74

## I–J

Ikeda, Mikio, 450–51, 457
International Business Machines, 296–98
Ivie, Robert M., 490
Jenkins, Creed H., 182
Johnson, James C., 108, 111
Johnson & Johnson Baby Products Co., 404, 416

## K

Kahler, Ruel, 433–34, 438, 455, 458, 461
Karasick, B., 412
Kast, F. E., 414
Kearney, A. T., Inc., 16–17, 22, 168, 170, 189, 211, 215, 373, 383–85, 406, 423–24
Keegan, Warren J., 435, 438, 462–63

## Index

Kirpalani, V. H., 470
Kolde, Endel J., 460
Kotler, Philip, 4–5, 8, 13
Kramer, Roland L., 433–34, 438, 455, 458, 461

### L

Ladores, Albert M., 536
LaFollette, W. R., 412
LaLonde, Bernard J., 12, 14, 22, 25, 31, 33, 47, 56–59, 62, 64, 73–74, 80, 97, 150–54, 214, 309, 311, 331, 448, 481, 483, 536
Lambert, Douglas M., 4, 16, 34–36, 65, 70, 78, 146, 181, 237–38, 250, 256–57, 261, 265, 328, 331, 333, 350, 369–73, 376–77, 405, 469, 478–79, 481, 487, 489, 501, 536
Lee, Lamar, Jr., 349, 357, 362
Leenders, Michael R., 342–43, 346, 353, 356, 358, 361, 363–64
LeKashman, Raymond, 36–38
Lesser, Jack A., 67
Lewis, Howard T., 21
Lewis, M. Chris, 94
Lewis, Richard J., 379–80
Lieb, Robert C., 121
Likert, Rensis, 424–25
Lineaweaver, F. R., Jr., 439, 453
Lipman, Rebecca, 341
Little, Arthur D., 314
Litwin, G., 412
Locklin, D. Phillip, 7

### M

McAdams, Tony, 491
McDermott, Dennis R., 403, 491
Magee, John F., 240
Mahoney, Thomas A., 422
Makridakas, Spyros, 296, 353
Mauro, George T., 121–22, 124–25, 155–58
Melnyk, Steven A., 340
Mendenhall, William, 247
Mentzer, John T., 78, 369–70, 373, 376
Miklas, W. E., 69
Miljus, Robert C., 491
*Modern Materials Handling*, 196–97
Morehouse, James E., 7, 33
Moskal, Brian S., 403
Mossman, Frank H., 21, 327–28, 470
Mueller, Paul M., 107
Murphy, Pat, 488–89

Murray, Robert E., 472–76
Murray, Thomas J., 404

### N

National Council of Physical Distribution Management, 9, 21, 31
Nevin, John J., 315
*Newsweek*, 33
Notman, James F., Jr., 108–9

### O–P

Orlicky, Joseph, 356
Ott, Lyman, 247
Pegrum, Dudley, 102
Perrine, Lowell E., 226
Potter, Ronald S., 157–58, 164–65, 176, 485–86, 492
Pritchard, R., 412
*Progressive Grocer: The Magazine of Super Marketing*, 65

### R

Ray, David, 34, 372
Rewoldt, Stewart H., 498
Rich, Stuart U., 543
Richard, Raymond, 56
Rimmer, Peter J., 449
Robeson, James F., 12, 25, 31, 33, 405, 491
Rosenbloom, Bert, 5–6
Rosenzweig, J. E., 414
Ross, Randolph E., 438, 442–43
Roth, Ronald D., 106–7
Ruppenthal, Karl M., 524

### S

Sabath, Robert E., 79–80
Sampson, Roy J., 106, 111–12
Schiff, Michael, 22, 148–49, 372, 378
Schneider, Lewis M., 33
Schultz, William J., 186
Shapiro, Stanley, S., 470
Shaw, Arch W., 21
Shumey, Mike, 190–93, 196
Shycon, Harvey M., 65
Sims, H. P., Jr., 412
Smykay, Edward W., 21, 24
Soderberg, Peter H., 404, 416
Spencer, John, 194–95, 198–99
Sprague, Christopher R., 65
Squibb, E. R. and Sons, Inc., 315–18

Steele, Jack D., 21
Steele, William R., 254
Steers, Richard M., 411–15
Stephenson, Ronald, 65
Sterling, Jay, 44, 46, 260
Stern, Mark E., 467–68
Stewart, Wendell M., 7, 33
Stock, James R., 8, 34, 112–13, 120, 150–54, 204, 403, 405, 424–27, 487, 507
Stolle, John F., 36–38, 74, 405, 407–8
Stringer, R., 412
Summers, Jefferson G., 296
Sutton, Robert M., 158, 164–65

### T

Taff, Charles A., 19–20, 209
Taylor, Donald A., 54, 501, 553
Taylor, Robert L., 408–9
Terpstra, Vern, 432, 437–38, 446, 452, 456
Tersine, Richard J., 16, 18, 349
Throckmorton, John F., 107
Tinghitella, Stephen, 226
Tompkins, James A., 190–92, 227, 229
Towle, Jeffrey G., 489
Transportation Association of America, 101–6, 108–10, 112, 136–42
*Transportation and Distribution Management*, 244
*Transport Topics*, 485

### U–Z

*U.S. News and World Report*, 487
Vreeland, Barrie, 159
*The Wall Street Journal*, 454
Walter, Clyde K., 67
*Warehousing Review*, 1, 216
Wayman, Wilbur S., 376
Weitz, Donald W., 129–30, 158, 164–65
Weitzel, William, 422
Wheelwright, Steven C., 296, 353
White, John A., 190–92, 227, 229
White, Phillip D., 344–45, 347
Whitehead and Partners, 372
Willett, Ronald P., 65
Williams, Frank J., 247
Williams, Rex R., 455
Wind, Yoram, 343
Wolk, Harry I., 470
Wood, Donald F., 108, 111
Zinszer, Paul H., 14, 22, 56–59, 62, 64, 67, 73–74, 80, 84, 97, 309, 517

# Subject Index

## A

Abbott Laboratories, 404
ABC analysis; *see* Customer service
Acme Office Products, Inc. case, 507–17
Air transport; *see also* Transportation
　carrier reform, 125–26
　characteristics, 104–6
　shipper response to carrier reform, 156–57
Airlift International, 105
Airline Deregulation Act (1977 and 1978), 121, 125
Aluminum Company of Canada, 424
American Institute of Certified Public Accountants, 242
American Society of Traffic and Transportation, 23
American Telephone and Telegraph Company (AT&T), 313, 325–26
American Trucking Associations, Inc., 106
Association of American Railroads, 156
Avon Products, Inc., 63, 240

## B

Bendix Corporation, 120
Bergen Brunswig Corporation, 190, 192, 315
Bill of lading, 147–49
Booz, Allen and Hamilton, Inc., 114
Borden, Inc., 41, 233
"Bottle laws," 278, 488
Bristol-Myers Company, 41, 233
Bureau of Labor Statistics, 8
Burlington Industries, 159

## C

California Growers Association, 202
Canadian National Railways, 117
Capital rationing, 236, 240–41
Carnation Company, 63
Celanese Corporation, 446
Cenex, 194
Channels of distribution
　cost reduction, 4–5
　defined, 5, 470–71
　development of, 4
　relationship with physical distribution, 5–7
　typical channel structure, 5
Civil Aeronautics Board (CAB), 125, 141
Clairol, Inc., 61, 66, 68
COGS (Consumer Goods System), 296
Colgate-Palmolive Company, 41, 233
Commodity analysis, 359–61
Communication effectiveness, 414–15
Consolidated Foods Corporation, 41, 44, 233
Consumerism, 487–88
Containerization, 117, 455–56
Cooperative Food Distributors of America, 315
Cost data
　budgetary practices, 382–83
　case studies, 373–76
　and control of PD activities, 372–73
　difficulties in obtaining, 376–77
　and distribution accounting, 480–81
　importance of, 369–70
　and MIS, 386–87
　and productivity standards, 383–86
Cost of lost sales; *see* Customer service
Cost/service trade-offs, implementation, 69–71
Customer order cycle; *see* Order cycle

Customer service, 149
　ABC analysis, 73–74
　activity/input matrix, 385
　audit, 71–78, 81–97
　cost of lost sales, 66–69
　defined, 14–15, 55–57
　elements, 57–63
　external market audit, 46–47
　impediments, 78–79
　importance of, 63–64
　improvements, 49, 79–81
　and international physical distribution, 449–50
　and inventories, 291–93
　posttransaction, 58–59, 62–63, 75, 80
　pretransaction, 58–60, 75
　reporting systems, 76–77
　standards, 74–78
　and the strategic physical distribution plan, 473
　transaction, 58–62, 75, 80
Customer service audit; *see also* Customer service
　example, 81–97
　goals of, 71
Customs house broker; *see also* Exporting
　functions of, 439
Cycle stock; *see* Inventory

## D

Dead stock; *see* Inventory
Delta Nu Alpha Transportation Fraternity, 23
Demand forecasting, 15
Demurrage and detention, 127
Department of Transportation (DOT), 125
Detroit Edison Company, 424
Distribution Centers, Inc., 202
Distribution communications, 15–16
*Distribution* magazine, 222, 439

**580** Index

*Distribution Worldwide; see Distribution* magazine
Diversion and reconsignment, 127–28
Documentation; *see also* Exporting
  examples, 443–44
Dow Chemical Company, 424
Dow Chemical Company case, 498–501
Drake Sheahan/Stewart Dougall, Inc., 122

**E**

Eastman Kodak Company, 404, 446
Economic order quantity (EOQ); *see also* Inventory management
  adjustments to the EOQ model, 286
  assumptions of the EOQ model, 285
  EOQ model, 283–85, 291
  inventory carrying costs, 282–83
  ordering costs, 282–83
80/20 rule, 295
Energy, 8, 117, 483–84, 486, 488
Ericson Company, 446
Export distributor; *see also* Exporting
  characteristics, 438
  function of, 438
  selection, 439–42
Exporting; *see also* International physical distribution
  advantages of, 433–34
  currency exchange rates, 461
  customs house broker, 439
  disadvantages of, 434
  documentation, 443–44
  export distributor, 438–42
  foreign-freight forwarder, 439, 443
  free-trade zones, 445–47
  terms of trade, 444–45

**F**

Farmers Union Central Exchange, Inc.; *see* Cenex
Favored Blend Coffee Company case, 517–23
Federal Council for Science and Technology, 8
Federal Energy Regulatory Commission (FERC), 125–26, 142
Federal Express Corporation, 102
Federal Maritime Commission (FMC), 125, 142
Ferle Foods, Inc. case, 559–76
Flexible budgets; *see* Standard costs
Flying Tiger Line, 102, 105
FMC Corporation, 145–47
Food Marketing Institute, 315

Ford Motor Company, 19
Forecasting
  physical distribution performance improvement, 49
  techniques, 353–55
  types of, 353
Foreign-freight forwarder; *see also* Exporting
  functions of, 439, 443
Foreign ownership; *see also* International physical distribution
  advantages of, 436
  disadvantages of, 436
  example 436–37
Foreign-trade zones; *see* Free-trade zones
Form utility, 10
*Fortune*, 405
Forward buying; *see* Purchasing and procurement
Free-trade zones; *see* Exporting
Freight forwarders; *see also* Transportation
  characteristics, 113
  types of, 113
Fuji Heavy Industries, 457
Fujitsu, 457
Functional shiftability, 205–6

**G**

General Electric Company, 13, 425
General Foods Corporation, 41, 233
General Mills, Inc., 293
General Motors Corporation, 164, 454
Genesco, 425
Giles Laboratories case, 536–42
GNP, 101–2
Goodyear Tire & Rubber Company, 446
Grocery Manufacturers of America, 315

**H**

*Handling & Shipping*, 122, 159, 164, 194, 198
*Harvard Business Review*, 240
Hooker Chemicals and Plastics Corporation, 404
Hurdle rate, 241

**I**

IMPACT (Inventory Management and Control Techniques), 296–97
Information systems; *see also* Order processing
  capabilities of, 326–27

Information systems—*Cont.*
  designing the system, 323–27
  need for information, 323
  sources of data, 325–26
Integrated physical distribution management; *see also* Total cost-tradeoff analysis
  and customer service, 66–71
  example, 44–46
  and international physical distribution, 458
  and PD organization, 404–6, 418
  and transportation, 147
Intermodal combinations
  fishyback, 104, 113, 117
  piggyback (TOFC), 104, 110, 113–17
International Business Machines Corp. (IBM), 13, 296–97, 425
International Paper Company, 120, 226
International physical distribution
  channel strategies, 432–37
  controllable elements, 448–58
  customer service strategies, 449–50
  export facilitators, 438–43
  exporting, 433–34
  financial aspects, 458–61
  foreign ownership, 436–37
  future trends, 486–87
  inventory strategies, 450–51, 459–60
  joint ventures, 435–36
  labeling, 456
  licensing, 434–35
  management of PD activities, 462–63
  packaging, 455–56
  sourcing of materials; *see* Purchasing and procurement
  transportation strategies, 451, 453–55
  uncontrollable elements, 446, 448
  warehousing and storage, 457–58
Interstate Commerce Commission (ICC), 125, 141, 485
In-transit inventories; *see* Inventory
Inventory; *see also* Inventory carrying costs *and* Inventory management
  control, 16
  and corporate profitability, 234–37
  critical business interfaces, 32
  cycle stock, 279–80
  dead stock, 282
  and international physical distribution, 450–51, 459–60
  in-transit inventories, 280, 450
  investment, 40
  and order processing, 311

Inventory—*Cont.*
  physical distribution performance improvement, 49–50
  positioning within the channel, 277–78
  purposes of, 275–77
  safety (buffer) stocks, 280–81, 292
  seasonal stock, 282
  speculative stocks, 281–82
  types of, 278–82
Inventory carrying costs, 7, 16, 237–60
  absorption costing, 242
  average cost of inventory, 243
  calculation of, 241–51
  capital costs, 241–44
  cost of money, 240–42
  direct costing, 241
  examples, 251–59
  FIFO, 243, 460
  and forward buying, 349–51
  and international physical distribution, 450
  and inventory turnover, 259–60
  LIFO, 243, 460
  risk costs, 246–50
  service costs, 244–45
  storage space costs, 245–56
Inventory management
  ABC analysis, 295, 374
  activity/input matrix, 385
  and customer service, 291–93
  economic order quantity (EOQ), 283–86, 291
  fixed order interval model, 287–88
  fixed order point, fixed order quantity model, 287–88
  forecasting, 295–96
  inventory models, 296–98
  inventory reduction, 294, 299–303
  and materials management, 357
  objectives of, 282
  order processing systems, 298–99
  and production scheduling, 293–94
  safety stock requirements, 286–91
  symptoms of poor inventory management, 294
  under certainty, 282–86
  under uncertainty, 286–88
Ishikawajimi Harima Heavy Industries, 457

## J–K

John Deere Tractor Company, 193
Johns-Manville Canada, Inc., 32, 318–22
Johnson & Johnson, 41, 233, 327, 404, 415–16
Joint ventures; *see* International physical distribution

Judgment sample, 295
Kaiser Aluminum and Chemical Corporation, 416
Kearney, A. T., Inc., 7, 22
Kraftco, 63

## L

Lever Brothers Company, 425
Levi Strauss & Company, 120
Licensing; *see also* International physical distribution
  advantages of, 434–35
  defined, 434
  disadvantages of, 435
Lilly, Eli, & Company, 315
Little, Arthur D., Inc., 314
LREPS model, 327

## M

McDonald's Corporation, 13
McGraw-Hill Book Company (A) case, 524–36
*Management Accounting*, 240
Management-by-crisis, 403
Management-by-objectives, 403
Maremont Corporation, 404
Marketing, 149, 487
  exchange process, 3–4
  marketing concept, 13, 21, 57
Marketing mix
  customer service, 63–66
  place, 36
  price, 34
  product, 34–35
  promotion, 35–36
Marketing and physical distribution audit
  external market audit, 46–47
  internal operations audit, 47–48, 84–94
Material handling
  objectives, 16
  scope of, 16
Materials management
  activities, 341
  definition, 339
  inbound transportation, 351–52
  inventory planning and control, 352–56
  MIS control, 352
  MRP (materials requirements planning), 340, 353–56, 361–64
  operating reports, 358–61
  performance measurement, 357–61
  and physical distribution management, 339–40
  production control, 351

Materials management—*Cont.*
  purchasing and procurement, 342–51
  salvage and scrap disposal, 19, 356
  warehousing and storage, 352
Matrix management, 409–415
Mead Johnson and Company, 66, 404
Michigan State University, 23, 327
Modular data base concept, 327–32; *see also* Order processing
  definition, 327
Motor Carrier Act of 1980, 120–21, 131–35, 485
Motor transport; *see also* Traffic management, *and* Transportation
  carrier reform, 121–24
  characteristics, 106–8
  shipper response to carrier reform, 155–56
MRP (materials requirements planning); *see also* Materials management
  advantages of, 362
  conditions underlying its use, 362
  defined, 354, 356
  disadvantages of, 362
  master production schedule, 354, 361–63
  objectives of, 362
  outputs, 363–64

## N

National American Wholesale Grocers' Association, 315
National Association of Retail Grocers of the United States, 315
National Council of Physical Distribution Management (NCPDM), 7, 9, 22–23, 45, 56, 167, 211, 218, 308, 372, 424–25, 448, 481
National Food Brokers Association, 315
National Wholesale Druggist Association (NWDA), 314
Nielsen, A. C., Company, 325

## O

Ohio State University, 23
OPEC, 467
Opinion Research Corporation, 413
Order cycle, 61; *see also* Order processing
  components of, 307–8
  defined, 307
  methods of order entry, 310–12

**582** *Index*

Order cycle—*Cont.*
   path of a customer's order, 312–13
   variability, 309–10
Order processing, 16–17
   communications function, 313–27
   and computers, 314–20
   cost justification of advanced system, 332–35
   and customer service, 80
   data base, 327–32
   financial considerations, 332–35
   initiates PD activities, 321–22
   order cycle, 307–13
Order processing and information systems, physical distribution performance, 49, 387
Organizational climate, 412
Ormont Drug & Chemical Company, 446

**P**

Packaging, 18–19, 198–201
   design of, 198
   functions of, 198
   and international physical distribution, 455–56
Parcel post, 167
Parts and service support, 17
Pet, Incorporated, 120
Physical distribution; *see also* Physical distribution management
   activities included within, 14–20
   audit, 473
   cost of, 11–12
   "five rights," 11
   as a function, 408–9
   and GNP, 7
   investment in, 7
   performance improvement, 48–50
   productivity, 7–8
   as a program, 409
   proprietary asset, 13–14
   reasons for growth, 33–34
   relationship with corporate profit performance, 40–44
   relationship with marketing, 10–11, 13
   role within the economy, 7–8
   role within the firm, 8–20
   significance of, 1
   size of workforce, 7
   strategic plan; *see* Strategic physical distribution plan
Physical distribution management; *see also* Physical distribution
   and cost data, 369–70
   defined, 9
   historical development of, 20–24

Physical distribution management—*Cont.*
   interest in the discipline, 22, 24–25
   and materials management, 339–40
   operationalizing of, 25–27
   and profitability of the firm, 12–13
Physical distribution organizations
   components of, 411–16
   coordination of, 406–7
   cost savings, 404
   developing an optimal PD organization, 416–19
   effectiveness, 411–16, 420, 422–27
   employee characteristics, 412
   environmental characteristics, 412
   examples, 420–22
   importance of, 404–6
   managerial policies and practices, 412–16
   operating characteristics, 425
   organizational characteristics, 411–12
   restructuring, 417–19
   types of, 406–10
Piggyback; *see also* Intermodal combinations
   TOFC service plans, 113–15
Pipeline transport; *see also* Transportation
   characteristics of, 108–10
Pizza Hut, Inc., 120
Possession utility, 10–11
Private warehousing; *see also* Warehousing
   advantages of, 186, 209, 211
   disadvantages of, 209–11
   performance measurement, 218–20
Procter & Gamble Company, 13, 41, 233
Procurement, 18; *see also* Purchasing and procurement
Production control; *see* Materials management
Productivity, 7–8
Productivity standards
   and control of PD costs, 383–86
   shortcomings of, 383, 386
*Progressive Grocer*, 65
Protective service, 128
Public warehousing; *see also* Warehousing
   advantages of, 201–4, 211
   disadvantages of, 204, 211
   and international physical distribution, 457–58
   performance measurement, 218–20
   services offered by, 204–8
   types of, 185–86

Purchasing and procurement; *see also* Materials management
   activity/input matrix, 385
   buying situations, 344
   defined, 342
   forward buying, 349–51
   goals of purchasing, 342–43
   international sourcing, 347
   quality control, 347–49, 357
   supplier evaluation, 344–47
   supplier selection, 343–46

**Q–R**

Quaker Oats Company, 32, 41, 233
Quality control; *see* Purchasing and procurement
Rail transport; *see also* Transportation
   carrier reform, 124–25
   characteristics of, 110–11
   shipper response to carrier reform, 156–57
   TOFC, 110
Railroad Transportation Policy Act (1980), 121, 124–25
Ralston Purina Company, 41, 193, 233
Rate bureau, 126
Reed-Bulwinkle Act of 1948, 126
Regression analysis, and inventory costing, 247–50
Return goods handling, 19; *see* Reverse distribution
Reverse distribution, 483
Revlon Corporation, 63, 240
Riverview Distributing Company, Incorporated (B) case, 553–58
Robinson-Patman Act, 78
Ronson Corp., 446
Ross Laboratories, 66

**S**

Safety (buffer) stocks; *see* Inventory
Salvage and scrap disposal; *see* Materials management
Seaboard World Airlines, 105
Sears, Roebuck and Company, 68, 120, 193
Seasonal stock; *see* Inventory
Simulation, 220, 327
Site selection
   plant, 17–18
   warehouse, 17–18
Smith Chemical Company case, 501–6
SOLIDS (Squibb on-line inventory and distribution system), 315–17
Spector Motor Freight, 130
Speculative stocks; *see* Inventory

Split delivery, 127
Squibb, E. R., and Sons, Inc., 315
Staggers Act, 156; *see also* Railroad Transportation Policy Act
Standard Brands, Inc., 41, 233
Standard costs, 377–82
 application, 392–97
 development of, 397–400
 and flexible budgets, 377–78, 382–83, 397–400
Sterling Drug, Inc., 296–98
Storage; *see* Warehousing
Strategic physical distribution plan
 broad-based management skills, 481–83
 and channel strategy, 468–72, 477–80
 components of, 477
 and consumerism, 487–88
 distribution accounting, 480–81
 energy/ecology issues, 483–84
 implications for management, 488–90
 inputs into, 472–73
 and international physical distribution, 486–87
 planning process, 473–77
 regulatory trends, 484–86
 types of, 467
Strategic profit model, 42–44
 asset turnover, 43
 examples, 44, 234–37, 299–303, 387–90
 financial leverage, 43–44
 net profit, 42–43
Strategy, developing a physical distribution strategy, 48
Sun Oil Company, 425
Sylvania Company, 23

**T**

Terms of trade, 444–45; *see also* Exporting
Thom McAn, 12
Time and place utility, 10–11, 13, 56, 277
 and transportation, 102–3
Total cost concept, 13, 31, 36–40
 and customer service levels, 38
 defined, 31
 inventory, 237
 inventory carrying costs, 40
 order processing and information cost, 39
 production lot quantity costs, 39–40
 transportation costs, 39
 warehousing costs, 39
Total cost-tradeoff analysis, 370–72
 cost tradeoffs, 370, 480–81
 example, 387–91

Total cost-tradeoff analysis—*Cont.*
 and integrated physical distribution management, 387–91
 and international physical distribution, 458, 460
 physical distribution organizations, 418
 and the strategic PD plan, 470
Traffic; *see* Transportation
Traffic management, 128–30
 evaluation of mode/carrier performance, 167–71
 and international physical distribution, 451, 452–55
 issues affecting future transportation decision making, 176–79
 leasing, 165–67
 mode selection; *see* Transportation mode selection decision
 private versus for-hire decision, 158–65
 shipment file, 148
 transportation audit, 171–75
Transit privileges, 127
Transportation, 19–20
 activity/input matrix, 384
 air, 104–6
 audit; *see* Traffic management
 common carriers, 118
 contract carriers, 118–19
 costs, 145–50
 economic importance of, 101–2
 exempt carriers, 119–20
 expenditures on, 7
 freight forwarders, 113
 inbound; *see* Materials management
 interface with PD and marketing, 103–4
 and international physical distribution, 451–55
 legal forms, 118–20
 modes, 104
 motor, 106–9
 and physical distribution performance improvement, 50
 pipeline, 108–10
 private carriers, 120, 123–24, 156; *see also* Traffic management
 productivity, 168–70
 rail, 110–11
 rate structures, 126–28; *see also* Transportation rates
 regulation, 120–28, 484–86
 regulatory agencies, 141–42
 water, 111–13
Transportation mode selection decision
 choice process, 153–54
 and international physical distribution, 453–55
 postchoice evaluation, 154–55

Transportation mode selection decision—*Cont.*
 problem recognition, 150–51
 search process, 151–53
Transportation rates; *see also* Transportation
 accessorial charges, 127–28
 class rates, 127
 commodity rates, 127
 exception rates, 127
 factors affecting, 128
 line-haul rates, 127
Transshipments, 61

**U**

Union Carbide Corporation, 425
Uniroyal, Inc., 404
United Airlines, 13
United Parcel Service (UPS), 102, 104, 167, 193
U.S. Steel Corporation, 11

**W**

Warehouse handling systems
 advantages of, 194–96
 automated (advanced) systems, 193–98
 disadvantages of, 194, 196
 standard (manual) systems, 193
Warehousing, 20; *see also* Warehousing operations
 activity/input matrix, 384
 cost tradeoffs, 181
 decision-making strategies, 201–26
 expenditures on, 7
 functions, 187–90
 importance of, 182
 and international physical distribution, 457–58
 and inventory carrying costs, 245–46
 layout and design, 190–92
 performance, 210–20
 physical distribution performance improvement, 49
 private, 185–87; *see also* Private warehousing
 productivity, 211, 214–16
 public, 185–87; *see also* Public warehousing
 site selection, 220–26
 S/R systems; *see* Warehouse handling systems
 standard costs and flexible budgets, 392–400
 types of, 184–87
 uses of, 182–84

Warehousing operations
 functions, 187–90
 handling systems, 192–98
 layout and design, 190–92
 packaging, 198–201

*Warehousing Review,* 216
Water transport; *see also* Transportation
 categories of, 111
 characteristics of, 111–13

Western Plywood Corporation case, 543–52
Whirlpool Corporation, 13, 32, 68, 276, 327, 404

*This book has been set VIP, in 10 and 9 point Zapf Book Light, leaded 2 points. Part numbers are 36 point Zapf Book Demi. Chapter numbers are 48 point Zapf Book Demi and chapter titles are 20 point Zapf Book Demi. The size of the type page is 36 by 48½ picas.*